Roads of Excess,
Palaces of Wisdom

The ancient tradition that the world will be consumed in fire at the end of six thousand years is true, as I have heard from Hell.

For the cherub with his flaming sword is hereby commanded to leave his guard at tree of life, and when he does, the whole creation will be consumed, and appear infinite. and holy whereas it now appears finite & corrupt.

This will come to pass by an improvement of sensual enjoyment.

But first the notion that man has a body distinct from his soul, is to be expunged; this I shall do, by printing in the infernal method, by corrosives, which in Hell are salutary and medicinal, melting apparent surfaces away, and displaying the infinite which was hid.

If the doors of perception were cleansed every thing would appear to man as it is, infinite.

For man has closed himself up, till he sees all things thro' narrow chinks of his cavern.

Roads of Excess, Palaces of Wisdom

Eroticism & Reflexivity in the Study of Mysticism

Jeffrey J. Kripal

THE UNIVERSITY OF CHICAGO PRESS
CHICAGO & LONDON

JEFFREY J. KRIPAL is the Vira I. Heinz Associate Professor of Religion at
Westminster College in New Wilmington, Pennsylvania, and the author of *Kālī's
Child: The Mystical and the Erotic in the Life and Teachings of Ramakrishna*,
published by the University of Chicago Press.

The University of Chicago Press, Chicago 60637
The University of Chicago Press, Ltd., London
© 2001 by The University of Chicago
All rights reserved. Published 2001
Printed in the United States of America
10 09 08 07 06 05 04 03 02 01   1 2 3 4 5

ISBN: 0-226-45378-2 (cloth)
ISBN: 0-226-45379-0 (paper)

Library of Congress Cataloging-in-Publication Data

Kripal, Jeffrey John, 1962–

    Roads of excess, palaces of wisdom : eroticism and reflexivity in the study of mysticism / Jeffrey J. Kripal.
    p.   cm.
    Includes bibliographical references and index.
    ISBN 0-226-45378-2 (alk. paper)—ISBN 0-226-45379-0 (pbk. : alk. paper)
    1. Mysticism—Study and teaching—History—20th century.   2. Sex—Religious aspects.   3. Homosexuality—Religious aspects.   I. Title.
BL625 .K75 2001
291.4′22—dc21   2001035571

For all the readers of *Kālī's Child*
who shared their own secrets with me,
having seen theirs reflected in mine.

The road of excess leads to the palace of wisdom.
> William Blake, *The Marriage of Heaven and Hell*

But if I was to report my own dreams, it inevitably followed that I should have to reveal to the public gaze more of the intimacies of my mental life than I liked, or than is normally necessary for any writer who is a man of science and not a poet. Such was the painful but unavoidable necessity; and I have submitted to it rather than totally abandon the possibility of giving the evidence for my psychological findings. Naturally, however, I have been unable to resist the temptation of taking the edge off some of my indiscretions by omissions and substitutions. But whenever this has happened, the value of my instances has been very definitely diminished. I can only express a hope that readers of this book will put themselves in my difficult situation and treat me with indulgence, and further, that anyone who finds any sort of reference to himself in my dreams may be willing to grant me the right of freedom of thought—in my dream-life, if nowhere else.
> Sigmund Freud, *The Interpretation of Dreams,* preface to the first edition

THE ROAD MAP

	Preface: Sex, Secrecy, and the Sacred	IX
	Introduction: Roads of Excess	1
ONE	Eyeing the Burning Wings: Analyzing the Mystical Experience of Love in Evelyn Underhill's *Mysticism* (1911)	33
	Secret Talk The Vajrāśva Vision	87
TWO	The Passion of Louis Massignon: Sublimating the Homoerotic Gaze in *The Passion of al-Hallāj* (1922)	98
	Secret Talk Heroic Heretical Heterosexuality	147
THREE	The Doors of Deception: R. C. Zaehner's Ethical and Erotic Challenges to Monistic Experience in *Mysticism Sacred and Profane* (1957) and *Discordant Concord* (1970)	156
	Secret Talk Writing Out (of) That Night	199
FOUR	Writing Out of the Light at the Center: Reading Agehananda Bharati's Tantric Trilogy (1960, 1965, 1976)	207
	Secret Talk The Descent	250
FIVE	The Mystical Mirror of Hermeneutics: Gazing into Elliot Wolfson's *Speculum* (1994)	258
	Secret Talk Svapna-Siddha	299
	Conclusion: Palaces of Wisdom	305
	Notes	331
	Bibliography	377
	Index	391

PREFACE

Sex, Secrecy, and the Sacred

We also admit that it is in the area of sex that we must search for the most secret and profound truths about the individual, that it is there that we can best discover what he is and what determines him. And if it was believed for centuries that it was necessary to hide sexual matters because they were shameful, we now know that it is sex itself which hides the most secret parts of the individual: the structure of his fantasies, the roots of his ego, the forms of his relationships to reality. At the bottom of sex, there is truth.

> Michel Foucault, *Hercule Barbin: Being the Recently Discovered Memoirs of a Nineteenth-Century French Hermaphrodite*

I shall take concealment, or hiding, to be the defining trait of secrecy. It presupposes separation, a setting apart from the non-secret, and of keepers of a secret from those excluded. The Latin *secretum* carries this meaning of something hidden, set apart.... [One aspect of the secret] is that of the sacred, the uncanny, and the mysterious. It is conveyed by words such as *arcanum,* another Latin word for "secret." The sacred and the secret have been linked from earliest times. Both elicit feelings of what Rudolph Otto called the "numinous consciousness" that combines the daunting and the fascinating, dread and allure. Both are defined as being set apart and seen as needing protection. And the sense of violation that intrusion into certain secrets arouses is also evoked by intrusions into the sacred.

> Sissela Bok, *Secrets: On the Ethics of Concealment and Revelation*

THIS IS A BOOK ABOUT eroticism and mysticism, as the subtitle clearly announces. But it is also a book about secrecy, which, perhaps appropriately, appears nowhere in the title of the book. Clearly announced or hidden, however, both eroticism and mysticism are surrounded and implicated in innumerable esoteric discourses and modes of experience. To write of either the mystical or the erotic, then, is also inevitably to write about the esoteric, about what I will call, in an intentionally open and multivalent fashion, the secret. A few words about secrecy, then, seem more than appropriate as we begin.

The philosopher and ethicist Sissela Bok and the literary critic Roger Shattuck, among many others, have written eloquently about the human experience of secrecy, in literature, government, science, art, and religion.[1] Shattuck has explored in particular the theme of "forbidden knowledge" in Western literature, that mythic and literary motif about forms of knowledge that are at once dangerous, strangely seductive, potentially liberating, and oftentimes destructive. From Adam and Eve in the garden, who dared taste the forbidden fruit only to know immediate sexual shame (secret knowledge and sexuality are entwined from the very beginning in the Western monotheisms) and quick exile from paradise at the hands of an angry and seemingly jealous God (hence the early Christian gnostics, who, in a relevant twist on the story, hailed the serpent as the true hero of the story and decried God as a petty obstructer of knowledge), through the scholar-wizard Faust, who sold his soul to the devil in order to know all, to the monstrous, murderous, and yet somehow touching Frankenstein monster, to modern science with its atomic bomb and human genome project, human beings have been acutely aware that culture and life itself depend, at least partly, upon how we approach forms of knowledge and truth that are felt to be somehow forbidden, secret, hidden, out of bounds.

Bok has explored these same themes, but on a much broader canvas and with a less literary and more specifically ethical or philosophical lens. How, she asks, are we to discern the ethics of concealment and revelation in the innumerable instances—secret societies, Catholic confession, psychotherapy, the trade secrets of the corporate world, police surveillance and undercover work, artistic expression, gossiping, scientific experimentation, social science research, and investigative journalism—in which human beings keep or reveal secrets? For Bok, secrecy is not something tangential or superficial to human existence, but ontogenetically integral to identity itself. We presume that infants, for whom the world is essentially one, know or keep no secrets. Only with the development of a relatively stable identity or ego can the phenomenological experiences of an "inside" and an "outside" develop and, with them, the experience of psychosocial boundaries and hence the need of controlling the flow of information across those same boundaries. Secrecy, then, implies psychological differentiation, that is, a self (or, more likely, a collection of selves) set apart and protected from the rest of the natural and social worlds. Such a psychological, indeed ontological understanding of secrecy allows Bok to avoid prejudging secret practices as inevitably deceptive, negative, or suspicious. But neither does she ever lose sight of secrecy's constant ability to degenerate into a cover for harmful deception, various forms of abuse, solipsistic delusions, self-deceptions, and premeditated lies (and perhaps it is no accident that her earlier book was on lying).[2] For Bok, human identity, freedom, and sanity itself are determined largely by how we negotiate with an always adaptable discretion some working balance between the two extremes of pure openness or absolute transparency and total solipsism or complete secrecy. It is never a matter, then, of always or never keeping or telling secrets, but of choosing discretely which secrets we tell or seek out and under what social circumstances.

I come to the same subject after two decades of being schooled in the telling, keeping, and conscious breaking of secrets, and hence my reading of such authors as Shattuck and Bok is a rather after-the-fact exercise of trying to make sense of myself and my writing—we are always, as Freud taught us so well, secrets even to ourselves, and so we need others and, even more strangely, our own self-expressions to understand ourselves. My training in the art of secrecy occurred largely within three Western cultural institutions, all of which focus in different ways on the positive speaking of secrets: the Catholic sacramental practice of confession and spiritual direction, the secular therapeutic discipline of psychoanalysis, and the academic practice of "professing" the truth as one perceives it. In each of these practices, first encountered and carried on, I might add, within the nurturing sacred confines of a Catholic seminary community, I was encouraged to tell all, or almost all. Significantly, the first two disciplines (confession and psychoanalysis) focused, like some moral microscope, on the vagaries, intricacies, and powers of sexuality and their undeniable connections to the spiritual life I found all around me and sensed so strongly working within me. As I will tell the story shortly, to speak and integrate such secrets within my conscious emotional and intellectual lives was to be profoundly challenged, religiously transformed, and physically healed. To speak the secret here was something excruciatingly difficult but also eminently positive. It was about truth.

Still, for all its power and beauty, there were real limits to what could be said within my faith tradition. Like any other identity, religious identities and their attending traditions need boundaries, which often become walls. I thus grew frustrated and sought more freedom to speak and to think. Encouraged by my spiritual mentors in the seminary, I found that freedom within the academy, where one is actively encouraged to say what one thinks, as long as one can support such claims with evidence and a convincing defense of one's method—that is, how exactly one arrived at one's conclusions. Here is an entire culture that exists, ideally anyway, for the sake of professing the truth, comfortably or uncomfortably.

All three disciplines (spiritual direction, psychoanalysis, and the intellectual life), moreover, were intimately bound up with a fourth esoteric technology of Western cultural history—the mystical life, that is, the quest for a felt and transformative union with the divine.[3] Etymologically speaking, the mystical *(mustikon)* is quite literally "the secret," "the hidden." Although it is certainly filled with its own secrets,[4] perhaps one of the defining features of the mystical life is its collapsing of the inside and the outside, a kind of fusion or boundary crossing that recognizes no ultimate differentiation from the rest of the universe, be it naturally or culturally defined. If human identity can develop and survive only through processes of psychic differentiation, here we have an ultimate denial of differentiation and, with it, an irrepressible desire to speak and write secrets, that is, to cross those boundaries and transgress those assumed customs, identities, and protective measures that give security to the ego, all the while affirming both the potential terror and suffering of this process and the power of this most radical of denials—the denial of (ultimate) difference itself. There can be no secrets in deep communion or unity, for a secret demands at least two separated selves. On this level, at least, the mystical is a kind of complete and troubling, even scandalous transparency.

It was this quadruple training—at once deeply religious and deeply suspicious—that made my hermeneutical encounters with the published "public secrets" of a Bengali textual corpus virtually inevitable and produced my first book, *Kālī's Child: The Mystical and the Erotic in the Life and Teachings of Ramakrishna*, a psychoanalytically informed study of the erotic mysticism of the Hindu saint Ramakrishna Paramahaṁsa (1836–1886). But none of these cultural practices—not confession, not spiritual direction, not psychoanalysis, not Christian mysticism—prepared me for the cross-cultural and theoretical complexities of what it would mean to study and write about someone else's secrets (another mystical denial of difference), even if (*a*) these were not private at all but were in fact published in texts available to quite literally millions of readers, and (*b*) they would soon become my secrets as well, as the texts transformed my own psyche, body, and life. The heart of the present book is the story of the latter hermeneutical-mystical process and how it informs my theorizing about the history of mysticism. It is about a kind of manic creative possession, a mildly dissociative trancelike state that was first induced by a hermeneutical encounter with the Bengali texts and out of which I would later think and write and speculate, "speculation" here understood not as a kind of groundless guessing, but as a type of intuitive visionary experience (*speculare,* "to see") in the necessary mirror (*speculum*) of the texts as both other and self.

It is difficult for me not to think of my thought as a kind of secret, at once alluring, beautiful, and necessary to tell, and yet also as something somehow to be feared, censored, denied, even slandered. This, after all, is precisely the way my thought has been received (or, more accurately, not received) in some circles. I am conscious, in other words, of participating intimately and historically in the esoteric discourses I set out to study. I am aware of what it feels like not only to reveal a secret but also *to become one.* I know it is a bold claim, but I nevertheless feel that this total hermeneutical experience of writing about and experiencing a series of secrets can legitimately be called "sacred," for it manifests all the characteristics about which Rudolf Otto wrote so eloquently to give some voice to the "numinous consciousness" of attracting mystery and repelling terror that has defined humanity's encounter with the divine from antiquity.[5] More to the point, this experience has taught me, in a deeply physiological way, about the sense of transcendence and sacrality that arises from revelations of sacred secrets, what Bok calls "intrusions into the sacred" and Georges Bataille, more accurately and traditionally, I think, referred to as transgressions of a taboo, transgressions, he thought, that were integral and necessary to any genuine entrance into the sacred as that mystical continuity or oneness that respects no social code and honors no moral distinction.[6] How closely, then, I can identify with the insight of Don Cupitt, who understands classical mysticism as a kind of "subversive and transgressive writing" performed in order "to write their way and ours to a condition of personal religious happiness."[7] That, anyway, is how it has been for me.

But why do I want to do this again? Why do I want to write about more secrets and, more strangely still, tell my own? Why expose myself in this way? Do I feel some need to redeem myself through an open confession of sins committed against God and tradition? These are difficult questions, and I realize that I have only conscious answers. My most basic response is to invoke the mystical texts themselves, for these are texts that invite us into their worlds, call us to take them seriously, and demand from us some honest answer to their claims about the most profound issues of life. Mystical texts, in other words, like all genuinely religious literature, demand to be read religiously, that is, as making some normative claim on our lives, and this normative thrust calls us, implicitly or explicitly, to decipher them, to speak our own interpretations of their obsessively spoken secrets. Foucault has written the same about any esoteric discourse, particularly one involving the subject of sexuality: "Is it not with the aim of inciting people to speak of sex that it is made to mirror, at the outer limit of every actual discourse, something akin to a secret whose discovery is imperative, a thing abusively reduced to silence, and at the same time difficult and necessary, dangerous and precious to divulge?"[8] The same, I think, can be said for mystical literature and its secrets. Why write about a secret if you want no one to know about it and try to interpret its import? Mystical secrecy, then, is not something we impose on the texts or the culture from without, but a discourse that we enter and participate in from within the texts and their narratives. It is the other that initiates the process. We answer the call.

I am wagering, of course, that it is good to enter such worlds, and that these worlds have something important to teach us today. I may be wrong. But this is precisely the risk one must take to learn anything of significance and depth. In this same spirit, if I am to err, and like all human beings I no doubt will, I would prefer to err on the side of openness, honesty, and public debate, for here at least there are those controls, balances, and challenges that prevent and address so much that is harmful to our societies, religious communities, and ourselves. I cannot quite go so far as Lord Acton, who once wrote that "[e]very thing secret degenerates ... nothing is safe that does not show how it can bear discussion and publicity,"[9] but I can certainly see inestimable value in his warning and acknowledge its truth in many of the discussions that follow.

The basic issue, it seems to me, is both an epistemological and an ethical one. The issue is epistemological because, even in the present academic milieu, where "truth" has all but disappeared into "power" and where theorizing too often boils down to a kind of simplistic identity politics or, worse yet, an elaborate ad hominem argument ("You are wrong because you are who you are or live where you live"), I genuinely want to know and understand—and, more radically, think we *can* know and understand—how the erotic and the mystical inform one another in that inescapable universal of the history of religions, that is, the human body. But the issue is also ethical, as I am convinced that our present religious orthodoxies regarding human sexuality produce far more suffering than they relieve, that they must appear fundamentally and dangerously misinformed in the light of contemporary biological, literary, and anthropological evidence, and that little of substance can or will change until we confront, together, the religious roots of our sexual ignorance. In more provocative terms, far from speaking secrets to amend some past sin against God or tradition, it seems more likely that I feel compelled to study and speak secrets in order to address the sins God (or whom we imagine to be God, anyway) and our traditions have committed against us.

I realize that these kinds of encounters with the esoteric and often erotic dimensions of mystical traditions and their modern study will be emotionally and doctrinally impossible for some of my readers. But I am not without hope, for I know that my voice is only one of many, and that I write within an invisible but very real community whose shared voices grow more eloquent and more convincing with each passing year. I also believe, with some experience in the classroom, in writing, and in public speaking venues, that people, whatever their backgrounds or cultures, can be and are routinely convinced by solid, well-documented arguments. In terms of the history of religions, if there is not something that we can call "historical truth," there is certainly something we can call "overwhelming historical probability," and so there are certainly better and worse constructions of the past, even if there is never a perfect or complete construction of that past. And these pasts, I need not add, matter, and matter a great deal, to us in the present, since as we reconstruct and reimagine our pasts we simultaneously recreate and reimagine our presents and futures.

* * *

It is common practice to list at this point in a book all the people who aided one in writing and thinking it into being. This happy task is complicated somewhat here, since, in a perfect world, many of the people who played central roles in the genesis of this book should actually appear in the body of the text within the autobiographical sections that follow each chapter essay. The perceptive reader will notice (the American writer Ginu Kamani was the first to point this out to me) that virtually no one except academic authors whom I cite appears by name in those sections of the book. My story and my acknowledgments are thus riddled with significant silences, peopled with persons of great influence and love who nevertheless have no names.

This is both intentional and, I think, ethically necessary. No one, after all, asked to be written about, nor do any of these people necessarily want to appear in a book, particularly one about secrets, my interpretations of which they may or may not share. I have thus gone to some lengths to keep specific names and places vague or entirely absent in my autobiographical text. This has, no doubt, weakened both the force and concreteness of the story, but it has also given me the emotional freedom to explore themes and events I otherwise could not have given myself the freedom to explore at this point in my life. To those who will nevertheless recognize clearly their persons or communities in my narrative, I ask their understanding. With Freud (see the second epigraph), I say to them: "I can only express a hope that readers of this book will put themselves in my difficult situation and treat me with indulgence, and further, that anyone who finds any sort of reference to himself [or herself] in my dreams may be willing to grant me the right of freedom of thought—in my dream-life, if nowhere else."

There are, however, also many people who contributed to the book whose names can be mentioned without reserve. My editor at the University of Chicago Press, T. David Brent, deserves the first mention, as it was he who encouraged me early in this project and guided it through all the important peer review, editorial, and production processes that make a Chicago book something much more than a book. If I may use the word, David believed in both the project and the spirit animating it, and that made all the difference. For early and later critical reads of the manuscript or parts of it, I owe a special thanks to Peter Chemery, Michael Sells, Mark Jordan, Ginu Kamani, Rachel Fell McDermott, Peter Fell, Sarah Caldwell, Sudhir Kakar, Jack Hawley, Kelly Bulkeley, Peter Homans, Steven Wasserstrom, Scott Holland, and Ken Arnold. I learned a great deal from each of them, even if I had to stubbornly dissent from some of their reservations in the spirit of Blake's proverbs, "in opposition is true friendship" and "without contraries there is no progression."

As this is a broadly comparative work and no scholar can hope to be even sufficiently learned, much less fluent, in every field and language, I have actively sought out the help of specialists for each of the chapter essays. For help with the Underhill essay, I would like to thank Michael Stoeber, who commented extensively on an early draft. For help with the Massignon materials, I owe an immense debt to Mary Louise Gude, both for her fine biography on Massignon and her personal support and encouragement with my particular take on the relationship between

Massignon's sexual life and intellectual work. Here too I benefited greatly from the wisdom and graceful advice of Sidney Griffith. Sidney disagrees with much that I have to say in this chapter and in this book, but this did not prevent us from having many fruitful conversations, and the book is far better for these. With the Zaehner essay, Lee Siegel shared numerous anecdotes and personal memories of Zaehner with me and commented extensively on an earlier draft (he also told me many very funny stories). I also received significant help from Mr. Adrian Hale, former librarian of Wolfson College, now at the Bodleian Library, who kindly invited me to examine Zaehner's Indological library stored at Wolfson and acted as a gracious host during my visit there, as well as Friedhelm Hardy, Julian Baldick, Sir Michael Dummit, and John Gurney, all of whom graciously pointed me down many fruitful paths of thought. For help with the Bharati chapter, I would particularly like to thank Susan Snow Wadley, chair of the Anthropology Department at Syracuse University, for allowing me to work in Bharati's library there, and Roxanne Gupta, for her many memories of the swami and her warm encouragement in pursuing this particular line of inquiry. Roxanne's conviction that I had captured something essential and essentially true about Bharati's spirit was especially comforting to me. Finally, for the Wolfson chapter, there is Elliot Wolfson himself, who agreed to the possibility of the chapter project in the first place and then graciously submitted to too many drafts and questions from me and came up to Cambridge to coteach a seminar class on his *Speculum* and my chapter essay on it.

I would also like to thank the administration, faculty, and staff of Westminster College for their invaluable individual and institutional support of my person and work, the American Academy of Religion for an individual grant to study the personal library of R. C. Zaehner at Wolfson College in the spring of 2000, and Diana Eck and Dorothy Austin, Co-Masters of Lowell House at Harvard University. Diana and Dorothy gave me a place to stay for the 2000–2001 academic year and graciously included me in the Lowell House Senior Common Room, a community of scholars and artists with whom I enjoyed many meals and conversations as I finished this project and thought it through again. Finally, I would like to thank my graduate students. I first taught this text in the fall of 2000 at Harvard Divinity School, where it functioned as the core text (in manuscript form) for my seminar, "Method as Path: The Scholar's Mystical Experience and Its Hermeneutical Reflection." As far as pedagogical experiences go, that seminar was magical for me, an almost effortless synergy between a rather green teacher and eighteen remarkable individuals, almost all of whom were eager to talk openly about the relationships among religious experience, sexuality, secrecy, and scholarship in their own lives. We laughed a lot. I realized then, in a way that I never quite knew before, exactly why I wrote this book. Whatever others might say, these student-colleagues taught me, and so also assured me, that there really are people in the world who have ears to hear and hearts to understand. It is to them and for them I profess the secret again.

Jeffrey J. Kripal
15 April 2001
Harvard Divinity School

* * *

Portions of the introduction and chapter 2 have been developed from an earlier essay, "The Visitation of the Stranger: Some Mystical Dimensions of the History of Religions," *Cross Currents* 49, no. 3 (fall 1999). Portions of chapters 3 and 4 appear as expanded forms of earlier sections taken with permission from "Debating the Mystical as the Ethical: An Indological Map," in *Crossing Boundaries: Essays on the Ethical Status of Mysticism,* ed. G. William Barnard and Jeffrey J. Kripal (New York: Seven Bridges Press, 2001).

INTRODUCTION

Roads of Excess

Although my body was asleep, resting almost anesthetized on its back, not unlike a corpse, consciousness was lucid and clear, fully awake. Suddenly, without warning, a powerful electric-like energy flooded the body with wave after wave of an unusually deep and uniform arousal. I tried to hold the energies in as *liṅgam*s spontaneously emerged and disappeared in a fluid dream space. At some point, the energies gathered together, as if they themselves were conscious, and erupted "in" in a kind of psychic implosion.

From an unpublished preface for *Kālī's Child*

I really don't know how it happened, but after some time I woke up sleeping, or, more precisely, I woke up in sleep, without having fallen asleep in the true sense of the word. My body and all my senses sank into deeper and deeper sleep, but my mind didn't interrupt its activity for a single instant. Everything in me had fallen asleep except the clarity of consciousness. I continued to meditate on fire, at the same time becoming aware, in some obscure way, that the world around me was completely changed, and that if I interrupted my concentration for a single instant, I too would quite naturally become part of this world, which was the world of sleep.

Mircea Eliade, "The Secret of Dr. Honigberger"

A FRENCH CATHOLIC ISLAMICIST attributes his dramatic conversion during a suicide attempt in the desert of Iraq to the parapsychological presence of his dissertation subject, the tenth-century Sufi al-Hallāj. A second French Islamicist—perhaps not accidentally, a gifted student of the former—claims an initiatic transmission from the eleventh-century Sufi Suhrawardi while hermeneutically absorbed in the mystic's writings.

2 Introduction

A precocious young Indologist "steps out of space and time" while studying yoga in India and later camouflages his mystical experiences in a supernatural novella about the *siddhi* or yogic power of invisibility. An early American psychologist goes out of his way to study psychic phenomena, analyzes his own religious experiences, and inhales nitrous oxide to theorize the simultaneous presence of multiple dimensions of human consciousness, some of which material he then records as third-party case studies in his own published work. A French playwright, novelist, and social activist writes Freud about his own "oceanic" experiences and the hermeneutical powers that they gave him in his work on the Hindu mystics Ramakrishna and Vivekananda, thereby initiating what would become the psychoanalytic theory of mysticism as a psychic regression to developmentally prior forms of consciousness. A Jewish scholar experiments with kabbalistic techniques as he worries about a "professorial death" rich in erudition but devoid of mystical contact. A Buddhologist draws from the existential riches of his own Tibetan scholastic training, homosexuality, and extensive meditative experience to locate the compatibility of orgasm and reason within the continuum of the "mind of clear light," which he confessionally describes as "so awesome when one newly becomes aware of it." An American philosopher of religion employs his own meditative experiences of neurological tubes "zipping" shut in the back of his neck and a subsequent (and quite permanent) awareness of a profound inner emptiness or silence dwelling behind his fluctuating personality and thought to philosophize about mysticism, mind, and consciousness. Finally, another philosopher of religion paints a number of visions, many of them involving the vaginas of naked Christian Madonnas and Native American goddess figures, and then ritualizes these in his own southern Indiana religious community within a sacred ritual dance (he would stand naked in the center, wearing a feather crown, as female devotees danced bare breasted around him) before legal charges and sexual scandal close the group down.

Perhaps we could overlook such unusual occurrences, or at least pass them over with a benign nervous smile, were it not for the fact that each of these figures—Louis Massignon, Henry Corbin,[1] Mircea Eliade,[2] William James,[3] Romain Rolland,[4] Gershom Scholem,[5] Jeffrey Hopkins,[6] Robert K. C. Forman,[7] and Frithjof Schuon[8]—has played a significant role in the twentieth-century study of religion. And their very different cases, each quite distinct in its rhetorical style, doctrinal content, and moral implications, nevertheless share a common emphasis, whether muted or made explicit, on the methodological centrality of subjectively felt mystical experience. Little wonder, then, that the Sanskritist and Indologist Frits Staal long ago made an eloquent plea for the "rational mystic," that student of mysticism who is willing to and capable of actually experiencing mystical states in order to study them.[9] Staal's plea still makes sound theoretical sense, although it has fallen largely on deaf ears, and this despite the utter commonality of such "rational mystics" in the academy, be they outspoken in their rational mysticism or, much more likely, hidden in the shadows of self-censorship, discretion, and whispered enthusiasms. Indeed, as I hope to establish in all that follows, the modern, and now postmodern, study of mysticism, from its early beginnings to its contemporary practice, has been largely inspired, sustained, and rhetorically formed by the unitive, ecstatic, visionary, and mystico-hermeneutical experiences of the scholars themselves. The mystical experiences of scholars of mysticism — no archaeology of the comparative study of mysticism can justifiably ignore this weirdly beautiful, if ethically ambiguous, source of inspiration, theory, and writing.

The Indologist, mythologist, and historian of religions Wendy Doniger has written in numerous contexts about "myths lived by scholars who study myths,"[10] always careful to point out that the relationship between art and life, scholarship and biography, is never clear-cut, resembling as it does a set of mutually reflecting "fun-house mirrors" that both distort and smooth out the features of the "real" scholar who stands caught between the mirrors of art and life.[11] In the present work I would like to extend Doniger's project from the study of mythology to the study of mysticism and discuss the role of subjective mystical and ecstatic experiences in scholars who study mysticism. More specifically, I want to address the twentieth-century study of mysticism as itself a kind of mystical tradition, with its own unique history, discourses, sociological dynamics, and rhetorical strategies of secrecy (for this, after all, is what the mystical always comes down to — something *mustikon*, or "secret").

I have striven to keep this study balanced in terms of both its religious foci and its chronological sweep. Hence, I have included chapters on the study of Christian, Islamic, Hindu, and Jewish mysticism as each has been practiced at a different moment in the twentieth-century study of religion (I begin in the early twentieth century with Evelyn Underhill's construction of Christian mysticism and conclude at the end of the century with the postmodern Kabbalah scholar Elliot Wolfson). By no means exhaustive, the result can be read as a kind of prolegomenon to or call for a fuller archaeology of the twentieth-century study of mysticism, in my mind an important cultural phenomenon in its own right and one in need of further theoretical reflection and analysis.

My own approach to both this intellectual movement and its religious subject is essentially comparative; that is, I assume that any adequate understanding of "mysticism" can be had only by a two-pronged approach consisting of a cross-cultural grasp of its many (often very different) forms and a critical self-reflexive analysis of the category itself as a product of Western modernity. As the reader will soon discover, my own particular "comparative style" has been deeply influenced by my early religious life and by my later professional training in the history of religions, an academic discipline with a distinct history in Western forms of thought and experience. Born in the nineteenth century as a means of ordering the numerous religious worlds that Europe was encountering in her political, economic, and missionary ventures, it has remained to this day a distinctively academic way of making sense of the foreign, the eccentric, and the strange, or in the terms of contemporary philosophical and theological thought, of the other. The historian of religions, and especially the historian of mysticism, almost by definition it seems, is someone who deals in the exotic and the erotic. Shamanic identifications with totem animals, ecstatic trips to the world of the dead, mystical unions with God, with the cosmos, and with the self, macabre visions of dismembered gods and disemboweled holy men, cross-dressing saints, ascetic practices that seem to alternate between the horrible and the ridiculous, male brides and virginal wives, saintly anorexic suicides, myths of bloodthirsty goddesses, gory, cruel sacrifices animal, human, and divine, and spiritual castrations metaphoric, apocryphal, and real—these are just some of the spiritual realities that the historian of religions seeks out in the texts, rituals, myths, and people of the world's religions in order to experience and understand them "from within."[12]

What happens to someone who willingly enters this confusing "labyrinth"[13] of strange beings and bodies? Much, it seems, depends upon who that someone is. Many scholars of religion, no doubt, remain relatively unaffected, protected as they are by a thick skin of skepticism, objectivity, relativism, and religious doubt (all more than reasonable responses, I should add). But other scholars harbor no such grudges against religion and possess, at the same time, unusual powers of imagination, receptivity, discipline, and experience that allow them to enter religious worlds in a different way. For these scholars, academic method and personal experience cannot be so easily separated. "Objectivity" is transcended not in a shallow subjectivism that yields little more than private experiences (however profound and personally meaningful), but in an interpersonal communion with the object of their study that produces, among other things, powerful insights into the nature of religion that stand the test of time and withstand the criticisms and researches of the larger academic community. There is something genuinely mystical about the work of such scholars, for their interpretations and writings issue from a peculiar kind of "hermeneutical union." They do not so much process religious data as unite with sacred realities, whether in the imagination, the hidden depths of the soul, or the very fabric of their psychophysical selves. Here in such moments, I will argue, the hermeneutical understandings and insights of such scholars clearly transgress the boundaries of academic study or speculation. In their subjective poles, these understandings became personally transformative; in their objective poles, they produce genuine insights into the nature of the phenomena under study. These are types of understanding that are at once passionate and critical, personal and objective, religious and academic. Such forms of knowledge are not simply academic, although they are that as well, and rigorously so. But they are also transformative, and sometimes soteriological. In a word, the knowledge of such a historian of religions approaches a kind of gnosis.

Mystical Experience as Hermeneutical Process

Here I want to look at this academic gnosticism as it manifests itself in the twentieth-century study of mysticism, particularly in the lives and works of five major figures: the Anglican spiritual writer Evelyn Underhill, the French Islamicist Louis Massignon, the English comparativist R. C. Zaehner, the Austrian-born Hindu renunciate-anthropologist Agehananda Bharati, and the contemporary Kabbalah scholar Elliot Wolfson. Each of the essays is meant to be more provocative than definitive; that is to say, I pretend to no exhaustive summaries or analyses of these scholars' works and the secondary literatures surrounding them. Rather, I seek to read these authors' primary texts in new ways, that is, as mystical texts in their own right (which, as will soon become apparent, is not quite to say that the authors themselves were necessarily mystics). I also intend, especially in the cases of Underhill's *Mysticism* and Massignon's *Passion of al-Hallāj*, to creatively misread their works, rather shamelessly at times, as rhetorical portals into my own theorizing about the mystical and the (homo)erotic and what this might mean for thinking about male subjectivity, masculinity, patriarchy, gender, and religion itself. Another way to describe it is that I will be approaching the mystical traditions not directly through their own primary texts and histories, but indirectly through these traditions' representations in the writings of historians of mysticism. My assumption here is twofold, namely, that (1) these textual representations are overdetermined aggregates of both the traditions themselves and the psyches and bodies of the hermeneuts who write about them, and (2) similar hermeneutical processes of mirroring and reflection have always been at work in the writing practices of the traditions themselves (I do not, in other words, make a clear distinction between historical or "canonical" mystics and contemporary historians of mysticism). My five chapter-studies, then, are not innocent descriptions of five scholars' works and lives; they are excuses to theorize, strategies to advance my own thought, shortcut ways of saying as much as possible about a range of mystical traditions in as little space as possible.

Of the authors themselves, I will argue not that they were mystics in the traditional understanding of that term (except perhaps for Bharati, who claimed that he was), but rather that their work was driven by implicit mystical concerns, that at certain points in their researches their hermeneutical encounters took on powerful and sometimes genuinely transformative dimensions, and that—most important—these "unitive" moments were later performed in the semantic, metaphorical, and theoretical events of their writings, if usually through the discipline of an esoteric strategy or rhetoric and within a discursive space hollowed out, as in some Lurianic creation myth, from an eminently modern experience of absence, contraction, and distance. Hence, each of these writers (as well as this one) could say with Michel de Certeau: "Ce livre se présente au nom d'une incompétence: il est exilé de ce qu'il traite."[14] But such an exile is never complete, and the original presence or originative experience always leaves traces or "sparks" of itself strewn glistening and glowing throughout these authors' texts. To employ a kabbalistic metaphor, it is my intention here to imaginatively recapture or re-collect at least some of these sparks, gather them together, and present them as examples of a type of modern or postmodern mystical discourse.

While doing so, I hope to demonstrate that the phenomenon of mystical experience as it is encoded in the lives and works of historians of mysticism can best be thought of as an esoteric hermeneutical process intimately related to both the biographical patterns of the scholars' lives and their hermeneutical interactions with the texts, people, and rituals they set out to study. Here I am always reminded of the Bengali Vaiṣṇava tradition, which coded a similar thesis in alliterative theological terms: "*Bhagavān, the bhakta, and the Bhāgavata*—these three are one,"[15] that is, the Lord *(Bhagavān)*, the devotee *(bhakta),* and the sacred text (the *Bhāgavata [Purāṇa]*) are one—all three, we might say, "make each other up" in a never-ending circle of interpretation. To my knowledge, the Vaiṣṇava tradition never read this hermeneutical triad in social constructive, deconstructive, or postmodern terms (with divinity and textuality as human constructions that in turn construct the human), but this is precisely what I will attempt to do in what follows. Mystical experience, hermeneutical insight, and the construction of "religion" (or "mysticism" or "God"), I will suggest, are indeed mutually constitutive processes that "make each other up" in a triadic process of self, divine other, and text, none of which appear to exist in any independent objective fashion.

Here I have been especially inspired by Michael Sells's artful literary studies of apophatic language, or "unsaying," in the history of Semitic mysticism, and particularly his fruitful notion of the "meaning event" as that moment in mystical texts "when the meaning has become identical or fused with the act of predication."[16] In reference to his own focus of study, traditional apophatic language, Sells shows that, since *apophasis* must always "unsay" any posited "object," "thing," or "what," apophatic language developed sophisticated semantic, metaphorical, and poetic ways to perform the unsaying of these same objects, things, and whats; consequently, the *how* or act of predication of the texts merges with the *what* of its meaning (a meaning which, in the case of apophatic texts, is always receding). The result is what Sells calls the aforementioned meaning event: "The meaning event is the semantic analogue to the experience of mystical union. It does not describe or refer to mystical union but effects a semantic union that re-creates or imitates the mystical union."[17] Such a notion allows Sells to move away from the modern concept of "experience" (with its unapophatic, dualistic subject-object structure) and to approach the mystical texts as literary devices designed to evoke semantically the meaning events which they encode: "The mystical writers . . . claim a moment of 'realization'—a moment in which, again, the sense and reference are fused into identity with event. In contrast to the realization as an instance of mystical union which entails a complete psychological, epistemological, and ontological transformation, the meaning event is a semantic occurrence. It can occur to readers within and without a particular religious community (though its significance may be different for two groups of readers)."[18] My own approach to the texts of Underhill,

Massignon, Zaehner, Bharati, and Wolfson is analogous to that of Sells. Instead of ancient and medieval mystical texts, I will be looking at modern academic and literary texts, and instead of apophatic language, I will be examining esoteric and erotic language. Moreover, I will not be able to abandon the concept of experience, for it is absolutely central to our twentieth-century understandings of mysticism and hence inescapable for any discussion of twentieth-century writers on mysticism. But my approach to the mystical in these texts is, like that of Sells, primarily literary, focused as it is on how the texts perform what they want to say, how they engage in different rhetorics of secrecy to hide or camouflage the already textualized "experiences" of their authors in the movements of their texts, and how the rhetorical occurrences of these mystical meaning events might then occur to readers of their texts—in short, I want to delineate and to practice a *mystical hermeneutics*. In Don Cupitt's terms, I understand mysticism to be "a kind of writing," traditionally a very dangerous kind of writing that bypasses institutional channels of salvation and "melts down" ontological assumptions and their attending psychological structures to produce a euphoric condition of religious happiness in the here and now.[19] Although I cannot go quite as far as Cupitt, who wants to argue that language determines religious experience "all the way down" (I am too committed to the body as matrix and shaper of the mystical),[20] I am particularly fond of Cuppitt's postmodern model, since it effectively collapses the mystical and the hermeneutical, the past and the present, into a single textual process. Here both the classical mystical author and the contemporary scholar of mysticism (who, of course, is often commenting on the classical mystical author) can be seen employing deconstructive, esoteric, and erotic hermeneutical strategies, often at considerable personal cost, "to write their way and ours to a condition of personal religious happiness."[21]

In exploring this phenomenon of the scholar of mysticism as a type of modern or postmodern mystical writer, I will be particularly interested in the hermeneutical and literary impact the mystical experiences of such scholars had on their texts—both the traditional texts they studied and the academic texts they themselves created (I see these two types of texts as inhabiting similar discursive, psychological, and physiological spaces). Hermeneutically speaking, the mystical experiences of such scholars had some rather profound influences on their choices and readings of traditional mystical texts and figures. In regard to the literary impact of these experiences, I will argue that, whatever else we can or cannot say about the phenomenologies of their subjective experiences (and sometimes we can say very little), we can accurately and legitimately class some of the writings of these historians as "mystical" in at least two senses: (1) such texts rhetorically both reveal and conceal the religious experiences of their authors, and (2) such texts have the power to semantically reenact analogous "experiences" in the hermeneutical events of their readings. Mark McIntosh, writing about the work of Sells and its application to mystical theology, makes a similar point: "So we might say that a given writer's possible mystical experience is only a part of an ongoing event of meaning which moves *through* (a) textualization to (b) the interaction of text and reader and so on to a new *enacted* 'textualization' in (c) the transformed practices and perceptions of the reader."[22] Here the mystical becomes what it literally is, the "secret" *(mustikon)*, the secret hidden this time not in a psyche or a body but in the texts generated by both the scholars' hermeneutical interactions with the traditional mystical texts and their own religious experiences (which are in turn hermeneutically related to their readings of the traditional texts, to their writing of their own scholarly texts, and subsequently, to the reading of their texts). What this creates is a kind of invisible hermeneutical community consisting of the historical subject, that is, the mystic (who, of course, is part of his or her own historical hermeneutical community), the hermeneutical-mystical experiences of the scholar, and the hermeneutical responses of the scholar's readers.

Secret Talk: Dreams, Mystical States, and Scholarship

My approach differs significantly from that of Sells in one important and obvious way. Both Sells and McIntosh have argued—correctly, I think—that we have no access to the experiences of historical mystics, and that, "even if we did, the author's act of discourse has constituted a new public world of meaning that is not bound by the author's experience."[23] This is another way of saying that a particular text's mystical quality does not ultimately depend on the author's subjective experiences; to assume that it does is certainly to misunderstand and misinterpret a great many premodern (not to mention postmodern) mystical writers, for whom the modern invocation of "personal experience" was not a particularly meaningful move. That applies quite obviously to the historical record and the reading of premodern texts. There is, however, one crucial exception to this important rule: us. That is, although we do not have access to the inner states of historical mystics, we do have relatively immediate psychological access to our own inner experiences and their modern forms of consciousness. And these modalities of consciousness, I must add, are as historically conditioned as any we have seen in the traditional texts. Consider, for example, the observation, made most famously by de Certeau, that, whereas premodern mysticism was historically embedded deeply in traditional forms of liturgical, scriptural, and doctrinal contexts, modernity has witnessed an increasing deracination of the mystical from the traditional forms of authority and faith and an ever-increasing psychologization of its meanings.[24] Appropriately, then, Jean-Pierre Jossua's recent, and quite beautiful, brief survey of Christian mysticism, *Seul avec Dieu: L'Aventure mystique,* merges towards the end into an honest discussion of the impressive analogues that exist between traditional Christian mystical phenomena and the research findings of early French psychiatry and Freud's psychoanalysis on psychosis, hysteria, and other altered states of consciousness.[25] Add to this the dramatic appearance in the nineteenth century of radically different types of mysticism in the West, particularly Theosophical, Islamic, Hindu, Buddhist, and New Age varieties, and the semiotic field of "mysticism" shifts yet again, this time into a register loaded heavily with the ecumenical, universal, and often Jungian concerns of the perennialist and transpersonal approaches that dominated so much of the twentieth-century discourse. Both this psychologization or reliance on "experience" and this implicit universalism, of course, have been heavily criticized as inappropriate lenses through which to examine accurately the past, but the point nevertheless remains: these are the very structures of our modern consciousness, and if we are to write a twentieth-century genealogy of "mysticism," we simply cannot avoid them. To write about the study of mysticism as itself a kind of modern mystical tradition, then, is to address the category of mysticism in a manner very different from what would be required by a historical study of, say, medieval Christianity or ancient India. It is to write within a radically pluralistic context about a deracinated, essentially "floating" category with often only the most tenuous connections to the historical traditions,[26] and all of this within a predominantly psychological, hyper-reflexive mode of consciousness. In other words, it is to write about us. And this, I will argue—for all its political, hermeneutical, and epistemological problems (and these, I freely admit, are considerable)—is of crucial importance, for whether we admit it openly or not, it is these kinds of psychological experiences, our experiences, which have driven and given shape to much of the twentieth-century study of mysticism.

Lest, then, I leave the safe and comfortable impression that it is appropriate to discuss the mystical only if it is enfolded into the texts of famous historical mystics or major scholars, most of whom are now ensconced (and so effectively silenced) in death, I will also attempt to address here these same issues in my own life and work. To this task I will return repeatedly in a series of interchapter minireflections on my own dream experiences and the mystical states that accompanied them. Such "secret talk" is drawn largely from the contents of the personal journals that I have kept over the past twenty years and the reflection, analysis, and interpretation that I have applied to their contents over the course of these same two decades.[27] In 1989, while I was living in Calcutta and reading a biography of Max Müller, I learned that the Sanskritist had intertextually connected his own journals to his work on the Vedas by giving his journals a Sanskrit—and essentially mystical—name, *Parokṣa*, or "Hidden."[28] I decided to follow suit and entitled my own after a central rhetorical form of the Bengali texts which I was studying at the time, *Guhya Kathā*, or "Secret Talk," Ramakrishna's phrase for those esoteric revelations of his Tantric and sexo-mystical experiences. This, it turns out, was a more-than-appropriate title for these confessional volumes, as Ramakrishna, the Bengali textual corpus on his life and teachings, and my own biography (the *Bhagavān-bhakta-Bhāgavata* triad again) have met repeatedly over the years, sometimes quite dramatically, at times surreally, in and through this very same esoteric structure, as I hope to show in the "Secret Talk" sections.

Although quite rare, if by no means impossible, within the history of religions,[29] there is considerable precedence for such an autobiographically reflexive move, for example, in some forms of feminist comparative theology,[30] psychoanalytic practice,[31] and postmodern anthropology, particularly in the latter's reflections on participant observation (or more radically and honestly, "going native"), the ambiguities of self-reflexivity, and the need for identifying and mining one's own subjectivity and its sociopolitical positioning for theoretical insight.[32] Indeed, a few anthropologists are now writing seriously about their own transformative cross-cultural religious experiences and what they call an "anthropology of extraordinary experience,"[33] and others have begun to address the epistemological riches and limits of erotic subjectivity in the field,[34] an inquiry of particular relevance for the present study. Along similar lines, I have been especially inspired by the work of Sarah Caldwell, whose *Oh Terrifying Mother* weaves diary entries on her personal history of sexual and physical abuse directly into an ethnography of Kerala ritual theatre to throw hermeneutical light on both.[35] I will attempt something similar here in a text whose existential concerns, rhetorical experiments, and lines of argument circle around and around, if never quite reaching, the flaming target of a single event,[36] that Night of ecstasy and descent signaled in the epigraph to this introduction and discussed at length below in "Secret Talk: Writing Out (of) That Night"—the mystical "heart" of the book, if you will. Let it be said up front that I am not so naive as to think that such subjective experiences can be universalized into a general theory of mysticism or religion, but neither am I so foolish as to think that such experiences have nothing to do with the events and patterns operating in the historical mystics and their own texts. It is this tension between absolute identity and insurmountable difference that I will try to maintain throughout all that follows.

As will become patently obvious, my interest in the erotic nature of certain forms of religious experience is largely a function of my own mystico-erotic experiences and my subsequent attempts to make some sense of them through the history of mysticism. To speak the secret, then, is to speak both out of and about my own sexuality. And this, to put it mildly, is a bit risky. Part of my reason for attempting such an experiment is that I have become convinced, with Don Kulick, that "erotic subjectivity *does* things."[37] In particular, I would argue that it is here, in what Freud would call the primary processes of the mind linked to the pleasure principle and its libidinal energies, that the powers of hermeneutical, poetic, and religious creativity flow most naturally. In the world of Blake as well, for whom male inspiration is always determined by a man's sexual situation and, in particular, by the reciprocity of his relationship with a woman, to write out of the sexual is to write "at liberty" and to write only out of the rational is to be "in fetters."[38] Precisely because of this Freudian-Blakean confluence of the sexual, the poetic, and the mystical, erotic subjectivity can be seen as a particularly important doorway into hermeneutical insight into texts, and, even more radically, into a temporary dissolution of the self that can open one up to unusual, creative, often aesthetically beautiful experiences, not unlike any number of traditional mystical practices. I am thus arguing for an expansion of what we normally mean by the intellect, one as close (if by no means identical) to the Plotinian *nous eron* (literally, the desiring intellect) and medieval Christian understandings of love and knowledge (*amor ipse intellectus est*, "love itself is knowledge")[39] as to modern academic models of rationality, linear thought, and objectivism.

A critical scrutiny of the erotic subjectivity of historians of mysticism also provokes in a particularly acute way a whole series of hermeneutical and philosophical questions that otherwise would likely remain unasked.[40] Among these we might list, again with Kulick, questions about the validity and stability of the self-other dichotomy (an illusory distinction in most mystical literature), the politics of desire and its possible imbrication in colonial structures of exploitation, one's emotional willingness to be challenged and transformed by the erotic subjectivities of a foreign culture, and the ethics of fetishizing and revealing another culture's sexual secrets. With regard to the latter, Kulick writes: "Ethnographic success is often measured, and anthropological careers often made, by the extent to which the anthropologist gets others to 'open up,' as this process is so benignly known, and reveal secrets—magical formulae, cult fetishes, esoteric myths, hidden rituals, private experiences, golden stools. But what about our own secrets? What would happen to the way we understand and practice our discipline if success was also seen to relate to the extent to which we revealed secrets of our own to the people with whom we work."[41] On one level, this is precisely what I want to do here: develop a different way of practicing the history of religions, that is, through the burning focus of a specifically erotic lens shared, described, and psychoanalyzed on the public page. The eye which sees and interprets the other now turns back on itself to see and analyze itself. The gaze bends back upon itself.

I am perfectly aware that some, maybe many, will read this exercise as narcissistic. And perhaps it is. But, in the spirit of the present work, I would quickly turn this observation back onto the mystical traditions themselves and suggest, with any number of other thinkers, that many forms of mysticism are by their very nature narcissistic to the extent that they concentrate intensely on the self (its structure, its dissolution, its divinization) and attempt to return to primordial structures of consciousness that psychoanalytic thinkers, from Freud to Heinz Kohut and Sudhir Kakar, have labeled "narcissistic" (indeed, I explore this very theme in my first "Secret Talk"), but which we might just as easily call, following William B. Parsons, primordial.[42] A similar half-insight can be heard in the joking jab often heard in this century that "mysticism" begins in a cloudy "myst," centers itself egoistically on the "i," and ends in "(s)c(h)ism" (note again the theme of excess). But again, joke or no, the adjective "narcissistic" need not be construed as negative judgment; it is simply a statement of seeming psychological fact. I accept it as such and proceed down the road.

Accordingly, I begin by discussing the personal and, more specifically, psychosexual genesis of my thesis that the history of male erotic mysticism privileges a homoerotic structure and "exiles" heterosexuality into a conservative social utility (the first and second secret talks, "The Vajrāśva Vision" and "Heroic Heretical Heterosexuality") and then proceed to describe my own visionary, ecstatic, and hermeneutical experiences of Śākta Tantra ("Writing Out [of] That Night"). From there, I reflect on the descent and therapeutic patterns of that experience ("The Descent") and finally on the relationship between dreams and scholarship and the dialogical nature of hermeneutical work and self-construction ("Svapna Siddha"). Through such personal and theoretical paths, my own "roads of excess," if you will, I hope to both tell my own story in dialogue with those of Underhill, Massignon, Zaehner, Bharati, and Wolfson and quite literally perform the basic thesis of the book, namely, that scholars of mysticism often have mystical experiences that they then encode or "hide" in their scholarship, reenacting in the process one of the original meanings of the mystical as the "hidden" or the "secret" *(mustikon)* dimension of the text. At the same time, by moving back and forth in the "Secret Talk" essays between explicitly autobiographical themes and a discussion of relevant scholarly literature on these themes (oddly enough, the autobiographical essays have notes), I hope to suggest not only that professional scholarship and personal religious experience can be mutually enlightening, but more radically, that our modernity and now postmodernity demand an honest and unflinching uniting of the two.

Obviously, then, this text is not intended to be read on any single dimension. Quite the contrary, the esoteric rhetorical structure that I will argue lies at the existential core of the modern study of mysticism is at least quadruply enfolded here. *Roads of Excess,* in other words, is not simply a study of scholars of mysticism who have had mystical experiences and enfolded them into their writing. Rather, this is a study of scholars of mysticism who have had mystical experiences and enfolded them into their writing (dimension one) that is itself enfolded by a scholar's mystical experiences (dimension two), which have in turn been influenced by the reading of scholars of mysticism (dimension three), and which I hope will catalyze other mystico-hermeneutical experiences or memories in its serious readers (dimension four). A text about the mutual enfoldment of the hermeneutical and the mystical in the history of religions that is itself enfolded by the mystical and the hermeneutical; secrets (of the mystical texts) glossing secrets (of the scholars) glossing secrets (of this author) glossing secrets (of his readers) glossing secrets (of the mystical texts) in a never-ending dialectic of mutual enfoldment, criticism, and hermeneutical insight—that is what I am after here.

Toward a Comparative Erotics of Mysticism

Roads of Excess is also a beginning essay toward a comparative erotics of the history of mysticism, here conceived and half developed not through the standard philological work and textual analysis of specific mystics that rightly lie at the center of the study of mysticism, but through the erotic subjectivities and texts of the historians themselves—not so much, then, "What does the history of erotic mysticism look like within or to itself?" but more "What does the history of mysticism look like when we view it through our own sexualities and contemporary discourses about the same?" Again, my focus is on what we might call a psychology of the study of mystical eroticism and the hermeneutical reflexivity that makes this project possible, not on the historical texts themselves. What appears when we adjust our lens in this specific way? I will be especially concerned with the following: the consistent sexualization and gendering of religious language, the virtual nonexistence of heterosexuality in the mystical or its "exile" from the mystical, the recurring homoerotic structures of male erotic mysticisms, the ontologies of eros produced by different doctrinal systems, and the ever-present ethical problems of gender binarisms, projections, essentialisms, and hierarchies that in turn have produced a stunning, if often quite subtle, array of mystical misogynies. I will approach each of these topoi in at least three mutually imbricated contexts: (1) their appearance and interpretation in classical mystical texts and traditions as these have been studied by our five authors; (2) the manifestations and transformations of these themes in the modern lives of these same authors; and (3) their subjective, idiosyncratic embodiment and partial denouement in my own life and work. I must ask that none of these contexts be read in isolation from the others: they are all intertextually related. Consequently, no single dimension can be removed from the text without seriously compromising the remainder. In other words, my gendered and sexed reading of the history of mysticism and its twentieth-century study cannot be separated from my autobiographical trajectories, as it was the hermeneutical interaction of all three processes (history-study-life) that ultimately produced both my theorizing and self-construction in the first place. And something similar is true, I would argue, for each of the five authors studied here. The present work, in other words, should not be approached as a proper comparative history of erotic mysticism, as an exhaustive treatment of five different thinkers, or even as an adequate autobiographical essay. Rather, it tentatively participates in something of all three genres, advanced all at once with the wager that something of genuine significance (or at least interest) might emerge from this intertextual practice that would not, that *could* not, arise through any one of these three paths followed alone.

"The unfortunate part of trying to communicate (our spiritual) experiences," Evelyn Underhill once wrote, "is that we never manage it and at best only interest and at worse amuse or repel. Hence the deep wisdom of Saint Bernard's 'My secret to myself.'"[43] It is my hope that by taking the risk of merely amusing or repelling my readers I might throw some theoretical light on Bernard's *secretum* and demonstrate that, far from being simply a matter of British privacy or twelfth-century public etiquette, as Underhill supposed, Bernard's *secretum* more likely carries truths of deep theoretical significance for us, truths, moreover, to which we have some humble access through our own erotic subjectivities and their questions, that is, through our own secrets.

If, however, we are to use our own erotic reflexivity to make intelligent guesses about the history of erotic mysticism, it is important that we be as clear as possible about what our categories are, what theirs are, and how the two do or do not intersect. Accordingly, a few words of definition are in order, particularly with reference to my use of the categories of sex, gender, sexuality, homoeroticism, homosexuality, and the erotic.

Sexes, Genders, and Sexualities

Writing within the Anglo-American critical tradition, I will continue to use the problematic distinction between sex, sexuality, and gender.[44] Within this discourse, I understand sexuality to be a biologically driven instinct that, although perhaps genetically determined to some degree, is nevertheless open to the powerful forces of cultural and historical conditioning, which work dialectically with the biological givens (like a person's "sex" or anatomical genitalia) to produce a third, dialectical realm that is the human, essentially symbolic experience of sexuality. In David Halperin's always eloquent terms, "sexuality does not refer to some positive physical property—such as the property of being anatomically sexed—that exists independently of culture. . . . Unlike sex, which is a natural fact, sexuality is a cultural production: it represents the appropriation of the human body and of its erogenous zones by an ideological discourse."[45] Gender I understand as that culturally variable modal model of masculinity or femininity (or both, or neither), that is, the general meanings, values, and practices normally associated with being a man or a woman or a third gender in a particular culture or subculture. Certainly the biological rootedness of human sex and the cultural constructions of sexuality and gender are strongly correlated—hence, I cannot go as far as thinkers who want to opt for a pure constructionism,[46] although I find this position heuristically invaluable—but neither can biological sex and encultured sexuality or gender be facilely equated without serious distortions to the historical, anthropological, and scientific records (the ethical and political ramifications of such a conflation are equally disastrous). As we now know from innumerable studies, physical genitalia, gender identity, gender role, and object choice are all potentially independent variables that can be combined in any number of ways, as the history of mysticism, with its stunning array of same-sex communities, male brides, symbolic and real eunuchs, gender transformations, cross-dressing saints, androgynes, hermaphrodites, and other third genders so powerfully demonstrates. In Wolfson's terms, then, "we should speak of gender as a sociocultural construction that is a matter of semiology (reading cultural signs) rather than physiology (marking bodily organs)."[47]

Homoeroticisms and Homosexualities

One of my central contentions in reading the signs of this rich human sexual diversity is that mystical communities and literatures have offered some of the most successful, if still ethically ambiguous, venues in which alternative sexualities and genders have expressed themselves, and this often in otherwise quite repressive social systems—there are always alternative modes of being in a particular cultural order, however well defined it may be. I thus read mystical texts, first and foremost, as cultural sites of sexual and gender liminality, as semiotic openings to a more polymorphous erotic existence that would be impossible within the more orthodox parameters of the social register in question. Whereas sexuality is inevitably canalized into heterosexual procreation within most societies, here, in the mystical texts, it is freed, as it were, from such strictures and so is able to manifest itself in other, less "acceptable" ways. Among these the homoerotic certainly holds an important place, at least with respect to male erotic mystics in Western monotheistic traditions that posit an erotic encounter with a single male deity (the situation is very different in South Asian traditions, where a plethora of normative theologies of the goddess, that is, of a feminine divine, have allowed male heteroerotic mysticisms to flourish as integral developments within the traditions).[48] The history of male erotic mysticism, particularly in the West, then, is also a homoerotic history. By this, I do not mean to imply that most male mystics who employed erotic language to speak about their religious experiences also engaged in homosexual acts, or even that most of these same mystics would have desired such acts within some culturally and historically specific register: an individual's use or appropriation of a homoerotic symbolic structure does not necessarily reflect a subjectively felt set of same-sex desires or, more problematic still, a "homosexuality" as we tend to understand that term today, that is, as a relatively stable "state of being" or "orientation" (but neither does it preclude such a possibility). I am arguing, rather, that the historical processes of different male mystical traditions, with their constant tacking back and forth between individual psyches and public social structures, eventually created symbolic, doctrinal, and institutional structures that clearly privileged males who were inclined to homosexual desires and acts in their own historically and culturally specific ways. The issue, then, is not this or that case study (numerous exceptions can always be found), but the general orientation and sexual salience of the symbolisms as they were developed through countless individual psyches over large stretches of time. Put differently, what I am after here is what Gananath Obeyesekere, following Weber, would call "ideal typical situations," that is, those psychosocial contexts that occur with sufficient frequency and psychic intensity to find their way into a publicly shared projective system.[49]

Along similar lines, Wolfson has pointed out that it is notoriously difficult to discern whether or not we can posit actual homosexual practices behind the homoerotic structures of mystical texts and their communities.[50] I think that we must leave this question generously open.[51] My analysis, however, does not depend upon or presume the conflation of homoerotic symbolism and homosexual practice or orientation. It relies, rather, on a gender analysis of the symbols and gender identities that mystical texts employ. By "homoerotic," then, I mean to imply the textual existence of a male-to-male symbolic structure in which mystical encounters are framed along same-sex lines, often with the human male coded as female in a heteroerotically structured encounter. In Mark Jordan's humorous terms, "I am talking about rhetorical positions, not copulatory ones."[52] Put differently again, what I am after, then, is essentially a structuralist argument involving the formation of symbolic systems, not a dubious declaration about this or that historical mystic's subjective sexual psychology (although the latter will become important in my reading of at least some mystics and modern scholars of mysticism, for whom we have more than enough psychological and sexual evidence to draw reasonable conclusions about their psychosexualities). Even this qualified thesis, however, would have major repercussions on how we read male mystical literature, were it taken seriously, represented accurately, and not dismissed, as it so often is, through fearful ad hominem retorts, historical blindness, hopelessly naive, usually homophobic, models of male sexuality,[53] inadequate models of homosexuality that want to deny the adjective "homoerotic" or "homosexual" to any practice or pattern that does not fit modern egalitarian models of homosexuality,[54] and what Stephen Murray has so accurately called the cultural "will not to know."[55]

Accordingly, I would certainly not deny that any number of heteroerotic mystics and mystical theologies have existed within the Western monotheisms—in the Christian context, for example, one thinks immediately of Dante and Beatrice, of Jakob Böhme and the Protestant Sophianic tradition, of Blake and, more recently, of Pierre Teilhard de Chardin's essay "The Evolution of Chastity." But I would suggest that the specificities of such a list merely further establish my point. After all, Dante had to abandon Beatrice and follow the great Christian bridal mystic Bernard of Clairvaux, that is, a canonized homoerotic saint, for his final journey into the Godhead, Böhme's books were suppressed in his own time and became part of an important but largely underground esoteric tradition, Blake had to create an entire new mythological universe to express his heterosexuality (apparently, it could not be mapped onto the existing structures), and Teilhard was all too aware that in order to create a place for actual heterosexuality in Christian mysticism he had to overturn both the basic dualism of Christian matter-spirit ontologies and the gender logic of traditional symbolic conceptions of God as the male bridegroom of the female soul.[56] It is not, then, that heteroerotic mysticisms have not existed within Christianity, merely that they have inevitably been marginalized and ignored, if not actively persecuted, by the orthodox representatives of the traditions. Christian mystical heterodoxy and orthodoxy, in other words, follow gendered and sexed lines. The bottom line seems to be a theological and structural one: where God is imaged as a male with whom the male mystic erotically unites, the symbolism will, by definition, be homoerotic for males. If, then, we cannot speak of a "homosexual orientation" with these male mystics, we can certainly speak of a "theological orientation" and declare this orientation to be decidedly homoerotic.

In more radical terms, it is not necessarily the case that such a homoerotic theology attracted males who were already similarly oriented, as if such an orientation preceded the structures of society and language; it is just as likely that such a theology, embedded in an entire symbolic universe of doctrine, ritual practice, monastic institution, and social hierarchy, actually created, sustained, and transformed these very desires, desire being what it is, an intimate expression of collectivity, in Adrienne Rich's words, "shared, unnecessary and political."[57] Following Halperin again for a moment, then, we might say that instead of viewing mystical theology and bridal mysticism as an objectification of personal sexual psychology, as psychoanalysis would encourage us to do, we might instead see such symbolically expressed desires as an integral expression of theological doctrine and ecclesiastical and social relations. In this view, "[t]he social body precedes the sexual body."[58] I am not entirely convinced by such a move, as I prefer to keep the dialectic between body and society more balanced, but I do find it to be a position immensely fruitful to think with.

And things are more complicated still, for the homoeroticisms that we actually find in mystical literatures require considerably more sophistication from us than an unquestioned biologism that equates genitalia with gender identity and a sexual dimorphism that knows no thirds or boths. We also have to take into account the immeasurably important issues of political context, patriarchal authority, and social hierarchies. Once framed in this way, what we usually find in the literatures is what we might call, following Halperin and Winkler's work on ancient Greece, age- or status-defined homoeroticisms in which the male of greater age or status (in our case, God) penetrates the male of lesser age or status or, in the case of India, third-gender homoeroticisms, where the religio-sexual identity is formed through practices that are neither masculine nor feminine, such as we find among the Hijras[59] or in various mythological and saintly androgynous figures.[60] But most often, I think, what we find, both in the West and in India, is a simultaneously status-defined and gender-defined (or gender-variant) homoeroticism, that is, symbolically structured encounters between two males of unequal status (God being the greater) in which the subordinate male imagines or understands himself to be female in some sense. The obvious exceptions to this pattern, at least in South Asia, are the Tantric traditions, which seem to be, and I think actually are, structured around more heterosexual assumptions.

Some of the different sexual symbolisms and esoteric practices of Tibetan Vajrayāna Buddhism and any number of Śrī Vidyā and Śākta schools of the Hindu tradition come immediately to mind. But even these, I shall try to show, are more complex in their gender and sexual constructions than we might first imagine.

And the erotic complexities by no means end here. Quite the contrary; the further we move into the history of mysticism, the more fluid the erotic complexities become, as we encounter posited actual heterosexual encounters within a bisexual Godhead (Teilhard de Chardin),[61] male mystics uniting heterosexually with their wives in order to homoerotically arouse the divine male into activity (medieval Kabbalah),[62] male souls encouraged to abandon "lustful Venus" in order, secretly, to woo, kiss, marry, and experience spiritual coitus with the Virgin Sophia as the feminine aspect of the Logos or as the passive efflux of the Trinity (Böhmean Sophianic mysticism),[63] sublimated pederastic encounters designed to enflame the soul's polymorphous sprouting of philosophical feathers and wings through the excitement of a homoerotic gaze (Plato's *Phaedrus*) or to give witness to the beauty, love, and existence of God (medieval Persian Sufism),[64] third-gender returns to a primordial infancy that is neither male nor female *(The Gospel of Thomas)*, symbolic and literal sex changes (Christian gnosticism or Chinese Mahāyāna),[65] cross-dressing, transgendered *berdache* figures and the homosexual proclivities of shamans in various Amerindian, African, and primal traditions,[66] legends explicitly (and positively) linking the cultural origins of esoteric Buddhism and the introduction of homosexual love into Japan,[67] men imaginatively given spiritual breasts through textual interpretation (Bernard of Clairvaux),[68] women given penises through magical means or—the more usual method—reincarnation (Chinese Mahāyāna),[69] and eunuchs (who were often assumed in the ancient Mediterranean world to engage in passive homosexual activity) "castrated" for the sake of the kingdom of heaven.[70] This is the usual stuff of mystical literature, the "open secret" for those with the proverbial ears to hear.

The Erotic

By "the erotic" I refer to that specifically dialectical manifestation of the mystical and the sexual that appears in any number of traditions through a range of textual and metaphorical strategies which collapse, often altogether, the supposed separation of the spiritual and the sexual. In other words, I intend by "the erotic" a radical dialecticism between human sexuality and the possible ontological ground(s) of mystical experience. I thus use the category not as a reductive category to explain away mystico-erotic experience as simple sexual displacement à la Freud, but as a respectful, ultimately hopeful way of insisting on *both* the sexual rootedness of mystico-erotic events (with all the physical messiness and literal fluidity that rootedness implies) *and* the possible ontic source(s)[71] of those same remarkable experiences.[72] Here again my method is more Blakean than Freudian, although it certainly participates in both modes of thought. Sexuality for Freud, Diana Hume George has reminded us, "is the foundation of culture and consciousness."[73] To understand this properly, however, one must, in Freud's own terms, "conceive of the sexual function in its true range,"[74] that is, one must understand sexuality to extend well beyond the genital to the multiple erotogenic zones of the human body and to the various forms of sublimation we find in human thought and artistic expression. My own use of the erotic extends this "true range" even further down (or up) into the ontological. This is both a Tantric and a Blakean move and, subsequently, a kind of inversion of Freud's notion of sublimation or "making sublime," which derives the sublime from the instinctual instead of the instinctual from the sublime. George's discussion of Blake's understanding of the ontological roots of eros applies equally well to my own: "Blake reverses the causal relationship. We are sexual beings and live our lives, think our thoughts, in a sexual context. But intellectual energy was not originally sexual; sexual energy was originally intellective. 'The Treasures of Heaven are not Negations of Passion but Realities of Intellect from which All the Passions Emanate Uncurbed in their Eternal Glory.' ... He [thus] inverts the progression and derivation.... Freud thought that left to itself, sexual energy would not transform. Blake thought that only if left to itself could sexual energy build genuinely human cities and create fully realized relationships."[75] In this same spirit of sexual-spiritual expression, Blake "transforms the meaning of 'holy' from set aside, secret, hidden, mysterious, to its contrary: open, free, and fully disclosed."[76] In psychoanalytic terms, that which is unconscious must be made conscious, and that which is repressed must be expressed, since sexual repression too often leads to neurosis and human suffering. In Blake's "Proverbs of Hell," "[e]xpect poison from the standing water."[77] Nothing describes the spirit of the present work more fully than this movement from concealment to revelation, from unconscious dream and vision to conscious theorizing, from sexual suffering to personal healing. Only here, I will argue, in the freedom of disclosure and honest expression, can some adequate understanding of the mystical as the erotic begin to take shape.

As I will discuss more fully below in my "Secret Talk" essays, my own repeated experiences of the mystical and the erotic have made it intellectually and existentially impossible for me to read mystical eroticism in any other way. In the subjective light of those psychophysical events, both the traditional prudish allegorization of the mystical use of sexual language (as the metaphorization of an entirely "spiritual" or "transcendent" plane of experience) and the overt reductionisms of classical Freudian theory (as a pathological displacement of the sexual onto the religious) ring equally hollow. Although this may be putting it too baldly, I *know* them both to be false. What I do not quite know, and what the present work is all about, is how to bring into existence, that is, into a public theoretical language, a better, more inclusive model that can be faithful to the important half-truths of both of these positions without naively succumbing to either of them.

From Śākta Tantra to Critical Theory

Such a methodological quest, as will soon be clear, arises directly out of my hermeneutical engagement with the Bengali texts that have shaped my professional and personal lives over the past decade and a half. These texts, which record the life and teachings of the nineteenth-century Bengali Tantric mystic and Śākta saint Ramakrishna Paramahaṁsa (1836–1886), portray multiple and often conflicting visions of what the Śākta Tantra is about, but taken together they allow us to reconstruct a reasonably consistent picture of a radically deconstructive tradition in which a fearless hero *(vīra)* intentionally, systematically, and secretly engages in transgressive rituals, the use of impure substances, and illicit acts (often of a sexual nature) in an attempt to accumulate "power" *(śakti)* beyond the categories and purity codes of established Brahmanic society: divinity lies beyond, not within, the social constructions of caste, purity, morality, and the "rights" of dharma; consequently, power is accessed, increased, and assimilated by breaking the socio-emotional "bonds" of "shame, disgust and fear" *[lajjā, ghṛṇā o bhaya]*. "These three must not remain," Ramakrishna taught.[78] There are, moreover, commonly said to be two kind of Tantric traditions: a "right-handed" stream that interprets the famous antinomian rituals in purely metaphorical ways, thereby removing from them any real danger or risk (the Indian equivalent of the allegorization method discussed above), and a "left-handed" stream that refuses such sanitizing methods for a literal ritual engagement with the socially forbidden within a radical monistic affirmation of the sexual as the site of the mystical. Part of what I am doing in this text is trying to fashion a theoretical model of mystical eroticism out of my intellectual and imaginal engagement with this left-handed, transgressive tradition.

It must be said up front that these same Tantric traditions have functioned in ethically ambiguous ways in the discipline of the history of religions. As Hugh Urban has recently taught us, the Tantric hero has held a number of rhetorical, political and religious positions in the twentieth-century study of religion, from Heinrich Zimmer's warmly humanistic, Jungian yogin, who heroically projects and dissolves the gods within his own creative imagination and sensualized body, to Julius Evola's hysterical, fascist hate-monger, who "rides the tiger" of Tantra to catalyze Mussolini and Hitler's war campaigns against imagined Jewish conspiracies and the collapse of a hierarchical, racist, antidemocratic "traditional" worldview. Urban concludes from this:

> It is therefore all the more imperative, if we are to continue to study the complex traditions of Tantra in an intelligent and useful way, that we be as self-conscious and reflexive about our own "methods and paths." We need, in other words, to ask ourselves how our own personal lives and objects of study, our own political interests and scholarly products, are intimately entwined in everything we say and do. Why is it that so many of us—predominantly white, middle class, highly-educated scholars in the academy—continue to be so fascinated with the seemingly exotic, erotic, tantalizing and titillating world of Tantra? And to what conflicts and desires, what fantasies and failings—to what lingering "darkness"—does it seem to respond in our own troubled age?[79]

These, I think, are all important, if potentially troubling, questions. *Roads of Excess* is my attempt at a beginning, if still tentative, answer. Briefly, what I hope to show is that my own rhetorical use of the left-handed Tantric hero is united to a particular kind of mystico-hermeneutical experience, a dialectical type of psychoanalytic theorizing, and a distinctly modern ethical program involving the recovery and political support of socially and religiously marginalized sexualities and genders. I write left-handed, in other words, not to become a Tāntrika or advance a traditional religious answer, but to think *with* and *through* and finally *out of* the Śākta Tantric universe I hermeneutically encountered in such personally powerful ways within a particular Bengali corpus of texts. Obviously, then, whatever else *Roads of Excess* happens to be, it is a deeply personal document that I wish to present as such, without apology and without shame. I am perfectly aware that such a move is unorthodox (although, as I hope to show, not *that* unorthodox), and that it carries certain professional risks—this, after all, is one major reason that the mystical experiences of scholars inevitably become the unspoken secrets of their published texts—but I am convinced that such a strategy makes eminent sense.

Methodological and Historical Reasons for Studying Historians of Mysticism

I have often felt a need for some concrete way to demonstrate that the academic discipline of the history of religions can and sometimes actually does function as a kind of mystical tradition in modern (and now postmodern) dress. I have been struck and deeply moved for some time by the stories (Doniger might call them the personal "myths") that fellow historians of religions have shared with me over meals and telephone conversations and in hotel hallways and convention rooms across the country. I have always wondered how it is that these experiences, which seem to be so meaningful, energizing, and creative, are so seldom allowed a clear voice in public, published scholarship. It is not that I blame my colleagues for not revealing their own secrets. Far from it. The political dynamics that the academy, perhaps necessarily, imposes on us and the subsequent, and eminently understandable, desire to retain confidentiality render it difficult at best to discuss our own cases with any degree of openness—the secret is replicated again, not in the more traditional forms of indirect scriptural commentary or symbolic vision or, more tragically, torture and persecution (let us never forget that some historical mystics actually died for their revealing of the concealed), but in the intricacies of what I will call an *academic esotericism.*

Such an esotericism is necessitated, at least partly, by the fact that it is considered improper and in bad taste to share such "subjective" things in the academy. We talk *about* religion. We don't do it. I recall here a piece of graffiti I once saw scribbled on a study desk in the basement of Swift Hall at the University of Chicago, where I did my graduate work. A sticker was neatly pasted to the carousel. It read: "Please report any suspicious activity to the Dean of Students Office." Someone crossed out the word "suspicious" and penned in over it the teasingly rhyming word "religious." There is a certain wisdom in this minor piece of humorous vandalism. Professionally speaking, it is not wise to appear too religious. Religiosity, for various historical and social reasons, is too easily equated with fuzzy thinking, rampant subjectivity, and theological dogmatism. So recent was its birth from confessional theology and so omnipresent are the bestsellers of quacks and dilettantes that many scholars in religious studies still cling desperately to the scientific ideal of complete objectivity, as if it could somehow remove our troublesome humanity and allow us to study human beings as classifiable plants and minerals. This profoundly ambivalent attitude to personal religious experience creates a social context which in turn produces different strategies of secrecy and silence among scholars, most of whom must pass dissertation committees, get jobs, publish articles and books, survive anonymous peer reviews, get accepted onto conference panels, and so on. Secrecy in the academy, in other words, like any type of secrecy, is socially constructed. It has a particular history and a particular social context.

If this is so, it follows that this secrecy can be exposed to theoretical scrutiny only through means that challenge and displace and at least temporarily dissolve the social structures that support it. To put the matter differently, if secrecy is socially constructed, its breaking must necessarily involve a deconstruction of the social forms that keep it in place and constitute it as a viable and meaningful practice. But this in turn involves embarrassment and nervousness and a certain sense of risk, all emotions that come to us human beings naturally in situations, such as this one, where our common social structures are momentarily violated.

But this raises a further question: *Should* such structures be violated? Should scholarly secrets be revealed at all? My own position is that, in at least some cases, they should be, not because the public has some right to know this or that juicy detail about the personal life of so-and-so (that is only sensationalism), but because these secrets often carry far more than personal significance, that is, the mystical secrets of historians of religions are methodologically and historically important for the study of mysticism.

Methodologically speaking, we can locate at least three defensible reasons for studying such secrets. First of all, such mystical experiences often function biographically as crisis-events within which the scholars feel "called" to a particular path of study. In James Horne's terms, such experiences function as creative, problem-solving events that resolve, if only *in nuce,* some intellectual, moral, or religious dilemma and so determine everything that comes after them, including the scholarship that flows from these initial visionary events.[80] Expanding on Horne's thesis, I would go so far as to argue that, without these subjective experiences and the creative energies they release in the psyches (and bodies) of the scholars who undergo them, there would be no study of mysticism, at least as it has been practiced for the past one hundred years.

But it is not just that these experiences are methodologically important because they provide the historian of religions with the energy to carry through a particular project. Second, and more important, they are methodologically significant because they structure, inform, and even determine the hermeneutical choices of the historians who have undergone them. Which texts are studied, which passages "come alive" and so receive hermeneutical attention, which theoretical tools the hermeneut employs, what interpretations are finally reached—all of these are profoundly influenced by the mystical experiences of the historians themselves.

Third and finally, it seems to me that the legitimacy of studying a particular scholar's secrets hinges upon how significant and influential that scholar has been in the study of mysticism. The five figures I have chosen for this study are hardly insignificant personalities in the twentieth-century study of mysticism. Each of them enjoys considerable stature in his field of specialization. To study such scholars, then, is not simply to study five more individuals. In some sense, it is to study the modern study of mysticism, figure out how it works, how it does not work, and how perhaps it could work better. These are all theoretical issues that transcend any interest in the personal lives of this or that scholar.

But the mystical experiences of historians of religions are also *historically* significant. The levels and degrees of contemporary academic training, the range of theoretical sophistication, the physical accessibility of other cultures, and the sheer volume of information at our disposal is most likely unique in the history of human civilization. The fact, then, that historians of religions often have profound religious experiences in the midst of this training, between these cultures, and absorbed in this information is of some historical significance. In bald terms, the mysticism of scholars of mysticism represents something new in the history of mysticism, that is, a kind of culturally aware, psychologically reflexive, and theoretically rigorous religious positioning that struggles openly, if agonistically, with issues of reductionism, relativism, and religious pluralism, and this in a liberal cultural milieu that, for all its faults, nurtures and protects freedom of thought and expression, even—and especially—when it calls into question time-honored authorities, be they human or divine. How much did Bernard of Clairvaux really know about the biology and psychology of homosexuality and its structuring of his own bridal mysticism? Was Emanuel Swedenborg aware of the cerebral lateralization that shut down his voices and visions after his apoplectic stroke?[81] Could Ramakrishna have recognized the oedipal roots of his teaching that sex with any woman is to be avoided as a deplorable act of incest?[82] Could the Zohar have been written had its author(s) known of and understood a historical-critical approach to the biblical texts? Or were Hildegard of Bingen and Julian of Norwich fully aware of the patriarchal underpinnings of their theologizing and visions? The answer in each case is certainly no, not because Bernard, Swedenborg, Ramakrishna, the zoharic authors, or Hildegard and Julian were lacking in intelligence or wisdom, but because the very terms of the questions—"homosexuality," "cerebral lateralization," "oedipal," "historical criticism," and "patriarchy"—did not exist before nineteenth- and twentieth-century theory. Obviously, historians of mysticism, even as mystics, are in hermeneutical, existential, and psychological positions very different from those of the traditional mystics they study. In many ways, then, these historians of religions as mystics become even more interesting (and certainly more relevant for many of our own contemporary concerns) than the traditional mystics themselves.

A Blakean Spirit

Rhetorically speaking, I want my own text—its consistent lapses into what Massignon liked to call a "testimonial style,"[83] its choice of words, its theoretical leanings—to replicate or perform my thesis that academic writing can also be a form of mystical writing; that is, I want it to function as a kind of "meaning event" in its own right. In essence, then, my general method might be described as mimetic, reflexive, and literary. And although I am quite aware of the ethical and political abuses the existential position of the mystical scholar is prone to and will spend some time looking seriously at similar problems in the work of Massignon, Zaehner, and Bharati (as well as my own), my approach to the scholar as mystic is unabashedly positive, poetic, and romantic. Indeed, my ultimate hope for this book is a Blakean one, as hinted at in my chosen title, *Roads of Excess, Palaces of Wisdom*. The dual expression is taken from one of William Blake's "Proverbs of Hell," collected, as Blake tells us, "walking among the fires of hell, delighted with the enjoyments of Genius." "The road of excess," Blake writes amid these devilish flames, "leads to the palace of wisdom."[84] No one can be certain about what exactly Blake had in mind when he first inked these words around 1794 in what I like to call "Blake's English Tantra,"[85] his *Marriage of Heaven and Hell* (although his own psychopathological, emotional, sexual, poetic, and visionary excesses are well known and amply documented),[86] but it has always struck me as a particularly apt motto for the study of mysticism. For whatever else the mystical might be, it is more often than not that which exceeds and transgresses and goes beyond the normal workings of human consciousness. It is that religious technique which employs excess on the road to new forms of consciousness and their subsequent wisdom. Such excess may be located in seemingly sadistic ascetic practices (or conversely, in a hedonistic libertinism), in actual violence, be it physically or psychologically defined (extreme illness, car wrecks, and sexual abuse are particularly effective inducers of the mystical), in the cultivation of extreme states of consciousness, in antinomian rituals and behaviors, in the deconstructive powers of a pure apophatic reason, in the ecstatic joys of human love, in the use of psychedelic drugs or solitude or sleep deprivation, or simply in the psychological and physical rigors of a disciplined piety that refuses all compromise with the normal needs of any socialized human being.

My sense is that the philosophical and theological concerns of the twentieth-century study of mysticism—particularly the common core or perennialist discussion and the Kantian debate about the epistemological nature of mystical knowing—have tended to obscure the violence and sexuality and general excess of the mystical traditions, a recurring pattern captured succinctly by one common medieval Latin term for the ecstatic rapture of mystical love, *excessus*—quite literally, the excessive, the ecstatic, that which erotically enraptures one out of the normal boundaries of egoic consciousness in order to "liquefy" the soul in the male beloved.[87] I am thus frankly suspicious of the religious, epistemological, and philosophical conservatism that underlies much of the project. One reason I have chosen the scholars I have is that each of them, in his or her own way, has managed to preserve and theorize about the excessive and the extreme, not just as some "distortion" or "perversion" of mysticism that needs to be prudishly explained away or dismissed as irrelevant because it interferes with some ecumenical or disembodied epistemological agenda, but as something lying at the very core of these religious experiences, their psychophysiological generation, and their reenactment in text and interpretation. Such an excessive gaze will also allow me to anthropologize Western academic culture,[88] to make the supposedly familiar strange again, and to collapse the difference between the scholarly us and the foreign them; they are not so foreign, and we are just as strange. The roads of both the mystics and the scholars who study them, then, are often joined through this common motif of the excessive. Whether as a traditional mystical path or as a theoretical method—which is also literally a "path" *(meta-hodos)*—these are "roads of excess" that merit our closest attention.

The well-informed reader will note the fact that I am not the first writer to steal a passage from Blake's *Marriage of Heaven and Hell* to title a book on mysticism (here too we have a kind of history of the twentieth-century study of mysticism collapsed into a Blakean mode). Aldous Huxley did the same for his *Doors of Perception,* that revolutionary little tract written out of Huxley's own mystical-mescaline experiences whose theological implications so troubled R. C. Zaehner and so delighted Agehananda Bharati, as we shall soon see, and Huston Smith has recently drawn on the same discursive history with his recent collection of essays on the same topic, *Cleansing the Doors of Perception.*[89] *Roads of Excess* knows of no mescaline, but it does resemble Huxley's *Doors of Perception* in its creative reliance on a series of differently induced mystical experiences, which I will discuss in my "Secret Talk." Hopefully, as with Huxley's book, Blake's proverb of hell can be fruitfully applied to our task here, and when we are finished walking down five (really six) such roads we might finally arrive at our own "palaces of wisdom" and be able to address the questions that set us down those strange roads in the first place:

How are the cross-cultural, cross-religious mystical experiences that scholars often know in their researches possible at all? How common are they? And what do they suggest about the alleged independence of cultural systems of meaning and practice?

What relationship do such events have to the exegetical or hermeneutical work of reading and interpreting religious texts? Of reading and interpreting academic texts?

Can the history of religions, as an academic discipline, function as a modern (and now postmodern) mystical tradition? Should it? Does it already?

How might we interpret the consistently erotic nature of both the mystical traditions themselves and their refraction in the lives and works of historians of mysticism? Can these phenomena add anything important to our contemporary moral debates? More generally, what can our academic tradition offer us in terms of ethical reflection on the mystical?

Finally, what constitutes the historian's paradoxical "place," at once "inside" and "outside" the mystical traditions he or she studies and attempts to understand?

For most of these questions, I have often felt a certain Lacanian alienation, as if I were born into a linguistic register or symbolic system that is foreign to my own experience in the world. In different (and more positive) terms, the fact that some of these are questions without any obvious answers signals to me that they are important questions, since they seem to point to truths beyond or outside of our present theoretical paradigms, linguistic categories, and forms of knowledge. One could, I suppose, opt for silence and a certain despairing obfuscation before such seemingly anomalous experiences (the traditional, anti-intellectual "spirituality is beyond reason" answer), but such a response is not in my nature. Categorical confusion and seemingly unanswerable questions can just as easily lead to new paths, new understanding, and new forms of experience. I take as my motto here another line from William Blake, my poet patron of the mystical, who wrote in *Jerusalem* (10:20–21): "I must Create a System, or be enslav'd by Another Mans/ I will not Reason and Compare; my business is to Create." When one's experience finds no place in the systems of others (or much worse, in one's own), it is certainly time to create another. And although I will do my share of "Reasoning" and "Comparing" in the pages that follow, this book is first and foremost an attempt "to Create," to help fashion a language that can speak more adequately to the kinds of mystical, hermeneutical, and sociopolitical experiences that have defined the genesis, development, and social reception of my own work and, I suspect, the work of many other historians of religions. In doing so, I am wagering, in a Ricoeurian fashion, that such an unabashedly autobiographical exercise, so profoundly indebted to those who have written and thought before me, will speak deeply to other thinking, feeling human beings whose lives and works are driven by similar psychological processes, intellectual questions, and moral and cultural dilemmas. If this happens at all, my general thesis that the history of mysticism as an academic discipline shares in the history of mysticism as a historical phenomenon will be confirmed, and I, now rooted in a century-long community of like-minded human beings, will feel a little less lonely and a little less strange. And that will be enough for me.

ONE

Eyeing the Burning Wings

Analyzing the Mystical Experience of Love in Evelyn Underhill's *Mysticism* (1911)

> When Dionysius the Areopagite divided those angels who stand nearest God into the Seraphs who are aflame with perfect love, and the Cherubs who are filled with perfect knowledge, he only gave expression to the two most intense aspirations of the human soul, and described under an image the two-fold condition of that Beatific Vision which is her goal. . . . The wise Cherubs . . . are "all eyes," but the loving Seraphs are "all wings." Whilst the Seraphs, the figure of earnest Love, "*move* perpetually towards things divine," ardour and energy being their characteristics, the characteristic of the Cherubs is receptiveness, their power of absorbing the rays of the Supernal Light.
>
> <div align="right">Evelyn Underhill, <i>Mysticism</i></div>

> Only mystics can really write about mysticism.
>
> <div align="right">Evelyn Underhill, <i>Mysticism</i></div>

> Istiusmodi canticum sola unctio docet, sola addiscit experientia [Only an anointing can teach a song like this, only personal experience can make it understandable].
>
> <div align="right">Bernard of Clairvaux, <i>Sermons on the Song of Songs</i></div>

MYSTICISM'S ETYMOLOGICAL and discursive patterns can be traced back as far as the Greek mystery religions, where the adjective *mustikon* (from the verb *muo,* "to close" the eyes or lips) was used to signal the hidden or hushed quality of the ritual secrets. From there it entered both Neoplatonic thought—"Shut your eyes and . . . evoke another way of seeing which everyone has but few use," Plotinus wrote[1]—and Christianity, where it was picked up by the early church fathers, still as an adjective, to describe the "hidden" objective and transcendent world that the Scriptures secretly revealed through Christ (here again the mystical and the hermeneutical were fused) and which could be entered ontologically through the mysteries of the church's sacramental life.[2] From this philosophical, hermeneutical and liturgical matrix the term entered Christian intellectual history, winding its way through the centuries, always as a Christian adjective, until the sixteenth and seventeenth centuries, when, after revolutionary shifts in European religion, economics, and politics and the subjectivities that both defined and were defined by these shifts, the term finally became a French noun, *la mystique*. As Michel de Certeau has taught us, "mysticism" was now understood to be a realm of subjective experience independent of church and tradition and open to rational exploration. In effect, a new tradition of "mystics" was created, with "mysticism" now framed not as an encounter with a personal God or, much less, an orthodox Trinity, but "as an obscure, universal dimension of man, perceived or experienced as a reality hidden beneath a diversity of institutions, religions, and doctrines."[3] Mysticism had become "psychologized."

The modern study of mysticism flows directly out of these historical processes and the psychologization of mysticism that was their result. Thus, the twentieth-century study of mysticism begins with the publication of William James's *Varieties of Religious Experience* (1902), which defined religious experience as personal experience, "of individual men in their solitude,"[4] as James put it, and understood the theological, liturgical, and institutional features of tradition as secondary derivations of the primary stuff of this same personal mystical experience. One fruitful way to understand Evelyn Underhill's *Mysticism* (1911) is to read it as a transitional or ambivalent text struggling, never quite successfully, to reconcile these traditional and psychological, these premodern and modern framings of "mysticism." Is the term an adjective best used to describe the substantively prior revelations, Scriptures, and liturgies of Catholic Christianity? Or is it a noun that stands in for a universal human potential for a particular type of psycho-religious experience? Underhill's answer in *Mysticism* is clearly a double, if not duplicitous, yes. She thus can argue on one page that the mystics encounter an objectively real transcendent God and on another employ a whole host of psychological categories to interpret mystical conversion or visionary experience (the latter often rather reductively). It seems, then, that she wanted to psychologize mysticism, but not too much. Or better, she wanted to show that the traditional mystics had out-psychologized the psychologists, that they were "psychologists before their time" and, moreover, were better at it than those annoying modern amateurs, who could only see sex and the subconscious in the mystic's experiences. In effect, Underhill wanted to take mysticism back to its traditional, premodern roots, but enriched now with the intellectual gifts of modernity. That this would be a difficult, and perhaps impossible, task Underhill seemed to sense, and it is of some significance that she spent much of her life struggling to establish and nurture doctrinal, liturgical, and social ties to institutional religion. Here we might place her early (and failed) attempt to convert to Roman Catholicism around 1907, her later return to Anglicanism in 1921, her four-year relationship (1921–1925) with the great German Catholic theologian of the mystical Baron Friedrich von Hügel, and her later public vocation as spiritual director, retreat master, and wartime pacifist (she died in 1941). In modern terms, she had become something of a "public intellectual," always trying to make "mysticism" relevant, practical, psychological, moral, defensible, ecumenical, evolutionary, and—after all of this— somehow still traditional.[5]

But *Mysticism* is more than a transitional text, more than a casualty of our rough passage from premodern to modern forms of consciousness. It is also a literary record of its author's mind and heart. From the very beginning, the book's romantic, deeply personal engagement with the materials was obvious to its readers and, like the charismatic sanctity of the mystics who preached and prayed in its pages, strangely contagious; hence the book's phenomenal success in sales, longevity, and cultural influence. Strikingly, the book is still in print and widely available ninety years after its initial appearance. Never the equal of James's *Varieties* in phenomenological analysis or psychological depth and certainly far surpassed in philological expertise, historical scope, and theoretical sophistication many times since,[6] Underhill's *Mysticism* nevertheless remains something of a religious phenomenon, the power and influence of which demands an explanation beyond and beside all the obvious criticisms that have been leveled against its methodological and epistemological assumptions. Christopher Armstrong put the situation this way in his biographical study of the writer: "Evelyn Underhill's greatest book is distinguished by the very qualities which make it inappropriate as a straightforward textbook or *vade-mecum* to anything connected with mysticism. This is why it will probably continue to be read after numerous so-called objective or scientific treatments of its subject have long been replaced and mouldered into oblivion. The spirit of *Mysticism* may be summed up by saying that it is romantic and engaged rather than dispassionate and objective, empirical rather than theoretical, actual rather than historical."[7] In the terms of the present study, we might reiterate Armstrong's insight by suggesting that the text's rhetorical power and cultural influence reside in the book's ability to communicate something of its author's own experiences, doubts, and struggles. Although its author, trained by her upper-class society to keep the private and public worlds carefully separated, never openly discusses her own religious experiences in its pages, the text is imbued, from beginning to end, with her spirit and obvious passion for the topic. Plato and Plotinus, Meister Eckhart, Johannes Tauler, and Jan van Ruysbroeck, Richard Rolle and Dame Julian of Norwich, John of the Cross and Teresa of Avila are given a voice again and again within the text, but always with the permission of Underhill's selective and highly interpretive pen—in the end, this is *her* soul on the page. Evelyn Underhill's *Mysticism*, then, was, quite literally, her mysticism—a discursive art or textual practice where her own religious experiences and deepest existential concerns could come to know and express themselves, if always implicitly, always "in secret," through the selection, ordering, and interpretation of what she often called simply "the mystics." Little wonder, then, that the book's publication initiated a series of correspondences, with awed readers treating Underhill as their veritable spiritual director. She often accepted the role early in her writing career and eventually accepted the mantles of retreat director and spiritual guide as primary personas later in life. *Mysticism,* it seems, marked Underhill as a director of souls.

Underhill has been blessed with at least three fine biographers (Margaret Cropper, Christopher Armstrong, and Dana Greene) and a very large chorus of interpreters, dissertation writers, editors, and critics. I will not repeat or even attempt to reproduce their many accomplishments here.[8] Rather, my goal is to "read again" Underhill's *Mysticism* as a literary expression of her private religious life, examining in particular her developmental, psychological, comparative, and hermeneutical understandings of "mystical experience,"[9] especially as these relate to my own interests in gender studies and what I have called a comparative erotics, that is, the study of the different ways that mystical traditions employ, deny, construct, deconstruct, realize, and transform human sexualities. Consequently, after a brief discussion of Underhill's early life (part 1), I will turn to a set of three internal themes or rhetorical features of the text that structure its form, provide its movement, and establish a muted but nevertheless very real experiential subtext (part 2): Underhill's organizing metaphors of quest, road, and map and the role her mystagogic "mystical Christianity" played in constructing both this "Mystic Way" and its destination; her liberal use of and struggle with the early psychology of religion; and the analogous "illuminations" of the poet, artist, and mystical writer. I also want to address two external themes that I believe are of particular importance for any contemporary reading of Underhill's *Mysticism* (part 3): the problematic nature of her understanding of "mystical experience" as a "fact" more or less independent of the conditionings of doctrine, language, and history ("transcendent" or "supernatural," in her terms); and the central, if unacknowledged, roles that gender and sexual orientation play in the mystical experience of love as it is expressed and discussed within Underhill's text. Finally, I will conclude with a few words on Underhill's life after *Mysticism* and the increasingly incarnational signposts that largely determined its direction.

Many of these issues—for example, the artificial nature of all maps and stage theories or the analogously "illuminated" nature of mysticism and creative writing—Underhill was quite aware of and dealt with explicitly. Others—the epistemological complexities of "experience" or the informing influences of gender and sexual orientation on mystical language—did not enter the study of mysticism in their present forms until the last quarter of the twentieth century and so naturally did not engage Underhill in any explicit or open way (although both were present in different forms in early French, American, and German psychology of religion). Certainly it would be grossly unfair to expect a writer of 1911 to presciently address the concerns of one of 2001. Still, I have my questions, and these I will ask of her text. Such questioning, I would argue, is a perfectly appropriate response to Underhill as author, for this, after all, is precisely what she herself does in *Mysticism:* she dialogues with dead mystical authors, quotes them, romanticizes and idealizes them, criticizes them, occasionally makes fun of them (she was particularly hard on Madame Guyon, whom she once described as "basking like a pious tabby cat in the beams of the Uncreated Light,"[10] an image which she no doubt knew well from her own quite developed love of cats, those "purry," lazy, and often seemingly sadistic creatures of the domestic space and garden),[11] and asks them questions (some of which they could not possibly have answered), all finally to tease from their fantastically disparate voices her own, eminently modern answers. I cannot approach Evelyn Underhill as she approached Ruysbroeck or Jakob Böhme, but I can, I hope, say something about the modern study of mysticism by showing how Ruysbroeck and Böhme appear in Underhill's text when it is "read again" from our own time and our own perspectives.

1. At Thirty-Six

Underhill published *Mysticism* when she was just thirty-six years old, an impressive accomplishment for any age, but one especially unusual for a reasonably young woman of Edwardian England with no advanced training in the field. How did she do it? And, more important, why?

Evelyn Underhill was born 6 December 1875 to Lucy Iremonger and Arthur Underhill, a Wolverhampton lawyer. Evelyn grew up a happy, bright, and gifted girl in a well-to-do English suburban family. Neither parent was particularly religious. She absorbed, from her agnostic father in particular, a certain liberalism in things religious. Hence, on the eve of her seventeenth birthday she could write in her little black notebook that "it is better to love and help the poor people round me than go on saying that I love an abstract Spirit whom I have never seen" and confess that "I do not believe the Bible is inspired, but I think nevertheless that it is one of the best and wisest books the world has ever seen." "When I grow up," the same self-description went on, "I should like to be an author because you can influence people more widely by books than pictures."[12]

Evelyn seems to have known no dramatic revelations or out-of-body experiences in her youth, as many traditional mystics and modern writers on mysticism have, but she did know the reality of other types of consciousness. One in particular she described to a correspondent many years later (1911) as a result of what she called her "fainting spells": "in those I used to plunge into some wonderful peaceful but quite 'undifferentiated' plane of consciousness, in which everything was quite simple and comprehended." "I always resented," she goes on, "being restored to what is ordinarily called 'consciousness' intensely." She compared such events to the "'still desert' of the mystics" but expressed doubt "whether this is a very *high* way of apprehending reality" (L, 122–123). More significantly for our present purposes, she used such altered states to intuitively understand both poetry and literature through a kind of hermeneutical union. With regard to Blood's line "my grey gull lifts her wing against the nightfall" and Stewart's "Myths of Plato," she could thus write: "I recognized at once that they had had exactly the same experience"

(L, 122). Moreover, and more fascinating still, Underhill seemed to be able to capture something of this hermeneutical union in *Mysticism,* whose lines could then catalyze similar experiences, or at least powerful memories of such events, in some of its more sensitive readers. Hence Underhill's description of a twenty-one-year-old woman whose reading of *Mysticism* made her "restless and miserable" because she knew that she had once known the reality of which it spoke under an anesthetic only to have forgotten it later, much to her dismay (L, 123). The young Underhill, then, had had mild mystical experiences before she published *Mysticism* (1911) but was still questioning their epistemological value, even as her book on the same subject appeared. This questioning, as we will see, did not disappear as she matured.

Philosophically, Underhill went through at least three stages before writing *Mysticism:* atheism, philosophical theism, and Christianity. As she put in a letter, "[F]or eight or nine years I really believed myself to be an atheist. Philosophy brought me round to an intelligent and irresponsible sort of theism which I enjoyed thoroughly but which did not last long. Gradually the net closed in on me and I was driven nearer and nearer to Christianity—half of me wishing it were true and half resisting violently all the time" (L, 125). Unmentioned here but of some importance was a fourth influence: occultism (Cropper, for example, gives the subject only three passing, dismissive sentences).[13] Underhill joined, probably around 1903, the Hermetic Society of the Golden Dawn, led by the Catholic occultist Arthur Waite, whose many books, Armstrong reminds us, appear liberally throughout *Mysticism.*[14] Underhill, appropriately known as Soror Quaerens Lucem, "the Sister Seeking the Light," within the community, seems to have taken quite a bit away from her experiences with Waite's brotherhood. This, Armstrong concludes "is undoubtedly the moment when she first encountered and explored in a fellowship of like-minded seekers, the possibility of communication with the ultimate mystery."[15] No doubt as a result of such experiences Evelyn published in 1907 "A Defence of Magic" in the *Fortnightly Review*[16] and dedicated an entire chapter, "Magic and Mysticism," to the subject in her later classic. Underhill's early work, then, was influenced by those usually unclaimed cousins of Western religious thought—the occult, the gnostic, and the magical.

Also of great psychobiographical significance was Evelyn's early attraction to and struggle with Roman Catholicism, the tradition she considered to be her "ultimate home." Evelyn had been attracted for years to the church's liturgy, its architecture, and its art (particularly on two trips to Italy in 1898 and 1899), but her real conversion came suddenly in what she herself describes, rather elliptically, as a vision. It occurred shortly after a brief stay at a French Franciscan Convent of Perpetual Adoration, Saint Mary of the Angels, in Southampton. On a secret retreat (her family would have certainly objected to such "Romish" pursuits), Underhill had to finally flee (her verb) after four days, "otherwise I should have submitted there and then."[17] After apologizing to her correspondent for her "egoistical confidences"—"the honestest way is to be a bit autobiographical and explain, and then you can choose if you care to go on with me"—Underhill describes in a letter dated 14 May 1911 what happened next: "The day after I came away, a good deal shaken but unconvinced, I was 'converted' quite suddenly once and for all by an overpowering vision which had no specific Christian elements, but yet convinced me that the Catholic Religion was true. It was so tightly bound up with (Roman) Catholicism, that I had no doubt, and have had none since (this happened between 4 and 5 years ago only), that that Church was my ultimate home" (L, 125–126). Underhill would later write to her spiritual director, Baron von Hügel, of a relatively constant, "on and off" sixteen-year religious feeling that she doubted her mind could construct on its own and which she traced back to this same "conversion experience of a quite definite sort, which put a final end to a (very uncomfortable) period of agnosticism."[18] The vision, it seems, had permanently altered something in her.

Still, even this experience was not enough, for Evelyn had serious intellectual and psychological concerns that the vision could not apparently resolve. In essence, she could not fully accept Catholicism because it insisted that its dogmas were historically and literally true, that they happened "like the Spanish Armada."[19] Evelyn from her youth had interpreted her Christianity symbolically and rejected, as we have seen, the notion that the Bible is inspired or somehow literally true. Later she would develop this symbolic understanding into a more sophisticated and complicated mystagogic approach, rereading again the dogmas as psychologically true descriptions of a universal mystical process (here she both echoes Waite and foreshadows Jung). Also, ever the reluctant psychologist, Underhill was very suspicious of the degree to which "self-suggestion" worked its magic in the Catholic convents and churches, and indeed in all religion. She went so far as to argue that prayer and worship were forms of self-deception, pointing out that some of her non-Christian friends could raise themselves to high states of prayer with techniques utterly devoid of religious context.[20] This was a psychological and natural process through and through, she seemed to suggest, and she simply could not bring herself to surrender her "intellectual liberty" to it for the sake of a happy piety.[21] Hers was a remarkable intellectual integrity.

Two events finally closed, if never really resolved, the dilemma. The first was Pius X's 1907 papal encyclical *Pascendi gregis* condemning the "heresy" of modernism (by which he meant practically everything then associated with modern thought, including and especially biblical criticism). Since Underhill understood herself to be a modernist, she was appalled by the church's hunting down of the Jesuit theologian Father George Tyrrell and its suspicions about von Hügel, both of whom she deeply admired (there is a touching passage in her letters in which she describes visiting Tyrrell's grave—sculpted into the tombstone was the chalice that had been taken from him [L, 134]). The anti-intellectual, ghetto-like mentality that was now the official order of the day made conversion virtually impossible for her. To make matters even more difficult, someone dear to Underhill stood solidly in the way: her childhood friend and now beloved fiancé Hubert Stuart Moore. Moore was appalled by the rituals and superstitions of Catholicism and feared that a priest-confessor would stand in between them as a very unwelcome third (interestingly, Cropper suggests that Evelyn never told Hubert about her later correspondence with von Hügel).[22] Despite her religious convictions, her novelistic description of marriage as a "lower road,"[23] and her growing love of the Catholic mystics, Evelyn finally decided not to convert and to marry Moore, which she did in 1907. She thus chose a human love over a divine claim, and her intellectual integrity over her "ultimate home." In effect, she chose to remain an outsider, exiled from the religious tradition that she loved most and to which she had been mystically converted in the postretreat vision.

Underhill's position was now hardly enviable, but hardly uncommon for twentieth-century historians of mysticism; in effect, she was now suspended between two religious worlds (in her case, Catholicism and Anglicanism), neither of which she could fully accept. The central mystical event of Underhill's life, in other words, occurred in a religious world to which she did not belong but to which she felt inexplicably drawn; indeed, it occurred after a literal flight from the contemplative attractions of a celibate, same-sex community of Catholic nuns. The result? She would now drift further and further into what she called "pure mysticism" and become more and more set against the dogmatic blindness and narrowness of institutional religion: "I went on for a long time going to Mass on Sundays as a sort of free lance and outsider: but gradually this faded out in favour of what I vainly imagined to be inwardness, and an increasing anti-institutional bias."[24] Evelyn Underhill had become a true modern mystic, more or less deracinated from the traditions and yet dependent on them for her very thought and writing.

Armstrong suggests that Underhill's decision to choose her marriage to Moore over her conversion to Catholicism was one of the most important decisions of Underhill's life, one that marked everything that followed. I would agree, for here were encoded a whole series of conclusions and sacrifices that marked her thought throughout: the "incarnational" element in mature mysticism that renounces "pure" mysticism for human reality, the eclipse of "experience" itself for the mature service and equanimity of the spiritual life, and a disappointing inability to grapple with the political issues of gender and authority. Of the latter, Grace Jantzen writes that "Hubert Stuart Moore's attitudes here are less than open-minded, and his behaviour shows all the marks of a spoiled boy determined to get his way," and, citing Underhill's letter to Moore in which she renounces her "fads" for his "real interests," questions the ancient "wisdom" of a woman sacrificing her most cherished ideals for those of her husband.[25] Armstrong's reading comes to differently toned conclusions, although it just as clearly sees the importance of what has happened here: "Called as she no doubt believed to a life of union," Armstrong observes, "she was also committed by her love of her fiancé to incarnation." Such a practical life decision was "the greatest of her life": "Her teaching on mysticism as well as her day-to-day life as Mrs. Stuart Moore in the large house in Campden Hill Square were the continuing reflection of this choice."[26]

Mysticism, which appeared a few years after this failed conversion and this decision to renounce a mystical marriage for a human one, was in great part a dramatic response to a series of events in Underhill's life that placed her squarely and painfully in a kind of religious marginality or homelessness. In Peter Homans's apt terms, its writing issued from a kind of mourning, a mourning of lost cultural and religious objects that deprived her of culturally shared sources of meaning and drove her back into the unconscious margins of both her psyche and her Christian culture.[27] Armed with such analytic probes, which were no doubt partially fashioned from her study of and fascination with modern psychology, Evelyn Underhill was able to create something both ancient and new, her own uniquely nuanced category of "mysticism." There is "a lot of religious loneliness about,"[28] she once commented, no doubt self-reflexively. This too is perhaps why she turned to Blake early in her career and preferred to begin *The Grey World* with a Blakean epigram or weave paraphrases of Blake's poetic prophecies into its narrative.[29] Here, after all, was a kindred soul that seemed especially "modern," that is, free from the troublingly medieval baggage of church institutions and dogma that Underhill found so unbelievable.[30]

Underhill once wrote of her halfway house between agnosticism and Catholicism as a kind of "border land."[31] Taking up this same theme, Dana Greene refers to Underhill's confluence of biographical exile and textual creativity as her "life and work on the borderland": "Having experienced the occult firsthand, she knew of its bareness. Having been blocked from entry into what she believed was her 'ultimate home' of Roman Catholicism, she found herself where she did not want to be, on the borderland. . . . Newly married, she could not share her religious intensity with her spouse. At this crossroad, she chose what was at hand—the exploration of mysticism. This decision was unintelligible by many standards, yet everything in her life had led her to this choice. She embraced it with extraordinary intensity and energy; mysticism became her life and work on the borderland."[32] It is these very borderlands—textual, doctrinal, psychological, and sexual—to which we now turn.

2. *Mysticism* as Mystical Text: Mapping the Road for Others to Follow

Especially in the borderland, one needs a map, some direction to get around and, hopefully, to get home. That Underhill felt lost and desperately desired such a guide is evident in the metaphors that fill and indeed structure her own text: those of quest, journey, road, way, stage, map, and home. Indeed, two-thirds of this massive text (its entire second part) is dedicated to mapping out in great psychological detail the many stages and crossroads, byways and highways (and wrong roads) of what Underhill calls "the Mystic Way" (perhaps not incidentally, she translated guidebooks for naval intelligence during World War I [L, 29]). Her method, then, is quite literally that, a *methodos,* a "road" *(hodos)* to "follow after" *(meta)* to get back home. If mysticism is "our homing instinct" (M, 23), then Underhill's method is a dual attempt to awaken us to this instinct through the poetic shock of both her and her mystics' prose and to direct us along the Mystic Way with a helpful map. Like a good spiritual director, she inspires and guides.

If we take the advice of the alchemical Hermeticists whom Underhill so appreciated and practice the "contemplation of the Metaphor set up"

(M, 142) in *Mysticism,* what we find is that mysticism here is a process, a movement, a kind of psycho-cosmic development of the *élan vital* that vaguely resembles not only Henri Bergson's philosophical speculations but the later theology of Pierre Teilhard de Chardin (and indeed Underhill adored Bergson as a mystical genius of the first rank [L, 146–147]). Evolution for Underhill was not a scientific threat to be rejected but a deeply significant spiritual truth to be pondered and deepened through reflection on mystical texts. Mystics are "the torch-bearers of the race" (M, 27), and mysticism is "the crown of man's ascent towards Reality" and "the orderly completion of the universal plan" (M, 34).[33] Underhill's text assumes such a secret or "universal plan" (M, 34) and seeks, with the help of the mystics, to uncover and reveal the plan's details to its readers. Accordingly, as the chapters on the Mystic Way proceed from "Awakening" to "Purification" to "Illumination" (interestingly, always "of the Self," an eminently psychological and quite modern category, and this despite her later dismissal of the category as too individualistic and "psychological" [L, 219]), so too does the reader's religious imagination, progressing with Underhill the spiritual master through and on beyond "Voices and Visions," "Ecstasy and Rapture," and the "Dark Night of the Soul" finally to arrive at the peace, glory, and beatific bliss of the "Unitive Life." As the text ends, so does the Mystic Way, for the goal has been reached, the bliss won, the hidden treasure found. The text thus mimics or performs its thesis about the Mystic Way, imaginatively taking the reader through this contemplative process as it rhetorically recreates it as text. Taken as a whole, *Mysticism* is what Sells might call a "meaning event," a textual performance of that of which it speaks.

Although Underhill clearly wants to claim an almost scientific status, even an objective transcendent existence, for what she calls "the Mystic Fact," a term which functions as both a code term for the ontological realism of mystical experience and as a title for the first half of the book, Underhill seems to know that her map of the Mystic Way is not a literal one, that the idiosyncrasies of historical mystics always frustrate any attempt to crunch them into neat theological categories. In Bergsonian terms, she knows that the creative impulse is "free and original, not bound and mechanical" (M, 167), and that any attempt to construct a "composite portrait" (M, 168) of the mystic is, in the end, more a comparative art than an objective science (hence the artistic metaphor). Although there are real tensions here, which I will get to shortly, for the most part Underhill does not seem overly troubled by the artistic nature of her endeavor, and this for two reasons. First, she clearly wants to read religious doctrines and beliefs symbolically instead of historically or descriptively. Certainly, with her mystics, she can find much "richness and mystery in doctrine," but she is equally adamant that the adventures of the mystic are not those of the ordinary believer and that, consequently, this doctrinal map, though always true for the mystic, is not enough, for there are other countries into which the mystic ventures, and these "unmystical piety must mark as unexplored" (M, 125). Underhill knows that as she ventures into these "other countries" she is stepping, to continue the spatial metaphor, on dangerous ground; hence, her language becomes ambiguous as she both argues for the necessity of Christian dogma and suggests its symbolic or psychological nature: "Whether the dogmas of Christianity be or be not accepted on the scientific or historical plane, then, those dogmas are necessary to an adequate description of mystical experience" (M, 107). Dangerous or no (and Underhill's orthodoxy was seriously questioned more than once in her life [L, 140]),[34] this symbolic method was exceptionally useful, since it freed Underhill from the icy grip of a dogmatic literalism or pious historicism that would make the art of comparison impossible, marginalize mystical authors to a heretical fringe, and exile the possibility of a real divine encounter to a remote past far out of reach of the modern Christian. This Underhill, always the defender of the mystics, would not allow. She thus quotes approvingly the poet Coventry Patmore (who was paraphrasing Eckhart's teaching on the Birth of the Word in the soul), who wrote of the Incarnation "not as an historical event which occurred two thousand years ago, but as an event which is renewed in the body of every one who is on the way to the fulfilment of his original destiny" (M, 118). Perhaps even more important, this same understanding of religious language as symbolic allowed Underhill to make some very fruitful links among the poet, the artist, and the mystic, all of whom, she pointed out again and again, alter their states of consciousness and employ symbolic paradoxes to express what they find. Maps, then, are not bad things. Like symbolic dogmas, poems, paintings, and mystical visions, they are the products of artistic genius and speak, if always in symbolic ways, of fantastic psychic lands yet to be explored.

Second, and more radically, the subjective nature of comparison and her mapmaking project does not trouble Underhill since, following Bergson, she believes that all human perception, including and especially that of the "real" world, is the result of a similarly selective activity. The brain is a kind of filter, and its senses are normally attuned to only a small fraction of what the human being is capable of experiencing. In essence, everything is already selection and comparison:[35] "This real world, then, is the result of your selective activity.... Let human consciousness change or transcend its rhythm, and any other aspect of any other world may be ours as a result. Hence the mystics' claim that in their ecstasies they change the conditions of consciousness, and apprehend a deeper reality" (M, 31). Or in more mythological and light-hearted terms: "Did some mischievous Demiurge choose to tickle our sensory apparatus in a new way, we should receive by this act a new universe" (M, 7). Underhill's *Mysticism,* I would suggest, functions as just such a demiurge, tickling through its literary art the reader's consciousness into a new phenomenal universe, the universe of the mystics.

Mystical Christianity as the Essence of Underhill's Comparative Method

Still, when we read any claim about "the mystics" that begins "They tell us chiefly, when we come to collate their evidence" (M, 335), we must ask ourselves at least two questions: Who are "the mystics"? And just how does Underhill collate their evidence in order to tell us what they say? Both questions, I think, can be answered by examining what Underhill calls "the essence of mystical Christianity" (M, 119).

The "essence of mystical Christianity," I would argue, is another way of talking about the "essence of Underhill's method." There is a certain ontology—symbolic, dialectic, and Christian—that structures, even determines, Underhill's interpretive choices, evaluations, and final normative conclusions in *Mysticism.* At times that ontology appears as a seemingly simple dualism, with the fallen "world of sense" set over and against the transcendent, supernatural "world of spirit." "We are amphibious creatures," she writes; "our life moves upon two levels at once—the natural and the spiritual," and everything hangs on which of these two worlds we choose to make central (M, 34); in scholastic terms, it is a question of "substance" and "existence" (see, e.g., her preface to the twelfth edition). But even here, Underhill is sophisticated, stressing the "amphibious" nature of human life and the "at once" of its two seemingly separate life worlds. Moreover, her own chosen lifestyle—a married woman living comfortably in a wealthy home—suggests that, ascetic temptations notwithstanding, she never did buy into a true dualism. What we find instead is a poetically gifted writer working, always in dialogue with her mystics, on Christian doctrine with a certain philosophical acumen (though she always denounced the abstract "stony diet of the philosophers" [M, 120] and declared to one correspondent that intellectuals too often "miss the bus" [L, 178]), a pronounced symbolic or anagogic sense, and the dialectical, "incarnational" theology of her model and eventual mentor Baron von Hügel, who had published his two-volume masterwork on Catherine of Genoa, *The Mystical Element of Religion,* in 1908.[36] These volumes sat on Underhill's desk, and no doubt preoccupied her mind, as she finished her own *Mysticism.*

In philosophical terms, Underhill sought to reconcile Being and Becoming, the One and the Many, the Transcendent and the Immanent within a single dialectic that nevertheless privileged the transcendent primacy of Being over the secondary immanence of Becoming. Expressions like "the Absolute," "the Utterly Transcendent," and "Pure Being" fill her pages. But so do her claims that the most mature of mystical visions do not relegate the world of Becoming to pure nothingness or insignificance ("the nihilism of Eastern contemplatives," as she called it [M, 40–41]), but rather insist on the "seething pot of appearances" as "the stream which set out from the Heart of God and 'turns again home'" (M, 40–41). Hence, citing Ruysbroeck, one of her favorite writers, Underhill can claim that "the full spiritual consciousness of the true mystic is developed not in one, but in two apparently opposite but really complementary directions" (M, 35). The goal of the Mystic Way is to embrace this paradox and "take up these apparent negations into a higher synthesis" (M, 41). Such is the "*ultimo sigillo*" of the greatest mystics (M, 36). According to Underhill, this "limited dualism," or what von Hügel had called a "two-step philosophy," is the only metaphysic capable of explaining the facts of mystical experience (M, 43). In more personal but still dialectical terms, she would encourage her correspondents to allow the tobacco smoke of the parlor and the incense of the chapel to mingle and mix (L, 217) or to learn how to enjoy both the passions of the spiritual life and the pleasures of a good cup of hot coffee (L, 78).

One of the primary ways Underhill describes this dialectic is through the symbolic or anagogic use of the Christian dogmas of the Trinity and the Incarnation. It is a "historical fact," Underhill claims, that the mystical process has found its best map in Christianity, and particularly in Neoplatonic Christianity, which took up and synthesized the ontological insights of Greece, India, and Egypt with the warm personalism of monotheism. "This," Underhill suggests in one of her more pious moments, "was the priceless gift which the Wise Men received in return for their gold, frankincense, and myrrh" (M, 104–105). The result was the doctrine of the Trinity, which synthesized the philosophical insights into the ontological ground and monotheism's divine Person, and the dogma of the Incarnation, which heals in its notion of the hypostatic union "the breach between appearance and reality, between God and man" (M, 119). The history of Christian mysticism for Underhill is essentially (and I use that word intentionally) a working out of these two eternal dogmas within the vagaries and compromises of time (M, 107). Indeed, for Underhill, Christianity was a mystical religion from the very beginning, and the New Testament can "only be intelligible from that standpoint" (L, 148).

All of this had an immense influence on Underhill's stage theory of mysticism, and particularly its handling of non-Christian mystics and non-Christian religions. To examine these, however, we must first have some idea of the Mystic Way itself. How does it begin? And where did it lead? Expanding on the traditional tripartite model of the purgative, illuminative, and unitive stages, Underhill posited a five-stage model: (1) the awakening of the self to the spiritual life, (2) purgation, (3) illumination, (4) the dark night of the soul, and (5) union. The brief raptures, ecstasies, and intellectual insights of illumination concluded what Underhill called "the first mystic life." Many, if not most, mystical paths end here. Only the greatest of the mystics venture further into the doubts and dryness of the dark night and the final equilibrium and permanent stability of the unitive life, where the soul's communion with God is as complete as it can be in this life.

Now what is important to recognize about this stage model is that it assumes a definitive end in union with a personal God, that is to say, the map is a Christian (or at least a theistic) map and is not terribly friendly to mystics who do not fit neatly into its final doctrinal assumptions. Underhill seems to realize this herself when she chides the orthodox for condemning as heretical or mad the geniuses of Böhme and Blake, whose experiences simply did not fit the traditional maps of Christian dogma (M, 104; cf. L, 156) (I will explain later why I think Böhme and Blake did not fit). But she is less than charitable and hardly fair when it comes to mystics who did not and cannot be fitted into her Mystic Way. "It is unnecessary to examine in detail the mistakes—in ecclesiastical language, the heresies—into which men have been led by a feeble, a deformed, or an arrogant mystical sense," she writes (M, 149). Thus, occultism and illuminism (by which, I assume, she means early-twentieth-century magic and Theosophy) are "perverted" spiritualities (M, 149), the initiates of Dionysius knew only a "mere crude rapture" (M, 236), the early gnostics possessed an "arrogant and disorderly transcendentalism," the Brethren of the Free Spirit practiced a "spurious mysticism," and the writings of

Paracelsus were "occult propaganda" (M, 149–150). Perhaps battling her own past, she is particularly hard on the occultists, whom she describes as intellectually arrogant, egocentric, devoid of love, and infected with a "touch the button" mentality (M, 162); theirs are "confusing and often ridiculous symbolic veils" and "grotesque laws and ritual acts" (M, 154), in the end a confusing "medley of solemn statement and unproven fairy tale" (M, 155). So too with the quietist, that false mystic who equates her pleasure and bliss with divinity and will not venture further into the dark night of the soul, a more humble communion with a transcendent God, and useful social work. Many of the modern "mystical" cults, Underhill claims (using quotation marks to show her disgust), are crudely quietistic in this sense and "might well provoke the laughter of the saints" (M, 324), who are now of course standing in as rhetorical devices for Underhill. In a phrase imbued with sexual and gendered connotations and a certain muted humor, all such religious styles are described as "the dilute cosmic emotion and limp spirituality which hang, as it were, on the skirts of the true seekers of the Absolute" (M, 300). So much for objectivity. Who wants to be "limp"?

Continuing this highly prescriptive and colorful discourse in the guise of scholarly description, Underhill tells her readers that the greatest mystics have not been heretics, but Catholic saints (M, 105), who, like true mystics, detest the eccentricities and excesses of the heretics and mystical dilettantes. To establish this claim, however, Underhill must read her mystical texts in highly original and radically selective, if not downright distorting, ways. What to do, for example, with al-Ghazālī, whose mystically converted heart, he tells us, "no longer felt any distress in renouncing fame, wealth, or the society of my children" (M, 211), or Angela of Foligno, who "though a true mystic, viewed with almost murderous satisfaction the deaths of relatives who were 'impediments'" (M, 216). Interestingly, Underhill will talk about the specifics of Angela's "impediments" only in a footnote, where, it turns out, they were her spouse and children. So too with the Curé de Ars, who would not smell a rose lest it tempt him away from his sanctity. Underhill feels justified in relativizing the Curé's prudishness by denying that he was a mystic at all (just a saint) and by contrasting it with the aesthetic sensibilities of Francis of Assisi, who loved flowers and had his community plant gardens of them (M, 215). But Francis was a man whose eccentricities lay elsewhere, in, for example, his public stripping before his horrified father, a boldly voyeuristic act which Underhill can read only in moral terms, that is, as a sign of the saint's detachment from worldly things (M, 212). As for the gustatory excesses of Catherine of Siena and Madame Guyon, who consumed the bodily fluids of sick patients, Underhill will not even talk about them (M, 225). And so on and so on, through excess after excess.

It would not be fair to suggest that Underhill denies excess in principle. She does not. Indeed, she acknowledges that the religious processes of mystics are unusually intense, and that the mystical psyche is often of the "highly strung" artistic type and defined by an "extreme sensitiveness" (M, 223). They have "surrendered themselves to the life-movement of the universe," and so they live "an intenser life than other men can ever know" (M, 35). So too with their conversions, which are "raised to the nth degree of intensity" (M, 177). Excess, then, is acceptable, at least as long as it is orthodox excess and fits into Underhill's general model of the balanced saint.

But nowhere do Underhill's Christian and theistic assumptions become more apparent than in her discussion of a possible "sixth stage" of the Mystic Way, that is, the mystic's total absorption into and identification with the divine Presence. Underhill admits that there does seem to be just such a sixth stage in Oriental mysticism (by which she usually means Sufism), but because the acknowledgment of such would relativize and subordinate the entire Christian structure of her five-stage theory by effectively positing a "higher" and more "mature" stage after and beyond its theistic consummation, she simply cannot let this claim stand. Instead, she suggests, with absolutely no training or specialized knowledge of these cultures, that European scholars have misunderstood the Oriental claims. To prove her point, she cites al-Ghazālī and a particularly polemic passage aimed at the monistic excesses of Sufi ecstatics.[37] "In this state," the Sufi intellectual writes, "some have imagined themselves to be amalgamated with God, others to be identical with Him, others again to be associated with Him; but *all this is sin*" (M, 171). The italics, I assume, are Underhill's.

Such a move, of course, works only if one avoids completely—as Underhill manages to do—the numerous mystical traditions of Hinduism and Buddhism that argue in a variety of different ways for the reality of just such a monistic identity or absolute absorption beyond theism. This Underhill can read only as "the nihilism of Eastern contemplatives" (M, 41) against which the Christian dogmas stand irrevocably and justly opposed: "Unless safeguarded by limiting dogmas, the theory of Immanence, taken alone, is notoriously apt to degenerate into pantheism: and into those extravagant perversions of the doctrine of 'deification' in which the mystic holds his transfigured self to be identical with the Indwelling

God" (M, 99). The doctrine of the Incarnation again stands as *the* symbolic expression of this most basic truth of Underhill's Mystic Way: "In the last resort, the doctrine of the Incarnation is the only safeguard of the mystics against the pantheism to which they always tend" (M, 120).

To further guard against the challenge of a "sixth stage" and the ontological claims of the "Eastern contemplatives," Underhill adopts—in concert with a host of other contemporary and future writers on mysticism—a clear and distinct perennialism, that is, the claim that all mystical traditions share a "common core" or central message, which of course, in her case, ends up sounding very Christian. Perennialist language appears throughout Underhill's text, usually connected to the absolutist terms "all," "every," or "always"; indeed, such expressions are too numerous to count here (for a start, see M, 3, 34, 49, 54, 55, 96, and 101). Within this perennialist enterprise Underhill's symbolic, comparative reading of religious doctrine was again of immense help: "Clearly," she writes on a topic that is not at all clear, "all these guesses and suggestions aim at one goal and are all to be understood in a symbolic sense" (M, 54). Here too one might place Underhill's careful avoidance of a whole host of pious Christian specificities. When, for example, she asked her friend Margaret Robinson to read Eckhart's German for her, she specifically asked for passages that did not contain references to such things as "Our Lord" and "the Blessed Virgin." So too, "bits flavoured with scraps of Scripture aren't much good: but those in which the same things are called the Eternal, the All, the Divine Love, etc. etc. will be useful.... I want to make a synthesis of the doctrine of Christian & non-Christian mystics—so no 'over-beliefs' are admissible."[38] In other words, she was looking for material that could be spun toward "the Absolute" and so would be acceptable to readers who were not pious Christians; in effect, she was constructing a modern ecumenical mysticism, not simply reporting on a past that was, by many measures, disturbingly violent, intolerant, and bloody. Such language and textual choices allowed her to suppress real differences among the historical mystics (many of whom were quite happy to see their fellow "infidel" or "heretical" human beings burn at the stake or die at the sword) and to present their historically divergent voices as a common harmonious song.[39]

It is also important to point out that Underhill could accomplish much of this partly because of what she did not do, that is, spend time on actual historical work. Indeed, it is striking to see just how little historical context there is in *Mysticism:* virtually none. She admits as much when she writes, "[W]e must know a little of accident as well as substance" (M, 96), "accident" being here a reference to historical context and doctrinal difference. Here it is also instructive to compare her text with that of von Hügel's *Mystical Element of Religion,* an immense two-volume work devoted largely to a single mystic, Catherine of Genoa. It would be difficult to imagine two more different approaches.

We can now, I think, answer our initial two questions: Who are the mystics? and How does Underhill collate their evidence to arrive at her map of the Mystic Way? It is striking that, unlike James, whose *Varieties* is filled with contemporary letters, James's own (often anonymously presented) mystical experiences (another substantiation of our thesis), and the publications of numerous contemporary mystical movements, Underhill seldom uses contemporary materials or personal acquaintances to make her points in *Mysticism* (see M, 227, for a footnoted exception). Here at least, to be a "true" mystic one must be quite dead; hence Underhill's appendix on the history of European mysticism that ends with the death of Blake in 1827.[40] Where, we might ask, are the following eighty-four years? But the mystics must be more than just dead. They must also be canonical or traditional, or at least not too weird, and certainly they cannot be heretics, gnostics, quietists or, God forbid, modern-day Theosophists. Once Underhill has liberated the mystics from this motley crowd, she can then proceed to arrange their texts in a way that supports the teleological movement of her map; that is to say, she knows where she is going before she gets there and she makes sure that the voices of her text support this destination. In domestic terms, that destination is "home," that "mystical essence of Christianity" which could retain its Christian pedigree without renouncing (or being renounced by) the convincing findings of biblical criticism, comparative religion, and modern science. We have now examined briefly Underhill's interactions with these three components of modern religious thought. Her fourth dialogue partner was more difficult, "by no means an enthusiastic witness" and at times "thoroughly hostile" as she once commented (M, 138, 183). To this fourth, more contentious and troubling partner we now turn.

*Saints in the Salpêtriére: Underhill's Struggle
with the Early Psychology of Religion*

French psychology, Underhill wrote in a moment of exasperation and humorous wit, "would, if it had its way, fill the wards of the Salpêtriére with patients from the Roman Calendar" (M, 267). We can laugh with Underhill here (even as we say to ourselves, "Probably so"), but we should not forget in our giggles that Underhill herself was deeply influenced and quite convinced by many of the claims of the early psychology of religion, particularly in its American and French forms. The names of William James, James Leuba, Edwin Starbuck, James Bissett Pratt, Morton Prince, Pierre Janet, Henri Delacroix, Richard Bucke, and Henri Bremond—all significant figures in the early psychology of religion—appear often in her text,[41] suggesting to us that Underhill was deeply and existentially engaged with these authors and their claims, particularly as they pertained to mysticism, one of their favorite topics. Certainly she had done her homework and knew what she was up against. Consequently, her thought is particularly nuanced, subtle, insightful, if also quite conflicted here.[42]

For our purposes, perhaps Underhill's most important insight was her general sense that traditional mysticism and modern psychology were analogous human enterprises, that they were two approaches to the same subject, one "from the inside," the other "on another plane," "on the outside," we might say. Accordingly, what is needed is a two-pronged methodology: "Now, in dealing with this, and other rare mental conditions, we are of course trying to describe from without that which can only adequately be described from within; which is as much as to say that only mystics can really write about mysticism. Fortunately, many mystics have so written; and we, from their experiences and from the explorations of psychology upon another plane, are able to make certain elementary deductions" (M, 49).

Underhill was certainly not shy about making such "elementary deductions." Hence, she interprets conversion, with James (although never quoting him), as a shifting and reunification of consciousness around a new psychological center (M, 54, 176), reads visions as human products of the religious imagination "raised to the nth power" (M, 270–271), interprets ecstasy as a temporary domination of the surface self by the transcendental self (M, 57), writes to a correspondent about unconscious spiritual nourishment (L, 73), draws parallels between the emotional upheavals of adolescence and conversion (M, 62; cf. M, 176–177, and L, 199), reads traditional emanation models of the universe as psychological projections of the mystical process (M, 102), acknowledges the psychological wisdom of occult and magical practices (M, 161), and understands meditation and contemplative practices as "psychic gateways" into other levels of consciousness (M, 49) linked to specific psychic temperaments (L, 73). These are hardly elementary observations; quite the contrary, taken as a whole they function as a convincing and coherent hermeneutic that ends up further psychologizing the mystical. Perhaps what she meant by "elementary" was "extremely convincing" or "obvious."

But to psychologize mysticism in such a way is to uproot it further from its traditional matrix of ritual, theology, and community life, and this Underhill would not have. She thus tries to relativize and defang the psychological hermeneutic through a variety of rhetorical and theoretical claims, even as she continues to employ it. One of her most common techniques is to argue that these "new psychologists," at whose hands mysticism has suffered so grievously (M, 53), are really just amateurs, wannabe mystics, perhaps, who lack the training and transcendental insight to get things right. In other words, the mystics were better psychologists than the psychologists, and the psychologists are just bad mystics. Mysticism thus becomes a kind of *praeparatio psychologica,* or better, psychology is demoted to a kind of *degeneratio mystica.* Thus, she can write, with a logic that foreshadows much that would come later in the century with the human potential movement and its intellectual wing, transpersonal psychology: "One by one the commonplaces of mysticism are thus rediscovered by official science, and given their proper place in the psychology of the spiritual life" (M, 47). Similarly, she can argue that modern psychology, in its doctrine of the unconscious, has simply confirmed and acknowledged what the mystical traditions knew all along, namely, that there is an immense range of psychic life lying outside the normal reach of awareness (M, 52). Within this same understanding, we are told that Augustine was a "born psychologist" (M, 250), Julian of Norwich anticipated the findings of modern psychology with her belief that "we are more verily in heaven than in earth" (M, 68), the occultists were "psychologists before their time" (M, 161), and psychotherapy is just a "magic art" with a polite title (M, 162). As for John of the Cross, he was "the sanest of saints and the most penetrating of psychologists," whose words "our modern unruly amateurs of the 'subconscious' might well take to heart" (M, 275).

Behind all of this name-calling, which looks quite silly today, lies a gifted woman with a great deal of intellectual integrity struggling mightily with what was, by all accounts, a powerful modern hermeneutic that had to be reckoned with. Underhill understood, in her usually perceptive way, that the battle must be fought on the level of language, rhetoric, and metaphor. She thus called into question the ways that psychologists literalized the *sub*s and *un*s that prefixed their major categories. Why must the levels of consciousness that appear in mystical experiences be understood as an "under," or, much worse, a "not"? Why not instead describe them with a *trans-,* as in "transcendent"? This, I think, is precisely what Underhill was getting at when she ridiculed the ugly, hard corners of "those comfortable words 'auto-suggestion,' 'psychosensorial hallucination' and 'association neurosis'—which do but introduce mystery in another and less attractive form" (M, 266). For Underhill, there is clearly a "real transcendental spark" in the human being that cannot ultimately be reduced to the libido (L, 241–242). So too, the God of the mystic's experiences is not, as Delacroix had argued with respect to Teresa of Avila, simply "the normal content of the subliminal mind" (M, 108); quite the contrary, this God is a God of the trans-, "utterly transcendent to the subject rather than 'set up within the soul'" (M, 109). As if to fight back with the same weapons, Underhill invokes Teresa again, this time to point out, long before Ernst Kris's notion of "regression in the service of the ego," that "even the sick come forth from ecstasy healthy and with new strength" and that "something great is then given to the soul" (M, 61). Both Teresa and Evelyn had a point.

Underhill's final compromise with the psychologists was to accept them up to a point, the point where they reduced God to a precritical name for the unconscious: "It follows, then, that whilst we may find it convenient and indeed necessary to avail ourselves of the symbols and diagrams of psychology in tracking out the mystic way, we must not forget the large and vague significance which attaches to these symbols, and the hypothetical character of many of the entities they represent. Nor must we allow ourselves to use the 'unconscious' as the equivalent of man's transcendental sense" (M, 53).

One way to grasp the workings of Underhill's difficult compromise with the early psychology of religion is to examine for a moment her psychological interpretation of visions. She begins her discussion by objecting strenuously to any simplistic or literal reading of their content, to that "materialistic piety" that "drags down the symbolic visions of genius to the level of pious hallucination" (M, 267). Such a literalism, however well intended, ultimately ends up making a mockery of mysticism by exposing it to the convincing interpretations of the psychologists; in its silly materialism, such a pious process is as fatal to the truth and beauty of mystical visions "as the stuffing of birds" (M, 268). Instead, Underhill proposes a psychological and symbolic reading of visions, which now become "forms of symbolic expression, ways in which the subconscious activity of the spiritual self reaches the surface-mind" (M, 271), that she was quite aware might hurt the "feelings of the pious" (L, 101). Even here, though, she is cautious and voices her own doubts through a careful qualification plopped down toward the beginning of a sentence: "Visionary experience is—*or at least may be*—the outward sign of a real experience. It is a picture which the mind constructs, it is true, from raw materials already at its disposal: as the artist constructs his picture with canvas and paint" (M, 271; italics mine).

But what about that "or at least may be"? How *are* we to decide finally on the truth of this or that vision? Underhill is perfectly aware of the "big question." She puts it this way: "[D]o these automatisms . . . represent merely the dreams and fancies, the old digested percepts of the visionary, objectivized and presented to his surface-mind in a concrete form; or, are they ever representations—symbolic, if you like—of some fact, force, or personality, some 'triumphing spiritual power,' external to himself?" (M, 268–269). Here, of course, we see the specter of psychological reductionism, whose haunting presence generated so much of the theoretical excitement and religious angst of the early-twentieth-century debates about mystical and visionary experience.[43] Underhill is quite happy declaring that induced mystical states are nothing but "psychic tricks" (L, 149), and that some visions are mere autosuggestions, that others are "morbid hallucinations" or "even symptoms of insanity," and that still others are a mixture of psychology and transcendence (M, 269). Her ultimate criterion for deciding between these options is what we might call the criterion of fruits: do they "infuse something new in the way of strength, knowledge, direction" (M, 270), or do they simply cause more anxiety and suffering? Two observations are in order here. First, such an answer is quite faithful to the history of Christian spiritual direction, which "discerned" between spirits with just this insight. Second, it is important to realize that the very same position was voiced before Underhill by the American pragmatist William James, who proposed a "fruits not roots" approach to the evaluation of mystical phenomena of all types in his *Varieties of Religious Experience*. Underhill, then, was hardly being original here. Just Christian, wise, and psychological.

There is a fascinating passage in *Mysticism* that sums much of this up. In its theoretical content and rhetorical form the passage is a synthesis of William James and Jakob Böhme, neither of whom is cited. "The business of the mystic in the eyes of these old specialists," Underhill writes, "was to remake, transmute, his total personality in the interest of his spiritual self; to bring it out of the hiddenness, and unify himself about it as a centre, thus 'putting on divine humanity'" (M, 54). Whereas the idea of unifying the consciousness around a new center is probably taken straight from James's chapter on conversion in *Varieties,* the phrase "the hiddenness" is from Böhme, whom Underhill elsewhere acknowledges but again does not properly cite (M, 57). "To bring it out of the hiddenness" and "unify himself about it as a centre" is thus Underhill's rhetorical linking of the mystical past and the psychological and therapeutic present within a single metaphor, with "the hiddenness" functioning as another name for "the mystical" and the phrase "to bring it out" suggesting both the psychological cathartic technique of making the unconscious conscious and the mystical practice of contemplation that can reveal—bring out— another transcendent "sense" (M, 49). Here, in a single sentence, we have a crystallization of both Underhill's power and her problem. Both, I would suggest, are ultimately a function of her rhetorical and theoretical linking of mysticism and a modern psychological method. To their further collapse into one another, this time in the illuminative and contemplative states of the mystical writer, we now turn.

Those Who Go with Him a Little Way:
The Illuminated Poet, Artist, and Writer

Behind most of Underhill's writing, and particularly its epistemological claims, lies the assumption that the human psyche is controlled by two general forces, those of love and knowledge. The soul's destiny, we are told, is determined by which of these forces it chooses to control the speed and rhythm of its internal cinematograph and, consequently, the shape and scope of its experienced phenomenological universe (M, 69, 30–31). As is her custom, Underhill illustrates this conviction for her readers by imagining it in the theological terms of an ancient mystical writer: "When Dionysius the Areopagite divided those angels who stand nearest God into the Seraphs who are aflame with perfect love, and the Cherubs who are filled with perfect knowledge, he only gave expression to the two most intense aspirations of the human soul, and described under an image the two-fold condition of that Beatific Vision which is her goal" (M, 46). The cherubs, Underhill tells us in a footnote, are "all eyes" and the seraphs are "all wings," for whereas the former may gaze on the supernal light the latter are able to actually move toward it, impelled by the force of love.

Underhill was adamant (almost too adamant, it seems to me) about the superiority of love over knowledge, of the seraph's burning wings over the cherub's gazing eyes, and equally insistent, in an almost antiintellectual fashion, that discursive, rational discourse is completely incapable of attaining the experiential heights of "true" mysticism. The mystics know, "not by the dubious processes of thought, but by direct perception" (M, 37); only they speak from "the most complete experience achieved by man" (M, 42), answering our questions "in the direct and uncompromising terms of action, not in the refined and elusive periods of speculative thought" (M, 42). Moreover, she claimed, it is love that guides and energizes the quest for knowledge, not the other way around: "None think for long about anything for which they do not care; that is to say, which does not touch some aspect of their emotional life" (M, 47).

And mysticism clearly touched Underhill's emotional life, on the deepest of levels. Little wonder, then, that she sometimes let down her rhetorical guard to reveal a basic confluence between the study of mysticism and its practice. Consider, for example, her description of the vitalistic command to "[c]ease to identify your intellect and your self" as the "primary lesson which none who purpose the study of mysticism may neglect" (M, 32). Such a comment makes little sense unless we assume a collapsing of theory and praxis in her thought. Here too we might place her obvious disgust with those who "merely have reasoned" about the experiences of others: "If we are to acknowledge that they 'knew the doctrine' they must have 'lived the life'; submitted to the interior travail of the Mystic Way, not merely have reasoned about the mystical experiences of others" (M, 82–83). Such a language implies, if it never quite actually declares, that Underhill identifies most closely with those who have "lived the life" and actually walked the roads of the Mystic Way. In the end, Underhill believed that "only mystics can really write about mysticism" (M, 49), a revealing confession from someone who wrote five hundred pages for *Mysticism* and would produce hundreds more after it. If experiencing the mystical and writing about it are connected, then Evelyn Underhill must have experienced a great deal indeed.

What, then, do we find in the text if we go looking for Underhill's "actual experience" behind or within it? First of all, it is important to point out that such a hermeneutical strategy is an appropriate, legitimate, and even obvious method to employ when approaching her *Mysticism*, since such a method "mirrors" or mimics Underhill's own hermeneutical style, which always proceeded from the base assumption that there was a definite experience—she went so far as to call it the Mystic Fact (and to drive the point home entitled the first third of her book after it)—behind and within the mystical texts. It is this mystical fact of actual psychological experience that gives the texts their unique poetic power, rhetorical magic, and sacred "fragrance" (M, 331).

But, for Underhill, this hermeneutical insight into the text's experiential core is a dialectical claim that applies to the reader of mystical texts as well, for the mysterious success of mystical writers in communicating to others something of "that veritable country" that they have discovered through their own contemplative roads can be explained only by "the supposition that somewhere within us lurks a faculty, a spark, a 'fine point of spirit' which has known this country from its birth; which dwells in it, partakes of Pure Being and can under certain conditions be stung to consciousness" (M, 332). In a different metaphor, the process of reading a true mystical text can become an act of remembering and an experience of nostalgia; hence, a passage from Böhme's *Aurora* is described as "one of those which arouse in all who have even the rudiments of mystical perception the sorrow and excitement of exiles who suddenly hear the accents of home" (M, 256). The reading of contemplative texts thus takes on a decidedly mystical function for Underhill, as the divine spark of the reader is ignited, or at least set aglow, by the divine spark of experience shimmering in the text. The hermeneutical experience thus becomes a kind of spiritual awakening, an ontological "shock" into new forms of awareness and being. And all of this is possible only because the writer of the text and the reader of the text are endowed with the same ontological gift of Pure Being. Properly seen, they are one and can know this oneness in the meaning event of the text that performs a hermeneutical union across space and time, hence the case of the young woman, recounted above, whose reading of *Mysticism* awakened in her powerful (and sadly nostalgic) memories of a mystical contact with reality that she had known in an anesthetic state and then forgotten despite her best efforts to the contrary.

Given such a hermeneutical mysticism, how do we as readers of mystical texts and academic texts about mystical texts determine which writers speak from experience and which do not? Underhill believed that the existence of an experiential core could be affirmed or denied by looking for the psychological detail, the personal touch, the rhetorical clue that identified a particular passage or text as "genuinely" mystical, that is, as pointing beyond mere poetic flair or amateurish suggestion to an actual psychological experience. In the end, what we are left with is a kind of personalized intuitive aesthetics and a privileging of the autobiographical text over the stylized and the formal one.

If we apply such a principle to Underhill's *Mysticism,* what do we find? On the surface, at least, not much, for Underhill never writes openly about her own mystical experiences, at least here[44] (but the same holds true, as McGinn has reminded us, for any number of classical mystical texts).[45] Nevertheless, there are numerous places in her writing—in terms of both rhetorical form and actual content—where the states of the writer and the mystic overlap and seem to implode into one another. The most obvious and least dramatic example of this is the manner in which Underhill's quoting style results in a rhetorical situation where her own text quite literally *is* a mystical text, or better, a series of classical mystical quotations strung together, often rather loosely, with Underhill's brief glosses and transitional comments connecting them. This may seem like a rather superficial observation, but its end result is nonetheless quite significant, for what the reader often ends up reading is not Underhill at all, but Ruysbroeck, Eckhart, and Teresa of Avila selected and arranged by Underhill. It is they who teach the reader the value of ascetic discipline, praise the beauty of illumination, explain the psychological necessity of introversion, and sing the joys of contemplation. Through this rather simple method of quoting mystical authors (often at considerable length), Underhill has created a text which is both hers and not hers. Moreover, through this same academic device (complete with footnotes and proper references) she can both identify her own authorial voice with those of the mystics (this is, after all, her text) and, at the same time, preserve a certain distance from those voices (she is, after all, quoting other authors). Rhetorically speaking, then, the mystical subjectivities that keep speaking through *Mysticism* both are and are not Underhill's.

This rhetorical tension is collapsed somewhat further when Underhill abandons her scholarly voice and adopts the plural first person pronoun of the "family of mystics," to which she no doubt understands herself to belong. Here the details of history and the very real differences of this or that individual figure are all effaced within a rhetorical "the mystics" or a simple "we," as the tone becomes hortatory, personal, and edifying. In terms of chapter structure, such passages often appear at the very end of the chapters as a means of calling the reader to appropriate for himself or herself the practices and truths of the chapter discussion. "[H]ere we are, a small family, it is true," Underhill writes at the end of chapter 1. "We cannot promise that you shall see what we have seen, for here each man must adventure for himself; but we defy you to stigmatize our experiences as impossible or invalid" (M, 24–25). Through a simple rhetorical device, that is, the use of the first person plural pronoun, Underhill identifies herself with the historical mystics and implies, if never quite claims, that she shares in their experiences. Compare the very last paragraph of chapter 2:

"Come with us," they say to the bewildered and entangled self, craving for finality and peace, "and we will show you a way out that shall not only be an issue from your prison, but also a pathway to your Home. True, you are immersed, fold upon fold, in the World of Becoming; worse, you are besieged on all sides by the persistent illusions of sense. But you too are a child of the Absolute. You bear within you the earnest of your inheritance. . . . Appropriate that divine, creative life which is the very substance of your being. Remake yourself in its interest, if you would know its beauty and its truth. You can only behold that which you *are*. Only the Real can know Reality." (M, 42–43)

Here again, Underhill's "she" disappears in a mystical "we." The text no longer describes or explains the Mystic Way. It beckons the reader to take it up. The end result is a piece of scholarship become mystical sermon, and again, a type of hermeneutical mysticism: "You can only behold that which you *are*."

But there are other places in *Mysticism* where the text's actual content witnesses to this same mystical hermeneutics. Foremost among these are her two contiguous chapters "The Illuminative State" and "Voices and Visions." It is here, I think, in the illuminative state, that most densely populated of stages (M, 239), where we can best locate Underhill's own personal voice, still admittedly "hidden" within the distance of her academic prose. Underhill admits as much in her stray comment, shared with a correspondent, that her chapter "Ecstasy" was a stage—interestingly, she uses the term to refer to both the book and the mystical process—of which she had no more "scraps of experience" to go on: "I am glad [the chapter] *Ecstasy* is not entirely illegible. I have done it very badly I think: it was altogether too much for me—just piecing things together and guessing in the dark. . . . The book gets more and more difficult. I am past all the stages at which scraps of experience could guide one, and can only rely on sympathetic imagination, which is not always safe" (L, 106–107). But this, of course, implies that she *had* some experience of the previous stages. Perhaps, then, Underhill's experiences at thirty-six reached as far as the illuminative state (the stage-chapter before "Introversion" and "Ecstasy and Rapture") and its related "Voices and Visions," but not much further.

This hypothesis—that Underhill identified most closely with the illuminative state and its attending phenomena—is in turn supported by another distinctive feature of her text, that is, its consistently aesthetic reading of mysticism as a phenomenon akin to the experience of poetry, art, and, to a much lesser extent, scientific invention, all processes Underhill explicitly associates with the illuminative state and the phenomenon of the "genius," whose secret, she adds, "still eludes us" (M, 65). When knowledge rules the self of a genius, we have the grounds for scientific greatness, but when love takes over in this same cell, "the self's reaction upon things becomes poetic, artistic, and characteristically—though not always explicitly—religious" (M, 44). Mystics are thus like all "intuitive persons, all possessors of genius, all potential artists" (M, 62). Underhill's use of "intuition" here is both Bergsonian (a type of creative contact with the universal *élan vital*) and psychological (a tapping of unconscious forces). In reference to the latter, she can write: "In all creative acts, the larger share of the work is done subconsciously: its emergence is in a sense automatic" (M, 63). It quite literally comes "from beyond."

Within the same aesthetic hermeneutic Underhill can compare the creative states of Raphael with the contemplative experience of Saint Teresa (M, 64) and describe the born musician and the poet as the mystic's "cousins" (M, 65). So too with the prophet and the dreamer. All alike go with the mystic "a little way," that is, to the illuminative state: "Those who still go with him a little way—certain prophets, poets, artists, dreamers—do so in virtue of that mystical genius, that instinct for transcendental reality, of which all seers and creators have some trace" (M, 233). At some point, a little further along the Mystic Way, however, the proficient becomes perfect (M, 234) and "the mystic swallows up the poet" (M, 235), but this is exceedingly rare. Most never get much beyond the illuminative state, where the vision is a mental painting that the psyche brushes out of the raw oil and canvas of its cultural and religious matrix (M, 271). The visions and voices of the illuminated, in other words, "may stand in the same relation to the mystics as pictures, poems, and musical compositions stand to the great painter, poet, musician" (M, 272). The vision thus becomes a "visualized poem" (M, 286), and Underhill is not at all surprised (much less scandalized) to learn that mystical visions often look a great deal like the actual frescoes and paintings that the visionary lives with (M, 289). Mysticism is a kind of art.

It is also a kind of writing. Underhill, as we have seen, understood creativity to be largely a function of unconscious forces; in her terms, it was "automatic." But ecstasy too erupts from these same levels of consciousness; it is a swamping of the surface self by the transcendent self, which again is the place of true genius. Logically, then, Underhill sees in mystical ecstasies and raptures the seeds of artistic, poetic, and especially literary genius. Ecstasy is a form of writing. "Thus saith the Living Light," as Saint Hildegard prefaced her own writings (M, 276). To prove this point—admittedly never made quite as explicitly as I have here—Underhill approvingly quotes William James describing the raptures of Philo, the great Jewish author, as examples of "a true creative ecstasy" (M, 64) and marvels at the "automatic writing" of Teresa of Avila, Suso, Böhme, Madame Guyon, and Blake (M, 276, 257, 66), all great mystics and writers who wrote, almost directly, out of their ecstasies in a mystical version of those possession states so well documented in anthropological literature, "a condition of consciousness resembling the 'trance' of mediums," as Underhill puts it (M, 294).

"Though the same was with me for the space of twelve years," Böhme writes in his typically difficult style, "and as it was as it were breeding, and I found a powerful Instigation within me, before I could bring it forth into external Form of Writing" (M, 257): writing is a kind of repressed sexuality ("it was as it were breeding" for twelve years) finally let loose in a stream of words. Or it is a kind of compulsive fickle passion: "[T]he burning Fire often forced forward with Speed, and the Hand and Pen must hasten directly after it; for it comes and goes as a sudden shower" (M, 297). "I am really drunk with intellectual vision whenever I take a pencil or graver into my hand," Blake writes, hinting with the metaphor of drunkenness that consciousness is palpably altered during such states (M, 235). With Blake's cup of intellectual vision and the writing it bestows we are back to the notion that mysticism and writing are linked through the psychological processes of artistic, poetic, and visionary creativity. Nowhere is this more apparent in Underhill's *Mysticism* than in her discussion of Teresa of Avila, who not only knew the gift of automatic writing but found herself, as writer and reader of what she wrote, reacting mystically to the words as they appeared on the page. Quite literally, she found herself entering the very states of consciousness she was describing on the page as she wrote their descriptions down (M, 294–295). Writer, reader, text, and mystical experience are truly one here in a particularly dramatic example of that hermeneutical mysticism I have made the focus of the present work.

Finally, there is still one more feature of Underhill's Mystic Way that suggests a linking of mystical experience and discursive knowledge, even if it insists on privileging the former over the latter. Enter the ancient category of "contemplation," perhaps the best traditional analogue for our own very modern term "mysticism." Contemplation for Underhill, like so much else about the spiritual life, is an "art" that manifests human genius on another plane of activity (M, 299). It is an "extreme form of that withdrawal of attention" that determines the creativity of musician, painter, and poet alike (M, 299). In most cases, contemplation requires considerable technical training, but, again much as we do in art, we occasionally encounter the born prodigy, the "sudden masterpiece" that seems to come out of nowhere (M, 299). Two epistemological features of the contemplative act are especially relevant for us here: its ability to unify and focus a person's powers within a single act of knowing, and its mystical ability to unify the knower and the known. Contemplation, Underhill tells her readers, is "a supreme manifestation of that indivisible 'power of knowing'" in which the human person's "'made Trinity' of thought, love, and will" becomes a Unity (M, 329). The cherub's eyes and the seraph's wings thus join forces in a "self-merging" that in turn effects a "real communion between the seer and the seen" (M, 300) and allows us to apprehend reality "by way of participation, not by way of observation" (M, 333). Pace Kant, a "'Mystic Marriage' has taken place between the mind and some aspect of the external world" (M, 302). Knowledge has become eroticized. It is a form of love.

Much to her credit, Underhill recognizes that such claims are difficult, if not impossible, to establish. Consequently, once again rhetorically mimicking her subject matter, she adopts a strategy that innumerable mystical writers had adopted before her, the strategy of esotericism: "Those who have seen are quite convinced: those who have not seen, can never be told" (M, 331). *Mysticism* thus falls silent, not for a lack of words (there are plenty of those to go around), but for a lack of a proper audience.

3. Reading *Mysticism* Today: Debating the Nature of (Sexual) Experience

Having contextualized *Mysticism* within the specific religious, intellectual, and marital details of Underhill's life and explored the various ways that her hermeneutical and rhetorical strategies interact and even merge within the Mystic Way, we come to the most basic issue of all in Underhill's writing, the category of "experience" itself. I approach the "mystical experience" of Underhill's *Mysticism* first as an epistemological claim and then explore its unacknowledged sexual dimensions.

The Problem of "Experience" in Underhill's Writings

Nowhere does Underhill appear more dated than in her epistemological understandings of mystical experience as a "fact" prior to the conditionings of text, doctrine, and community. We can hardly fault her for this, since this was the reigning assumption for much of the twentieth-century discussion of mysticism, and indeed still is in many corners. Nevertheless, if Underhill is to be appropriated at all for contemporary studies of mysticism, we must deal honestly and critically with this aspect of her thought.

Underhill's epistemological assumptions appear throughout *Mysticism,* where they are seldom disguised and often celebrated. The mystic, we are told, is superior to the materialist, the idealist, and the skeptic since he substitutes "his living experience for their conceptual schemes" (M, 26), the implication being of course that mystical experience is not structured by any such conceptual schemes. In this same vein, we read that the mystic solves the problems of life "not by the dubious processes of thought, but by direct perception" (M, 37), and we are taught to reject all abstract philosophical propositions as "hopelessly academic" (M, 110). Even mystical philosophy or theology, with their ancient and noble pedigrees, are merely "the comment of the intellect on the proceedings of spiritual intuition" (M, 95). The mystic "tastes supreme experience," whereas the mystical philosopher only "cogitates upon the data so obtained" by others (M, 95), we are told yet again in a passage that sounds more like a description of the digestive process than an evaluation of two different kinds of mystical texts. Underhill goes so far as to suggest that the "true" mystic hardly needs a map at all. His humility forces him to use the map of his own community to communicate with others, but in truth his discoveries are independent of any such necessity (M, 104). He wanders the country free, we assume. Here Underhill could not be further from contemporary interest in how what Underhill calls the "hopelessly academic" helps construct, if not actually determines, the country itself. Hans Jonas, the scholar of gnosticism, is often cited in this context. Interestingly, he employs the same base metaphor Underhill used—the way—but employs it with very different epistemological assumptions: "[W]ithout an antecedent dogmatics there would be no valid mysticism.... in order that certain experiences may become possible and even conceivable ... speculation must have set the framework, the way, and the goal—long before the subjectivity has learned to walk the way."[46] And indeed, Underhill's own spiritual director, Baron von Hügel, would make the same point when he pointed out to his directee that the church came first and the mystics later (L, 21), but this was well after *Mysticism.*

Underhill's rejection of mystical philosophy and theology in turn informs her choice of texts as well as her particular readings of them. Mystical literature is, by definition, literature "of the first-hand type" (M, 39);

hence, we must be especially careful to distinguish between mere poetry or suggestion and texts based "on a concrete and definite psychological experience" (M, 254). We must look for passages that have that "strange note of certainty," a "stranger note of passion" (more on this in a moment), and an "odd realism," all of which suggest a source in experience rather than tradition (M, 338). Catherine of Genoa's *Treatise on Purgatory,* for example, is "clearly founded upon first-hand mystic experience," and this "is all that our present purpose requires" (M, 202). What is clear about this we are never told.

Three different theoretical moves further undergird and support all of this: Underhill's symbolic understanding of religious language, her perennialism, and the Jamesian notion of ineffability. All three appear in the following passage: "[A]ll these transcendental theories are only symbols, methods, diagrams; feebly attempting the representation of an experience which in its fullness is always the same, and of which the dominant characteristic is ineffability" (M, 101). Unfortunately, to defend her perennialism from the specter of genuine difference, Underhill must condemn "the eccentric" (what, other than difference, makes him so strange?) and the individualist as either heretical or insane: "The best and truest experience does not come to the eccentric and individual pilgrim whose intuitions are his only law: but rather to him who is willing to profit by the culture of the spiritual society in which he finds himself, and submit personal intuition to the guidance afforded by the general history of the mystic type. Those who refuse this guidance expose themselves to all the dangers which crowd about the individualist: from heresy at one end of the scale to madness at the other" (M, 300). This, of course, all but guarantees a conservative, orthodox, and safe construction of mysticism. It also erases a great deal, perhaps most, of the history of mysticism from our view. This, no doubt, is also why Underhill tended to reject visions and auditions as inappropriate markers of the mystical: they, after all, were their own representations, their own authorities. As such, they stood apart from tradition and ecclesiastical authority as dangerously different and idiosyncratic.

In the end, what Underhill cannot see is that even the most orthodox of mystics are not reporting on some independent objective experience but interpreting a highly subjective state that may or may not be engaging noumenal ground, and all this with categories that not only describe the experience after the fact but help shape and form and guide the event within the experience itself. Experience itself is interpretation.[47] There are places in Underhill's text that can be read in this way, even if

Underhill herself fails to do so. Consider, for example, one of the many Suso quotes that appear in *Mysticism:* "If that which I see and feel be not the Kingdom of Heaven, I know not what it can be" (M, 187). Here, from a celibate man whose ascetic self-violence is virtually unmatched in the history of Christian mysticism, who suffered intensely from psychosomatic conditions, and who considered himself to be the bride of Christ, we have an honest "if," an open acknowledgement that "what I see and feel" might be interpreted along very different lines. Erotic lines, for example.

What the Seraph's Wings Conceal:
Tracing the Erotic through the Text

Dionysius's burning-winged seraph appears initially in the vision of the prophet Isaiah, where it hovers before the presence of Yahweh to announce the majesty, glory, and holiness of the divine Presence in the temple (Isaiah 6). A terrified Isaiah describes the strange angelic being in the text as possessing six wings, two with which it flies, two of which it uses to shield its face from the divine Presence, and two of which conceal its own "feet," a biblical euphemism for the genitals.[48] Underhill, as we have seen, used Dionysius's winged seraph to symbolize the superior powers of love, which moves the soul toward the divine. The cherub, we are told, being "all eyes," sees but cannot advance. It is winged love, not eyeing knowledge, burning passion, not lucid observation, that constitutes the secret heart of the mystical for Underhill. Still, if we read again her *Mysticism* in the light of current developments in religious studies, particularly those involving the gender analysis of texts, we can quickly detect something underneath and behind love's wings. We can "eye the burning wings" and see what they are concealing, even if Underhill herself would no doubt object—perhaps rather strenuously—to what we claim to see with the many eyes of our new methods.

We have already seen Underhill giving voice to and then silencing the American and French psychologists in her text, no doubt because of their infamous penchant for isolating psychopathological and sexual motifs in religious expressions of all types. The sexuality of the mystics in particular was something well outside the boundaries for her, a borderland she would not enter, a form of mystical excess she could not accept. Granted, Underhill seems quite comfortable with "love," even "passion," in the mystics and consistently analogizes the spiritual life as an experience of human love on a higher plane and to a greater intensity, "to the nth degree," as she liked to say. She can thus write that the mystic's "awakening to consciousness of the Absolute . . . does but reproduce upon higher levels those characteristic processes of conversion and falling love which give depth and actuality to the religious and passional life" (M, 232). That seems clear enough, and remarkably honest.

The problem, I think, resides in that word "passional." Why not "sexual"? The mystical life, we are told, is truly a kind of divine romance, a *Ludus Amoris,* or "Game of Love" (M, 227–228). A capitalized Love perhaps, but certainly not a lowercase sex. Seldom indeed do the words "sex" or "sexuality" appear in Underhill's prose. Interestingly, when the term "sexuality" does appear, it is connected, as we shall soon see, to the "prurient imagination" of modern scholars and is labeled "morbid" (M, 137). Genuinely abnormal physical symptom-signs, a Sufi who rejoiced at the deaths of his wife and children, "feeble-minded" mystics, a famous Christian saint who would not smell a rose, even hints of genuine insanity—all these could be discussed, debated, and ultimately defended. But any discussion of sexuality—and I mean *real* physical sexuality—had to be banished to vague footnotes at the bottom of the page, where such unspoken secrets could be revealed only in the contorted forms of euphemism, suggestion, simple denial, or, perhaps most commonly, bibliographic reference—"Let someone else talk about such things," Underhill seemed to say, as she cited another French or American psychologist (whom few of her readers, of course, would ever read). In the end, it is the body that is the problem. Only this can explain Underhill's strange refusal to take seriously the literally physical experiences of heat and fire that mystics report. "Often," Rolle writes, "have I grasped my breast, seeing whether this burning were of any bodily cause outwardly" (M, 194). Another mystic, contemporary to Underhill, describes "*waves of fire* succeeding one another for more than two hours*"* (M, 193; italics in original). Underhill's response? Such an experience is a "well-known but dubious concomitant of spiritual experience," and this despite her admission that both Walter Hilton and the author of the classic *Cloud of Unknowing* refer to a similar "sensible heat" (M, 193). Why, then, is this dramatic experience of the "Heat," as Rolle called it, so "dubious"? We are not told, but we can easily guess the reason—because it involves the body. Underhill's incarnational dialectic begins to degenerate here into a simpler dualism.[49]

This last discussion, I should add, took place largely in a footnote (recall the seraphic "feet"), the usual place in Underhill's text for discussions of controversial topics. When the discourse moves "above the waist" of the text, Underhill's prose becomes impossibly contorted and hopelessly bowdlerized. Consider, for example, her discussion of why the mystics so loved the Song of Songs:

> The sense of a desire that was insatiable, of a personal fellowship so real, inward, and intense that it could only be compared with the closest link of human love, of an intercourse that was no mere spiritual self-indulgence, but was rooted in the primal duties and necessities of life—more, those deepest, most intimate secrets of communion, those self-giving ecstasies which all mystics know, but of which we, who are not mystics, may not speak—all these he found symbolized and suggested, their unendurable glories veiled in a merciful mist, in the poetry which man has invented to honour that august passion in which the merely human draws nearest to the divine. (M, 137)

Here Underhill seems especially uncomfortable with the possibility that some mystics sought their bliss and pleasure for its own sake: without suffering, we are told, there can be no real gain (M, 222). Hence, even here, in the mystical use of sexual language, that place of pure pleasure, Underhill must posit "duties and necessities." And thank goodness for the "merciful mist" of mystical poetry that shields us, the readers, from "their unendurable glories," that is, from the sexual nature of these experiences. Little wonder that the language of mystical sexuality must also become the language of secrets—these are forbidden truths. Finally, to make certain that her readers do not attempt to understand such things, Underhill reminds them that these are matters about which "we, who are not mystics, may not speak."

But why not? Did not Underhill herself acknowledge earlier in the book that we can say a good deal about mystical states by studying together both the traditional mystical authors, who spoke "from within," and the psychologists of religion, who speak "on another plane"? Why not the same dual approach here? Because Underhill does not like, *at all*, the conclusions that had already been reached about the sexual nature of mystical eroticism. Hence her exceptionally defensive prose peppered with the loaded adjectives "great," "pure," "unearthly," "unique," "prurient," "morbid," "dangerous," and "spiritual":

> The great saints who adopted and elaborated this symbolism, applying it to their pure and ardent passion for the Absolute, were destitute of the prurient imagination which their modern commentators too often possess. They were essentially pure of heart; and when they "saw God" they were so far from confusing that unearthly vision with the products of morbid sexuality, that the

dangerous nature of the imagery which they employed did not occur to them. They knew by experience the unique nature of spiritual love: and no one can know anything about it in any other way. (M, 137)

"[A]nd no one can know anything about it in any other way." And with that she silences the mystical, returning it back to its "hidden" or "secret" status within or behind or below the text.

Prurient imagination or no, however, sexual metaphors do appear in Christian mystical literature with a remarkable consistency (mystical marriage, betrothal, wedding ring, union, consummation, kiss, embrace, piercing, wound of love, conception, etc.); indeed, even the virtues are sexualized by Ruysbroeck as the accompanying "ornaments of the spiritual marriage" (M, 199). As Denys Turner correctly notes, "[T]he language of the love of God in the western Christian tradition is notably erotic,"[50] and, with the exceptions of Genesis and Psalms, it is doubtful whether any book of the Old Testament was commented on more frequently in the Middle Ages than the Song of Songs,[51] that remarkably bald love poem of the Hebrew Scriptures that does not even have the decency to declare that the lovers praised there in such elaborate metaphors are married.[52] Moreover, despite both Underhill's defensively explicit rejections and Turner's ambiguous lack of interest in the power of a psychological hermeneutic,[53] we *can* know something about the experience of mystical love by critically examining such metaphors with our own psychological categories. What is particularly striking about such appearances from such a perspective, at least with respect to the male mystics, is the remarkable manner in which they line up along a rather clear homoerotic structure. This, of course, is a function of Christian theology, which posits a male divinity (usually in the form of the Father or of Christ) with whom the male mystic "unites." That a man's soul is imagined to be female in relationship to the divine does little to hide the fact that what we finally have, after all the usual adjectives are hurled at the psychologist and the reductionist, is a male mystic using sexual language to describe his uniting with a male divinity, that is to say, a homoerotic symbolism.

Consider, for example, the cases of the famous Cistercian monk and reformer Bernard of Clairvaux (d. 1153) and his older contemporary Rupert of Deutz (ca. 1075–1129). Bernard's *Sermones super cantica canticorum* holds a central place in the history of Christian mysticism, coming as it does at the beginning of the flowering of medieval mysticism in the twelfth century. Written in the form of eighty-six sermons allegedly delivered to his monks at Clairvaux, the text is actually an artfully wrought summa of medieval mysticism whose profound influence on later mystical thought and expression is unquestioned. Here, Bernard, inspired by the first line of the Song of Songs, "Let him kiss me with the kiss of his mouth," writes for pages on the kiss as the most appropriate symbol for the soul's union with God. Bernard is clearly uncomfortable with images of penetration and orgasmic fusion, probably not so much for their erotic content as for what they suggest theologically—ontological identity. He will thus allow no real penetration, even in the kiss. Hence, though the soul may be kissed "by the kiss of the kiss" *(ab osculo),* the interbuccal "kiss of the mouth" *(ab ore)* is reserved for the single instance of Christ's assumed human nature. In other words, only in the Incarnation is the erotic union of the human and divine fully realized. Only in Christ does the divine "deep kiss" the human. Everyone else, and recall that Bernard was addressing an all-male same-sex community, can receive only the "kiss of the kiss" from the male deity.

If we are too pious or prudish to see the distinctly homoerotic dimensions of a male mystic kissing a male Christ (deeply or no), we must remember that many of Bernard's contemporaries did not share our squeamishness. Consider, for example, the twelfth-century priest and poet Walter Map, whose clerical satire *Trifles* repeats a familiar joke told about Bernard. Mark Jordan summarizes the story for us: "Two Cistercian monks are talking piously about an incident in which Bernard tried to bring a young man back from the dead by stretching out on top of the corpse. Bernard did not succeed. Another clergyman, an anti-Cistercian, interrupts the pious story with feigned astonishment. He had often heard of monks throwing themselves on top of boys, but usually both the monk and the boy got up afterwards."[54]

Bernard's contemporary Rupert was familiar with this same distinction between the "kiss of the kiss" and the "kiss of the mouth," or what we today call, perhaps appropriately here, the "French kiss." But what is a rather abstract homoerotic trope in Bernard's text that can be drawn out only by a ribald joke becomes an explicit homosexual experience in Rupert that is more than apparent in the religious text. Consider, for example, Rupert's description of his vision of his divine lover, Jesus: "When I quickly entered [the altar], I took hold of him whom my soul loved. I held him, I embraced him, I kissed him for a long time. I felt how deeply he appreciated this sign of love when in the midst of the kiss he opened his mouth so that I could kiss more deeply."[55] Finally, in order to complicate things even further and call for a truly embodied reading of mystical texts, recall that Bonaventure, one of the tradition's great mystical theologians, was quite clear that the ecstasies of male mystics often produce real sexual fluids: "[I]n spiritualibus affectionibus carnals fluxus liquore maculantur," he wrote [Within the spiritual affections, they are stained with the liquid of the carnal flow].[56] Homoerotic or heteroerotic, the spiritual affections are also sexual sensations with real, physiological, fluid analogues. The term "metaphor," I would suggest, does not even begin to suggest what is actually at work here.

As I tried to make clear in the introduction, I am not arguing here that all male Christian mystics who employed such sexual imagery to describe their mystical unions were homosexually inclined in some culturally and historically specific sense. I happen to think that many of them were, but I freely admit that in most of these cases we simply do not possess enough intimate biographical information (that is, about their sexual lives) to make any reasonably comfortable conclusions. But we do have their texts, and their texts are often sexualized and gendered, often in quite personal and specific ways. Pace Underhill, who wants to claim that traditional descriptions of the mystical marriage are "singularly free from physical imagery" (M, 138), such texts are astonishingly and sometimes shockingly rich in just such imagery. Surely, then, it is not unreasonable to suggest that these textual sexualities bear some psychological relationship to the actual sexualities of the texts' authors. Ironically, Underhill's hermeneutic could be developed in precisely this direction (with or without her permission), particularly in its insight that the mystic's response to divine love will always be psychologically patterned after his or her specific response to human love: "It must never be forgotten that all apparently one-sided descriptions of illumination—more, all experiences of it—are governed by temperament. 'That Light whose smile kindles the Universe' is ever the same; but the self through whom it passes, and by whom we must receive its report, has already submitted to the moulding influences of environment and heredity, Church and State. . . . *The response which it makes to Divine Love will be the same in type as the response which its nature would make to earthly love: but raised to the nth degree*" (M, 252–253; italics mine). But even given such a hermeneutical principle, which I wholeheartedly accept, I am not suggesting that every male bridal mystic was homosexually inclined. What I am suggesting is that Christian male erotic mysticism is inevitably homoerotic *in doctrinal structure,* and that this doctrinal structure privileges a homosexual orientation, certainly in mystical textual expression and most likely in actual physiological response as well.

Speaking in far more psychohistorical terms, we might say that male mystics whose sexual inclinations or practices influence them to employ traditional (homo)erotic language to describe their experiences of the divine Presence can become canonical within the tradition only to the extent that their symbolisms deny the possibility of a heteroerotic approach to the divine (which, of course, would render the latter feminine). It is not, then, that mystical heterosexuality is actually denied to canonical males; it is that homosexually oriented or simply homoerotic males become canonical by virtue of their sublimated homosexualities, which happen to "fit" the textual, doctrinal, and symbolic structures of the Catholic tradition. Moreover, there are certainly definite psychological, social, and political forces at work here as well. Psychologically speaking, homosexuality, condemned as a horrible offense against God eventually associated with the "sin of Sodom," was probably always more likely to be repressed and driven under, where, like Böhme's breeding thoughts, it could, with a little psychophysiological luck, sublimate itself into other types of human expression, including mystical forms of eroticism. In more sociological terms, we might say that homosexualities are not "captured" by society for the purposes of procreation and social stability and so are more free to be sublimated, transformed, and "realized" on other dimensions. Politically speaking, these same sexualities, to the extent that they preserve a male object as divine and authoritative, do not overtly challenge the patriarchal structures of society and heaven. Nor—need I add?—do they threaten the possibility of procreation, that is, children, whose crying, smiling, hungry presence would of course definitively spell the end to a celibate religious lifestyle; homosexualities, in other words, whether effectively sublimated or actually practiced, function as perfect contraceptives. Thus, through a wide range of symbolic paths (sexual, doctrinal, social, political, and biological) homosexualities emerge as "the 'path[s] of least resistance' through which the tradition flows" (M, 105).[57] We are dealing, in other words, with a historical process determined by doctrinal, scriptural, sociopolitical, and biological constraints, not with some sort of "divine election" or iron psychological law about "true" mysticism.

Such a thesis can be demonstrated through an examination of the soul's gender, the gender of the divine, and the various sexual metaphors that are used with such enthusiasm throughout Underhill's text (both by her and her quoted mystics) to describe the "mystical marriage" of the two. I begin in the very beginning, with a provocative quote from Coventry Patmore, which Underhill sets directly opposite the very first page of chapter 1, "The Point of Departure." Patmore writes: "What the world, which truly knows *nothing,* calls 'mysticism' is the science of *ultimates,* . . . the science of self-evident Reality which cannot be 'reasoned about,' because it is the object of pure reason or perception. The Babe sucking its mother's breast, and the Lover returning, after twenty years' separation, to his home and food in the same bosom, are the types and princes of Mystics" (M, 3; cf. M, 135). Now the mystic here is clearly male, and the divine is imagined—in quite untraditional terms—as female, first as a breast-feeding mother, then as a wife whose domestic and nurturing qualities are understood again as a kind of breast-feeding. That the author understands the wife to *be* the mother (for the mystic returns to "the same bosom" after twenty years' of maturation) suggests that the male mystic's eroticism might reveal, on closer analysis, some rather clear oedipal dimensions.[58] Taken as a whole, the Patmore quote is both deceptive and revealing at the same time: deceptive because the divine is almost never imagined as a female lover in the Christian mystical texts; revealing because Patmore understands, in his own poetic idiom, that the mystical process involves some rather powerful regressive (back to the breast), sexual (the lover at his wife's breasts), and oedipal (the wife's breasts as the mother's breasts) forces. In both its deception and its insight, the quote functions, as most epigraphs do, as a kind of prophetic or precocious understanding of things to come.

Underhill's prose quickly confirms the theoretically rich confusion of her epigraph, for her very first lines open with the claim that "[a]ll men... have fallen in love with the veiled Isis whom they call Truth" (M, 3), a decidedly non-Christian feminine symbolism, and continue for another full page referring to "Reality" in the feminine, no doubt to continue the heterosexual structure set up by Patmore. But this is a very long book about Christian mysticism, where a mystical heterosexuality can only appear in the margins, in heretics, or, as here, in noncanonical poets, for Christ is the "true Bridegroom" of the female human soul (M, 109). Hence, by the third page, Underhill has slipped back into more traditional language and is referring to the soul, be it male or female, as "she" (M, 5). Tellingly, by the end of chapter 1, Patmore's heterosexual symbolism has disappeared altogether: the very same passage is quoted again to conclude a long, impassioned defense of mystical experience, but this time without its heteroerotic ending: there are no lovers, no bosoms here. We are back to mysticism as the "science of *ultimates*" or the "science of self-evident Reality," that is, a sexless metaphysical abstraction about which we are forbidden to reason, for, as we are told yet again, we know "*nothing*" (M, 25). Here, encoded into the rhetorical "frame" and gender transformations of this very first chapter, we have a kind of unconscious or unintended parable about the genesis and ultimate fate of the mystical, which inevitably begins in the psychological messiness of the sexualized body (in Patmore's case, with a shocking coincidence of lovemaking and breast-feeding in the bosom of the mother-lover), never quite stabilizes itself in a single gender identity, and ends in the "sublime," that is, sublimated heights of metaphysics and a disturbing anti-intellectualism that wants to shut off all thinking about what has happened here: "[A]nd no one can know anything about it in any other way."

Such patterns continue to be woven, almost imperceptibly, throughout the text by the individual strands of this or that quotation, by Underhill's glosses, and by the careful handling of controversy, alternate readings, and scholarly dissent. But when we finally step back (quite a ways back, I admit) from all of this and examine *Mysticism* as a whole, what we can see is a richly woven tapestry revealing some quite simple, but no less dramatic, designs. These, it seems to me, are defined largely by three Christian doctrinal responses to sexuality and gender. Specifically, mystical heteroeroticism is (1) affirmed and celebrated in canonical females, (2) denied to canonical males, and (3) tolerated in noncanonical, heretical, or marginal males.

1. *Female heteroerotic symbolisms* are not difficult to find in Underhill's text. Indeed, they are everywhere, a textual feature that is no doubt a function of both the traditional nature of such symbolism and Underhill's own comfort level with her own gender and this type of female sexuality. She is thus warm and effusive about Julian of Norwich's passionate response to Christ and her subsequent experience of being "oned with bliss" (M, 247). More than once she quotes Julian writing, "I saw Him and sought Him: I had Him and wanted Him" (M, 90), or more sensually, "Him verily seeing and fully feeling. Him spiritually hearing and Him delectably smelling and sweetly swallowing" (M, 268). So too with Mechthild of Hackborn, who heard the Lord say to her: "Come, My bride, and enjoy My Godhead" (M, 196). And then there is, of course, Teresa of Avila and her famous "transverberation," a traditional euphemism for an event that can only be described as a kind of mystical orgasm experienced, interestingly enough, at the hands of a burning angel, who seemed to be "all on fire." Underhill quotes: "I saw in his hand a long spear of gold, and at the iron's point there seemed to be a little fire. He appeared to me to be thrusting it at times into my heart, and to pierce my very entrails; when he drew it out, he seemed to draw them out also and to leave me all on fire with a great love of God. The pain was so great that it made me moan; and yet so surpassing was the sweetness of this excessive pain that I could not wish to be rid of it. The soul is satisfied with

nothing less than God. The pain is not bodily, but spiritual; though the body has its share in it, even a large one" (M, 292). Despite the fact that Underhill is quite clear that neither the "sense of God" nor the "illuminations" of the illuminative state should be taken as metaphorical—they are phenomenologically accurate descriptions of an objective presence and literal experiences of actual photisms (M, 242, 249)—she will make no such claim for the sexual language of the mystics. Unlike the mystics themselves, she seems quite uncomfortable acknowledging the "large" part that the body so obviously plays in Teresa's painfully pleasurable moans or Julian's sweet swallowings. Not surprisingly, then, when Underhill visited the Convent of the Incarnation in Spain, where Teresa had lived, she encountered there what she described to a correspondent as a "very bad picture" commemorating Teresa's spiritual betrothal. What she meant by "very bad," I suspect, was "obviously sexual"; hence her gloss on the experience: "[I]n fact, a good deal has to be passed over lightly!" (L, 180). This, of course, is exactly what she did in *Mysticism* as well: she passed over the sexual lightly. Not, however, lightly enough for all of her readers. One reviewer, for example, described the "transcendental eroticism" of the mystics who appeared in her text as "nauseating" (L, 125). Bowdlerization, it seems, is always relative to a reader's tastes.

Despite her Edwardian squeamishness about sexuality, which, by the way, did not necessarily extend to nonreligious contexts,[59] Underhill is hardly naive about the socially constructed nature of such experiences; hence her elaborate and insightful analysis of the "mystic marriage" of Catherine of Siena, who borrowed the imagery of her own nuptial vision from the hagiography of her namesake Saint Catherine of Alexandria, with whom she would have been familiar since infancy (M, 292). But as with her use of psychology, Underhill will go only "so far" with such interpretations. Thus, any attempt to glimpse within Evelyn's discussions the actual psychohistorical details of her mystics' emotional and sexual lives is, to mischievously borrow from Underhill her own frustrated analogy, which she applied to her friend's vague descriptions of a convent, "rather like constructing an antediluvian monster from a fossil of his back double tooth!"[60] Still, such paleontological feats are possible (indeed, they are the stuff of paleontology), and we too can glimpse something of the dinosaur's actual life from even the broken teeth that Underhill throws us. We can, for example, notice that one of the most consistent and striking features of these female mystics and their marriages to Christ is the fact that many of them began their spiritual careers after abandoning or, more likely, escaping from what Underhill euphemistically calls "unhappy" or "uncongenial" marriages (our fossilized teeth, if you will). Catherine of Genoa, for example, suffered years of loneliness and depression, "the result of an unhappy marriage," Underhill tells us (M, 181). "'O Love, no more sins! no more sins!'" she would cry. "And her hatred of herself was more than she could endure" (M, 182, quoting von Hügel). Certainly such an ambiguous cry (just whose sins are being lamented here?) and such obvious self-loathing might be interpreted in very different ways today, that is, as possible symptoms of sexual trauma. (On a lighter note, Underhill once commented that "[a]fter living in a hotel full of Italians I fully understand why St. Catherine shut herself in one room for three years—but it wouldn't have been much good unless she had a soundproof door" [L, 158]). She reacted similarly to Madame Guyon, whose beauty and sexuality (which Underhill subsumes under the phrase "fashionable appearance") caused her pious Franciscan confessor to be "filled with apprehension" (M, 184). Like Catherine before her, Guyon knew much mental anguish, "also the result of an uncongenial marriage" (M, 182). Sadly, she had signed (or was forced to sign?) the marriage contract without even being told her future husband's name: "[H]ardly was I married, when the remembrance of my old desire to be a nun overcame me" (M, 183). Could this be a coincidence? Underhill probably gets very close to the psychological truth of such scenes when she describes the marital and familial pain of yet another woman, Antoinette Bourignan. Reinforced "by the miseries of an unsympathetic home, still more by a threat of approaching marriage, the impulse to renunciation got its way" (M, 213). The dinosaur takes shape: the mystico-erotic bursts into flames from the ashes of the familial-sexual life, and the former cannot be more fully understood without confronting squarely and honestly the latter.

2. *Male homoerotic symbolisms,* like female heteroerotic symbolisms, are everywhere in *Mysticism,* although never of course acknowledged as such. Suso, for example, sees the heart region of his body become like transparent crystal. There a feminine Divine Wisdom appears, "and she was fair to look upon." But this ultimately is not the object of the soul's desire, for "by her side was the soul of the Servitor [Suso], full of heavenly desires; resting lovingly upon the bosom of God, Who had embraced it, and pressed it to His Heart." There, in the arms of a male God, it remained "altogether absorbed and inebriated with love in the arms of God its well-beloved" (M, 286). The same "object-choice" is enacted again in another passage, where Suso compares his desire to embrace "his sweet Friend" and press "Him to a heart overflowing with love" to the love a

baby feels for its mother, whose physical tenderness now becomes a symbol for the sweet ministrations of Divine Wisdom (M, 254). The gender of the divine is thus unstable or fluid, but whenever sexual metaphors are used (the beloved, the embrace), the divine quickly becomes masculine. So too with Tauler's "marriage from which the Lord comes" (M, 55), Ruysbroeck's "peace of the summits," that "dim silence where lovers lose themselves" (M, 304; cf. 48, 312–313, 356), Bernard of Clairvaux's kissing of Christ (M, 137–138), and Rolle's experience of being kissed by a strange lover (M, 354), whom he identifies elsewhere with "Christ my Jesu," the "spouse of my soul by all this present life" (M, 194) — each time the object-choice is another (divine) male. Turner at least is to the point: "Bernard is in love with God erotically."[61] Exactly. And, if we can leave Underhill for a moment, the kiss that Bernard receives from that male deity both feminizes him and penetrates him, rendering him mystically pregnant: hence, Bernard can describe how the groom's kiss causes the bride's breasts to grow with a "milky abundance" and her womb to swell with life. "Men with an urge to frequent prayer will have experience of what I say," Bernard insists.[62] No one, though, has written more eloquently, passionately, and personally about such homoerotic encounters than John of the Cross: "Lover to loved, in marriage of delight!" he sings (M, 352). In another passage he explains the psychology of such mystical accomplishments: "We require a more ardent fire and a nobler love — that of the Bridegroom. Finding her delight and strength in Him, the soul gains the vigour and confidence which enable her easily to abandon all other affections" (M, 203). Such a renunciation is not too difficult, we might imagine, for those for whom such heterosexual "affections" hold little meaning and even less passion and whose homosexualities could not possibly find expression in society or the church anyway, that is, homoerotic mystics.

Rhetorically and textually speaking, what all of these male mystics have in common is their desire to celebrate their unions with Christ in the terms of a mystical marriage — they are *brides*. And indeed, there is really no other choice, as long as one wants to remain in both a sexual and a Christian register. As Origen put it so starkly, the inner man has only one legitimate bridegroom, the Word of God, that is, Christ, even though he may choose to abandon him for "some adulterer and seducer."[63] In bald terms, a man's erotic love for God is inversely related to his sexual love for a woman. In Turner's more careful terms, "All . . . depends upon our choosing God as the object of love, for human beings, having the power of choice, can divert that *eros* away from God altogether and can, as it were, reduce the power of human love as likeness [to God] virtually to zero."[64] Little wonder, then, that traditional interpreters disapproved universally, "without exception," Turner notes, of an interpretation of the Song of Songs as being about what it so clearly seems to be about, that is, a human heterosexual relationship. That reading, Turner points out, amounts to a kind of "*hermeneutical* adultery."[65] Why? Turner does not say so, but I would: Because there simply is no place for a heterosexuality within this male mystical universe.

Since this homoerotic language is so traditional, indeed almost second nature, Underhill seems comfortable quoting such authors at great length, at least until the traditional language becomes more personal and takes on a decidedly physical sexuality. Ruysbroeck apparently went a little too far when he wrote that "[t]his driving and drawing we feel in the heart and in the unity of all our bodily powers, and especially in the desirous powers" (M, 48), since Underhill quickly, and rather bizarrely, glossed this last clause as referring to "the business of the Will" (M, 48). At other times the censorship is self-imposed by the mystic. This is a rather common phenomenon, Underhill tells her reader in a footnote, which we encounter in souls who fear that they have revealed "matters which might not be spoken of." What these matters are we are never told, but we certainly have our guesses, especially when we are told, in the very next line, that Coventry Patmore destroyed his masterpiece for these same reasons. Its title? *Sponsa Dei,* "The Spouse of God" (M, 143).

3. Not surprisingly, genuine *male mystical heteroeroticisms* appear nowhere in *Mysticism,* except in a few marginal or heretical poets and a decidedly nontraditional Protestant mystic, the shoemaker, merchant, family man, and theosophist Jakob Böhme, whose writings, not surprisingly, were banned in his own day.[66] At the very end of her chapter "The Purification of the Self," Underhill takes up the self's passage from the new to the old, from purification to the illuminated life, and places there, at the threshold, the figure of Böhme, the heretical heteroerotic mystic. Because of its virtual sexual uniqueness, the passage is well worth quoting at length:

> When Christ the Corner-Stone [i.e., the divine principle latent in man] stirreth himself in the extinguished Image of Man in his hearty Conversion and Repentance . . . then Virgin Sophia appeareth in the stirring of the Spirit of Christ in the extinguished Image, in her Virgin's attire before the Soul; at which the Soul is so amazed and astonished in its Uncleanness . . . being ashamed in the Presence of its fair Love. . . . But the noble Sophia draweth near in the Essence

of the Soul, and kisseth it in friendly Manner, and tinctureth its dark Fire with her Rays of Love, and shineth through it with her bright and powerful Influence. Penetrated with the strong Sense and Feeling of which, the Soul skippeth in its Body for great Joy, and in the strength of this Virgin Love exulteth, and praiseth the great God for his blest Gift of Grace. I will set down here a short description how it is when the Bride thus embraceth the Bridegroom, for the consideration of the Reader, who perhaps hath not yet been in this wedding chamber. It may be he will be desirous to follow us, and to enter into the Inner Choir, where the Soul joineth hands and danceth with Sophia, or the Divine Wisdom. (M, 230–231; Underhill's gloss in brackets).

This, of course, can be read as both Böhme's and Underhill's call to "the Reader, who perhaps hath not yet been in this wedding chamber," to read further and, by that same hermeneutical experience, imaginatively enter that very chamber in the later chapters of *Mysticism,* which of course will treat the more advanced stages of the contemplative life, including and especially the mystical marriage. But, as with the opening Patmore quote, what is most interesting about this rhetorical use of Böhme is the way the quoted passage fits only uncomfortably into the sexual and gender patterns of Christian mysticism. For here, after dozens of human brides and divine bridegrooms (with many more to follow), we meet a human bridegroom and a divine bride, imagined alternately as Virgin Love, Sophia, or Divine Wisdom. Not surprisingly, this mystical event causes some anxiety in Böhme, who writes of the soul's "being ashamed in the Presence of its fair Love." But Sophia draws near the male soul, kisses it, and so initiates an encounter that will result in "a strong Sense and Feeling" or "great Joy" in which the body shares.

I cannot help wondering about the possible oedipal dimensions of such an originally shame-filled encounter, for Virgin, Sophia, and Divine Wisdom are all, of course, common epithets for the Virgin Mary, "the Mother" par excellence of Christian tradition. But this, after all, is a Protestant, not a Catholic, mystic, and such things seem muted at best, rather like the passage's sexual symbolism, which speaks of only kissing and dancing and a strong "Sense and Feeling" in what is, after all, a bridal chamber, that is, a place of passionate sex. Regardless, is it any wonder that the only significant male mystical heteroerotic passage in Underhill's text was composed not by a celibate monk or a canonical saint, but by a married man who made shoes for a living and wrote banned books? Böhme, Underhill explains, was the least ascetic of the mystics (M, 226). That he seems to have been the least homoerotically inclined of our male erotic mystics treated by Underhill is probably no accident. Böhme was simply not a bride.

Concluding Reflections: Evelyn's Progressive Incarnation

Before we leave Underhill's *Mysticism*, it is necessary to say at least a few words about what came after it in terms of both Evelyn's work and life. In terms of the work, the answer is simple: practically everything, since *Mysticism* was her first work of scholarship and dozens more were to follow, including her second well-known work, *Worship* (1936). As suggested by the title of this second classic, the movement of Underhill's religious life also changed and shifted after *Mysticism*, even if this is more difficult to track and read. *Mysticism* made her famous, but it by no means marks the "last word" for its author. Quite the contrary, Evelyn's thought continued to evolve and change as it moved further and further away from a fascination with the strange and singular experiences of the mystics to a more and more pastoral concern for the quite ordinary lives of her readers and listeners and the institutional and liturgical matrix in which these lives developed. Such a pattern can be detected in her book titles. *The Mystic Way*, a kind of simpler and shorter synopsis of *Mysticism*, appeared in 1913, still very much in line with the nontraditional approach of *Mysticism* and addressed to what Cropper calls, quite accurately I think, the "unorthodox seeker,"[67] that is, the modern aspiring mystic deracinated from tradition and authority. *Practical Mysticism* appeared in 1914 as Underhill's attempt to address religious readers with no clear institutional affiliation, and *The Essentials of Mysticism* appeared in 1920, with Underhill now forty-five. As Cropper insightfully points out, this would be the last of her books to contain the word "mysticism" in its title.[68] Very much in line with this transformation from "pure mystic" to a deeper appreciation for tradition, Evelyn returned to the Anglican communion of her childhood a year later, at forty-six, and there evolved gradually and gracefully into a beloved retreat master, a serene and wise spiritual director, and a public pacifist.

There was certainly no greater influence on these important turns in her road than the Catholic lay intellectual and scholar of mysticism Baron von Hügel, who became her spiritual director in 1921 (the same year she returned to Anglicanism), "my 'final court of appeal' on all questions of the inner life," as she once described him (L, 319) . Cropper's biography is particularly rich here, as it includes much of the correspondence that took place between these two important scholars of mysticism. As noted above, von Hügel's massive study of Catherine of Genoa, *The Mystical Element of Religion* (1908), had appeared shortly before Underhill's *Mysticism* (1911). Von Hügel had read *Mysticism* and responded to it warmly, a fact which gave Underhill immense satisfaction.[69] Warmly, but not uncritically, for Underhill's text made the Baron "anxious" for its author. What finally emerges from their correspondence and von Hügel's direction is a meeting of two very different understandings of the spiritual life: one (Underhill's) modern in its approach to the mystical as something essentially apophatic, only metaphorically connected to doctrine, vaguely hostile to institution and authority, eminently psychological (despite her protestations to the contrary), and, most important, ultimately separable from the historical faith traditions; the other (von Hügel's) insistent that the mystical is only one element of religion (hence the title of his book), and one that cannot be removed from the broader context of liturgy, Scripture, and institutional authority without serious negative consequences (von Hügel, in other words, sought to return to the ancient understandings of the mystical as the secret exegetical dimensions of Scripture and the liturgy). The modern psychologization of mysticism about which de Certeau has written and which Underhill's early work had enacted thus met its challenge in the liberal but still traditional Catholicism of the baron, all under the shadow of what Rome was calling, quite significantly I think, the heresy of "modernism." Underhill would ultimately submit to this return to tradition, at least partially. The later twentieth-century study of mysticism would find it much more difficult to do so.[70]

The correspondence itself is quite touching—my personal favorite is when Underhill recalls von Hügel's commenting that the sacrament of penance cannot absolve one from not having a sense of humor (L, 331)—and deserves far more attention than we can give it here as a paradigmatic moment in the modern study of mysticism. In her own letters to the baron, Underhill struggles honestly and openly with the effects of historical criticism on miracles and the central tenets of Christianity,[71] the "terrifying" possibilities of scientific materialism and an ironclad deterministic universe,[72] and what she calls the "horrors" of psychological reductionism. In terms of the latter, Underhill confesses that she often suffers from a "terrible, overwhelming suspicion" that her own religious experiences are "only subjective,"[73] illusory, or "imaginary."[74] "There are times," she admits in a particularly revealing passage, "when I wish I would have never heard of psychology."[75] But here too she describes experiencing a Teresan "prayer of quiet"[76] and relates to her director a dramatic auditory experience in which she heard a voice (in both English and Latin) that resolved for her a vocational crisis.[77] More often, however, we find her bemoaning her "Quakerish" and "Unitarian" leanings, that is, her tendencies to a "pure mysticism" defined by an exclusive theocentric and transcendent focus. To this the baron always responds with the counsel to return to a more incarnational, Christocentric, and sacramental spirituality. Specifically, he asks her to attend regular liturgies, monitor her devotional excesses, visit the poor, and develop some nonreligious hobby. In one of the more delightful of these "incarnational" moments, this time in a P.S., von Hügel reflects on their mutual love for domestic pets, specifically her cats and his little dog. Even here, however, theology has the last word: "Again it was God incarnate, it was Jesus of Nazareth, of Gethsemane and Calvary, and not pure Theism that taught this. De-Unitarianizing, if you please!"[78] And in the end, Evelyn would submit to the baron's direction. Hence, whereas before she had had no experience of Christ, read Christocentric piety through reductive psychological lenses, could make no sense of the New Testament, and took communion only out of obedience (L, 26–28), later in life she became a more or less orthodox Anglican, emphasized a Christocentric piety to her directees, encouraged them to read the New Testament each day, argued against Anglican divines who rejected the adoration of the Blessed Sacrament (L, 69), and confessed that the Feast of Corpus Christi was her "secret love" (L, 77). However we might want to judge this development, Evelyn had come a very long way from the days of *Mysticism*.

But perhaps such a "descent" from the mystical heights, cats and all, was there all along in Underhill's person and writing. Had she not sacrificed her heartfelt desire to "be received" into the Roman communion for the sake of her husband and marriage?[79] With such a happy, well-adjusted marriage, it is extremely unlikely that she could have ever become a bridal mystic; she simply lacked the sexual conflict and social suffering that provide the psychological catalyst for such pursuits. And did she not continually insist, even in *Mysticism,* on the dialectic systole and diastole of the mystical life (M, 173), which in its fullest forms always descends back into the social world after, indeed *because of,* its ecstasies and unions? In more traditional terms (that is, in the usual sexual metaphors of the mystical life), had she not taught that divine fecundity must follow betrothal and the mystical marriage if the spiritual life is to be truly consummated (M, 172)? Indeed she had. Armstrong refers to this life process as Underhill's "progressive incarnation": "From this point of view her story has seemed to emerge more and more as a process of what one can only call a progressive incarnation, a gradual mitigation then transmutation of her early other-worldly mystical values, until we find in her at the end someone whom experience has taught the triviality of seeking Experience. . . . it took Evelyn many years to see how in practice the satisfaction of the 'metaphysical thirst' at the heart of all living religion . . . could be reconciled with the renunciation of such satisfaction for the higher value of 'an overflowing love to all in common.' "[80] Just as the contemplative mystic "swallowed up" the illuminated poet along the Mystic Way, here the ethical and the social finally "swallow up" the transcendent for the sake of a newly framed mystical humanism. Or in more traditional mystagogic language, with such a sacrifice, "the mystic has worked out in [her]self mystically the life-story of Jesus and is re-united with the vision, no longer as mere spectator but as part of it."[81] She had written the map and then used it herself to walk the life. Or did she walk the life, and then write a map of it? Regardless, *Mysticism* was not simply a literary expression of her religious life at thirty-six; it also contained the "seeds" of much that would follow. Like a dream, it was wish fulfillment, truth telling, and personal prophecy rolled into one.

These final notions of a "progressive incarnation," of a "sacrifice" of the divine for the human, even an eclipse of experience itself, are especially important for us to keep in mind as we proceed down our own roads of excess. Such themes will appear again on these roads, until an independent "experience" disappears entirely within a final mystical hermeneutics of language and text. Evelyn Underhill, in both her romantic glorification of the lone "mystical experience" and her later renunciation and relativization of that same singular event, is thus an appropriate place to start, for in this she contains hidden within herself both the signs of a romantic past and the seeds of a still-contested postmodern future: "[T]he past can indeed speak to the present and to listen is not necessarily to retreat."[82]

The artist is but a perishable image of what the saint may become: the free and living instrument of the one Poet, the creative Power. . . . This attitude is explained very well at the end of Plato's *Gorgias* (sec. 79): ". . . Listen, then, as they say, to this very lovely story. Perhaps you will believe it is a fable, but for me it is a *true story,* and I wish you would regard all I am going to tell you as the truth." The mystics conceive the parables of their catechism as true prophecies that will be verified in time, but which can only be said to be "true" insofar as they have been realized. The truth of their parables is observed *a posteriori* in what they produce in society, in the swarm of imitations, the teeming variety of images, synonyms, and viable applications they provoke in those who have listened to them attentively.

Louis Massignon, *Essay on the Origins of the Technical Language of Islamic Mysticism*

Hodie in libro experientiae legimus
[Today we read in the book of experience].

Bernard of Clairvaux, *Sermones super cantica canticorum*

SECRET TALK *The Vajrāśva Vision*

vajra: "(thunderbolt) = *liṅga* [phallus] = *śūnya* (emptiness)"
Mircea Eliade on the Tantric symbolism
of the *Dohakośa*s *(Yoga: Immortality and Freedom)*

aśva: "a horse, stallion"
Sir Monier-Williams, *Sanskrit-English Dictionary*

> I went to the Garden of Love,
> And saw what I never had seen:
> A Chapel was built in the midst,
> Where I used to play on the green.
>
> And the gates of this Chapel were shut,
> Thou shalt not. writ over the door;
> ....
> ....
>
> And I saw it was filled with graves,
> And tombstones where flowers should be ...
>
> William Blake, "The Garden of Love"

MY FAMILY on my mother's side (Wiedel) are mostly farmers, German Catholic settlers who, like most American immigrants, found themselves settling down by accident or by plan (or more likely, a little of both) in a very particular place at a very particular time, in their case, in the middle of the nineteenth century in the rich soil of southeastern Nebraska, where they have since grown into one of the largest families in the area, "like grasshoppers," they like to say with a grin and a gleam in their eyes. My father's father, that is, my paternal grandfather, immigrated around 1911 from a small village in southern Czechoslovakia called Sviny (literally, "Pigs"), just a few miles from Freiburg, the birthplace of Sigmund Freud. John Kripal was a blacksmith who served briefly in the Great War before being honorably discharged. Later he would run a Chrysler garage in a small town with a biblical name, Hebron, and instill in his children a love of cars, mechanics, and engineering. My father can fix just about anything that doesn't run on a computer chip.

The name is intriguing. Kripal. Forget the correct pronunciation. My immediate family pronounces it "cry-pl" (with the accent on the first syllable), relatives in northwestern Nebraska say "cripple" (despite the unfortunate connotations), while other relatives in southern California insist on pronouncing it "kri-pel" (with both vowels short and the accent on the second syllable). In terms of its likely historical and etymological origins, we are probably all wrong. After all, it is a most unusual Czech name and is almost certainly derived from another language altogether. Significantly, it is a relatively common Indian name, especially in northern India, where it would be pronounced kri-paul (with the accent on the second syllable). Happily, as a Sanskrit-based name, it connotes the presence of the gods' "grace" *(kṛpā)*—much better, I tell my cousins, than the crippled homonym of our commonly pronounced English name. Such etymological musings take on more meaning and more than a little substance when family tradition, completely unaware of Sanskrit vocabulary and backed up with some recent ethnographic research in Sviny, has our distant ancestors settling the village with another family in 1656, provocatively, as a Gypsy family with its ultimate origins in India.[1]

* * *

"Tell me about your earliest memory," my seminary analyst, who also happened to be a monk, said to me at one of our first sessions. "You won't believe me, if I tell you," I answered. "Tell me anyway." "O-o-okay," I stuttered nervously, "I remember—not intellectually or pictorially, mind you—but I remember the *feeling* of being inside my mother's womb." "What did it feel like?" "I felt cramped, and I wanted out, desperately, and then I came out and everything was fine."

To this day I am not sure whether this "memory" is in fact a memory or a kind of projected parable of my lifelong engagement with the mystical as something to merge with *and* be born from. I did not know at the time of that conversation, but I know now that Freud thought mystical experiences are regressive returns to early stages of psychological experience, particularly to those earliest months of intense bonding between mother and child that give rise to a feeling of "primary narcissism," that is, a oneness between the child's psychic state and the numinous presence of the mother.[2] Such a model, Freud thought, might reveal "connections . . . with a number of obscure modifications of mental life, such as trances and ecstasies."[3] Indeed it might. It also helps explain why the motifs of unity, oneness, and merging are so common—dare we say "universal"?—in the history of mysticism: such experiences are essentially memories of that most basic and universal of human experience—the experience of infancy—now transformed through ritual, doctrine, and psychological maturation into something sacred. Or was it always sacred, and do the mystical traditions simply give us elaborately coded ways to re-member, to embody anew this lost Presence of mythological proportions?

Provocatively, more than one mystical tradition has adopted a similar assumption to out-Freud Freud and argue, or at least suggest, that the mystical be traced further back along the life cycle to the uterine state of the fetus. Hence Ramakrishna's equation of birth with a fall from the cosmic bliss of Brahman and the Bengali proverb he used to gloss this teaching: *garbhe chilām yoge chilām* [When I was in the womb, I was in mystical union]. Here too we are reminded of the architectural fact that the innermost sanctum of the Hindu temple, which as a whole is often likened to a many-tiered mountain hiding a dark interior cave, is traditionally called the *garbhagṛha,* or "womb-chamber." It is here, in this darkest and most secret space of the temple, where the deity can be seen in a ritually formalized "vision" *(darśana).*[4] Here too we might place the Shingon stage model of a developing Buddhahood as a series of fetal states, where human gestation is treated "as a privileged period of nirvanic experience spent in a pre-samsaric pocket universe" and physical birth, once again, becomes a kind of ontological "fall."[5] By implication, to become the Buddha is to become a fetus again, to return to the pocket universe of the maternal womb where all is one.

I find all of this quite compelling, perhaps partly because of my own narcissistic memories and their impact on my thinking and life arc. But what is particularly significant for me about my own "memory" is how different it is from the mystical model of a blissfully complete fetal state that knows no lack and wants no "fall." The memory, after all, speaks of a deeply felt desire *to get out,* to be born, to enter the world, to exist as a separate being outside the womb and beyond the mother. As such, the memory was prophetic of much that would follow. It held the future in its representation of the past.

*   *   *

As a boy of three or four, I found one of those graphically illustrated books on human gestation and birth in my parent's room, hidden in a dresser drawer. I had stumbled upon a secret, a literally hidden vision, couched in incomprehensible medical jargon but more than adequately illustrated with what I took to be some very bizarre pictures. I remember thinking that the baby looked an awful lot like a lizard at a certain stage; it was really quite terrifying at the time, as if I had encountered something primordial and basically nonhuman. And the birth process—it looked so painful to me. I definitely did not want to be a woman, I said not so confidently to myself, because they had to suffer the pain of childbirth (apparently, my four-year-old brain assumed that I could have been a woman, had I wanted to). But neither did I want to be a man, because they had to go to war, fight, and die (it was the mid-1960s and I had no doubt absorbed something of the media's coverage of the Vietnam War). I was caught in an early gender dilemma. At three or four I was struggling, and not very successfully, with what I would later learn to call human sexuality, gender identity, suffering, and death. Babies looked like lizards, birth was eerie and traumatic, and war was very, very scary. There were no obvious answers, only irresolvable dilemmas. Luckily, I was perfectly capable of forgetting such thoughts. And I did.

* * *

When my little brother and I were four and five, our parents bought us two gray kittens. He named his King Kong (it seemed very incongruous and funny then too), and I named mine Magic. A few years later he was collecting The Incredible Hulk comic books and would soon become a very large college football player and, later, a successful bodybuilder. I went on to collect The Amazing Spiderman comics (with those Kaliesque eyes), become a seminarian and aspiring monk, and, later, a historian of mysticism. Two lives presciently known in two little cats.

* * *

It was the middle of December 1989. I had just returned to the States for a Christmas visit in the middle of an eight-month research stint in Calcutta. As I looked around at the drab bathroom stalls that surrounded me somewhere in JFK Airport, a powerful memory suddenly flashed into my mind. It had not appeared for a very long time, perhaps for as many as ten years, and now here it was again, but this time, unlike all of its other appearances, it appeared with a clear and definitive interpretation. The memory involved a waking fantasy that used to torment me as an adolescent, very much as Jung's fantasy of God shitting on a cathedral used to torment him as a boy.[6] The fantasy was constructed out of the symbols of my Catholic culture: I would see a naked ithyphallic Jesus on the cross with myself and the Virgin Mary standing beneath him. I felt terribly guilty about this fantasy as a boy, but I could never quite shake it, and I certainly did not understand it. Eventually, as the years went on, I forgot about it, but the problems which it announced shortly after puberty would haunt me for years and in the end would almost take my life. In that bathroom stall in JFK I finally understood its original meaning and the ominous announcement it was making: at puberty I was about to "crucify" my sexuality for its unresolved oedipal dimensions. The divine erection, I realized, was aimed, if always unconsciously, at (the Virgin) Mother, and for this it had to be crucified, it had to be killed. And kill it I did. For the next six years, from shortly after puberty to my junior year in the seminary, I would engage myself in various ascetic practices, mostly involving different forms of fasting, until my once athletic 6' 1" frame was reduced to a skeleton-like 125 pounds, a mere shadow of my former physical self—a modern American case of what Rudolph Bell would call, appropriately I think, "holy anorexia."[7] In the meantime, I would enter a Benedictine seminary and begin to consider the monastic life my chosen vocation. Fortunately, the monks who ran the seminary were very wise, highly educated, and knew a neurosis when they saw one. At their gentle but consistent prodding, I entered psychoanalysis with a professionally trained monk at the beginning of my junior year (the fall of 1983) and, on the point of starvation, began to dream dreams.

It all took only a few months. Almost immediately I began to dream about women, women bearing milky, rich food (I especially remember the milk shakes and the banana cream pies). I did not understand why, but I always felt guilty in the dreams for accepting the food. At some point in the course of our sessions, it suddenly "hit" me: on some unconscious level, I was making the symbolic, and incestuous, equation: food = mother = sex. This was not a difficult realization for me, since I distinctively and clearly remembered falling in love with my beautiful mother as a small boy. By anyone's standards, mine was an idyllic childhood, filled with love and happiness and emotional warmth. Ironically, it was this very happiness that set me up for an adolescent crisis, for this was an "Eden" I had absolutely no desire to leave. But the "fruit" of sexuality would come, bidden or no, and with it the shame and guilt of this newfound knowledge. Freud's oedipal theory, then, was not just another piece of speculation for me: it was the most obvious and healing of truths. I also, of course, then understood what had been happening to me for the past six or seven years. To cope with my unacknowledged oedipal feelings, I had effectively attacked the source of my illicit desires, the body, with a piece of deadly symbolic logic: you desire the mother, the mother is food, you cannot have the mother, you cannot have food. The fact that starvation effectively destroyed my sexual attractiveness (who can love a skeleton?) and depleted my physical and sexual energies to almost nil only added to the deadliness and efficiency of the ascetic logic. The problem was thus "solved," if at an exorbitant cost.

Now twenty-one years old and exhausted with being exhausted, I decided that the cost was too high and the solution was in truth not much of a solution. For some reason, I could now eat, on all sorts of levels. Moreover, something deeper than simple consumption was now happening, as if my metabolism suddenly slowed down and my body began finally to accept the food. Consequently, I gained seventy pounds over the course of the next five months. Something had "clicked" inside, and the body responded with an extraordinary zest. Freud, compassionately and deftly mediated through the structures of an enlightened Catholicism, literally saved my life.

* * *

But that is not the end of the story. Freud was undoubtedly right, but he was also limited, for something other than an Oedipus complex was being revealed in my nights. This "something more" soon crystallized itself, not surprisingly, in another dream about the same time as the oedipal fantasies were being seen and analyzed. Actually, I hesitate to call what happened a dream. In its numinous quality, its energy, and its striking symbolism, it was more of a vision; in a paper I wrote on the experience in graduate school for my mentor Wendy Doniger (who appropriately loves horses both mythical and real and all things religious and sexual) I called it a "myth-dream,"[8] for its meanings were all mythical in the classical sense of that term: definitive, foundational, creative, paradoxical, revelatory, true. The dream involved three presences: myself, a young, attractive maiden dressed in the manner of a Greek or Roman woman,[9] and a winged unicorn whose literally burning body appeared like brilliant black lightning. The maiden said nothing but simply smiled and led me to the edge of what looked like a very deep, very turbulent black sea. Just below the waters burned the fires of a terrifyingly beautiful winged horse with a single horn coming out of its head. Neither the horn nor the wings were fully grown. The Fire fascinated me—dangerous, dark, and yet filled with light. I instinctively knew that it was my task to get this mysterious being out of the water, and so I entered the waves and tried to pull him up, but to no avail. The scene then shifted and I saw myself as a youth riding naked on the now fully winged and fully horned being into the sky.

I woke up with a start and knew that something significant had just been spoken. Over the next few months I researched the symbolism of the dream with all the resources I could find in the monastic library: the Pegasus myth, the history of horse symbolism, the unicorn in the Western artistic and religious imagination, the symbolism of water, the Jungian notion of the anima, and so on. My tentative conclusions were at once troubling and liberating. Among other things, I understood that to get the unicorn out of the water I would have to engage the maiden of the dream as my lover; the unicorn of the classical myth, after all, could only be captured by enticing him to lay his "horn" in the lap of a virgin. The Greek maiden was thus a transitional symbol for me, in that in her virginal state she bridged two distinct symbolisms: that of the Virgin Mother of my Catholic upbringing (who, I might add, was often actually identified as the maiden of the unicorn myth in Christian allegorical glosses on the story)[10] and that of the virgin lover of the pagan unicorn myth.[11] Most important, I realized that the dream was structured around a profound *coincidentia oppositorum* that would engage me for years to come, that between the mystical and the sexual, or what I would later call the erotic. The winged fiery unicorn, after all, embodied at least two sets of opposites in its single form: it was sexual (it had a phallic horn) and yet somehow spiritual (it had wings and flew), and it mysteriously burned under the water. If this was sex, it was God's sex. Later, I would decide to call this dream-vision the *vajrāśva* vision, as the Tibetan symbol of the *vajra*—at once ritual object, thunderbolt, diamond, phallus, and marker of nirvanic emptiness—mirrored in a striking way the glistening brilliance and felt energies I experienced in the dream of the horse's *(aśva)* horn *(vajra)* and its surrounding images of dark fire, amorphous water, and transcendent wing.

God's sex or no, however, the vision was still structured around oedipal themes (even God cannot escape Freud): the small-horned unicorn can be read as a self-representation of the little boy and his feelings of sexual inadequacy before the Mother, the fearful waters can be seen as a symbol of the Mother and what it might feel like to be absorbed back into her womb,[12] and the virgin maiden, as I have already pointed out, was operating as a transitional figure between the Mother and the Lover. Accordingly, the dream's resolution would depend ultimately on my facing and resolving these same oedipal themes.

* * *

The dream troubled me deeply, for as hard as I tried, I could not discover any adequate resources in my inherited religious tradition to appropriate the truths I had seen that night. Granted, there was the bridal mysticism of the medieval church, in which the male mystic "married" Christ in an ecstatic union; here I read John of the Cross and Teresa of Avila and tried to pray with an uncensored version of the Song of Songs that one of the monks had translated. But this did not help much, for I quickly realized that the symbolism of the bridal tradition was in clear conflict with my own sexual nature: how could I, a heterosexual man, erotically engage a male Christ? It was not that I found the implied homosexuality of the symbolism morally troubling; it was simply that I found it unengaging; I, after all, was not homosexually inclined. Desire, sexual or spiritual, needs an object appropriate to its own "natural" movement, be that movement socially constructed or genetically determined or, more likely I think, a little of both. Deeper still was what I would later recognize as the problem of ontology. Here in the dream-vision there was no division between spirit and sex—they were one and the same. But in waking life, in my religious tradition, these two realms of being were clearly set apart, separated through innumerable symbolic, doctrinal, historical, and institutional structures. What could a sermon on the sacrality of marriage or the holiness of sexuality possibly mean coming from a celibate institution that systematically excluded women from its ranks and held up a virgin mother and a sexless savior as the ideal woman and man? Despite what anyone said or could say, it was patently obvious to me that to be holy was to be sexless.

A powerful visionary experience, my own sexual orientation, and an ontological crisis, then, all joined forces to lead me into a clear and seemingly irreconcilable conflict with my own cherished traditions; at some point I had to admit that there simply were no adequate symbolic resources within Christianity to nurture and eventually realize the union of the mystical and the sexual I had known intuitively in the dream-vision. Ontologically, the tradition's dualism (with a God set apart from the created order) rendered any attempt to divinize eros, as my dream had so clearly done, impossible. Symbolically, the male nature of God made a heteroerotic approach to the divine through this eros equally impossible. These uncomfortable conclusions were only confirmed when I tried to speak of the vision to my spiritual director. He had successfully guided me through any number of emotional, psychosexual, and spiritual crises, but now, in a very atypical fashion, he had absolutely nothing to say. But what *could* he say? In its heterosexual engagement with the divine, its explicitly pagan roots, and its deification of sexual energies,[13] the dream-myth could hold only the most tenuous of places in his, and my, religious world. The dream had exploded my Catholic world and pushed me beyond the comfortable boundaries of that ancient practice which guarded, defined, and identified those boundaries—the art of spiritual direction.

When I further researched the history of the unicorn myth in graduate school, I discovered that the creature's first appearance in the West was in a fourth-century-B.C.E. Greek text, the *Indika* of Ctesias, who located the geographical origins of the *monoceros* in India. Still, significantly, whereas "the western unicorn legend was very probably born out of the Indian myth of Ṛṣyaśṛṅga [the sexually innocent ascetic who had sublimated his semen into a 'horny' head], it is only in the west that the hunting of the unicorn . . . and the transmutative properties of its horn are brought to the fore."[14] The myth-dream thus acted as a transitional mediator for me, joining European and South Asian cultures within a single haunting narrative. I would learn much later that India also possesses a rich history of myths about Bāḍava, "the name of the submarine fire . . . which originated from Śiva's third eye when he incinerated Kāma, the Hindu Eros."[15] It is said that Bāḍava now dwells at the bottom of the ocean, where it burns continuously under the waters until it finally dries up the sea and erupts to consume time itself. Śiva's asceticism, like my own, had destroyed the sexual only to find it reappearing "under the waters" as the erotic, burning apocalyptically. Interestingly, the medieval Siddha traditions employ this same flaming horse under the waters as a symbol for the *kuṇḍalinī*, the dormant "coiled" energies said to dwell at the base of the spine that the yogin attempts to awaken through psychophysiological discipline. Hence, the *mūlādhāra cakra* at the very base of the spine is sometimes called "the submarine fire" *(vāḍavānala)*.[16] Here, I thought, was a culturally developed analogue of what I had experienced as the horn. In my own life and experience, then, the unicorn myth has resonated powerfully, if largely unconsciously (that is, under the waters), with Indological, Tantric, and mystico-erotic themes. Not surprisingly, this same myth-dream would play a central role in my choice of India and Hinduism as objects of study and practice, well before many of these resonances were identified and named.

At the same time of the *vajrāśva* vision, I was beginning to discover that there were other religious symbolisms out there, some of which actually affirmed a heterosexual approach to the divine. Indian Tantra seemed the most developed; here was a tradition in which a heterosexual male could remain a heterosexual male and approach the divine in an explicitly erotic fashion within a tradition that was philosophically sophisticated, iconically striking, and mythologically complex. What I found in my first halting studies of things Indological at times bore an almost uncanny resemblance to the truths of my myth-dream. I had discovered an affinity, a contact with someone and something outside my own subjective experience that confirmed my own vague intuitions; the unicorn's fire became a hermeneutical fire, a way to make contact with the texts I was studying.

* * *

The following year, when I returned for my senior year and asked the same monk for his spiritual direction, he refused. I would be leaving the seminary, he told me, and I needed to become my own spiritual director. Distraught, I asked him again. He refused again. I was thus thrown back upon the resources of my own soul and mind, and I did what he suggest I do: I became my own spiritual director through the only art and practice that still made sense to me, the comparative study of religion. I graduated from the seminary and its nurturing monastic tutelage and went to Chicago to study the history of religions.

* * *

8 May 1999. The *vajrāśva* vision is interesting. The beginning was clear enough (get the horse out of the water), and the end was clear enough (fly away on the horse), but the middle, the how-to-do-it part, was completely missing, as if I was supposed to stumble through this on my own, making it up (quite literally) as I go. The dream-vision, in other words, demands interactive participation and interpretative choice. It can only be fulfilled through a hermeneutical process.

20 June 2000. Looking back on this process again, I am struck by the degree to which my memories have been filtered through a distinctively psychoanalytic framework. Clearly, a certain "smoothing" has taken place, a secondary revision that has created its own narrative, its own world of meaning. In effect, psychoanalysis has become my spiritual map through which I have traveled back along my own developmental arc to earlier and earlier levels of my psychic palace. In effect, it has functioned as a

modern or postmodern mystical path for me, back to the oedipal father, the preoedipal mother, and the narcissistic self. How much of this is "real," and how much is constructed by the categories themselves? That is virtually impossible to say, at least for me. But isn't this precisely how all mystical traditions function, as elaborate constructions of meaning, as maps that are as much fictions as reflections?

TWO

The Passion of Louis Massignon

Sublimating the Homoerotic Gaze in *The Passion of al-Hallāj* (1922)

> Not that the study of [Hallāj's] life, which was full and strong, upright and whole, rising and given, yielded to me the secret of his heart. Rather it is he who fathomed mine and who probes it still. A brief allusion to him on the margin of Khayyām's "quatrains" set down by an uncertain hand, a simple sentence by him in Arabic in the Persian "memorial" of ʿAttār, and the meaning of sin was returned to me, then the heart-rending desire for purity read at the start of a cruel Egyptian spring. It is with lowered eyes, *markhiyā ʿaynayyā,* that I hail from afar this lofty figure, always veiled for me, even in his tortured nakedness.
>
> True sanctity is necessarily excessive, eccentric, abnormal, and shocking.
>
> Louis Massignon, preface to the new edition of *The Passion of al-Hallāj*

> Come, give me wine to drink and say "It's wine." And don't give me to drink in secret, when it is possible to do it in public.
>
> Abū Nuwās, quoted in "Vision and Passion: The Symbolism of Male Love in Islamic Mystical Literature," by Jim Wafer

I SUGGESTED IN THE previous chapter that the Christian experience of mystical love and the "mystical marriage" cannot be divorced from the issues of gender and sexual orientation. To the extent that a male mystic encounters the divine as a masculine Presence and uses sexual language to express the experienced truths of that encounter, those expressions will, by definition, be structured along homoerotic lines. This is not necessarily to suggest that such male mystics were homosexually oriented along their own culturally and historically specific lines, much less our own, but the thesis does grant these questions a greater salience and probability.

And the same is true of scholars of mysticism. They too are sexual beings. They too routinely use sexual language to describe both the texts they study and their own experiences of those texts. There is, however, one major difference, but it works in our favor here: when we are dealing with a medieval mystic (say, John Ruysbroeck), we are told precious little, if anything, about his sexual life and nothing about his sexual orientation (this being a modern category); when, however, we move into the twentieth century and examine scholars who are trained to see and describe just these sorts of things, we are often, if not always, told immeasurably more. Here again the historian of mysticism becomes more interesting and theoretically useful than the historical mystic. Certainly this is the case with the life and work of the French Islamicist Louis Massignon (1883–1962), a figure who has played a particularly central role in the development (and experience) of my thesis on the mystical potential of scholarship. I will explore Massignon's life and work in four movements here: a brief synopsis of his eventful life up to his conversion in the deserts of Iraq in 1908 (part 1); a discussion of the historical methodology and hermeneutical assumptions, particularly in regard to the interpretation of mystical texts and theopathic utterances, that formed the backdrop of his four-volume masterwork, *The Passion of al-Hallāj* (part 2); a literary analysis of *The Passion,* analyzing in particular its treatment of Sufi homoeroticism in the light of Massignon's struggle with his own homosexuality (part 3); and a short study of his later life of social action in the context of his belief in the *abdāl,* that chain of apotropaic saints whom God has called to suffer vicariously for the salvation of humanity (part 4).

A personal confession is in order here: with Massignon I am especially aware of being in the presence of a kind of oceanic humanity whose powerful currents and depths I do not pretend for a moment to be able to navigate safely. I fear being drowned here, primarily because of the mystery of Massignon himself, but also because of my own relative ignorance of Islamic histories, languages, and cultures. I am also acutely aware that the secondary literature on this scholar is especially vast, and that I enter this subject as a hopeless neophyte who may turn out to be nothing but an unwelcome dilettante. And yet, if there is a fault here, I would suggest that it ultimately lies with Massignon himself and his weirdly beautiful prose, whose florid flashes of a romantic, almost decadent eloquence simultaneously reveal and conceal the intimacies of the soul who penned them. In the words of Herbert Mason, Massignon was a man "of profound and eccentric desire."[1] His writings certainly support such an evaluation. Composed in a style that Mason describes lovingly but honestly as "herky-jerky,"[2] they move back and forth—usually with little warning—from rigorous historical prose on the most mundane and ordinary of topics to impressive flights of lyricism and mystical insight. At numerous points in his oeuvre, especially in his later "minor works," the Arabist abandons altogether the scholarly objectivism and didacticism of "the orator who is more or less an actor playing the God of modern biblical exegesis" (whom he obviously scorns) and returns to a more intimate, and for him more natural, "testimonial" style.[3] And even in *The Passion,* within those hundreds of pages of excruciatingly technical discussions of Persian banking practices, caliphate histories, and Islamic theology, there lie hidden, "like the spark in dry flint" (PH, 1:lxvii), numerous, seemingly anomalous paragraphs of a genuinely mystical, deeply personal, and sometimes downright eerie nature—oneiric revelations of personal destiny, speculative discussions of the "intersigns" that parapsychologically punctured Hallāj's (and Massignon's) life curve, morbidly elaborate, almost obsessive, descriptions of the tortured, incised, bludgeoned, and decapitated male body, idiosyncratic (and strangely psychoanalytic) reflections on the sexual natures of flowers, and deeply ambiguous, burnt essays on the nature and meaning of mystical love.[4] The text haunts, fascinates and repulses all at once, like the sacred itself. The text, moreover, was written, published, rewritten, republished, and translated for its readers, including and perhaps especially those who do not know Arabic or Persian but nevertheless want to think deeply and passionately about mysticism, love, sacrifice, suffering, and death. The text, if not the man and his culture, thus belongs to no one. As long as we stick close to this text, then, as a published, if still opaque, documentary of both al-Hallāj's and Massignon's Passion, we have every right to think, to wonder, to ask out loud. And fortunately, at least here, there is much, almost too much, with which to speculate, through which to see things in the mirror of the text.

Not accidentally, a similar type of intimate, specularizing vision could be found among certain circles of eleventh-century Baghdadian Sufi mysticism, which claimed to see God in the reflected beauty of the human (usually young male) face, that seductive visage that was said to give "witness" to what Massignon called the unimaginable, superintelligible Presence (PH, 1:280). This is what the Sufi tradition called the "witness practice" or "witness play" *(shahid bāzī),* a suitably ambiguous term even in

English, suggesting a mirroring dialectic between the subject, who "witnesses" the Presence, and the object, who gives "witness" to the Presence. Such a contemplative, essentially homoerotic gaze bothered Massignon deeply (as it did orthodox Islam), despite the fact, as we shall see, that it helped form the first few centuries of Hallāj's name and survival among Sufis after his death. Consequently, Massignon sought desperately to transform it through his hermeneutical choices into a more respectable, orthodox, and formless intellectual mysticism of "pure" love and sacrificial suffering. In Jim Wafer's terms, he sought to replace the Sufi "visionary complex" of seeing God in the immanence of the beloved's beauty with that other, perhaps even more central pattern, the "passion complex" of suffering and death for and in the beloved as transcendent other: "Whereas in the vision complex," Wafer writes, "the relationship between lover and beloved is mediated symbolically by the faculty of sight, in the passion complex it entails a symbolic physical interaction in which the lover is wounded or killed by his beloved."[5] The two complexes, of course, often interact in the same texts (consider, for example, the moth that sees the attractive flame, feels drawn to its beauty, and perishes in it [PH, 3:91]). So too here in *The Passion of al-Hallāj,* where the naked tortured body of Hallāj on the gibbet is always the paradigmatic "witness" for Massignon. Hallāj was the scandalous, excessive, excommunicated outlaw-saint in whose male human form the scholar could see, could *witness* and *give witness to,* both himself as crucified homoerotic mystic and the divine male Presence reflected in a mutual dialectic of ontic Essential Desire (he always capitalized the expression) and mystical love. The Sufi Bistāmī, we are told, "expressed desire" for the divine Presence, Shustarī "repeated this desire," and Hallāj's own disciple, Shiblī, claimed that he saw this Presence in the body of Hallāj on the day he spoke his most famous theopathic utterance, "Anā'l-Haqq," that is, "I am the Truth" (PH, 1:280). There is little doubt, I think, that, in his heart of hearts, Louis Massignon claimed to see, like Shiblī, the same divine Presence witnessed in the physical form of al-Hallāj, even if this vision could only become legitimate after the male bodies of both Hallāj and Massignon had been sufficiently tortured and indeed physically sacrificed for the male God as beloved. Massignon's was thus a "witness practice" of sorts, a homoerotic gaze more or less successfully sublimated[6] into an elaborately coded, exquisitely performed hermeneutical mysticism of four volumes, fifteen hundred pages, and five decades of male writing, suffering, serving, and loving.[7]

1. The Life of a Scholar-Saint

It is not at all uncommon when scanning the secondary literature on Louis Massignon to encounter writers referring to the scholar as a Christian mystic or even as a saint.[8] He certainly had and still has his critics—and there is much in his thought for us to be uneasy about[9]—but the fact remains that in thinking about Louis Massignon's life we are thinking about a most unusual human existence, in whose dramatic events and religious genius many see a very real, palpably felt sanctity. And indeed, Massignon was able to fuse, with more than a little vocational anguish and doubt, an especially focused, distinguished intellectual career with what was, by all accounts, a deeply personal and highly idiosyncratic search for God. His lifelong work on the eleventh-century Sufi mystic al-Hallāj and his own theology of mystical substitution, sacrifice, sacred hospitality, transforming mystical union, and social activism were inseparable—each informed the other within a developing hermeneutical spiral that continued to deepen and radicalize as what he liked to call his "life-arc" proceeded through the years. Yes, he could refer to his scholarly work as "this empty labor which absorbs the best of my energy"[10] and was seriously tempted to abandon his career to join Charles Foucauld in the deserts of North Africa in a hermit's existence of Christian witness and suffering, but he continued to write "empty" scholarship until the very end and elected to remain where he was, at the pinnacle of French, and indeed international, scholarship on Islam. His was not an easy, unproblematic union of the intellectual and mystical lives, but it *was* a union.

Mary Louise Gude has recently given us a comprehensive, critically balanced, and psychologically astute biography of the scholar, upon which I will lean heavily and gratefully throughout this essay. Gude divides Massignon's life into two basic periods: his life up to the end of World War II, which was dominated by an early and then abandoned agnosticism, a moral-sexual crisis followed by a dramatic conversion back to Catholicism, the search for a vocation, and the development of his scholarly pursuits; and his last nineteen years, which were progressively given over to social activism, explicitly religious writing, and public demonstrations against French and European atrocities committed against Muslims during the Israeli crisis and the Algerian War. Following Gude, I will treat the first period, focusing particularly on his conversion, as an entry into my biographical reading of *The Passion*, after which I will briefly treat the second, political activist, period as a reflection on the unique fusion of the mystical and the ethical that Massignon was able to effect through his scholarship, his understanding of mystical union as a transforming union of the will (as opposed to a monistic identity of substance), and his Islamo-Christian theology.

Early Life

Louis Fernand Jules Massignon was born on 25 July 1883 to Marie Hovyn and Fernand Massignon. His was a privileged world of wealth, education, and cultural access. His father, though trained as a physician, left medicine to become a recognized and successful sculptor under the pseudonym Pierre Roche. Roche moved in the elite circles of Parisian culture, befriending other artists, novelists, and intellectuals, including the sculptor Auguste Rodin and the decadent novelist turned pious Catholic J.-K. Huysmans (the latter, as we shall see, had a particularly profound impact on the younger Massignon). Significantly, however, Roche was a firm agnostic when it came to things religious, while his wife was a fervently pious Catholic. This familial dualism would show itself later in their son's remarkable life. As Gude puts it, "[T]he sensitive young boy was in some sense caught between the two, because no choice he might make about religious belief would please both his parents" (LM, 6). It was not simply, however, a choice between piety and agnosticism, for, as Gude observes, the father's artistic sensibility, with its insistence on hidden meanings and other modes of knowledge, was a far cry from the reigning positivism of the time and in many ways set the young Louis up for his later symbolic and religious researches (LM, 8).

After obtaining a baccalaureate in philosophy, Massignon entered the Sorbonne to study mathematics, a course of study which he completed in 1901. That same year he traveled to Algeria, at his father's proddings, and came into close contact with Muslim culture for the first time. The next year he studied mystical literature, particularly Eckhart, Ruysbroeck, and John of the Cross,[11] as he prepared for his *mémoire* for the *licence dès lettres*, which he completed in 1902 on the vocabulary of love in the seventeenth-century novel of Honoré d'Urfé *L'Astrée*. He then served in the army, after which he decided to pursue a university career. He obtained the *diplôme d'études supérieures* in history and geography in 1904, writing on Leo Africanus.

Having studied Arabic for his essay on Leo Africanus, Massignon decided in 1906 to travel to Cairo in order to spend a year among Arabic speakers. On board ship he met a twenty-nine-year-old Spanish aristocrat by the name of Luis de Cuadra, who was returning to Cairo, "where he had quit Christianity for Islam so as to continue adoring God without remorse for his life, in the manner of Omar Khayyam."[12] The two became lovers. Massignon was always explicit about the nature of his relationship with Cuadra, as "for his friends he made hardly any mystery about the most secret things."[13] The relationship, though intimate and intense, produced a profound moral crisis in the young Massignon. Interestingly—and I do not think we can overemphasize this fact—it was this same homosexual conflict that led, both indirectly and directly, to Massignon's abiding interest in Sufi mystical literature. Indirectly, Massignon detected in the literature powerful expressions of love that, though structured along homoerotic lines (that is, between a male Sufi and a male God), were nevertheless sufficiently removed from the moral dilemmas of actual homosexual contact as to cause him little moral pain.[14] Here, in the mystics, Massignon could both indirectly express his homoerotic yearnings and feel good about them.

More directly and dramatically, it was his lover, Luis de Cuadra, who literally put into Massignon's hands sometime in March 1907 the maxim that would psychologically catalyze his lifelong quest. It was a verse from Hallāj recorded in 'Attār's *Memorial of the Saints* that read: "Two moments of adoration suffice in love, but the preliminary ablution must be made in blood" (LM, 23). Somehow, the Hallajian verse awakened emotions in Massignon akin to religious conviction, sexual guilt, and a painfully felt desire for "purity." Years later, in the prologue to *The Passion* he still could recall the details of an emotionally traumatic spring and the noble specter of a naked, tortured male body: "A brief allusion to him [Hallāj] in the margin of Khayyām's 'quatrains' set down by an uncertain hand, a simple sentence by him in Arabic in the Persian 'memorial' of 'Attār, and the meaning of sin was returned to me, then the heart-rending desire for purity read at the start of a cruel Egyptian spring. It is with lowered eyes, *markhiyā 'aynayyā,* that I hail from afar this lofty figure, always veiled for me, even in his tortured nakedness" (PH, 1:lxv–lxvi). The passage is overdetermined with multiple allusions, as was Massignon's wont. The reference to Omar Khayyām must have recalled for Massignon his lover Cuadra, who had converted to Islam to resolve the Christian contradictions of his homosexual lifestyle and to continue worshiping God "in the manner of Omar Khayyam." The reference to "an uncertain hand" or, better, to "an ambiguous hand" (Gude's translation of *une maine equivoque*) is also a clear reference to Cuadra's crucial role in initiating the forty-year process of scholarship, conversion, and sanctity centered on Hallāj. The "meaning of sin," the piercing desire for "purity," and the reference to a "cruel Egyptian spring" all speak of considerable moral suffering and sexual conflict. Hallāj's tortured, naked body only adds to the erotic complexity of the passage, standing in, no doubt, for both Massignon's desire for the male body as object and his guilty crucifixion of this same desiring body as subject. The image of a crucified male, of course, also recalled for him another sacrificed body, that of Jesus: "I will never forget that springtime of 1907. . . . I saw bending towards me in the midst of all those past figures of Islam, this crucified effigy, a striking double of the Master whom I had loved when young."[15] Finally, it is only with "the meaning of sin" and a subsequent "heart-rending desire for purity," that is, with the advent of homosexual conflict, that Massignon's religious life begins.

The Visitation of the Stranger

But these Hallajian maxims delivered by an ambiguous hand that sparked so much in Massignon's youthful body and mind were only the beginning. Much more was to follow the very next year on an archaeological mission in Mesopotamia. Events came to head on 28 April 1908, when an argument broke out between one of Massignon's servants, a man named Weli, and Massignon himself. Significantly, the catalyst was again the scholar's sexuality: "In the evening, having overheard my escorts' reflections, attributing to me effeminate manners, I questioned Weli, who said that he himself had proffered these rumors."[16] Massignon became furious, an argument broke out, and Weli left the caravan, taking the group's money with him. A series of complicated events followed, with the result that Massignon, now accused of espionage by the local ruler to whom he had gone to resolve his dispute with his servant, had to abort the mission and board a Turkish steamer on 1 May for a return trip to Baghdad, where he was living.

Massignon was the only European on board the steamer. The other passengers stared at him "brutally," as Massignon described it, "less for being suspect of espionage than for loose morals."[17] Later an officer told him that he would be dead by morning, as he claimed to know that Massignon had been part of the assassination attempt against Nazim Bey (the Ottoman minister of justice) and that he was in fact a French spy. Massignon was, of course, terrified. He went to the captain, gave him his revolver, and tried to convince him that his mission was of a strictly archaeological nature. He then fell asleep, his mind "still haunted by impure desires," his inner ear filled with voices announcing his execution and suggesting that "a Christian should kill himself rather than endure such shame."[18] Terrified by the threats to his life, literally haunted by sexual shame, and suffering intensely from a probable case of malaria and sunstroke, Massignon began to behave erratically on 2 May (the accounts actually differ somewhat on the exact dating and sequence of these events). He threatened his own and the other passengers' safety (he had pointed a gun at the captain and then at his own head and swallowed two or three lit cigarettes and would later become delirious and incoherent). When the boat stopped near the ancient ruins of Ctesiphon, Massignon, fearing for his life, tried to escape but was wrestled to the ground and bound. The next day (3 May) Massignon made a weak attempt at suicide, wounding himself superficially near the heart with a knife. But he was not to die that day, for around 2:30 P.M., the despairing Massignon, still bound hand and foot in the captain's cabin, was suddenly struck down by what he would later call "the lightning of revelation."[19] There are numerous, usually passing, references to this event in his writings. Certainly one of the fullest and most beautiful occurs in his piece "Visitation of the Stranger: Response to an Inquiry about God": "The Stranger who visited me, one evening in May before the Taq, cauterizing my despair that He lanced, came like the phosphorescence of a fish rising from the bottom of the deepest sea; my inner mirror revealed Him to me, behind the mask of my own features. . . . The Stranger who took me as I was, on the day of His wrath, inert in His hand like the gecko of the sands, little by little overturned all my acquired reflexes, my precautions, and my deference to public opinion."[20] "Like the phosphorescence of a fish rising from the bottom of the deepest sea . . . like the gecko of the sands": the ocean and the desert paradoxically meet in the passage as the tininess of God rising in the waters of Massignon's soul becomes the tininess of Massignon himself, now fearfully cupped "like the gecko of the sands" in the awesome hands of God, "on the day of His wrath."

Dreams of guilt and horror, however, continued to haunt him to the point that he kept his eyes closed for two solid days. Finally back at Baghdad, his eyes still shut tight, he was transported to the civil hospital, where the spiritual ordeal continued as he felt himself "pursued by nothingness" and his very identity questioned: "A series of terrible mental images continued to pass before my retinas against a background of Hallajian flames (a burst of sunlight, transposed)," he wrote.[21] Massignon arrived at the hospital on May 5 and did not awake until the morning of May 8. During that time the supernatural Presence visited him again. This time he clung to a beloved name, an almost certain reference, Gude believes, to Luis de Cuadra: "Then, taken up for the second time into the supernatural, I felt myself warned that I was going to die.... I clung to a beloved name, repeating it to myself, declaring to myself, 'if he has betrayed me, I want to be sincere for two and carry his name with me always.'"[22] When he finally awoke on May 8, he heard the doves cooing, "haqq, haqq," a soothing sound which reminded him of the legend of Hallāj's death that spoke of the doves' perennial pious repeating of God's name—"haqq, haqq"—in commemoration of that terrible holy event and the sanctity that it sealed. Since he had taken a young girl to task months before for showing him similar doves that would not coo, Massignon, always attuned to synchronistic hints in his environment, believed that the cooing that helped awaken him this time was a sign signaling the role of Hallāj's martyrdom in the dramatic events of the previous days: "And, in an instant, in the suspense of silence, I understood them: the Truth of my pardon came out of the broken talisman, from the veil of the torn Name."[23] Massignon's ordeal was over.

Almost. The strange Presence continued to visit him. It returned on June 24 and again the next day on a train, the latter time to convince him that the truth he longed for could be found in Catholicism. He immediately fell to his knees in the train and begged a priest with whom he was traveling, Père Anastase, to hear his confession then and there. The priest agreed to hear his confession as soon as they arrived at their destination. Unfortunately, however, even then Massignon could not receive the Eucharist, since his sins were such that their absolution had to be reserved for the local bishop. Still in anguish, still not fully forgiven, still with his party, he visited the Church of Saint Joseph in Beirut on June 28 and decided to make the Way of the Cross by extending his arms to form a cross and lying on the ground, face down in intense prayer. In this posture, Massignon's mind was haunted again by his past deeds and present spiritual condition. He clearly recognized his sufferings in those of Jesus on the cross, as he attempted to crucify and so redeem his forbidden sexual desires within a traditional Catholic ritual acted out on the hard floor of an actual church. Understandably, a young Frenchman stretched out in the form of a cross on their church floor troubled some of the parish onlookers, and they summoned the priest. The priest arrived, but Massignon refused to respond, having made up his mind to answer only to Père Anastase: this, he had decided, would signal that his sins had been absolved by the local bishop. Père Anastase indeed asked him to stand up, he did, and his mental visions instantly disappeared. Full absolution was his, exactly as he expected (LM, 50–51). Massignon's conversion was finally complete, if not yet fully realized in a long life of textual scholarship, ecumenical work, and political activism.

Analysis of the Conversion Experience

How are we to understand such events? One way to get at this question is to ask the simple question: What was Louis Massignon converted from? The answer at first appears to be double—his agnosticism and his homosexuality—but with closer analysis, these two existential problems reveal themselves to be two dimensions of the same cultural dilemma. How, after all, could Massignon have possibly accepted his own homosexuality within the orthodox doctrinal world of his early-twentieth-century Catholicism? For Massignon, at least, an agnostic position was a natural and reasonable corollary of his homosexuality. He solved his existential dilemma by removing one side of the contradiction—his Catholicism. The fact that his father himself was agnostic no doubt also gave a certain convenient weight to the position. There were, however, other solutions. Cuadra, for example, solved the problem by converting to another religious worldview, in his case, Islam. And even within Christianity, ingenious and bold souls such as the Catholic and Anglican decadent authors that Ellis Hanson has studied found multiple symbolic, mystical, and liturgical resources for their homoerotic existences within the very heart of Christianity.[24] But for whatever reasons, neither a clear conversion to Islam nor a decadent Catholicism were viable options for Massignon: his homosexuality thus required his agnosticism. The two were of a piece. Consequently, in order to convert from his agnosticism he had to convert from his homosexuality. Hence the powerful religious *and* sexual dimensions that run intertwined all the way through the conversion narrative recounted above. However we choose to read these events, one thing is unmistakably clear: they were linked—psychologically, morally, even physically—to the conflicted energies of Massignon's homosexuality (and the category seems entirely justified here).

Consider for a moment the Hallajian quatrain that sparked the process. Most obvious, of course, is the fact that it was literally given to him by an "ambiguous hand," that is, by his lover Cuadra. Less obvious is its actual content: "Two moments of adoration suffice in love, but the preliminary ablution must be made in blood." But why? Why are love and death, as we shall see, continually, often morbidly, connected in Massignon's mind? Why this verse and not some other? What was it about Massignon's experience of love that led inevitably to reflections on a bloody death?[25] Why, in what was called "The Discussion on Sin" (5 March 1944), did Massignon describe the visitation of the Stranger to Georges Bataille as a kind of "spiritual death"?[26] My own conviction, and I will expand on this below, is that this linkage of love and death allowed Massignon to deal with his own sexual desires through a kind of deathlike sublimation of them—a symbolic crucifixion, if you will, that he could enact within a lifelong pursuit of (sexual) purity, sacrificial sanctity, and the asceticism of scholarship. Certainly Massignon's comments on his symbolic "crucifixion" in the Church of Saint Joseph supports such a reading: "[T]o carry my own cross," he wrote, meant "first of all to endure myself, such as I had been made, with my habits of body and spirit: that is heavy to do alone."[27] We could hardly ask for a clearer connection between crucifixion and sexual sublimation. Here too I would place such incidents as his promotion of the canonization cause of the Ugandan convert Charles Lwanga and his companions, all of whom were martyred in 1886 when they refused to submit to the sexual advances of their nominally Muslim ruler. Gude points out that Massignon believed that such saints could act as an antidote to the sexual immoralities of religious same-sex communities and the Catholic priesthood. He thus celebrated a monthly mass in the martyrs' honor and lobbied for their canonization among church leaders and the African bishops. The entire group was canonized in 1964, two years after Massignon's death (LM, 206; cf. TP, 51–52). The case is particularly instructive in light of Massignon's own linking of love, homosexuality, and death. Here was yet another solution to Massignon's deepest problem: canonize a group of converts who had opted for a literal death over a homosexual act and then use their example as a bulwark against one's own (and some of the church's) innermost proclivities—a deeply ambiguous legacy indeed.

It is perhaps also worth noting here Cuadra's ultimate fate. Significantly, Massignon would make a dramatic vow to suffer vicariously for the salvation of his former lover's soul; that is, he would mystically "crucify" himself to free Cuadra from his homosexuality (and/or conversion to Islam?), as he had done in the church in union with Christ for his own conversion. However, despite such prayers and a remarkably faithful weekly correspondence that went on for years, Cuadra would eventually commit suicide in a jail for reasons never made clear. Did he finally despair of combining his sexual and religious aspirations and seek a final resolution in his own annihilation? Or did he kill himself after committing some serious crime to avoid imprisonment or execution? We will probably never know. Regardless, here again, a homoerotic love was linked in Massignon's life to a dramatic death, this one quite real and self-inflicted. It is sad, but perhaps not incidental, that Cuadra's father would kill himself as well.

Although I suspect that he would never put it quite this way, that is, in the terms of a psychologically informed analysis (a hermeneutical style against which he could be defensively dismissive [PH, 1:292 n. 118]), Massignon himself was quite aware and quite explicit about both the reality of his homosexuality and its relationship to his scholarship. Indeed, sometimes he found the key precisely where I would locate it, in what we have come to call, following Freud, the mystery of sublimation (cf. PH, 3:116). In the following passage, as often is the case, Massignon only alludes to the sexual dimensions of the process through a vague reference to "our common misery," but he provocatively, and I think quite accurately, identifies the psychological dynamic of sublimation as the key to both his motivations for beginning *The Passion* and the almost bottomless reservoir of energies needed to carry such a massive project through: "[I] considered that a significant life, a total human experience containing substantial allusions [to mystical experience] and linked to examples of heroism, all within a divinely planned scenario, could make dawn in others the desire to sublimate our common misery and the secret of how to do it, and that there was no higher lesson to pass on."[28] The facts that Hallāj's mysticism was read homoerotically by both his contemporaries and immediate descendants, that he desired a male God, and that he passionately interacted with any number of male disciples rendered the secret of Hallāj's sublimation all that more significant for Massignon. Here indeed was a saint who knew how to accomplish exactly what Massignon himself so desperately needed.

A Virginal Conception of Scholarship

But there is another theme hidden within the conversion account, that between the stranger and the friend. Massignon would later reflect at some length on such themes, often in a specifically testimonial style. Since he is utterly transcendent, God is "the Stranger" for Massignon: when "He comes into our midst, it is as a Stranger who interrupts our normal life, like a moment of rest from work, and then passes on."[29] These visits of the Stranger carry homoerotic overtones for Massignon (never, of course, quite stated as such), and sometimes hints of scandal. The Virgin Mary, "Mary of Nazareth, who offered herself to the Stranger, becoming an object of suspicion all her life," seems to be the scholar's model here.[30]

Writing in a long tradition of Christian mystical thought, which we have examined briefly above in our first chapter, Massignon claims that the soul too must become such a virgin: "Before the Lord who has struck the blow, the soul becomes a woman.... She starts only to commemorate in secret the Annunciation, viaticum of hope, that she has conceived in order to give birth to the immortal." She has been visited by "a mysterious Stranger whom she adores."[31] Or again, following Hallāj, the final sheath of the heart deep inside the feminine lower self or *nafs,* "whose appetite is lustful," is the *sirr,* "the latent personality, the implicit consciousness, the deep subconscious, the secret cell walled up [and hidden] to every creature, the '*inviolate virgin*'" (PH, 3:19; gloss and italics Massignon's). Indeed, cognition itself results from the intelligence dividing and opening itself up like a flower in order to be fecundated by an "exterior shock" (PH, 3:173). The intellectual-mystical life thus carries a definite homoerotic structure for Massignon, with God as the active, if invisible, male Presence, or "Stranger," and the soul as a feminine virginal creature, "who intends to remain passive, in the embrace of the real, in order to conceive it."[32] The homosexual element that seems to have helped initiate the visitation experience for Massignon is thus carried over into the experience itself. Here too, I might add, we could place Massignon's comment that the apostle John, the beloved male disciple of Jesus, is always designated in Arabic as "the virgin."[33] Such symbolic patterns are further enriched and made even denser by Massignon's understanding of fasting, which he links to abstinence from food, sexual activity, and speech (the mystical returns as a multiple "shutting" *[muo]* of the mouth); here again, it is the Virgin Mary who is his model, she who took a vow of silence that she might be impregnated by the Word.[34]

This Stranger, who "penetrates" the "one single Virgin" of our hearts,[35] is balanced in Massignon's account of things by the figures of the guest and the friend. These figures would enter deeply into Massignon's thought, to the point where he would later claim that one gains access to Semitic mysticism "only through perfect hospitality."[36] Friendship, religious experience, and research thus became virtually indistinguishable in his thought. And in his conversion. For there were many friends present at the conversion, invisible friends that Massignon somehow sensed in his soul: "I felt with certainty a pure, ineffable, creative Presence suspending my sentence through the prayers of invisible persons, visitors to my prison, whose names disturbed my thought."[37] According to Massignon, these disturbing names belonged to five people, four of whom Massignon knew personally and one of whom had been dead for almost nine hundred years, al-Hallāj himself: "I would write my doctoral thesis about him begun then in Cairo."[38] Research flowed naturally out of religious experience, as if Massignon, the woman, had conceived that night in May. "Discovery antecedes theory," he would write, "commotion precedes denomination."[39] That is to say, the experience of the scholar, however confused and at first unbelievable, nevertheless constitutes the seed of all that grows out of it. And more *must* follow, for such a believer must not only become a woman and conceive God in the secret "virginal point"[40] of the soul; unlike the woman, who conceives "blindly," this believer must also "explain the notion one has of Him."[41] In other words, it is not enough to have the experience, however profound. It is not enough to conceive blindly. One must also strive to articulate it, to express it, to make it known, for language itself, if handled properly, can anagogically draw the reader "toward the real author of the article beyond the personality of the one who signs it"[42] (cf. PH, 3:175–176), and the proper technical terms, gleaned from the biographies of the mystics, can enable the researcher "'to enter into the presence' of the One whom no Name *a priori* dare evoke."[43] Such "inspired" articles and mystico-linguistic studies began for Massignon shortly after the visitation of the Stranger. They would continue to flow for over fifty years, the varied fruit of the scholar's mystico-erotic "conception" before the male Presence.

Behind many of these writings was Massignon's deep conviction that somehow a tenth-century mystic had reached across history and helped effect his conversion. Indeed, Massignon believed that all five invisible intercessors had the power of reaching across time and space through their "transmissive compassion"[44] and prayers. Nor were they alone in their powers. According to Massignon, there is an elite corps of human beings who by their willing assumption of "the blind anguish of living multitudes" understand the efficacy of vicarious suffering and announce "its transcendental glory." It is this line of hidden saints that constituted for Massignon "the secret of history."[45] Al-Hallāj, "who died crucified for the pure, inaccessible love of God"[46] and in order to unite his fellow Muslims in the Unity of God was one such hidden ruler of history. Certainly he was the most important and influential presence in Massignon's life, a fact to which the scholar's immense magnum opus on the mystic and martyr amply testifies.

Massignon admitted that such a claim might seem "queer"[47] to those who have not experienced its reality,[48] but he nevertheless continued to apologetically[49] share in print with his fellow historians of religions the strange instances of his own "premonitorial dreams"[50] and experiences of this transmissive compassion and continued to insist that such cases of vicarious suffering possess a real "parapsychological genuineness."[51] Perhaps he was speaking out of his own experience of that desert May afternoon of 1908. Years later, as if still struggling to find a vocabulary with which to "conceive Him," he would write out whole paragraphs filled with words drawn from disciplines and fields as disparate as Sanskrit symbolism, parapsychology (cf. PH, 2:337, 3:278), modern cosmology, Greek theology, and Jungian depth psychology in order to communicate this deepest of his convictions: "Here lies the ford, the wade *(tirtha),* for crossing—from parapsychological research to the invisible realm. Here we get on from the 'orderly' material world, through a distortion (Einsteinian) of Space *and* Time to an 'overorderly,' chrono-grammatically personalized 'constellation' of human events: no longer casualized, but as Jung says, 'synchronized' by their intelligible meaning; which appears *apotropaic,* i.e., transmissible—not genealogically, but as a chain of spiritual rings."[52] "A distortion of Space *and* Time": Massignon intentionally emphasizes that "and," for he knows and proclaims that the single most significant presence of his life is a man who has been dead for over nine hundred years: "Not that the study of [Hallāj's] life . . . yielded to me the secret of his heart. Rather it is he who fathomed mine and who probes it still" (PH, 1:lxv). The researched had become the researcher, the "reader of hearts" who knew Massignon across the centuries and now guided his life. This mystical *correspondance*[53] over time, with which Massignon simultaneously plumbed both his own biography and that of Hallāj, constituted the secret of his lifelong research on the "Passion of al-Hallāj." Certainly the very title of Massignon's magnum opus speaks of this hermeneutical union between the researcher and the researched. For al-Hallāj's Passion was not only an "essential, insatiable, transfiguring divine Desire"[54] that united his soul to the divine beloved; it was also an anguished suffering, a literal crucifixion, that by its very intensity and mystical efficacy somehow united the mystic to Massignon himself across the farthest reaches of space and time. Such an event, Massignon writes, fulfills "the 'hope against hope' of a miracle appearing in the center of the universe, which could change our hyperextension through an involution, and unite us as freedmen of a Hidden Guest, half-veiled as before dawn."[55] With this miracle, this "hole" in the fabric of space and time, the goal of Massignon's "mystical hermeneutic" had been reached. The Stranger, through a Friend, had become the Guest.

2. Massignon's Mystical Method

Massignon had to develop a very specific methodology for reading and writing the history of religions in order to pass Hallāj's higher lesson of sublimation on to the future. There are at least two primary places in Massignon's corpus in which he engages in explicitly methodological discussions: in his *Essay on the Origins of the Technical Language of Islamic Mysticism,* where he discusses what amounts to a linguistic mysticism; and in the preface to the second edition of *The Passion,* where he specifies "the working hypotheses actually underlying the initial plan" of the project, set forth here "in the manner of a methodology of the history of religion" (PH, lx). I will focus on the first here, as it deals explicitly with the theme of the present work, the possibility of reading contemporary scholarship as mystical literature.

A Sufi Discipline, the Power of Arabic, and Ecstatic Speech

As Benjamin Clark points out in his translator's introduction, Massignon's *Essay* advanced two major theses, both of them new to their day: that Sufism is based primarily on the Qur'ān and cannot be read as a foreign import, say, from Hindu monism (cf. PH, 3:14);[56] and that Hallāj was the summation and crystallization of the Sufi tradition before him, a tradition which, again according to Massignon, went into gradual decline after Hallāj, particularly in the aesthetic and overly speculative metaphysics of Ibn al-'Arabī and the Persian school (EO, xxi). A third project of the *Essay,* and one most relevant for our purposes, involved the development of what can only be called a mysticism of language.

Here Massignon expanded on the Sufi discipline of *istinbāṭ,* the frequent recitation of the entire content of the Qur'ān in an attempt to assimilate something of the full power of the words and their revelatory content. The sacred words are thus "chewed" and eventually "swallowed" so that the text, like food, can literally become part of the reader (EO, 35; cf. PH, 3:3). Massignon extends this Qur'anic method of recitation and assimilation to the reading of mystical literature. He can thus write of "wishing to savor" the works of mystical writers and warn his colleagues that they will not succeed in truly understanding the texts until they move well beyond the classification of technical terms and the nuances of doctrinal statements. In his own words, "he must personally redo the moral experiment, reliving the experience by putting himself, at least hypothetically, in the place of his subjects, in order to gain a direct, axial understanding of the consequences of their rules for living" (EO, 40). We can safely remove the "at least hypothetically" in Massignon's case, for this is precisely what he attempted to do with the Hallajian corpus—master its grammar and syntax, trace its prior history and later survivals, savor its mystical messages, pray with its words, and literally incorporate its maxims and teachings and narrative in his own body and life. Such a hermeneutical practice, of course, could have major repercussions in the consciousness of the hermeneut. Massignon knew this and clearly expected others to follow him in his radical method. As Pierre Rocalve puts it in his study of Massignon: "Massignon was the first in the West to provoke a kind of 'Copernican revolution' and, according to an expression dear to him, a 'decentering,' and even a 'mental stripping,' which led researchers following his example in regard to Sufism, to proceed through attempts at internal reconstitution and no longer by examinations 'from the outside' to which their 'patient erudition' was limited."[57] Massignon is explicit about such a method: "I have discarded any descriptive concept that does not expressly belong to the mental experimentation that I have wished to absorb, to reproduce in myself, and to transpose in French" (PH, 3:xiii).

Perhaps here the key term in Massignon's thought was *expérimental,* which, Clark reminds us, should be translated "experimental" instead of "experiential" to avoid the passivity of the latter term and to emphasize the active, exploratory nature of the Sufi's discipline (EO, xxv). And, by extension, the hermeneut's: "The habit does not make the monk, nor the note the song: we could not infer, simply because two authors have used the same words, that there was even an understanding between them; *experimental* verification is required" (EO, 42; italics in original). In somewhat different terms, because Massignon's criterion for judging the value and genuineness of a mystical author (and he clearly was about making such normative judgments) was ultimately social or ethical, there was only one sure way to determine the final meanings of his writings—live them out and see where they lead and what their socio-ethical consequences are (EO, 41). It is certainly also relevant here that Massignon understood salvation to be a communal affair effected through social action and not an individual accomplishment gained through individual meditation or ascetic practice (EO, 62). He could be extraordinarily dogmatic about this. By their fruits you shall know them.

More radical still, Massignon believed that entire metaphysical orders were implicated in the grammars and vocabularies of different language groups. Hence he can claim that Indo-European languages present a verbal system that is relative to the speaker and thus both "egocentric" and "polytheistic" (EO, 47). Semitic languages, on the other hand, display absolute verbal tenses that concern only the action, stress the first person under the influence of the Spirit (PH, 2:58), and hence give witness to a profound theocentric order that affirms the transcendence and imminence of what Massignon calls the "One Agent" (EO, 47–48). The Semitic languages, moreover, use a word order that is "lyrical, with phrases parceled into staccato formulas, condensed and autonomous" (EO, 48), a phrase, by the way, that could just as easily be used to describe Massignon's own writing style (cf. LM, 14).

And yet there was an even more intimate link between language and mystical experience for Massignon, for the scholar believed that the highest form of mystical union, the kind of transforming exchange of wills that he detected in Hallāj, inevitably led to inspired, ecstatic speech, the grace of *shaṭḥ*, "the divine speech that attacks the soul directly through the unwitting reciter's voice, in the form of the consecrated words" (EO, 73; cf. PH, 3:342). It did not matter to Massignon at all whether or not such ecstatic speech was accompanied by ecstasy, and he scoffed at the idea of judging mystical states by the presence or absence of "altered" states. Indeed, he had only condemnation for the "secret pleasure or spiritual lust" that he saw, with Hallāj, in the ritual techniques of the Bagdhadian Sufis ("these esthetes' acrobatics," as he derisively called them [EO, 75]), and he could speak of Indian teachers who used hashish, coffee, and opium only as "charlatans" (EO, 74) (here he resembles R. C. Zaehner). What counted in the end was whether the mystical state led to revelatory utterance that the hermeneut or believer could take, chew on, swallow, and be transformed by: the "absolutely essential thing" was *shaṭḥ* (EO, 74). It was as if the transforming union produced linguistic food for the faithful by which they could then be gradually transformed into what they eat—a kind of eucharistic reading, if you will.

Massignon had an almost absolute reverence for the bread of such words, for he saw crystallized in them the spiritual lives of their authors, the realities of which they spoke "minted" or conferred therein by the transcendent God (cf. PH, 3:79–80). Sometimes he would use the analogy of the poetic process to explain how this crystallization comes about: "The ability, which poets possess, to engrave the characteristic mark of personal experience of the universe onto common words, is even greater in mystics" (EO, 82). Like the poet's, the mystic's words possess no meaning outside their proper context (for there they are just words), but seen as "distant markers on the road" to God they become immeasurably valuable, their meanings deepening as the "mystical experiment" of the one who utters, and now the reader, progresses. Their "anagogic sense" is a "divine call" away from a false understanding of the world to a divine one, a call that must be answered by a conversion of language itself: the soul, Massignon tells us, must "reform its vocabulary in the image of the divine speech" uttered in the experience of *shaṭḥ* (EO, 82). And this linguistic conversion, this mystical transformation of language, is, in the end, a sign of the more radical exchange of wills and agencies that has taken place in mystical union, which, provocatively, is also an erotic possession: "An exchange, a switching of roles through love, is offered; the consenting soul, without suspecting it, is invited to desire, and to express in the first person, the point of view of the Beloved Himself" (EO, 83). Once again, the mystical experience is homoerotically structured for Massignon.

The Writing and Reading of Literature as Religious Experience

Also important here is the deep and abiding influence of J.-K. Huysmans and Stéphane Mallarmé on Massignon, a theme that Gude has explored in an important article on the language of mysticism in all three writers.[58] Through his trilogy of autobiographical novels, *Là-Bas* (1891), *En Route* (1895), and *La Cathedrale* (1898), Huysmans had popularized Mallarmé's poetic theories for a broader public. He also happened to be a friend of Pierre Roche, Massignon's father. Through these two channels, one literary and one personal, Huysmans "led Massignon to reflect on the role of language in transmitting mystical experience and how such experiences, by definition ineffable and discontinuous, can be cast as narrative."[59] Huysmans's influence on Massignon can also be seen in the former's insistence on what he called a "spiritual naturalism," a kind of dialectical faithfulness to both the full force of the historical document in all its realism and an ability to "sound the mine shaft of the soul and not attempt to explain mystery by the ills of the senses."[60] Such a dual method carried over into the writing style of Massignon, who, like Huysmans, adamantly refused to soften or bowdlerize the necessarily excessive lives of the saints and engage in what he called, no doubt with something of a disgusted sneer, "the proper *toilette* of the 'acta martyrum'" (PH, 1:lxvi). For Massignon, "true sanctity is necessarily excessive, eccentric, abnormal, and shocking," and to bind it within the "prison of common courtesies" is a lie, a failure to understand, and, much worse, a refusal to follow (PH, 1:lxvi).[61] Nowhere perhaps does this Huysmans-inspired naturalism come out more dramatically than in Massignon's numerous descriptions of torture, incision, decapitation, and execution that appear, again and again, throughout Massignon's retelling of Sufi history.

More radically still, Massignon was deeply sensitive to poetic theory, particularly that of Stéphane Mallarmé (1842–1898), a poet who had developed a theory that words, handled properly, that is, by a knowing poet, had the power to lead their readers beyond themselves into the absolute itself. Huysmans had described Mallarmé's alchemy of words as "an attempt to abolish the signifier or the materiality of language and thereby [allow] the poet to define the function of poetry as a spiritual one, existing beyond language."[62] In the words of Des Esseintes, his was "a condensed literature, a liquid essence, a sublimate of art."[63] As indeed was the artful style of Massignon, who believed that certain gifted writers (who, by the way, could also be scholars) were capable of communicating something of the original experiences of the mystics to their readers, who could then recreate the experiences for themselves within their hermeneutical encounters with the scholarly texts.[64] In effect, for Massignon, the mystical hermeneut was indeed a kind of godlike Hermes, a winged mediator between the divine and human worlds who through his grace-filled art could bring something transcendent down in and as his text. Translation became a genuine "carrying across" (*trans-latus*, literally, "carried across"). Clearly, this is what Massignon's style was all about on some level: "An array of images: oxymorons, comparisons, and metaphors often clothe an unyielding yet explosive syntax that is the despair of a translator. Such a style disrupts readers' expectations and serves as an invitation to the kind of 'decentering' that Massignon observed in the writings of the mystics and which was central to his own life. However, unlike many accounts of mystical experience, whose interest is solely documentary, much of Massignon's writing is inseparable from the unmistakable signature of his prose."[65] Seldom, if ever, in the twentieth-century study of religion have the mystical and a scholar's writing style been so deeply intertwined into a single process of reading, writing, and reading. This was a man who "longed for a fullness that could be realized only through an experience of divine life, and his writing is the trace of that longing."[66]

3. Rereading *The Passion of al-Hallāj*

How exactly was such a deeply personal mysticism woven into a four-volume, fifteen-hundred-page work of historical scholarship? Where exactly can we detect these traces of longing? A psychologically informed analysis of *The Passion of al-Hallāj* reveals that the very themes that defined the experience of the visitation of the Stranger—conflicted homoerotic desire, the suffering *abdāl* or chain of apotropaic witnesses, the theme of atoning sacrifice, and a desperate search for sexual purity—also structured Massignon's reading of al-Hallāj. Fortunately, such mystical-hermeneutical threads are not difficult to spot in the text, as they often announce themselves through a dramatic shift of genre and tone. The prose becomes passionate and lyrical, as if appearing from nowhere, and the readings become unusually idiosyncratic, eccentric, even bizarre. We are through with famine and political corruption and sophistic legal arguments surrounding Hallāj's eight-year trial. Suddenly gone are all those unbelievably long lists of caliphs, scholars, and military leaders with their dates. We have now arrived at the erotic and its implosion in a kind of mystical autoeroticism, or what Massignon and the Sufis more traditionally called the "love of God."

The Ontology of Desire

Desire is ontologically grounded in *The Passion,* for, as Massignon never tired of pointing out, Hallāj's metaphysical position was both original and heretical in its absolute insistence on identifying Desire (*'ishq*),[67] which Massignon always capitalized, with the Divine Essence itself (PH, 1:lix). Very much unlike traditional Islamic scholasticism, which denied that God could love himself within such an Essential Desire (PH, 1:362), Hallāj boldly "shows us [note the inclusive "us"] the Essential Desire of God, of Love, Lover and Beloved together, in His primordial solitude" (PH, 1:345). Indeed, we are told by Massignon that many of the Sufis of Hallāj's time claimed to see in human desire "a pure transnatural attraction" (note again Massignon's sanitizing use of "pure"), which they claimed descended from God himself (PH, 1:343). It was this very attraction, this Essential Desire, that Hallāj was developing, purifying, radicalizing, passing on to future generations, generations, I might add, that, particularly in Persia and Turkey, would continue to collapse the mystical and the erotic into each other within increasingly dialectical discourses and poetic traditions. Schimmel's oft-quoted comments on the poetry of Hāfiz, Jāmī, or 'Irāqī seem particularly important here as well, with Hallāj the master and Massignon the disciple: "It seems futile," she writes, "to look for either a purely mystical or a purely profane interpretation of the poems. . . . their ambiguity is intended, the oscillation between the two levels of being is consciously maintained"[68] And again, to restrict oneself to the "heavy and usually quite tasteless theological interpretations"[69] is to miss the very real possibility that, in Wafer's reading of Schimmel, "the poets may be trying to suggest the unreality of the distinction between eroticism and spirituality."[70] The same, of course, could and should be said of any number of other male mystical traditions, from Christian bridal mysticism to Indian Tantra.

Though such a dialectical mysticism often threatens to veer toward a monistic or pantheistic metaphysics, Massignon was insistent that, at least with Hallāj, it never did; hence his repeated distinction between what he called an "existential monism" *(wahdat al-wujud)*, which collapses the identity of the soul and the divine into a single transcendental unity, and a "testimonial monism" *(wahdat al-shuhud)*, which effects an "exchange of wills" (PH, 1:126) and bestows the essential "Ipseity" or "I" of God upon the soul while at the same time mysteriously preserving its distinction from the Divine Essence (PH, 3:47–51). Testimonial monism, a kind of "possession" state, if you will,[71] retains the sacrality of the person and is dialectical to the core. It also, just as importantly for Massignon, preserves enough duality to make a theology of sacrifice—with a single heroic saint or savior figure suffering for the sins of humanity—sensible and workable. Within a true monism, an existential monism, such a strangely brutal and sadistic (if eminently and troublingly traditional) logic is both meaningless and a bit silly, as some Sufi traditions saw quite clearly (PH, 2:227–28). This same dialectical monism, I should add, also makes love itself possible, for without duality of *some* kind there can be neither desire nor love. The erotic and the monistic are mutually exclusive registers.

Interestingly but hardly surprisingly, Massignon's allegedly academic description of Hallāj's testimonial monism employs a deeply personal language that calls us back, through a series of familiar associative images and allusions, to his own mystical conversion. In his usual, halting style, Massignon abandons the impersonalism of scholarship and speaks testimonially here of a "you" and a "me," thereby calling his reader to join him in the sacred encounter that he is presently recounting: "in the shock of a sacred visitation, which places Desire between 'you' and 'me,' by the chaste veil of tears; thus bearing witness to this divine Tertium Quid. *Asrārunā bikrun,* 'our hearts, in their deepest recesses, are a single Virgin,' who conceives thus, in the eternal present" (PH, 1:lvi–lvii). The metaphor of the visitation, the suffering of chastity, the virginal point of the heart—these are all Massignonian themes rooted deeply in his conversion and consequent life experiences.

In one of his fullest descriptions of this same testimonial monism, Massignon advances a position that is very close to Underhill's comments on the "psychic tricks" of induced mystical states and, as we will see in our next chapter, is virtually identical to R. C. Zaehner's reading of mystical monisms. Interestingly, both employ erotic language to describe the state. Zaehner's will be Christian and so will insist on feminizing the soul within a mystical marriage register. Massignon's, more faithful to Hallāj's homoerotic world, retains the masculine genders of both the human lover and the divine beloved:

> The effect of divine unity is not the destruction of the mystic's personality, by crushing it with rites *(sabr, sahu)* or disengaging it through ecstatic intoxication *(sukr)*; divine unity perfects it, consecrates it, exalts it, and makes it its own living agent. . . . He cries out his joy having reached . . . "the One who is at the heart of ecstasy," . . . beyond the cult of enthusiasm that inspires others to work themselves into ecstasy through created objects and human means; the outcome of these practices is the idolatrous destruction of one's individuality at the feet of an indifferent divinity. But the true mystic, according to Hallāj, does not end that way. The divine union in which it is consummated is the amorous nuptial in which the Creator ultimately rejoins his creature, in which He embraces him and in which the latter opens his heart to his Beloved in intimate, familiar, burning, and flowing discourse. (PH, 1:274)

And, as if he senses the reasonable conclusions of his readers, Massignon immediately adds that "[t]here is no Arab mystic whose passionate longing is both more ardent and more pure than Hallāj's; no transposition of symbols of profane love occurs in it to confuse the impulse" (PH, 1:274). What is genuinely absent here is the dialectical sophistication of Schimmel's reading of Sufi poetry as simultaneously erotic and mystical. Massignon's sexual-spiritual dualism (which again I would read as a product of his own sexual-religious conflict) made such a hermeneutic simply unthinkable for him.[72]

Sublimating the Homoerotic Gaze: The Sufi Witness Practice

Massignon tells us that, unlike the angels, whose natures are defined by a formless "intellectual ecstasy," human nature is ruled by sight, that is, by a kind of "visionary ecstasy" (PH, 1:350). And although Massignon himself certainly preferred the angelic intellectual ecstasy beyond forms (hence his rejection of Christian mystical symbolism as "weighted down" with the weight and profuseness of physical images),[73] he had much to struggle against in the Baghdadian Sufism of al-Hallāj's era. As Massignon himself pointed out in considerable erudite detail, certain poetic, artistic, and religious circles of Baghdad had taken this visualizing human nature and developed it into a specifically homoerotic form of mysticism, with the experience and even expression of human sexual desire functioning as a kind of mirror into which one gazed in order to catch a glimpse, however flickering, of God himself. Hence the homoerotic gaze that the Sufis called the "witness practice," that is, that spiritual discipline of seeing God in the unveiled beauty of the unbearded (that is, young) male face and form.[74] Massignon explains: "The unacknowledged ideal of Baghdadian high society at that time was the search for ecstasy: in the presence of an image of beauty that transfigures the human form and illuminates divine meaning. This is what is meant by the *shāhid,* the 'present witness,' who verified the fact that God *is*" (PH, 1:280).[75] Massignon, it should be immediately noted, was not disposed to thinking much of this practice and pointed out that, at least as an explicit practice (as opposed to an organizing mystical theology), it is absent from the reliable biographies of Hallāj (PH, 3:228, 239–242). Significantly, however, he could sometimes write of the practice in neutral or even vaguely positive terms (PH, 2:388–89; cf. 3:100), and he never could quite discount it completely: "[T]he beauty of the human face was unveiled so that the ultimate ideal meaning might be read in it: an unveiling that, too often, ended up, by offering itself to all, only to destroy, through the lure of the feminine face, natural family relationships, and to degrade, through the brilliance of the virile face, intellectual relationships" (PH, 1:279). The practice, then, involved an erotic dialectic of teasing concealment and dramatic revelation (hence the recurring image of the veil) that worked through a kind of sublimated sexualized gaze, often of a distinctly homoerotic type among the all-male Sufi communities; hence Massignon's linking of the brilliant virile face and intellectual community. Such practices, we are told, cost any number of young artist singers and poets what Massignon calls, no doubt thinking of his own youthful past, their "masculine purity" (PH, 1:280). Once again, Massignon's obsession with sexual purity surfaces in his prose.

In passing, I might note that the gender patterns we saw in Christian bridal mysticism—with the problem of a union between a male mystic and a male God—are here as well, but with the Sufi witness practice they are more open, more honest, and, quite simply, more resolved in an explicit homoerotic pattern. The human Sufi can retain his male gender before a male Beloved because the model of love is defined, from the beginning, as explicitly homoerotic. What was implied but still opaque in the Christian case is thus made obvious and redundant in the Sufi one. Sufism, we might venture to say in the mirror of comparison, is more honest about its homoerotic roots than Christian bridal mysticism ever could be.

Still, it is important to keep in mind that such practices were always suspect in the eyes of the orthodox Islamic community, and it would be a serious mistake indeed to suppose that all Sufi mysticism is homoerotic. Far from it. There is the famous *ḥadīth* of the Prophet, for example, according to which the pleasures of perfume and women were dear to him and prayer was his consolation. Schimmel suggests that it was out of this tradition that the school of Ibn ʿArabī—who composed his Meccan love lyrics after being inspired by a beautiful Persian woman in whose translucent beauty he seems to have seen a revelation of God—developed the idea that, in Ibn ʿArabī's own words, the "love of women belongs to the perfections of the Gnostics, for it is inherited from the Prophet and is a divine love."[76] Still, it would be equally problematic to take Ibn ʿArabī's heteroerotic mysticism as normative, for, in Schimmel's terms again, "the appreciation of women in this form is no more the rule in Sufism than is the full appreciation of conjugal life." Quite the contrary, "[w]omen were generally seen as the lowest rung of the spiritual ladder, as expressed in the well-known saying by Jamāl Hānswī . . . 'The seeker of the world is feminine, the seeker of the otherworld is a hermaphrodite, and the seeker of the Lord is masculine.'"[77] Once again, the homoerotic register takes over as finally normative, at least within specific Sufi circles.

Heteroerotic Punishments and Homoerotic Friends

Even if it is impossible, then, to generalize this homoerotic structure into Islam or even Sufism, it is an undeniable fact that a homoerotically structured mysticism runs throughout both Hallāj's life and Massignon's treatment of it, with page after page delineating the minutest psychological, doctrinal, and political consequences of "loving Him." And it is here alone, within this restricted Hallajian-Massignonian focus, that I advance my thesis about the homoerotic structuring of male mystical eroticism. Here at least, one can read for dozens, even hundreds of pages through *The Passion* and never run across a single woman (or even a feminine divine pronoun) as the object of a male Sufi's desire. It is as if "woman" as sexual object did not exist in this religious universe, or at least in Massignon's textual representation of it. One comes across an occasional exception, but these only end up proving the general rule. Consider, for example, the passage describing the human lover as a valiant knight pursuing his soul as his beloved (PH, 1:87). On first glance, we might assume that we have found at last one of those rare heteroerotic male images in mystical literature. And we would be wrong. For it is the soul, not the divine, that is feminized here. Hence, the human male mystic can assume a heterosexual relationship only to him/herself in a kind of internal autoeroticism. God is markedly absent, pushed out by the logic of the male heterosexual register, as it were.

Moreover and more telling, when a woman finally does appear in the text as an object of a man's sexual gaze, she can bring only disaster, and in the most famous case, Hallāj's very death. Not surprisingly, the crime involves a kind of gaze, this time an explicitly heteroerotic one. The legend, as Massignon recounts and studies it, begins with a disciple named Mūsā walking behind Hallāj through the alleyways of Bayda. A shadow falls on Hallāj. The saint looks up to see a beautiful woman standing on a roof. He immediately turns to his disciple and predicts his own execution for that single, accidental glance. The same disciple happens to be present years later when Hallāj is about to be executed. Hallāj has never forgotten his past mistake and explicitly links his neck "stretched" to be chopped off to his former neck "stretched" up toward the woman on the roof (PH, 1:57). The message is clear enough: Hallāj's execution is blamed on a heteroerotic glance, and, indirectly, on a woman.

Definitively not so with the homoerotic gaze. Indeed, quite the contrary, as we have already seen, the homoerotic gaze, far from being deadly, is developed into an entire mystical theology through the "witness practice" of the Baghdadian Sufi circles. Any number of figures and scenes could be cited for pages here, almost endlessly it sometimes seems, like the slow, disorganized development of Massignon's own text. To take just a few examples, consider the figure of Shiblī, Hallāj's disciple whom legend has denying his master to save his own skin and then throwing a red rose at Hallāj on the cross in an act of devotional love. As a youth, Massignon tells us, "Hallāj appeared to him . . . as the chosen witness of that divine splendor that transfigures the human face" (PH, 1:36). In other words, Hallāj became the object of Shiblī's homoerotic gaze and mystical practice, the "witness" of God's very glory. It was this same Shiblī, we are told, who transmitted to future Sufi novices, "in secret, the worship of Hallāj's memory: as a jewel of forbidden beauty, not as a sacrament of immortality to be distributed to everyone" (PH, 1:36). In his jolting and sexually suggestive style, Massignon describes the union that Shiblī "passionately sought by the most bizarre means" as "an instantaneous shock, a contact impossible to maintain, a throbbing jealousy" (PH, 1:85). Among these unusual, eccentric means we find Shiblī threatening a youth (Massignon refuses to tell us whether it was a young man or woman) whose beautiful form Shiblī believed was created only to tempt others (PH, 1:85).

Then there was Ibn ʿAṭāʾ, who, unlike Shiblī, *was* put to death for defending his beloved master. Massignon writes of "the level to which their pure friendship soared" (PH, 1:93), careful again to define this intimate relationship as "pure," a code word for Massignon that, as we have seen, usually carries connotations of homosexual abstinence. Among other documents and stories, Massignon includes two touching letters from Ḥallāj to ʿAṭāʾ. Ḥallāj writes and Massignon translates (with careful parenthetical glosses and well-placed capitalizations to defuse the passage of its obvious homoerotic charge): "[B]etween the (divine) Spirit and His lovers,—there is no disjunction owing to the difference between persons," Ḥallāj writes (PH, 1:94). And again: "This thought toward him (= Ibn ʿAṭāʾ) is my passion for You—O You, to Whom our allusions turn. We are two spirits that desire has joined together—there, near You, and facing You" (PH, 1:94). Here the homoerotic and the mystical have become inseparable, two manifestations of the same Essential Desire that joins three lovers—Ḥallāj, Ibn ʿAṭāʾ and God—in a single, all-male trinity.

Here too we might recall, among other examples too numerous to list, Abū Hamza, who cultivated with his young handsome disciples what Massignon calls a "Platonic gaze" bordering on homosexuality (PH, 1:80), Baqlī, credited by Massignon with a pure form of the witness practice, who sees angels with long feminine hair, earrings, and necklaces of pearl (PH, 2:388–389), Jibrīl (in Baqlī's dream-vision?), who strips naked before the throne of God "in a delirium of love" (PH, 2:389), and a fascinating little associative footnote on the word "shroud" that appears in the text: "The last wish of Qūsī: to be buried without a shroud so as to appear naked before God" (PH, 1:361 n. 71). The last example is particularly instructive of how Massignon's mind worked—through multiple associations and allusions that, if patiently followed, eventually lead us back to the single, all-defining Passion of Massignon's life and scholarship— a sublimated homoerotic relationship with the living male God.

Ibn Dāwūd and the Problem of ʿUdhritic Love

But no figure plays a more central role in the homoerotic subtext of *The Passion* than Ibn Dāwūd, a "sensitive personality, frail and effeminate"

(PH, 1:358), who extolled a form of sublimated homoeroticism and played a major role in calling for (and eventually winning) Hallāj's grisly execution. What is so striking about Ibn Dāwūd's place in Massignon's text is the fact that the most sustained and impassioned discussion of mystical homoeroticism within *The Passion* occurs in a twenty-page section on Hallāj's *indictment* by Ibn Dāwūd (PH, 1:348–368). If Hallāj's execution was not linked to his own form of homoerotic love—and the political, legal, and doctrinal dimensions of the case indeed render it much more complicated than this—Massignon's text certainly wants to suggest this, if only by the way it sets the execution up through a lengthy discussion of Ibn Dāwūd and his understanding of love.

Unlike the Sufis, who, as we have seen, claimed to discern the Divine Essence in their erotic desire, Ibn Dāwūd considered desire to be an aberration of the will and understood the Sufi desire for God to be essentially an illusion (PH, 1:342). Since God is formless for Ibn Dāwūd, any form of devotion that "loves" God must, by the very logic of that expression, render him anthropomorphically, which is idolatrous. Thus, from a strictly doctrinal perspective, God cannot be loved (PH, 1:345). Ibn Dāwūd rejected, in other words, not only the Sufi mystical doctrine of an ontologically based desire, but the very possibility of loving God. Certainly he struggled with the problem of homosexual love, but on an essentially secular and ultimately ascetic plane. Hence, Ibn Dāwūd's solution to what Massignon calls the two problems of "seductive beauty and of intellectual [that is, male] relationships" was to experience the homosexual passion without giving in to it (PH, 1:339). His was a quite conscious attempt to deny and sublimate his homoerotic desires.

Ibn Dāwūd, we are told, extolled a form of "uranism,"[78] Massignon's negative term—the scholar can write of being "contaminated by" it (PH, 1:343)—for the attempted sublimation of homosexual desire in Baghdadian literary and religious circles that we examined briefly above in its specifically religious aspects. Massignon's discussion of this theme with respect to Ibn Dāwūd is, to say the least, unusual, overdetermined, and highly idiosyncratic, reflecting no doubt his own deeply ambiguous position vis-à-vis his homosexuality. Massignon, for example, often writes of this uranism in ʿudhritic terms, an Arabic-based adjective coined from the phrase *hubb ʿudhrī*, literally, "gentleness of heart" (PH, 1:348). He also insists on linking it with that familiar complex of male love, death, and monotheism: "[A]nd if [the Arab] prays, his prayer, born out of a burnt monotheism, can only hasten his death, through desire to see the veil of beauty rise, to discover another Face" (PH, 1:348). Here Massignon specifically evokes the language of the witness practice, with God, "another Face," as the proper object of the homoerotic gaze. Such a gaze, however, inexplicably leads to one's physical death. Insightfully, Massignon locates the logic of all of this within a "burnt monotheism," that is, the belief in a single male God for whom the human male lover burns with desire.

Massignon is astonishingly clear that it was precisely this kind of love that defined both the social milieu of the time and Hallāj's mystical sublimation of it: "[W]hatever may have been Hallāj's position, thoughtful minds believed it possible to make the unsocial 'crise de sauvagerie' of 'udhritic love develop gradually into the 'crise de sauvagerie' in God as is the Hallājian Desire" (PH, 1:348). Such a transformation is signaled in Massignon's text by a number of rhetorical signs, among them the use of lowercase and uppercase letters; hence, in the previous passage a lowercase "love" is transmuted into an uppercase "Hallājian Desire." At other times this transubstantiation of love into Desire is marked by a dramatic shift in tone and a sudden poetic flourish. Hence, as if he knew precisely what the experience felt like, Massignon describes what it meant to "transmute uranism into divine love, to harden the look of the lover to the point of making him see God through his tears drenching the created face of the beloved" (PH, 1:280). 'Udhritic love, we are told again in a clearly personal passage, "suggests that love is not a stratagem of the reproductive instinct, but a divine annunciation. It is not an external revelation of the Law, but an internal one of Grace" (PH, 1:350). But surely we are not told this in quite this way in any Muslim text: rather, Massignon is telling us this, in his own words and within his own barely concealed convictions. The language, after all, is strikingly Christian, punctured by an erotic "divine annunciation" (we recall his repeated references to the "virginal point" of the soul) and a clear, capitalized Pauline distinction between law and grace.

As if to drive the uranian-Hallajian synthesis home further, Massignon tells us that it was through two Hallajians that the *hubb 'udhrī* was textually transmitted to future generations as the attribute of an Arab tribe that was, again in Massignon's purity register, "preeminently pure." This was the Banū 'Udhrā, whose people "died when they loved" and believed that "to die of love is a sweet and noble death" (PH, 1:348), hence of course the adjective "'udhritic," that is, "of the tribe of 'Udhrā." In one of the more revealing (and concealing) passages of *The Passion,* Massignon tells us that this notion of *hubb 'udhrī* originates in Yemen and is linked to a specific archetype involving the appearance of a kindred soul and the clarification of one's vocation or destiny: "[T]his 'kindred soul,' the sign of our calling, is above all (and sometimes totally) a spirit, and the spiritual relationship in which it sustains us avoids any physical and sexual contact" (PH, 1:349). Such a nonsexual love, we are told, is "angelic" and reveals one's predestination (PH, 1:349). Massignon's use of the pronoun "us" personalizes the passage, and his insistence that this experience avoids any "sexual contact" suggests again a personal grounding in Massignon's own sexual struggle. Is he speaking autobiographically here of his experience of Hallāj?

Massignon then twice breaks into an even more elaborate paean to the virtues of homosexual sublimation in the mirror of the kindred angel that has appeared to reveal one's destiny and salvation: "More profoundly, shouldn't the human nature of the two lovers, in the care of a single angel, be marked with the sign of a predestination of unimaginable unity, and, for their salvation, mustn't the two lovers go beyond the mutual image of their beauty in the angelic mirror, in order to adhere to the *fiat* of the Essential Desire?" (PH, 1:349). Strikingly, this same passage is repeated, almost verbatim, two pages later (PH, 1:351), as if to signal its importance in Massignon's mind. But of what (and more importantly, of whom) is he writing here? References to the "angelic mirror" and Massignon's encouragement to "go beyond" the mutual images seen there suggest that he is employing the language of the witness practice in an attempt to sublimate it into something more pure. The mirror image is also striking for its possible homoerotic connotations here, as the visual means to a kind of male doubling. In any case, the style and lilt of the passage, dramatically reinforced by its repetition, marks it out from the larger text, if only to encourage us to ask questions that cannot, in the end, be answered.

What, for Massignon, finally separates the "pure" love of the Banū 'Udhrā tribe from the moral "contamination" of a decadent and cosmopolitan uranism? Briefly and perhaps too simply, we might say that whereas the former renounces images and remains dialectically theistic, the latter is idolatrous to the extent that it worships an icon, a human being, a creature instead of the Creator, and veers inevitably toward a kind of narcissistic absorption. Hence Massignon's call for lovers to enjoy their beauty "in the angelic mirror" and not to become lost, "like Narcissus, in a cloudy mirror" (PH, 1:351). The mirror as the visual means to a kind of male doubling thus returns, this time as a trope for the assumed literal narcissism of homosexual love. Here Massignon is simply following his master, Hallāj himself, who, when he was told about the death of two "inseparable uranian lovers," responded that they are now united "in a single thought which has made them sink in the cloudy water of a double consciousness" (PH, 1:351). In Massignon's own terms, the homoerotic has failed to move beyond itself to the Virgin's fiat, that is, to a celibate position and a mystical exchange of wills. The register, on the contrary, remains distinctively autoerotic, a doubled male mirror reflecting shared homoerotic gazes into infinity.

Mystical, Sexual, Textual, and Political Secrets

Another major theme in *The Passion,* again often if by no means always linked to homoerotic desire, is that of secrecy. Like many mystical traditions, Sufism itself can be fruitfully approached through a study of its multiple patterns of revelation and occultation, of revealing and concealing, that is, through its esoteric practices, for, by its own textual confession, "Sufism is built on secrecy" (PH, 1:87). But esoteric claims can easily become thinly disguised political claims, and political claims are often dangerous claims. There was sometimes hidden in Sufi esoterism, then, a very serious challenge to authority, for to take seriously the mystically democratic claims of such a one as Hallāj was to turn the prophetic authority upon which the law was built into a sham (PH, 1:295). Hence the traditional debate about "the saint" (whose claims sometimes conflicted with those of Qur'anic society) and "the prophet" (whose claims usually were those of Qur'anic society) and which was greater. One solution to this problem was to bifurcate the tradition into two more or less separate dimensions, an exoteric legal domain and a more private esoteric domain. Massignon could thus write of a basic dualism between "a purely external literal law and a purely individual mystic esoterism" (PH, 1:295). So too with the apotropeans, those suffering saints "who must remain hidden" (PH, 1:131), the traditional hiddenness of the imam (PH, 1:305–322), and the Shi'ite principle of *taqīya* or "dissimulation" (PH, 1:305)—all were elaborate esoteric strategies to gain and protect power of different kinds: mystical, political, and other. Similarly with the place of the secret dream: it was the "embryo of prophecy," outside the law, and beyond the waking intelligence's censorship (PH, 3:337–338). Not everyone, of course, agreed with such strategies. Hasan Basrī, for example, railed against those "who made Hell stink" because they concealed knowledge (PH, 1:191 n. 7).

Hallāj himself seemed to be closer to Hasan Basrī than to the more traditional Sufis who insisted on keeping secrets. Indeed, his very name, Hallāj (literally, "carder" of cotton or wool), was sometimes read metaphorically and applied to his ability to "card" or read the secret contents of the people's consciences (PH, 1:153), and he was executed precisely because he refused to honor the traditional arcanal discipline of the initiated Sufis, that is, he spoke publicly of a love and an identity that other Sufis no doubt knew but prudently insisted on keeping secret in order to avoid legal prosecution (PH, 1:li, 1:23, 2:101, 105). In this same revelatory spirit, according to one textual witness, he had many friends who often came to him in secret to speak of forbidden things (PH, 1:469). Similarly, in one of the few accounts we have of Hallāj in ecstasy, he can be seen dancing as he recites the telling line: "Whoever has been told a secret in confidence, and then tells it . . . " (PH, 3:239). And then there is the Hallajian legend that tells of him stealing an esoteric book from Makkī and publishing it (PH, 2:101). Not surprisingly, Hallāj's disciples practiced a similar rejection of secrecy. Hence Junayd's complaint to Shiblī that the doctrine that they had prepared and safely hidden he had exposed and thrown "to the vulgar minds" of the public (PH, 1:86). Little wonder, then, that the immediate history of Hallāj's writings was one of censorship and official bans. Indeed, his texts could not be freely published and distributed due to an official ban on his works that was in place between 922 and 1258, and some people were even executed for violating this silencing (PH, 1:lvii, 2:5–9, 32). The mystical returns yet again as the dangerous textual secret *(mustikon)*.[79]

For still others, secrecy was a means to carve out a psychological space in which they could feel more or less free to pursue their sexual and mystical lives at peace and in harmony with God. Dhū'l-Nūn, for example, could write: "Whosoever familiarizes himself with God, is familiar with every beautiful thing, face, voice, perfume; underneath it all the mystics have secrets, that can only be revealed to their intimate friends, under penalty of chastisement and retribution" (PH, 1:81). So too with Ibn Jāmi', Ibn Dāwūd's lover, who, "though confused and anguished at an early age over this forbidden affection," was unable to deny the power of his desires and so created out of his memories of *'udhritic* poems he had learned as a child an "ideal of life in which the very Platonic desires of his love were made to harmonize with the practical requirements of his faith" (PH, 1:357). The cornerstone of this reconciliation was a famous *hadīth* that his father had, quite wisely it seems, shared with him: "The one who loves, but remains chaste and does not divulge his secret, and dies, such a one is a martyr!" (PH, 1:357). Massignon's feelings about such a solution come out on the same page. Here, in the context of a long footnote, Ibn Dāwūd visits a dying Niftawayh and asks him how he is feeling. Niftawayh responds that "[t]he love you know about has put me in the state you see me in" (note again that the themes of homoeroticism and death are explicitly linked). Ibn Dāwūd asks his dying friend what prevented him from fulfilling his desires. Niftawayh responds (and Massignon parenthetically comments): "The satisfaction of love has two aspects: the pleasure of the eyes, which is licit (on the contrary, *illicit!* [Massignon goes on to quote "Sufism and reason" to prove his point]) and sensual pleasure, which is no longer licit. And, from the latter I have been averted by the *hadīth* that my father recited to me: 'The one who loves, does not confess his secret, remains chaste and forbearing, may God pardon and open the gates of Paradise to him'" (PH, 1:357 n. 54). But this was not Ibn Dāwūd's solution. His was a touching and poignant "unfulfilled embrace" (PH, 1:358) that could find its satisfaction only in the mind, and finally in death.

Two Ways to Die of Love

Massignon puzzles over the fact that, although Ibn Dāwūd and Hallāj differed so radically in their teachings about love, their memories are intertwined for the Muslim community (PH, 1:361). But how really different were their teachings? Massignon, for example, quotes two touching homoerotic scenes with Ibn Dāwūd involving the unveiling of the beloved's face, one of which reads: "[O]ne night when I was sleeping in his house, he [Ibn Dāwūd] lifted the veil from my face and said, 'God, You know that I love him, and that it is You whom I behold in him'" (PH, 1:362–363). Now how really different is such a sentiment from that expressed by Hallāj to Ibn ʿAtāʾ quoted above? In another text Massignon examines, Ibn Dāwūd refuses to look at a lover's face because the lover had first looked at it in a mirror. This again is strikingly similar to Hallāj's (and Massignon's) position on homosexual love as a narcissistic gaze into a "cloudy mirror," that is, as an inappropriate form of autoeroticism. Provocatively, however, the text in which this scene is embedded is ambiguous about such a negative reading. The preacher using the incident of Ibn Dāwūd's lover and Ibn Dāwūd's reaction to his mirror gazing concludes: "Such must be the behavior of the believer vis-à-vis (his) God" (PH, 1:363). Massignon leaves the passage uninterpreted. But should we? What is the preacher getting at here? That the believer must renounce an autoerotic gaze to preserve his visage for God alone? That the love of a male monotheistic God is essentially homoerotic for human males? To what does the "such" refer? Significantly, we are never told— we are back to a double reading and yet another secret.

As for the deaths of Ibn Dāwūd, the accuser, and Hallāj, the accused, according to Massignon, both men died for love. But how very different were these deaths: the saint's bloody, gory, and shockingly violent; Ibn Dāwūd's quiet, controlled, and sexually frustrated until the end. Massignon describes in elegant detail the final hours of Ibn Dāwūd. A dying Ibn Dāwūd lies on a divan, "before a cage that holds a blinded twittering nightingale." His body, we are told, is going to be ritually bathed by Ibn al-Mughallis (instead of by the "filthy Niftawayh," whose filthiness, I should add, is never explained). "What was of concern to him," Massignon tells us (but based on what?), "was that he was allowed in this way to carry the mental conception of the forbidden pleasure intact, since it was unsatisfied, to the paradise of the uranians" (PH, 1:361).

How puzzling for Massignon, then, that the tradition insists on employing the theme of *hubb 'udhrī* to characterize the saint when in fact this was closer to the teachings of his executioner. Hallāj thus becomes (or was he always?) a uranian or satanic lover of God in the memories of the earliest Hallajians: "What Ibn Dāwūd had been, at heart, they reclothed his victim in" (PH, 1:365–366; cf. 3:239–242). Indeed, it took two full centuries for this comparison of the *'udhritic* and the satanic to be effaced by the Sufi tradition, as many of Hallāj's closest followers, including his beloved Ibn 'Atā', "were convinced of the therapeutic excellence of the sublimation of *'udhritic* desire to the Desire of God" (PH, 1:366; note again use of lower- and uppercase letters to signal the transubstantiation). This is a particularly astonishing moment in Massignon's argument, striking both for its honesty in discussing what must have been a painful historical truth for the scholar and for its ultimate failure to provide a better solution to the problem of Hallāj's original homoerotic legacy to Sufism.

Massignon's solution to this history and this early "satanic" identification works out of an assumed equation between the homoerotic gaze and a sterile narcissism (quite literally, as we shall see) and an equally clear equation between a vaguely Christian heteroeroticism (the "virginal conception" of the mystic) and a kind of internal divine procession that more than resembles Christian Trinitarian thought. He develops this idea in two long passages, both of which deserve our attention for their dramatic display of Massignonian themes and autobiographical tropes. In the first, the scholar is commenting in his typical staccato style on how "God loves Himself in an Essential Desire" (PH, 1:362) and contrasting this with the "lonely" position of the uranian lover Ibn Dāwūd:

It is true that if divine transcendence excluded the possibility of God's communicating to Himself and submitting to Himself, in His essential life, then the perfection of Tawhīd, of pure Islam, is Tafrīd, the proclamation of the Jealous Solitude, which the Zāhirite theologians, following Ibn Dāwūd, analyzed correctly in the pure uranian love sung by classic Arabic poets: in the "disinterested" gaze of morose delectation that Ibn Dāwūd considered licit, directed at forbidden beautiful faces (of beardless youths: *nazar ilā'l-murd*). (PH, 1:362)

In the second passage, Massignon goes further and, after comparing Ibn Dāwūd's uranism to a kind of narcissistic, intellectualized masturbation, makes his point through a rather bizarre discussion of two types of flowers in Sufi thought ("Contrary to animals," he tells us in an associative footnote, "plants hold their sex and not their head toward the sky" [PH, 1:368 n. 82]): the white narcissus and the red rose, the latter which the homoerotic Rūmī mocked and which Shiblī threw at the dying Hallāj. Once again, it is the phenomenology of the gaze that finally captures our attention as the defining feature of Massignon's text:

> The jealous glance, winking from within, at the swerve of Divine Transcendence just as it "draws near," is the "rear view" glance of intellectual onanism, of narcissism, enamoured of no one else but its own ideal, in the mirror of its mind. In fact, the poets of Ibn Dāwūd's time, Platonized narcissists, celebrated the lordship of the narcissus *(narjis)* flower, which the uranian Sophocles portrayed blossoming at the edge of the magic shadow, a thick and hardy snow flower whose polygonal sexual bud undergoes invagination, speared toward the inside. Meanwhile their spokesman, Ibn al-Rūmī, mocks the rose *(ward)*, a flower of the glade, for the bloody dehiscence of its sex, ingenuously blossoming out toward the sky, in dazzling display. If it does not close again over its enraptured vision of the sun, it is because it is like a crystal of it which becomes opalescent through a virginal conception. (PH, 1:368)

The homoerotic, narcissistic, masturbating gaze—again, in the same "cloudy mirror" of the uranian lovers that Hallāj had condemned—is thus contrasted with the virginal conception of the sun and the blood-red rose, a symbolic complex which at least in principle maintains a vague heteroerotic structure even as it hints at the violence ("the bloody dehiscence of its sex") that always accompanied true mystical love for Massignon. The narcissus flower is "invaginated," that is, autoerotic, enclosed within its own cold sexual solipsism. The rose, on the other hand, looks to a warm, transcendent sky god, the sun, for its enraptured vision.

Unlike the narcissus, which grows in the shadows, the rose blossoms toward the sun and becomes a crystal that can refract its bright rays through a heteroerotic encounter. And yet the complex of sun and rose is not really heterosexual at all, as the flower's conception is still "virginal," that is, without actual sexual contact. The only actual sexual act mentioned here is, depressingly, onanism, that is, a condemned masturbation, which Massignon wants to implicitly link here to homosexuality as twin forms of a sterile autoeroticism. Massignon thus at once affirms (in a symbolic polarity) and denies (in virginity) the heterosexual register in a passage clearly designed to deny the homoerotic structure of Sufi mysticism through a feigned Christian heterosexuality—bizarre indeed as a piece of historical analysis, but ever so revealing as a revelation of Massignon's own conflicted soul.

And yet, despite all of this, Hallāj's naked tortured body remains, even in Massignon's purified prose, the legitimate object of the homoerotic gaze, for he captured in the voice of his heart and offered up for all who can see what Massignon calls "the unimaginable Presence." The scholar is remarkably clear about all of this: "This superintelligible Presence is what Shiblī believed he perceived and saw again in 309, personified in the human form of Hallāj, in the mosque of al-Mansūr, on the day when 'Ana'l-Haqq' was uttered. Indeed it must be admitted that, during his visits to the Baghdadian salons of Madā'inī, Sāwī, Bahrām, even more than in the markets, Hallāj was boldly offering to manifest this Presence" (PH, 1:280). How does Massignon deal with this admission? Essentially, he argues that such a scandal was mitigated by the spectacle of the saint's gory martyrdom: "The scandal of his bearing witness in this way was tempered by the desire he expressed to die accursed for the whole body of believers to whom he exposed himself" (PH, 1:280). In other words, the homoerotic gaze is legitimate, even holy, as long as it "sacrifices" and kills that which it admires and loves as a reflected substitute, still in the mirror, of the desiring embodied gaze. Or more baldly still, homerotic desire is appropriate to the extent that it culminates in the death of both the object and the subject of that desire.

Leaving The Passion

I cannot help reading here a Massignon who implicitly acknowledged through a poetic form of textual scholarship his own homoerotic desires only to "kill" and "curse" them through the tortured body of Hallāj, the vicarious victim of his own conversion from homosexuality and agnosticism. If the link between a guilty homosexuality and a violent spirituality of death was not present in Hallāj, it was certainly present in Louis Massignon. Indeed, if we follow Massignon's own rhetorical lead and engage in our own exercise of poetic and theoretical excess, we might rightly speculate that the phenomenon of *The Passion* can and should be read as an intricately developed homoerotic gaze on the tortured male body, crucified for its radical (and assumedly illicit) love of a male God. Through this remarkable textual project of five decades, Massignon could both crucify and sublimate his own homosexual desires, driving them into another plane of experience that found more than enough legitimation, not in the symbolically heterosexual world of Christian mysticism, but in the explicitly homoerotic universe of Hallājian Desire.

4. From Mystical Union and Sacrificial Substitution to Political Activism

There were many features of Massignon's thought that made his late political activity both theologically possible and ethically necessary. We have seen, for example, that he believed that the only way to verify the reality of the Sufis' experiments and ecstatic experiences was to examine their social consequences and to see what curative effect they had, or did not have, on Islamic society (EO, 10–11). Foremost among his theological justifications for political action were his understanding of mystical union as an exchange of loving wills rather than an identity of substances and his theology of suffering as mystical substitution or sacrifice for the other. Indeed, the argument can be made that mystical love and sacrificial suffering were the twin pillars of both his thought and his life, hence the double entendre of his masterwork: *The Passion of al-Hallāj.* Indeed, the foreword to the 1914 edition makes this link explicit in its description of Hallāj's "teaching of mystic love and true sacrifice" (PH, li)—the phrase could just as easily be used to summarize Massignon's life and teaching. We have, of course, examined the notion of mystical love at some length above, but we have not yet related it to Massignon's understanding of mystical union or substitutory suffering. A few words on each are thus necessary before we conclude. But first we must finish the story of Massignon's life.

Picking Up the Life

Massignon's life, of course, did not simply end with his dramatic conversion back to Catholicism in the deserts of Iraq in 1908. He would return to Paris and finish his dissertation, according to him, at the demand of his spiritual director and as a debt to Hallāj for effecting his conversion (LM, 61–62). He would also struggle mightily with a vocational crisis between an ascetic life in the desert of North Africa with Charles Foucauld, who kept asking him to join him, and an intellectual life in Paris. Whether to marry or not was also a major issue. Finally, he opted for the intellectual vocation and a married life, the latter at the prodding of his spiritual director (LM, 135) and with the stated desire to transfigure it "to a life of union with God."[80]

Gude notes three defining strands in Massignon's life, only two of which we have treated so far: the intellectual and the mystical. Equally important, especially for his later life, was Massignon's extensive experience in the military and diplomatic realms of French culture (LM, 88), what we might call, for lack of a better word, the political. In World War I, Massignon first served as a minister of foreign affairs, reading and summarizing Arab newspapers. His real desire, however, was to serve on active duty in the army and, more specifically, in the trenches of the front lines. Massignon had a "deep-seated need to risk everything" (LM, 89). And he did. Despite the attempted interventions of his family and Paul Claudel, the young scholar finally arrived at the trenches on 9 October 1916, where he spent the next four months, at times in direct enemy contact, a feat for which he won the Croix de Guerre and numerous citations (LM, 89–90).

Massignon then was in the diplomatic service from 1917 to 1920, gaining firsthand knowledge of how French and British diplomats dealt with Muslims and negotiated, tricked, and forced their vision of the postwar Middle East into existence over the Islamic desires for religious unity and political autonomy for the Arab countries. He was deeply affected by this diplomatic experience, as it was a theater on which he saw played out his own deepest political ambivalences stemming from his dual commitment to France's mission in the world and his dramatic and repeated rejection of its colonial enterprises (LM, 90–91). He thus could neither unequivocally endorse French policy nor fully uphold Arab nationalism. He sought instead a mutual transformation of cultures through contact and exchange among equals (LM, 101–105). It was an idealistic and inconsistent, even self-contradictory position (for how could there be an exchange of equals between colonizer and colonized?), but it was Massignon's position.

In 1919, at the age of thirty-six, Massignon was named the successor of his mentor, Alfred le Chatelier, to the chair of *sociologie et sociographie musulmanes* at the Collège de France. He would remain in the position for thirty-five years. On 26 March 1922, exactly one thousand years after the death of al-Hallāj, Massignon deposited his two dissertations on the saint at the Sorbonne, perhaps one of the clearest and most dramatic examples of what Massignon called the "intersigns" of his life, those synchronistic matches between internal religious realities and external historical events through which the scholar created the meanings and discerned the direction of his life arc (and indeed, in this case it was a conscious construction, as the documents had been more or less finished for some time and Massignon was no doubt timing his completion and rewriting of them—they had been partially destroyed by bombs during the war—for the auspicious date). Constructed or no, however, his was a universe of secret signs that had to be decoded and then acted on through intuition, grace, and intense involvement in the spiritual-political world of his faith. What might appear as coincidence or pious wish to an outside observer often appeared to Massignon as potent intersigns of a destiny that could only be realized through interpretation and committed action. Places and events thus "converged for Massignon in an intricate pattern of symbol" (LM, 134).

Later, Massignon became increasingly familiar with Gandhi and his notion of *satyagraha*, or "grasping the truth," through nonviolent protest and conscious suffering. The two finally met in Paris on 5 December 1931 at the apartment of Mme. Louise Guieyesse, who the next year would found the group Amis de Gandhi, to which Massignon would later attach himself and his work for Muslims in France and the French colonies so closely (LM, 128–129). In 1936, he had another significant meeting, this time with Monsignor Montini, who would later become Pope Paul VI (perhaps not insignificantly suspected of his own secret homosexuality).[81] Montini became a friend and a supporter of the Badaliya, a community Massignon founded based on the concept of substitutory suffering. As pope, he would later support and promote Christian-Muslim dialogue at the Second Vatican Council (LM, 145). In 1937, Massignon lectured for the first time at the Eranos Conference in Ascona Switzerland, where he came into close contact with a generation of European scholars (Jung, Eliade, Scholem, and Corbin, among others) whose writings would do so much to define the shape of religious studies in the West.

As a personality, Massignon was often described as pious, ascetic, eccentric, and astonishingly talkative. Claudel's journal note is typical: "Holy Saturday. Massignon, still ascetic but a more joyous air. He's suffering from a knee inflammation, the 'malady of monks,' the result of too protracted prayers. He talks incessantly."[82] He also had a reputation for blurting out things that others found inappropriate, unusually insightful, funny, or all three. Consider, for example, the delightful anecdote of Massignon at the wedding ceremony of the shah of Iran and King Farouk's sister (Massignon was attending as a French diplomat). Solange LeMaître tells the story of finding himself behind a general and another French minister and next to a very animated Massignon, who was becoming increasingly passionate as he spoke to him about the gospel, the love of God, and the story of the Samaritan woman at the well. At some point, Massignon forgot where he was and shouted, "Don't forget; the prostitutes are the ones who will enter first into the kingdom of heaven." The general and the minister, LeMaître notes, turned around quickly.[83] On an equally humorous and lighthearted note, Joseph Kitagawa once told me about an incident that occurred when Massignon came to the University of Chicago in 1952 to deliver the Haskell Lectures. During a question and answer period, someone asked him to say something about Islamic sects. His French ear mistakenly heard "sex" for "sects" and quipped: "Well, of course you know that I'm a homosexual." The audience was stunned. It was, after all, 1952.[84]

Massignon stayed in Paris during World War II, preoccupied with the safety and health of his family and mourning the loss of his many colleagues and friends, some of whom fled abroad, some of whom, such as his dear childhood friend Henri Maspero, were killed in the war or in the concentration camps (LM, 153). After the war, he resumed his diplomatic activities, travelling to Egypt, Palestine, Syria, Lebanon, Turkey, Iraq, Iran, and Afghanistan on a mission to renew France's ties with these regions (LM, 155). From then on, he became increasingly active in the political sphere, taking a number of unpopular positions, always in light of his defense of Islamic populations that he saw as victims of European colonization and cultural aggression. His later stance against the Algerian War, for example, won him many enemies and sometimes put him in genuine physical danger (he was punched in the face at one speaking engagement and narrowly missed a bomb at another [LM, 226, 222]). But probably his most controversial position was the one he took against the founding of a separate Jewish state. Because he came to equate Zionism with French practices in North Africa (both excluded and denied Muslim populations), he opposed the idea of a separate Israel. In his own passionate words, "Israel wanted to return to the land, and from 1918 onward I supported that aspiration, but it was not in order to make other Displaced Persons!"[85] Many criticized Massignon for failing to fathom the depth of Jewish suffering and the desperate need for a homeland. Others pointed out that Massignon's theology was excessively abstract and atemporal, continually returning to an ancient patriarch, that is, to Abraham, as the ground for monotheistic unity and looking toward a wishful future for a coming eschatological solution (LM, 166–167). Still others were simply baffled by all his talk of suffering saints and the mystical efficacy of personal sacrifice. All of these criticisms still seem more than apt.[86]

The 1950s and early 1960s saw Massignon deeply involved in a country torn by the drama of decolonization and the Algerian War (he retired from the Collège de France in 1954). Even as this political activity and religious practices became more furious and controversial (he took up, for example, a Gandhi-inspired fasting), his health began to ebb away. And his contradictions became even more apparent. As Raoul Girardet points out, the Algerian crisis, in particular, caused him considerable conflict almost until the end (he died at the end of October 1962, just a few months after the war ended on March 18), since, even as he risked his reputation and safety for Muslims, he remained faithful to the idea of an Algeria as part of France and as a special site of Christian-Muslim exchange: "And probably," Girardet notes, "one can speak of the contradictions in the old man divided between his inflexible moral principles and his lack of adaptation to the new historical conditions of his time."[87]

Massignon was writing an article for the twelve hundredth anniversary of Baghdad when he died of a massive heart attack on 31 October 1962 at the age of seventy-nine. It was ten o'clock in the evening, just two hours before the very day Massignon had wished he would die, November 1, All Saints' Day. His friends were shocked by the coincidence, or what Massignon would call yet another "intersign," a mysterious confirmation of his union with that community of saints through time who have suffered for others and so preserved, at great personal cost, the stability and ultimate salvation of the spiritual and physical worlds.

At the end of her biography, Gude quotes a beautiful journal entry from François Mauriac, which he wrote after learning of Massignon's death. The letter is an especially appropriate way to end our biographical sketch as well, for its fusion of the mystical and the intellectual, for its mournful but grateful synopsis of the scholar's life, and for the Massignonian spirit which imbues its stuttering style and graceful lilt: "I know no more striking example of knowledge transformed into love. Massignon next to my fireplace in 1911 or 1912, recounting the story of his miraculous conversion; Massignon the friend of père de Foucauld, the Massignon of Al Hallaj . . . Massignon secretly ordained; irreplaceable Massignon! He was an Arab story-teller who had to recount his life. At least he received the grace of seeing the last colonial war end and the dawn of the [Vatican] Council emerge. Now he will intercede for us."[88]

The Notion of Mystical Substitution and the Abdāl

As we have seen, Massignon believed that there were silent witnesses to his conversion, specific historical souls who had suffered for the event. One of these was J.-K. Huysmans, the decadent novelist turned pious Catholic who had prayed for Massignon's conversion on his deathbed. Massignon believed that Huysmans's dying prayer was efficacious and so sought to explore the writer's work shortly after his return to France. It was here, in Huysmans's writings, that he found developed the idea of mystical substitution, that is, the theory that God calls certain individuals throughout history to suffer willingly for the salvation of the world (cf. PH, 3:111–121). Huysmans had borrowed the idea from the writings of Joseph de Maistre (1753–1821) to whom he had been introduced by the occultist turned Catholic priest Joseph-Antoine Boullan (who had contributed occult material to Huysmans's first novel, *Là-Bas*). Huysmans then developed the idea in 1901 in his biography of Saint Lydwine de Schiedam (d. 1443). Gude points out that it was through such ideas that Massignon came to understand his mysterious encounter with Hallāj, who, like Christ and Saint Lydwine, had willingly offered himself up for the salvation of the Islamic community (and, it seemed, Massignon himself).

It was Hallāj's example, Gude goes on, that gave Massignon both a historical subject to which to dedicate his intellectual life and a religious model to imitate with all his soul. *He* now in turn would become a sacrifice, an intercessor for Islam, one of the aspiring *abdāl* in this ancient chain of mystical substitutes for the salvation of the world (LM, 60). Hence his later desire to be ordained a priest as a married man, a most unusual wish that was in fact granted when he was given an indult from Pius XII in 1949 and was ordained a priest the next year in the Melkite rite of the Greek Catholic Church. Even here, the homoerotic is central, for, in Massignon's own words, this vocation to suffer and sacrifice began in 1908 with his desire to save the soul of his former lover, Luis de Cuadra (LM, 179). Was Massignon suffering to save Cuadra's soul from the damnation of homosexuality? Or his own? Or more likely, both? From this distance, it appears likely that the salvation such substitutory suffering effected, for Cuadra and presumably for Massignon, was a salvation from the guilt and conflict of a religiously tortured homosexuality. And what was Hallāj's role in all of this? What should we make, for example, of the tradition that Shiblī, Hallāj's disciple, hurled what Massignon calls a "terrible reproach" at Hallāj on the cross concerning the "secret of Sodom" (PH, 2:309; cf. TP, 44 n. 4)? Along similar lines, consider also the fact that Massignon identified Abraham, who interceded "on behalf of Sodom, the City of Perdition" (PH, lxiii), the first of the *abdāl*. Indeed, in an article that may throw more than a little light on Massignon's conversion experience, Abraham is described as a "stranger" or "guest" of the Sodomites, and Sodom "is the city which loves itself, which refuses the visitation of the Angels, of the Guests, of the Strangers or which wishes to abuse them."[89] The chain of apotropaic witnesses and substitutory suffering, in other words, literally begins with Abraham's "prayer for Sodom," which Massignon explicitly connects with the sin of homosexuality. One could hardly ask for a clearer and more dramatic connection between Massignon's vocation to suffer sacrificially and his conflicted homosexuality. If Massignon's vocation, then, was one defined by *la substitution pour Sodome,* and I think it was, this Sodom stood in as *la substitution pour Louis Massignon.*

A brief examination of Massignon's privately distributed text "La Prière sur Sodome," which was published after his death in *Les Trois Prières d'Abraham,* adds considerable detail to such a thesis.[90] Here Massignon states clearly that Abraham's sacred vocation functions as a precise "antitype" of the crime of Sodom (TP, 35): as I have argued above, the two patterns (a condemned homosexuality and the mystic's/Massignon's vocation to suffer vicariously) are mutually imbricated. Drawing on an impressive list of ethnographic, psychological, sexological, biological, and historical scholarship, Massignon goes on in the same essay to construct his own religious history of homosexuality, demonstrating in the process just how central same-sex desire is to the history of religions.[91]

In brief, Massignon detects three "stages" in what he clearly considers a disease (the metaphors of contamination, state of virulence, disinfection, therapy, immunization, and epidemic are omnipresent in the essay):⁹² (1) the stage of legal codes enacted for or against homosexual practice, as we find, for example, in Hittite or Cretic law (which allowed it), or Assyrian or Incan law (which prohibited it), or Indo-Buddhist culture, which "restrained" the contamination to certain castes or "depraved cloisters" (TP, 39); (2) the second stage, the classical type of which is best seen in ancient Greece, which benefits from what Massignon calls the crisis of polytheism that pushes it to abstract language and into a true "uranism," that is, a "desire for heaven, without the desire for God" (TP, 40); and finally, (3) the psychology of inversion that appears after the monotheistic revelations and the messiah and leads to a kind of "latent contradiction" within the believing soul (TP, 40). For Massignon, this final stage is best captured not by the pagan category of uranism, but by the theistic notion of 'udhritic love that we examined above, that is, a resignation to suffer the carnal desire without giving in to it in an attempt to meditatively arrest thought and immortalize the desire (TP, 41). According to Massignon, a similar psychology develops within Christianity. His description of this last and final development of homosexuality within the Christian world could not be more pertinent to my thesis: "[T]he uranian crisis arrives in an explicit, decisive and explosive fashion at its logical conclusion: no longer, finally, the sterility of the tribe or the city, but the following: the despair and suicide of the individual" (TP, 41).⁹³

In its origins, however, such desire is pure, and this "human connaturality is not 'unnatural.'" Indeed, if it can be deepened into modesty and chastity and arrive at a vow of virginity, it becomes "complementary to transnatural love which unites us with God."⁹⁴ Thus, we arrive at the exemplar, the Virgin herself, the human homage to whom is mysteriously devoid of any natural sexual attraction and whose Immaculate Conception is the very reason that "God has foreseen in permitting Sodom to exist" (TP, 57). Thus it is that Massignon's "Prayer for Sodom" ends not with a fiery destruction, but with a female Virgin, a male Host, and a pure homoerotic posture: "*Omnia propter Electam.* All for Her whom the angel has hailed at Nazareth, who has accepted in her breast, for us all, the gift of the Spirit, the Consoler of tears: the Guest (the Friend on whose heart John has reclined his head)" (TP, 57).

And all of this, of course, was built on a very particular ontology, essentially a Christian theism that posited a transcendent God and an order of salvation that somehow demanded the intense sufferings of at least a few of its paradigmatic participants. On a purely psychological level, trauma was central to the mystical life. Had not Junayd described the mystical state of *fanā'*, or "annihilation," as God possessing the soul with a "supreme violence" (PH, 1:77)? Was not Ibn ʿAtāʾ correct to see pain itself as the true sign of the soul's passage into transcendence (PH, 1:92)? And indeed, is not Sufism itself a "ritual experimentation with pain" (EO, 10)? Little wonder, then, that Massignon more or less equates the mystical life with asceticism, abnegation, and sacrifice (PH, 3:353) and finally ends *The Passion* not with a hopeful hymn to beauty or human goodness, but to an anticlimactic discussion of a series of plates on Hallāj's gory execution and cremation. The volume (and the expository work) ends with these words: "A vague stream of blood, from his mouth to his navel, depicts more the flexing of the chest muscles than the wound in the side" (PH, 3:360).

Less rhetorically but more radically, especially intense, often grossly unjust suffering was required of a few select souls for the order of salvation. In Massignon's own terms, "the transnatural distance that separates the divine essence from humanity can only be bridged by force." Hence the brutal logic of Hallāj's prayer: "So, kill me . . . and I shall be freed at last" (PH, 2:86). Such is the logic of transcendence. At other, even more telling, times, this desire to suffer is combined with a certain barely muted phallic eroticism that seems to take sexual pleasure in suffering itself; hence the bandit in Ahman Ghazālī's *Intuitions of Lovers*, who sings the provocative lines, "He, He is going to kill me,—and I, I am enraptured in Him; In the thrust of His sword,—there is such beauty" (PH, 2:166), or, still more telling, Massignon's paraphrase of Faris's descriptions of Hallāj in *fanāʾ* (mystical annihilation) as the *shāhid* or witness whose carnal self is not eliminated "but enclosed in a sheath of joy and aroused at the sight of suffering, like the onlookers enthralled by Joseph's beauty" (PH, 2:199).

Little wonder, then, that Massignon reacted so strongly and so negatively to ontologies or mystical traditions that called into serious question this dark vision of transcendence, suffering, and death. Certainly, Sufism was not without such skeptical voices; hence the following exchange between two Sufis: "They crucified Mansūr [Hallāj], and he did not run away from it; but you, you jump out of the way of an ordinary stick!" mocks the first. "That proves that Mansūr was not perfect," retorts the second, "otherwise he would have fled, for, in the sight of God, it is all one and the same!" Monism, in other words, renders illogical the necessity of suffering and sacrifice. Massignon is quick to pass immediate judgment on such a crystal-clear logic: "This dialogue," he quips, "reveals the ingenuous arrogance of monistic mysticism and its incomprehension of the meaning of martyrdom" (PH, 2:227–228). Incomprehension? Arrogance? Only if one assumes a violent monotheism and a subsequent violent mysticism of suffering, blood sacrifice, and death.

But monistic Hinduism, which seemed to deny altogether any genuine distance between the human and the divine, offered one of the greatest challenges to Massignon's sacrificial vision. Little wonder, then, that Massignon rejected the thesis that Sufism had been deeply influenced by Hindu monistic strands, read yogic states in a purely psychological fashion, and responded so enthusiastically to Gandhi's *satyagraha*, which with its theistic base and emphasis on vicarious suffering resembled in a remarkable way Massignon's own notion of the suffering *abdāl*. For Massignon, the problem of Hindu mysticism, as represented in the Upaniṣads and systematized in Patañjali's Yoga-Sūtras, was that it dwelt primarily on "preliminary meditation, the negative eradication of all mental images or intellectual movements *ad extra*" (EO, 62). Its mystical experience was thus too often "strictly confined to the psychological consciousness" (EO, 62). Moreover, and more damning, there was no real place in it for a "living, threatening, transcendent, and personal God," as is witnessed to in Islam and the Western monotheisms (EO, 59). Hence Massignon's purely psychological glosses on various technical terms of Patañjali's Yoga-Sūtras: *nirodhapariṇāma* (literally, "the full development of [mental] cessation") as "this perilous leap from the mental trampoline, this rapture into the void," *samādhi samprajñāta* (literally, "union with awareness") as "conscious psychological ecstasy," and *samādhi asamprajñāta* (literally, "union without awareness") as "unconscious psychological ecstasy" (EO, 64). The true position of Patañjali's system, then, is that it has no genuine conclusion: in the end, it can offer only "a glimpse of a negative state obtained by high-frequency cycles of thought that remove all images from the consciousness" (EO, 66). In simple terms, yoga can produce only psychological states of the mind. There is no God here, and thus there can be no genuine transformation of the will within a true mystical union. That can be found only in the three Semitic monotheisms, which posit a transcendent God, the reality of the immortal, individualized soul, and so the possibility of a transforming exchange of wills (EO, 67). We cannot allow ourselves, he insists, to be dazzled by the unusual ecstasies of those mystics who "boast, in their solitude, of forgetting in God to have pity for men" (EO, 11). There can be no pure delight, no bliss for bliss's sake (PH, 3:25–26).

As we shall see in our next chapter, this ethical rejection of the ecstatic and the monistic is essentially the position of R. C. Zaehner as well. Comparatively speaking, it is not a very helpful position, as it works from the a priori ontological assumptions of Western monotheism. But—and this is my point—it is an absolutely necessary position for Massignon, for if the Hindu yogīs are right to locate the ultimate mystical state in *samādhi*, then his notion of the mystical substitute and the salvific efficacy of suffering become dubious at best and a kind of dangerous justification of trauma and human injustice at worst. The stakes were very, very high for Massignon. Hinduism, or at least this form of Hinduism, had to be rejected.

Concluding Ambivalences

Against the backdrop of such Hallajian flames, Massignon's life and thought appear to me as a vision both eerily beautiful and deeply problematic. In terms of the beauty, it seems apparent enough (and I am here expanding on Gude again [LM, 248]) that Louis Massignon was the son of his father the artist, that through an unusually gifted imagination and religious-artistic sensibility he was able to create an entire universe of meaning from the profound energies of a sexually conflicted body, mind, and soul (if we should speak of these three separately at all), the symbols and technical terms of the mystical literature he loved and knew so well, and the intersigns he so deftly interpreted out of the seemingly synchronistic events of his life. If there is a historian of mysticism that truly lived an art form, Louis Massignon is it.

But my own admiration for this art is equivocal, ambiguous, and disjointed by the eras and subsequent moral sensibilities that separate us. Speaking confessionally for a moment, I was born the evening of October 10, just a few hours before the Second Vatican Council convened on the morning of October 11 and just a few days before Massignon died. This I might take as my own meaningful "intersign." And how it separates us.

Let me voice my discomfort in an exaggerated, excessive form—that is, let me propose a little "road of excess" for us to walk down—and then gloss it in order to explain where it might lead us. I would put this road in the form of a question: "What do we do with a palpable sanctity that was psychologically derived from what many of us now take to be a serious moral mistake?" That is, how are we to understand the holiness, the felt energies, of a man such as Louis Massignon when we believe, as I do, that those energies were sublimated forms of a morally tortured homosexuality? Both Massignon's hermeneutic of medieval Persian mysticism and his own life rest largely on a single assumption, namely, that any active homosexual expression is sinful, damnable, something to be converted from. What happens, for our readings, for our lives, when we no longer believe this, when, on the contrary, we conclude through strong textual, biological, anthropological, and historical research that traditional religious condemnations of homosexuality are themselves morally damnable to the extent that they produce—as they so clearly did in the life of Louis Massignon—untold human suffering, anxiety, and repression (not to mention what they seemed to produce in his lover, the ultimate and all too common "solution" of suicide)? Is not this, to misquote Massignon completely out of context, an "aesthetics of despair," a "paradoxical eulogy of a sadistic victim devotion" (PH, 2:166)?

The paradox, of course, is that this very repression produces, in some rare cases, the beauty and power of a sublimated art or mysticism. Would Louis Massignon have been so taken with the Essential Desire of al-Hallāj, with the saint's sensualized sacrifice of his own body and life, and with the general asceticism of Sufism had he believed that his homosexuality was a grace of God to be expressed in a loving context and not a damnable curse to be eliminated through an attempted suicide and a dramatic conversion? The answer, of course, is quite simply no. And this presents us with a dilemma, the dilemma of evaluating a beautiful life based on a moral mistake. There is something essentially tragic about all of this, something powerful and human beyond our grasp—a saint sacrificed, morally tortured, and then canonized by his own religious tradition. Little wonder that Louis Massignon loved Hallāj so. They shared a common Passion.

SECRET TALK *Heroic Heretical Heterosexuality*

[Christian churches] seem cunningly designed to condemn same-sex desire and to elicit it, to persecute it and to instruct it. I sometimes call this the paradox of the "Beloved Disciple": "Come recline beside me and put your head on my chest, but don't dare conceive of what we do as erotic." Perhaps it is more clearly seen as the paradox of the Catholic Jesus, the paradox created by an officially homophobic religion in which an all-male clergy sacrifices male flesh before images of God as an almost naked man.

Mark Jordan, *The Silence of Sodom*

> Love's a guillotine
> where a man
>   Must lose his head
> or else
> he is not shriven
>   in the Church of Love.
> "Well," you say,
> "I'd like to love—but
>   can't I keep my head?"
> Keep it then—
> but I fear you're not
> destined for much success.

Awhad al-Dīn, poet and friend of Ibn ʿArabī, quoted by Jim Wafer in "Passion and Vision: The Symbolism of Male Love in Islamic Mystical Literature"

Opposition is true friendship.

William Blake, *The Marriage of Heaven and Hell*

THERE WAS SOMETHING I just didn't understand. I had been led to believe by the celibate structure and transcendent monotheism of my own religious tradition that profound and transforming religious experiences come primarily to those who renounce the active expression of sexuality. Jesus had spoken mysteriously of those who willingly become "eunuchs for the kingdom of heaven," that is, (symbolically?) castrated males. Paul was even more clear that the state of virginity was the most appropriate mode of being for this, our eschatological age. The influence of Neoplatonism on early Christian thought only served to emphasize this Jewish ascetic-eschatological strand with its dualistic emphasis on the body *(soma)* as a tomb *(sema)* to be delivered from. Consequently, much, if by no means all, of the history of Christian spirituality can be read as an amplification of this most basic of mystical teachings, namely, that the kingdom comes when the sexual doesn't. This anyway was clearly the message I received, through any number of explicit and implicit liturgical, scriptural, institutional, and iconographic channels, from the Catholicism of my youth.

Why then, I kept asking myself, did the timing of my preliminary mystical experiences (about which I will have more to say below) and dream-visions coincide precisely with the active expression of a long dormant, long repressed sexuality? My own life experience, it seems, stood in direct contrast to my tradition. It wasn't supposed to happen this way. Moreover, I asked again, why couldn't I, as hard as I might try, imagine myself into the male erotic-mystical models of Christianity? Teresa of Avila? I could understand her vision of a flaming angel plunging a fiery arrow "deep within" her until she moaned in an intense pain that was also unspeakably pleasurable. Being a woman, I thought, posed no problems for Teresa's religious imagination; her gender "fit" into the tradition and its image of the female soul as bride being penetrated by a masculine divine. But Bernard of Clairvaux and John of the Cross? What could I make of Bernard's psycho-theological descriptions of being kissed or penetrated by Christ the bridegroom?[1] Or what could I make of John's poetic glossing of the "delightful wound" of his poem, *Llama de amor viva?* "[W]hen the soul is transpierced with that dart, the flame gushes forth, vehemently and with a sudden ascent, like the fire in a furnace or an oven when someone uses a poker or bellows, to stir and excite it. And being wounded by this fiery dart, the soul feels the wound with unsurpassable delight. . . . The fire issuing from the substance and power of that living point . . . is felt to be subtly diffused through all the spiritual and substantial veins of the soul in the measure of the soul's power and strength."[2] This was a symbolic language, highly reminiscent of the phenomenology of orgasm, that made little sense to me; here, after all, was a man being entered. It was all very confusing to me. Only later would I see that the male bridal mystics had formed the tradition, however consciously, around an essentially homerotic structure, a point similar to those advanced by scholars such as John Boswell and Mark Jordan and which I have developed in my own way above in chapter 1.[3]

But again, what else could such mystics have done? In a monotheistic tradition in which God is male, any relationship with the divine that is cast in sexualized language or experienced sexually must, by definition, be homoerotically structured for males. It is as if society "captures" heterosexuality for biological reproduction and the maintenance of public social structures and will allow only the homosexual or the bisexual, really anything *but* heterosexuality, to "escape" into the liminal realms of mystical experience, ecstatic excess, and liturgical leisure. All sorts of alternative sexualities are at once symbolically nurtured and officially denied in the fantastically rich symbolic traditions of Catholicism: both males and females (not to mention the church) "marry" Christ, nuns are routinely given transsexually masculine names, priests wear what are essentially liturgical dresses, men and women live in celibate same-sex communities, the virtually naked body of a divine man (the crucifix) is artistically and ritually privileged, this same male body is consumed in the central rite of the Eucharist, and religious devotion is continually cast in what can only be described as a highly eroticized adoration of a divine, physically perfect male. To "love Jesus" or feel "the love of Christ," then, are often emotionally loaded, overdetermined sexual-spiritual experiences within Catholic piety, and the symbolic, vocational, liturgical, and mystical resources are rich and generous for virtually any sexual orientation, except male heterosexuality.[4] Consequently, the heterosexual Catholic male, as heterosexual, as male, as Catholic, and as mystically inclined, is in a very real dilemma. Whether he knows it or not, whether he admits it or not, he is an existential, almost ontological stranger to his own tradition. As much as he might want to, he does not fit.

Howard Eilberg-Schwartz has convincingly demonstrated a similar thesis in the case of Judaism: there too God is male, Israel is imagined as his bride, and any male representative of that bride (and in such a patriarchal tradition, it is inevitably the male who represents the collective) becomes cast in an implicit homosexual role vis-à-vis the divine: "The primary relationships in Israelite imagination were between a male God and individual male Israelites, such as Moses, the patriarchs, and the prophets.... Men were encouraged to imagine themselves as married to and hence in a loving relationship with God. A homoerotic dilemma was thus generated, inadvertently and to some degree unconsciously, by the superimposition of heterosexual images on the relationship between human and divine males."[5] But this can be a problem only for men who are heterosexually inclined and who want to give their love to real historical women, for "being a husband to a wife is in tension with being a wife of God."[6] Granted, such a symbolism is particularly rich for male mystics who are homosexually inclined or who feel drawn to a homoerotic spirituality, but the same structure tends to generate only anxiety and confusion for those who are not, Eilberg-Schwartz argues; hence the well-known injunctions against seeing God's body, particularly his front side (that is, his phallus), in the biblical texts. The homoerotic gaze focused on God's phallus is simply too much for a tradition that must generate a homoerotic symbolic structure and deny that structure at the same time.

* * *

I came to a remarkably similar conclusion in the seminary. It was as if "being called" (the literal meaning of a "vocation") to the priesthood was more or less synonymous with "being gay." No one, of course, put it that way, and most Catholic leaders would certainly passionately deny this, but this is precisely the effect the church's celibate all-male institutional structure and condemnation of homosexuality have on its official ranks.[7]

Consider the following thought experiment. What are the options of a young, pious, homosexually oriented Catholic male who wishes to remain faithful to the church's present teachings? He can live in secular society as a repressed homosexual man (for any active expression of his sexuality would only result in damning guilt and public, and most likely familial, condemnation), or he can join one of the church's innumerable same-sex communities and be richly rewarded—religiously, socially, and, usually more humbly, financially—for sublimating his homosexuality into religious expression and activity. Individuals, of course, will choose individually, but it is not difficult to guess what might happen statistically over large populations of Catholic gay males. Often, of course, the human realities are not statistically anonymous but personally tragic. Consider my friend William, whom I met in the seminary. He was gay, very gay, and he was Catholic, very Catholic, and he couldn't possibly put the two together. His solution? Remove the contradiction, that is, himself. He was in a coma for eight days after swallowing an entire bottle of sleeping pills. Luckily, he awoke. Sanely, he left the seminary and, I gather, the official church to live out his sexuality in integrity elsewhere.

And what are the options of a pious, heterosexual, Catholic male who likewise wishes to follow the church's teachings? Unlike his gay counterpart, there are no dramatic obstacles to the active, social expression of his sexuality, at least within the bounds of marriage; hence, he is much more likely to choose a sexually active lifestyle. Moreover, and just as important, he is likely not nearly as skilled as his gay brother in hiding and repressing his sexual orientation; after all, he doesn't have to. Not surprisingly, then, celibacy makes little sense to him.

When we put these two "imagined" scenarios together, the demographic conclusion is unavoidable: the seminaries, and consequently the ranks of the priesthood, fill up with a largely gay population. The irony is clear enough, if morally unacceptable: a profoundly homophobic institution creates, by the very facts of its condemnation of homosexuality and its insistence on celibacy, a rich, if deeply ambiguous, homoerotic culture.

* * *

It was not that I found the homoerotic culture of the seminary or even the church morally objectionable. It was not that I objected either to homosexuality itself or to a sublimated homoerotic spirituality. Quite the contrary. I have seldom witnessed such profound and loving human relationships as I witnessed in the seminary, and I have only gratitude and a feeling of deep nostalgia for the individuals I came to know and love there. Sublimation is a powerful matrix of spirituality, piety, and human community, when it works. What hurt, and what still hurts, was the awareness, dimly felt in my thoughts but clearly seen in my dreams, that the church's homoerotic structure excluded my very being from its most intimate forms of community. I could not possibly fit. I was a religious exile by virtue of my heterosexuality. And what is worse, almost no one can admit this in public. I am thus exiled by a denied truth, a stranger by virtue of an unacknowledged secret at the heart of my own indigenous mystical tradition.[8]

* * *

I knew nothing of John Boswell, Howard Eilberg-Schwartz, Mark Jordan, or Ellis Hanson at the time (and indeed only Boswell had published his work by the early 1980s), and even had I known of these ideas, I am not sure that they would have helped; I was, after all, looking for a heteroerotic mysticism, not a historical thesis about a homoerotic tradition. What was a source of immense mystical power and even therapeutic resolution for someone like Louis Massignon, whose sexual orientation fitted this theological gendering, could only be a problem of ontological dimensions for someone like me. Consequently, I eventually turned to Hinduism because I found in its beautiful mythologies, striking iconographies, and mystical doctrines a fantastically rich source of mystical eroticisms of all kinds, including and especially heteroerotic systems. The Hindu goddess traditions, unlike my own failed Catholic bridal mysticism, could be explicitly heterosexual and deeply mystical at the same time. In the mirror of these same traditions, moreover, I could see even more clearly the homoerotic lines of my Catholicism: where was the goddess here? In essence, Hinduism saved me by giving me back who I was, by assuring me that being heterosexual and aspiring to a sexually expressed mystical life were not mutually exclusive options. I was struck in particular by the Hindu Tantra, as I saw it as the mirror opposite of Christian bridal mysticism. Here, after all, was a tradition that saw the human aspirant as masculine and the divine as feminine. Here, I believed, was a tradition in which I could find an erotic mysticism that made sense, that is, one in which males had erotic encounters with females and not other males. Here, finally and most important, was a tradition that had developed an entire spectrum of monistic and nondual ontologies that, at least in theory, promised to make some sense of the intimate connection between sexual and mystical experience I had seen so darkly in my dreams. Such nondualisms, I hoped, devoid of the usual theistic assumptions about God's transcendence, did not have to "split" the body and soul apart in a dualistic fashion. The sacralization of sexuality seemed to be a genuine possibility here.

Thus, I began my studies of the Hindu Tantra after being somewhat frustrated with the consistently homoerotic structures that I found working in my own mystical traditions; finding myself heterosexually oriented, I had had enough of male mystics becoming women to marry a male Christ. Sadly, I was thus something of a misfit in my own mystical tradition. Consequently, I turned to the study of Tantra because I imagined it to be a tradition structured around heterosexual rituals, divinities, and experiences. And what did I find? I found Ramakrishna, another male mystic "becoming a woman" in order to engage male divinities (and other human beings) in erotic and quasi-erotic encounters. In short, I was back to the very homoeroticism I thought I had left behind. I discovered, moreover, that the heterosexual symbols and rituals that first attracted my attention Ramakrishna himself rejected. And why not? Much as I had perceived Catholic bridal mysticism, Ramakrishna found such symbols to be structured around a sexual orientation that he did not share, in his case a heterosexual one; Ramakrishna and I, in other words, were in a very similar structural dilemma, if for opposite reasons—I understood him precisely because I was both like and unlike him. My search for a heteroerotic mysticism thus ended in a rather spectacular, and deeply ironic, failure.

Heroic Heretical Heterosexuality 153

But was such a fruitful failure really so surprising? The heterosexual Tantric mystic, after all, is consistently described as a "hero" *(vīra)*, his sexual encounters with the goddess are understood to be fraught with great risk, and Tantra itself is copiously described as something dangerous and terrifying—strange terms indeed for a heterosexuality that many men experience as a source of pleasure, beauty, and well-being. It is as if the male Tāntrika must fight for this heterosexuality against great odds. Such a hunch is confirmed when we remember that Tantric goddesses, Kālī foremost among them, often appear in mystical traditions dominated by the emotional-devotional states of the infant or child, the oft-stated goal of mystically merging with the mother, and a bewildering symbolic complex of motherliness, sexuality, grace, and violence. It is in such a context, I think, that we can best place, understand, and appreciate the striking prominence of transvestism and decapitation as symbolic castration (lots of male horned animals lose their heads in the goddess traditions) in her cultus. "The rapture of recognizing (and being recognized by) the mother's affirming presence together with the ambivalent anguish in response to her individuality-destroying embrace are the complementary affects evoked and condensed in the worship of Kali,"[9] Sudhir Kakar writes, following what can only be described as a very strong, if always controversial, scholarly consensus.

The Tāntrika's heroism, in other words, lies in his courageous refusal to renounce his adult heterosexuality before the mother and her individuality-denying, if sexually blissful and loving, presence. Even here, then, a mystical heterosexuality cannot be assumed; it must be fought for and won from a kind of maternal annihilation. We must also keep in mind that these heteroerotic traditions are considered to be radically heterodox, esoteric traditions that go directly against the more public, orthodox concerns of the culture. Once again, it is a mystical heterosexuality that does not fit the religious norm; hence its heroic, essentially heretical status.

This same pattern of a heterodox heterosexuality and an orthodox homoeroticism is also seen in the case of Bengali Vaiṣṇavism, where the ultimate goal is to share in the bliss of Kṛṣṇa's love play with Rādhā in Vrindavana. The key question, however, is *how*. In the orthodox, or Gauḍīya, tradition, the male devotee can never take on the persona of the male god Kṛṣṇa, for this would render him guilty of the "pride of being male" *(puruṣābhimāna);* he can participate in Kṛṣṇa's eternal *līlā,* or "play," with Rādhā only through a feminine identification, that is, by becoming a *sakhī,* or female attendant, of Rādhā. Hence the popular folk saying in Bengal that "except for Arjuna and Kṛṣṇa, everyone has nipples"; that is to say, we are all women in relation to the divine. In the heterodox Sahajiyā tradition, on the other hand, the male devotee can take on the nature of Kṛṣṇa; that is, he can assert his own male heterosexuality within his mystical *sādhana* or practice with a human woman now understood to be Rādhā.[10] Interestingly, it is precisely this practiced heterosexual masculinity that renders him both Sahajiyā and heretical. As with the Christian materials, it is what we today would call sexual orientation that determines both orthodoxy and heresy, and, once again, it is heterosexuality that is heretical.

* * *

1 November 1999. I remember distinctly a dream I had in the seminary. I was in the water and sexually aroused. On one side was a beautiful woman, on the other Christ. It was clear to me in the dream that I had to choose between them. The choice, then, was both between a celibate religious or a secular sexual life and a homoerotic or a heteroerotic orientation. Interestingly, the dream set the choice up in a way that allied or analogized the religious and the homoerotic—*the dream knew*. In any case, the choice, if it ever was one, was made for me, as it were, for it was the woman, not Christ, who ultimately attracted my libidinal energies—this was the direction of my desire, toward the feminine and hence away from Christ(ianity). The dream knew perfectly well then what I have since come to know only gradually and with considerable pain and mourning—that Catholicism is homoerotically structured, and that I, as an active heterosexual male, do not and cannot fit into its present symbolic and institutional system.

9 June 2000 (University of Notre Dame). I am surrounded here by Madonnas, on the sidewalks, on the buildings, on the golden dome overlooking this beautiful campus. I was standing in front of the administration building yesterday. On top of it stands a remarkable golden Virgin Mary perched on a golden dome that sparkles in the sun. Exactly opposite her, down on the ground, stands an androgynous-looking, longhaired Jesus and his Sacred Heart, his hands uplifted, a Latin verse etched below him: "Venite ad me omnes" [All come to me]. (On a humorous note, the less pious students note the upraised hands and the statue's position before the perched Virgin to dub this statue the "Don't Jump Ma! Jesus." "Touchdown Jesus," his arms raised, like a referee's signaling a touchdown, to bless the world, graces the library and overlooks the football stadium. "First-Down Moses," his index finger raised high, stands before

another entrance to the library. And "Christ Teaching (Ballet)" wears a dainty nightgown-looking garment on the other side of campus.) I looked up at the Virgin and turned around to look again at the Jesus wanting to embrace me, and I thought to myself: "This is just perfect—I'm caught again between a sexless Virgin and a homoerotic Jesus. That pretty much sums up my experience of Catholicism."

And yet, that's not quite fair. An adolescent Catholicism may have almost killed me, but a more mature one possessed certain "openings" through which I could pass to be healed (a Freudian monk) and to explore other religious worlds (my seminary classes in the history of religions and the Vatican II document *Nostra aetate*). And even the Virgin herself, if I can speak for a moment about her as if she possessed a subjectivity apart from ours, was hardly oppressive. Indeed, although the Virgin Mary operated in ways almost entirely pathological in my adolescent mind (as an illicit object of my unconscious incestuous desires), "she" gracefully transformed herself into a Greek maiden to heal me and eventually (as we will see after chapter 3) into a Hindu goddess to unite with me as a lover. It is very difficult for me to be bitter about all of this. It is very easy for me to feel mournful and nostalgic.

20 June 2000. My struggle with Catholicism has never been simply a matter of belief. It has always been a matter of (sexual) being, a profound crisis or conflict between two orders of being: my heterosexual existence and the tradition's homoerotic structure.

3 March 1986 (Chicago). Deep in the night, two brief but powerful raptures. I'm not sure if they were "real," that is, if they affected my psychophysical organism, or if they were pure dream projections. In any case, they happened. There was a sense of pleasure, an energy; by a sheer movement of the will, the power was directed toward a rapture in which my body was flooded with a pleasure sensation and my mind was propelled into a light that was dark. No one taught me the mechanics of the "flight"—I instinctively knew what to do. A certain degree of fear was involved. The dream state was very deep. The experience reminded me of the other incident in which by a sheer movement of thought I found my consciousness leaving my body in a half-sleep—then fear brought me immediately back. Last night, a certain *raptus* was effected, despite the fear. The flight, however, was within. It was as if desire, directed inward, "broke through" some level of my psyche and body and, projected onto inner space, created a sort of inner radiance.

THREE

The Doors of Deception

R. C. Zaehner's Ethical and Erotic Challenges to Monistic Experience in *Mysticism Sacred and Profane* (1957) and *Concordant Discord* (1970)

> Contemplatives are not likely to become gamblers, or procurers, or drunkards.
>
> Aldous Huxley, *The Doors of Perception*

> Or dope addicts?
>
> R. C. Zaehner's penciled gloss to the above in his personal copy

> Obviously, the layman who is a stranger to mystical experience is in no position to distinguish between the various "states" of the mystic.
>
> R. C. Zaehner, *Hindu and Muslim Mysticism*

R. C. ZAEHNER (1913–1974) was a trained specialist in ancient Iranian languages and the study of Zoroastrianism who spoke numerous modern European and Middle Eastern languages and taught himself many ancient ones, including Arabic and Sanskrit. Once hired to fill the distinguished Spalding Chair in Eastern Religions and Ethics, which Sarvepalli Radhakrishnan had just vacated (an odd choice, Sir Michael Dummett points out, since Zaehner had no formal training in the standard "Eastern" religions),[1] Zaehner made it clear from the very beginning that he could accept neither Radhakrishnan's perennialism nor his generous and hopeful universalism. On the contrary, Zaehner's vision emphasized radical difference, a certain dark and critical eye on things religious, a brave, if incomplete, willingness to employ psychological reductionism as a convincing hermeneutic, and an acute, decidedly Roman Catholic theology (I was told in graduate school that R. C. stood for "Roman Catholic"). Indeed, Zaehner made it something of his lifework to show exactly why monistic forms of mystical experience, wherever they are found, are ethically, psychologically, and theologically inadequate, if not outright deceptive or pathological. His disarming, slightly scandalous honesty, his humorous and irreverent rhetorical style, his unabashed theologizing, his clear normative vision, and his acute sense for the amoral and even immoral nature of much of mysticism all make Zaehner a fascinating and entertaining, if never quite popular, thinker to study.[2]

"Looking, with his glasses and his academic cap, very like an owl" (CWH, xii), Zaehner began his inaugural address at Oxford with a frontal attack on what he perceived to be the simplistic and theologically erroneous universalism of Spalding and Radhakrishnan, whose money and chair he had just taken and whose writings he was now quoting to deny. Dummett assesses the emotional and political impact of Zaehner's inaugural address this way: "Probably it was in bad taste; it certainly was very witty, and it certainly also gave great offence" (CWH, xii). But it was vintage Zaehner. Twenty-two years later, reflecting on the stated aims of Spalding that the chair might have the "aim of bringing together the world's great religions in closer understanding, harmony, and friendship," Zaehner could admit that "I am painfully conscious of the fact that I have totally failed to achieve any (or almost any) of the objectives Mr. Spalding had in mind" (CWH, 1–2).

Not that he ever wanted to achieve such objectives, for Zaehner's "failure" was, by his own admission, primarily a function of the scholar's honesty, his insistence on the distinct integrities of the religions he studied (what we might today call their irreducible "otherness"), and what he called, not inappropriately I think, his stubborn "pedantry," by which he meant a more or less objective eye for detail and an uncompromising insistence on precision (CWH, 2), qualities that he felt were sorely lacking in the perennialist-dominated comparative study of mysticism. In the course of those twenty-two years of marvelous "failure," one book stands out in particular need of our attention, Zaehner's *Concordant Discord* (1970). Contrary to what one might be led to believe by the secondary literature on Zaehner, much of which privileges his *Mysticism Sacred and Profane* (1957), it is here in *Concordant Discord,* his 1967–69 Gifford Lectures concluded just five years before his death, that Zaehner's vision of a genuinely comparative and genuinely mystical method is rendered most clear, most moving, and, as we shall soon see, most erotic. Consequently, it is this text that will focus much of my study of Zaehner's religious path and the comparative method from which it cannot be distinguished. I will begin with a brief biographical sketch (part 1). I will then proceed through his system, beginning with a discussion of his influential *Mysticism Sacred and Profane* and its tripartite developmental typology of mysticism, which would stay with him, in various versions, until the very end (part 2). After that, I will turn to two deeply significant themes—one might almost call them obsessions—in Zaehner's thought and life, the problematic ethical status of monistic mysticism (part 3) and the essentially erotic nature of the highest stages of the mystical life (part 4). Finally, I will conclude with what I think was Zaehner's most developed and mature comparative vision, a mysticism of matter, the future, and then despair, delivered through the voices of a Balzacian androgyne, a censored Catholic priest-scientist, and the French novelist Georges Bernanos (part 5). What I hope to bring to life through all of this is a passionate, quirky, deeply religious, even pious man (he chose the color of his ties to match that of the liturgical season)[3] who knew personally and well the beauty of different types of mystical experience but nevertheless felt that he must warn of the moral and doctrinal dangers inherent in many of them. In his case, these defensive mechanisms were primarily intellectual and theoretical, with Jungian depth psychology, Catholic theology, Sufi polemics, and the modern comparative study of religion being his usual lines of defense (or means of polemical attack). For Zaehner, mysticism, at least in its more monistic forms, was a strangely seductive force that must be fought off and ultimately denied for the sake of stable moral, social, and doctrinal needs and the more ultimate truths of theistic encounter.

In some ways, Zaehner was a tragic figure, for, as we will see, even his passionately held moral and doctrinal truths sometimes seem to waver, if not apocalyptically collapse, and for all his talk of a "mystical marriage" and the transports of love he seemed to know very little of either in his actual historical life, a fact that supports the very thesis he would fight so hard against, namely, that mystical eroticism, for whatever else it may or may not be, is a sublimation of the sexual instincts built on the ruins or absence of a socialized sexual-familial life. Zaehner struggled openly with this idea, on the page, in the public's eye, at the very center of Western academic life for over twenty years. Precisely because of his open struggles with the ethical, the erotic, and the mystical, Zaehner is, in the end, an always controversial but nevertheless endearing and, I think, important personality whose honesty and forthrightness on the page have seldom, if ever, been matched in the modern study of mysticism. Clarity, he once wrote, was the only genuine academic virtue he recognized, and he despised those academics, particularly German theologians, it seems, who confused their obfuscation and bad writing with profundity.[4] One gets the sense, and his friends and students certainly confirmed this for me, that what he thought and felt he more or less accurately and fully put on the public page (thousands of them, I might add). This same sense was confirmed for me again when I studied the Indological and theoretical sections of his personal library, paying special attention to his penciled marginalia and sometimes elaborate annotations on the blank pages at the backs of the books in order to get a feel for what the man read (and did not read) and how he read and thought off the page, as it were. What I found "reading Zaehner reading" is that he thought off the page as he thought on the page: comparatively, passionately, and humorously, returning consistently to the same themes over and over again: the phenomenology of nature mysticism, or what he called, following Richard M. Bucke, "cosmic consciousness,"[5] comparative bridges between Hinduism and Christianity, the problematic moral status of mysticism, the nature of love, the psychology of religion, and so on. This intimate and confessional presence on the public page, no doubt, partly explains both his success as a writer and his controversial status as a religious and theoretical thinker. R. C. Zaehner, after all, was a man who often sarcastically said what many no doubt have thought but would not dare say, much less sarcastically so. He did not go quietly into the night, at all. When he dropped dead on the street from a heart attack suffered on his way to mass in the fall of 1974, he had written and taught and spoken more "mystical criticism" than anyone before or since. It is this persona of the "mystical critic"—understood doubly and ironically as a mystic who is also a radical critic of mystical literature—through which I will approach the life and work of R. C. Zaehner.[6]

1. A Zoroastrian Life: From Telling Lies to Professing Truths

By anyone's standards, R. C. Zaehner led a rather remarkable academic life.[7] Born Robert Zaehner on 8 April 1913 (his college buddies would call him both Robbie and, prophetically, Prof, the latter for his bottle-thick glasses) to Swiss immigrant parents, he entered Christ Church, Oxford, in 1932, where he studied classics and Oriental studies with a special focus on Old and Middle Persian, Old Iranian, Pahlavi, and Zoroastrianism under Harold Bailey. While an undergraduate at Christ Church, he also taught himself Arabic and Sanskrit. Later, when he was asked by

Oxford University Press to write a textbook on Hinduism,[8] he agreed on the condition that he must first read the entire *Mahābhārata* in Sanskrit. Accordingly, he would retire each day after lunch to his room, there to read through the gargantuan text on his own, noting, as he went, this or that grammatical point and becoming, as he progressed, more and more taken with the character of Yudhishthira.[9]

During the war, from 1943 to 1947, he was assistant press attaché in the British embassy in Tehran. It was here, in Iran, that he converted to Roman Catholicism in 1946, taking the name Andrew as his confirmation name. In 1950 he returned to Oxford to lecture in Persian. He did not lecture long, however, for in 1951–1952 he was granted a leave of absence to return to Tehran as acting counsellor. In 1952, partly because of the powerful influence of his ally and mentor, Sir Morris Bowra, Zaehner became the Spalding Professor of Eastern Religions and Ethics with a fellowship at All Souls College. His early work focused on Zoroastrianism, but with the appearance of *Mysticism Sacred and Profane* in 1957 he quickly and permanently entered and then helped define the comparative study of mysticism, a field in which he published over a dozen books over the course of the seventeen years before he died on 24 November 1974.

Zaehner's charisma, personality and idiosyncracies are all fondly remembered to this day. Ann Lambton's intimate portrayal of Zaehner's spirit resonates especially well with all the funny stories and fond memories former students and colleagues shared with me: "He did not, perhaps, suffer fools gladly, but for the serious student he would take immense pains. . . . He had a strong sense of the incongruous—one of his favorite books was *Alice through the Looking-Glass*—and those who were privileged to work with him found him an entertaining companion, and will remember not only his scholarship and learning, but also his loyalty and the delight of sharing with him many wildly funny incidents." "He was also," she concludes, "a man of great originality, not to say eccentricity."[10] Lambton's passing reference to Lewis Carroll's classic fantasy tale is significant, particularly with reference to Zaehner's oft-repeated invocation of the White Queen, who, we are told, could believe in "as many as six impossible things before breakfast." Zaehner playfully applies the White Queen persona to the Roman Catholic curia in *Zen, Drugs and Mysticism*.[11] In private, he was also known to apply it to himself, after which he would chuckle madly.[12] At other times the White Queen was replaced by the spirits of alcohol. "I'm having a *crise de foi*," Zaehner once told his student Lee Siegel, "Or is it a *crise de foie?*" Faith *(foi)* or a nearly pickled liver *(foie)*? Zaehner was willing to keep the question jokingly open and, in the meantime, took a certain ironic delight in making fun of his own doctrinal and religious (not to mention alcoholic) excesses. Along similar lines, former friends and students endearingly spoke to me of his many, always-changing obsessions: with an early British pop star named Tommy Steele, whom Zaehner adored and went to see numerous times when he appeared in concert at Oxford; with different foods—skate, for example—that he would eat many times a week for months on end; with Charles Manson, about whom he insisted on lecturing (along with Aristotle!) when he was invited to the University of California at Santa Barbara, despite the baffled protests of his academic hosts; and with many other things.

What did Zaehner have to say about his life? The closest he ever came to writing autobiographically was his first Gifford Lecture, which appeared in *Concordant Discord* as chapter 1. There he suggests that it was not irrelevant that before he was called to the Spalding Chair he was in government service for ten years, a service "in which truth is seen as the last of the virtues and to lie comes to be a second nature." Academic life, then, came as a relief, for, "if ever there was a profession concerned with a single-minded search for truth, it was the profession of the scholar" (CD, 6). Although he does not say so here, what Zaehner is alluding to is the fact that he worked in British espionage before he became an academic. R. C. Zaehner was a spy. More specifically, he worked for MI6 counterintelligence while he lived and worked in Persia during World War II. Peter Wright, who has studied Zaehner's personal file, describes Zaehner's work in espionage this way: "It was difficult and dangerous work. The railway lines into Russia, carrying vital military supplies, were key targets for German sabotage. Zaehner was perfectly equipped for the job, speaking the local dialects fluently, and much of his time was spent undercover, operating in the murky and cutthroat world of countersabotage."[13] By the end of the war, Wright goes on, Zaehner's work became even more risky, as now the Russians were trying to gain control of the railway and Zaehner was working behind Russian lines at great risk to his personal safety. When Wright interviewed Zaehner at All Souls to explore a rumor that he had in fact been a KGB plant, Zaehner was deeply hurt, visibly wept and spoke at great length about what he might know about the defector. Wright was deeply moved by Zaehner's integrity and charm and felt bitter at the ease with which the charge he had come to explore was made. When Zaehner died, Wright sent a wreath, "anxious to make amends; but I could never forget the look on his face when I asked him if he was a spy. In that moment the civilized cradle of Oxford disintegrated around him; he was back behind the lines again, surrounded by enemies, alone and double-crossed."[14]

Although I do not want to make too much of the thesis, it sometimes seems as if Zaehner's extraordinary truth telling—whatever we want to make of these truths, and however politically incorrect they may seem to us today—was in some sense a redemptive or compensatory act for him, as if he sought through his various professions of truth and faith to answer and redeem his earlier career in dissimulation and deception: "[O]ne thing at least Zoroastrianism had taught me, and that was that the Lie is the very principle and fountain-head of evil," he proclaimed in his opening Gifford Lecture (CD, 8). Zaehner was referring here to his woefully inadequate knowledge of Eastern religions when he assumed the Spalding Chair, but I think the sentiment can just as easily be read as reflective of his own dualistic life, unevenly divided as it was into two professional halves—the dissimulating spy and the too truthful professor.

The truth comes to play a central role in his rhetorical style, even if, as we will see, there is much that remains hidden and unspoken between the lines. As I have already noted, his inaugural Spalding address, "Foolishness to the Greeks," became famous for its open attack on the very principles of the chair which he just accepted (the fact that the chair came with a five-year probationary period makes this frontal attack all the more remarkable). As Zaehner tells the story in 1967, he had just returned from a "career of professional lying," and so it seemed to him that to tie a chair to such unacademic goals as interreligious dialogue and cultural harmony was a serious mistake, another lie, for such goals could only set serious limitations on the objective pursuit of truth (CD, 6). In what were perhaps the address's most remembered lines, he proclaimed: "Such a procedure [seeking harmony where none exists] may well be commendable in a statesman. In a profession that concerns itself with the pursuit of truth it is damnable" (CD, 429). Toward the end of his life, in the opening lecture of his Gifford Lectures, Zaehner expresses regret for the "unfortunate impression" that these very words caused in his listeners. He thus chooses to soften his language, but not much: now (in 1967), he confesses, he would replace the expression "damnable" with "to be deplored" (CD, 7). But even then he insists on keeping that word "damnable" to describe Radhakrishnan's Vedantic, proof-texting perennialism, as "in the long run, it leads not to understanding, harmony, and friendship, but to misunderstanding, discord, and a friendship which, however sincere it may appear to be, is ultimately valueless because it is based on a fundamental misunderstanding: it is based on a lie" (CD, 7). The damnable lie thus appears again. So much for mellowing with age.

2. The Doors of Deception: The Hallucinogenic Catalyst of Zaehner's Entrance into the Field

As conservative and dogmatic as Zaehner often sounds, it must be remembered that he saw himself writing and thinking within a religious context of loss and absence. If, in Peter Homans's apt sense, Zaehner himself failed to mourn the cultural loss of religious objects,[15] he was certainly aware of what had been lost, and he insightfully saw that the rise of the comparative study of religion was linked inextricably to the decline of religion itself in the West. Convinced that we now live *sous le soleil de Satan,* or "under the sun of Satan" (a line from Bernanos, one of his favorite French writers), where everything is "rottenness and gangrene," Zaehner can write of departments of religion as mushrooms growing in this religious rot: "[T]he old certainties have gone, and so departments of religion are springing up like toadstools throughout our demented Anglo-Saxon world. The less we believe, the more we talk about what other people believed" (CD, 382). In another telling line, he refers obliquely to modern scholarship as that upon "which our youth is crucified" (CD, 352) and wryly notes that since Christ detested respectability he must be taken seriously, "unless, of course, he is simply ignored or made the subject of academic study" (CD, 355). In similar terms, Zaehner is convinced that the modern study of mysticism, and in particular the Western world's turn east, stems from Christianity's failure to nurture and proclaim its own mystical riches alongside its more developed prophetic character.[16]

This turn east makes more than a little sense for Zaehner, who was hardly against such a comparative move, as long as it was handled properly, which for him of course it seldom was. The Indian religions, in particular, have something to teach Christians about their own tradition, something that can help them deepen their own religion and "open up insights that were only dimly perceived before" (CD, 19). This "something" is clearly mysticism for Zaehner. Hinduism, after all, is the mystical religion par excellence: "Hinduism," he writes, "is both the fountainhead and the typical manifestation of mystical religion in all its forms" (CD, 194). Such a Hindu hermeneutic runs throughout Zaehner's writings and can be seen as well in his marginalia, which are often nothing more than Sanskrit or Arabic terms used to gloss Christian ones, or vice versa: "love"/"*bhakti*/*shauq*" "ecstasy"/"*samādhi,*" "*vairāgya*"/"dark night of the soul," "swooning"/"*fanā'*," "salvation"/"*mokṣa,*" "*jñāna*"/ "contemplation," and so on. The study of mysticism, then, may be growing in the rot of modern secularism and the confusion of cross-cultural communication and interreligious borrowing, but it is all a terribly fertile rot, a place of potential renewal as much as certain death. And it speaks, quite literally, from the margins.

Mystical Experience and the Writer

Although Zaehner eschewed the lonely roads of excess, which he consistently resisted when they appeared to him in the forms of the 1960s counterculture or in the antinomian practices of historical mystics, for the surer and wider "highway" of orthodox Catholicism, he assumed that at least some twentieth-century studies of mysticism originated in the mystical experiences of the scholars themselves (CD, 41) and was quite clear that this mystical-hermeneutical pattern replicates a similar process in the genesis of traditional mystical literature (CD, 46). But this same reliance on subjective experience is a potential problem for Zaehner, since the mystical experience often brings with it a quite unwarranted sense of certainty and a tendency to attach itself to any intellectual content that it finds handy, not to mention the "irritating" habit of mystics to speak of infinite knowledge despite the fact that their experiences so obviously add nothing of substance or content to their specific knowledge (CD, 43; cf. 78). Zaehner, for example, points out that Richard Bucke, the Canadian psychologist whose *Cosmic Consciousness* had such a powerful and long-lasting influence on both scholarly and popular discussions of mysticism, confused his own "intuitional experiences" with his reading of evolutionary theory to come up with some at best bizarre conclusions about the increasing frequency of mystical experience, about the identity of the Buddha's and Walt Whitman's experiences, and about the supposed moral elevation that cosmic consciousness brings (CD, 46–48). Zaehner's conclusion is biting: "[H]is shattering experience had warped his rational judgment in the matter of the experience itself" (CD, 49).

In some very real sense, Zaehner is much more interested, as is this study, in those writers who were able to maintain a critical distance from the experience in order to create and write out of an absence that was also a remembered presence. Foremost among such writers for Zaehner was the French novelist Honoré de Balzac, whose refusal to submit to a natural mystical state was precisely what made him into a great novelist. In Balzac's *Le Comédie humaine,* for example, we have "the story of Balzac as he might have been, had he allowed cosmic consciousness to get the better of him instead of himself canalizing and utilizing it to produce perhaps the most grandiose literary monument the world has ever seen. Perhaps it was because he was so firmly rooted in the world that is beyond time, multiplicity and passion that he wrote with such superb authority and compassion about the miseries, the passions, and the infinite diversity of the world we know only too well" (CD, 50). I cannot help seeing a self-portrait of Zaehner in this warm description of a beloved novelist. Certainly Zaehner was no novelist, but this model of the creative writer who can write and think and love only because he has *not* fully submitted to the mystical resonates almost perfectly with the persona we see taking shape in Zaehner's published writings and their practice of a mystical criticism.

Once we emphasize this distance aspect of Zaehner's hermeneutic, it is equally important to point out that he just as clearly valued an originative presence, as long as this presence did not overwhelm the critical faculties and turn its vessel into a public idiot or moral disaster. One of his former students, for example, made it quite clear to me that Zaehner felt that this student had no business studying mysticism since he had had no mystical experiences himself, and when another student traveled to Iran and was blessed at the hands of a sheik, through hypnosis or hallucinogens, with a visionary experience of the twelve Imams, Zaehner was utterly fascinated. Here too we might recall Zaehner's single-paragraph attack on Stace: "Buber had had an experience and, so far as is known, Stace had not" (CD, 200). So too in his laconic handwritten annotations on Hans Jacobs's *Western Psychotherapy and Hindu-Sadhana:* "161. Presumably he has no practical experience of *samādhi."* We need not assume or guess that Zaehner had such experiences. He tells us himself that he had. We need only to recognize this fact for what it is: an entrance into the hermeneutical practice of R. C. Zaehner and, to a much larger extent, the twentieth-century study of mystical literature.

The Doors of Deception

In the spring of 1953, the novelist Aldous Huxley swallowed four-tenths of a gram of mescaline under the supervision of a psychiatrist in order to explore the mystical potential of the hallucinogen, for "short of being born again as a visionary, a medium, or a musical genius," how else "can we ever visit the worlds to which, to Blake, to Swedenborg, to Johann Sebastian Bach, were home?"[17] In short, Huxley wanted to know "from the inside" what the mystics were talking about: he wanted to experience their texts from within. What the writer expected from the drug was an elaborate visionary show within the solipsistic confines of his own chemical brain. What he got instead was an apocalyptically tinged revelation of the external world—"The great change was in the realm of objective fact" (16)—and the creative genesis of a little Blakean tract, *The Doors of Perception*, that would become a kind of cult classic for the 1960s counterculture movement, inspire a generation of writers on the mystical, including Timothy Leary and Agehananda Bharati, and provide a catchy name for the rock band The Doors. But Huxley was not thinking about the 1960s or rock music at the time (it was, after all, 1953). He was thinking about ancient Greek philosophy, Platonism to be exact, and medieval Christian mysticism:

> *Istigkeit*—wasn't that the word Meister Eckhart liked to use? "Is-ness." The Being of Platonic philosophy—except that Plato seems to have made the enormous, the grotesque mistake of separating Being from Becoming and identifying it with the mathematical abstraction of the Idea. He could never, poor fellow, have seen a bunch of flowers shining with their own inner light and all but quivering under the pressure of the significance with which they were charged ... a transience that was yet eternal life, a perpetual perishing that was at the same time pure Being, a bundle of minute, unique particulars in which, by some unspeakable and yet self-evident paradox, was to be seen the divine source of all existence. (17–18)

This dialectical, paradoxical experience was also profoundly hermeneutical, as it both issued from his reading of Hindu and Buddhist mystical texts and in turn affected those same, now revolutionized texts. Interestingly, the texts of a famous twentieth-century scholar of Zen Buddhism, D. T. Suzuki, mediated Huxley's interpretation of the experience within the experience itself:

> The Beatific Vision, Sat Chit Ananda, Being-Awareness-Bliss—for the first time I understood, not on the verbal level, not by inchoate hints or at a distance, but precisely and completely what those prodigious syllables referred to. And then I remembered a passage I had read in one of Suzuki's essays, "What is the Dharma-Body of the Buddha?" ... the Master answers "The hedge at the bottom of the garden." ... It had been, when I read it, only a vaguely pregnant piece of nonsense. Now it was all clear as day, as evident as Euclid. Of course the Dharma-Body of the Buddha was the hedge at the bottom of the garden. (18–19)

Leaving the garden that was the Buddha, Huxley now entered his study and saw a vision that could easily function as a kind of imaginal motto for the present study of the mystical dimensions of certain types of scholarly texts. "I saw the books," Huxley noted, and "what impressed itself upon my mind was the fact that all of them glowed with living light and that in some the glory was more manifest than others" (20).

Much of *The Doors of Perception* is concerned not with the experience itself, but with Huxley's speculations on what it all might mean. Huxley wonders, for example, whether the brain's function might be primarily eliminative, filtering out every sensation and bit of information that is not important to human physical and social survival. Through mystical or hallucinogenic experience, however, something Huxley calls Mind at Large "seeps past the no longer watertight valve" and "all kinds of biologically useless things start to happen" (26). Among these useless things are an apocalyptic entrance into reality itself beyond the cozy symbol and linguistic sign and a subsequent indifference to human relationships and social concerns. Such mystical states, Huxley admits, cannot be reconciled with active charity and practical compassion (35, 40–41).[18] Under the influence of mescaline, then, Huxley confesses that he knew contemplation "[a]t its height, but not yet in its fullness" (41). In the end, a more dialectical position is needed, one that knows the ontological ground but can still insist on the integrity, even holiness, of the individual and human reason. Hence, for Huxley, to be enlightened is "to be aware, always, of total reality in its immanent otherness—to be aware of it and yet to remain in a condition to survive as an animal, to think and feel as a human being, to resort whenever expedient to systematic reasoning. Our goal is to discover that we have always been where we ought to be" (78). So too with the person—the writer, the scholar, the historian of mysticism, we might add—who has glimpsed something of the mystical and has returned to the realm of the intellect and the symbol: "But the man who comes back through the Door in the Wall will never be quite the same as the man who went out. He will be wiser but less cocksure, happier but less self-satisfied, humbler in acknowledging his ignorance yet better equipped to understand the relationship of words to things, of systematic reasoning to the unfathomable Mystery which it tries, forever vainly, to comprehend" (79).

Huxley's little book and the Door in the Wall it attempted to jar open for its readers both had a very significant impact on R. C. Zaehner and the future course of his writing career. Zaehner begins his *Mysticism Sacred and Profane* with these words: "It should be said at the outset that this book owes its genesis to Mr. Aldous Huxley. Had *The Doors of Perception* never been published, it is extremely doubtful whether the present author would have been rash enough to enter the field of comparative mysticism. Mr. Huxley left us no choice."[19] Huxley's book, which had documented the novelist's claim that his own mescaline-induced mystical experiences were of the same nature and order as the experiences of the classical mystics of the history of religions, strikes "at the roots of all religion that makes any claim to be taken seriously," Zaehner argued (MSP, xiv). Why? Because "if mescalin can produce the Beatific Vision here on earth . . . the Christian emphasis on morality is not only all wrong but also a little naive." Mescaline thus "presents us not only with a social problem,—for how on earth could a society composed exclusively of ecstatics possibly be run?—but also with a theological problem of great magnitude" (MSP, 13). From the beginning, from the very first pages, Zaehner understood the mystical as a serious ethical problem and a profound theological challenge.

Zaehner is clearly struggling with his own demons here, for he himself had known the profundity and overwhelming reality of the mystical at the age of twenty shortly after reading Arthur Rimbaud's poem *Saison en Enfer*. This experience "combined all the principal traits described in *The Doors of Perception*" (MSP, xiv-xv), Zaehner tells us, although, very much unlike Huxley's, it came unsought and without the use of drugs. It was what Zaehner liked to call a "natural mystical experience," which "may occur to anyone, whatever his religious faith or lack of it, and whatever moral, immoral, or amoral life he may be leading at the time" (MSP, xv). As Zaehner would never tire of saying, mysticism, at least this type of mysticism, has nothing to do with ethics, or God, or religion for that matter.

But after his conversion to Catholicism in 1946 Zaehner had to set this earlier event beside "an experience of what I can only assure Mr. Huxley is of another order,—the attempt, however bungling and inept, to make contact with God through what Catholics call the normal channels of grace" (MSP, xv). Clearly, Huxley's book had made a potential mockery of this entire tradition, for if he were correct, "then it follows that the vision of God is a natural concomitant of mania, that it can be induced by drugs, and that since the vision makes nonsense of common morality, let alone of the virtues of humility and charity, then the picture of God which we derive from the teaching of Jesus of Nazareth must be false" (MSP, 124). And so a very Catholic Zaehner, catalyzed by the social, ethical, and theological problems Huxley had made all too clear, proceeds from the depths of his own confessed mystical experiences, both "sacred" and "profane," to construct a sophisticated model of mysticism that could rescue his Catholicism from the shipwreck Huxley's little book had unquestionably exposed it to. "Obviously," he tells his readers in another book, "the layman who is a stranger to mystical experience is in no position to distinguish between the various 'states' of the mystic."[20] This scholar was no stranger to mystical states of consciousness, and he made it his business to distinguish between them.

The Typology

Zaehner's comparative model implies a universal psychic substratum and a set of psychic experiences that are differently (and often wrongly) interpreted in specific cultural contexts. There is, in other words, a "grand pattern of the universal mystical tradition" (CD, 337) or a "common mystical tradition of mankind" (CD, 140) that can be detected and studied with the proper hermeneutical lenses. His model is a developmental one that is tripartite in structure and psycho-theological in approach, that is, it combines both psychological and theological models to explain different types of mystical experience that constitute different stages along a normatively constructed "path" or developmental trajectory (in this, it replicates numerous traditional typologies of mystical experience constructed by the various traditions themselves). Accordingly, there are three distinct stages of the mystical path for Zaehner, each of which corresponds to a different type of mystical experience and a different psycho-theological level.[21]

1. The Panenhenic Experience, or Nature Mysticism. The first stage is that of the panenhenic[22] mystical experience, in which the mystic experiences himself or herself as identical to the natural world in a manic-like state of positive ego inflation. Such states can come naturally, as Zaehner's came to him at twenty after reading Rimbaud or as Bucke's came to him reading Whitman (CD, chap. 2), or by the use of drugs, as Huxley's came to him late in life under the influence of mescaline. Ethically speaking, such "natural" or "profane" monistic states work against any human relations (MSP, 8–9) and are inherently amoral, as are both the collective unconscious (whose surges into consciousness manifest themselves in these states) and nature itself. Zaehner thus often refers to this kind of mysticism as nature mysticism. Not surprisingly, these states are often associated with immoral behaviors, particularly those involving the sexual powers, which are so often loosened by the ego's absorption in the unconscious (MSP, 148). "Moral problems, it is clear, have no meaning once one obtains this 'higher' vision, and personal relationships too cease to have any importance" (MSP, 13).

Zaehner does not hesitate to employ both mythological precedent and psychological reductionism to explain these natural forms of "downward transcendence" (MSP, 140)—what he will elsewhere, following Louis Gardet, call forms of a "finite absolute" (CD, 203). Thus, he liked to quote Indra's reply in the Chāndogya Upaniṣad to a traditional description of the experience of Brahman in deep sleep: "Surely he might as well be a man annihilated. I see nothing enjoyable in this" (CD, 91). Echoing Indra, Zaehner suggests again that *nirvāṇa* may mean "nothing less than death, the final extinction of the flame of life" (CD, 66; cf. 99). In a more psychological vein, he often points out the striking analogies between natural mystical states and manic-depressive illness (MSP, 88, 106), a disturbing but nevertheless provocative and potentially fruitful diagnosis that deserves, I think, a very serious look, especially after the work of Kay Reed Jamison, who has convincingly demonstrated the illness's organic connection to literary and poetic genius.[23] Zaehner's tactic here is especially insightful and sophisticated, as he does not practice a simple layman's psychologism but rather turns to the mystical texts themselves and demonstrates that the classical Sufi distinction between *basṭ* and *qabḍ*, "contraction" and "expansion," impressively replicates the depressive and manic states of the modern diagnosis, and that at least some Sufis were quite aware and critical of the manic's error of identifying his "expansion" as an ontological identification with God. In numerous other places, Zaehner employs a Jungian model and reads these states, when uncontrolled, as an absorption of the ego into the collective unconscious,[24] or, when controlled, as an integration of the conscious and the unconscious. Such an integration is the psychological end point of this first stage of the mystical path.

2. The Isolation of the Self or the Mysticism of Isolation. Beyond these natural states of absorption in nature and psychic integration Zaehner finds a "mysticism of isolation" and those experiences in which the soul comes to know itself as absolute beyond and outside of the phenomenal world through ascetic discipline (MSP, 150). Zaehner places much of classical Indian mysticism here, and especially Advaita Vedānta, Sāṁkhya, and, to a lesser extent, Mādhyamika Buddhism, all of which for him, although quite distinct in their doctrinal formulations, amount to more or less the same thing phenomenologically (that is, "so far as the experience is concerned")—the stripping of the soul of its psychophysical attachments resulting in an experience of the soul's own immortality in isolation from the world (MSP, 135). Thus, for Zaehner, "Sāṁkhya ... marks an advance beyond nature mysticism in that it makes a clear distinction between Nature on the one hand and the immortal soul or spirit on the other" (MSP, 125). Zaehner compares such an immortal spirit *(puruṣa)*, "above both the conscious and the unconscious" (MSP, 125), to the state of the amoral, newborn child: "it has reverted to original innocence in which there is neither good nor evil" (MSP, 128).

3. The Return of the Self to God or the Mysticism of Love. Such states are profound for Zaehner, but they are also ultimately dead ends on the mystical path, and dangerously seductive ones at that, for the soul experiencing its own inherent bliss and immortality can all too easily mistake this eternal nature with the divine itself and so deify itself as God, as Brahman, and so on. Such states, however genuinely transcendent, must themselves be transcended in God (CD, VII), for this is "the soul's delusion that it is God" (MHM 157), that "colossal exaltation of self" (MHH 125) that Zaehner, backed by a select group of famous Hindu and Sufi mystics, condemns as erroneous. Employing the same comparative method that he did with the manic-depressive diagnosis, in which he turned to Sufi mystical texts to find support for his own position, Zaehner does not simply issue this normative judgment from the arbitrary height of his own theological assumptions (which, by the way, he freely admits, puts on the table [MSP, xv], and openly questions [CD, I]). Rather, he turns (and returns in a much fuller fashion in *Hindu and Muslim Mysticism*) to the Indian theistic mystic Rāmānuja and the Sufi polemicists Qushayrī, Junayd, and ʿAṭṭār to critique the monistic excesses of the Bhagavad Gītā and the ecstatic utterances of that most "outrageous" of Sufi mystics, Abū Yazīd: "Abū Yazīd, then, like the Yogin of the sixth chapter of the Bhagavad Gītā, reached a state in which he thought that 'there was no bourn beyond it,' but, according to Rāmānuja in India and ʿAṭṭār in Persia, *they were perfectly wrong*" (MHM 128; my italics). For "whether you call your soul an individual *puruṣa* or the Absolute *nirguṇa* or qualityless Brahman makes no difference. All you can achieve is the isolation of your essence, thereby denying yourself the presence of God" (MSP, 146).

How, then, might the eternal soul be delivered from its own seductively blissful isolation? Zaehner's answer is provocative. Theologically put, the answer is "grace," which is, phenomenologically speaking, often experienced as a form of mystical eroticism. For here the soul must realize that, if it is to proceed any further, its only role can be "that of the bride: it must play the woman, because, as far as its relations with God are concerned, it must be entirely passive and receptive" (MSP, 151). In effect, the soul must undergo a symbolic sex change, a gender transformation at its ontological core. Zaehner did not seem to be aware of what this might imply about the mystic's sexual orientation and gender identification—at least here in *Mysticism Sacred and Profane*—but, to his great credit, he did not hesitate to affirm the essentially erotic nature of the very highest mystical experiences: "There is no point at all in blinking the fact that the raptures of the theistic mystic are closely akin to the transports of sexual union" (MSP, 151). Despite such courage and his earlier willingness to submit natural and isolation mystical experiences to a reductive psychological hermeneutic, Zaehner will have none of the psychologist's insights here (which would seem to be more than a little relevant) and chooses instead to adopt an *imago Dei* theology that effectively reverses the psychologist's thesis that the divine experience is a projection and sublimation of the human organism (not to mention orgasm): "[I]f man is made in the image of God, then it would be natural that God's love would be reflected in human love, and that the love of man for woman should reflect the love of God for the soul" (MSP, 151). The final bliss of the theistic mystic in this life thus "consists in the total surrender of the whole personality to a God who is at the same time Love" (MSP, 169). At the very heights of mystical experience, at the end of the path, the sexual, once denied by the ascetic, returns as the erotic. Or in more traditional theological terms, without love, it is impossible to reach "the God who *is* love" (CD, 136).

The Serpent's Gift: Adam and Eve as Evolutionary Myth

Zaehner also thought mythologically. The Hebrew myth of Adam and Eve functioned as a particularly rich source of thought and reflection for him. In this he stands in an especially long line of Jewish, Christian, and Muslim exegetes.[25] Elaine Pagels, for example, has written of ancient Christian gnostic exegeses of this story as a move from interpreting the text as "history with a moral" to "myth with meaning." "Read this way," she writes, "the text became a shimmering surface of symbols, inviting the spiritually adventurous to explore its hidden depths, to draw upon their own inner experience . . . to interpret the story."[26] Such a hermeneutics certainly fits the temperament and intellectual commitments of R. C. Zaehner, who ridiculed biblical literalism as that "absurd near divinization of the Bible" (CD, 348), privileged mystical modes of knowing in his own hermeneutics, and did not hesitate to resort to allegorical methods when they suited his own polemical or apologetic purposes.[27] In many ways, R. C. Zaehner was a gnostic who did not hesitate to read and understand orthodox Christian dogma through his own mystical-psychological exegeses.

Not surprisingly, then, his reading of the Genesis myth, with the serpent functioning as the antihero of the story, is an essentially gnostic tale, refashioned anew for twentieth-century readers through Charles Darwin, Richard Bucke, Henri Bergson, C. G. Jung, Sri Aurobindo, and Pierre Teilhard de Chardin, the latter two figures receiving the extended attention of an entire comparative monograph late in Zaehner's life (1971).[28] The Adam and Eve myth, Zaehner writes, "lends itself to evolutionary interpretation, but with embarrassing results for the theologian, for it is not God who personifies the forward thrust of evolution, but the serpent; it is the serpent who propels man into a state of self-consciousness, and Yahweh who would hold him back" (CD, 327). We are immediately reminded here of the rich sources of rebellion and reflection that the Christian gnostic texts represented for early Christianity. These texts, after all, often portrayed the serpent as the protagonist of the story, the bestower of a "knowledge" *(gnosis)* that a petty, envious God tried to prevent. Consider, for example, *The Testimony of Truth:* "What kind of God is this? First, he envied Adam that he should eat from the tree of knowledge.... And afterward he said, 'Let us cast him [out] of this place lest he eat of the tree of life and live forever.' Surely he has shown himself to be a malicious envier. And what kind of God is this?"[29] Zaehner's point, then, is hardly new. What makes it especially interesting, even original, is his ability to support this ancient gnostic insight with theoretical buttresses constructed from a wide range of comparative, psychological and mystical materials. As it also can function nicely for my own rhetorical purposes—that is, as a lead-in to my analyses of Zaehner's ethical and erotic critiques—a brief discussion of Zaehner's handling of this ancient myth is in order.

Zaehner's fascination with the story was not some late, quirky blip in his thought and writing. Quite the contrary. He used it a number of times to interpret the natural mystical states of the purified soul. It appears as early as *Mysticism Sacred and Profane,* where, in describing the isolation of the self, Zaehner argues that such preliminary states—both those of the natural panenhenic and the more spiritual, isolation experiences—can be compared to Adam's childlike innocence in Paradise or to the blissful state of souls in Limbo (MSP, 101, 128, 129, 151). The myth would reappear throughout his middle writings and appear again in his late *Concordant Discord* (1970) and *Evolution in Religion* (1971). The former opens after an introductory chapter with an essay on Bucke, whose sense of religious history Zaehner deplores as utterly useless and silly but whose insights into the Adam and Eve myth he appreciates as still valuable (CD, 327). Essentially, Bucke had understood Adam and Eve's fall as not a fall at all but a rise into self-consciousness, as a psycho-spiritual development that could be completed only in the "cosmic consciousness" that Bucke now heralded as the true Christ. So too with Zaehner: "The serpent . . . is the spirit of rationality, the immanent will inherent in the evolutionary process, if you like, which urges the human race to grow up" (CD, 328).

In another comparative move, Zaehner argues that a Taoist interpretation of the story is most natural and useful, for Taoism, unlike any other religion, saw that "the serpent's gift of discursive reason" (CD, 334) could only exile humanity from the bliss of Edenic union with what the Taoist tradition calls "the Uncarved Block," that is, nature before the meddlings of ego and analytical reasoning, both of which slice the Block up into warring bits and pieces. Zaehner, in a fascinating display of comparison as normative theology, clearly appreciates the Taoist desire for such a "return to the womb" mysticism (CD, 218) but ultimately sides with the "human, humane, humanistic, Confucian point of view" that reads such a fall in positive terms, as a "break-through from group-consciousness into self-consciousness" (the expressions are Bucke's). "This," Zaehner observes, "is man's refusal to form one piece for ever with the 'Uncarved Block,' even though this participation means a blissful unawareness of physical death because the Block itself can never die" (CD, 224). Whereas Taoism refused to face the reality of humanity's emergence from a "nebulous, collective consciousness," Confucianism accepted this fact and argued that it is best to develop the Tao now in the best interests of the human community (CD, 257). To be a self, then, is *not* to be one with nature; to accept one's self-consciousness is to renounce one's cosmic consciousness for the sake of the larger social community and a new cultural refashioning of the Way.

Two contrary characteristics of Zaehner's comparative-mystical reading of the Adam and Eve myth strike me as worthy of comment. First is his lucent insight into the ethical-intellectual components of the story, with the fall more or less equated with the "knowledge of good and evil," that is, with a discriminating moral intelligence. This seems unproblematic enough. But what should we make of his subsequent refusal or inability to see and comment on the sexual components of the story? Clearly, the Jewish, Christian, and Muslim exegetes saw sexual meanings in the story. In Jewish exegesis, for example, the snake sometimes copulates with Eve,[30] and the "knowledge of good and evil" could be identified with sexual awareness.[31] As for Christianity, Augustine virtually equated humanity's "original sin" with the sexual act when he suggested that this "sin" is passed on through the semen.[32] Not that we needed such exegetical inventions. Zaehner once rhetorically asked whether we really needed a God (in this case, Kṛṣṇa of the Bhagavad Gītā) to tell us that becoming one with nature is not the same thing as becoming one with the self in the love of God (CD, 301). To borrow this same Zaehnerian question, we might ask if we really needed a Freud to tell us that the Adam and Eve story—sexual differentiation, the snake, the fruit, the immediate shame connected to an awareness of nakedness (that is, of sexuality), and the fertility punishment (pain in childbirth, suffering in the fields)—is about sex. Why didn't Zaehner see or comment on *any* of this? Before I attempt an answer, let us examine for a moment what he did see and what he did so clearly understand, namely, that humanity's "fall" from mystical absorption in nature was also a "rise" into ethical consciousness.

3. The Ethical Critique

Zaehner's ethical critique of mysticism runs throughout *Mysticism Sacred and Profane* and only increases in tone and conviction in his later writings. Such a critique, however, always functioned as a logical and necessary outcome of his original, tripartite, developmental stage theory, which he first set out in *Mysticism Sacred and Profane*. To the question, "Is mysticism moral?" Zaehner's answer is unmistakable: "It depends." It depends on what *type* of mystical experience one is discussing, and Zaehner is refreshingly clear about which types are moral and which types are not.

As we have seen already, the first, panenhenic stage is a union with a nature that is amoral and, more often than not, decidedly antihuman. Here Zaehner quotes approvingly the honest and uncompromising humanism of the nature mystic Richard Jefferies: "How can I adequately express . . . my contempt for the assertion that all things occur for the best, for a wise and beneficent end, and are ordered by a humane intelligence! It is the most utter falsehood and a crime against the human race" (MSP, 45). Nature is utterly indifferent to humanity (MSP, 45), and so to look to such natural experiences for any kind of reliable human ethics is folly, a project doomed to fail. How much sense Zaehner's beloved Rimbaud made, then, when he envisaged a materialist future in which his mystically experienced universal mind was the "substratum of the material universe" and his absolute a materialist absolute (MSP, 65). Perhaps there are more consoling and encouraging ontologies, but none more honest and unflinching. "Will you cure our ills by daring to deny them?" Zaehner pointedly asks. "That is the crunch," and that is precisely what such mystics ask us to do (CD, 345).

It is not that mystical participation in such a materialist universe must be immoral or necessarily evil. Far from it: "Theologically it means a return to Eden, a return to the primitive condition when man had not tasted of the Tree of the Knowledge of Good and Evil, a return to the innocence of childhood" (MSP, 82). Unfortunately, however, nature mysticism does not often reside in this edenic innocence, for, especially in its more manic phases, nature mysticism inevitably weakens the will, releases unconscious libidinal forces (MSP, 148), and loosens the moral sense, with all too predictable social results (MSP, 89, 106). This first stage, then, is at best amoral and at worst, and too often, blatantly immoral.

It is more difficult to define the moral status of Zaehner's second, isolation, stage, for it can be said to be both moral and amoral at the same time. True, such states require moral and ascetic discipline to reach, and in this sense they "possess" a moral dimension, at least as a prerequisite or as a preparatory stage. But in their own phenomenological structures they are not properly moral, for, by definition, they are experiences of isolation and so bear no relationship to other selves, moral agents, or the world. Once again, monism, even a monism of the self, precludes a true ethics, for "in monism there can be no love" (MSP, 172).

More disturbingly, this same loveless monism of the self can become decidedly immoral. Consider, for example, Zaehner's reading of Upanisadic amoralism, particularly that of Bṛhadāraṇyaka Upaniṣad 4.3.22. Zaehner translates the passage this way: "In this land 'a father becomes no father *(a-pitā)*, a mother no mother, the worlds no worlds, the gods no gods, the Vedas no Vedas. There a thief becomes no thief, the murderer of an embryo no murderer of an embryo . . . a mendicant no mendicant, an ascetic no ascetic. (The Brahman which the released soul becomes) is accompanied by neither good *(puṇyena)* nor evil. He (the soul) has passed beyond all the troubles of the heart'" (MSP, 116–17). Zaehner, ever the comparativist, provocatively places this scriptural passage beside the self-induced madness of Rimbaud and the manic psychosis of John Custance (both of whom said more or less the same thing), only to put the sensitive reader in a very difficult interreligious situation. After setting up the phenomenological analogy, Zaehner then points out that we are dealing here with neither a mad French poet nor an even more obscure and manic Custance but "with the sacred books of one of the world's greatest religions" (MSP, 117). Zaehner does not flinch before the obvious implications of such a phenomenological comparison and suggests here, and in a far more developed way in his *Hindu and Muslim Mysticism* insists, that the Upanisadic writers, exactly like Rimbaud and Constance, were "perfectly wrong" about both their self-deification and their alleged transcendence of morality. Thus the Advaita Vedānta, and with it much of Hindu mystical thought, is rejected as ontologically false and as morally inadequate, if not downright dangerous. But Zaehner is quite clear that it is a serious, even "monstrous generalization," a "travesty of Hindu mysticism as it developed in history" (CD, 153), and a "condescending" act to equate Hindu mysticism with monism,[33] and he has much to say, most all of it deeply appreciative, about the *bhakti* movement and the love mysticisms it generated within the Hindu devotional traditions.[34]

Only the third, theistic stage of the mystical path, then, is properly and genuinely moral for Zaehner, and this for both ontological and ascetic reasons. Ontologically speaking, it makes no sense to talk about ethics without some sort of duality, as we have already noted (MSP, 144), and true duality appears only here in the theistic stage. Moreover, ascetically speaking, theistic mystical experience requires moral perfection, whereas nature mysticism is quite possible without effort of any kind (MSP, 104). Natural mystical experiences, then, unlike theistic encounters, have no inherent or essential moral value and will only "make the good man better and the bad man worse" (MSP, 104). Thus "when all is said and done," sanctification, holiness, and ascetic practice are the only adequate methods we have of judging between divine and natural forms of mysticism (MSP, 105). It is ethics, and ethics alone, we might conclude, that separates "mysticism sacred and profane." Or put differently and devotionally (and erotically), *it is love*. Once again, Zaehner turns to a traditional mystic—in this case, the great Hindu theologian Rāmānuja—to make this, perhaps his ultimate ethical point: "Any mystical state which is one of undifferentiated oneness is the experience that one individual soul enjoys of its own individual self: it has nothing to do with God. Thus in any form of mystical experience from which love is absent, there can be no question of God: he is absent too. To interpret the experience as being identical with the One or the All is absurd; beguiled by the beauty and apparent infinity of its own deep nature, the liberated soul—so Rāmānuja holds—mistakes the mustard-seed for Mount Meru, the drop for the sea."[35]

The Universe through the Looking-Glass: Zaehner's Comedic Monism

Both this essentially ethical vision of a true "sacred" or theistic mysticism and the inadequacies of natural, "profane," or monistic mysticism come out dramatically in appendix B of *Mysticism Sacred and Profane,* where Zaehner relates a tape-recorded session he arranged to record and analyze his own reactions to Huxley's mescaline. I know of no funnier episode in the twentieth-century study of mysticism than this one and no funnier scholar than R. C. Zaehner on mescaline (although his students and friends told me repeatedly that he could be equally hilarious as simply himself). The appendix is also one of the best-documented cases of a historian of mysticism intentionally inducing an altered state and taking great measures to record and analyze it accurately from both the "inside" and the "outside." I must add, however, that I was told by acquaintances of Zaehner on more than one occasion that something more happened during the experiment that did not make it into the appendix, that is, that was intentionally left out. I do not know and so cannot say what this "more" was, but I can say that the claim does not surprise me at all. Once again, the mystical is precisely that which is kept "silent," "hidden," or "repressed."

The experiment was carried out on 3 December 1955 at Oxford in the company of a psychiatrist, a researcher of psychic phenomena, two Oxford students, and another fellow of All Souls. Zaehner was given 0.4 grams of mescaline (the exact dose delivered to Huxley) at 11:40 A.M. He confesses that he became increasingly apprehensive as the day approached, dreamed about it for three consecutive nights, and feared, irrationally, he admits, that it might prove fatal to him. He spoke throughout the experiment of a cold sensation in his extremities (especially his feet) and his genitals and described, quite in line with other Western reports on *kuṇḍalinī*-like phenomena, a tingling sensation that began at the base of his spine. Custance had reported the same as signaling his manic bouts, and Zaehner, perhaps following Custance here, employs the expressions "manic" and "mania" to describe his own drug trip. Although Zaehner does not himself say so, it seems that he had rather carefully planned the event to produce distinctly Christian mystical experiences (he was, after all, trying to prove Huxley wrong). Hence, he was quite eager to lead his troupe to Christ Church and Tom Tower. Unfortunately, at the "moment I had been eagerly anticipating, nothing happened at all. Tom Tower stood there as he always has done, looking precisely the same" (MSP, 214). The cathedral was a bit more interesting, as the choir loft undulated and the rose window throbbed. A pillar he looked at, however, "remained absolutely motionless. I respected it for that" (MSP, 216).

Once the party returned to Zaehner's room in All Souls, however, things started to cook up and became increasingly funny. Noting that Dr. Allison's right ear had "expanded quite considerably," Zaehner notes wryly that "I somehow felt it would be impolite to draw attention to this" (MSP, 217). Again imitating Huxley's experiment, his observers offered him various art books to observe under the influence of the drug. He was first asked to look at Gentile da Fabriano's *Adoration of the Magi*. As Zaehner gazed at the picture, he noticed that the second magus was trying to take his crown off: "He's bringing up the . . . no. (Testily) Come on, come one, come on (encouraging the Magus)" (MSP, 217). Things got better (and funnier) when his guests shone a light on the same piece. Zaehner now realized that the magus couldn't take his crown off, as hard as he tried, because of course *he was stuck in the painting*. Zaehner now broke into uncontrollable fits of laughter that were to last for over an hour. When asked what was so funny, he replied ecstatically: "'Nothing.' This was true: everything had suddenly become so totally funny that to single out one thing rather than another would not at all have conveyed this experience of total funniness" (MSP, 217). Things only got funnier when he noticed the infant Jesus trying to push away the magus who was bending down to him. The magus, it turns out, was actually trying to bite the infant's toe!

After more pieces of art, which Zaehner refused—"I just wanted to laugh on in peace, 'laughing at nothing' as I described it" (MSP, 218)—the experimenters, again imitating the Huxley account, offered him specific books to look at or try to read. After reading a bit of Frazer's *Golden Bough*, which he found to be one of the great "comic classics" (a real stretch for anyone who has tried to wade through it), Zaehner found himself amazed that people could be so silly and stupid as to believe in causes and effects, and he hesitated to reveal his "great thought," which, it turns out, was that "[e]verything is much funnier than it seems" (MSP, 220). A bit later, in a book of Picasso paintings, he saw "the good old collective unconscious looking out," which of course he found quite funny: "That's the trouble with Jung, he doesn't realize how dull his collective unconscious is" (MSP, 223). Finally, they tried to get him to listen to some music, which he eventually did—Berlioz's *Te Deum,* one of his favorite pieces. The moment it began, he became absorbed in its rhythms and he finally settled down: "[A]t that stage," he wrote, "I felt the manic phase had passed sufficiently for me to think about religious things." And indeed, even in the manic state, he would express discomfort at looking at a praying figure of Francesca, for "[i]t's a holy thing not to be looked at when you're drugged" (MSP, 225).

In other words, Zaehner's theistic dualism was hardly challenged by what Huxley had described as a profoundly nondual mystical experience under the same dosage of the same drug. "In Huxley's terminology 'self-transcendence' of a sort did take place, but transcendence into a world of farcical meaninglessness. . . . the quality of 'funniness' and incongruity had swallowed up all others." Zaehner ends the appendix with the following telling line: "The fact that I am an assiduous reader of *Alice through the Looking-Glass* is probably not irrelevant to the nature of my experience" (MSP, 226). Nor, of course, are the facts that he undertook the elaborate experiment to prove Huxley's experience fundamentally misguided, that he went into it with a very developed and very sophisticated model of what "sacred" and "profane" mysticism are, and that he considered drugs to be capable of producing only the latter. In the end, I think, Zaehner's Oxford on mescaline is significant not because it proves Huxley (or Zaehner) right or wrong, but because it offers us one more example of how mystical experiences are profoundly influenced, perhaps even determined, by their emotional, doctrinal, and psychological contexts. In the process, moreover, and perhaps more important, such an experiment shows us that historians of mysticism are often quite willing to use their own bodies and minds as tools to understand the mystical, that Zaehner had a wonderful sense of humor (with or without mescaline), and that Zaehner's Oxford on mescaline was not nearly as good as Huxley's Southern California on the same.

4. The Mystical Marriage: Ontology, Gender, and Homoeroticism in Zaehner's Life and Work

Most commentators on Zaehner have focused either on his justly famous debate with Huxley and the American counterculture, his tripartite typology of mystical states of consciousness, or his ethical critique of monism, and this is entirely proper, as these were indeed the overriding concerns that structured and gave force to much of his writing. But such a triple focus obscures and hides from view another aspect of Zaehner's thought that was, in many ways, just as central and just as important—the erotic,[36] that mysterious *numinosum* in which "spirit and matter are indissolubly linked, merging into one, making whole and therefore holy" (CD, 56). The erotic functioned on numerous levels in Zaehner's work and life: as an ontological critique of Augustinian dualism and what he perceived to be the deleterious effects of Neoplatonism on Christianity, as an understanding of gender that grounded and more or less reified femininity as the proper sign of the human soul and its creaturely passivity and masculinity as the proper sign of the divine and its primary agency, as a struggle with psychoanalysis and its own reductive reading of religious eroticism as essentially libidinal and conflictual, as the end and summation of the mystical life in a normative and universally true "mystical marriage" of the female/passive human soul and the single male/active God, as a proper eschatological language with which to speak about the end of history and humanity in a final cosmo-erotic unity-in-diversity modeled after the Trinity itself, and, finally, as a personal psychosexual struggle carried on in the secret spaces of Zaehner's emotional and sexual life. About the last we know only a little, but even it is hermeneutically significant. About everything else—in a very real sense, the hermeneutical reflection of that secret intimate life—we know a great deal indeed.

There is no better text to examine this aspect of Zaehner's work than *Concordant Discord,* his 1967–1969 Gifford Lectures, published in 1970, just four years before his death. All the major themes of Zaehner's thought are here, summarized, developed, repeated, and delivered, as always, with acerbic wit and punch, but this time through a specifically mystico-erotic vision. Zaehner himself tells his readers in the preface that this text can be read as a more developed version of his earlier writings (CD, 1). Along these same lines, Zaehner includes the full text of his Spalding inaugural lecture as an appendix, as if to frame his career with this first and last text. As it turned out, *Concordant Discord* would not quite be his last text, but it nevertheless appears that Zaehner understood it to be something of a final testament.

The text itself moves along the same developmental line that Zaehner had been proposing all along, beginning with the more or less "solitary" and monistic visions of India (lectures 1–10) to Taoism (11) to the "solidary," communal vision of Confucianism (12–13I) to Zen (14) and finally to the solitary-solidary, mystical-ethical synthesis of Catholic Christianity

(15–20),[37] which he approaches through a series of what he calls his "fringe Catholics"—foremost among them Charles-Pierre Peguy, Balzac, Bernanos, and Teilhard de Chardin. Significantly, the text begins and ends with love; indeed, Zaehner tells us quite explicitly and many times that he found the title and inspiration for the defining rhetorical metaphor of the volume, "concordant discord," in the first lines of Saint Francis de Sales's *Traite de l'amour de Dieu* (CD, 1).

The Mystical Ground of Eros:
Zaehner's Ontological Critique of Ascetic Christianity

It is certainly no accident that our final guides into Zaehner's vision, revealed only in the last pages of the volume, are an androgynous literary figure (Balzac's Seraphita/Seraphitus) and a Catholic "mystic of matter" whose books were systematically suppressed during his lifetime (Teilhard de Chardin). Sex and scandal thus appear respectably throughout Zaehner's slightly heretical text. And why not? After all, Zaehner's phenomenology of eroticism is grounded in an essentially ontological understanding of human sexuality and a passionate critique of traditional Christianity and its spirit-matter dualism. Theologically speaking, Zaehner is hardly conservative here, especially for his time (which, we must remember, was well before most of feminist and all of queer theory), although certainly after the last forty years of gender studies, political action, and postmodern deconstruction his ontological understandings of gender and sexual orientation must appear grossly inadequate today. Contextualized in its own culture and time, however, that is, in a cold-war, post–Vatican II Catholic England pondering the counterculture excesses of American and British youth and the impressive successes of "Eastern religions" in the West, Zaehner's erotic thought is, to say the least, unusual, striking, and conflicted, and, to say the most, highly creative, visionary, and mystically generated.

Zaehner understands human eros to be metaphysically grounded in both the cosmic and divine worlds. Consequently, mystical eroticism can always "spill" or "slip" over (Zaehner's Freudian slips: CD, 161) into actual human sexual relationships, and, conversely, sexual relationships, or at least idealized ones, can be used to induce genuine contemplative or protomystical states (CD, 53–54). Indeed, in some places, for example, in his discussion of Walt Whitman's earthy, sexualized poetry, Zaehner wonders aloud whether the sexual metaphors are metaphorical at all: "what he means and what his most frankly sexual poems express is that the sexual act not only symbolizes the union of the opposites and the harmony of the spheres but in a sense *is* them" (CD, 55). So too with the lush sensuality of Indian Vaiṣṇava poetry. Zaehner gently but firmly chides Hindu apologists for insisting that there is nothing "erotic" in all that scratching, biting, and beautifully described lovemaking; this "can scarcely be true, for the kind of love depicted is simply sexual passion transported on to the spiritual plane" (CD, 161). Zaehner never quite puts it this way, but it is as if the erotic is the "door," or, perhaps better, the fluid "stream" (my Freudian slip) that links the human and divine worlds.

He will thus have none of the traditional Christian condemnation of the flesh as somehow evil or corrupt. In a genuinely Zoroastrian spirit, which he explicitly defines as such, Zaehner insists that evil is of the spirit, not of the flesh (CD, 390), and that the flesh and matter are essentially good, or, at the very worst, simply neutral. Moreover, he flatly condemns the spirit-matter dualism as an essentially deleterious heresy that crept into Christianity from Neoplatonism and Manichaeanism, primarily through Augustine (CD, 52), whom he cannot seem to forgive for this (CD, 405). Because the very technique and mechanics of Christian mysticism is to join these two orders, Zaehner argues that to deny this "marriage of spirit and matter" is to be less than a Christian (CD, 360), for "if the Incarnation means anything, it means the sanctification of ordinary life" and especially "the sanctification of marriage and of the reproductive instinct on which marriage is based" (CD, 387). To the extent that Christians—particularly Protestants and Puritans, who have always been suspicious of mysticism (CD, 159), perhaps partly because of its undeniable connections to eroticism—have identified the flesh with the devil, they have grossly misrepresented the radical nature of Jesus' teaching; much worse, by doing so, they have "made him respectable" (CD, 387).[38]

But Zaehner has not and will not. He genuinely believes the Incarnation and its predictably disrespectful ontological implications, and he is absolutely convinced—probably through his comparative studies—that certain types of mystical experience and sexual language are phenomenologically inseparable. He thus privileges human sexuality as the locus classicus of the very highest stages of mysticism and sexual language as the most appropriate expression of these states. Indeed, Zaehner can get downright precise in his physiological and phenomenological descriptions of that "awkward resemblance between the raptures of divine love and sexual orgasm" (CD, 162): "In sexual intercourse as in ecstasy the human ego melts away and is, so to speak, lifted out of itself," for both "involve the total concentration of the whole personality on to one point ['the heart' in the case of ecstasy, 'the phallus' in the case of orgasm]: both are a kind of 'yoga' or integration" (CD, 161–162). What writer, other than perhaps Bataille, has gotten quite this specific? The comparison to Bataille seems apt, if only here, in Zaehner's eroticism, which sometimes ends in a kind of mystical death or annihilation. Thus, describing his own position in his typical style through a discussion of another mystic, in this case Francis de Sales, Zaehner writes that mysticism and sexuality "are opposite and contrary poles of that oddest of human instincts, self-transcendence, the very negation of the instinct of self-preservation" (CD, 163).

But lest we make Zaehner too hip and sexy, it is important to recall his understanding of gender, which was anything but fluid and sophisticated. Zaehner thinks about gender as he thinks about eroticism in general—ontologically. Here, as in so many other places, Zaehner's thought works in and through a meditation on the Upaniṣads. In this sacred context, gender identity is fluid only at the beginning, at the *very* beginning, before there was a world: "In this purely mythological phase this state of oneness is regarded as being an unconscious state: it is beyond all dualities and all distinctions regarding sex. When consciousness is attained there is discontent: the One desires variety," and an elaborate series of incestuous rapes take place to create the different species (CD, 76). After this primordial oneness and its sexually violent diversification, gender quickly solidifies for Zaehner, who again uses Indian philosophical terms to make his points. The word for spirit in the dualistic philosophy of Sāṁkhya, we are told, is *purusha*, "meaning a human male" (CD, 98). And so, "[i]f God is both transcendent and immanent, so too is man; both are *purushas,* that is, males, and as such both stand over against *prakriti,* material Nature, which is the *one* female" (CD, 113). Now Zaehner never actually says that he agrees with this kind of cosmic gender essentialism, but it is quite clear that he does, since wherever he goes in the history of mysticism, he returns to this most basic and reified understanding of gender. Indeed, "the emergence of the gentler, creative female principle is ... consistent with a general tendency in all religions," hence *śakti* in Hinduism, *yin* and *yang* in Chinese religions, wisdom in Judaism, and the Virgin Mary in Catholicism (CD, 347). In his defense, Zaehner saw such comparative moves—it *was* the 1960s—as a radical move out of an oppressively masculinist theistic system: "Some of us are getting a little tired of 'the Lord God of armies' who plagued the Jews in olden times and is plaguing us still in our deeply divided world" (CD, 348). Still, the power differential and dynamics of submission and control are unmistakable, and Zaehner, in his usual style, refuses to mince words; hence, with reference to traditional Jewish language feminizing Israel, he writes: "[T]his implied a relationship of master and servant, later to be converted into one of husband and wife. Both relationships imply submission on the part of Israel and on the part of the individual Jew" (CD, 349). In other places, he goes out of his way to point out that the term "rapture" and its French equivalent "ravissement" both imply a kind of divine "rape" of the soul (CD, 321).

Still, he resists as "ridiculous and wicked" the simple equation of feminine, matter, and evil so common in Jungian (not to mention religious) discourse—let us not be duped by silly grammatical games involving the gender of nouns, which shift and reverse from language to language anyway (CD, 390–391)—and so he returns again and again to androgynous and even hermaphroditic themes in the history of religions. For example, he returns to the Upaniṣads, this time one of his favorites, the Śvetāśvatara, to make the point: "Thou art woman, thou art man: thou art the lad and the maiden too," but, as if to correct itself, "It is not male, not female, nor yet hermaphrodite" (CD, 141). Hinduism, we are told, is the "religion of the 'coincidence of opposites,' to borrow the phrase of Nicolas of Cusa," who, Zaehner proudly adds, was a Catholic cardinal. But nowhere, he adds again, is Cusa's dictum more dramatically displayed and plain than in the iconography of Śiva, the ascetic whose symbol is the phallus (CD, 163); it is thus Hinduism, not Christianity, that has perhaps seen most clearly the "discordant concord" of the sexual and the spiritual (CD, 171). Once again, it is Hinduism that is the mystical religion par excellence, here precisely because of its dramatic and sophisticated display of the erotic.

Zaehner and the Psychology of Religion

We have already seen Zaehner making liberal use of Jungian psychology in his tripartite stage theory. He seems to have generally admired Jung, even though he could be quite critical as well (CD, 390). He also understood and accepted much of Freud's theorizing, although here he was significantly more ambivalent and dismissive; hence his curt and humorous response when handed a particular book while under the influence of mescaline: "Take it away, it's psycho-analysis" (MSP, 219). Things were not always so black and white, though, within the reason of normal consciousness. Zaehner, for example, clearly understood the Christian notion of the kingdom of God in psychological terms; it may be true, he wrote, that the kingdom is "within us," but "few of us are ever conscious of it" (CD, 42). He could be even more reductive when it came to the regressive nature of natural mystical states: "In seeking a form of consciousness which eliminates the ego," Zaehner writes again, "it is very possible that one will not rise to an angelic state but fall to that elemental state of consciousness which must have existed before man learnt to say 'I'" (CD, 103). In another place he suggests such states can best be interpreted as regressions into Jung's collective unconscious (CD, 46), and he comes terribly close to object-relations theory and its notion of cosmic narcissism when he writes that "the child is near the kingdom of God because he is near the beginning, near to the ineffable simplicity of the Tao" (CD, 233).

He certainly was not against employing a psychoanalytic reductive hermeneutic when it suited his own ideological purposes. For example, he suggests that ascetic misogyny is both a perversion of early Christian teaching and proof of the "inner unsureness" of the celibates themselves (CD, 391), and he repeatedly insists that mystical love reveals the closest possible affinities with sexual love. Still, he was obviously uncomfortable with the idea that mystical love is "simply a sublimation of the sexual instinct" (CD, 161), and he reads Freud as a simplistic pansexualist who must be rejected (CD, 343). Zaehner never quite says so, but my reading of his personal library suggests that he was most familiar with psychological reductionism not through Freud, but through James Leuba's *Psychology of Mysticism*. He seemed particularly incensed by Leuba's (rather accurate, I think) observation that "[n]ot one of the prominent representatives of mysticism lived a normal married life."[39] This, it turns out, was one of the few passages Zaehner noted in his handwritten annotations: "119. No normal married life!" And his marginal note on page 119 itself suggests more sarcasm than reflection (and a certain Catholic privileging of celibacy?): "Of course they didn't." One cannot help wondering whether he was not struggling here, in the margins of both the book and his own psyche, with his own "No normal married life!"

A typical example of how this ambivalent relationship to the psychology of religion worked out on the printed, published page is Zaehner's discussion of the Spanish mystics Teresa of Avila and John of the Cross. Zaehner clearly recognizes the heteroerotic, even sexual, components of Teresa's moaning transverberation (who hasn't?) but misses (or remains silent on) the more disguised homoerotic element in John's writings: "St. John of the Cross," we are told, "speaks of these wounds as arrows or as a fiery spear. St. Teresa uses the same symbol to the great satisfaction of the Freudians. . . . To deny that the symbolism is phallic is quite unrealistic, for this is clearly the consummation of the spiritual marriage which is itself the climax of a long betrothal" (CD, 320). One might wonder why a woman being delightfully if painfully pierced is sexualized, while a man employing "the same symbol" is not. Regardless, Zaehner will comment only on the first fact, and even then only with a cheap jab at "the Freudians." It is as if he knows that "the Freudians" are onto something important here but will not quite admit it to himself or his readers.

Gender Bending in the Mystical Marriage

As I hope is clear by now, mystical eroticism was not a side interest or a minor category in Zaehner's thought. Quite the contrary, the erotic was rooted in a dialectical ontology of spirit and matter. It crowned the mystical life in his model and dwelled at the very summit of his developmentally conceived religious path. It is where Zaehner's thinking and religious belief and personal passion all ultimately meet and conclude. We might briefly recall again his tripartite model of nature mysticism, the mysticism of isolation in the soul/psyche, and the mysticism of love of God. Such a model demands a sexual language, for "[o]nce mysticism admits the existence of a God who is distinct from the self and who is felt to be supremely lovable, erotic imagery cannot be avoided, for there is a certain harmony between the physical and spiritual worlds" (CD, 159). And for Zaehner, this relationship will always define the human as both female and passive. In other words, for any human male Zaehner's theory posits an ontologically necessary feminization or passive mystical homoeroticism, as it insists on a basic dualism, a sexual dimorphism between the human soul (feminine/passive) and God (masculine/active). "The human role in relationship to God is always that of the female to the male" (CD, 160), or again, "[i]n all mystical traditions the love of bride for bridegroom is taken as the most satisfying symbol for the love of the soul for God" (CD, 160). Thus, Zaehner finds it rather obvious and uninteresting that the South Indian poet-saint Nammalvar "considers himself as a woman, and through the pangs of love loses consciousness" (CD, 205) and does not blink (I presume) to write: "In human love, as opposed to human lust, sexual intercourse is the normal climax of the whole process of self-giving which is love: it is a sacrament, the seal of divine approval set on a life of self-dedication. In the very nature of things it is the woman who sacrifices herself and gives herself to the man because this is the instinct of the female in the whole natural order. Similarly in divine love the soul abandons herself entirely to the will of the divine Lover who is therefore necessarily conceived as male—*Purusha,* a 'male Person.' So too in Christian mysticism one speaks of 'ravissement' and 'rapture,' both of which are euphemisms for rape" (CD, 161). Since monism or isolation collapses this natural dimorphism, it can only result in a "dead" asexual state that Zaehner admires as a preparatory stage but abhors as a final goal. In short, *monism cannot love.* Nor can asceticism, for love implies both passionate attachment and a fervent commitment, which of course renders ascetic detachment nonsensical (CD, 156). Hence Zaehner's ultimate desire is a mystico-erotic one, to encounter sexually and spiritually—for, again, the two can never be separated for Zaehner—the divine male, the supreme *Purusha.*

Zaehner certainly understood the homoerotic implications of his gendered theorizing on the mystical life and its erotic goal, but—always constitutionally allergic to Freud and psychoanalysis—he could never quite admit this to himself, at least in print. And so he writes of the Śaiva Siddhānta tradition, as if addressing, if in a somewhat distorted and exaggerated form, my own working thesis: "As in the sect of Caitanya, the soul is regarded as the bride, God as the bridegroom. This is always so when the symbolism of the spiritual espousals is used. To say that mysticism of this type is no more than a sublimation of sex is really rather absurd since the majority of the mystics in all traditions—a vast majority in the case of the Muslims—have in fact been men. Anyone rash enough still to put forward this theory must carry his theory to its logical conclusion, namely, that all male mystics must be, whether they know it or not, pathic homosexuals. If you believe this, you can believe anything" (CD, 168). Zaehner, of course, has set up a rhetorical straw man here, for "all male mystics" do not use homoerotic language to induce and describe their mystical encounters. One thinks immediately of Zen, Theravāda Buddhism, and Advaita Vedānta, for example. Zaehner was quite aware of this and even insisted that such writers do not use sexual language because it is not reflective of their monistic experiences (CD, 294), but this is precisely what bothered him so much about these traditions. In psychoanalytic terms, we could say that erotic language is not salient to these mystics because their religious experiences are rooted in more primordial, essentially narcissistic psychic structures that were developmentally prior to their oedipally structured sexualities, whatever these may or may not have been. In any case, Zaehner's theological assumptions prevented him from taking such traditions too seriously. Since a male God dwells at the end of his normative stage theory, and since the spiritual and physical dimensions of the human being normally interpenetrate and spill over into one another, *any* male mystic that gets beyond the isolating psychological monism of Zen or Advaita Vedānta to a grace-filled sexualized encounter with the living God "of Abraham, Isaac and Jacob" (or Kṛṣṇa or Viṣṇu or Śiva) *must* ultimately use homoerotic language.

Putting aside for the moment the rather large blind spot of Zaehner's ideological refusal to take nonsexualized monistic states more seriously, let us restrict ourselves to those male mystics who do in fact use homoerotic language to describe their encounters. What is Zaehner's evidence for the now qualified thesis that many male mystics who use homoerotic language were likely homosexually oriented in some culturally specific way? Significantly, although he promised us earlier in the text that he would address the psychoanalytic sublimation thesis (CD, 161), he offers us here only a single counterexample, which demonstrates, again, a basic misunderstanding about homosexuality: "It would be difficult to imagine anyone more virile than Meister Eckhart, and yet it is he who tells us that not only must we become virgins, that is, free from all earthly attachments, but that we must also become women in the full sense of the word—wives, *Weib*—so that we can conceive Jesus in the soul and bring forth fruit" (CD, 168). That is all we get—a single Christian mystic describing the mystic (and himself, I presume) as a pregnant virgin-wife who, we are told, could not have possibly been homosexually oriented because he was "virile." I can only mischievously answer back in Zaehner's own polemical spirit: "If you believe this, you can believe anything."

The Work of a Life

How should we read such passages in the light of what we know about Zaehner's own homosexuality? Despite the fact that Zaehner was a very private man who tried to deflect attention away from his own mysticoerotic experiences with the divine—"it is a personal relationship between the soul, the bride, and God, the bridegroom, in which obviously no one else can share" (CD, 210), he once wrote in reference to mystics in general—the general outlines of the scholar's sexuality are hardly mysterious, much less controversial. When I interviewed former students and friends, many of them spoke of his homosexuality spontaneously and freely (without my asking about it; indeed, I did not know about it). Lee Siegel, who worked with Zaehner in the early 1970s as a graduate student in Indology, had the most to say. Zaehner shared with Siegel, among many other things, his first memory of sexuality. He was a young boy when he witnessed a cock mount a hen. Thinking that something horrible had just happened, he ran to his mother in terror. And even as an adult, Zaehner confessed to Siegel, the sight of a woman's breast would "send him running." Not that his own homosexuality left him much less conflicted; far from it indeed. Siegel reads his former mentor as an unwilling gay man who used his Catholic piety to struggle more or less successfully against his own sexual desires (we are reminded of Massignon here). Siegel speculates that Zaehner himself understood these desires to be essentially evil; hence his lifelong obsession with the reality of Satan and evil, beliefs which Siegel reads as displaced or projected forms of homosexual guilt. Symbolic support for Siegel's thesis appeared during Zaehner's mescaline trip, when he was shown "a distorted version of Michelangelo's 'David' as far as the navel" on a record dust-jacket. Zaehner described the naked body of the young king sculpted by the famous (and now widely recognized as homoerotic) artist as "interesting in a sinister kind of way" (MSP, 213). Along these same lines, Siegel points out that whereas Zaehner's sitting room was sumptuously decorated with Persian rugs, art, and personal curios, his bedroom was completely bare, except for a single crucifix hanging over the bed. The proverbial bedroom, it seems, was for Zaehner a place not of pleasure and procreation, but of celibacy, sublimation, and suffering. Like the crucifix hanging on his wall, he had crucified the naked male body of his desires. Accordingly, Zaehner told Siegel that he had had no sexual relations since his conversion to Catholicism, "except once, and that didn't count since I was drunk." "But that leaves one with a question," Siegel mischievously adds, "since Zaehner was always drunk."[40] Even after the humor and assumed grins, Zaehner's confession is a remarkable one, since he converted to Catholicism in 1946. Twenty-five years of conflicted, pent-up sexuality will have its way somehow. In Zaehner's case, that way seems to have been writing about (and experiencing) erotic mysticism.

Not surprisingly, Zaehner, to my knowledge, never spoke openly about his homosexuality in print. It does come through at times in his rhetorical handling of certain homo-mystical traditions and figures. His description of Walt Whitman, for example, is utterly devoid of condemnation or judgment (CD, II); indeed, he reads Whitman's bisexual poetry ("I am the poet of the woman the same as the man, / And I say it is as great to be a woman as to be a man") through Hindu Tantrism's Śiva/Śakti and Śiva's subsuming of the male and female principles within himself (CD, 52)[41] and, again, through Persian mystical poetry: "As in the mystical poetry of the Persians the imagery is so frankly sexual that one wonders whether it is imagery at all. We know that in the case of the Persian Sufis what started as the mystical love of God sometimes degenerated into something all too human, the love of a human boy. This was a development of which the orthodox did not approve, yet even the great Al-Ghazali conceded that the contemplation of youthful male beauty was a legitimate first step on the way to the contemplation of the divine" (CD, 53–54). This is an especially interesting passage, both for its clear awareness of the homoerotic dimensions of Persian Sufi mysticism and for its gentle handling, almost defense, of the Sufi "witness practice" we have encountered above in our study of Massignon. The discussion ends, after all, not with a loud Zaehnerian denunciation (and it is important to recall that he seldom held these back when he felt they were warranted), but, as was his rhetorical custom, with an implicit defense through a revered traditional author, in this case "the great Al-Ghazali." In effect, Zaehner is defending Sufi homoeroticism through Sufi homoeroticism.[42] Interestingly, with another homoerotic text, this one Christian and admittedly less explicit— a passage from Saint Francis de Sales comparing the natural mystical state to Saint John's "bodily sleep on his dear Lord's breast" (CD, 305)— Zaehner fails completely to comment on the implied same-sex intimacy of the passage. Indeed, I know of no passage anywhere in Zaehner's writing where he discusses Christian homoeroticism. Sufi homoeroticism, certainly (was this what attracted him to Persian studies in the first place?). Christian homoeroticism, definitely not. Such a double standard, of course, makes good sense in the light of Siegel's thesis about Zaehner's defensive employment of Catholicism as a pious bulwark against his "evil" homosexual desires.

At first glance, it might seem a bit strange that a man who wrote so obsessively about the mystical marriage and the pleasures of mystical eros was never in fact married and, by many accounts, never appeared to have, much less enjoy, any lasting intimate relationships. But is this really so strange, given what we know about the broken sexual lives of historical mystics? Zaehner's marginal outrage at Leuba's comment that "[n]ot one of the prominent representatives of mysticism lived a normal married life" makes more than a little sense if we locate that outrage in the conflicted, seemingly lonely, intensely mystical context of Zaehner's own intimate life, which was defined by anything but "a normal married life." Once again, Leuba was right. Would Zaehner have been so interested in erotic mysticism had he not been so sexually conflicted? Would he have been so hard on the isolation of monism and stressed the necessity of love had he not been so isolated and lonely himself? Would he have come to different conclusions about the homoerotic roots of theistic male erotic mysticism had he been writing in the late 1990s rather than the late 1960s? And what role did his Catholicism play in helping him to deal—positively or negatively—with his own homosexual orientation? However we want to answer these questions, I think we are on very solid ground with the suggestion that, here at least, the life throws a great deal of light on the work.

Certainly there is something defensive and hurried about his assertions that there is nothing homoerotic about a male mystic marrying a male God or becoming a pregnant wife-virgin. Surely it is also significant that, in a very untypical fashion, he has virtually nothing to offer to counter such a thesis, although it is quite clear that it bothers him, that it irritates him a great deal. Potshots at Freud litter his texts, even if he knows, on some level, that much that Freud had to say is more than borne out in the mystical literature. His inconsistent employment of psychological reductionism is especially obvious, for it is not at all clear why theistic mystical experiences—which, according to him, are structured along gendered and sexual lines and clearly replicate more or less universal social relationships (father, child, husband, wife, etc.)—should escape a psychological hermeneutic. Indeed, I think the argument can be made (and it certainly has been made in numerous monistic traditions, not to mention modern psychological traditions like object-relations theory) that it is precisely *these* theistic experiences that are constructed out of the relative bits and pieces of mundane social life.

Little wonder, then, that understanding theology as unconscious psychology bothered Zaehner so. A psychoanalytic or feminist lens, for example, calls into serious question Zaehner's assertions that God is the supreme *Purusha*, that the human soul is always female and passive in the mystical encounter, and that the mystical marriage is the normative end and summation of the mystical life. Once the psychoanalytic and feminist hermeneutical perspectives are taken seriously, Zaehner's claim appears indefensible, as we can see that such divine and human genders (and the specific mystico-erotic experiences to which they give rise) witness not so much to the metaphysical nature of the deity or to the normative end of some objectively real and universally true spiritual path as to the psychosexual biographies of the mystics in question and, more importantly, to the larger psychosexual patterns of the cultures that produced the historical mystics' psyches in the first place and preserved their teachings as valuable reflections of their own patriarchal systems and axiologies. In blunt terms, for whatever else it may or may not be, the male mystical marriage is clearly a psychosexual product of patriarchy, which defines divinity as male, essentializes women (and secondarily, male souls) as passive, denies actual historical homosexualities any livable social reality or legitimacy, and permanently exiles male heterosexualities from the realm of erotic divinity, where they could function only as threats to a single male God. Seen anthropologically, that is, as if it were an external, observable culture, bridal mysticism wants to produce a symbolic system in which a single alpha male can have sex with anyone and everyone (of whatever apparent gender), but only after he has denied to these same sexual partners (through institutional celibacy, asceticism, sexual suffering, or, more likely, all three) any semblance of a normal sexual life with each other. And this, we are asked to believe, is the ultimate goal and summation of the religious life. One does not now whether to laugh or to cry.

Or be a bit envious. There is, after all, a genuine emotional and sexual beauty in much mystical literature, a certain supernatural reverie, a sumptuous delight, in Lacanian terms, an unmistakable *jouissance* beyond the phallus. Certainly, many of the polymorphously erotic states described in mystical texts render "normal," socialized sexuality boring at best. As Ellis Hanson has recently put it with respect to the "decadent" elements of Catholic mysticism: "Anyone who has learned about sexuality from the Bible or the lives of the saints must surely be in for a grave disappointment upon encountering the real thing. Like libertines, Christians must necessarily spice up their scenes of sin, no less than their flights of spiritual eros, lest we think their swooning anything but sublime. There is nothing more decadent than the sensuality of the chaste."[43] Even then, however, one cannot help noticing, through the lines as it were, all the personal suffering and questionable ideological assumptions regarding gender, agency, and power within which such mystical pleasures are psychophysiologically generated. In the end, we cannot help noticing that the mystical marriage, however sublime or pleasurable, is inevitably consummated on the ruins of a once (or never) active sexual life. Zaehner's troubled cry haunts us from the margins of the page: "No normal married life!"

5. The Corpus Written: Erotic Sublimation as Creative Process and Cosmic Redemption in Zaehner's Penultimate Vision

As central and important as both Zaehner's ethical and erotic critiques of religion were, they can both be subsumed within his ontological vision and its most basic insistence that matter cannot and should not be expelled from the spiritual life. But this again is to return to a certain kind of eroticism, for it functions as a sacralization of what the Christian tradition has contemptuously calls (and for Zaehner, mistakenly condemned as) "the flesh." Zaehner's eroticism, in other words, was not restricted to his selection and reading of mystical literature or to his normative theologizing about the mystical marriage of the individual soul with God. More radically (and problematically), eroticism also functioned for Zaehner in a genuinely eschatological fashion, as the driving force of evolution and salvation history worked out within what he liked to call, following Marx (who, interestingly enough, may have been following Böhme), the "throes of matter" (CD, 413). It was in the "hot embrace" (CD, 413) of such a sexually violent matter that Zaehner's final vision takes shape for us.

And the Flesh Will Become Word

Zaehner also had a rather profound, if never quite clear, sense that eroticism has something to do with writing, creative inspiration, and insight. We have already had the occasion of noting Zaehner's fondness for the mystical novels of Balzac. Balzac, Zaehner suggests, was a consummate writer precisely because he both knew and refused the monistic absorption of cosmic consciousness. It is from Balzac again that Zaehner borrows a literary metaphor to develop what is essentially a Teilhardian or Bergsonian view of evolution, namely, that it is only in and through matter that consciousness can develop into its full flowering in Christ.[44] Appropriately, then, *Concordant Discord* is framed by two evolutionary mystics: it begins with some critical reflections on Richard Bucke and ends with an appreciative treatment of Teilhard de Chardin. Toward the very end of the text, Zaehner sums up his comparative mystical vision (which reflects quite closely, I should add, the chronological development of his professional career), beginning this way:

> In Hinduism and in Buddhism the soul or self is willy-nilly enmeshed in matter, in its blood, its sweat, and its tears. It is there much against its will and it can see salvation in no other terms than escape. The Zoroastrian and, following him, the Christian see that matter itself is involved in the redemptive process and that until the trend of the Incarnation is reversed and the flesh in its turn becomes Word, as Balzac puts it, we cannot see the final significance of the Incarnation, matter transformed into spirit in what the Zoroastrians call the Final Body, the mystical body of Christ which is the Church brought to

fruition in the all-embracing cosmic Christ which Teilhard de Chardin saw as the consummation of the world. (CD, 392)

"[A]nd the flesh in its turn becomes Word"—this is perhaps the final key to both Zaehner's vision and, if I may read such language psychologically again, to the erotic dynamism of the writing process itself. Every written corpus is also a corpus written, a sublimation of psychosexual forces into personal meaning, social communication, and intellectual insight.

Appropriately, then, the final lecture-chapter of *Concordant Discord* is entitled "The Flesh Will Become Word." Here Zaehner develops further the Balzacian theme he had announced in the earlier, penultimate lecture. Jung and Teilhard are now joined by a most unusual presence, the androgynous Swedenborgian angel of Balzac's *Seraphita*, Seraphita herself (CD, 410). Everything that we have heard in these last nineteen lectures, we are told, is here in *Seraphita* as well, "except Satan" (CD, 412). But Seraphita is also Seraphitus. Once again, the mystical is revealed only when the sexual-social categories of the acceptable social world are denied. Appropriately, then, s/he is "not of this world" but sent to the world, like some gnostic savior, "to reveal the inner structure of the universe and the manner of its ascent to God" (CD, 410). Long passages from the novel follow, summarizing the angel's guidance of Wilfrid, who loves Seraphita as a woman, and Minna, who loves Seraphitus as a man, to the throne of God, where they see that "from the greatest to the least of the world, and from the least of the worlds to the smallest particle of the beings that compose it, all was individual and yet one" (CD, 410). The two souls rise still further. Not bound by cyclic time like the lower creatures, they follow together the "straight line of the infinite, aiming unswervingly at the unique centre" (CD, 411). Bringing the imaginative visionary experience back to his own comparative researches, Zaehner comments:

> Cyclic time, which is the curse of the Orient and which conditions their religion, is broken, and the soul of man, and in the course of time the soul of the All-man, 'the Soul of the world', is destined to follow the straight line of the infinite, aiming unswervingly at the unique centre.... In the still centre spirit and matter, male and female, strength and love, are reconciled.... And as love reaches ever higher degrees of expression, it not only unites ever more closely but it also differentiates every more sharply. This is a truth that every lover knows: with the Trinity, we may assume, it is absolutely true. (CD, 412–413)

It is not difficult to see why Zaehner loved *Seraphita* so. The novel is structured around the very same homoerotic system of the theistic mystical traditions Zaehner loved. Hence, when Seraphitus is addressing Minna, he can speak of God as the "Best-beloved"[45] and, later, as the "Celestial Bridegroom,"[46] and he can describe (to a quite jealous Minna) "how I love Him." "Whom?" Minna innocently and nervously asks. "God!" a still male Seraphitus boldly answers.[47] Predictably, however, the quite human (and, more importantly, quite heterosexual) Wilfrid never uses such language and can only direct his sexual desires to a beautiful feminized angel, that is, to Seraphita herself. The angel can be bisexual and appear to Minna and Wilfrid as male and female respectively, but God can *only* be male. Exactly as Zaehner argued, at the height of the mystical encounter the human soul is always female and the divine is always male, or so it would seem.

Within this same ontology, Zaehner ends his Gifford Lectures with a kind of Last Judgment, with the nature mystics, monists, and "those who believe in nothing" condemned to a form of inert unconsciousness and the theists enjoying a redeemed universe through an at once unifying and differentiating ecstasy of forms and essence: "Ecstasy there will be—in concord, the knitting together of all spirits in one Spirit and through the Spirit into God: or in discord, the dissolution of the personality into its material fragments. On the one hand, 'the inert mass of those who believe in nothing.' . . . On the other, 'the last word of the enigma, the dazzling utterance which is inscribed on the brow' of matter redeemed." And, finally, quoting Balzac to sum it all up: "The obverse of *Et verbum caro factum est* will become the new Gospel which will be summed up in the words: 'And the flesh will become Word: it will become the living Word of God'" (CD, 427). So ends Zaehner's comparative mysticism, with a kind of reverse Incarnation, a sublimation of the erotic flesh into the Word of God.

Our Savage God: The Final Case of Charlie

But that is not quite where things ended for R. C. Zaehner, for he would soon grow skeptical of Teilhard's pseudoscience as a "pipe dream and a mockery of human distress" (DZM 141; cf. 178–180), and his Balzacian vision of unity in diversity and ecstatic transfiguration would be overshadowed by two final Zaehnerian obsessions that, taken together, eerily replicated at the end of Zaehner's life the radically dualistic ethical system of Zoroastrianism that gave structure and meaning to its beginning. One last time, Good met Evil and did battle in the mind of R. C. Zaehner, this time in the persons of the ancient Greek philosopher Aristotle, whom Zaehner affectionately called "our father Aristotle," and the American serial killer Charles Manson, whom Zaehner insisted on calling simply Charlie. Both figures appear in *Our Savage God*,[48] Zaehner's last and in many ways most provocative book, and in the collection of posthumously published essays *The City in the Heart*. In the latter, for example, we find the essay "The Wickedness of Evil," in which Zaehner argues that Manson had had a "classic enlightenment experience" (CWH, 38), and that it was the monistic logic of this enlightened consciousness that logically justified his gruesome murders. In Charlie Zaehner found a dramatic summary and terrifying crystallization of his own lifework on the ethical criticism of monistic states of consciousness: "The secret of Charles Manson," he wrote, "is that he knew this timeless moment can at least be simulated by LSD and in a 'total' and brutal exercise of the physical sexual act. Lucidly he drew the obvious conclusion which most of our modern Zen Buddhists do all they can to hush up. Where he had been, all things were One and there was 'no diversity at all': he had passed beyond good and evil" (CWH, 41).[49] And in this Manson was living out the brutal logic of the Bhagavad Gītā, which states clearly that "[o]n the absolute plane . . . killing and being killed are equally unreal" (CWH, 37). Or in the impeccable logic of Manson himself: "If God is One, what is bad?" (quoted in CWH, 35). So obsessed was Zaehner with Manson that he asked a lawyer of one of the victims' families, whom he met while staying with the Siegels in Santa Barbara, if he could arrange a meeting "with Charlie," even as he phobically feared that Charlie would come after him in California for speaking and writing about his case.[50] Charlie was Zaehner's last obsession.

Here too, at the end, Zaehner's theistic worldview begins to show signs of genuine collapse. Once again, it is the ethical that ultimately shipwrecks the world. Consider, for example, Zaehner's stinging and bitter criticism of the "savage" and genocidal biblical God who appears as "an irrational and sometimes brutal tyrant" (CWH, 29–32), his comments on the "obnoxious doctrines of Incarnation and the Holy Trinity" and their specious fulfillment of Judaism (CWH, 80–81), the "repulsive" doctrine of the Atonement (CWH, 82), and the demeaning nature of religious belief: "To be religious is to be a slave, and not only to be a slave but to be the slave of monsters you have yourself thought up" (CWH, 46). So too with his essay "Tantum religio potuit suadere malorum." Here the professor passionately argues that the monotheistic assertion of the absolute unity and supremacy of God "raises far more problems than it solves," for "if there is only one God who boasts of having created good and evil, and glories in the destruction he wreaks, then what chance has man but to bow to the will of the divine Monster?" (CWH, 52). And lest he be charged with an unthinking anti-Semitism, it is good to recall Zaehner's remarks in this same essay about "all that mealy-mouthed claptrap about 'Gentle Jesus meek and mild,'" which denies all the hard sayings and antifamily values of the preacher (CWH, 53). Indeed, Zaehner's barely submerged disgust with theism knows no Christian sectarianism, for there is "no Semitic religion without violent paradox," and "theology is little more than a pathetic effort of human reason fettered by irrational faith to reconcile divine inconsistencies with something that has the specious appearance of rationality" (CWH, 53). Hence his concluding lines on religion in this article: "Perhaps, after all, we are better off without it" (CWH, 56). Certainly this "R. C." cannot stand for an unthinking Roman Catholicism.

In the spring of 1974, just back from the University of California at Santa Barbara, where he had lectured on Aristotle and Manson despite the baffled objections of his academic hosts, Zaehner fell asleep, smoking and drinking in his reading room. He woke up to the smell of smoke and found his chair on fire; he had dropped his lit cigarette onto the chair. After putting it out (some say with a glass of water, others speculate that it was more likely gin), Zaehner went upstairs to bed only to awake later to the sound of cracking fire and the smell of more smoke. The fire destroyed much of the fifteenth-century room, destroyed almost all of his personal belongings, damaged some of his library (I thought of Mircea Eliade, whose death seemed to be prefigured in his own self-inflicted library fire,[51] as I paged through Zaehner's slightly charred, smokey books), and threatened to spread to other sections of All Souls before it could be put out. By all accounts, this was a major event in Zaehner's life and contributed significantly to a mood of deep depression. A few months later, on 24 November, R. C. Zaehner died suddenly of a heart attack on his way to mass, the final result of a heart condition that he had successfully hidden from his closest friends.

SECRET TALK *Writing Out (of) That Night*

Obtaining the nature of Śiva is not the last word of the Tantra. When one takes on the corpse-state of Śiva, then a direct experience of the cosmic goddess can be obtained; the state of death or *samādhi* is also realized in this condition, and the image of Kālī is a special example of it.

Ram Chandra Datta, *Śrī Śrī Rāmakṛṣṇa Paramahaṁser Jīvanavṛttānta*

The vision is fixed in his mind and inscribed in his intellect and burns in him like fire.... The vision that the soul sees occurs at the time that a person sleeps, and his soul ascends and draws down from above the life force.

Kabbalist Azriel of Gerona

Ego dormio et cor meum vigilat [I sleep, but my heart stays awake].

Song of Songs 5.2

26 SEPTEMBER 1989, 2:30 A.M. (Calcutta). A ghostlike woman (modeled after a figure I had drawn a few days before in my notebooks) appears over my bed in a dream and merges with me. I wake up, my body tingling and my heart racing. I can clearly feel a spot that is in my heart.

29 October 1989, Kālī-*pūjā*, 1:30 P.M. Exhausted from a long night of visiting *pūjā* pandals (temporary tentlike structures erected for the celebrations), I slept until 8:00 A.M., shuffled down to breakfast, came back up to my room, and slept again until 12:30 P.M. Sometime this morning I had a very beautiful Śākta dream. No real images, just a powerful sense of an ecstatic existence before, indeed in, an utterly loving Presence (I sensed when I awoke that what I was in fact remembering were the joys of my early life with my mother), which then transformed itself into the similar but different bliss of a lover's body, my wife's body, wrapped around mine—in both cases, an intense pleasure everywhere, a slight sense of "I," a slight sense of "her," but no real boundaries. Then I began to "fall." I felt more and more separated, more and more just "I," alone, cut off, a self. Eventually, I woke up, and I felt genuinely depressed. How peaceful and pleasurable it all was, and yet no real desire moving somewhere

to die, to be released; just pure, formless, total pleasure circling back on itself—*ānanda*.

* * *

As hinted at in the previous journal entries, while researching Ramakrishna's secrets in Calcutta, I encountered not a few of my own, most of which, not surprisingly, were given to me in the Tantric images of the texts I was then working on. More specifically, I had a series of highly symbolic ecstatic experiences that were unmistakably sexual and mystical and whose meanings seemed to point in powerful, if still hidden, ways to the ontological identity of human sexuality and the psychological realities experienced in ecstasy, vision, and mystical union. This is what I would later call "the erotic." This idea, of course, had for some time been the most compelling "secret" of my own biography. I had known *raptus* well before going to India. But with this series of mystical experiences in Calcutta and my simultaneous discovery of Ramakrishna's own "secrets" in the texts, this union of the mystical and the erotic also became the central thesis of my research on Ramakrishna. The lives of the researcher and the researched had begun to mingle in strange, confusing, and wonderful ways. Consider, for example, the journal entry dated 29 October 1989. I had returned late the previous night from some street celebrations of Kālī-*pūjā*: "A night of images—Tantric yogīs with waist-long matted hair dancing and singing *Śyāmā-saṅgīta* [a kind of devotional song to the goddess], Ramakrishna and Bamaksepa [another Śākta saint], a bloody slaughter post (with half a cucumber sitting beneath it), and four bloody goat heads bowing to Kālī." The next morning I had the Śākta dream recorded above.

A few days later (4 November) I visited Kalighat, the most famous temple dedicated to the goddess, with some friends: "On the way way to find an auto rickshaw [to leave], we saw a young man carrying a tiny little corpse to the cremation ground—a baby, not more than a few months old." I had bought a black stone *liṅgam* there; it was "indestructible," the vendor told me. "We couldn't all fit in the rickshaw, so Catherine sat in my lap. All I could think of was my 'indestructible' *liṅgam* tucked away under her in my [traveling] pouch."

That night the erotic returned, this time mixed with fear, death, and a quite literal *ex-stasis*, or "standing outside." In a draft for the preface to *Kālī's Child* I tried to relate the power of this event and delineate its

Writing Out (of) That Night   201

theoretical implications for the writing of the book. Here is the pertinent selection from that unpublished draft:

> But *Kālī's Child* is not just a research project. It is also an integral part of my own biography. Looking back, I can see clearly that my methods were not simply linguistic or theoretical; they were also experiential. At one point in my Calcutta researches, shortly after the autumn festival of Kālī-*pūjā,* that which I studied even entered a waking dream state in a strange and striking way. The safe, comfortable lines between the researcher and the researched dissolved in an encounter that looked—and, so I imagined, felt—much like the mystico-erotic states I was then uncovering in the Bengali texts. Although my body was asleep, resting almost anesthetized on its back, not unlike a corpse, consciousness was lucid and clear, fully awake. Suddenly, without warning, a powerful electric-like energy flooded the body with wave after wave of an unusually deep and uniform arousal. I tried to hold the energies in as *liṅgam*s spontaneously emerged and disappeared in a fluid dream space. At some point, the energies gathered together, as if they themselves were conscious, and erupted "in" in a kind of psychic implosion. As I felt my "I" being sucked up into an ecstasy that felt entirely too much like a death, I watched my legs and torso float uncontrollably towards the ceiling. Quite unaccustomed to death or weightlessness (be they physical or symbolic), I desperately grabbed the bed frame and, in a scene that seemed as bizarre then as it sounds now, instinctively tried to embody the energies in order to bring them "back down" into my physical frame. After much gymnastic twisting and turning and holding on, I finally awoke. Actually, it wasn't a waking up at all, for the "I" had never been asleep, but it was at least a "sitting up," and this with a buzzing body that, thank goodness, was no longer an anesthetized corpse or a floating balloon.
>
> When I later reflected on this powerful, if half-humorous, experience, I often thought of the sleeping but sexually aroused Śiva-corpse lying prostrate under Kālī and of the deathlike fear Narendra felt under Ramakrishna's electric foot as the walls dissolved into an "I"-less emptiness around him. As I continued to study the texts, I quite naturally added this strange and yet unmistakably real experience to my otherwise perfectly normal academic toolbox; there was historical criticism, there was philology, there was textual analysis, there was psychoanalysis, and then there was that Night. It didn't seem to fit at all, but there it was. The experience was unimportant and even irrelevant to those aspects of the study that could be established through historical, philological, or analytic methods; dream states, after all, are no substitute for historical knowledge, language study, and theoretical sophistication. But the

experience did have methodological implications, for it made me very wary of methods that would reduce Ramakrishna's own mystico-erotic experiences to the "nothing buts" and clinical jargon of classical psychoanalysis. Without that Night, I am quite certain that I would have been quite happy with such reductionisms and would have painted the saint as hopelessly neurotic; that, after all, is what he and his strange states often look like from the outside. But I had been, somehow, "on the inside" of similar states, and I suspected that the neurotic saint I saw was only a half-truth.

This is all to say that what follows possesses, in Eliade's terms, both a discursive, conscious, or "diurnal" dimension, which can and should be judged by normal academic methods, and an intuitive, unconscious, or "nocturnal" side, which I cannot defend but can only state as my own "secret talk."

This vision, like all visions and dreams, is overdetermined; appropriately, no single event receives more interpretive energy and reflection in my journals than this one, and much of my subsequent life can be read as a kind of "living out" of the dream's descent pattern, that is, its opting for the domestic and the human over the mystical and the transcendent (the details of which I have omitted here). For our present purposes—an examination of the hermeneutical potential of mystical experience— certainly one of the most striking consequence of the event's nocturnal dimension (as opposed to "emission") was its hermeneutical impact on my work, and more specifically, on the literary form of the book itself and its five chapters, each of which was structured around a particular iconographic feature of Kālī erotically astride the supine Śiva, whose seeming unconsciousness under her feet is variously interpreted by the tradition as sleep, death, mystical ecstasy, and sexual bliss (I could relate to all four). Taken together, from chapter 1 on Kālī's sword, which inflicts death and grants liberation, to the oedipal themes of chapter 2 on Kālī as Mother and Lover, to the final three chapters on various aspects of her erotic position "on top" of Śiva, the chapters unconsciously recreated— "performed" in Sells's terms—the phenomenological shape of that Night, embodying anew the symbolic form of my experience of Śiva's mystico-erotic sleep "under the goddess." It was as if the chapter essays were written "looking up" at the goddess from below, remembering the Fire in an attempt to capture it again, this time in a text instead of a physical body— a corpus in every sense of that term: written text, physical body, supine "corpse."

Looking back now instead of up, I would not claim any necessarily transcendent, objective referent for the experience or the subsequent writing of the book. Rather, I see the entire process as a function of my own autobiographical trajectories and their creative meeting in the theorists I had studied and the symbols and teachings of the Bengali texts I had at that time immersed myself in (which, of course, I had chosen for largely autobiographical reasons in the first place).[1] Speaking theoretically, I would say that the experience of that Night was a profoundly hermeneutical one. And it became only more so when I recreated it again in my own text (and now again, in this text). Such a process originated in the context of my study of the history of religions at Chicago, and more specifically, in my readings of the scholars whose lives and works grace this book's chapters. I was particularly taken with Massignon's mystical experience of "the visitation of the Stranger" while researching the life of the tenth-century Sufi al-Hallāj, who, as we have seen, he believed played an actual intercessory role in the experience. Massignon's parapsychological dissertation experience led me to believe that it was psychologically possible to gain access, somehow, to the inner truths of another tradition, or even of a dead saint. Eliade's yogic experiences, which he had mischievously "camouflaged" in his supernatural thriller "The Secret of Dr. Honigberger," and Scholem's cryptic remark about the possibility of a profound philology possessing "a certain mystical function"[2] also figured heavily in my hopes and expectations before I went to India. Indeed, I had written two research papers on these very themes before I left for India. Finally, when I experienced my own "visitation of the Stranger" in Calcutta, it inevitably and naturally led me back to the texts with new insights and convictions. And, of course, it then helped to generate my own text, which in turn became part of my subsequent biography.

There is no objective, replicable science here, nor is there any simple ontological dualism that could render meaning to a word like "transcendent." Rather, there is a kind of mystical reading and writing, a labyrinthine textuality, a creative hermeneutical spiral that advances only by turning back on itself, from the text to experience and back to the text, in a continual act of living reflection. Certainly a similar conviction lies behind Massignon's belief (here summarized by Jacques Waardenburg) that "the spiritual realities to which [Sufi technical] words allude can be rediscovered through the study of the words themselves—and that the researcher at a certain moment finds himself confronted precisely with that reality to which the mystic testifies,"[3] no doubt a bold, almost fantastic, claim, but I believe a defensible one. Traditional mystics, after all, like traditional hermeneuts, are reading and listening to texts in the lights of their own lives, recreating and refashioning those texts in the energies of their own psychophysiological experiences, using those experiences to reread the original texts of their traditions, and then creating their own new texts (either themselves or through others). In both the mystical and the academic cases, there does not seem to be any identifiable or recoverable experience "before" language or textuality but a kind of spiraling, infinitely looped textuality, a mystical hermeneutics: a text of living fire.

* * *

25 April 1999. The sheer intensity of that *śakti* cannot be adequately spoken in any single expression or text, but it can be "spread out" over many years and many books, which together, taken as a whole, can indeed approach an appropriately comprehensive expression of the Fire.

19 July 1990. I ran across a passage in Mark Dyczkowski's *Doctrine of Vibration* that captures well both the aesthetic catalysts and phenomenology of my own mystico-erotic states, my "Blakean delight," as I like to call it:

> [T]he yogī is instructed to seek this higher state of consciousness in the wonder *(camātkāra)* or delight *(ānanda)* he feels in moments of intense physical pleasure.... Occasions for this practice are, for example, the sense of satisfaction one feels after a good meal or the aesthetic delight one experiences when listening to good music or the pleasure of sexual union with the Tantric consort or even solitary sexual excitation. In these moments of delight the yogī can penetrate momentarily into his own authentic Śiva-nature *(sambavāveśa)* through the empowered contact *(śāktasparśa)* he makes with it in the freedom of the pure subjectivity of the Fourth State.[4]

Indeed, I distinctly remember knowing something akin to this state after eating half a pizza, drinking two beers, and falling asleep in front of a fireplace—absolute satiation, and then, suddenly, there it is, pulling me up and out of myself.

9 November 1990. I spoke with Wendy Doniger yesterday about contradiction in Claude Lévi-Strauss, Eliade, Jung, and her own work. Lévi-Strauss and Wendy do not believe real contradiction can be transcended. Eliade and Jung do. Wendy's "erotic ascetic" is really not about contradiction, or if it is, only on a lived, existential level. As she said when I explained to her my project of determining how sexual energies are

employed in mystical experience (the "erotic mystic," if you will): "But they are not truly contradictory, because *they are the same.*" Tonight I opened up the Kathāmṛta and read in the fourth volume: "tāke pete gele bīrjo dhāroṇ korte hoe" [in order to attain him, you must retain the semen] (KA 4.85). The rhyming translation captures well my discussion with Wendy: to attain, retain, for that which you are attaining is precisely that which you are retaining, transmuted now into another type of sexual experience—the erotic. The English rhyme (not to mention the Bengali text) signals an ontological identity between the semen (or better, the libidinal energies that accompany its release) and God.

9 October 1994. To imagine the sexual and then, from within, remove its imagined object is to allow it to realize itself as the erotic. Every external object must fail to fulfil that which eros is. The erotic is the sexual with its intentionality removed. The erotic is nonintentional sexuality achieved through the religious imagination.

10 February 1990. What fascinates me is an eroticism that does not spend itself in dualism, that does not objectify itself so completely that it dies, that on some level is *nondual,* that turns back on itself to experience deeper and deeper dimensions of itself. It is precisely this kind of eroticism that I find in mystical texts.

21 March 1991. It is the night raptures that I try to ritually recreate in my meditations and writing. Plato's *Phaedrus* also comes to mind—realizing that the Beauty one is attracted to is projected from within, and that one will never truly possess it until it is reabsorbed back into its projecting source and "imploded" into an inner space and an inner radiance. Is this what the Sufi "witness practice" was all about?

27 November 1991. "Śibatva lābh koriya sabābastha prapto hoiyale kālīr sādhan pāoyo jāe [When one obtains the Śiva-nature by attaining the state of a corpse, the Kālī-practice is accomplished]" (Gopinath Kaviraj, "The Secret of Kālī"). A perfect Indological description of my mystical life—the sleeping body-corpse aroused into a creative trance by a feminine energy.

17 October 1994. Kālī, for me, has two forms—that beautiful "form of sexual desire" *(kāma-rūpā),* and that nondual state of arousal in which

the pleasure, the object, and the subject melt, dissolve, and implode into a realm of dark light, ecstasy, and electric awareness.

24 November 1994. I had a dream a week or so ago. I was bending a Plexiglas window back on itself. When I touched the two ends together, my body shook with sexual pleasure and I woke up. Energy turns back on itself, a perspective (the window) becomes nondual, "bent back on itself."

FOUR

Writing Out of the Light at the Center

Reading Agehananda Bharati's Tantric Trilogy
(1960, 1965, 1976)

> Is it not more austere to renounce generalization on the basis of one's private mystical experience instead of talking about it? And furthermore, is not the suspension of judgment more austere than conferring upon the experience of the Supreme the status of objective existence and then preaching that objective existence? On embracing a woman, is it not more difficult to restrain one's sperm than to ejaculate? And yet, yogic teachers teach us to restrain it. I take this as the best analogue, because it is so pungent: I may know the agonizing urge of the mystic to teach the God he has seen, to go out and teach all the people after his experience—and yet I must control the urge and keep the experience to myself.
>
> Agehananda Bharati to the Śaṃkarācārya during the Kumbhamela of 1954 upon being asked whether asceticism is necessary for salvation

I DO NOT KNOW if they ever met, but I suspect that there are few figures in the modern study of mysticism who would have gotten along worse than R. C. Zaehner and Agehananda Bharati. Zaehner was a homosexually conflicted apologist for Catholic theism who employed Sufi polemics and Jungian psychology to reduce Hindu monism to narcissistic delusion and gross ego inflation and considered it something of his lifework to delegitimate the mystical potential of drug-induced states of consciousness. Bharati, on the other hand, was a heterosexual, self-professed hedonist who despised Catholicism (he proudly called himself an apostate), employed Hindu monism and modern psychology to reduce theistic experience to an oppressive delusion, and made it something of his lifework to legitimate the use of LSD and Tantric sexuality within a newly conceived modern monistic mysticism. One of the few things they could have perhaps agreed on is that monistic mysticism has little or nothing to do with ethics (Zaehner was appalled by the fact; Bharati reveled in it). But that is about it.

And this is precisely what makes them so interesting to study and compare. It also witnesses to the fact that the modern study of mysticism is a large affair capable of encompassing a number of different, often irreconcilable, perspectives. I am interested in Bharati for a number of reasons, foremost among them his unique blending of the mystical and the theoretical. Bharati, perhaps more than any other twentieth-century Indologist, explicitly combined his subjective mystical experiences—which, contrary to what the opening quote might suggest, he wrote and talked about extensively—and his technical theorizing and philosophizing about mysticism. He thus offers us a powerful exemplum of this study's basic theme—mystical path as source and catalyst of theoretical method.

I will approach Bharati's life and work primarily through his writings and, more particularly, through what I think we can recognize as his Tantric trilogy: *The Ochre Robe* (1960), *The Tantric Tradition* (1965), and *The Light at the Center* (1976). An autobiography, a comparative or thematic monograph on Indo-Tibetan Tantric traditions, and a work of modern religious polemics, these are three very different kinds of books; nevertheless, they are held together, and rather tightly so, by Bharati's constant reference to what he called "the tantric tradition," which will in turn become my reference point. I will focus my gaze on these three major texts as modern—at times almost postmodern—Tantric texts, supplementing them, where necessary, with Bharati's numerous professional journal articles, popular magazine and newspaper essays, book reviews, and other publications, which number over six hundred by one postmortem count.[1] I have also drawn occasionally on Bharati's scribbled marginalia, which are available to us in the books of his personal library now preserved at Syracuse University, as well as a rather remarkable (and racy) oral tradition that still surrounds his memory among contemporary Indologists and former students, colleagues, and friends, which I have not drawn on explicitly but which nevertheless informs both the spirit and content of the essay.

There are many possible keys to understanding Bharati's corpus, understood here—in true *sandhā-bhāṣā* fashion[2]—in both a sexual-physical and a textual-spiritual sense. His abysmal early family life and barely concealed hatred of his father ("I am a son by accident as far as I am concerned," he once wrote),[3] his aesthetic disgust with Christianity and its gory central symbol (OR, 227), his experience of Hitler's Germany and his subsequent hatred of fascism, nationalism, and cultural chauvinism in all their many forms, his ecstatic love of classical music, his struggle to establish against almost insurmountable odds the legitimacy of his unusual bicultural monastic identity, his high intellectualism ("which you are free to call snobbery" [OR, 212]), his polyglot training and consequent linguistic elitism, his preference for the precision of British linguistic analysis and Ludwig Wittgenstein, his call for a kind of mystical or monastic humanism that emphasizes individualism, rationalism, and cosmopolitanism, his practice of a radical type of "cultural criticism," and his final identity as an established American anthropologist—all of these are appropriate and fruitful entries into the monk's thought and personality. But none, I would argue, are quite as useful and provocative as his mystical commitment to the Indo-Tibetan Tantric traditions and the manner in which this commitment colored—and radiantly so—much of what he wrote, of who he was, and of what he tried to accomplish in his life and writings.

What Bharati called "the Tantric tradition" is actually a complex of mystical traditions indigenous to a number of South Asian, East Asian, and Himalayan cultures that emphasize, among other things, (1) a variety of decidedly esoteric hermeneutical strategies to achieve, ritualize, protect, and textually record various mystical-ecstatic states of consciousness; and (2) antinomian ritual techniques that work against much orthodox philosophy and praxis, including, in the classical Indian tradition, the ingestion of drugs, the eating of meat, and the ritual use of sexual intercourse, all highly polluting to an orthodox Hindu (and all quite central to Bharati's writings and life). As we will see, Bharati liked to refer to this aspect of Tantra as "psycho-experimentation" and emphasized its importance for any future renaissance of mysticism in the West. It is clear that Bharati understood himself as writing and living within this broad Tantric tradition. It is also clear that what he had to say about "mysticism" (and he had much to say) was in essence Tantric, issuing from the dual corpora of the Tantric texts, which he knew and read in their original languages, and the intimacies of his own physical body and its desires, about which he wrote more than a little. Finally, and perhaps most relevant for our present concerns, it is clear that a certain kind of Tantric esotericism defined the parameters—both negatively and positively—of how Bharati read mystical texts and subsequently wrote his own.

After a brief biographical sketch (part 1), I will approach Bharati the Tāntrika in roughly this order, examining, first, the general antinomian ritual theory that defined his experimental and theoretical approaches to the mystical (part 2); second, the explicitly erotic and hedonistic nature of these same psycho-experiments and his subsequent theorizing out of them (part 3); and third, some of the exoteric and esoteric rhetorical strategies of legitimation, interpretation, and encoding that Bharati employed to read and to write (and to not write) about his Tantric experiences (part 4). As it would be impossible to write anything remotely accurate about the phenomenon that was Agehananda Bharati without engaging in intimate discussions of sexuality, drugs, and unflinching culture criticism, I hope that the candor and content of what follows will be read in the spirit in which they were written: as attempts to reflect as accurately as possible the ambiguities, contradictions, charisma, honesty, and humor of the human being born Leopold Fischer, renamed Ramachandra, and initiated into Hinduism as Agehananda Bharati. Bharati once wrote that he considered the ability to make fun of oneself, which he called "self-persiflage," a necessary characteristic of any sophisticated human being, and he bemoaned the fact that so many religious people insist on taking themselves so terribly seriously.[4] Perhaps we can still call ourselves "sophisticated" if we do not laugh both at ourselves and at Bharati in what follows, but we will have no right or reason to claim any understanding of this man or his writings without more than a little laughter and more than a few smiles. "This takes us into one of those very intimate types of speculation which scholars tend to pass on to other scholars or to future research," he once wrote in another context.[5] So let us begin.

1. Writing Out of a Life

Agehananda Bharati was born Leopold Fischer on 20 April 1923 in Freud's Vienna. Of Czech and possibly Jewish descent (OR, 40), Leopold was an apostate from Catholicism by age thirteen and at fourteen was sitting in on the classes of the Sanskritist Erich Frauwallner ("his audience . . . consisted of an average of three oddities, thus increased by another" [OR, 39]). At sixteen he was formally accepted into Hinduism as Ramachandra by an itinerant Indian preacher who was visiting the Indian Club in Vienna, which Leopold piously frequented and where he would soon make a private vow to fight for India's freedom ("it was another ten [years] before I realized the ridiculousness of any form of nationalism" [OR, 46]). When drafted into the German army, Ramachandra found his way into the Indian Legion, where he served disguised as a Hindi-speaking, unusually pale Indian until he was incarcerated in a prisoner-of-war camp, where he remained for the rest of the war. After the war, he studied Indian history, Buddhism, and Sanskrit under Herbert Guenther[6] and eventually sailed for his beloved India, arriving in Bombay on 30 January 1949. There Ramachandra almost immediately joined the Ramakrishna Math and Mission, whose literature he had absorbed and been inspired by in Vienna. But eventually frustrated with the order's anti-intellectualism (OR, 129–130; LC, 96), censoring prudery (OR, 137), and insistence that Ramakrishna be recognized as a literal *avatāra* or "descent of God" (OR, 141–143, 221–222), a disappointed and slightly disillusioned Ramachandra left the order after two years and traveled to Benares to search for another monastic tradition. There, after being turned away by over one hundred monks in three dozen different establishments (traditionally, one must be born a Hindu to take *sannyāsa* or renunciation), he finally found an independent renouncer by the name of Swami Visvananda to give him initiation into the more ancient, more traditional, and more intellectual Daśanāmi sect, the monastic tradition founded by Śaṅkarācārya, the great eighth-century systematizer of Advaita Vedānta. Ramachandra was initiated in 1951 by Visvananda, who gave him the monastic name of Agehananda Bharati—roughly, "the Indian *[bhāratī]* (who is) blissful being homeless *[ageha-ānanda]*." Almost postmodern in his cosmopolitan, cross-cultural, quasi-rootless personality (and this despite his hatred of eclecticism), Bharati would live up to his name, passionately preaching the mystico-erotic nature of his "bliss" and struggling to the very end with his religious "homelessness," particularly as it influenced the nature of his own religious authority and right to represent the tradition. Visvananda astutely predicted the latter struggle and its racial roots: "Do not expect too much recognition, Agehananda. This big white body of yours may be fine for almost any other purpose, but it is an obstacle in your recognition."[7] And indeed, much of Bharati's written corpus can be read as a defense of his physical corpus, that is, as a lifelong attempt to justify his conversion and legitimate and establish his chosen identity as a "big white" Hindu.

Bharati lived in India for another six years after his initiation, wandering its roads the length of the country from north to south, interacting with hundreds of *sādhu*s (holy men) of all stripes, taking a secret Tantric initiation in Assam, writing popular pieces for the papers, and teaching philosophy first in New Delhi and then at Benares Hindu University (1951), where he interacted with Guenther again[8] and tried with limited success to introduce Wittgenstein and Continental philosophy to his

Indian colleagues and students. Bharati left the university in 1954 after a dramatic sexual scandal (about which he says nothing in his autobiography). He remained in the country for another two years, when he left to travel in Thailand and Japan. He arrived in the United States in 1958, where he took a research position at the University of Washington. It was at Washington that the psychoanalytic anthropologist Melford Spiro convinced him that he needed to take up a traditional academic discipline to survive in the American academic world; Bharati chose anthropology. The choice would change him radically yet again; hence, he describes his new love of the discipline as a kind of "conversion" from text to context (OR, 279–280), from written scripture to living human beings. In 1961 he took a post in anthropology at Syracuse University, a position which he held (without a Ph.D.) for thirty years, until his death on 14 May 1991. Writing and speaking (the latter in fifteen languages)[9] as a one-of-a-kind monk-anthropologist, Bharati was a colorful and well-known American Indologist whose works gained both academic and popular audiences in the 1960s' and 1970s' American counterculture, a cultural and temporal space which, not coincidentally, coincided with the height of Bharati's career and writing.[10]

2. An Archaeology of Bharati's Antinomianism: From Viennese Antiauthoritarianism to Tantric Ritual to Academic Theory

"I can resist anything but temptation," Bharati once wrote (DL, 54), quoting the flamboyant British decadent writer Oscar Wilde.[11] Indeed, this quip was what he mischievously described as his *mahāvākyam*, his "great saying," which he rhetorically elevated with this Sanskrit compound—surely with a smile—to a truth of ultimate importance with the classical "great sayings" of the Vedantic tradition: *brahmāsmi*, "I am brahman," *tattvamasi*, "You are That," and so on. This same mischievous willingness to stand a religious tradition on its head out of the authority of his own experiences can also be seen in Bharati's humorous reworking of the Latin paternoster that forms the subtitle to chapter 7 of *The Ochre Robe*: "Et nos inducas in tentationem—ad majorem dei gloriam" [And lead us into temptation—for the greater glory of God]. The prayer is a Tantric prayer, for this is the same chapter in which Bharati defends his Tantric position that asceticism is not the only way to salvation before one of the premier authorities of his own monastic tradition, the Jagadguru Śaṃkarācārya of Govardhanapīṭha, at the Kumbhamela (a large gathering of ascetics) of 1954. In another context and on a more serious psychological note, Bharati once wrote that mystics seek out temptation, because it reminds them of the mystical (LC, 59), and he italicized the word "reminds," as if to signal that there was something more here than mere symbol—a category, by the way, which he hated as too weak and indirect[12]—some deep identity between the psychology of transgression and the phenomenon of mystical experience.

Freudian, Fascist, and Catholic Vienna

Bharati's antinomianism is a complex phenomenon, displaying clear psychological patterns that reach back into his childhood and adolescence; Bharati, we can safely say, did not develop his lifelong penchant for transgression, apostasy, and virtual blasphemy out of nowhere. It began, in more ways than one, in Vienna. Our task of constructing an archaeology of his personal antinomianism is made immeasurably easier (and its success more probable) by the facts that Bharati grew up in a Vienna in which Freud was "all the rage" (OR, 27), that he knew more than a little about his fellow famous Viennese, and, although clearly ambivalent about psychological reductionism (OR, 178, 219)[13] and psychiatric diagnostic categories (LC, 98, 119, 143, 196–197), that he did not hesitate to apply a psychoanalytic hermeneutic to himself (OR, 33, 78, 168–170), to his fellow monks (OR, 102, 171; LC, 88), to historical mystics (OR, 92–96)—"gifted" and "pathological" were virtual synonyms for him when speaking about mystics[14]—and even to entire religious traditions or cultural institutions (OR, 31, 165–166, 244; LC, 160, 166). Moreover, his repeated insistence that mystical experiences can confer no ontological status on their objects,[15] his stated desire to interpret the phenomenology of yogic powers *(siddhis)*, subtle physiology, religious visions, reincarnation, and ecstatic states nondiscursively as strictly psychological in nature (OR, 168–170, 189, 235; LC, 79, 84–85, 164–166),[16] his famous and controversial hypersexualization of religious experience and language, his reading of mystical traditions as therapeutic (LC, chap. 7, 225–227, 232),[17] his understanding of the guru-disciple relationship and the phenomenon of conversion as types of transference (LC, 227),[18] and his willingness to submit his own visionary and mythological experiences to a psychological analysis all place his interpretive perspective quite close to a psychoanalytic hermeneutic, as does his appreciative, if mixed, comments on and reviews of psychoanalytically inclined anthropologists and Indologists, such as Wendy Doniger O'Flaherty,[19] Gananath Obeyesekere,[20] G. M. Carstairs,[21] and Philip Spratt (LC, 230),[22] and his occasional use of categories such as the "Freudian slip."[23] Thus, after astutely psychoanalyzing the sexual phobias and subsequent asceticism of a young monk, Bharati could write, "I had not been born and brought up in the home of Sigmund Freud for nothing" (OR, 102). No, he had not been; hence, despite Bharati's own rhetorical objections, Freud appears often in his writings (and occasionally on his walls—Joseph Campbell reported seeing a photo of Freud on Bharati's office wall at Benares Hindu University in the fall of 1954)[24] and seems central to his general project.

It thus seems more than natural to ask psychoanalytic questions about Bharati's antinomianism and his more general rejection of authority in all its forms. We can begin with his early family life. Bharati sarcastically tells us early in his autobiography, as if to poke fun at Freud, that he supposes that this is the point where he is expected to tell us about his childhood and whether it was happy or not, "but the fact is that I do not know" (OR, 26). But he does know, and all too well. The next few pages proceed to paint a starkly negative picture of an alcoholic father, whom he never missed when he left the house, and a sharp-tongued mother, who drove him to celibacy. "This short and negative description of my family life was absolutely necessary for an understanding of my subsequent development" (OR, 29), he then states, confirming the very psychological paradigm he had supposedly rejected.

In terms of specifics, I would suggest that his contentious and bitter relationships to his parents were important psychological factors in his subsequent asceticism. One could easily read his repeated jabs at boring, monotonous marriages, his comment about "the dark seventies of the twentieth century" when people thought "that you have to smile politely when people talk about their children at parties,"[25] his sarcastic criticism of American fathers who think that eight hours at work and eight hours at home with the family is a "very admirable arrangement" (OR, 11), and his insistence that thankfulness for one's parents is not something that can be forced out of one (OR, 28) as defensive mechanisms against his own negative family life. But such sophistication is unnecessary, for Bharati himself was open about his hostility; indeed, he was quite willing to admit that he bore a lifelong grudge against his father for beating him on Christmas Eve morning for peeking at the Christmas tree; he "had a hangover that morning," Bharati bitterly adds (OR, 26).

I cannot help reading his later apostasy from a paternal Catholicism in similar terms. It is probably no accident, for example, that this apostasy crystallized in his relationship with a local priest, who embodied in his symbolic persona "the father" as paternal parent, father-God, and the entire patriarchal religious tradition (OR, 31–32). Bharati never makes such explicit connections himself, but he does imply as much in his comments that he detested the word "father" in Christianity (OR, 142), and that father figures "like the Judeo-Christian God" repelled him.[26] Equally revealing is his list of "pervasive Judaeo-Christian value-orientations" that surround and smother Western man: "his family, the psychiatrist, the hospital."[27]

Moreover, Bharati does engage in self-analysis about his relationship to his mother. Here Bharati suggests that it was his mother's annoying Freudian insistence on the necessity of sexual indulgence which laid the psychological seeds, "if only unconsciously," for his later celibate lifestyle; he rejected an active socialized sexuality, in other words, because his mother tried to force him into an indulgent direction (OR, 28). The oedipal irony here is overwhelming, with a negative childhood reaction to a mother's Freudian sexualism leading to a form of adult celibacy that, by all accounts (including and especially his own), was itself hypersexualized. He was his mother's Freudian child here, ten times over.

Perhaps even more important, the political climate of Bharati's youth embodied in Nazi ideology and the Führer himself only radicalized Bharati's rejection of authority in all its forms, including and especially the religious. And here we need not speculate at all, for Bharati states clearly and unequivocally that he associated the hated authoritarianism and unthinking dependence that Nazi ideology demanded with Catholicism: "With both teachings . . . I experienced the same thing: the prohibition of interest on the one hand, and the imposition of interest on the other" (OR, 42). Or again: "[T]he fact is that Catholic religious education and Nazi political education produced identical results in me, the same traumatic conditions, the same spiritual nausea. . . . 'You must, because someone else wants you to!'" (OR, 41). Bharati later identified his dual rebellion against these two patriarchal traditions as a major cause of his conversion to Hinduism (which, we should remember, was defined in part by his love for the Tantric mother-goddess and India as Mother).[28] We could thus read Bharati's enthusiastic apostasy from Christianity and equally passionate conversion to Hinduism in classical oedipal terms as religiously encoded responses to the psychological dynamics set up in his home and culture: such a dramatic transformation in his identity and emotional life could both "kill" the hated father of home, church, and state and win the mother over as a sexual partner (something, as we shall see, Bharati did in fact accomplish through the medium of Tantric ritual and mythology).

Such an early identification between Nazism and Christianity—and what he would later call the "god-king-country-establishment" (LC, 208)—also helps explain one of the most troubling pieces of marginalia that I found in the swami's Syracuse library: black swastikas boldly penned in over pages of a Bible, clear evidence that he saw biblical monotheism as one of those dangerous universal solutions that insisted on imposing itself on others, regardless of their psychological or emotional differences. Here we might also recall a passage in *The Ochre Robe* in which Bharati wryly describes a scene in which he witnessed a pious Catholic woman shamefully catching herself making the sign of the cross before a poster of Hitler, an image which she instinctively mistook for a religious icon (OR, 41). Finally, it probably did not help matters that Bharati and Hitler shared the same birthday (20 April), and that this association was further cemented in Bharati's memory by the school holiday that was observed every year on that day in honor of the Führer (OR, 45). It would be a mistake, though, to suggest that Bharati facilely conflated Nazism and Catholicism, and I think that we can make too much of his biblical swastikas. He knew that there were important differences between the two traditions, and he clearly hated Nazism more than Catholicism, as he refused to formally abandon Catholicism in his youth and adolescence since too many people were doing just that "for reasons I didn't approve" (OR, 46). Such reasons become immediately clear when we learn that he finally did leave the church in 1947, "when there was no longer a Hitler to embarrass me" (OR, 45). It must also be remembered that Bharati wrote extensively about and radically criticized fascist and protofascist elements of modern Hinduism; noted repeatedly and with considerable concern that uninformed Hindus admire Stalin and Hitler (OR, 202);[29] criticized the hero worship implicit in much popular Hinduism (which he considered to be the "master-key to the understanding of the modern India which is now emerging" [OR, 54; LC, 216]), along with the doctrine of the *avatāra* or "incarnation," as tending toward a certain fascist direction (OR, 223–224; LC, 214); openly rejected the normative worldviews of "Hegel, Marx, and Hitler" (OR, 10); wrote articles on Hindu fascism and Subhas Chandra Bose,[30] whom he met in a secretly arranged Nazi rendezvous in Berlin (OR, 48–49); passionately resisted a group of historians (accompanied by three American neo-Nazi officials) who wanted to write off "the so-called holocaust" as an exaggerated fiction;[31] warned about the dangers of Indian nationalism and the "dormantly Hindu-fascist view of things" of the popular Indian gurus (LC, 171, 185); argued strenuously about the fascist, potentially dangerous elements of the Bhagavad Gītā (OR, 133, 214; LC, 199, 214–215); and repeatedly argued for the virtues of cosmopolitanism and humanism and against nationalism, patriotism, or "any scale of values . . . which does not put the individual human being in the first place" (OR, 14; cf. OR, 44). It was not for nothing that he was accosted in the dark by two young Indian men, who threatened to kill him one day for openly insulting the Russians and Chinese and "the great giant Hitler" (OR, 202). Bharati's relationship to and understanding of fascism, in other words, was overwhelmingly negative, a lifelong struggle with his own personal past, birth culture, and political history. In a passage that sums up his overwhelmingly negative assessment of Vienna as both familial origin and Nazi culture, Bharati wrote that home is where you are born and never go back to (OR, 77). We cannot deny his fascist past—and any future, fuller study of Bharati will have to struggle with it mightily—but we must also remember that he vehemently "renounced" it, rendering himself in effect "homeless" *(ageha)*, and blissfully *(ānanda)* so.

Tantric Transgression

Such are some of the psychological, familial, and political foundations of Bharati's later antinomianism. But these, I would stress, are only the beginning, for what makes Bharati so fascinating is the manner in which he was able to build something extraordinary and culturally significant on this early, rather dark, psychic foundation. Bharati, after all, did not stop with resentment toward his father, disgust with his mother, anger at Nazism, and religious apostasy. He moved on, literally to India, psychologically to a new Indian identity, and spiritually to new forms of ritual, symbol, and consciousness that could better answer his own intellectual questions and psychological needs. It is no accident, I think, that he eventually found a spiritual home in the Tantric traditions. Here, after all, were mystical traditions whose very raison d'être was to deny religious and social orthodoxy and to transgress accepted norms in an attempt to gain power *(śakti)* and effect a mystical union, symbolized this time not by a stern and authoritarian father-God or a male Christ-bridegroom (Bharati's heterosexuality rendered the latter symbolism meaningless), but by a beautiful goddess embodied in an actual, physical woman. The father was now symbolically dead, left at a home Bharati had renounced. The Mother as Lover had returned, embodied anew in an oedipally informed Tantrism: "For me, as a votary of Śakti [the Tantric Goddess], she [India] is both mother and the ever-beautiful, divine, beloved princess" (OR, 173).

I will get to the Mother as Lover in due time. But first it is important to treat the theme of transgression, or antinomianism. Along with eroticism and esotericism, antinomianism played a major role in Bharati's theory of mysticism, but I think a case could be made that, psychologically speaking, Bharati's antinomianism precedes both his famous penchant for eroticism and his lesser-known but equally important insistence on concealing (and revealing) secrets. My basic thesis here is that Bharati, psychologically and politically conditioned by a personal history of antiauthoritarianism, experienced aesthetic profundity and genuine mystical experience in Tantric ritual transgression and subsequently theorized out of this personal history and ritual experience to create a radically transgressive, amoral model of mysticism. The first part of the thesis—the link between Bharati's early antiauthoritarianism and his later attraction to Tantric antinomianism—is speculative and will always remain so. I have dealt with it, if too briefly, above. The second part of the thesis—that Bharati built on his early antiauthoritarianism and employed the model of Tantric ritual transgression to advance an amoral model of mysticism—is somewhat easier to demonstrate. To it I now turn.

Academic Theory: An Amoral Model of Mysticism

Bharati tells us that he began his religious life with the usual assumption that the religious is the ethical, and that being religious was essentially about achieving some type of moral goodness: "I was, you would not believe it did I not tell you repeatedly, an ethicist, i.e., I believed moral values stood above all other values" (DL, 57). Only years of monastic training and his own mystical experiences disabused him of this faulty notion. Bharati himself locates the origins of his position that ethical values are equivalent to aesthetic judgments and have nothing to do with mystical experience per se around the year 1951 (DL, 57). After that, he would hold an uncompromising position on the amoral nature of mystical experience until his death forty years later.

Bharati's mature position on the amorality of mysticism could not be much clearer—or more repeated; I counted over forty statements on the issue in *The Light at the Center* alone, and he monotonously returns to the same theme in his other writings. "The apologists on behalf of the silent mystic majority . . . have a stake in claiming and believing that the mystic is *ipso facto* a sublime human being, a wise man, etc. This error I must dispel," Bharati writes (LC, 53). The monk does his dispelling through a variety of paths, all of which can be traced back to his definitions of mysticism and the mystic, both of which, as we shall see below, are marked by Bharati's emphases on the aesthetic, nonontological, transgressive, and hedonistic nature of the mystical experience. Far from being some mark of wisdom or sublime morality, mysticism for Bharati is "a skill[32] which confers delight" (LC, 75), a kind of art learned through experimentation with the pleasure principle (LC, 30), that is, through the experiences of ecstasy and euphoria induced by any effective means. It is quite irrelevant precisely how someone comes to his or her experience, Bharati tells us, immediately adding his own humorous (and largely autobiographical) random list: "through fasting, prayer, drugs, self-mortification, fornication, standing on his head, grace, listening to *Tristan and Isolde* unabridged three times in a row, etc." (LC, 209).

Along similar lines (minus the classical music), Bharati claims that mysticism entails no ontological implications of any sort—that is, it is of a psychological nature—and it has absolutely no effect on one's moral character. Indeed, to the extent that its methods employ the illicit and the forbidden—and the mystic is by definition a transgressor who plays with temptation (LC, 59), an embarrassment to the established order (LC, 20), a being inimical to the ecclesiastic, the establishmentarian, and the moralistic (LC, 21, 199–200), and a "marginal person" (LC, 206)— the most effective means to the mystical is often an explicitly immoral one. Mysticism, accordingly, is what is *illicit* in both its motivation and its pursuit, an "anathema in any specific social and religious tradition" (LC, 200). By a different argument, "if observation shows that the zero-experience [Bharati's term for mystical experience] is triggered by meditational procedures, by drugs, by orgasm, by fasting, or by anything else, then moralistic assessments about its genesis are out of place" (LC, 112). Bharati's conviction, boldness, personal authority, and delightful hubris are truly impressive here: "[F]or at least two and a half thousand years, yogis, mendicants, and mystics have thought that the specific technique they used and transmitted to their disciples was necessarily bound to the style of life which they led and which they recommended. Again, they were and are wrong: any technique can and is used along with any type of religio-mystical life" (LC, 132).

Bharati will offer only two qualifications, but they are important ones: (1) adjectives such as "illicit" and "immoral," he tells us, have no meaning within a community of consenting adults who choose to participate in the mystical experiment (LC, 212–213); and (2) mystical experience does result in a permanent change in the psychological experience of the individual who has had one, making him or her virtually immune to "the vicissitudes of life, against boredom and despair" (LC, 75). Bharati describes this latter transformation as producing an autonomous individual who begins—and here he sounds remarkably like Foucault—"to use his body as he wishes, withdrawing it from the public reservoir of bodies" (LC, 208; cf. LC, 200–203). In this latter sense, and in this latter sense only, mystical experience may be construed as "moral."

Still, Bharati is far more concerned with dispelling any and all notions that mysticism is moral in the commonly understood sense of "socially useful" or "licit" or "good." "[T]he genuine mystic as a person," he insists in his typically humorous, jolting style, "remains the person he was before—a king, a knave, a dentist" (LC, 53). Here a sanctimonious medievalism—and by implication, all pieties—meets its funny end in the utter banality of the modern, anesthetic-wielding cavity filler. By far, the majority of mystics were of an "asocial, even anti-social, autocentric, self-indulgent kind" (LC, 87), for the mystical life tends to disengage one from the social world (LC, 71); indeed, "some of the best mystics were the greatest stinkers among men. Self-righteous, smug, anti-women, anti-men, politically fascist, stubborn, irrational" (LC, 91).

Here he hints that the mystical is not just the amoral, but often can develop into the immoral or the socially dangerous. The mystical experience, he claims, possesses nothing of merit beyond itself, and granting it any outside value, including any moral value, is both wrong and dangerous (LC, 74). Why? Because "it is just as possible that the mystic, following some teaching which he wrongly holds . . . is authenticated by his zero-experience, may choose an ideology that kills and tortures" (LC, 74). The prophet who has had no mystical experience is even more dangerous, for he simply "reiterates the ideal image of his society" (LC, 83).[33] Bharati's concern with separating the ethical from the mystical, then, carried with it—paradoxically—genuine ethical, even political, concerns. He was all too familiar with monks and mystics who did not hesitate to quote the Gītā to justify murder and war (OR, 133, 214; LC, 199, 214–215).[34] He had experienced firsthand the dangers of Nazi fascism, and he worried out loud—and often—that such a thing could happen again, especially in India.

Where then should people look for social advice, ethical guidance, and political wisdom? Certainly not to mysticism. Rather, it was better to seek out the "wise men of the West,"[35] that is, the classical texts and teachers of Western political and social thought. Bharati was also particularly clear that India could and should learn from Western humanism, particularly that of Bertrand Russell, Wittgenstein, G. E. Moore, and T. S. Eliot (OR, 13): "To be a better human being you have to think better. There's no other answer. To be moral means to be rational."[36] Similarly, Western man should develop a "mystical correlative" to its humanism by learning from India and her "clearly-defined and long-practiced mystical traditions . . . (Yoga, Vedānta, Tantra) which will allow him to be a humanist and a mystic at the same time" (OR, 14). Interestingly enough, for Bharati, it is humanism that constitutes a "spiritual attitude," whereas mysticism is a "physical matter" (of technique, I presume). Because they inhabit different spaces within the same individual, the two can happily coincide,[37] even if they can never quite meet on the same ground. Thus he called for a meeting of the East and the West in the individual (OR, 16). The ethical here enters Bharati's thought, but through the category of a cosmopolitan, cross-cultural humanism, certainly not through mysticism, which is always in itself amoral, which can effectively be approached through antinomian techniques, and which is capable of both great good and great evil.

3. From "Tantrism" to "Mysticism": Theorizing Out of the Erotic

Closely related—philosophically, psychologically, and ritually—to Bharati's antinomianism was his famous and always controversial eroticism. Here was a monk who had numerous lovers throughout his life, who spoke and wrote openly about his sexual life, and who used the phenomenology of human sexual experience to theorize about the philosophical, ethical, ontological, and aesthetic import of mystical states. But his was not a simple, "natural" sexuality expressed for the sake of mental well-being and aimed teleologically toward procreation; any talk of sexual expression as a necessary component of mental health reminded him of the early Freudianism that his mother had propounded and that he himself despised, and he had little, if anything, positive to say about children, parenthood, or a stable family structure, all of which he clearly saw—in true ascetic style—as a kind of "mask" behind which people can hide from true autonomy (LC, 203). No, Bharati's sexuality was a Tantric sexuality, a ritualized, aesthetic, mystical sexuality out of which he attempted to construct a cross-cultural synthesis of what he considered to be the best of Western and South Asian cultures,[38] that is, an individualistic, rational, and cosmopolitan humanism and the stunning beauty and transformative power of mystical experience, "[e]ros and charitas rolled into one," as he described it at the very end of *The Light at the Center* (234). His was thus an actual, physical "left-handed" sexuality (as opposed to a "right-handed" safely imagined or merely metaphorical sexuality) deeply imbued with the mystical as postulated[39] ontological substratum of reality.

"I felt that I had been too close to the core," Bharati noted after a tense and breathtaking debate on the possibility of an erotic mysticism with the Śaṃkarācārya, one of the highest authorities of the renowned Daśanāmi monastic tradition (OR, 241). In terms of Bharati's Tantric thought and experiences, however, there can be no question about the erotic being "too close to the core," since the erotic *was* the core of Bharati's life and thought. We are dealing, after all, with a set of traditions for which the code term *bodhicitta* can and does mean both the "mind of enlightenment" (its literal interpretation) and "sperm"[40] and which routinely refer to the ascetic as the *ūrdhvaretas,* "he whose semen is [turned] up."[41] It seems not only appropriate but necessary, then, to invoke the category of the erotic again here with Bharati, this scandalous man who saw clearly that religious practice and sexuality are often bound up with all sorts of pathological symptoms (LC, 102), who recognized that some types of mystical practices (particularly those that concentrated on sexual symbol and/or expression) could be healing (LC, chaps. 7–8), and who insisted that the most intimate and intense pleasures of the human body, far from being a hindrance on the mystical path, are in fact potent and potential sites for some of the most emotionally staggering and aesthetically beautiful revelations that human experience has to offer. "[T]he monastic and mystical life," Bharati forcefully argued from both the Hindu scriptural tradition and his own mystical experiences, "are entirely based on a particular set of experiences which are, in the last analysis, erotic" (DL, 50).

Arguing out of this same erotic position, Bharati suggested to the Śaṃkarācārya that celibacy is often a positive hindrance on "the path of deepest intuition" (OR, 99). Here he no doubt had in mind the Tantric traditions, those traditional Indian paths that reject sexual asceticism for the revelatory powers of sexuality. Bharati understood his own vocation as a call to walk these paths, to theorize out of them, and to promote them as viable alternatives to the monotheistic traditions of the West. "If one of the most beautiful and worthwhile themes of the Indian tradition is to be preserved and if it is to be a medium of placing India on a level with the achievements of occidental humanism, the modernized, intelligent tantric will have to [be] given an honourable place," he wrote.[42] It is clear that this is a self-description and that Bharati understood himself to be just such a rational, modern, intellectual Tāntrika whose task it was to resuscitate and legitimate that which was most beautiful and valuable in Indian culture—the Tantric.

The Category of Tantrism in Bharati's Thought

What, though, did Bharati understand by the terms "Tantrism" and "Tantric"? To contextualize Bharati's own understandings of Tantrism, it should be pointed out that the project of defining Tantrism is a contested issue among contemporary Indologists and Buddhologists. The Indo-Tibetan Tantric traditions have long been (in)famous for their explicit and implicit eroticisms, and more specifically, for their provocative and relentless linking of human sexuality and religious experience. It is clear that early colonial administrators and Christian missionaries in India latched onto this aspect of the traditions in order to denigrate and demonize them. Early-twentieth-century attempts by such figures as Sir John Woodroffe (a Roman Catholic judge of the High Court at Calcutta who published volumes on various aspects of the traditions with his "ghost translator" and collaborator Atal Behari Ghosh)[43] to legitimate and popularize the Tantric texts were not enough to reverse the earlier discourse, but they did go a long way in constructing the modern category of "Tantrism" in the minds of both Indians and Westerners alike. Indeed, it is likely, as Andre Padoux and more recently Hugh Urban have suggested, that the modern connotations of the categories of "Tantra" and "Tantrism" are as much products of Western colonial, scholarly, and popular discourse as they are continuations of South Asian traditions and texts.[44] There were certainly Tantric texts, Tantric rituals, and Tantric practitioners well before the British ever arrived, but it is doubtful whether they would have understood themselves as belonging to something called "Tantrism" or "the Tantra"; that would come later, with the British, the Indologists, the traveling swamis, and the Western popularizers.

In any case, this early, highly romantic discourse was developed further in the second half of the twentieth century in the West, when a combination of the Western 1960s' countercultures and an efflorescence of discourse on sexuality and gender created a new social space for the discussion of things Tantric. Bharati's career can best be understood as an early manifestation of this renewed, culturally supported interest in the Tantric traditions; indeed, an argument could be made that he did more than a little to encourage, nurture, and extend this cultural appropriation. Certainly he wrote during a time in which there was a plethora of popular works on Tantra being published but very little solid scholarship available to the general public (according to Bharati, Eliade, Guenther, David Snellgrove, and Giuseppe Tucci were the only real exceptions; there were also a few Indian scholars, but, according to Bharati, they could not write about the subject without demonstrating their own considerable discomfort[45] [TT 10]). It was this popularized, embarrassed state of things that Bharati sought to redress with the publication in 1965 of his self-described magnum opus, *The Tantric Tradition*.

The Tantric Tradition

Much has happened since Bharati wrote *The Tantric Tradition* almost forty years ago now, and one can now see the signs of a more mature, more critical, and more technical literature. Within this new discourse some scholars have sought to distance Tantra from its earlier association with sexuality—and there are some textual grounds for doing so, for, statistically speaking (probably not the best way to approach a sacred text), many Tantric texts themselves dwell relatively little on the details of sexual ritual and theory—but Bharati was certainly not one of these scholars. He more or less equated the Tantric traditions with a kind of mystical hedonism.[46] In a talk at Naropa, the Tibetan Buddhist center in Boulder, Colorado, for example, Bharati defined Tantrism as "a technique or techniques towards the achievement of the ecstatic, coded in scriptural terms, defined as a short-cut method of achieving a theologically postulated freedom, by harnessing, rather than subduing, the sensuous equipment present in all people."[47] Here his language is unusually subdued and abstract. In other contexts he had no qualms—theoretical, textual, personal, or religious—about being more specific about Tantric "harnessing," equating it with what he called "psycho-experimentation," Bharati's term for a certain doctrinal agnosticism (philosophy, theology, and doctrine are all secondary, even unimportant, for Bharati)[48] coupled with an unhampered willingness to experiment with one's body and mind through everything from yogic *prāṇāyāma* (breath control) to enjoying classical music, taking hallucinogenic drugs, and engaging in ritual sexual intercourse (with a very heavy emphasis on the last three, preferably to be practiced together; LC, 205).[49] Tantra could thus be described as "total sensuous indulgence guided by certain esoteric controls."[50] As "instruments of opposition and criticism of the official religious establishments,"[51] these traditions were "antiestablishmentarian,"[52] for they defy "traditional moral claims almost axiomatically."[53] Interestingly, Bharati compares them in passing to Western psychotherapy and Jungian creative imagination.[54] We could not be any further away from Underhill's position that the mystical can be properly appropriated only within a community and an established historical tradition.

Bharati believed that this desire for experimentation and this ability to bracket dogma and doctrine were valuable characteristics of Hinduism that were uniquely suited to a skeptical and radically freethinking Western modernity.[55] And this, of course, was all quite incompatible with Western monotheism and its laws: "[T]en commandments are nine too many for a mystic," Bharati joked (LC, 205). This spirit of bold experiment and free thought is omnipresent in Bharati's writings. In one particularly significant passage, in which Bharati is debating with a senior abbot, Bharati goes so far as to suggest that mystics should be freely experimenting before they are given any doctrinal instruction at all to allow them to come to their own idiosyncratic discoveries unconditioned by previous dogmas and orthodoxies (OR, 239). Except for one important exception—his first mystical experience at age twelve during a hypnagogic state[56]—Bharati was certainly well indoctrinated before he experimented, but he experimented with a vengeance as if to make up for this orthodox fault. Again and again (and again), Bharati returns to sex, drugs, and classical music (instead of rock 'n' roll, which he predictably despised as "piss music")[57] as close parallels and so effective inducers of the mystical state. And he is quite precise, almost pharmaceutical in his prescriptions: "In hedonic, erotically charged, musically supported, ritualistically informal LSD sessions, with unworried, concerned, mystically inclined people around, and with a dose of 200 micrograms of pure unblended LSD, the average taker enters the deepest place roughly four and a half hours after the take" (LC, 47–48). In this same spirit he described the ancient Upanisadic seers—whose writings constitute the core of traditional Hinduism—as "mystic-rebels" whom he compared to Timothy Leary (LC, 69), praised "Leary and Huxley and the tantrics, all of whom seemed to get to the zero-experience by some measure of fun" (LC, 66), and mischievously described five eight-hour LSD-25 sessions he had with the Trappist monk and writer Thomas Merton, whom he convinced to join him (probably news to most Merton scholars).[58] Such experimentation knew few bounds;[59] indeed, he even goes so far as to describe a Black Mass he witnessed, complete with the head priest dressed up as Satan and sexually entering a prostrate hierodule (LC, 69).

For Bharati such radical experimentation was made possible by the basic monism of Tantrism. Theism and a personal God could result only in guilt, pity, and fear—all products of the dualism and alienation implicit in theism; the liberating logic of monism, on the other hand, enables the radical mystic to use his own body without fear of reprisal. Bharati believes that the Christian mystic's fear of drugs and sex and "his habit of self pity" stem ultimately from an axiomatic ontological dualism between the mind and the body. Once this dualism collapses in monism, however, the body, sacral sexuality, and the employment of hallucinogens all lose their negative connotations (LC, 126). Indeed, for Bharati, there is a real correlation between mysticism and monism. With impeccable logic, he points out that there are no good grounds to reject pleasure as long as one adopts a monistic ontology, for there can be no such thing as secular pleasure, "if you understand the universe as a spiritual unit" (DL, 16). Moreover, in the Indian context he believed, following Ninian Smart, that history showed a positive, if rough, correlation between theistic thought and philosophical naïveté (LC, 191–193).

Bharati, however, was not naive about the "dark side" of the Tantric traditions, and his writings presciently display a deep and insightful concern for the categories of gender and power well before such categories came to dominate religious studies in the last decades of the twentieth century. On numerous occasions he expressed his moral indignation at Indian culture's patriarchal oppression of women, misogyny (OR, 131), fear of sexuality, and phobic reactions to female sexuality (OR, 165–166, 203, 261; LC, 230). Moreover, and more to the point, he was quite aware of the gendered, drastically asymmetrical nature of Tantric ritual and its troubling objectification of the female ritual partner. Resisting any naively romantic treatment of the tradition, he rejected completely the popular American counterculture notion that Tantra somehow inculcates mutual feelings of love, respect, and tenderness between the partners, that it was, if you will, a mystical form of romantic love: "Nonsense. The sex of Tantra is hard-hitting, object-using, manipulative ritual without any consideration for the person involved."[60] He acknowledged that a future American-generated Tantrism might well include these emotions[61] (and, as we will see below, he certainly wanted there to be such an American Tantric tradition), but he had no patience for those who wanted to project such emotions onto Indian culture: "[T]here is no place for emotional or interpersonal commitment in any Asian contemplative tradition. *Everybody* is a male chauvinist in the official Hindu and Budhhist Indian tradition.... It is the man who controls the seminal upward and downward flow. What about the woman? That's the most embarrassing question you can ask any tantric, who is an Indian male."[62] To complicate things further, Bharati also recognized that Tantric practice was structured around a heterosexual orientation, that a homosexual orientation would not "fit," as it were,[63] and that the rituals and their general esoteric spirit could take on abusive qualities, as they did in the case of Charles Leadbeater, who Bharati asserts used his own brand of theosophical esotericism to seduce young men.[64]

The Category of Mysticism in Bharati's Thought

This erotic, transgressive, ambiguously gendered, ethically problematic understanding of Tantrism naturally and obviously flowed over into both Bharati's theoretical understanding of mysticism and his discussion of historical mystics. But not immediately. His initial definitional project is more indebted to the monism of Advaita Vedānta. Consider, for example, his definition of "mysticism" in the opening pages of *The Light at the Center*. Mysticism, he writes, is "the person's *intuition of numerical oneness with the cosmic absolute, with the universal matrix, or with any essence stipulated by the various theological and speculative systems of the world*" (LC, 25; italics his). A person who pursues such experiences as his or her primary goal in life and who simultaneously states that he or she is on this quest is a mystic, for Bharati (LC, 25). Mystical experience, moreover, unlike discursive knowledge, is not accumulative (LC, 66) or teleological (LC, 76). Moreover, it is autonomous (LC, 112, 174, 189), that is, although orgasms and LSD and classical music (Bharati's three favorites) can and do clearly initiate or "trigger" the mystical, the experience itself cannot be reduced to sexuality or a chemical compound or to the notes on the page. Bharati is particularly sophisticated and honest here. Writing about the last of his major mystical experiences and mentioning the previous two (recall that he normally spoke of only four),[65] he writes that LSD was indeed the trigger, but that so was the initiatory ritual phase in the Tantric community in Assam (the third experience), as was the confinement cell in the Indian Legion (the second experience). It was not, then, that orgasm actually triggered this last experience with a woman named Matsuko (the fourth experience), yet Bharati doubts that the experience would have happened at all had either Matsuko or the LSD been missing (LC, 44). The mystical thus both is and is not related ontogenetically to the sexual and the hallucinogenic.

Here, in the LSD and the lover, we meet another aspect of Bharati's understanding of the mystical: his insistence that ecstasy or enstasy (a term he borrows from Eliade) is also "part of the objective description" (LC, 27). A refusal to acknowledge or experience such euphoria does not disqualify a person from the category of "mystic," but such an individual does fall into a marginal category vis-à-vis the mystical (LC, 27). Hence, Bharati adds a very important addendum to the above definition: a mystic is now "*a seeker of intuitive union with the cosmic ground, who chooses experiments which would lead to such intuition,* preferring the available enstatic or euphoric experiments to available less ecstatic and less euphoric ones" (LC, 28; italics his). Once again, Bharati's Tantrism shows itself in his definitional insistence that it is psycho-experimentalism that is "the hallmark of the mystical endeavour" (LC, 35).

In terms of his own Hindu traditions, such an experimental, intuitive euphoria is best captured by the code term *ānanda* (bliss or pleasure). Its frequency in the scriptures, Bharati tells us, tends to "blunt" its hedonistic edge, but it nevertheless remains hedonistic to its ontological core: "[T]he basic content of the Hindu doctrine *is* hedonistic, the canonical scriptures talk overtly about delight and pleasure, and even the last five centuries of puritanical subversion have not quite succeeded in suppressing them" (LC, 29). Thus, the mystical life becomes a training for what he called a "skilled bliss" (OR, 142). All of this, Bharati writes (in a Freudian register, I might add) "is sensuous in the very real sense that it measures spiritual growth by the pleasure principle" (LC, 30). According to Bharati, however, the scriptural passages that support such a reading are consistently ignored, allegorized away, and bowdlerized by practically all the leading thinkers of the Hindu Renaissance (I suspect Bharati would object to my "practically"), who are well-meaning reformers but nevertheless poor textual historians (LC, 34, 192). Such an attitude is epitomized most dramatically by the Harvard Brahmin economics professor who assured Bharati that the sixteen thousand "*married* milkmaids" (Bharati's emphasis) with whom Krishna made passionate love were in fact the sixteen thousand verses that Krishna had piously memorized (LC, 215). Bharati will have none of this, not just because it does almost infinite violence to the historical texts, but also because it distorts the very nature of the mystical mind, which inevitably "zeroes in on the orgasmic situation," a fact which is "as distasteful to the committed Hindu ecclesiastic as it is to the fundamentalist Christian" (LC, 30).

Bharati, in other words, was not just fighting an internal turf war with the Hindu Renaissance (although he was certainly doing that).[66] He was also trying to make a theoretical point about a comparative category, that of "mysticism" itself. He was thus more than a little perturbed when he saw major Western theorists—particularly his old Benares Hindu University colleague and friend J. L. Mehta and R. C. Zaehner, who offered to write the preface for *The Light at the Center* (LC, 9)—denying the euphoric core of mysticism. Bharati postulated psychological origins for this theoretical timidity and the subsequent faulty scholarship that it produced: "No, mysticism cannot be pleasurable, orgasm-linked, flesh-linked. . . . Mehta and Zaehner appreciate mystical *writings* in which erotics, drugs, ecstasy-metaphors abound, but they will not have drugs, erotics, and ecstasy. . . . I have a feeling that actual ecstasy scares them. . . . I am certain that the erudite stratagems of profound secrecy—theological codes, better literature, deeper speculation, etc.—are so many mantles protecting the anxious savant from the zero-experience" (LC, 63). Bharati responded to such official and scholarly prudery with what we can only call a radical sexualization of mysticism. The mystic, he wrote, is the one who "creates what no husband, lover, or lecher succeeds in doing: he makes orgasm permanent, uninterrupted" (LC, 200). Certainly this was Bharati's goal, for he did not flinch from describing himself as a hedonist who measured the value of his life by how much pleasure it could give him (OR, 202; LC, 194; DL, 15); he became a monk, he wrote, not to deny himself pleasure but to increase it, to deepen it, to extend it to the postulated depths of the universe (OR, 173).

Within this same hedonistic worldview and in the spirit of Tantric *sandhā-bhāṣā* (intentional language), the code language of the Tantric texts that simultaneously "intends" both a sexual and a mystical meaning, Bharati sexualized practically everything. Mysticism is rather like virginity, he once quipped: you either possess it or you do not (LC, 95). Similarly with the unconnected nature of mysticism and ethics: "The zero-experience cannot generate sanctity anymore than an orgasm can make one a good parent" (LC, 110; cf. LC, 99). So too with the mystic in his mystical states, who, contrary to pious belief, cannot be aware of the world. Certainly a person in love might become particularly sensitive and open to the external world, "[b]ut in sexual intercourse?" (LC, 50). Still in the same sexual register, all mystical literature says more or less the same thing, just as the most "beautiful orgasms" of women—Bharati interviewed them—are identical (LC, 80). Almost monotonously (Bharati's humor always rescued him from monotony), the swami compares the mystical experience to "certain drug experiences, or those supreme orgasms with expected and unexpected sexual partners" (LC, 100; cf. 101, 212, 218). Thus, he can describe a man who once had a mystical experience but never nurtured it to a businessman who hires a whore in a city to which he will never return (LC, 115).

Indeed, Bharati even sexualized, quite literally, "nothing." Consider, for example, his discussion of the "zero-experience," his coined and central expression for the monistic mystical experience before and beyond any interpretive schemas. "Toward this point of the blastoff countdown," he writes, "all else has been preparatory in the Space Center." In less dramatic terms, he wants to apply the same zero-expression to philosophical ratiocination, where "there is zero content of a cognitive sort in the experience," as in, for example, the solving of a mathematical problem, and then (of course) to the sexual context, where the orgasm is (the rocket-like) zero-experience (LC, 48). Houston and the NASA Apollo program can be detected in the historical background of such a discourse (recall that it is 1976), as can the Buddhist traditions with their emphasis on the category of "emptiness" (śūnyatā, literally, "zero-ness") and Bharati's insistence that genuine mystical experience is doctrinally "pure," that is, devoid of interpretation. But such technological, religious, and hermeneutical connotations quickly fade into the background for Bharati, who chooses, in his usual fashion, to highlight the sexual within a rhetoric that can be accurately read as a type of American-English *sandhā-bhāṣā*, intending at once both mystical and sexual meanings.

Such free and shocking rhetoric did not go unnoticed, especially in India, where there was no counterculture or drug revolution to support it. "Why is it, Agehananda," a brother-monk asked, "that you so often bring similes from the sensuous sphere into your argument and speeches? . . . it appears to people that you flaunt this symbolism in order to annoy them; you use it, it seems, with a vengeance. Why?" (OR, 240). Bharati had an answer: "to exhibit the delicate intimacy of spiritual experiences" (LC, 240). What he actually intended to say, I think, was something along the lines of this: "to rescue the mystical from the abstractions of philosophical code words and prudish censorship and enflesh it in real bodies with real organs." In a fascinating passage he explains just how difficult and countertraditional such honesty is: "If I say, 'In a particular yogic state, the devotee saw the Goddess of the Universe enter his body'—these are the words of a particular text, then there can be no objection; it is like a poet's description of his lady's embrace. But if I say, 'In my yogic state, and, if you follow my instructions, then eventually in your yogic state, I see, and you will see, the Goddess enter your body, or you entering Hers,' then this is bad taste, in the same way as it would be bad taste for a poet to write, 'When I embraced Mrs. X, of 1120 Marine Drive" (OR, 240). I suspect that this passage is autobiographical, and that Bharati had sexual experiences with goddess-presences as well as human women. The latter is beyond doubt: he had numerous sexual partners, and he comes perilously close to actually naming Mrs. X or giving her address on different occasions (LC, 39–43). The former, mythological, encounters are more difficult to establish, but he does drop some fascinating hints. For example, in his fictional letter to his (fictional?) Bengali lover Lalita he brags that "[a]s to the woman, it never mattered to me whether she had two arms or four,"[67] and then, as if to signal this comment as his own mystical *guhya kathā* or "secret talk," he adds, "meam mysticam audi vocem," that is, "Hear my mystical voice" (DL, 29). He hints at a similar mythological eroticism in *The Light at the Center,* even if he wants to distance it from the monistic experience per se. After reflexively interpreting such experiences as psychological projections, he writes that they gave him evidence that he had indeed emically entered Hindu mythology, but that this should not be equated with having entered Hindu mysticism, since even though one meets the gods face to face, makes love to them, and talks to them, one has not become a mystic. For that, one must become these very gods (LC, 41). At this point the deities disappear, but the erotic euphoria remains. Indeed, the euphoria is intensified as the deities coalesce into their substratum and manifest their true natures as projected imaginalia, ecstatic forms of the erotic itself, of the Brahman. In Bharati's quite beautiful prose, the deities are "converted ecstasies," and the universal absolute is "nothing but the totality of these gods, of these ecstasies within" (LC, 151). Thus, not unlike William Blake, who bemoaned the fact that men, confusing poetic tales for literal truth, have forgotten that "[a]ll deities reside in the human breast,"[68] Bharati can assert his own deconstructive vision. Comparing modern academic truths to those of the ancient Upaniṣads, Bharati is clear that the modern truths are more sophisticated, more convincing, and more relevant. Indeed, with immeasurably more zero-experiences, psychology, and comparative religion behind us, we can now see that "first, we created our gods and our god; then we forgot that we created them; then, by the zero-experience and by calling to our minds that we (our ancestors, that is) created them, we realized that these divine creations are we ourselves" (LC, 152).

As for specifics, Bharati is clear that he took Tantric initiation in 1953 in Assam, a traditional locus of Tantric practice and culture, although, in true esoteric fashion, he refuses to reveal the actual location of the sect in order to protect its members from legal and political persecution. It was after one of the initiatory rites that his third major mystical experience took place. The sun was rising and the practitioners were separating from their partners. As Bharati walked back to the ashram he felt a strange sensation, "as in a dream, with the orectic lines between the will and the body disconnected as it were." At first he interpreted it as simple fatigue (the rituals had apparently lasted all night), but then something else happened: "I did not walk but I was the universe moving in itself. I saw my legs and all, but these were just two rather unimportant instruments among millions of unseen instruments that made the universe move; but I was the mover" (LC, 42).

His fourth mystical experience occurred five years later, in 1958, during his first year as a research associate at the University of Washington. After a long night session with LSD-25—he brags that he was one of the first to experiment with the chemical compound—and "a very beautiful woman" in the company of friends, incense, and "no psychiatrists" (he *hated* psychiatrists), Bharati and his lover went to bed around four o'clock in the morning. The next morning brought more sex, a Tantric vision, and another mystical experience of oneness. More specifically, when he saw millions of fishlike beings inside his lover's glowing womb copulating in perfect rhythmic motions, he thought immediately of the *brahmāṇḍa*, the Egg of Brahman of Indian cosmogony:

> Now, of course, this was simply a comeback of the drug . . . but when this spectacle subsided and I withdrew from her, I was again all *that*, with nothing whatever excluded. . . . . For a second or a fraction of a second, I feared that Matsuko was being left out, but as I tried to communicate this to her I noticed I couldn't, for she was *not* left out—she was me, or better, I was she, too. I did not recall Assam [his third experience], nor the army cell near Bordeaux [his second], nor the chintzy flower-paintings on my Vienna childhood wall [his first]; I did not recall India, nor any other history of geography. I was it—not *again*, but always. (LC, 43)

It is important to note that of the four major mystical experiences Bharati records in *The Light at the Center*, two of them—the Assam initiation and hallucinogenic sex with Matsuko—occurred in explicitly Tantric contexts.

Finally, before I leave the topic of Bharati's Tantric eroticism, it should be pointed out that the monk-anthropologist's program to advance a Tantric model for the mystical as the erotic was more than an academic argument, for Bharati was clearly interested in establishing a kind of

Tantric mysticism within American society. At the beginning of *The Ochre Robe* he compares himself to Śaṅkara, who we are told founded four monasteries, traveled the length of India twice, and wrote about eighty books. Bharati notes that he too has published about eighty tracts and has traveled further than his master, even if he has not yet founded any monasteries, "though I intend to. I also desire to preserve and further the Brahmin-Hindu tradition, though with the addition of other, newer, and possibly more embracing methods" (OR, 9). Here Tantrism enters again. Bharati knows he stands virtually alone against some four million Asiatic monks in his belief that the Tantric tradition "more accurately reflects the essence of the spiritual tradition of India and Asia" (OR, 12). He also notes with dismay that none of the modern mystical movements in the West have been founded by a "recognized Indologist or Orientalist" (OR, 20); this is a bizarre statement (what Indologist would *want* to found such a movement?), unless we remember that Bharati understood himself as just such an Indologist and just such a potential Tantric founder.

Bharati did not believe that Tantra could be established in India at any time in the near future (FA 128). Only the West could supply the necessary radical thought, freedom of expression, and unflinching hedonism necessary for such a mystical project. Left-handed Tantra is a real alternative to the more ascetic forms of yoga (LC, 230), he argued, particularly in the "affluent, hedonistically liberal, increasingly dedogmatized West" (LC, 233), where there is an intellectual tradition of radical criticism and dissent. In India, which historically lacks the secular traditions necessary for such radical thought, there can be no such radical criticism of parents, religion, and society (LC, 231). America, however, and especially the Boulder of the Tantric Buddhist Naropa Institute, offer other possibilities: "Tantrism may happen here and maybe it has started right here in Boulder, Colorado 80302."[69] Hence, "by historical accident so to speak, Occidental man today is situated nearer to the Hindu ideal of indifference to social censorship than the Hindu practicioner who has to work so much harder to attain it."[70] Moreover, he lacks, almost completely, any ritual taboos of purity codes regarding sex and food that could block his way along the Tantric path. For Bharati, then, the Western individual is a most potent, if still potential, site for that Tantric Renaissance for which he hoped and worked.[71]

But such a Tantric migration to the Western world will work only if the tradition of scholarship and intellectual sophistication, which had constituted the bases of the Tantric traditions in their original cultures, accompanies the Tantric traditions in their migration to the West. Without such a scholarly base, any American Tantra becomes "fraudulent" for Bharati and is doomed to die.[72] Consequently, nothing of any lasting value can be created until the enthusiast abandons his facile anti-intellectualism and the expert becomes the sympathetic scholar. Or in more explicit terms, the popular neo-Hindu model of the traveling swami must be rejected for a more intellectual project: "[I]f the tantric camel is to enter at all and with profit it must enter through the eye of the needle that sews in Sanskrit and Tibetan, and that probes in terms of modern anthropology and analytical philosophy, and not through the offices of any non-intellectual, anti-academical, albeit spiritual eastern proselytization."[73]

Bharati's closing lines to *The Light at the Center* sum up his position on the amoral, erotic status of mysticism and his call for a new American-Tantric approach to the Light at the Center that is more than a hippie-style eclecticism, more than anti-intellectual pretext:

> With the rise of intellectually disciplined non-squares, non-puritans who would absorb and transmit the primary sources unsanctimoniously, meditating, studying, *and* copulating as they do these things, there may well come a time when a rational mysticism is generated by modern people who love to think, read, learn difficult grammars, and make love to consenting adults. A rational mysticism is not a contradiction in terms; it is a mysticism whose limits are set by reason: a quest for the zero-experience without any concomitant claim to world-knowledge, special wisdom, or special morality. These latter three must be directly generated by reason, and by reason alone (LC, 234).

A high intellectualism, a privileging of language (here as language study, elsewhere as linguistic analysis), rationalism, free sex, and a clear separation of mysticism and morality—these are the hallmarks of Bharati's Tantric thought on mysticism. In the end, then, it appears that there is no easy way to separate his antinomianism, his eroticism, and his mysticism. As in the Tantric rituals themselves, these three appear together—naturally, we might say—as potent psycho-mimetic reminders of the Light at the Center.

4. Bharati's Textual Hermeneutics: Exoteric and Esoteric Strategies

As is apparent by now, one way to understand Bharati's life and thought is to see them as passionate attempts to rescue the "light in the center"

(LC, 187, 200) from what he considered to be the "pompously glib," anti-intellectual, and even dangerous culture of the gurus and their particular brands of mysticism (LC, 200). He also clearly wanted to rescue this light from the dysfunctional eclecticism of the American New Age scene, an eclecticism which he considered to be a real hindrance to mystical practice; such eclecticism, which can unthinkingly join "Aloha" and "Amiga" on the same record album (LC, 11) or blithely offer Tai Chi and Jungian therapy under the same institutional roof,[74] deeply offended Bharati's aesthetic tastes and his desire for some measure of philosophical consistency and serious commitment. Not only are such combinations logically ridiculous; more importantly, and more damning, they remain only "pretext,"[75] for they prevent a person from any serious engagement with the rituals, doctrines, and languages of a particular mystical tradition (much of which, he liked to point out, is inevitably boring). Popularizations of all sorts he despised as intellectually vacuous exercises that delude people into thinking that they have mastered a tradition and so prevent genuine appropriation of what is in reality a foreign, often profoundly foreign, body of teachings.[76] Syncretism, by its very logic, "precludes genuine quest" (LC, 11).[77]

The Modern Intellectual and the Future of Mysticism

As noted above, Bharati believed that the hard work of such assimilation and cultural borrowing could be accomplished only by the modern Western intellectual. He thus liked to point out the fact that Western radical intellectuals—he was thinking in particular of Herbert Marcuse and Norman Brown (interestingly enough, both psychoanalytically informed thinkers)—often demonstrate a genuine mystical interest in merging with some larger dimension or reality but nevertheless seldom actually participate in what he liked to call (in true 1970s fashion) "the mystical scene" (LC, 21). "I muse," he wrote, "about the chances for a mystic who is also an intellectual by modern standards, who thinks hard and directs his capitations to diverse topics, including mysticism" (LC, 214). Such broad-minded, curious intellectuals do not seek total, totalitarian solutions for life's problems and refuse to surrender their critical powers of doubt, skepticism, and questioning; resisting any and all simple ideologies, they are thus a potent and indispensable bulwark against any future fascism, be it politically or religiously construed (LC, 94, 96). They also offer what Bharati believed no religious dogma, guru, or institution can deliver: true intellectual integrity (OR, 43). Bharati argued that any mystical tradition that hoped to survive and flourish in the West must build on just this kind of intellectual sophistication and radical honesty; otherwise, it was doomed to dissolve as soon as it tried to enter the intellectual center of Western culture—the university. There are two audiences, he noted, with which modern gurus significantly "do not score": professional Indologists and analytic philosophers (LC, 178, 221, 223). Both groups of people would have to be respected, if not actually convinced, if any modern mysticism of lasting value were to be built here.

But it was not just that traditional mysticism needs the university and its intellectuals to survive in American culture. It was that modern intellectuals actually *know more* than the mystical traditions themselves. Bertrand Russell, Bharati notes, may have been a better logician than Śaṅkara, and C. G. Jung may have in fact known more about psychology than Patañjali, the ancient author of the *Yoga-sūtras* (OR, 196). These, of course, were and still are unpopular, politically incorrect things to think and say, but Bharati thought them (as many no doubt do); moreover—and this is what sets him apart—he also *said* them.

He clearly and understandably wanted some more company here, even as he saw himself as a kind of leader, a paradigmatic model, if you will, for this more intellectual, radical, and mystical future: "It [the study of mysticism] must now be done by one who is an insider, an initiate, a professional in the field of mysticism, but who is also a professional social scientist and hence a social critic. Voilà, here we are" (LC, 11). Moreover, Bharati bragged, still in his voilà, that he didn't practice the usual anthropological compromise of participant observation: "this book *[The Light at the Center]* . . . is the result of *participation* rather than 'participant observation'" (LC, 11; italics his). Bharati, of course, knew that he had many predecessors in the study of mysticism "from the inside" (even if none were quite as strange as he was). Indeed, he sensed—quite correctly, I think—that much, if not most, of the modern study of mysticism was ultimately driven by the mystical experiences, working behind the scenes in subtle ways, of the scholars themselves. He thus did not flinch from putting modern scholars of mysticism in the same list with founding figures in the history of Christian mysticism, but interestingly, he saw both groups as rhetorically compromised by their social, religious, and professional contexts. Their zero-experiences thus became theology or mere echoes heard among the technicalities of acceptable scholarship advanced most recently by such people as Evelyn Underhill and R. C. Zaehner (LC, 68). He also deeply respected Alan Watts, primarily for his experiment-prone, hedonistic nature and his success in translating difficult Asian ideas into a quasi-scholarly prose that was also accessible to a popular audience (LC, 92): "Here was a man," Bharati declared, as if from the authority of his own mystical experiences, "who knew what he was talking about" (LC, 81). And indeed, one sometimes gets the impression that Bharati saw himself as a more learned and authoritative Alan Watts addressing the American counterculture and the universities.

As for other scholars, his reactions were more ambivalent. He obviously respected R. C. Zaehner as the "best educated and the shrewdest apologist for Christian mysticism" (LC, 50), and he suspected strongly that Zaehner had actually had at least one zero-experience (LC, 51), but he resisted vehemently Zaehner's well-known attempts to subsume Indian monism into a decidedly Catholic theistic theological vision, as well as his pious resistance to Huxley's hedonistic and aesthetic claims for parallels between hallucinogenic and mystical states.[78] Still, he obviously liked the fact that such scholars of mysticism were almost never only mystics, that is, that they had other interests, both intellectual and cultural. In James Horne's terms, Bharati was clearly arguing for the superiority of the "mixed mystic," the mystic who does not allow mysticism or its techniques to become ends in themselves but uses them to struggle with some intellectual, artistic, social, or scientific problem.[79] "The mystics I have known or read were not mystics pure and simple," he wrote. "They also happened to be theologians, ecclesiastics, musicians, scientists, and anthropologists" (LC, 60). Such a mixed state is especially apt for those to whom the zero-experience comes only occasionally, for then it becomes necessary to "fill in the gaps" with interesting and rewarding pursuits of a different nature. Bharati understood himself as just such a mixed mystic; he is clear that his anthropological and academic profession would have been psychologically impossible had he experienced ecstatic states as many times as, say, Ramakrishna, whose psycho-neurological condition he considered to be more or less unique (LC, 96). Pleasure, especially mystical pleasure, is just too seductive, and there can be no discursive thought within monistic states of absorption (LC, 38). Moreover, emotional distance, at least some distance, is crucial for discursive, rational, objective thinking (LC, 213), and religious enthusiasm usually submerges one's critical and rational faculties, especially at the beginning (OR, 211). The mixed mystic is thus preferable to the pure mystic when it comes to adequately interpreting such states.

But, paradoxically, being "inside" the experience is just as crucial as the objectivity that scholarly distance provides. There is no question here of being *either* an "insider" *or* an "outsider" for Bharati; both are necessary for genuine insight into the nature of mysticism.[80] Bharati thus argued that any mystic who happens also to be a scholar must live in the world in a "schizophrenic" manner (LC, 82), thinking both "outside" the experience in a discursive, rational fashion, and existing—usually rather sporadically—"inside" the experience in a nondiscursive, emotional, ecstatic way. Such a dialectical existence may border on the schizophrenic — for one can never exist "inside" and "outside" the mystical state at the same time[81]—but it also creates a psychic condition and a hermeneutical perspective uniquely attuned to understanding the nature of mysticism.

Language and the Mystical:
Speaking Inside and Outside the Light

Of course, such talk about being on the inside and/or the outside is not something new in the history of mysticism; indeed, it replicates a quite traditional esoteric structure present in many of the historical traditions, often for the very same antinomian and erotic reasons that necessitated Bharati's own esotericism (which, if the truth be told, he wasn't very good at). Similarly, Bharati's "schizophrenic" scholar-mystic finds many parallels in the history of mysticism, particularly in India, where such Tantric sects as the Vaiṣṇava Sahajiyās and the Kartābhajās developed elaborate ritual and textual devices to create a *Homo duplex* who could exist simultaneously—or at least serially—in both the socially constructed dharma and in the ritual dissolution of that same dharma within the Tantric community.[82] What makes Bharati particularly interesting for our own present purposes—an exploration of the problems and promises of the interpenetration of the scholar's subjective religious experience and his or her subsequent public theorizing—is that he was quite aware of the paradoxical nature of his existential situation, and that, consequently, he developed some rather sophisticated rhetorical strategies, hermeneutical devices, and philosophical positions to "bridge" the chasm that yawned between Bharati the mystic and Bharati the scholar. He knew, in other words, that he was a *Homo duplex,* but he also strove "to become one." Much of this striving to bridge the chasm and to turn the two into one involved the philosophical analysis or technical use of language. That is, once again, he theorized out of his own existential situation and subjective experiences, which he proposed to use as a kind of methodological control point (LC, 38). His academic method thus flowed out of his mystical path, and his mystical path was part of his academic method.

Of course, in one sense, there is very little about Bharati's personality and writing style that could be called "esoteric." Quite the contrary, pace his own occasional rhetorical nods to the contrary (see, for example, "Speaking about 'That Which Shows Itself'" and the epigraph to OR), there was very little indeed about which the man would not speak, and speak all too clearly. I suspect the reasons for this disarming honesty and penchant for scandal were largely psychological, as I suggested above. But it is also true that Bharati learned sometime in midlife to justify his no-nonsense approach with insights gleaned from Wittgenstein and the Anglo-American school of analytic language philosophy that he inspired. Perhaps this is why both *The Ochre Robe* and *The Light at the Center* begin with epigraphs from Wittgenstein on the esoteric, that is, nonlinguistic, nature of the mystical: "Worüber man nicht sprechen kann, darüber muss man schweigen" [One must be silent about that about which one cannot speak]; and "das zeigt sich. Das ist das Mystische" [Mysticism is that which shows itself].[83] I think that Bharati read and propounded analytic language philosophy in general as a kind of intellectual apophaticism, as a way to "clear the deck," as it were, for genuine quest. Certainly he approved of its radical nominalism and rejection of ontological referents, for here, Bharati thought, it approached the cathartic insights of Buddhism.[84]

More significantly, however, Bharati ceaselessly invoked the analytic distinction between etic and emic speech, the former being the objective, descriptive, "outsider's" understanding of the phenomenon under study, the latter the subjective, emotional, "insider's" view. Bharati loved to use this simple distinction to lambaste and deconstruct people's assumptions about what is obvious and real, including and especially the nature of mysticism. "Talking, thinking, and writing about mysticism is not mysticism, just as talking, thinking, and writing about poetry isn't poetry" (LC, 37). That is to say, etic, scholarly speech about mysticism is just that—descriptive speech *about* mysticism. It is important and helpful and perhaps even propaedeutic, but it is not the real thing. It is not emic speech arising "from the inside" of the practice and experience. On the other hand, purely emic speech that issues from within the traditional doctrinal vocabularies of the mystical traditions is problematic as well, for it inevitably tends to reify its own emotionally laden categories and to treat them as objective descriptions of objectively real structures. That is to say, emic speech, especially in mystical traditions, often tends to want to pass itself off as literal description. And this is clearly wrong. Mystical language must be recognized for what it is—a kind of beautiful poetry issuing from intense subjective psychological experiences which may or may not have an ontological referent outside the human subject. Bharati refused, adamantly and passionately, to assign any necessary ontological implications to mystical experience: *"[T]he mystical experience does not confer ontological status upon its content."*[85] All mystical talk of "reality" and "unreality" possesses only psychological significance and has no ontological reference. It does not, however, follow that the mystic realizes that his or her reference is psychological (LC, 79). Bharati, in other words, adopted a clear psychological hermeneutics of suspicion to understand and interpret the traditional mystic, who, lacking the self-reflexivity and categories of modern psychology, inevitably confuses the emic with the etic. Such a move may be understandable—for the experiences often display euphoric, expansive, narcissistic characteristics of mythological proportions (LC, 216)—but it is also bad philosophy, for the move collapses the all-important distinction between etic and emic speech and advances a claim that cannot hold up to careful critical analysis.[86] There are thus for Bharati two kinds of mystics, and subsequently, two kinds of scholars of mysticism: "wise" mystics and scholars, who do not claim any objective referent for mystical experience; and "unwise" mystics and scholars, who do.[87] Any scholar or believer who thus confuses the etic for the emic, or vice versa, can only end up producing a discourse that Bharati liked to humorously describe, following G. D. Berreman, as "anemic" and "emetic,"[88] that is, bloodless and pukey.

This is where we should also place Bharati's important category of "postulation," which he contrasted with the more traditional cognitive process of "belief." The distinction runs throughout Bharati's corpus but is most clearly explained in his short piece "Religion for the Thinking Person." There he explains in clear terms that belief in any traditional religious object, god, or principle is naive, for it must again confuse emic language with etic explanation. What then to do with the simple fact that all the major religions come with some fairly heavy ritual, doctrinal, and mythological "baggage," even if this baggage is simply the historical consequence of their origins in distant places and times? Interestingly enough, Bharati argued that the modern religious person does not have the option of "picking and choosing"; one must either adopt the religious tradition in some form of its wholeness or surrender any hope of being genuinely religious. But how can the former be accomplished today with integrity? One should *postulate* the existence of the gods or whatever the religious doctrine posits, acting and thinking and feeling *as if* they existed. "To postulate means to accept, believe, assume a thing, state of affairs, doctrine *as though* it were true, existent, *as though* it were 'the case.'"[89] Bharati argued that the emotional, aesthetic, and psychological effects of such an intellectual act are identical to those produced by naive belief, that the process can be therapeutic,[90] and that one need not sacrifice the intellect's own innate integrity to practice it. On a biographical note, even as a Hindu chaplain at Syracuse, Bharati, true to this postulating but not necessarily believing form, would firmly resist all attempts to pry from him his own beliefs. When pressed by students for his own beliefs, "None of your business" was reported to be his usual reply.[91]

Since this recommended method strongly resembles the *epoché* of the phenomenologists (as well as Paul Ricoeur's related "second naïveté "), we might be surprised to learn that Bharati despised the discipline of phenomenology[92] and had some critical things to say about its contemporary practice, which he seemed to more or less equate with the Chicago school of Mircea Eliade, Joseph Kitagawa, and Charles Long.[93] In particular, he objected to the modern category of the "symbol"—the liṅgam is not a "symbol" of Śiva, he argued, it *is* Śiva—perhaps because it allowed an emotional and intellectual distance that his own notion of postulation and participation denied.

Such a "bracketed" phenomenology was not enough for Bharati. He wanted genuine and radical *engagement*. He wanted, in his deepest philosophical and mystical heart, a future postulating mystic who could schizophrenically talk both emically and etically,[94] some rare and unusual soul that would need neither the God talk of theology nor the protective indirectness of scholarship to talk about the zero-experience pure and simple: "The Christian mystic, until this century, could not possibly isolate his zero-experience report from other Christian talk, since such isolation was totally alien to the analyses and reporting strategies. Today the mystic who happens to be a social scientist can feel reasonably certain that future mystics will learn to reject the stylistic shell of their environment when they report their zero-experiences" (LC, 99). Bharati thus recognized that there were and still are political issues at work in the construction and preservation of emic speech and the suppression of etic language, for in the past to speak etically about such experiences would have in effect amounted to a radical challenge to both the church and the political authorities, both of whom built their right to rule on the emic-etic confusion of theology and objective truth. Etic speech about the mystical is thus not simply a dry exercise for the professorial analytic philosopher or anthropologist. It is "a relentless analysis" that can lead to "the possible loss of one's own cherished traditions."[95] It is thus, potentially at least, radical politics. It is power.

It is obvious by now, I think, that Bharati would have strenuously resisted what we now call constructivism, best exemplified in the work of Steven Katz, and would have argued for some form of universal essentialism (LC, 80),[96] as it has been variously defined by W. T. Stace,[97] Ninian Smart, and, more recently and more subtlely, Robert Forman.[98] Bharati was clear that there is only one zero-experience, although there are many mysticisms that are generated by the cultural, linguistic, and doctrinal contexts of this experience (LC, 141). He also liked to invoke Noam Chomsky here; there may indeed be some innate human given about the mystical experience (as Chomsky argued for language), but there nevertheless must be some particular tradition or linguistic grid in which to express it.[99] There can be no general or universal mysticism, just as there can be no general or universal language,[100] and all abstract talk of ontology is beside the point for the practicing Tāntrika, who wants to taste and drink the forbidden: "[T]he mystical adept is interested in *filet mignon* and sparkling burgundy, the ontologist is interested in food and drink."[101] Moreover, unlike Louis Massignon, who believed in the mystical potentials of language and textual study, Bharati stated clearly that he did not believe that studying Sanskrit and Tibetan could generate mystical experience.[102] He consequently maintained a clear, outspoken nominalist position throughout his writings (DL, 57), asserting that we must never mistake our words and concepts for actual things. In the end, learning is like a beautiful vase in a princely courtyard, a wonderful place to hold and even aesthetically enhance the flower of mystical experience but in itself quite unable to produce that flower, which is identical in the learned and the unlearned (OR, 61). Or, in a more Bharatian metaphor, which he learned from a woman-saint, learning is said to be like red hibiscus on a beautiful woman; she is most lovely nude, but when she dresses up and puts red hibiscus flowers in her hair, "something seems to be added to her perfection" (OR, 124).

Esoteric and Mystical-Hermeneutical Strategies

Still, there *are* places, quite a few of them actually, in Bharati's corpus where this almost absolute distinction between etic and emic speech, between the philosophical precision of scholarship and the aesthetic pleasures of religious experience, breaks down, where the vase and the flower, the woman and the red hibiscus begin to merge. The swami does, after all, insist on linguistic study as a prerequisite for serious mystical praxis among American students,[103] and he constantly invokes his own linguistic capabilities to assert his own cultural and religious authority to speak on things Indian. Moreover, despite his essentialist views, it seems apparent that many of his own mystical experiences were imbued with linguistic-doctrinal structures, and that his extensive reading in Indian mystical literature and, later, in the Sanskrit sources, played more than a little role

Writing Out of the Light at the Center 243

in his experiences. But more important, even if he did want to hold that language could not lead to the mystical (as his Wittgenstein quotes seem to suggest), he clearly did believe that mystical experience could and does lead to a more profound understanding of language. Indeed, for Bharati, mystical experience can grant the cognitively gifted scholar[104] both a rhetorical power for writing his or her own texts and a certain hermeneutical gnosis for reading those of others. The mystical overflows into the hermeneutical. "Literally, or obliquely, mysticism seems to remain his central theme—and the zero-experience lingers at the back of his mind and his speech. I believe it is precisely this that gives charisma to even the driest mystic" (LC, 54). Or the driest scholar of mysticism, I would add. Consequently, there are certain "linguistic cues" that the mystically gifted can hermeneutically detect in the writings of both the mystics and, more interesting still, scholars of mysticism, Jung and Zaehner in particular. A problem, however, arises here, particularly with the latter academic writers, as the technical and theological language of these modes of writing so obfuscates the zero-experience that only someone who has actually had a zero-experience will be able to determine if a particular historian of mysticism has had the experience as well, and this from other textual clues that Bharati unfortunately does not specify for us (LC, 57). In very similar terms, Bharati argued that one could recognize a true mystic by his or her *monolexis,* that is, by the idiosyncratic, nontraditional hermeneutical strategies that he or she used to read the traditional texts, in effect transforming the historical scripture into a symbol or metaphor for his or her own mystical experiences. Such a move is necessary, Bharati thought, to prevent any overly dysfunctional break with the tradition and cultural surround (LC, 67). Bharati himself no doubt practiced this hermeneutical technique with his privileging of the Tattirīya Upaniṣad's *ānanda-mimāṃsa* ("analysis of bliss") as a means to establish his own hedonistic reading of the scriptures (LC, 29–30; DL, 16),[105] with his idiosyncratic reading of state of the *brahmacarya* (traditionally understood as "one who is celibate" but which Bharati read literally, in what he claimed was a Tantric fashion,[106] as "one who moves in Brahman"; DL, 50; LC, 229), and, more radically, with his experience of legitimating the ancient Upaniṣads by means of his own monistic experiences: "I felt that I had authorized the scriptural statement *aham brahmāsmi* [I am the Brahman] . . . that in an irreverently anachronistic fashion, I had authenticated the Upaniṣad" (LC, 41). Indeed, Bharati's entire written corpus can be read as an example of just such an act of *monolexis,* a "singular reading" that maintained its connections to the historical tradition primarily through the ingenuity and sheer persistence of the monk's personality and charisma.

Bharati also proposed that not confusing the emic and the etic does not imply that an anthropologist or historian of religions should not take the emic corpus seriously as a possible source of truth and theory,[107] much as Paul Feyerabend suggested that physicists draw on anything and everything—from astrology to witchcraft—to think about their problems.[108] "[T]he yogi's or other mystic's talk about time, space, homunculi and their removal must be taken for their etic potential as well, since they may contain important scientific truths, albeit couched in scientifically quaint terms."[109] Bharati is quite modest and humble about what these important truths might be (arguing for their therapeutic, psychological, and apophatic potentials), but he nevertheless suggests that the emic can generate etic truths, that is, that the boundary can and should be crossed by those with the proper philosophical training.

Along similar experiential-hermeneutical lines, Bharati privileges scholars who have had the zero-experience over those who have not and confesses that he would have never written either *The Tantric Tradition* or "Śākta and Vajrayāna" without his own active participation in the "nondiscursive, 'spiritual' patterns of quest" within these traditions: "I hope that sensitive readers will feel rather than spot my own personal commitment to them," he writes.[110] Here, of course, we enter a kind of "soft esotericism" that gently pushes back the uninitiated and the outsider. Such an outside realm may be ruled by W. T. Stace, the greatest of the outsiders (LC, 60), but it still remains the outside. Only the scholar-mystic who could speak about the mystical in both an emotionally warm, even ecstatic, emic fashion and in an analytical, descriptive, and philosophically astute, etic way will finally be able to "crack the code" (LC, 174).

But perhaps nowhere does Bharati's esoteric hermeneutics appear more clearly than in his numerous treatments of that uniquely Tantric use of language called *sandhā-bhāṣā* (literally, "intentional language"), a "code language," Bharati tells us, "understood only by the tantric group."[111] Consisting of a set of sexual metaphors or similes encoded in ontological or mystical terms, the terminology can be interpreted either literally (as sexual) or metaphorically (as referring to some mystical state of consciousness), depending—and this is the important part—on the aspirant's state of advancement.[112] The highest (or deepest) hermeneutical levels, however, seem to be reserved for those practitioners who can read and use the language to refer to both levels *at the same time*. Eliade put it this way in his classical study of Tantric yoga: "The *sandhā-bhāṣā* . . . seeks to . . . project the yogin into the 'paradoxical situation' indispensable to his training. The semantic polyvalence of words finally substitutes ambiguity for the usual system of reference inherent in every ordinary language. And this destruction of language contributes, in its way too, toward 'breaking' the profane universe and replacing it by a universe of convertible and integrable planes."[113]

Also important here—and something almost never commented on by too serious scholars—is the intended mischievousness and delightful sexual humor of the Tāntrikas and their doubly "intentional" texts. Sudhir Kakar, one of those rare scholars who knows when to smile in print, captured this aspect of *sandhā-bhāṣā* beautifully in his description of his encounter with some Tāntrikas and their playfully paradoxical understanding of *ānanda,* or "bliss": "Whenever the term *ananda* came up in the text—and *ananda* comes up often, since it is the name of the state in which every tantrik must aspire to live perpetually—and I translated it as 'supreme bliss,' I was told to forget all the mystical balderdash since *ananda* was the pure and simple pleasure of intercourse. If I took the concrete meaning . . . then I was invariably chided for my literal-mindedness since the word in that particular context just happened to stand for 'enlightenment.'"[114] Bharati, like Kakar, "got the joke" (and told it as well) in both its literal and spiritual senses. He relates a famous example of *sandhā-bhāṣā* from Tarkālaṁkāra's commentary on the Mahānirvāṇa Tantra: "mātṛyonau liṅgaṃ kṣiptvā bhaginīstanamardanaṃ gurumūrdhni pādaṃ dattvā punarjanma na vidyate." Literally, the sentence reads "having slipped [his] penis in [his] mother's vagina, fondled [his] sister's breasts, and placed [his] foot on [his] guru's head, he will not be born again," but it can also be read in code language as a description of the *kuṇḍalinī*'s ascent through the interior *cakra*s, or in Bharati's rendering: "Having first meditated on the *śakti* located in the coccygeal center, then on the female energy represented in the heart region, he penetrates with his meditation into the uppermost center located in the cranium and experiences enstasis."[115] Obviously, there are easier, less scandalous (and less oedipal) ways to say such things; hence, one might also conclude that such language also is meant to function as a kind of outrageous shock technique, both for the prudish outsiders, who need to be scandalized off, and for the initiated, who are seeking liberation through precisely this kind of transgressive linguistic-emotional experience. Little wonder that Bharati understood the Tantric traditions themselves as esoteric traditions—persecuted, subversive, always to be denied by the social order.[116]

"Dear Lalita": A Bharatian Esoteric Text?

Clearly, there are numerous places in Bharati's corpus where esoteric hermeneutical principles are literally invoked, but none perhaps are as fascinating as the case of his fictional letter-book to a Bengali lover named Lalita. I discovered this text in his personal library. Significantly, it does not appear in the exhaustive bibliography of his works published in the *Syranthropy* memorial issue, nor have I found any references to it in his later writings. Moreover, the copy I found displays physical characteristics that suggest (but cannot prove) possible censorship, either on Bharati's part, which I personally cannot imagine, or on the part of someone else (which I can): its cover and publication page are ripped off, leaving us without any reliable publication details (except a date—1962), and the entire second half (?) of the book, which treats the nature of Tantric practice (DL, 50, 63), is completely missing, again ripped right from the two simple staples that hold the entire document together. The typescript suggests an Indian publisher. The text is directed, we are told, "to those who are interested in the sort of experimentation that follows from the traditional modes of *sādhana*, particularly tantric" (preface page). The entire text is written in the form of a personal letter to Lalita, perhaps in the tradition of the Tantras themselves, many of which advance as an intimate colloquy between the god Śiva and his consort the Devī. Also an exercise in what Bharati called "cultural criticism," the text was "bound to antagonize many, and to enthuse a few." "But this," Bharati quickly and unapologetically adds with his usual confidence, "is the hallmark of any important book" (preface to DL).

The book is indeed important, if most for its deeply personal revelations of Bharati's heart and mind. Here Bharati confesses that he has failed, almost completely, to win a following in India for his hedonistic reading of the scriptures (DL, 13) and identifies himself as a Tāntrika (DL, 14) and hedonist whose goal in life is "to experience as much pleasure as possible, and as little pain as possible" (DL, 15). For this, he confides to Lalita (and so to us), he has been ostracized as a heretic from both "pious India" and "philistine Europe." Significantly, only a few academics and those who love him take him seriously (DL, 15). Bharati, as a good hedonist, then proceeds to outline the things that he most hates, that is, those that bring him suffering, and those that he most loves, that

Writing Out of the Light at the Center 247

is, those things that bring him the most pleasure. "I shall, as a skilled pedagogue, begin with what I hate," he writes (LC, 19). But before he begins, he notes, in a very revealing passage, that his hatred of things that are so commonly loved by so many people makes him "much hated with so many people—far more than you may be knowing" (DL, 20). Here we catch a hint of just how problematic a man he was within his own Hindu tradition.

Bharati's list of hated things revolves around what he calls "ugliness," culminating in the category of puritanism (DL, 37–40), which "mars or destroys beauty, which I love most of all things" (DL, 38). The three most beautiful things in the world for Bharati were—in this order, I think— women, classical music, and anthropology (DL, 25). If the last member strikes the reader as a bit odd, remember that Bharati was a humanist at heart, a lover of human beings; hence, he glossed his trinity of beauty this way: "comparing human beings with each other, enjoying them and giving them enjoyment" (DL, 25). Still, the emphasis was unmistakably on the enjoyment of human beauty, particularly as it was manifested—in traditional Śākta theology—in the body and person of a woman. And here, in this text, Bharati writes openly about his own sex life and its importance in measuring the richness of his life. "Great men," he begins in one of his many memorable moments of *hubris,* "like Cicero, Sri Krishna, or Agehananda measure their own worth not by the tape used for them by others, but by the richness of their own life," and "no life," he immediately adds, "can be rich without sex" (DL, 50). He goes on: "I constantly harp on and recur to sex, because I hold that the erotic part of it is the prototype and in a way the consummation of the rich life. I shall show you later that the monastic and mystical life are entirely based on a particular set of experiences which are, in the last analysis, erotic" (DL, 50). Unfortunately, this is the very part that some (offended?) reader literally ripped from our historical grasp. "I shall yet have to tell you about the constant ordinance of *cherche la femme* as a possible *sādhana* toward the end of this letter" (DL, 63), but alas, we *cherchons la femme* in vain. Still, much of Bharati's Tantric eroticism survives, both here in his letter to Lalita and strewn throughout his later writings. I have dealt with it in some depth above. Here it is necessary only to point out that Bharati did not hesitate to comment on the embarrassing and unaesthetic proportions of the male organ (DL, 61–62), speculate on the hormonal and biological origins of sexual orientation and arousal (DL, 61), write about the techniques and psychology of sexual practice, much along the lines of the *kāma-śāstra* literature of India, and share in print the details of his own sexual-religious fantasies (DL, 58–60); indeed, he scolded his fellow Tāntrikas for engaging in their elaborate techniques only for the sake of *mokṣa* or *mukti:* "[M]y stipulation is that all these various pursuits, including sadhanas towards *Mukti,* and *Mukti* itself (whatever that may be, and it may be so many various states)—must be just items in the rich life" (DL, 52). If Bharati was a Tāntrika, then, he was first and foremost a humanist Tāntrika who insisted on the secular and physical components as themselves worthy of respect, dignity, and sacrality. I might also point out here Bharati's lifelong love of Indian erotic sculpture and the simple fact that his library was particularly rich in eroticism: there I found many Indological works on various sexual aspects of Indian mythology, ritual, and practice, as well as the usual coffee-table presentations of Indian eroticism, and even a few more technical but still popular sexological books on the biological nature of human sexuality and reproduction, one of which (tucked away in a cabinet) was entitled simply *The Secret.*

Indeed it was, at least of Bharati's life and writings.

Conclusion: Disappearing into the Light at the Center

Like the picture book on sexual reproduction tucked away in the cabinet, Bharati too has been "shelved," at least for the moment, by Indologists and historians of religions. One does not hear his name much anymore, and a recent search on my part for secondary sources on his life and/or work turned up very little indeed.[117] Perhaps it is just too early. Or perhaps Bharati's spirit has become what his work argued so passionately for all those years: an intellectual form of transgression. Bharati's thought and person, after all, stand solidly against contemporary anti-Orientalism and its virtual demonization of Western scholarship. Strangely, this need not be the case, for Bharati's very existence powerfully deconstructed the categories of "East" and "West" in a kind of postmodern ecstasy of cultural confusion. Still, Bharati remains a problem, and for the very reason that was predicted long ago by his own guru, Swami Visvananda—Bharati, as Visvananda put it, had a "big white body," and this would make it difficult for him to win recognition and the authority to speak. To make matters even more problematic, this man in the big white body was a vehement critic of the Hindu Renaissance and its modern gurus, and he insisted on writing about a long list of politically incorrect, potentially explosive themes throughout his life (eroticism, fascism, fraudulent religious figures, drugs, etc.).

It is worth noting here at the end, however, that with age came a certain emotional mellowing, a settling down, and a new, more generous openness to syncretistic forms of religion as legitimate forms of tradition worthy of intellectual consideration. Perhaps related to this late transformation is the fact that in the mid-1980s he went on a strict diet and lost over one hundred pounds. As his body changed and aged, so too, it seemed, did his mental and emotional attitudes. And he began to dream of a specifically Western Tantrism that would be committed to women's equality and liberation in every sense of that word, that would recognize women not as ritual objects to employ for some strictly soteriological end, but as human subjects and agents worthy of dignity and respect in their own right. Of this he saw clear signs in the 1988 Society of Tantric Studies conference that one of his graduate students, Roxanne Gupta, had arranged at Syracuse. The ethical was informing the mystical more and more.[118]

Bharati may have indeed stood "in the Light at the Center"—I have no doubt that he had a series of profound mystical experiences and thought in and out of their Light—but it was a Light few seem willing to gaze into. Bharati, of course, would not have been surprised by this; indeed, he more or less predicted it with his understanding that the mystical is transgressive to its psychophysiological core. Perhaps, then, we should read the cross-cultural wonder and sexual scandal of Agehananda Bharati as unusually clear signs that this man lived up to both his name—"the Indian Blissful Being Homeless"—and his own Tantric understandings of the mystical, that antinomian, erotic, amoral presence which must always remain an embarrassment to those who stand outside the Light at the Center.

SECRET TALK *The Descent*

For Blake, unconsciousness and instinctual impulses are not categories that exist only below consciousness, but above and beyond consciousness as well. The portion that exists beyond consciousness is, however, the visionary perspective of the fourth fold. . . . Freud classed the intellectual processes among displacements of sexual energy. "The energy for the work of thought itself must be supplied from sublimated erotic sources." From the visionary or fourth-fold perspective, the formulation must be reversed. But from the natural perspective, Blake would agree that Freud's formulation is exactly correct.

Diana Hume George, *Blake and Freud*

What was attempted at the end of the last century, in Freud's time, what all sorts of decent souls around Charcot and others were trying to do, was to reduce mysticism to questions of cum *(affaires de foutre)*. If you look closely, that's not it at all. Doesn't this jouissance one experiences and yet knows nothing about put us on the path of ex-istence? And why not interpret one's face of the Other, the God face, as based on feminine jouissance?

Jacques Lacan, "God and ~~Woman~~'s Jouissance"

If . . . we claim that the *yoga* and *sādhanā* pattern may provide a replacement for the analyst or even for psychotherapy, the highly specialized techniques of tantrism, especially of the [left-handed] *vāma*-divisions might *a fortiori* help resolve that wide range of puzzles and agonies which centre in the libido, or more specifically, in the sexual component of the human individual. The *ācāryas* [teachers] . . . constantly speak of their method as methods of healing, and of their systems as essentially therapeutic systems. . . . There is no reason why the modern thinker should not translate this into modern idiom—not only through a postulational "as if," but by taking tantric suggestions as seriously as he would take the analyst or the psychiatrist seriously.

Agehananda Bharati, "Śākta and Vajrayāna: Their Place in Indian Thought"

OBVIOUSLY, THE ECSTASY of that Night did not appear out of nowhere. It was powerfully, if by no means completely, contextualized within any number of emotional, cultural, and religious spaces, and hence it can be read on any number of levels and with any number of evaluative conclusions: as the fantasy of a foreigner suffering in a distant land from the minor traumas of culture shock, loneliness, and simple physical exhaustion; as an elaborate dream translation of the Bengali texts in which I had absorbed myself almost completely; as a romantic expression of the now highly criticized orientalist frame of mind in which India is seen as the archetypal site of spiritual pilgrimage, visionary odyssey, and mystical experience; or simply as an unusually intense erotic dream linked, like most dreams, to the previous days' events, in this case my trip to Kalighat and participation in the aesthetically overwhelming events of citywide Kālī-*pūjās*. And all of these readings would capture something of the experience.

But as with all individual symbolic experiences, the most significant truths inevitably rely on the ideas and meanings that the person having the experience spontaneously associates with the event. My own associations were organized around a single mythical complex: that of ascent and descent. And these, of course, were implicated in the vision itself, which clearly understood itself not as a descending to a subconscious realm of darkness and dumb instinct, but as an ascending to a superconscious dimension of terrifying emptiness and noetically charged erotic energies. Very much like Blake's fourth-fold visionary perspective, then, the vision wanted to claim that the mystical and the erotic are mutually enfolded, but that it is the mystical as the empty ground of consciousness itself that is ontologically prior, or in Blake's more poetic terms, that "[t]he Treasures of Heaven are not Negations of Passion but Realities of the Intellect from which all the passions Emanate Uncurbed." Somehow, however, it was the erotic that had provided the plumb line into this treasured intellect.

Other less metaphysical, more personal meanings were supplied by the vision's own images. Specifically, as I was descending from the ecstasy, I saw a demon-baby appear in front of me. Instinctively, I stared at it until it dissolved into the psychic space from which it had emerged. The image made sense, since the previous day I had been to Kalighat and witnessed a family carrying its dead baby to the goddess, a sign for me of the fear and dread that every hopeful parent must feel. My heart was torn in two for the family as I gazed at the tiny limp corpse they carried with such love and pain. The act of dissolving the demon-baby immediately after a descent from the "high" of the rapture thus spoke of a definitive turning around from the safe, if terrifying, absorption and annihilation of the mystical back into the always uncertain world of social and familial relationships, that is, into human life. To love another human being is to set oneself up for the pain of death and separation. Solitude is safer, but it is also loveless.

As with my archaic "memory" of wanting out of the womb, the patterns of this mystical experience thus spoke of a turning *from* the mystical *to* the social, to life in the world, outside the womb, outside the ecstasy. Significantly, the rapture ended not with some beatific vision, but in my wife's brother's living room, with Erica, our golden retriever, licking me in the face—an archetypal American domestic scene, if ever there was one (in "real" life, I should add, Erica's effusive affections annoyed me to no end). Practically, the descent also meant returning to a dissertation, which would become a book, which, as I have tried to show, was itself psychologically, hermeneutically, and mystically connected to that Night. Although well on its way by the time of this event, the dissertation was "conceived" in some sense on that Night within a supersexualized encounter between a young graduate student and a numinous Presence. It was indeed "Kālī's Child."

I finished the first half of my researches in Calcutta energized by the glow of that event and returned to the States to see my wife over the Christmas holidays. On my return, as I entered a dingy bathroom stall in JFK Airport, I realized that during the last few months I had somehow, through dream and ecstasy and textual study, resolved the crisis of the crucified erection that had almost taken my life. I now understood the fantasy. I could quite consciously interpret it. And because I could interpret it, I could also transcend it. Consequently, I no longer desired to deny my sexuality and all that it expressed (or did not express) about my engagement with and disengagement from the world. The incestuous connection between Mother and Lover had been severed, and both the Virgin Mother of my Catholic upbringing, whose impossible oedipal structure almost killed me, and the Tantric goddess of Bengal, whose erotic-noetic energies I was literally stunned by but whose promise of maternal merger I had to refuse, had been transformed into an imaginal Presence far closer to the Lover of my original myth-dream, whose noetic-erotic truths both healed me and pushed me to write. And in fact, even she was gone now, having been happily replaced by a real woman, my wife. In essence, I now saw that the patterns of my life were not directed toward the intensely terrifying pleasures of ecstatic absorption; hence that Night that was both a refusal to merge with the Mother and an insistence to descend from the mystical into my own individuality, my own heteroerotic existence, my own destiny seen darkly now in the myth of the original dream-vision of the darkly burning unicorn that had to be freed from its watery fury. I would keep my head, for now. I would love a woman, not a goddess. The Tantra, mediated through Freud, had helped to heal me.

And yet, in another, very real sense, I never did descend (and perhaps never will), for in everything I write the Fire somehow returns, and this often quite despite my best efforts to keep it away or suppressed or at least safely muted. It speaks despite me and yet in and as me. I do not think. I am thought. And in this I sense her fiery form again—laughing, dancing, burning, sticking that long tongue out at us and all our little box-like socialized egos. The written text, even as scholarship, thus has a mystical life of its own, and it is her life, somehow still flowing out of the noetic-erotic energies of that Night. It is the corpus come alive beneath the goddess.

*   *   *

24 May 1994. My "holding on" that Night—it was a turning back, a refusal to let go, but it was also a descent, an embodiment, an act of incarnation. From the perspective of transcendence, it was a failure of sorts. From the perspective of this world, it was a coming back, an affirmation. From the perspective of reality as a whole, *it is all the same*—transcendence, immanence, ecstasy, descent, ascent . . . these are all relative terms, relative, that is, to an ego.

3 January 1995. Last night the Fire visited me again. This time it was a bit different, an overall intensity with nowhere to go and yet focused in my head, pouring out, pointing out, like a long channel of fire or an immense horn. I saw myself lying in bed with this immense horn of energy extending seven or eight feet out of the top of my skull. I tried to be absorbed into the abyss, but I couldn't, because I . . . because I knew I belonged here.

12 November 1999. Were the *liṅgam*s I saw floating in my dream space that Night signs of intense sexual arousal? Or severed phalluses functioning as threats of maternal absorption or castration? Or Bataille-like

images of orgasm as ecstatic death *(le petit mort)*, beheading, and release into a cosmic continuum? Or Lacanian castrations moving me into a jouissance "beyond the phallus"? Or something of all four? In my present mind, the fact that I turned from the mystical absorption and descended back into egoic consciousness signals a phallic position, a "heroic" decision not "to become one." I thus emerge from the Mother a man. (Interestingly, I slipped here and wrote, "I *merge* from the Mother a man.")

8 July 2000. The *śakti* or power of that Night was both erotic and noetic, that is to say, its energies carried both an unbearably intense pleasure, which I can still feel in my body, and an intuitive grasp of the texts and their doctrinal content, which still often almost physically overwhelms me. I am reminded here of the story told in Saradananda's *Līlāprasaṅga* (1.2.1). Narendra had already developed what the text calls the power to transmit religion *(dharma-śakti-saṃkramana)* to others through touch. He decides to use this new power on a meditating brother-disciple in order to teach him about the secret truths of nonduality, which Ramakrishna had shared with Narendra by giving him scriptural texts he explicitly forbade others to read. Narendra asks the brother to touch his knee. The disciple does and feels a distinct shock, which he compares to touching an electric battery. This allows the disciple to meditate more deeply, but, unfortunately, he is not ready for such an ontological revelation and, consequently, cannot assimilate the energy's innate doctrine. Ramakrishna scolds Narendra for giving to the disciple something for which he was not yet intellectually and religiously ready (interestingly, he compared Narendra's attempted *śakti-pāta* (initiatory transmission) to a forbidden sexual act, that is, the impregnation of a woman already six months into her pregnancy—such an act, we are told, destroys the delicate development of the pregnancy and ruins everything). Saradananda then informs us that, because the teaching came too suddenly and without the proper preparation, the disciple misunderstood the doctrine of nonduality and used it in an immoral fashion (we are told no details). The story fascinates me, both for what it clearly implies and for what it does not quite say, namely, that the energies of *śakti-pāta* somehow carry doctrinal content or intellectual force (that seems clear enough), and that these energies possess definite erotic dimensions—hence their "immoral" use in what I suspect was a sexual practice of some sort (and that is not at all clear, but "immoral" is often a euphemism for "sexual" in the texts). This noetic-erotic force makes perfect sense to me, but only because I have known something similar, which is to say that this is an esoteric truth

that can be neither explained nor defended with reason alone. It can only be "confessed" as a secret.

19 December 1989, 4:15 P.M. I could say with perfect honesty and amazement that I am a Śākta and that I have experienced, many times now, "what Ramakrishna called Kālī." But why? How? Why is it that my religious experiences, though nurtured in a profoundly Christian setting, have never been comfortably Christian? I've gone from a burning unicorn and a Greek maiden to mystico-erotic encounters with a Hindu goddess—this is very odd, "strange" *(adbhūta)* as my texts say.

22 September, 8:30 A.M. Karen was explaining to Jyoti how when she was a child she insisted on squatting exactly like Indians squat and would only eat with her hands. She often wonders if her being an anthropologist in West Bengal isn't related to that, and perhaps to an earlier life. I had a strange experience yesterday. I was drawing Kālī's eyes, all three of them, for my calling card I want to have printed. I suddenly realized, as I drew my own version, that these sexy eyes were very close to Spiderman's eyes, over which I fussed so as a child artist. Why this uncanny affinity with things Bengali? I've made up a story, which I half believe, to explain to puzzled Bengalis why I have a seemingly Punjabi or Sikh name. I tell them that in my previous life I was in fact a Hindu, and that, mistaking the name for an Indian one, I thought I had reincarnated in an Indian family. I was wrong. I have thus spent much of my life trying to get back to my Indian roots, to my Hindu nature. This explains a lot for my Indian friends, and they alway laugh, partly because the story is intentionally funny, partly out of joy that a pale American identifies so with their religious culture. I laugh too, for the same reasons.

21 March 1990. I just returned from Darjeeling today, the "Land of the Thunderbolt." Kanchenjunga, at 28,156 feet (or something like that), is spectacular. This pilgrimage was inspired partly by my fondness for Thomas Merton and his own romance with this mountain and this place. Strangely, as the train pulled in and the clouds lifted a bit, I could have sworn, absolutely sworn, that I saw a perfect image of Merton's face carved into the mountain's snow with a series of perfectly placed, perfectly timed shadows. A 28,000-foot Rorschach test made of rock and ice. Imagine that.

2 January 1993. If it were not for the decidedly mystical moments of my life, I would have easily turned Ramakrishna into a pathological case

study, which of course is precisely what many of his contemporaries very reasonably did and what some scholars still do, and with more than a little evidence. Only because I have experienced something uncannily similar to what I see operating in the texts—a *śakti* both sexual and not sexual at the same time—do I have the faith to hold to my dialectic of affirming both the sexual and the mystical elements in Ramakrishna's life. This is all to say that the dialectical nature of my work depends upon, rests on the mystical. But will readers without such experience see this in my work? Will they be able to hold the dialectic in its proper tension? Will they be able to see, I mean *really* see, the *coincidentia*? Probably not.

9 June 2000. I often remember Jason, puzzled by the infernal method of *Kālī's Child*, at once reductive and mystical, asking me about what I *really* think about Ramakrishna's ecstasies. I told him, quite honestly, that on Mondays, Wednesdays, and Fridays I read Ramakrishna's ecstasies reductively, on Tuesdays, Thursdays, and Saturdays I am quite certain about their ontological ground, and on Sundays I just can't make up my mind.

7 April 1995.
> Thus the tradition is esoteric in large measure because ultimately it is necessary to undergo the process of experiential replication before the symbols will speak to us completely.
>
> Paul Muller-Ortega, *The Triadic Heart of Śiva*

There is a "secret" dimension of *Kālī's Child* that few of my readers will understand, that intangible something in it that witnesses to my own "experiential replication" of the texts and their world in my body.

29 March 1996. I talked to Anand at some length on the phone last night. He told me to "keep my pen nib sharp" despite my critics (a humorous phallic image for him), and that I should see the pain of the controversy as the beginning of a wonderful journey that will deepen and develop my and Ramakrishna's emotional lives. Astonishingly, he thus mirrored back to me, in his own distinctively Bengali warmth and affection, my own "memorable fancy" about the work *for* the saint.

30 May 1991. "Can the power that produces children be the same power that results in the experience of God?" Ramakrishna asked this rhetorical question to denigrate domestic life and the procreative expression of human sexuality and to protect himself from an indigenous, essentially

Tantric, thesis that would have changed everything. The answer of course is yes.

24 October 1998. My wholeness, even if only glimpsed, renders many of the ecstasies of the mystics pathological. That is to say, my psychic inability to disorder myself again, to imbalance myself, to induce ecstasy or vision is a function of the psyche's stubborn desire for some stability and balance. Ecstasy, vision, and trance are "pathological," not in the sense of "bad," but in the sense of "trying to heal and put back together." My health, in other words, passes judgment on the mystical "from the other side," having gone through it, touched it briefly, and emerged from it to live whole.

23 November 1999. Isn't it telling that Ramakrishna often spoke of certain mystical states becoming impossible later in life, as if they had served their therapeutic purposes and so no longer appeared? So too with me.

25 June 1999. If the mystical is a remembering of the maternal Presence, then isn't it terribly sad that human beings seek out this state (which seems to be decidedly out of place in adult life) by renouncing and often even degrading the very realities that created that state in the first place, namely, woman, the family, and sexuality?

7 December 1998. The mystical life is not a selfish hankering after this or that extraordinary experience, although such experiences are integral to it and without them there is no mystical life. Rather, the mystical life is a *process* in which the psyche (or God, if you prefer) grants such experiences at crucial, meaningful moments in order to push one further along his or her specific life arc. There is, in other words, a certain teleology here, a wisdom that knows or at least hopes for a future healing.

FIVE

The Mystical Mirror of Hermeneutics

Gazing into Elliot Wolfson's *Speculum* (1994)

> The temptation to read oneself into the text poses itself equally to the scholar who on the face of it is functioning independently of a faith community and to the member of that community. Indeed, in the case of both, the act of reading may be portrayed as a double mirroring. The text is a mirror that reflects the reader and the reader a mirror that reflects the text.
>
> Elliot Wolfson, "Lying on the Path: Translation and the Transport of Sacred Texts"

> O Human Imagination O Divine Body
>
> William Blake quoted as an epigraph to *Through a Speculum That Shines,* by Elliot Wolfson

NO CONTEMPORARY HISTORIAN of religions has thought more deeply and written more eloquently about the hermeneutical experience and its potential mystical dimensions than the American Kabbalah scholar Elliot Wolfson. As I hope to demonstrate in this final chapter, his masterwork on medieval Jewish mysticism, *Through a Speculum That Shines,* can be read on at least two levels: as a textual-historical study of medieval kabbalistic erotics and hermeneutics, which posited the event of revelation in and as the act of reading Torah; and as a postmodern, postcritical performance of this same erotic and hermeneutical mysticism in and as *Speculum.* There is, in other words, something both genuinely erotic and mystical about *Speculum* itself, a place where traditional kabbalistic hermeneutics, critical theory applied to this hermeneutics, and the psychoanalytic gaze all collapse into one another, not in a dramatically obvious and singular psychological experience located in the person of Elliot Wolfson (as we saw, for example, in the case of Bharati), but through the mirroring mystery of reading and interpreting texts, including and especially *Speculum*, that text which is, quite literally, a shining "mirror" *(speculum)* for us to gaze into in order to discover (and lose) ourselves in the otherness of the medieval kabbalists and their imaginal worlds.

In relation to the four that preceded it, this fifth and final chapter is unique in at least three ways. First, it is not an essay about an admired but deceased scholarly ancestor with whom I have had no personal contact; it is an essay about a contemporary living scholar who also happens to be a colleague and friend. Apropos our present hermeneutical concerns, this friendship began through a mutual reading of each other's work. I had read *Speculum* on the recommendation of another colleague in Jewish studies and was quickly struck by what I have here called a hermeneutical mysticism working within it as both method and object of study. When I shared this reading experience with Wolfson in a letter, he responded enthusiastically, affirming my sense of what he called "the 'unspoken' subtext of *Speculum*." He went on: "You are the first person who has expressed the matter in this way, which I believe is an accurate reflection on my creative process."[1] From there our dialogue developed as we located and reflected on the uncannily similar homoerotic conclusions we had each arrived at with such different material, he working on medieval kabbalistic texts and I on early modern Bengali Śākta material, and on the politics of reception through which we both had to suffer, at about the same time, for our gender analyses of sacred traditions. Very much related to this relational quality of what follows is the second distinguishing feature of the essay, that is, the fact that whereas the theses of the earlier chapters could not be reflected in the minds and hearts of the authors under study (not that this would completely resolve the interpretive issues, for a text can never be completely equated with the conscious intentions of its author), the present thesis can and has been. This is not to suggest that Wolfson necessarily agrees with everything that follows. Nor do I mean to imply that such a reflection should close debate on the issues. I simply want to make immediately clear the dialogical nature of what follows. Third and finally, there is the chapter's deeply personal and self-reflexive ending, a final "double mirroring" that reaches quite beyond any standard academic or professional parameters to reflect on the nature of my own hermeneutical mysticism and its specific refraction through Wolfson's *Speculum*.

It is particularly appropriate that I end with Wolfson's thought and work, and this for two reasons. First, medieval Jewish Kabbalah offers what appears to be the strongest case in the Western monotheisms for a systematically heterosexual mysticism. The kabbalist, after all, unites with the Shekhinah, the divine Presence or feminine aspect of the Godhead, in both his exegetical activities and in his Sabbath conjugal unions with his wife in order to repair the Godhead and the historical world. Moreover, the covenant that binds him to his God is literally inscribed on his penis through the ritual of circumcision, and it is this opening that in turn gives him access to a visionary experience of the divine pleroma. If we are looking for a phallocentric, seemingly heterosexual mystical tradition, this is it. Kabbalah can thus provide us with a particularly strong and dramatic case study with which to test our working hypothesis about the homoerotic privileges of male erotic mystical traditions. Secondly, my own understanding of hermeneutics as a mystical practice is best reflected in, and indeed has been enriched and deepened by, Wolfson's own hermeneutical understandings and philosophical acumen. To end with Wolfson, then, is not only to end in the present; it is to end with a genuine, if still tentative, shared conclusion.

I will proceed to this conclusion through five movements: a synopsis of Wolfson's life and work up to the present (part 1); an analysis of his recent discussion of the relationship between scholarly and pious approaches to the act of reading sacred texts (part 2); a discussion of his early work on the hermeneutical, erotic, and visionary dimensions of circumcision, writing, and reading in kabbalistic thought (part 3); a reading of his *Through a Speculum That Shines* (part 4); and some personal reflections in the text's mirror (part 5). My goal throughout will be to present another hermeneutical-mystical model for us to consider: the rhetorical eclipse of "experience" itself within what we might call a mysticism of reading and writing. Appropriately, what we have here is not a mystical Christianity mythically formed around a descending, dying, and rising savior figure, or a Muslim desert mysticism of transcendence, or a Hindu insistence on a nondual Brahman before and beyond all linguistic registers, but a distinctly Jewish form of language mysticism in which the sacred appears within the mystery of the text and its noetic-erotic interpretation.

1. Along the Path

In both personal communication[2] and in his published scholarship, one of the most common ways Wolfson has chosen to talk about his life and work is in terms of the metaphor of the road, as an intellectual and spiritual journey "along the path," as he likes to say.³ Reflecting this same quality, Pinchas Giller has written of the "restless, searching spirit" so evident in Wolfson's scholarship.⁴ Even a brief glance at Wolfson's religious and intellectual development more than confirms the accuracy of such a judgment.

Elliot Wolfson was born on 23 November 1956—the birthday, he points out, of one of his intellectual heroes, Paul Celan—in Newark, New Jersey. He grew up, however, in Brooklyn in an Orthodox household, the son of a rabbi. He was educated in Orthodox schools *(yeshivot)* and was exposed to classical Jewish learning, especially talmudic study (which he loved), from the very beginning. One of the many emotional resonances of these years involved the fact that most of his teachers were Eastern European refugees, survivors of the Holocaust. Wolfson speaks of this experience as the experience of a ghost: "The Holocaust haunted every corner of my childhood. . . . The synagogue I attended as a child was replete with survivors. I recall the tailor I went to was a survivor, many of the shop owners, and so on. There was no escape."⁵ The Jewish culture of his childhood, in other words, was all encompassing and strongly tinted with an aura of religious difference, historical memory, and cultural survival. As Giller points out, such a training stands in rather sharp contrast to that of Gershom Scholem, who adopted Kabbalah, at that time an ill-respected topic equated with superstition and occult nonsense, in open opposition to the acculturating patterns of his German family but nevertheless took a position vis-à-vis the mystics that was often marked by a cool distance or emotional indifference. For Wolfson, on the other hand, "the texts and tropes of Jewish tradition were mother's milk,"⁶ and so a sympathetic understanding of mystical forms of subjectivity came more easily. Interestingly, whereas Scholem would become an ardent Zionist, Wolfson has long resisted the identification of a text's boundaries "with the lines drawn on a map" and has explicitly called for a place at the table of Jewish studies for the non-Jew.

But however all encompassing Wolfson's early Orthodox upbringing was, mother's milk or no, this was Brooklyn, and genuine openings to the outside secular world were just around the proverbial corner (and there were many corners). Wolfson's mind quickly embraced the secular world, if still a Jewish secular world, particularly in its psychological and philosophical modes. By the seventh grade he was reading Freud. Consequently, when it came time for his teacher to capture each student's spirit in a pithy end-of-the-year epigram, she caught Wolfson's in three words,

"Sigmund Freud's Adverbs," a clear witness to an early interest in language and psychoanalysis that would follow the young student into his later adult work.

A personal passion for mysticism quickly followed. In high school he was reading the literature and attending the lectures of two prominent Hasidic groups in Brooklyn, Lubavitch and Bratslav, and was particularly fascinated by the paradoxical nature of Nahman of Bratslav. Giller attributes Wolfson's marked "understanding of the mystic's subjectivity" to this early exposure to Hasidism on the streets of Brooklyn.[7] Certainly such influences can still be glimpsed. During our shared sufferings at the hands of offended critics, for example, Wolfson would quote Nahman to me: "The deeper the truth, the greater the controversy it creates in the world."

During Wolfson's last years in high school he studied in *yeshivot* in Jerusalem for a year and a half and then returned to Yeshiva University in New York, where he studied for three more semesters—Talmud from 9:00 to 1:00 and secular courses after 2:00. It was after those 2:00s that he was first smitten by what he calls the "serpent of philosophy." Against his father's wishes, he left Yeshiva and enrolled in the B.A./M.A. program at Queens College and the City University of New York. There he focused on the history of philosophy, with special emphasis on ancient Greek thought, existentialism, and phenomenology, and wrote an M.A. thesis on the theory of the self in Edmund Husserl and William James. After graduate school he continued his studies on his own, this time focusing on Martin Heidegger, whose *Discourse on Thinking* opened him up to a new interest in Eastern religions, especially Zen Buddhism. About this same time he also began to read Kabbalah and became interested in the occult. Such systems of thought gave him alternatives to the "personal, willful God" of orthodox Judaism, an image of Deity which he no longer found convincing.

Now disillusioned with the surface "pots and pans" quality of American Judaism, disturbed by Orthodoxy's aversion to philosophical reflection, and seeking a spiritual discipline that did not rest on an intellectually impossible personal theism, Wolfson finally decided to pursue a path in religious studies. Accordingly, he applied to University of California at Santa Barbara to study Eastern religions and to Brandeis University to study Kabbalah. Accepted into both programs, he ultimately chose the latter on a long walk through Baltimore as he held in each hand a letter of acceptance to one of the schools. By the end of the walk, he had decided that the deeper he would get into the study of a particular religion the more of its myth he would have to incorporate and, consequently, the more of its ritual. Since he was already more than familiar, kinesthetically as it were, with the myths and rituals of Judaism, he decided on Kabbalah, tore up his letter to UCSB, and put his letter of acceptance to Brandeis in the mailbox—his path was thus determined on a literal walk. At Brandeis he wrote his dissertation on Moshe de Leon's *Sefer ha-Rimmon* (Book of the Pomegranate) under Marvin Fox and Alexander Altmann. Wolfson defended his dissertation and graduated from Brandeis in 1986. From there he moved to New York University, where he has taught ever since.

Wolfson's early public work consisted of a number of long, dense essays on the many mystical and gendered themes that would soon crystallize as *Speculum*—those of mysticism, esotericism, eroticism, the feminine, visionary experience, hermeneutics, and the phallocentric nature of Kabbalah. His publishing career began effectively in 1987, with the appearance of two articles on circumcision: "Circumcision and the Divine Name: A Study in the Transmission of Esoteric Doctrine"[8] and "Circumcision, Vision of God, and Textual Interpetation: From Midrashic Trope to Mystical Symbol."[9] From there his fifty-plus essays ranged widely—treating zoharic hermeneutics, female imaging of the Torah, the German Pietists, the theurgical dimensions of prayer, negative theology, Martin Buber, Shabbetai Donolo, Franz Rosenzweig's mystical eschatology, Sabbatianism, ecstatic ascent—always returning, as if drawn by the gravitational force of his own existential center, back to the central themes of gender, hermeneutics, and mysticism.[10] Giller points out that since his dissertation Wolfson has more or less abandoned the literary historiography—identifying authors, dates, and places, creating critical editions, isolating lines of influence, and so on—that dominated the methodology of Scholem and his students and has followed instead his own interests and insights—his own path, he would no doubt say—creating in the process a new set of powerful heresies for the field to struggle with.[11] And this is, for the most part, true. It is, however, important to point out that Wolfson has continued to work on and publish critical editions of texts, even as he has indeed turned his energies mainly to hermeneutical concerns and gender analyses.

Scholem's heresies became the discipline's new orthodoxies. It remains to be seen what will become of Wolfson's heresies. Certainly his work has challenged, if not called into serious question, many of the orthodoxies and common assumptions of an earlier generation of Kabbalah scholars, particularly as regards the structuring nature of gender in kabbalistic culture. As we shall soon see, sexuality is a defining feature of

Kabbalah for Wolfson, and much of what he finds in the texts in this regard resists, absolutely, any attempt to fit it into religiously palatable or socially acceptable categories. Mystical eroticism for Wolfson is an ontological force that is at once religiously profound, aesthetically beautiful, sexually ambiguous, and morally troubling—*awe-ful* in the original sense of that term. Particularly in regard to the feminine, Wolfson's feminist gaze, inspired by Luce Irigaray, has explored sexual and ethical crevices of kabbalistic thought and vision that few could have imagined and fewer still probably want to imagine. Giller is wryly to the point: "In uncovering this tradition of phallocentric ocularism [much more on this below], Wolfson inadvertently outraged a gender orthodoxy in kabbalistic studies that nobody knew was there. It seems that the *Shekhinah* has her own lobby in both academic and popular Judaism."[12] Indeed, "[i]n a former age, he might very well have been ostracized or excommunicated for revealing the tradition's innermost secrets."[13]

What Giller does not say here is that Wolfson, in some very real sense, *has* been effectively ostracized, if not by an external body of elders or an Orthodox tenure committee, then by the logical force of his own hermeneutical work and its intellectual power. To return to his own chosen metaphor, he is "on the path," constantly moving, constantly searching, forever asking questions that many segments of his own contemporary tradition will not allow to be asked, much less be answered. The existential result—much as we saw in Massignon and Bharati but in an entirely different intellectual key—is some very powerful scholarship and a searching sense of religious homelessness on the margins, along the path. As he shared with me:

> I could never go back to the Orthodox belief system, although in some ways (somatically perhaps) I feel comfortable in an Orthodox setting. I suppose ideologically I am closer to Conservative than Reform or Reconstructionist, but frankly none of the denominations works for me. I have never found my way back. . . . I have never overcome the displacement, although I have come to terms with that displacement and I see it as a form of homecoming in a tradition wherein being home means being on the path. For me, Judaism is a textual community . . . and not a religion marked by place. I do not deny the importance of place in Judaism, but the space of the text has been far more important, in my judgment.[14]

And with that it is time to arrive "at the space of the text" and walk Wolfson's path with him through it.

2. Lying on the Path

In the midst of the communication cited just above, Wolfson referred to one of his most recent essays, "Lying on the Path: Translation and the Transport of Sacred Texts."[15] He writes there: "The questioning of the path of tradition, however, entails that when one seems furthest off track one is actually at home. To be centered in the tradition is to discover oneself in the margins of the text, to affirm as old that which is new by affirming that which is old as new." Again Wolfson describes himself on a path that is both "off track" and "actually at home." The quote and the essay in which it is embedded are particularly important for us for many reasons, foremost among them the fact that it is here that Wolfson begins to address directly our own present questions about the mystical potential of reading and writing academic texts. Let us begin Wolfson's path, then, right here, lying on it.

"Lying on the Path" is a typically Wolfsonian title-metaphor that works on at least two levels, intending both the meanings of physical and emotional exhaustion (the piece was written shortly after the scholar had been attacked on various fronts for his homoerotic readings) and the connotations of possible deception, on the part of both scholar and believer alike, I gather.[16] The piece opens with the assertion that the academic study of sacred traditions brings with it "an implicit danger and a challenge to the scholar and the practitioner" (LP, 1). For the practitioner especially, the historicizing methods of the study of religion can become extremely threatening as sacred events are "unmasked in the light of historical scholarship" and revealed to be products of "the masquerade of mythical thinking" (LP, 1). Wolfson does not give any concrete examples of this process in the essay, but in person he has suggested the example of the fate of Jewish sacred history within secular scholarship. For example, by most scholarly accounts, the Exodus never took place and appears, on a historical level at least, to be pure fiction, a founding myth designed to stabilize and legitimate a national community long after the "fact" of the alleged divine event. And yet this mythical event that never happened grounds the most basic meanings and possibilities of Jewish belief and practice. How to reconcile these seemingly irreconcilable positions?

Although Wolfson never spells it out clearly in this essay, the danger and challenge for the academic scholar in all of this certainly lies in this same historical scandal, not as offended believer but as the object or target of the offended believer's anger. In essence, the scholar speaks the historical truth, in the best form we have, and then suffers at the hands of the traditional community for speaking such a truth. We are reminded here of Evelyn Underhill, who could not accept Catholicism's insistence that the Ascension happened, "like the Spanish Armada." Much like the Exodus, it did not, but anyone who is courageous enough to say so suffers before the scandalized who cannot, for whatever developmental, religious, or cultural reasons, process such a reasonable truth.

Nor is this danger restricted to the scholar's historicizing methods. The contemporary critical focus on sexuality and gender is even more likely to result in open conflict between the academic and pious communities. Here again, I would suggest, academic experience mirrors (this time in a reverse fashion) mystical praxis and experience, particularly in the latter's traditional emphasis on esotericism, that is, the praxis of keeping secrets (many of them sexual) from the public both to avoid threatening the common good and to protect the gnostic, whose truths would threaten, if not actually dissolve, those of the orthodox community. Wolfson, pace more recent interpreters who have tried to stress the conservative and orthodox nature of mysticism,[17] develops in great detail this line of thought in *Speculum*, returning repeatedly to the felt danger and risks of mystical gnosis. Consider, for example, the story of the child who literally self-combusted the moment he understood Ezekiel. The point of the parable? "Exegesis," Wolfson comments, "provides the context for ecstatic experiences that may be harmful or lethal."[18] Hence the traditional rhetorical strategy of esotericism: "The sages did not speak of this explicitly so that people would not come to contemplate what is above. . . . Therefore they would transmit this matter to their students and sages in a whisper and privately, through [oral] tradition *(qabbalah)*" (S, 151). Books, especially mystical books which record such deconstructive and/or sexual secrets for an indiscriminately mixed audience, are very dangerous things, for an inanimate book, unlike a wise master or rabbi, cannot withhold itself from an unauthorized or unprepared reader. The results can be deadly, we are told again by a traditional source: "We have heard strong rumors that some people who have been occupied with these [books] immediately perished" (S, 157).

None of these kabbalistic parables and "strong rumors" can, I think, be taken at face value (children do not self-combust and people do not die because they read a particular book), but they do convey a very important hermeneutical truth that is directly relevant to our present concerns, namely, the fact that certain mystical convictions and experiences—particularly those involving sexuality—are indiscriminately shared with others only at considerable personal risk. Not everyone can understand; indeed, probably few are capable of emotionally and intellectually processing such secrets at all, much less understanding them. Mysticism as a body of esoteric truths, then, far from being "practical" (as Underhill wanted to argue), is in fact radically elitist, or, put differently, "esoteric." Wolfson defines the latter as "that which cannot be communicated fully in writing and which should be only alluded to partially in written form and transmitted orally" (S, 189).[19] And here lies the crux of the problem. For what happens when a major contemporary Jewish scholar not only cracks the code of a medieval visionary tradition and reveals its esoteric sexual nature, but also publishes a major work of scholarship on these same hidden truths? If these are things that "cannot be communicated fully in writing and which should be only alluded to partially in written form and transmitted orally," then how are we to assess an eminently public work, selling in the thousands and piling up book awards as it goes along, which so clearly violates this traditional ban on full, written, open disclosure? Are its ill-prepared readers bursting into flames?

The short answer to all of this, of course, is that Wolfson is not living in thirteenth-century Spain, he is not a member of any of the kabbalistic communities he studies (that would be rather difficult since none of them have survived), and so he has violated no trust, no initiatory vow to secrecy, no ethnographic ethic. Sociologically speaking, he is entirely innocent. But this is not quite the issue, and Wolfson has been quite clear that what makes the kabbalistic secret so secret is not its potential political fallout but its graphically sexual content—esotericism and eroticism are always linked for Wolfson; they go together. Clearly, however, there is also a very powerful ethical subtext running throughout Wolfson's sexual revelations as well, for the erotic he recovers in the kabbalistic texts inevitably ends up erasing the feminine through various symbolic and theological strategies. It is precisely this ethically charged sexual revelation, not any hypothetical moral lapse on his own part, that has won Wolfson both his greatest admirers and his most insecure and consequently most vocal critics. Metaphorically speaking, readers *are* bursting into flames. Wolfson hints at this in the very last lines of his "Occultation of the Feminine and the Body of Secrecy in Medieval Kabbalah":

> In the case of the *Zohar* and related kabbalistic literature . . . the secret did not involve esoteric knowledge that had to be suppressed for political reasons. Rather, the erotic nature of the union necessitated the concealment of that

which was exposed.... By contrast, in modern scholarship, this secret has assumed another connotation, for it has become dangerous to uncover that which is hidden in the symbol of the concealed woman. Alas, in what can only be called hermeneutical revenge, the secret has hid itself precisely from the very scholars who have undertaken the systematic exposure of the mysteries of the tradition. The disclosure of this secret on my part has not been without a price, but it is a price that must be paid if the notion of secrecy in kabbalistic esotericism is to be properly understood.[20]

"Lying on the Path" was written within this experience of "hermeneutical revenge"—enacted, strangely, exclusively by fellow scholars—and can be read as an attempt to give some answer to the seemingly unbridgeable chasm that separates the academic scholar and the pious believer (scholar or lay). Wolfson turns to literary theory and hermeneutics for his answer, and particularly to the mysteries of language, translation, and interpretation, all of which, for him, issue from a dialectic of distance and intimacy, absence and presence. Drawing on the thought of Rosenzweig, Walter Benjamin, and especially Hans-Georg Gadamer, Wolfson attempts to construct a philosophical position that stems not from some Platonic ideal or ontological absolute far beyond the reaches of language, but, in Gadamer's phrase, from the very "centre of language" (LP, 4). Within such an existential stance there is no pure experience outside of or before language, and one need not escape the text to know transcendence, for the text itself calls one out of oneself by the very fact of its hermeneutical distance. "A person who is trying to understand a text," Gadamer writes and Wolfson quotes, "has also to keep something at a distance, namely everything that suggests itself, on the basis of his own prejudices, as the meaning expected, as soon as it is rejected by the sense of the text itself" (LP, 4). What is required, then, is a kind of "uninterrupted listening" and a certain ascetic approach to the act of reading as the process through which one loses oneself in the world of the text. It is only here, in the self-cancellation of the hermeneutical experience, that the meaning of the text can assert itself. This distance and this self-cancellation, moreover, are invaluable safeguards against the nationalistic and chauvinistic poses now so common in contemporary religious studies: "Meaning does not arise ... through the dogmatic, imperialistic or triumphant possession of a text, a posture that we regrettably find in the case of some scholars who mistakenly compare the boundaries of a text to the physical space of national entities that are drawn upon a map.... Belonging to a text is not achieved by possessing a passport that declares one's national identity" (LP, 5). Wolfson is clearly thinking of Jewish studies here, which often, if by no means always (and Wolfson does cite important exceptions), demand that one be Jewish if not actually Zionist, but his comments could apply equally well to any number of other fields, and particularly present postcolonial Indology, where being a Westerner or having white skin is often implicitly or explicitly equated with colonial collusion and political guilt, and this, bizarrely, within a Foucauldian or Derridean philosophical system that is of distinctively Western origins.

To counter such contemporary thinking and its explicit political posturing, Wolfson turns to one of his favorite thinkers, Martin Heidegger, and redefines belonging to a text as the experience of being taken up by and gathered into it: "Belonging, therefore, is the very opposite of possessing; it involves being possessed" (LP, 5). The "truth" here is always constituted by a conflict between disclosure and concealment, or in Heidegger's etymological turn, the *aletheia* (Greek for "truth") is quite literally an "un-covering" *(a-letheia)*, an attempt to reveal the meaning of the text by stripping away, through the act of interpretation, its many meanings. Wolfson points out that the kabbalists understood the act of interpretation in a similar way, analogizing their speculations on the Torah as consecutive acts of removing the garments of Torah, who, as we will learn below, was often imagined as a lovely maiden hidden behind seven palaces or levels of meaning. Hermeneutics thus, in typical mystical fashion, becomes eroticized, an act of denuding a lover—a kind of intellectual striptease.

It is within this Heideggerian-kabbalistic notion of truth as that which is uncovered or denuded that Wolfson introduces his central dialectical insight: "The contextual meaning of the text is disclosed only when the layers are discarded, but the layers cannot be discarded unless they are unfolded" (LP, 7). That is to say, the sacred text is *already* a concealment, a coded distance, but the concealed cannot be revealed nor the distance made intimate unless one begins with the concealment and works from the distance. In hermeneutical terms, the mystical can only be known within the particulars of the text, even if it always escapes and transcends these same particulars. There can be no general or anonymous mysticism utterly devoid of context.[21] In another related mystical analogy, this one of Sufi origin, God is said to be concealed behind a paradoxical veil: "The veil conceals the secrets, but no secrets can be grasped without the veil."[22] Both poles of the dialectic—the presence and the absence, the revealed and the concealed—are crucial, and if either is missing, revelation (in either a religious or an academic sense) cannot take place. Such is the nature of the mystical secret—a secret that cries out to be told, a secret that once told demands to be hidden again.

This same dialectic of distance and intimacy, moreover, controls the process of self-discovery that is implied in every scholarly act of reading. Such reading, Wolfson writes, "involves receiving, which is a paradoxical emptying of self to become who one is" (LP, 7). Through the sacred text, "the reader discovers him/herself, but only insofar as the distance is maintained between text and reader" (LP, 7). In a different metaphor, the act of reading can be thought of as a double mirroring, with both text and reader mirroring and giving being to the other. There is no text without a reader, and there is no reader without a text (LP, 7). Both "make each other up" within the mystery of the hermeneutical act. As Maurice Blanchot put it, the book does not become "the work" until someone reads it and the word "being" is pronounced: "This event occurs when the work becomes the intimacy between someone who writes it and someone who reads it" (LP, 10). We are very close here to what I have called a hermeneutical mysticism.

What Wolfson objects to in the pious reading of sacred texts is the very real possibility that the distance and resistance of the text will be denied or collapsed and the reader will identify completely with the text, claiming it in effect as an exclusive and absolute possession. Here reading becomes pure projection or political coup, and the hope for a true communication across space and time is defeated before a naive fundamentalism. Here too, in hermeneutical forms, are many of the dangers that haunt both our contemporary world and academy: the dangers of nationalistic chauvinism, political exclusivism, the oppression of minorities, and the silencing of marginal voices (here appearing as divergent readers and creators of alternate meanings). This is a disaster for Wolfson on both the academic and traditional levels, since tradition itself proceeds and survives only through the "ongoing process of critique and reflection, which in great measure are based on misreading and creative deconstructing" (LP, 11). Tradition itself, in other words, implies distance, and it can survive the continual ravages of time and changing cultures only if it can preserve and nurture the same distance *in itself.* Ironically, then, to be at odds with the tradition is traditional, despite all appearances and protestations to the contrary. Wolfson's penultimate appraisal of the situation sides with the academic position as both more faithful to this understanding of tradition and more amenable to human justice and well-being: "The hermeneutical dialectic of the scholar requires the distancing of the reader from the text so that the reader can hear the word of the text, whereas the hermeneutical dialectic of the pious seeker demands a narrowing and eventual obliteration of distance" (LP, 11).

All this has some rather major and obvious implications for the question of the scholar's own mystical experiences and the authorization they give (or do not give) him or her. Here Wolfson's tone becomes more personal, frustrated, and humorous:

> How often have I heard in my life from members of the traditional Orthodox community that I could not possibly understand the texts I am studying since I am neither a kabbalist nor one who has received teachings directly from a master of the tradition! The insistence that only one from within can understand the texts is especially prominent in the case of mystical sources. Indeed, virtually every time I teach my introduction to Jewish mysticism or lecture at some adult education setting, I am asked whether or not I have had anything resembling a mystical experience. The assumption hidden in this question is very revealing: If I have not had some such experience, surely I am not qualified to teach about mysticism. My stock response to this question is, "My mother was a mathematician and no one ever asked her if she were a triangle." (LP, 12)

Wolfson suggests that this insistence that one must have had a mystical experience to teach about mysticism is similar to the more general claim that only a member of a faith community, an "insider" in popular parlance, should be able to speak authoritatively and academically about the tradition. Neither position, Wolfson believes, should be tolerated, much less advocated, in the academy. To establish his point, he draws an analogy with the state of Jewish studies and what he believes to be the "ultimate litmus text" of its intellectual integrity: the professional success of someone in the discipline who comes from completely outside the culture. Such success, he implies, is very hard to come by.

The politics of cultural identity and the innate chauvinism of religion (any religion) thus combine to create a situation in which the academic study of religion is equated with a specific cultural or religious identity, that is, being Jewish or Christian or Hindu or whatever. Distance has been erased, and with it the possibility of new insight and knowledge. Such a pattern is to be particularly mourned in Jewish studies, Wolfson points out, since Jewish history witnesses to the very cross-cultural fertilization, encounter, and challenge that the discipline seeks to silence among its own ranks (the same, I think, is again true of the postcolonial study of Hinduism). Wolfson's rhetoric takes on mystical suggestions here of the kabbalistic notion of *tikkun,* or "repair," of the world through mystically intended ritual acts: "In order for the process of reading as the repair of the tradition to be realized," he writes, "it is necessary to secure a legitimate place at the table of study for the non-Jew" (LP, 15).

Wolfson ends "Lying on the Path" on a hopeful note that a convergence between the scholar and the practitioner, between the modern and the postmodern, may evolve in the future: "[P]erhaps things will evolve to the point that the two paths shall converge to forge a new way on the journey that will lead to a spiritual renewal that is both culturally specific and universally applicable" (LP, 15). And even if they do not, the effort and the journey will not have been wasted, for, in the words of Sanford Budick, "[e]ven if we are always defeated by translation, culture as a movement toward shared consciousness may emerge from the defeat" (LP, 15). In the end, then, whether recognized or not, the critical study of religion participates in the reconstruction of tradition, which has always been the "writing of continuous displacements." Such a recognition, Wolfson hopes in his dialectical style, might help us close the gap between scholar and practitioner, "for the former will discern that what has been lost is indeed what will be gained, and the latter that what has been gained is what will be lost" (LP, 16). In terms of the path, to be home is to be lost, and to be lost is to be home.

Academic method and pious community, then, both are and are not related, but, ironically, it is the academic approach, particularly in its hermeneutical practices, that is more faithful to the actual historical dynamics of tradition. Believer and scholar alike may, and probably will, take revenge on the hermeneut for revealing the sexual secrets of the tradition (and their ethical implications), but in the end it is precisely this revelation of the hidden that constitutes the rhetorical heart of most mystical traditions. The secret can be concealed again through the processes of pious outrage, professional review, or official ban, but paradoxically this very concealment will only call forth yet another revealing, and another concealing, and another revealing . . . Such is the rhetorical logic of the secret *(mustikon).*

3. Phallic Beginnings

How, then, does this all work out when we come to the actual interpretation of sacred texts? How does Wolfson position himself within his own texts vis-à-vis the medieval mystical fraternities and figures he studies? Does he identify in any way with their religious worlds? Does he practice a kind of hermeneutics that collapses in some fashion—rhetorically, confessionally, or psychologically—into mystical experience, as we have variously seen in the cases of Underhill, Massignon, Zaehner, and Bharati? The best place from which to begin answering such questions is Wolfson's masterwork on kabbalistic visionary experience, *Through a Speculum That Shines*. To its dense pages I will soon turn. But first a few words on Wolfson's earlier essays and their development of his central thesis of the phallocentric orientation of kabbalistic thought.

Wolfson has consistently argued, from his first published essays on the visionary potential of circumcision to the full working out of his hermeneutic in *Speculum*, that kabbalistic thought is defined by an all-encompassing androcentric phallocentrism. Not surprisingly, indeed all too predictably, he has been criticized for seeing the phallus everywhere through an anachronistically applied Freudian hermeneutic.[23] One does not, however, have to read the kabbalistic passages Wolfson translates at such length for long to realize, with a certain amazed shock, that these medieval authors were applying "Freudian" principles within their own distinctively mystical worldview centuries before Freud.[24] Given this, it seems to me far more likely that the line of sexual reading in fact develops in precisely the opposite direction that the prudish critics suppose, that is, *chronologically,* from medieval kabbalah to Freud's psychoanalysis. I am reminded here of David Bakan's provocative thesis, advanced almost a half a century ago now, that psychoanalysis—with its oral initiatory ritual structure, its emphasis on esotericism, its understanding of sexual symbolism, its antinomian engagement with the "lower" or "infernal" powers of instinct, its strange fascination with numerology, and its rabbinic-like exegetical style—functions as a kind of secularized Kabbalah, and that the former in fact may find its deepest intellectual roots in the latter.[25] Seen in this light, a psychoanalytically informed hermeneutic such as Wolfson's, far from projecting the modern back onto the medieval, is in fact mining the medieval for the veins of the modern, using the medieval, as it were, to render more explicit and exoteric what could be for us moderns only implicit and esoteric. Here the genuine revelations of a hermeneutical method arise from a profound structural or cognitive sympathy between two apparently foreign systems of thought—the kabbalistic and the psychoanalytic, the medieval and the modern, the mystical and the theoretical. We are back, once again, to hermeneutics as a hidden or camouflaged mystical practice.

Regardless of where we stand on such a thesis—I find it convincing but do not want to make too much of it here—one thing is clear enough after a study of Wolfson's written corpus: the kabbalistic phallus emerges from within an astonishing display of exegetical skill and scholarship, the symbolic complexity and intertextual richness of which I cannot possibly do justice to here, as the central pillar of this mystical-hermeneutical worldview. And indeed, Wolfson's prose often reads remarkably like the kabbalistic texts themselves, moving effortlessly, as in a free association session, from scriptural citation to mystical gloss to contemporary critical theory and back to scripture again. Granted, we always have an opening theoretical discussion of the relevant scholarly literature and a historical treatment of the specific theme in biblical, rabbinic, and early kabbalistic writers, and we are constantly reminded through cultural anthropology and historical-critical methods of the contexts and associations through which a particular passage should be read, but from there on out, usually until the end of the essay or monograph, we inevitably find ourselves convincingly lost in a complex web of meanings, associations, insights, and images, most of them charged with sexual connotations. It is as if we are caught in the very texture of Kabbalah, thinking, reading, imagining our way through a modern Zohar with Wolfson.

Consider, for example, the three kabbalistic themes of writing, creation, and circumcision,[26] each of which refers constantly to the other two (and innumerable others) in a kind of Derridean production of mystical meaning, always receding, always deferring, here, however, working their way in the very end, in a decidedly un-Derridean fashion, to what is always their ultimate goal, the transcendent signified, the divine phallus. We could thus begin almost anywhere in the texts (of the kabbalists or Wolfson) and find our way back to this final phallic center, but for the sake of illustration and in the spirit of the present work, let us begin with the act of writing and the production of mystical texts. Significantly, these very themes are quite literally primordial for the kabbalists, going back to the very beginning, both cosmologically and textually, to the very first words of the Zohar, the central work of thirteenth-century Spanish theosophical Kabbalah that describe the Godhead's first creative impulses at the very height of the *sefirot,* those ten shining spheres that constitute together both the divine *anthropos,* that is, the dynamic manifest side of God, and the object of virtually all of the kabbalist's speculations and exegetical labors. Commenting on the very first word of scripture, the Zohar begins thus: "[I]n the beginning of the will of the King the hardened spark began to engrave engravings in the supernal lustre" (CS, 60). By means of this "hardened spark," God engraves the ten shining spheres, nine visible and one, the uppermost, "hidden and unknown," along with the twenty-two letters of the Hebrew alphabet, the mystico-linguistic forms of all that will emanate in the later stages of the creation (CS, 61).

Wolfson performs an exegesis of this passage by placing it alongside other related zoharic passages and medieval anthropological notions to show that the Zohar, following standard Greco-Roman, Near Eastern, and medieval understandings, identified the writing instrument with the phallus and the tablet or page with the female: writing was thus homologized to phallic penetration, an inscription that becomes in other linguistic contexts a "knocking against" (CS, 62) or even, as one kabbalistic text puts it, an engraving "in the womb of a lustre in which the point is inserted" (CS, 67). The medieval Galenic view of the semen's origin in the cranial cavity also becomes significant when we learn in another passage that the Hebrew letters became punctuated when this same hardened spark struck against the ether of the brain. Wolfson can thus identify from cultural context and kabbalistic linguistic practice the "homologous structure of the brain and the penis" (CS, 63). Hence both the penis and the brain are depicted as the letter *yod* in kabbalistic thought (CS, 63), the same letter that is the sign of the covenant inscribed on the penis in the ritual act of circumcision (CS, 64). Similarly, the Hebrew *yedi'ah* can connote either cognitive activity or marital intimacy: *noesis* and *eros* are thus ontologically related activities, since "in zoharic theosophy there is a correspondence between contemplative experience and seminal emission; indeed, the *semen virile* is homologized to the light-seed of the brain."[27] Hence the theosophical image of the head of the divine *anthropos* as the ultimate origin of a seminal creation, the fount of letters and vowels, and that which gives form and life to the spherical lights that emanate from the primordial darkness of the infinite, the Ein-Sof (CS, 66–67). Bolstered by these and dozens of other kabbalistic associations, word plays, and glosses, Wolfson can conclude that in zoharic literature the act of writing is "a decidedly erotic activity: the active agent of writing is the male principle; the written letters are the *semen virile;* and the tablet or page upon which the writing is accomplished is the female principle" (CS, 68).

As mentioned above, this same eroticized writing of the hardened spark onto the lustrous female tablet is central to the kabbalistic creation myth of the universe's emanation from the very highest of the *sefirot*. "Before all the emanation the Ein-Sof was alone delighting in himself," declares one Lurianic text (CS, 69). Again, through a rich weave of kabbalistic texts, the androgynous nature of the infinite, and the hard spark that corresponds to the penis, Wolfson is able to read God's primordial delight in himself as a sexual metaphor for a kind of divine autoeroticism and the original moment of divine inscription as a mythologized "act of sexual self-gratification" (CS, 69). Consider, for example, the following text from Vital:

> Indeed, in the first time of the first copulation, the male was aroused by himself *(nit'orer ha-zakhar me-'aṣmo)* without arousal of the feminine, and there arose in him the will and the desire to copulate *(raṣon we-ta'awah lehizdawweg)* even though as of yet there was no aspect of the female waters. Therefore, this copulation is very hidden and it was not in the aspect of the intercourse of his genitalia with her genitalia, for the feminine was still not created in the world. . . . Therefore, this first copulation was in the supernal will, thought, the upper brain, in the secret of the supernal will that is entirely masculine and without any mark of the feminine, and understand this.[28]

God, then, toys with himself to produce what the texts call a "shaking" *(ni'anu'a)*. "What is essential for this analysis," Wolfson points out, "is the fact that the shaking that results from the self-pleasure is a decidedly linguistic act, indeed the graphic act of writing" (CS, 71). More specifically, the primordial autoerotic act yields the linguistic structures of the Torah, of the created order, and of human language itself. In this remarkable mythological vision, God, language, and the entire created universe are erotic to their shared ontological core. Wolfson's summary of the very first lines of the Zohar draws out this mystico-erotic correspondence between writing and God's creative activity:

> The most powerful myth in zoharic kabbalah, textually placed in the beginning of the *Zohar*, which mirrors the ontic beginning of existence, involves the characterization of God begetting himself through the process of inscription that unfolds through the upper phallus etching the supernal tablet. . . . By extension, human writing too is endowed with sacred significance as a mode of *imitatio dei;* that is, the act of writing involves the unification of the masculine and feminine achieved by the former striking against the latter. This function of writing is especially applied to the composition of kabbalistic texts that expound secret matters. The purpose of such writing is to unite the male and female aspects of the divine. The salient theurgical component here should not obscure the mystical dimension, for from the kabbalistic vantage point, writing of secrets is a decidedly phallic activity that ensues from an ecstatic state wherein the mystic is united with the feminine divine Presence. (CS, 74)

In order to illustrate this further, Wolfson proceeds to describe a most remarkable medieval ritual in which the kabbalist prepares ritually for two consecutive evenings (Friday and Saturday) before he can inscribe an interpretation of the *sefirot* on Sunday. Having completed the proper purifications and preparations, he wraps himself in a prayer shawl on Sunday and places the crown of the Torah scroll (representing, as we shall soon see, both the Shekhinah and the corona of the penis) on his head, thereby symbolically uniting with the divine feminine Presence and empowering himself to write. Wolfson makes clear the remarkable phallic implications of this ritual: "Having united with the Presence, depicted by the placing of the crown of the Torah scroll upon his head, the scribe can assume the position of the phallus to disclose the secrets of the divine" (CS, 75). Nowhere perhaps have the erotic underpinnings of the mystical and its linkage to the act of writing texts been more dramatically and clearly displayed than here.

Circumcision also expresses in a particularly powerful and specifically Jewish way the phallic nature of writing (CS, 75). Indeed, the incision itself is seen as an act of writing, a semiotic mark, an inscription of the sign of the covenant (*'ot berit*) on the (sexualized) flesh of the infant boy. The cut, moreover, inscribes a physical opening that in turn corresponds to an ontological opening within God through which the visionary can witness the divine pleroma, thus, "[C]ircumcision provides the author of the *Zohar* with a typology of writing/reading that is at the same time a typology of mystical experience understood in a sexual vein" (CS, 30). In Wolfson's reading, hermeneutical activity is thus seen as an opening of the text that corresponds to the opening of the penile flesh: "Through exegesis, that which was concealed, hidden, closed—in a word, esoteric—becomes opened, disclosed, manifest—in a word, exoteric" (CS, 30). And this same complex of openings is in turn related to another, the opening of God to the kabbalist in visionary experience. Without circumcision, there can be no vision of God—it is the phallus, "the flesh," that grants mystical vision; hence the kabbalistic reading of the Jobian claim, "But I would behold God from my flesh" (CS, 31), that is, from the circumcised phallus. Related here as well is the common kabbalistic connection between the penis and the eye, for "only one who is circumcised has an eye that is open" (CS, 35). Little wonder, then, that kabbalists specified acts of writing as rectifications for sexual sins; both, after all, were understood to be products of the penis (CS, 76). So too with the facts that the word *sod*, "secret" or "mystery," is associated specifically with the sphere of *Yesod*, that is, the phallic gradation of the *sefirot* (S, 47), and that such phallic secrets—indeed the secret *as* the phallus—cannot be revealed to anyone who has not been circumcised (CS, 45).

The nature of mystical hermeneutics, then, is defined by a movement from closure to openness, from uncircumcised and unseeing penis to circumcised and seeing penis, from esoteric and hidden meaning to exoteric and revealed meaning. In Wolfson's terms again, "[d]isclosure of what has been concealed—through the opening of the flesh—is the basic structure common to visionary experience and mystical hermeneutics" (CS, 48). Just as writing and the creation of the universe were coded in symbolically phallic terms, mystical exegesis becomes a kind of erection, an ejaculatory experience of ontological openness, one-eyed vision, and esoteric revelation. Let us turn now to *Speculum* and see how these same themes are expanded, developed, and problematized there.

4. Gazing into Wolfson's *Speculum*

In traditional Jewish mysticism, the mystic is said to pass through seven palaces *(hekhalot)* on his way to the throne of glory *(kisse' ha-kavod)* or, alternately, to the chariot *(merkavah)* seen in Ezekiel's famous vision; hence the historical designations of Hekhalot and Merkavah mysticism given to this visionary tradition by modern Kabbalah scholars (S, 74). In the famous zoharic reworking of this ancient motif, the Torah is compared to a beautiful princess or maiden hidden away behind seven *hekhalot* (S, 157).[29] From there she beckons to her lover, the mystical exegete, who must pass through the seven interpretive layers of Scripture—a process that is often analogized as an erotic-exegetical "denuding" of the sacred text—in order finally to reach the king's daughter, who, to make matters even more allegorically complex, often stands in as a parabolic figure of the Shekhinah, that feminine Presence of the Godhead and last of the ten *sefirot* (and so first to encounter on the way "up") through which the male kabbalist approaches the divine pleroma. Hermeneutical experience is thus framed in both a sexual and a mystical way, as the kabbalist interprets his way to a much-longed-for sexual encounter with an erotically charged divine feminine Presence (I might briefly note the familial complexity of the symbols as well, since the Shekhinah is technically both a mother (as wife of God) and a lover of the kabbalist, and the maiden, as the king's (God's) daughter, is also the kabbalist's sister). At last we have found a true heteroerotic mysticism. That seems clear enough. Is not this the point of Wolfson's phallocentrism thesis and the kabbalist's erotic search for the textual maiden and the Presence? What could be more clear, more provocative, more male, and more heterosexual than this?

But it is not in fact clear at all. And that, put far too simply, is the point of Wolfson's *Speculum*. This text, much like the traditional parable of the erotic exegete and his royal lover ensconced within the palaces, imaginatively moves its readers through seven stages ("chapters," as we usually call them), repeatedly losing and finding us again through a chronological treatment of Jewish mysticism from the early biblical, apocalyptic, and rabbinic sources to the medieval Rhineland-German Pietists and the Provençal-Spanish kabbalists. In this historical process, we encounter Wolfson's theoretical reflections on the contextual and structural natures of "mysticism," symbolic and gender analyses of visionary phenomena, and ministudies of individual kabbalists and their schools (and hundreds of lengthy footnote-essays, often complete with Hebrew script, that seem to wrap around the text like some ancient talmudic commentary), until we finally arrive at the vision of the Godhead itself in the final and seventh palace-chapter. Once again, then, we encounter a two-dimensional text that performs its subject, intuitively recreating on the level of scholarship and rhetorical structure the mystical journey and final visionary experience it sets out to study discursively.

We are implicitly promised such a performative vision in the very title of the text, for "the speculum that shines" is a traditional kabbalistic reference to the historically unique vision of Moses, who alone among human beings saw God without images, that is, directly, through "the speculum that shines." All other prophets, sages, and seers, however great, saw only images through "the speculum that does not shine," that is, through the "cloud" or empty "mirror" of the Shekhinah. As the mystically inclined rabbinic exegete Hananel put it: "All the prophets saw [the glory] within the speculum that does not shine, and it seemed to them that they had seen a visible object.... the vision that they saw was an image and not the actual [entity]. Moses gazed upon the glory and the splendor of the Shekhinah through the speculum that shines from behind the Shekhinah" (S, 148). Inasmuch as the tradition defined such a shining vision as the exclusive property of Moses, the revelation is, by definition, a religious impossibility after him. But Wolfson reminds us that the rabbinic or kabbalistic figure of Moses, far from representing some actual historical figure, is in hermeneutical fact always a stand-in for or self-portrait of the mystical text's author (S, 332). He who sees through the speculum that shines in a particular mystical text is not Moses, then, but the author of the text himself.

Perhaps, we might conclude, the author of *this* text, like a modern kabbalistic Moses, may know something about the vision attained "through a speculum that shines" and, if we are fortunate enough, lead us to it through his own exegetical-mystical practice. This, in fact, is exactly what Wolfson does—he takes us through seven palace-chapters of astonishing erudition and hermeneutical skill to finally show us in the seventh the meanings of both the feminine Presence (the now denuded princess in the palace) who is "the speculum that does not shine" and, through her, the formless glory that glows behind or within her that we can make out, however darkly, "through a speculum that shines." Paradoxically, as we shall see in due time, such a final effulgence is not formless at all, and Wolfson is provocatively clear about what the kabbalist sees within his secret gnosis. Moreover and more radically, through Wolfson's interpretations we see with him what the kabbalist sees; as readers, we participate imaginatively in the specular accomplishments of the kabbalistic texts under study.

Visionary Experience in the Kabbalah: The Erotic Gaze

Before we can see, however, we must ask how the medieval kabbalists saw. The question already assumes the methodological canvas of Wolfson, who has framed his art along the borders of imagination and visionary experience or, in a more appropriate metaphor, has tilted his methodological mirror to pick up just these sorts of ocular secrets. The method thus becomes a metaphorical mirror, which, appropriately, mirrors back its subject, the kabbalistic speculum: "I have privileged the use of visionary experience as providing a speculum through which the scholar can gaze upon the religious texture of the various currents of Jewish mysticism" (S, 394; cf. S, 9). *Speculum,* then, is first and foremost a study of vision, of the ocular, imaginal, and specular modes of religious experience, particularly as they pertain to God's body. Indeed, the book's imaginal, visionary, and bodily foci are announced in a Blakean epigraph to the introduction that dialectically identifies and mystically unites humanity and divinity in the creative mysteries of the imagination: "O Human Imagination O Divine Body," the poet sings and Wolfson begins (S, 3). Visualization, image, enlightenment, illumination, hermeneutical in-sight, the aesthetics and ontology of light, reflection, mirror, flame, fire, flaming eyes, rainbows refracted through clouds, and the divine glory itself—these are the radiant terms of both kabbalistic mysticism and Wolfson's refracting study of it. In this, he moves away from both the orthodox position in Jewish studies, which, following Scholem, has tended to understand Judaism as a primarily auditory tradition (S, 50), and a very common position in studies of mysticism (which most likely derives from Christian apophatic mystical authors such as the Pseudo-Dionysius and John of the Cross) that wants to marginalize visionary phenomenon as "nonmystical," that is, as purely psychological or even delusional. Here, on the contrary, vision appears in the center of the mystical mirror within what Underhill so beautifully and appropriately called those "gleams of ecstatic vision" (quoted in S, 60); thus, it is only here, dazzled by these same reflected and refracted gleams, that we too can begin to see.

According to Wolfson, the kabbalists tended to understand the imagination as a mediating organ that works in terms of the visionary's psychological and cultural matrix. Like the Shekhinah itself, the imagination appears to be empty in itself. It always receives its particular forms from without, even if it insists on shaping these into common, perhaps even universal, structures. As one kabbalistic text puts it, "the glory appears to the prophet not in actuality but [according to] the image of the appearance" (S, 216), that is, according to the time and character and place of the visionary (S, 155). This does not, however, render the imagination simply "imaginary," a source of fantasy or purely fictive knowledge, for in the kabbalistic world the symbolic imagination is that "divine element of the soul that enables one to gain access to the realm of incorporeality by transferring or transmuting sensory data and/or rational concepts into symbols" (S, 8). And in this translation mode, Wolfson points out, its function is essentially hermeneutical; like the Greek god Hermes himself, after whom the discipline of hermeneutics is named,[30] the imagination has "carried across" *(trans-latus)* divine secrets "down" to the human realm. Employing Corbin's notion of the *mundus imaginalis* and the imaginal, as well as the phenomenological conclusions of Husserl, Heidegger, and Maurice Merleau-Ponty that there is no phenomenological difference between an experienced object and an imagined one (S, 53, 109), Wolfson can thus distance himself from psychological and political reductionisms[31] and insist that the imagination is "the organ that puts one in contact with spiritual realities that are perceptible to each individual according to the dominant images of one's religious and cultural affiliation" (S, 119). Such appearances, then, are not simply images that appear in the mind. Like the Hebrew term *dimmuyot* or the Latin *figurae*, these "images" "reflect the inherent nature of that which is visualized"; they are "ontological realities" or "ontic paradigms" that can be seen within the imagination (S, 39–40). Again, they are "diaphanous symbol[s] through which the opaque reality shines" (S, 62), genuine "hierophanies" of the sacred (S, 118). As such, the realm of the imaginary is at once real and illusory, for God is both definitively outside the image and yet somehow within it (S, 207). The imagination thus becomes "the divine element of the soul that enables one to gain access to the realm of incorporeality through a process of symbolization" (S, 63); strikingly, it is not at all clear that the modern reader should not include himself or herself among that "one." The text invites one in.

It is similar with the current debates on the constructed or universal nature of mystical experience. Wolfson rejects both the simple universalism of the perennialists, who want to assert a common essence or core of the world's mystical traditions, and what he calls the relativism, nominalism, or hyper-Kantianism of the contextualists, who insist on the constructed nature of all mystical experiences down to their ontological bases. Instead, Wolfson opts for "an intermediate position that seeks out common structures underlying the manifold appearances" (S, 56), a "modified contextualism" practiced in the light of structuralist assumptions (S, 54). "That there remains a common characteristic it would be absurd to deny" (S, 55), and this is predictable given the dynamics of the imagination—which, in Richard Kearney's words, is "neither an Argus of a thousand glances nor a Cyclops of one eye" (S, 7)—but equally significant, and perhaps far more relevant for the textualist and historian, are the culturally informed signs and images through which the mystic always understands and experiences the divine, "through the speculum that does not shine," as it were. Here too a dialectical theory of the symbolic imagination as a hermeneutical organ linking the physical world with the spiritual realm and the specificities of culture and language with a shared, indeed universal, psychological ability to imagine seems especially useful and apt, particularly for the historian of religions, as it is only here, in the middle, in the linguistic, symbolic, and imaginal details of the mediating imagination (of both the kabbalist and the historian), that comparison and historical understanding become possible at all.

*Hermeneutical Mysticism and
the Final Vision in the Seventh Palace*

What, then, do we see through in this imaginal world? What constitutes the vision of the kabbalists through the speculum that does not shine? And most important, what constitutes the vision through the speculum that *does* shine? It is of considerable theoretical, rhetorical, and religious significance that Wolfson waits until his seventh and final chapter to treat most fully the kabbalistic version of hermeneutical mysticism. It is also here, in the seventh, that we finally get to gaze on the princess and learn the erotic secret of the kabbalistic gnosis. Chapter 7, then, is the place where visionary revelation, textual hermeneutics, and mystical sexuality all collapse into one another within a single textual experience. It is here, then, in the seventh palace, that we must look for our answers.

Not that Wolfson did not isolate and name something of this hermeneutical mysticism early on, indeed from the very beginning: "The gap between revelation and interpretation is fully closed inasmuch as interpreting Scripture is itself a revelatory experience," Wolfson writes in the very first pages (S, 11). Vision too is ultimately a hermeneutical event, for "insofar as the visionary experience is hermeneutically related to the text, it may be said that the way of seeing is simultaneously a way of reading . . . a 'visionary hermeneutics'" (S, 53). Wolfson can thus write of a kind of infinite textuality or hermeneutical loop that issues from the nexus of scripture, mystical experience, and visionary event; hence, "the shaping of the text by the experience, which is itself informed by previous textual tradition, in fact precludes any dichotomization of revelation and interpretation" (S, 120). There is no "experience," then, to isolate apart from the texts.

But, just as important, neither are there any texts to isolate apart from the kabbalists' experiences. Wolfson is thus quite clear that underlying the elaborate theosophical, allegorical, and symbolic strategies of kabbalistic hermeneutics we can and should find actual psychological experiences. He can thus write alternately of an "exegetical mysticism" (S, 122), of an "experiential mysticism" (S, 122), and of the "active mystical nature of exegesis in general" (M, 124). Hence, with reference to the interpretation of apocalyptic and *merkavah,* or "chariot," texts: "Study should not be reduced to mere exegesis devoid of any experiential component; on the contrary, one must assume that the visions and revelatory experiences recorded in the apocalpyses are not simply literary forms but reflect actual experiences deriving from divine inspiration. . . . That a similar claim can be made about the chariot mystical texts should be self-evident" (M, 124). This is essentially the thesis of the present study, applied here to the kabbalistic texts. I might reword Wolfson's insight with respect to our present concerns as follows: "That a similar claim can be made about many contemporary studies of mysticism should be self-evident."

Even more radically—and here we are reminded immediately of Underhill's Teresa of Avila, who entered particular states of prayer at the very moment she was describing them with the pen in her inspired, automatic states of composition—the interpretation of sacred texts can actually generate in the hermeneut the mystical reality expressed in the texts. With the Zohar especially, "theosophical ruminations are practical means for achieving a state of ecstasy," and "there is indeed a genuine ecstatic experience underlying the hermeneutical posture of the *Zohar*" (M, 330). Or, in a different formulation, the Zohar is "inscribed within the circle of experience and interpretation: the vision that generated the text may be reenvisioned through interpretive study" (M, 331). There is a very thin, perhaps dotted line, then, between the original recorded vision and the imaginative recreation of it in the mind of the reader, and, under the right circumstances, the latter may actually lead to an experience of the former, always of course refashioned in terms of the visionary's culture and psyche. Wolfson tells us, for example, that as a result of their hermeneutical activity the kabbalists often experienced paranormal states of consciousness that frequently involved the phenomenon of fire (M, 122): "Ben Azzai was sitting and interpreting, and the fire surrounded him" (M, 327). Here too we learn from the Zohar (1:94b) of a fraternity of kabbalists sitting in a blazing house as they interpreted the Scriptures, connecting passage to passage among the mystical flames of the divine feminine Presence: "Thus it was that on that day the colleagues . . . saw the face of the Shekhinah and they were encompassed by fire. The face of R. Abba was burning like a flame from the joy of the Torah. It has been taught: that whole day none of them left the house and the house was bounded by smoke. Among themselves they were innovating words of Torah as if on that very day they had received the Torah on Mount Sinai" (M, 355–356).

The phenomenon of a hermeneutical mysticism and its connection to visionary experience are thus well-documented characteristics of the kabbalistic traditions. What is of particular interest beyond this is Wolfson's further claims that this hermeneutical mysticism was also an erotic mysticism, that the exegetical process was sexualized and gendered (and rather complexly so) down to its ontological core, and that seeing itself was an essentially phallic act. In Wolfson's technical terminology, kabbalistic mysticism was defined, especially in its later medieval forms, by a particular "phallocentric ocularcentrism" (CS, xii). Such technical brevity hides the complexity of Wolfson's argument, which advances simultaneously through a number of exegetical and symbolic paths. Again, it bears repeating that, as in the Zohar itself, there is no simple linear argument here but a complex of symbolic connections, traditional associations, and psychoanalytically informed textual interpretations, all of which together produce for the reader who has advanced this far the final vision "through the speculum that shines." Here, in the seventh, the princess in the palace is in sight.

But in what kind of sight? Much of Wolfson's argument is based on the feminist theory that the male gaze is a double phallic gaze, "the eye substituting for the penis and the object of vision signifying the externalized, representable form of the phallus" (M, 104). As we shall soon see, it is this very argument that defines for Wolfson the final vision through the speculum that shines, so it is of some importance that we understand how he arrived at it. Precisely because of its importance, Wolfson marshals a number of different subtheses to establish this major claim. For the sake of illustration we might divide them into those that treat the phallus as subject/seer and those that treat the phallus as object/seen.

Foremost among the former, that is, those treating the phallus as the subject or organ of imaginal vision, is Wolfson's argument that circumcision and visionary experience are often connected in the kabbalistic imagination through the ritual of circumcision, which serves as "an initiation that results in the specularization of God, the penis functioning as the organ that facilitates vision" (S, 104), hence again the Jobian claim that "[f]rom my flesh . . . I will see God" (S, 342), a motif which we have examined above.[32] Also important here, however, are Wolfson's exegesis of the phallic eyes "seized by pulsations" and emitting "flames of fire" (S, 92–93), a theme which he had developed earlier in two important articles;[33] his interpretation of the kabbalist, uncovering his head to "derive pleasure" from and "feast on" the splendorous Presence as an intensely erotic experience, with the uncovering of the head symbolizing "the disclosure of the male organ, perhaps in an ejaculatory state" and the act of voraciously eating standing in as a metaphor for sexual intercourse (S, 42–43); his analysis of sight itself as sexual, according to which the kabbalist is rewarded with a vision of the face of the Presence for refusing to look at an obscene scene, the former mystico-erotic experience acting in essence as a sublimation of the latter sexual experience (S, 43 n. 130); his interpretation of Moses who hid his face, that is, who "sublimated his sexual arousal vis-à-vis the divine" (S, 43) and, according to rabbinic sources, separated from his wife after he had received the Torah on Mount Sinai;[34] and the idea that it is in the phallic gradation of *Yesod* that the imaginal forms actually appear (S, 315). Wolfson can thus write: "The contextualizing of the imaginative faculty in the phallus is a central tenet of zoharic theosophy; indeed, one might very well speak of the phallic imagination as the critical element in the ecstatic-mystical experience underlying many of the homiletical and theoretical discussions of the *Zohar*" (S, 316). It is the phallus that sees, that imagines, that knows.

Just as the phallus is the kabbalistic organ that sees, so too is it that which is seen (this subject-object nondualism functioning as a kind of self-cycling autoeroticism, we might surmise), for "it is by virtue of the phallus that the mystic is granted permission to see what is obscured in the ordinary field of human experience and that which is seen is the divine phallus disclosed in the moment of coitus" (S, 286). Hence the kabbalistic gloss on Isaiah 33.17 to "behold the King in His beauty *(yofi)*," that is, in his phallic form (S, 85–86 n. 50); the kabbalistic injunction against viewing the sign of the covenant as the "bow" in the clouds corresponding to the *Yesod,* that is, the phallic gradation (the phallus in the Shekhinah; S, 337; cf n. 40); and the ancient understanding of the enthronement of God as a form of *hieros gamos* that the visionary might finally witness (S, 99).[35] Such seemingly outrageous claims become significantly less unbelievable when we find similar suggestions made in the kabbalistic texts themselves. Consider, for example, the *Sefer ha-Yiḥud* (the "Book of Unity") describing visionary gnosis as that moment when the "permission to see and to contemplate is attained by those worthy 'to behold the king in his beauty' (Isa. 33:17). They enter the chamber of the king and 'eat of its luscious fruit' (Cant. 4:16), and they delight in the entertainment of the bridegroom and bride" (S, 286). Or Elijah ben Solomon Zalman, the Gaon of Vilna (d. 1797), writing that "[i]t is known that all union is dependent on sight, as it is written, '[When the bow is in the cloud] I will see it and remember the everlasting covenant . . . [the sign of the] covenant I have established' (Gen. 9:16–17). It is known that the establishment of the covenant *(haqamat berit)* is in sexual copulation" (S, 286). Or consider Joseph of Hamadan: "The covenant *(berit)* that is seen in the cloud on a rainy day signifies the colors of the attribute of the Saddiq. . . . Ezekiel the prophet, may peace be upon him, alluded to this when he said, 'Like the appearance of the bow which shines in the clouds on a rainy day. . . . That was the appearance of the semblance of the Presence of the Lord. When I beheld it, I flung myself down on my face' (Ezek. 1.28). From here [it is deduced that] it is forbidden to look at the phallus *(berit)* and the one who sees the phallus should fall on his face" (S, 340). The sexual connotations of the king's beauty, the eating of fruit, and the delights of the bridegroom and bride, as well as seeing the union of the rainbow and cloud and immediately connecting this to the covenant consummated in sexual intercourse—these are hardly wild

Freudian anachronisms. Freudian they may be, anachronistic or inappropriate they definitely are not.

Most significant, however, is the final vision of the kabbalist at the very height of the *sefirot,* a mystical experience which, for Wolfson, constitutes a vision of the divine phallus through the medium of the Shekhinah or divine feminine Presence, often, we are told, "through a nocturnal dream-vision" (S, 307). In Wolfson's language, "the feminine aspect of the Godhead is the optical apparatus through which the masculine aspect, and particularly the *membrum virile,* is seen" (S, 306–307)—hence "an opening, an optic hole, by means of which the concealed is disclosed" (S, 307). Here, following the French feminist and psychoanalyst Luce Irigaray,[36] Wolfson is playing on the double meaning of the term *speculum* as both "mirror" and gynecological instrument or optical device through which one explores the sexual crevices of the female body. Strikingly, and in a typically androcentric fashion, what the kabbalist sees through this female orifice is not the female womb or even the feminine nature of God (for that is the speculum that does not shine, she who has no form of her own, who is erased), but the divine phallus inside, hidden as it were by the encompassing or containing vagina. This is the inner glory that pulses, shimmers, and shines within the feminine cloud-mirror when it speaks to the righteous prophets: thus, "the concealed phallus, the ultimate and obsessional object of the mystic's gaze, is specularized through the speculum that resists representational form, as it has nothing of its own" (S, 274). The divine feminine Shekhinah is thus an optical apparatus that refracts the divine phallic light and renders the invisible visible, like the rainbow that becomes apparent in the mist of the formless cloud (S, 274).[37]

But it is not just that the divine phallus is seen inside the feminine. In the world of Kabbalah, where innumerable gender transformations and transsexual processes routinely render the male female and the female male or collapse both within an unequally shared androgyny,[38] it is also the case that the feminine *crowns* the phallus as its exposed corona. "The vision of the Presence is ultimately a seeing of the corona of the divine phallus" (S, 342). She is the sheath through which the male form erotically appears (S, 275), the Sabbath "crown of beauty" that sits on the dew-covered heads of the kabbalists who had invoked her the previous evening as their beloved bride (S, 275 n. 14). Such an understanding stems from the theosophical understanding of the bifurcation of the Godhead (and subsequently the human) from its original androgynous state into the separation and fissure of historical exile. The male longing for heterosexual union, then, is interpreted by the kabbalists as a desire on the part of the separated male to reunite with that aspect of himself that was separated from him. The site of this reunited androgyny is the phallus itself, the organ itself corresponding to the male and the corona corresponding to the female.[39] In a particularly complex gender dynamic, then, the divine, reintegrated phallus is both male and female, or better, its femaleness is included in and in some sense occluded by its maleness, or better still, its femaleness "crowns" its more basic and foundational maleness. The kabbalistic phallus is a *male androgyne*. It is the phallus that thus acts as the site of gender union within a one-sex theory; ontically speaking, the masculine is more basic (S, 358).

The Enlightened Will Shine:
Mystical Hermeneutics as Erotic Mysticism

It is a kabbalistic commonplace that the study of Torah is an illuminative experience, not simply in the metaphorical sense, but in some mystical sense: whereas unprepared hermeneuts burst into flames and even die, pious exegetes are said to glow, surrounded as they are by the Presence, light streaming from their heads. This is the crowning "splendor" *(zohar)* of the Shekhinah, the masculine potency that corresponds in kabbalistic thought to the *Yesod,* the phallic gradation refracted through Torah and its study. Wolfson can thus write: "Mystical enlightenment thus consists of the illumination of the divine phallus on the heads of the kabbalists, which results in their ability to comprehend mysteries of Torah that emerge from the feminine Presence" (S, 357). Hence, the word *'aṭarah,* or "crown," is used as both a technical term for the penile corona and as a symbolic designation for the Shekhinah (S, 358). This, Wolfson points out, implies some subtle crossing of gender boundaries, for when the kabbalists are crowned by the Presence, they are also implicitly feminized (S, 357). Such a crowning, moreover, harks back to the ritual of circumcision, for in both cases it is the corona that is exposed and highlighted. We are back to circumcision as the moment of mystical vision and hermeneutical insight.

Such a crowning carries eschatological meanings as well, for in the world to come, we are told, the righteous will be crowned with diadems and derive pleasure from the Presence (S, 361). It is thus the crown that symbolizes the soul's phallic union with the divine, a union that is often described in intensely erotic terms. Consider, for example, what happened to Ben Azzai in the rabbinic legend of the four sages who entered

Pardes. Ben Azzai's vision would literally kill him: "Thus it happened to Ben Azzai: the light that he gazed upon overwhelmed him from his great desire to cleave to it and to derive pleasure from it without interruption, and after he cleaved to it he did not want to separate from that sweet radiance, and he remained immersed and hidden within it. His soul was crowned and adorned from that radiance and splendor to which no creature can cleave and afterwards live" (S, 362). The crown for Wolfson thus "represents the unification of the male mystic with the feminine Presence by virtue of the effulgence that encircles and envelops the head of the mystic. In such cases the crown symbolizes the corona of the penis that unites with the Shekhinah" (S, 363).

Summing up, then, we might say that when this feminine crown or corona is exposed, through circumcision and/or erection, the divinity itself can be seen through the speculum that does not shine, that is, through the Shekhinah as corona. Which is to say that the speculum that shines is the exposed, possibly ejaculatory phallus (S, 43). And all of this is effected not simply through the kabbalist's ritualized sexual intimacy with his wife on the Sabbath eve, but through exegetical activity that is understood to be a kind of sexual union with the feminized Torah/Shekhinah. It is through her as the speculum that does not shine, that is, as a kind of piercing mirror, that the final vision of the Godhead within the womb can be won.[40] Here, then, is the final hermeneutical vision of the kabbalist according to Wolfson:

> [T]extual study is presented as an intensely erotic experience. The exegete stands in the position of the phallic *Yesod* and the text corresponds to the feminine *Shekhinah*. But here again it is necessary to point out that the feminine is localized as part of the phallus. When one appreciates this transmutation of gender symbols, it becomes evident that through textual study the kabbalist is visually contemplating the divine phallus. Reading is a double mirroring: the words of Scripture are a reflex of the *Shekhinah* which, in turn, is a reflex of *Yesod* [the sefirotic phallus]. The hermeneutical task is thus to penetrate beneath the textual surface so that one beholds the phallus of God, the ontic source of secret gnosis. . . . The hermeneutical circle is inscribed in the biblical verse "From my flesh I will see God," that is, from the sign of the covenant engraved on the penis the mystic can imaginatively visualize the divine phallus. The movement of the imagination is from the human body to God and from God back to the human body again. (S, 397)

Finally, it is not without some significance, for our own present Blakean reflections and for the rhetorical structure of *Speculum* itself, which we might remember began with a line from Blake ("O Human Imagination O Divine Body"), that Wolfson concludes *Speculum* the way he began it: "Thus my path returns to Blake," Wolfson concludes in his very last lines, and ends his monograph on the kabbalistic imagination with our own patron poet:

> The Eternal Body of Man is The Imagination
>   God Himself
> That is
>   The Divine Body . . . (S, 397)

The Homoerotic Turn

One important implication of all of this is that the kabbalistic vision is, much like Christian bridal mysticism and Sufi eroticism, unmistakably homoerotic in its final structure. Unlike all of our previous authors, however, Wolfson sees this clearly and states it explicitly. He knows the secret, and he refuses to deny it: "[I]n the Jewish mystical texts it is always the male mystic visually confronting the male deity" (S, 396). Indeed, he radicalizes it with his insistence that the phallocentric nature of both the mystic's sight and the object seen render the encounter doubly homoerotic, for "the singular bond that connects the male deity and male worshiper is the penis" (S, 370). Granted, there is plenty of heterosexual symbolism in the kabbalistic universe—again, just as there was in the Christian and Sufi worlds—but it is all predicated "on the ontological reintegration of the feminine in the masculine. That is, heterosexuality is transformed by kabbalistic symbolism into a homoeroticism: the union of male and female is a reconstitution of the male" (S, 396). In different terms, although erotic yearning for the female is indeed a sign of the beginnings of the redemptive process, that is, the theurgic uniting of the male and female principles in the sefirotic Godhead, the consummation of that process "is marked by the restoration of the feminine to the masculine, which entails the transformation of the Shekhinah from feminine other to the sign of the covenant on the corona of the phallus."[41] And this crossing of gender identities has the inevitable effect of shifting "the texture of the erotic experience from the heterosexual to the homoerotic."[42] We should not, then, naively mistake heteroerotic symbolism for heterosexual identities, orientations, or even meanings. The presence of the former by no means guarantees the latter.

Consider, for example, the complex gender dynamic implied in the kabbalistic notion that the kabbalists should unite with the Shekhinah and their wives so that the "female waters" might be stimulated. This seems like a clear heteroerotic dynamic, until we learn that the ultimate purpose of this act was to arouse the upper "male waters." The kabbalist's heterosexual union with the feminine, in other words, had an ultimate homoerotic purpose, to arouse the upper male and cause the divine phallus to become erect. They united with the divine male through the divine and human female—a mystical homoeroticism effected through heterosexual activity: "Come and see the secret of the matter: When the righteous man is in the world, the Shekhinah does not depart from him, and her desire is for him. Consequently, the desire of love for her from above is like the desire of a male for a female when he is jealous of her. . . . From the righteous above the supernal waters flow and from the righteous below the feminine emits fluid in relation to the masculine in complete desire."[43] And this, in turn, masculinizes the Shekhinah in kabbalistic thought, for by her insemination she is "sweetened," that is, in the complicated symbolism of the *sefirot,* through her union with the righteous male the gradation of feminine judgment is ameliorated by that of masculine mercy. Such gender complexity, Wolfson points out, makes it impossible to argue simply that the mystic is masculine in relationship to the feminine divine. What we in fact have is a sexual union between the male kabbalist and the Shekhinah that feminizes the male (in relationship to the upper male, since he is included in the feminine Presence) and masculinizes the female (in relationship to the lower male, since by her insemination she is "sweetened" with masculine mercy),[44] and all the while a human male mystic is arousing a divine male God. Nothing is as it seems.

Such a latent homoeroticism spills over onto the sociological plane, where it helps define charisma (as sexual attraction) and intimately bonds males to one another within an all-male mystical community. In Wolfson's eloquent terms, "[h]omoeroticism is the carnality of celibate renunciation," and "[a] prolepsis of the eschatological transmutation of erotic energy from the bisexual to the monosexual is found in the fraternity of mystics whose study of Torah takes the place of sexual mating with their female partners."[45] Thus, the Zohar states (2:94b): "R. Hiyya and R. Jose met one night in the Tower of Tyre. They stayed there as guests and took joy in one another. R. Jose said: How glad I am that I saw the face of the Shekhinah" (S, 370). Wolfson goes below the surface of this passage to point out that the mystical vision of the Shekhinah is connected "to the joyous bonding of the two male mystics," and this in a phallic tower (S, 370).[46] Thus, heterosexual desire (for one's wife and the Shekhinah) is "fulfilled in the homoerotic bonding of the mystic to the male body of God, which is constituted by the members of the kabbalistic fraternity."[47]

And this homoeroticism in turn develops into a divine autoeroticism, for God "takes delight" in the righteous mystics who study Torah, who are in fact his own sons created in his own image: "The erotic bond between God and the righteous, therefore, is not incestuous, but narcissistic: God's love of the righteous is an expression of self-love. God delights in his own image reflected in the faces of the mystics even as the mystics delight in their own image reflected in the face of God. From this perspective, moreover, it can be said that the homoeroticism is an aspect of divine autoeroticism."[48] And here, of course, we have come full circle, from the original autoerotic creation of the universe from an androgynous male deity to the full eschatological completion of humanity's union with God in the autoerotic experience of a divine mirroring of the male as both subject and object of vision and delight. Strikingly, nowhere is there a woman to be seen. From her allegedly "formless" status as the speculum that does not shine (males have seldom been able to figure out the shape of a woman's genitalia) to her instrumental use by the kabbalist to arouse the upper male to her final eschatological incorporation or subsumption in the divine phallus, she is always and everywhere erased. So, in the end, we have not found a simple heteroerotic mysticism at all. We are back to a conflicted, essentially misogynistic homoeroticism at the heart of the mystical. Christian bridal mysticism, the Sufi witness practice, Ramakrishna's Śākta Tantra, and now medieval Kabbalah—they have all brought us here.

5. The Double Mirror of Scholarship: A Personal Reading

Is there some special way that *Speculum* is able to mirror back to its readers the visionary and mystical experiences that focus and define its content? Does it, can it function as a visionary experience in its own right, on at least a literary or hermeneutical plane? I want to approach these questions—which lie at the very heart of the present study—from two poles, a subjective or psychological pole and an objective or theoretical pole. In truth, this is a false dichotomy, and I do not want to make too much of it, for, as I am about to demonstrate, the objective or comparative fruits of my hermeneutical interaction with Wolfson's *Speculum* flow directly out of some deeply subjective psychological experiences whose independent normative implications I would set at nil. Still, there is something to be said, both rhetorically and theoretically, for keeping the subjective and objective relatively distinct (as another version of the text's "resistance," perhaps), and in the end the comparative conclusions that constitute the latter, which can effectively be applied elsewhere, are more theoretically useful than the former, which have infinite personal value but little if any external application.

The Subjective Pole

Let me begin by asking whether we have been able to locate something that we can safely call Elliot Wolfson's mystical experiences. Certainly we have discovered more than enough evidence for the kabbalists' mystical experiences and their genesis in hermeneutical activity, but what of this man and his exegetical work? In the end, I think, we must admit that there is little that we can say about the personal religious experiences of Elliot Wolfson. But this, I must add, is exactly what we would expect with a Jewish mystical writer, for, as we have learned above, the dichotomy between revelation and interpretation collapses in Jewish mysticism within an infinite textuality or hermeneutical circle in a manner that effectively renders the very categories of our essentializing question inappropriate, even a bit silly. To reiterate once again, hermeneutics itself is a kind of mysticism.

But still, why did I sense so strongly a mystical subtext working within Wolfson's *Speculum*? What did I see, if not at least something of Elliot Wolfson? Looking back, I would now say that what I saw when I gazed into Elliot Wolfson's *Speculum* was not so much Elliot as myself. This is, after all, a speculum, a *mirror*. Certainly the kabbalists themselves understood that what they saw in the speculum of the Shekhinah were reflections of their own divine souls, which, paradoxically, were also reflexively understood to be mirror-like. As Wolfson described their understanding, "[H]uman imagination is a mirror that reflects the divine mirror in such a way that by imaging the image of the divine anthropos the visionary, in effect, is seeing his own pneumatic being projected outward" (S, 352). A certain psychological reflexivity, a Ricouerian second naïveté, if you will.

Certainly this is what happened to me when I read Wolfson's *Speculum*. Subjectively speaking, what I saw glimmering in Wolfson's hundreds of visionary accounts, exegetical insights, and homiletic stories were reflections, many of them stunningly accurate, some of them almost exact reproductions, of my own mystical experiences and hermeneutical conclusions. The palpably felt inner "fire consuming fire" (S, 158), the *lingam*-phallus that grants and initiates a vision (not to mention hermeneutical activity), the ambiguous inside-outside phenomenology of the ecstatic ascent, the bright dream as place of vision ("they see the light in several images *[dimmuyot]*, visions, or dreams," as one kabbalistic text puts it [quoted in S, 152]),[49] phallic feet, the hermeneutical-textual nature of mystical experience (this was certainly the clearest reflection for me), the phallic head (in the kabbalistic sense a glowing crown or diadem, in my case a unicorn's horn often felt as a tingling sensation or bursting at the top of the skull), a feminine divine Presence, the overwhelming erotic quality of the encounter with this Presence, a kind of "visionary thinking" evolved from "mystical inspiration" (S, 285), the union of eros and noesis, the consequent emotional notes of danger, fear, and risk, and the final ecstatic death as the moment of mystical rapture (S, 335–336)—these *all* found deep and powerful resonances and reflections in my subjective experiences and hermeneutical conclusions, not metaphorically, but phenomenologically, psychologically, actually. Indeed, I could take any number of Wolfson's quoted kabbalistic texts or, often more helpful, his own hermeneutical glosses on them, replace their specifically kabbalistic or theoretical terms with Tantric or personal ones, and use them, almost verbatim, as accurate phenomenological descriptions of what I saw and felt that Night and many nights before and since. And sometimes even this replacement is not necessary, as when, for example, Wolfson describes the kabbalistic understanding that the "writing of secrets is a decidedly phallic activity that ensues from an ecstatic state wherein the mystic is united with the feminine divine Presence" (CS, 74). I recognize this. I remember this. I *know* this. Dare I admit such a truth? But I already have.

The hermeneutical experience of reading *Speculum*, then, was quite literally a mystical one for me, not because it recorded the confessionally shared mystical experiences of Elliot Wolfson, but because it reflected back to me my own mystical experiences through the mirrors of the kabbalistic texts and Wolfson's sympathetic mirroring of them in his own eloquent prose. Exactly as the kabbalists (not to mention Underhill, Massignon, Zaehner, and Bharati) claimed and Wolfson made so clear, the act of reading a text was capable of reproducing, at least on the levels of memory and nostalgia, something psychologically akin to the visionary experience that first ecstatically produced it. In Sells's terms, the text encoded a meaning event that in turn could hermeneutically reflect a whole series of mystical experiences, in this case, my own.

I fully realize that this is hardly a traditional way to read, much less evaluate, an academic text, and in the end I cannot adequately defend my reading in any of the usual rational or discursive ways. All I can do is assert as clearly and as unequivocally as I am able what it is that I hermeneutically and mystically experienced. Underhill would call this the indubitable "fact" of my psychological experience, and although I am perfectly aware that such a fact is open to multiple interpretations and can be deconstructed through any number of possible critical channels (most of which I welcome and some of which I have practiced on myself above), in the end I cannot object to the appropriateness of her term. I can only assert what the mystical traditions have so often insisted themselves, that there is an intuitive, nondiscursive way of reading and understanding mystical texts and the authors who wrote them, and that this gnosis is something that can only be "received" outside the normal channels of the rational mind; hence the claim of many kabbalists that they possess an esoteric lore attained not through reason but through a received tradition, that is, through "Kabbalah." I interpret such a claim as a phenomenologically accurate description of the reception of textual-hermeneutical vision beyond the realm of reason from an imaging unconscious that has been prepared by intense hermeneutical work. The "tradition," then, is essentially a textual phenomenon working its magic independently of discursive ratiocination, that is, in the hidden depths of the psyche and its imaginal powers.[50]

To my knowledge, Wolfson has never addressed the issue in quite this way, and I certainly do not want to suggest that my reading even begins to exhaust the many hermeneutical, historical, and mystical implications of his text. There does, however, seem to be a rather solid symbolic place for me to stand within the parameters of his own discourse—before what he himself calls the double mirror. We have already encountered this double mirror many times. We saw it encoded into the final vision, where a phallic gaze encountered, and found itself mirrored in, a phallic object. We saw it again at the very end of *Speculum*, where it appeared as a sexual dimorphism between the words of Scripture, which were understood to be a reflection of the Shekhinah, and the *Yesod,* or divine phallus, of which the Shekhinah was herself a reflection—divine text mirroring divine feminine mirroring divine phallus. Wolfson returns to the same metaphor in "Lying on the Path," this time in order to apply it closer to home, to the scholarly and pious reader: "The temptation to read oneself into the text poses itself equally to the scholar who on the face of it is functioning independently of a faith community and to the member of that community. Indeed, in the case of both, the act of reading may be portrayed as a double mirroring. The text is a mirror that reflects the reader and the reader a mirror that reflects the text" (LP, 7). If the metaphor is at all accurate, what we have here is a mirror mirroring another mirror, that is, a kind of infinite regress of reflections, none of which, I must add, are "really real." That, after all, is the nature of a reflection: it both is and is not. It is a presence and an absence at the same time, a refraction that both reproduces and reverses the original within a phantom appearance.[51] Hence, although I am perfectly aware of the unusual fashion in which I have personally read and appropriated Wolfson's *Speculum,* I would suggest that much of the academic scandal is relativized and muted somewhat by my equally acute awareness that the text will mean and be something quite different to another reader-mirror. My reading, in other words, is just that, *my* reading, a subjective hermeneutical-mystical experience relative to my own life and work, in Wolfson's apt phrase, a "creative misreading" or traditional "deconstruction"—in the end, a *double reflection* that calls both the text and myself into being.

The Objective Pole

But I reject the notion that what we have here is pure projection, mere reflection, romantic illusion. Projection, reflection, illusion? Yes. But also hermeneutical insight into the very similar processes that have produced the historical mystical texts and their authors. Am I creatively misreading the medieval kabbalists (and the Bengali texts) in the light of my own psychological experiences? Yes. And this is exactly what the historical mystics were doing with their own textual inheritances. Am I reading them again through the lenses of my own socially constructed sexuality and gender and their questions and conflicts? Yes. And this is exactly what they were doing, again in their own culturally specific ways.[52] In this, we as historians of mysticism are no different than the mystics we study, and we can use our own embodied hermeneutical-mystical experiences to understand and recover theirs. It is the hermeneutical *process,* not the doctrinal content, that is similar (although, given our shared neurobiologies, even the latter is often strikingly similar). And this, I suppose, is yet another way of asserting the basic thesis of this study.

But there is something more here, for there are real theoretical payoffs to such an imaginative engagement, genuine comparative insights that would have been impossible without the original subjective connection. Take, for example, the topic of mystical eroticism. There was one particular aspect of *Speculum* with which I could not personally identify—the homoerotic nature of the kabbalistic symbolism. As I pointed out above in my "Secret Talk: Heroic Heretical Heterosexuality," this had made no existential sense to me when I first encountered something similar in Christian bridal mysticism, and it makes no more existential or sexual sense to me now. It does, however, make perfect theoretical sense, as I tried to demonstrate in chapter 1 with respect to Underhill's bridal mystics and in chapter 2 with Massignon's Sufis. Such a homoerotic model is only strengthened when similar patterns are found to be independently operating in entirely different mystical traditions. I was thus happily stunned to see just how close Wolfson's gender analyses of the kabbalistic fraternities were to my own analyses of Ramakrishna's mysticism and its homoerotic patterning of his devotional Tantric community. Both of us, quite independently, had demonstrated a whole series of theses with entirely different material: that the symbolic systems set up a male mystic to sexually encounter a male deity; that the former fact inevitably transforms symbolic heterosexuality (female soul/male divine) into a lived homoeroticism (human male/divine male); that the sexual nature of the mysticism results in a distinctively esoteric structure; that such esoteric-erotic systems, while seeming to affirm a feminine aspect of the Godhead, actually end up erasing woman almost entirely from the system; that psychoanalytic reductionism, while helpful as a hermeneutical tool, in the end collapses within the symbolic world of the tradition, since the ground to which the kabbalists or Tāntrikas reduced their own visionary and mystical experiences was posited as divine (in the kabbalistic case, the divine soul; in the Tantric case, the goddess's divine *śakti*); and that, in Wolfson's terms, the "renunciation of heterosexual carnality and the concomitant affirmation of the homosocial rapture of mystical ecstasy"[53] expresses itself in terms of an erotic passion that binds together a mystical fraternity, in the kabbalist context through the phallic gaze encountering the divine phallic object, in Ramakrishna's case through the symbol of the self-born phallus *(liṅgam)* that generates devotional love between the *avatāra* and his all-male community.[54] And so on and so on, often down to precise mystico-physiological theories (e.g., the experience of a palpably felt fire, the phallic foot, or the cerebral location of the semen).

In terms of my own life and work, none of these insights would have been possible without my own subjective engagement with these issues both in my own Catholicism and in the Bengali traditions. In effect, I needed some concrete way to work through these problems, both religiously and intellectually. I needed texts. In Wolfson's dialectical terms, hermeneutical revelation required a prior occultation in the specificity of the texts, which in turn assumed a prior revelation in the mystico-erotic experiences of the figure of the texts, which of course in turn were formed by other texts, and so on. To enter the opaqueness of the texts, then, is to enter a psychohistorical process of revealing and concealing *and to participate in it.*

But such a hermeneutical process need not imply a complete identification. I am not a Hindu, much less a Tāntrika. In Wolfson's terms, the texts and the traditions have always shown a very real "resistance" to my attempts to understand them, and, in the end, my understanding ultimately issues from a genuine sexual and cultural distance and a consequent realization that, inasmuch as I understand the texts and their subject, I understand them because they are what I am not. Or, more accurately, inasmuch as I understand the texts and their subject (and there is much that I do not understand), *I understand them because they are and are not what I am.* That is to say, to return to our mirror metaphor, I am able to understand something of the mystery that was Ramakrishna and the texts that record his experiences, both because we share a common mystico-erotic set of experiences *and* because these experiences appear in our bodies and in the texts as sexual opposites, reversed images of one another in the double mirror of our shared humanity. Remove either pole, the subjective or the objective, the sympathetic identification or the textual resistance, and hermeneutical understanding collapses. Our mutual images are thus momentarily caught in a double mirror for us to ponder, reflect on, and ultimately lose again. Such is the nature of the scholar's mystical experience and its hermeneutical reflection.

SECRET TALK *Svapna-Siddha*

Blessed is the person initiated in a dream *[svapna-siddha]*.
                    Ramakrishna, in Ram Chandra Datta's *Jīvanavṛttānta*

These dreams can be very exactly described as "initiatory." . . . doctrines later developed in many writings are inseparable from the teachings thus received in dreams.
                    Henry Corbin, "The Visionary Dream in Islamic Spirituality"

How many times have I just escaped "losing" myself—losing my way in that labyrinth where I was in danger of being killed, sterilized, "emasculated" (by one of those terrible mother goddesses, for example). An infinite series of intellectual adventures—and I use that word "adventure" in its primary sense of existential risk. They were not, all those things, mere items of "knowledge," acquired piecemeal and at leisure from books; they were so many encounters, confrontations, and temptations. I am perfectly aware, now, of all the perils that I skirted during that long "quest": first and foremost, the danger of forgetting that I had a goal, that I was directing my footsteps toward something, that I was trying to reach a center.
                    Mircea Eliade, *Ordeal by Labyrinth*

RAMAKRISHNA TAUGHT THAT it is possible for a certain type of aspirant to be initiated or "perfected" in a dream. The Bengali and Sanskrit compound he uses here, *svapna-siddha* ("perfected in a dream" or, with a little imagination, "a dream to perfect"), has been an especially fruitful one for me, both hermeneutically and mystically.[1] Accordingly, I would like to spend a few final moments reflecting on this idea and what I believe that it can offer us in our search for an intellectually adequate and mystically inspiring hermeneutical practice.

If we look for such perfecting/perfected dreams in the Bengali texts on the life and teachings of Ramakrishna, we very quickly find them, and practically everywhere. Specifically, devotees are constantly dreaming of Ramakrishna, and later of his wife, Sharada, and of being initiated by them. But, interestingly enough, however auspicious or "perfect" the initiatory dreams are seen to be, they are never enough for the dreamers. Inevitably, the disciple feels compelled to act on the dream, to live it out. Specifically, the dreamer feels driven to seek out in waking life the living presence seen in the dream. In short, he or she must make the psychological "dream" *(svapna)* "perfect" *(siddha)* in social reality, ritual, and public discourse. Freud's notion that every dream is a wish fulfillment is here given its distinctly Indian flavor: the dream-wish, already fulfilled or "perfected" in the dream, must nevertheless be perfected again through the ritual of initiation, the giving of a mantra, and the perfecting "practice" *(sādhana)* that both the initiation and the mantra imply. What began as a wish in the night is now an integral part of social reality, human identity, and religious institution.

What is more—and this is the key—from a historical perspective, the dream affects not just the dreamer but the dreamed, for it is inevitably the dreamers who end up encoding their dream-experiences in texts, constructing in the process the image and identity of the dreamed (in this case, Ramakrishna) for posterity's sake—dreams create texts and, with them, saints.

Certainly this has been true in my own life, for what have I done but try to "perfect" a series of dreams, to "write them out" in my own texts on a saint in order to give them a public, social form, a "body" or corpus, as it were, that might stand up to the critical scrutiny of my colleagues and readers? Once again, the nocturnal and the diurnal cannot be separated; they are two movements of the same life. Dream becomes scholarship, and scholarship becomes dream. In truth, the written corpus is a corpus written.

Consider again the flames of the incandescent unicorn under the dark waters. It has been my vocation to call, pray, plead, and coax it out. It is a scandalous, terrifying creature—and I have known much fear—but it is also a beautiful being. And although its paradoxical truths were in some sense already "perfected in the dream" *(svapna-siddha)*, they also constituted a "dream to be perfected" *(svapna-siddha)* in intellectual work, social discourse, and texts, like this one. Like nonduality itself, everything is already accomplished, and yet it must be realized as such. The mystical appears here not as a series of isolated "peak experiences"—although these are very important—but as a lifelong process of interpreting the world and oneself into being. We are narrative paths, not stable mountains.

And by narrative paths, I do not mean to suggest that we write our own stories or fully determine our own paths. Not at all. Certainly in my own case I had *no* idea where my own thought and dreams would lead me. I know I am in their story, but I also know that I have little control of its direction and conclusions. To create is to surrender to these intellectual and imaginative forces in one's life and head, to become a cipher or vessel for energies well beyond one's conscious control. Only then might one become a "hole" in space-time through which the secret might be spoken anew.

* * *

But what if I am just plain wrong? What if the roads of excess I have chosen are existential dead ends, the unfortunate results of some disastrously mistaken directions? (That damn Freud.) More specifically, what if my interpretations of the crucified ithyphallic Christ, the submarine Fire of the seminary, and that Night in Calcutta, which together have determined so much of both my life and my work, are all simply misplaced?

Such understandable questions, I would suggest, are themselves mistaken, as they issue from the assumption that dreams and religious experiences have objectively real, stable meanings that can be more or less definitively determined with the proper, preferably social-scientific, methods. If hermeneutical theory has taught us anything, it is that this is patently not so. My dreams and mystical experiences, like those of the historical mystics, have no meaning apart from my own subjectivity and its cocreative hermeneutical interactions with them and the cultural traditions in which they appear. Had I been living in West Bengal rather than western Missouri, for example, I can well imagine that I would have come up with some very different interpretations of my dreams and anorexic sufferings (which, of course, would have been structured quite differently in West Bengal, if they had occurred at all). And different interpretations would have resulted in different sexualities and, consequently, different forms of life or accepted fictions. To "perfect" a dream, then, does not involve finding the one and only "correct" interpretation; rather, it involves accepting responsibility for one's own existential interpretations as these are performed in relationship to that which is given by the unconscious and the cultural and physical environment. It is like learning to paint with what one has at hand. A painting is not "right" or "wrong." It just is.

Psychoanalytically speaking, the wisdom of the unconscious always leaves room for the ego's interpretations and interventions. Meaning is by no means infinitely plastic, for much is indeed given by biological, psychological, and cultural forces well outside the "I," and this can be ignored only at considerable risk. But the possibility of meaning remains remarkably open, nonetheless, very much in need of the subject's hermeneutical engagement; hence, my own life lives neither in the clarity of the submarine Fire (the beginning of the *svapna*) nor in the certainty of the final naked flight (the end of the *svapna*), but in the silent, unspoken space between the two where everything remains to be seen and written and read.

Our hermeneutical union with the mystics we study, then, does not so much lie in the phenomenological similarities of our experiences, which are always seriously compromised by cultural and linguistic particularities, but in the shared realities of our sexualized bodies and in the hermeneutical processes through which we all create meaning. It is not that we create the same symbolic worlds but, rather, that we all create symbolic worlds. It is the process, not the product, that we share.[2] Consequently, the fact that the scholarship that we create through our hermeneutical interactions with the texts and people we study often displays more or less clear signs of our own psychosexual experiences and personal histories is not a "problem" to bemoan, a "stain" to remove, or, more bizarrely, an act of "imperialism" to deny, but the very place of our hermeneutical union with these historical human beings and the best promise of our coming to some, always tentative, understanding of our shared humanity. Why? Because the physiologically grounded, deeply personal, hermeneutical processes that have driven the twentieth-century study of mysticism are but modern variants of the processes that have always driven the history of mysticism. There is no way to remove ourselves from this shared religious history, no Archimedean place to stand outside the hermeneutical circle (or is it a spiral?). There is no way to escape the *mustikon* of our most intimate involvement with that which we interpret and so become. We *are* it. In the end, then, the mystical, for whatever else it happens to be or not be, is a profoundly hermeneutical process, a road of excess, a palace of wisdom along the way, a text of living fire in which we all, historian and mystic alike, burn and love and see and write in that Night.

* * *

3 May 1995. I'm reading Wilhelm Halbfass's *India and Europe*. His hermeneutical reflections have helped me remember why I became an Indologist in the first place—not to study scientifically, that is, sociologically, another culture, not to convert the heathen, not to make money or extend an empire, not to prove the superiority of my own culture, *but to be transformed.* Part of this process involves delineating the manner in which I

have been spiritually colonized or converted by India and, consequently, how I try to master and make sense of this conversion through theory and the normative disciplines of sociology, psychology, and the history of religions. Comparison for me is not an intellectual exercise or a methodological option. It is an existential dilemma.

24 September 1991. Last night another fiery visit. Again, my body and mind in a continual state of excitation, an arousal that went on and on. It was really quite frightening, a crescendo to who knows where. I awoke to find a space heater humming loudly, as if it was on the same frequency as the energies—a kind of technological mantra or meditation bell, if you will.

5 February 1994. I have always wondered how "real" my experience of Kālī was in Calcutta. Did it fit in anywhere into the tradition? Or was it a purely private and idiosyncratic affair? Today I ran across the following passage: "Two or three days before Shri Ramakrishna's passing away, She whom he used to call 'Kali' entered this body. It is She who takes me here and there and makes me work.... he called me to his side one day ... looked steadfastly at me and fell into samadhi. Then I really felt that a subtle force like an electric shock was entering my body!" (Swami Vivekananda, *Collected Works*, 8:206). This is *exactly* what the energy felt like in Calcutta and what it still feels like when it comes. Given the precision of the phenomenological similarities (recall also that I immediately saw the Calcutta experience to be similar to Narendra's famous experience under Ramakrishna's foot), I cannot help believing that something profound happened in Calcutta, and that that power, which Vivekananda and Ramakrishna both understood to be "Kali," is now in this body and continues to visit me in my nights. This anyway has become my personal mythos. I am reminded of Massignon's visitation of the Stranger and the manner in which this "axial event" focused and gave shape to his hermeneutical vision and scholarship on al-Hallāj. But note Vivekananda's language: "She whom he used to call 'Kali.'" If this is a personal myth, it is a postcritical myth, a myth that is recognized and loved *as a myth*. Here I part company with Massignon, who clearly believed in a way that I do not and cannot.

6 February 1994. Given that the shock experience was so similar to Narendra's experience, both in its structure and in its emotional tone, it would not be difficult to see the Calcutta experience as an initiation or

śakti-pāta under Ramakrishna's phallic foot. This, of course, would make it a homoerotic experience as well.

14 April 1994. "Profound philology can have a genuine mystical function" (Gershom Scholem). Profound philology is not mastering a grammar and a dictionary and being able to put the two together to produce a more or less accurate translation. Profound philology involves the imaginal and analytic powers working in tandem in order to understand, from within *and* without, the symbols and categories and energies of a text. It involves, on its deepest level, not simply a translation of words, but a translation of the realities of the text into the life of the translator and, indirectly, into the lives of his or her readers, often with stunning consequences.

20 May 2000. Never imagine that a mystical hermeneutics changes only the hermeneut. It also changes the interpreted. Like Blake's *Jerusalem*, inspired, we are told, by a dead, disembodied Milton entering Blake's left foot (!) to allow himself to be converted from his former misogynistic ways within Blake's visionary poetry,[3] every work of mystical hermeneutics transforms both the interpreter and the interpreted. It is an act of mutual conversion and shared hope.

CONCLUSION

Palaces of Wisdom

Much of our happiness as human beings derives from our re-experiencing *[Nachfühlen]* of alien states of mind. . . . Human studies have indeed the advantage over the natural sciences that their object is not sensory appearance as such, no mere reflection of reality within consciousness, but is rather first and foremost an inner reality, a coherence experienced from within.

Wilhelm Dilthey, "The Rise of Hermeneutics"

All whatever is spoken, written, or taught of God, without the knowledge of the signature, is dumb and void of understanding; for it proceeds only from an historical conjecture, from the mouth of another, wherein the spirit without knowledge is dumb, but if the spirit opens to him the signature, then he understands the speech of another.

Jakob Böhme, *The Signature of All Things*

In Blake, we recover our original state, not by returning to it, but by recreating it. The act of creation, in its turn, is not producing something out of nothing, but the act of setting free what we already possess.

Northrop Frye, "The Keys to the Gate"

THE PRESENT STUDY emerged from the dual conviction that the modern study of mysticism contains hidden within itself dimensions of experience, hermeneutical reflection, and writing that can accurately and fruitfully be described as "mystical," and that these esoteric and erotic structures, however suppressed or camouflaged they might be, deserve to be uncovered, explored, and openly discussed. Like Böhme, I have attempted to "bring out the hiddenness" with the hope that this might tell us something important, not about the metaphysical structure of the Godhead, but about the modern study of mysticism. In the terms of our Blakean proverb of hell, I proposed to explore or map out five scholarly roads of excess, and in the process relate my own, in an effort to arrive finally, if still tentatively, at some few palaces of wisdom. I suggest here where on these roads we might catch a glimpse of those ever-elusive palaces. Writing well within traditional Western mystical discourse—from Jesus' "kingdom of God" (for what kingdom is there without a palace?), to Jewish Hekhalot mysticism with its seven palaces of Torah interpretation that, one by one, lead to the maiden in the tower, to Teresa of Avila's "interior castle" with its seven dwelling places—I will briefly visit my own seven interior palaces of wisdom here and end with some final reflections on the "infernal method" that has largely determined both the direction and ultimate destination of these wanderings.

The First Palace: Excess

In some sense, the road of excess is itself a palace of wisdom, for looked at historically, both the history of mysticism and the twentieth-century history of the study of mysticism are nothing if not histories of indeterminate, open-ended excess. Evelyn Underhill and a whole host of modern followers may wish to believe that mysticism is "practical," that it can easily be adjusted to the normal mundane workings of the human mind and the societies this mind both continuously creates and is created by, but if the historical record means anything, we can only pronounce (and excessively so) such a perspective hopelessly rose colored and naive. Granting the existence of the usual exceptions that prove the rule, it seems reasonable to conclude that when we are looking for mysticism what we usually find is some form of psychological, physical, sexual, or moral excess. Human beings, after all, do not normally unite themselves with the universe, nor do they routinely leave their bodies to become one with the divine. Consciousness is structured in such a way as to protect itself and to maintain a certain equilibrium. A healthy ego is a stable and strong (if by no means singular) one; hence, many forms of contemporary psychological theory measure mental health through such measures as the ego's ability to attach itself to objects and other people, a far cry indeed from the traditional mystical metaphors of death, detachment, and annihilation. Given the psyche's natural tendency to preserve itself, it should come as no surprise that it is usually—if by no means always—necessary to employ some sort of violent means to alter or destroy this equilibrium in order to induce a mystical state. Psychoactive drugs, sexually transgressive practice, sensory deprivation, paradoxical teachings, sleep deprivation, fasting, and ascetic violence are among the more common means in the history of religions, but psychological and physical trauma of any sort are often equally, if not far more, effective.

Certainly we have seen this truth manifest itself in the lives and works of our scholars of mysticism. In Underhill's case, such excess appears in the text quite despite the author's protestations to the contrary. Underhill can thus claim that the true mystic, like the great Catholic saint, always shuns excess and eccentricity, but her sources witness powerfully against her. From her opening epigraph on the breast-feeding mother-lover to her final reflections on the mystical marriage, which inevitably encodes either genuine social suffering ("unhappy" marriages as Underhill euphemistically puts it) or overwhelming experiences of pleasure and pain (Teresa's moans that she thought would kill her or Suso's many dramatic illnesses), excess is everywhere, just behind the corner, in the footnote, between the lines, in what is not said. Certainly we can understand Underhill's desire to defend mysticism against the detractors of her day, but in the end we must declare her mistaken, at least here. Nor is it an accident that Massignon's visitation of the Stranger, that mystical center and axial event of his life, came to him not in a peaceful, orthodox, and ordered piety, but in a malaria-induced fit and an attempted suicide, the latter inspired by terrible guilt over his profound homosexual desires, and all this within the terror of a death threat. Four volumes of detailed historical and philological scholarship on a single marginal mystic and a personal life of risky, sometimes dangerous activist ventures followed, excess answering excess. Excess reigns in Zaehner's life and work as well, if in an opposite direction, for what was his *Mysticism Sacred and Profane* if not one long attempt to fight off the doctrinal implications of Huxley's mescaline visions of Mind at Large? So too with his homoerotic reflections on the mystical marriage as the pinnacle of the religious life. What was this, if not his own way of denying, sublimating, and sacralizing his own guilt-ridden homosexuality? And then, of course, there is Agehananda Bharati, the mystical hedonist who entered his mystical states in the darkness of military solitary confinement, with the help of hallucinogenic drugs, or through the secret practice of Tantric sexual rituals. He, perhaps more than any other theorist, knew and proclaimed that the mystical is the excessive. Wolfson's work, if not his life, is marked by many of the same themes as central hermeneutical conclusions reached through an extensive philological, philosophical, and psychoanalytic study of the kabbalistic texts. The phallocentric gaze, the troubling misogyny of the texts, the dramatic sexual fantasies of the kabbalists encoded within their sefirotic speculations—these are all manifestations of mystical and erotic excess. Here too, finally, we must place his notion of "hermeneutical revenge," the reaction of society and the orthodox academy against the excessive hermeneut. Excess upon excess. Without Blake's "road of excess" there would be neither mysticism nor any reason or call to study it.

We might also say that there is something "excessive" about creativity itself, for one can advance knowledge or cast new light on a subject only by going beyond, by *exceeding,* that which is already known and accepted and seen. And this can be both a scary and a very lonely experience. The creative thinker, then, dwells, by definition, outside the acceptable. He or she *must* be a scandal, a controversy, an annoying gadfly on the butt of the comfortable and the sure. Not unlike the Tāntrika meditating in his cremation ground in order to free himself from the bonds of shame, disgust, and fear, the intellectual too must step out and beyond the socially acceptable through the powers of the imagination in order to see and to profess the new truth.

The Second Palace: Absence

But to perform the minute tasks of day-to-day scholarship, this palace of excess must eventually give way to the palace of absence, for scholarly creativity demands both a closeness and a distance from its subject—both a remembered presence and a present absence. Northrop Frye has put it as well as anyone in his rejection of "mysticism" as an appropriate term for the study of Blake's poetry. Mysticism, Frye points out, implies a religious technique of spiritual communion with God that is, by its very nature, incommunicable. As such, it is "difficult to reconcile with anyone's poetry," for the poet may indeed catch a glimmer of some "direct apprehension," but "to the artist *qua* artist, this apprehension is not an end in itself but a means to another end, the end of producing the poem. The mystical experience for him is poetic material, not poetic form, and must be subordinated to the demands of that form. From the point of view of any genuine mystic this would be somewhat inadequate, and one who was both mystic and poet, never finally deciding which was to be the adjective and which the noun, might be rather badly off. If he decided for poetry, he would perhaps do better to use someone else's mystical experiences, as Crashaw did St. Teresa's."[1] If we simply substitute the word "scholar" for Frye's "poet" here, we meet a by now very familiar character, the historian of mysticism who "is both mystic and scholar" and, consequently, appears especially liminal, neither quite here in the tradition nor there in the academy—in Frye's colloquial judgment, "rather badly off." And although Richard Crashaw's method is indeed the usual rhetorical solution to this problem, it is, as we have seen, by no means always quite that simple.

It is significant to note, however, that Frye did not see these problems as entirely insurmountable. He suggests another, specifically Blakean term to better capture these mystics who were also poets—the "visionary." A visionary, unlike many traditional mystics, never relinquishes "the visualization which no artist can do without"; hence, the visionary's method is primarily perceptive and symbolic instead of apophatic and unitive. Thus, whereas mysticism and art may be mutually exclusive, "the visionary and the artist are allied."[2] In our own terms, we might decide— depending upon our values—to call the visionary a "failed mystic" or, conversely, to call the radical mystic an "artist without talent." Moshe Idel thought the former was an appropriate description of Gershom Scholem,[3] and both R. C. Zaehner and Agehananda Bharati did not hesitate to declare any number of genuine mystics to be genuinely bad poets, philosophers, and moralists. Closer to the point, Bharati speculated out loud that his career as an intellectual, which he took real delight in, would have been psychologically impossible had he known the mystical more often and more permanently; to think and create culture requires real distance. Wolfson, moreover, has discussed at some length how the kabbalistic theory of *tsimtsum,* or "contraction," that primordial moment in the Lurianic creation myth in which the light of Ein-Sof withdraws from itself in order to create a womblike vacuum within the divine pleroma in which the world of difference and individuality might exist, is itself analogized as a phallic act of inscription or writing: "To write is to mark, to mark to demarcate, to demarcate to delimit by measure and boundary. From this vantage point the divine writing stems from the suffering that lies at the core of God's being."[4] Hence God's textualization in the Torah and his further demarcation in the hermeneutical process. Writing and reading, in other words, can arise only from a contraction, a suffering, an absence that is also, paradoxically, a presence. To read and to write, then, is to share in divine creation, and to suffer with God.

The point remains much the same in all of these cases: in order to create art or scholarship or culture out of the mystical, some distance is necessary. It seems more than apparent that mystical experience may often act as a powerful hermeneutical catalyst but that it is *not* sufficient to produce sound scholarship. In the end, there simply are no substitutes for philological training, fieldwork, theoretical sophistication, peer criticism, and, above all, radical self-reflexivity. And to be self-reflexive is already to be two, to be distant from oneself.

The Third Palace: Art

Very much related to this wisdom of absence that refuses the absolute of ontological union for the relative joys of a poetic creativity is what we might call the wisdom of art, the awareness that what one is doing is both fictive and beautiful, both illusory and profound, both literally false and existentially true. Little wonder that Freud admired nothing more than the artist, the writer, and the creative process itself. Before such human mysteries, he confessed, even the psychoanalyst must lay down his armory of psychological categories and stand in respectful awe. William Parsons describes Freud's view in these terms: "Art . . . never made epistemological assertions about reality, nor was it able to construct a worldview. It was an 'illusion,' but pretended to nothing more. Artists, moreover, existing at the margins of culture, seemed to have an unusual access to the unconscious and the talent to represent unconscious processes in symbolic, experience-distant ways. Art could be therapeutic in providing an outlet for institutional gratification and edifying when it stirred the imagination and ignited introspection. Thus conceived, art had a special relationship to psychoanalysis."[5] Even, however, if the intellectual, very much like the artist, renounces all certain closure and opts instead for the honest beauty of uncertainty and an open-ended quest,[6] there is something here that escapes, transcends, bursts all our notions and frustrates all our hermeneutical skill, perhaps because it is precisely from here, from this unconscious *mustikon,* that our deepest hermeneutical insights ultimately arise. And how can an effect plumb its cause?

Certainly we have seen this palace of art appear again and again on our textual horizons. Underhill, for example, consistently invoked the analogies of the artist, the poet, and the painter to portray the mystic as a kind of consummate artist of infinity. And Massignon, although he may not have quite seen it this way, was certainly following in his father's artistic footsteps when he created, out of the most unusual moments and synchronistic events, a most remarkable "life-arc," an almost mythical narrative of heroic risk and intersigns for both him and us to decode, each in our own way, art following upon art. We might also recall here Zaehner's love for French literature and the fact that his first mystical experience was induced by reading a French poet, Rimbaud. Similarly, Bharati counted classical music or a good opera among hallucinogens and eroticism as one of the most effective means of inducing mystical states and resolutely rejected any and all ontological claims for mysticism as philosophically naive, opting instead for a hedonistic or aesthetic appreciation of this eminently human experience. Indeed, the wise mystic for Bharati is precisely the mystic who does not make ontological claims for his or her experiences and can laugh at both the self and its pious worldview. Wolfson shifts the register again to the explicitly hermeneutical act, here analogized as an art form, hence his metaphor of the historian of religions as artist and his chosen subject as the "canvas" on which to paint a four-hundred-page treatise on what can only be called the artistic organ par excellence, the human imagination. Little wonder, then, that he compared the prophetic-mystical experiences of the kabbalists with the fury of poetic inspiration and framed his "mirror," his *Speculum,* with Blakean hymns to the divinity of the imagination and the body.

Sudhir Kakar suggested something very similar when he wrote that mystical experience is "the preeminent way of uncovering the vein of creativity that runs deep in all of us," as it engages the "unknowable ground of creativeness as such."[7] This is very close to what I have been trying to find and then express through the winding roads of excess I have stumblingly followed throughout these present pages. There is a Presence rooted in our erotic forms, which we boringly call bodies, and in our nocturnal visions, which we banally call dreams, within which, out of which we think and write. We have become too familiar with ourselves and our strange existences; it is time to become strange again, for there is something about what we do as scholars of mysticism that is itself mystical. But the mystical here has abandoned its metaphysical pretensions, its historical literalisms, and especially its premodern, authoritarian ethical systems. It has become a kind of mystical humanism or postmodern psychology. It can laugh. It has become the palace of art.

The Fourth Palace: The Erotic

As I tried to tell the story, I began my quest for an erotic mysticism with the conviction that my own Roman Catholic heritage possessed precious few, if any, genuine resources for a heteroerotic male mysticism. In effect, I went looking for a more or less stable, late-twentieth-century, Western, exclusive heterosexuality in the premodern texts of the Western and South Asian mystical traditions. I didn't find one. The joke, it seems, is on me. But jokes are often forms of wisdom and always, at their best anyway, transgressive, extreme, excessive, standing outside the social register in order to criticize, even mock it. Looking back with a grin, I would describe my search as a fruitful failure to the extent that it has convinced me of the constructed, historically conditioned natures of all sexualities, including and especially my own. Very much like the illusory, constructed nature of my own ego, which showed itself as ephemeral and nonexistent that Night in Calcutta, human sexualities appear, after the search, as fluid, plural processes of an ever-changing present, not stable and easily identifiable binary things that we can somehow find mirrored in the texts and cultural practices of the past. For me to imagine, then, that I could find a single, stable, binary heterosexuality in mystical texts, those expressions of human fluidity par excellence, was to go looking for something that never in fact existed, at least there, in those paradigmatic manifestations of sexual excess, nondualism, and polymorphous pleasure. In the mirror of the history of erotic mysticism, what needs explained is not their homoeroticisms but our "heterosexuality."

It is in this ironic, seemingly negative sense (it is really not negative) that I believe my project to be successful. Suspended between the eroticisms of the history of mysticism and the reflexivities of our own twentieth-century knowledges and disciplines, perhaps we can now see a little more clearly what constitute both the similarities and differences of our shared humanities, that is, perhaps we can now practice a more precise comparative erotics of mysticism. Halperin has put it this way with reference to the study of classic antique cultures: "The real issue confronting any cultural historian of antiquity, and any critic of contemporary culture, is, first of all, how to recover the terms in which the experiences of individuals belonging to past societies were actually constituted and, second, how to measure and assess the differences between those terms and the ones we currently employ." "Such an analysis," he goes on, "will probably lead us (and we must be prepared for this) into a plurality of only partly overlapping social and conceptual territories, a series of cultural formations that shift as their constituents change, combine in different sequences, or compose new patterns."[8] This project of analogy instead of identity, difference instead of sameness, family resemblance versus universalism seems a wise one. It certainly mirrors well my reading of the methodological journey mapped above.

But why, I ask myself at the end, did I feel so drawn to these traditions in the first place? If their own sexual mappings are so different from my own, why the attraction? Perhaps what I was after all along was a way out of the box, a way out of the binary, rather unbelievable categories and hypermoralizing tones that define and surround our discourses on male sexuality and trap modern men within a set of more or less restricted models of masculinity. Here is where the palace of the erotic ends as a historical thesis and becomes a normative vision, a social critique, a hope for a kind of masculine transfiguration. For this, I find Kaja Silverman's Lacanian analysis of male subjectivity particularly helpful,[9] primarily because it can be employed simultaneously within a mystical and sexual register. In Silverman's terms, the "lack of being is the irreducible condition of subjectivity." "If," she goes on, "we were in the possession of an instrument which would permit us to penetrate deep into the innermost recesses of the human psyche, we would find not identity, but a void."[10] Mystical experience, I would suggest with Freud[11] and, more explicitly, with Irigaray,[12] can function as precisely this kind of psychic probe. And what do we find with such a probe? As Silverman reminds us, for Lacan the subject of the unconscious is "acephalic," that is, headless, symbolically castrated; hence, I would immediately add in my own Indological and subjective terms, Kālī's decapitating sword and gory garland of heads and the floating *liṅgam*s (literally cut off from their bodies) that appeared in my dream space to announce the ego's entrance into this unconscious, egoless, acephalic space.

For Silverman, the ideological reality and dominant fiction of our symbolic order is created primarily by the positive Oedipus complex, that is, the social construction of a relatively unambiguous male heterosexuality and its attending patriarchal social structures (that is, the very heterosexuality I went looking for in the mystical texts), what Lacan called the Symbolic Order or the Law of the Father. Masculinity is thus a "crucial site" for not only creating but also renegotiating our own dominant fiction, our *vraisemblance*. Accordingly, any attempt to reconfigure male subjectivity in order to make room for a more justly structured gender order must also effectively "render null and void virtually everything else that commands general belief."[13] This sounds extreme, but I think it is essentially correct, at least in terms of religious realities, those "dominant fictions" par excellence. For how much sense can a father God who demands the sacrifice of his own son make in a social world not defined by the dark emotional saliences of the Oedipal complex? And how much sense can a blissful union with a divine mother make in a social world not constructed through especially intense mother-infant bonding and a subsequent nostalgia for pre-Oedipal merger? Very little, I think. So too with purity codes, ethical systems, gender identities, marriage practices, social hierarchies of all sorts, authority and submission, power itself—they are *all* built on (if never quite determined by) the foundations of very particular Oedipal constellations. With whom does the child identify (and how intensely)? To whom does the child submit (and how completely)? And when in the developmental process does what take place (and how successfully)? Weston La Barre is thus onto something important when he suggests that "arguments about the nature of 'God' are an irrational hurling of individual oedipal convictions at one another" that is ultimately both fruitless and misguided, since "each is talking about ontologically somewhat different phenomena."[14] But to accept this is to accept the constructed nature of *all* "dominant fictions," and especially those of our very psychosexual selves and the social orders they in turn help create (and are created by). It is to enter the void and experience a sexual-social apocalypse. It is to return, if only for a moment, to what Lacan called the Imaginary, that pre-Oedipal, prelinguistic, essentially mystical realm of maternal merger where one can, as in *The Gospel of Thomas*, "make the two one and make the inside like the outside and the outside like the inside and the above like the below . . . so that the male might not be male nor the female be female."[15] Significantly, it is precisely the repression or forgetting of this imaginary kingdom that creates, that *is*, the Lacanian unconscious.

Developing Silverman's Lacanian analysis of "perverse" masculinities that call into question the dominant fiction of the positive Oedipus complex, I would suggest that mystical masculinities, equally "perverse" in their rejection of socialized heterosexuality, call into question not only conventional heterosexual male subjectivity, but "reality" itself, for this "reality" is always defined, preserved, and sacralized by the social constructions of this same sexual identity. Conversely (and rather ironically), heterosexual masculinities do the same once they are placed in the many homoerotic subcultures of these same traditions, for there they can only call into serious question the patriarchal maleness of God as they seek a more feminine divine Presence. Anyone who doubts either need only stand up in a conservative Christian church and declare that homosexuality is one of many natural, God-given outcomes of our biology and socialization, or think about what it might mean for Roman Catholicism to abandon its all-male, same-sex, celibate authority structure—the world might as well be ending.

It is this temporary dissolution of male sexual identities and their attending subjectivities and reality-fictions in the mystical and maternal realm of the Imaginary that constitutes our fourth glimpsed palace of wisdom, the palace of the erotic, of the sexual collapsed back on itself in a kind of psychic implosion or nondual pleasure, in what Lacan might call "a jouissance that is beyond," that is, a jouissance of the whole body and of being that is beyond the phallus and its less-than-polymorphous concentration on itself.[16] Handled properly, the erotic as jouissance can become a place of masculine transfiguration where the self, having been apocalyptically dissolved, can be refashioned anew in a form that remains more porous and open to other modes of sexual subjectivity, including and especially those that we normally label "mystical."

But a difficult palace this is, and how few have genuinely entered it. Hence, Underhill and Zaehner, constricted by their own dominant social constructions of sexuality and gender, were each unable to deal with the homoerotic structures of Christian bridal mysticism: in essence, they refused the transfiguration. Massignon, on the other hand, saw as clearly as any the apocalyptic nature of sexuality. He knew that any active public expression of his own homosexuality could only dissolve the orthodox Catholic world in which he chose to live. His original "solution" was both radical and tragically logical: he would remove the offending subjectivity, himself, first through a half-attempted suicide and then in a life of homosexual renunciation. He too was blinded by the light on the mountain. Bharati's solution to a socialized masculinity was quite different: he chose to live as a Tantric monk beyond the conventions of society and within the antinomian erotics of the Tantric traditions he loved so well. His was a heterosexual masculinity that refused to be fully socialized, a mystical hedonism that sought transcendence and transformation through energies freed by hallucinogens and sexual ritual. Consequently, he seemed to know the Imaginary quite intimately as what he liked to call "the Light at the Center" (or should this experience of the mystical be placed even further back, beyond the Mother, in the Self?). Wolfson's work offers yet another response to the socially defining character of masculinity, for he shows dramatically that the sexually fluid, heteroerotic, and homoerotic symbolisms of kabbalistic masculinities, though certainly "perverse" in Silverman's sense, are nevertheless hardly models of sexual justice in our present terms. The world may be apocalyptically destroyed and reconstituted within the *sefirot,* but this world of phallic visions, concealed misogynies, and male androgynes is hardly a world that many women would want to live in. Indeed, they barely exist in it at all. To dissolve one patriarchal world, then, is often simply to create another one, and in the end a masculinity that can love a woman as a woman or a man as a man (and not as a goddess or divinity or metaphysical abstraction) seems to be the only real way out of a troubling religious history of misogyny and misanthropy.

The masculine transfiguration[17] of which the erotic hints here, then, is a masculinity that has seen itself dissolved within the ecstatic space of the Imaginary and reconstituted again within the Symbolic Order of language and society. Both sides of the dialectic, the deconstruction and reconstruction, are necessary for the transfiguration, but it is the latter that, critically and self-reflexively approached, ultimately brings the process to some measure of completeness, for it is only here, outside the mystical merger, as it were, that the masculine psyche can both remember its own ecstatic existence before and within the Presence and know that such bliss is implicated deeply, ontologically, within the human experience of love, the love, however imperfect, of a flesh-and-blood human being. The transfiguring response to such a gnosis is not an ascetic retreat into an ontological abstraction or, worse yet, some version of the innumerable mystical misogynies that the religions provide in such disturbing abundance, but a warm, willed embrace of that very space in which he first knew the Presence—the space of human love.

The Fifth Palace: Ethical Criticism

Such a masculine transfiguration ultimately demands and relies upon not the delights of mystical union, but the always agonistic processes of ethical criticism. Mystical merger, however profound, however blissful, is never sufficient, is never enough, for the social worlds in which we live are defined and determined not by union, but by *difference,* and difference is the realm, the only realm, of ethics. Hence the need to submit both the mystical traditions themselves and our own hermeneutical interactions with them to a serious and prolonged ethical critique. This willingness, I would suggest, is our fifth palace of wisdom.

In terms of our hermeneutical practices, no one has advanced a more insightful and sustained critique of the paradoxical position of the historian of mysticism outlined here than Steven Wasserstrom in his recent *Religion after Religion.* Wasserstrom's concerns are many and complex, but they can be crystallized into two major points: (1) that the comparative nature of the historian's methods lands one squarely outside any and all traditions in an overly abstract, pseudotranscendent space that claims to speak for all religions but in fact speaks for none of them, lacking as it does any solid grounding in history, scripture, law, or community; and (2) that the mystocentric focus of the history of religions has tended to obscure if not erase the ethical dimensions of religion, particularly of the monotheisms, for the more mysterious and seductive workings of myth, symbol, paradox, and antinomian mysticism. Examining the lives and works of Gershom Scholem, Mircea Eliade, and Henry Corbin, Wasserstrom is able to identify a shared idea that he calls "religion after religion": "A paradoxical idea on many levels—a non-religious religiosity, a secular antimodernism, a metarationalism operating within academic discourse—*religion after religion* speaks for the mystical traditions they represented from within and without at the same time."[18]

Certainly there is much in my own method that is open to Wasserstrom's criticisms—its paradoxical insider/outsider status, its mystocentric focus, its fascination with symbols and myths and everything strange—but there is also much in it that answers this same important critique. Certainly the roads outlined here do not shy away from asking hard ethical questions of both the traditions and the scholars who study them. Nor does it follow the examples of Eliade and Corbin, who intentionally hid their initiatic experiences, denigrated social-scientific methods for the sacred irreducibility of religious experience, read religious symbols as tautological (that is, as representing themselves), and rejected the project of modernity as a fall from a kind of theosophical "tradition" or perennialism.[19] Quite the contrary, I have revealed my own initiatic secrets, employed both psychoanalytic and historical methods to uncover the sexual and socially constructed dimensions of scholarship (including and especially my own), read religious symbols as expressive of something other and more than religious truths, and accepted both the modern condition and its postmodern, essentially paradoxical possibilities as inevitable and at least potentially positive.

Along the way, moreover, I have asked serious ethical questions of Christian bridal mysticism, Sufi eroticism, Roman Catholic homophobia, Hindu monism, and Jewish Kabbalah. Indeed, the ethical import of the hermeneutic I have developed here and elsewhere—with a psychoanalytic focus uncovering traumatogenetic triggers and a recurring homoerotic structure—would, if acted on systematically, have some rather profound consequences on the mystical as it is usually defined (as a series of extraordinary ecstatic, unitive, or possession experiences). Consider again the cases of Louis Massignon, R. C. Zaehner, and Agehananda Bharati. I cannot imagine any of these men dedicating their lives to mystical texts after an unproblematic embrace of a fully socialized, integrated sexuality. Nor do I think it an accident that Underhill's quite comfortable married life and established place in British society led, quite naturally it seems, to a nonexcessive fantasy of the Christian mystic as emotionally balanced and sexually integrated. Only Wolfson's hermeneutic contains within itself a radical ethical criticism of kabbalistic eroticism as something ambiguous, contorted, and ultimately misogynist in its androcentric erasure of woman. Only Wolfson really embraces an ethical critique of mystical eroticism in the fifth palace.

Sexual suffering, *real* sexual suffering, seems to be the "trigger" by means of which we might truly see something about the real. But can we affirm the mystical at the cost of the human and the ethical? Much as the search for a modern heterosexuality in the premodern mystical literature has failed, I am convinced that any search for a modern, workable sexual or social ethics in this same literature is doomed from the start. The mystical is *not* the ethical. The former arises from the death or temporary disappearance of the ego; the latter emerges from the affirmation of the ego among many other egos, that is, from an uncompromising privileging of the human person within a community of persons. The mystical cannot lead to the ethical without considerable help from outside and elsewhere, that is, from reason, political theory, moral debate, and a love of human beings, not as ciphers for grand metaphysical realities ("Christ," "Brahman," "emptiness," or whatever), but as human beings in all their mundane and messy glory. Mystical experience may thus give us a unique access to the ontological dimensions of human experience, but this ontological level cannot help us with our social and ethical tasks. It is certainly possible that we may find its apophatic and deconstructive powers helpful in our initial task of calling into question our own dominant fictions, but in the end we must turn elsewhere, well outside the mystical, for the tools we will need to construct another, more adequate fiction. I am struck, at the end, by how similar this position, which is my position, is to that of Bharati, who argued more or less the same thing thirty years ago.

But I would go further and argue that the moral status of the mystical is more ambiguous and more complicated still. After all, it is often not just the case that a particular mystical experience is itself structurally nonmoral, but that the means of inducing such states of consciousness are, at least from a social perspective, positively immoral, physically dangerous, or emotionally tragic, as we have seen again and again throughout this present study (hence our first palace of excess). This is *not* to say that traumatogenetic states entered through something like repeated sexual abuse or the death of a loved one are themselves immoral or even inauthentic; rather, I am simply arguing that it is often the case that certain types of altered states of consciousness are psychologically accessible only because of clearly and decisively tragic events, few of which we would want to call "moral." As I have argued elsewhere, the house of the mystical cannot be reduced to its various doors.[20] How one got in and what is inside are two very different issues. Certainly, for example, we can affirm the erotic energies of the mystical as some of the most beautiful, sublime, and valuable experiences available to us, but we must also, I think, recognize that such states have their own epistemological limitations, that they often are distorted cries for healing and sexual justice, and that very often their ultimate goal is not more "experience," however seductively profound, but human wholeness and love. Consequently, near the end of my own road of excess lies the palace not of divinization or divine love or transcendence from this world, but of a mystically enriched humanism and a passion for social and sexual justice within *this* world. The kingdom, Jesus says in *The Gospel of Thomas,* is spread out on the earth and people do not see it. It is not "up" there but "in" here, in the human, in the world, in this world.[21]

The Sixth Palace: Paradox

Philosophically, then, what I am left with in the end is a kind of paradoxical, cross-cultural "mystical humanism" that acknowledges, values, and even seeks out the ontological ground(lessness) of human being, but that also insists on acknowledging, protecting, and nurturing the social, ethical, and physical well-being of historical individuals, even if this means forestalling, for the moment at least, those mystical truths of personal dissolution and union with the universe that, with the physical deaths of these same individuals, become undeniable and absolute. "Heaven and earth are not kind: / The ten thousand things are straw dogs to them," sings the *Tao Te Ching* in a different land. So too with the Sage: "People are straw dogs to him."[22] Hence the necessity of asserting our humanity, our capacity for "kindness," before all three.

This same paradoxical structure carries over into the actual practice of scholarship. As I have represented him or her, the historian of mysticism must practice two seemingly mutually contradictory moves: he must imaginatively relive or even replicate the symbolic world of the texts or community being studied, *and* he must step back and outside this world to analyze it with the critical tools of the modern study of religion. She must be both an aspiring gnostic *and* a radical skeptic. In this, I am clearly working out of a double heritage deeply informed by both the romantic, phenomenological, and hermeneutical traditions of Friedrich Schleiermacher, Wilhelm Dilthey, Gerardus van der Leeuw, Rudolf Otto, Joachim Wach, and Mircea Eliade, each of whom proposed in his own way an essentially mystical method through which one could "bridge the gulf between subject and object,"[23] and the Enlightenment-inspired reductionistic methods of Sigmund Freud, Émile Durkheim, and Karl Marx, who all ultimately privileged causal "explanation" *(Erklärung)* — be it psychological, sociological, or economic — over sympathetic "understanding" *(Verstehen)* and provocatively exposed levels of meanings of which the religious believer or insider inevitably remains unaware. I do not think that these two broad interpretive traditions within the present practice of the history of religions are necessarily exclusive, although I do believe that the epistemological tensions that exist between them are both unavoidable and necessary. What I would propose, then, is a kind of hermeneutical spiral (rather like a unicorn's horn) that advances through these very centripetal and centrifugal forces, always working in tandem and *in tension* as they move toward a fuller and more radical in-sight (a term that happily encompasses both "understanding" and "explanation") into what we have come to call "mysticism."[24] The trick, of course, is not to point out what is obviously already the case in the academy as a whole, but to preserve and even nurture this paradoxical tension, this spiral path, within the same hermeneutical practice.

Of particular interest to me here, then, has been the existential places and theoretical practices of historians of mysticism who have imaginatively allowed their own worldviews to be turned "inside out" by the traditions, even as they turned the traditions "inside out" through critical theory, rational discourse, and ethical critique. Ideally in such a situation (and there are few, if any, *ideally*s in the world of religious studies), a mutual transformation takes place, and both the scholar and the tradition find themselves transcended in a moment of understanding that is neither here nor there, neither clearly inside nor quite outside, bad news perhaps for the dogmatist (whether devotee or theorist) but a positively giddy experience for the imaginative and open minded. Such is the ideal anyway. The actual is, as always, a glorious mess, both "glorious" and "messy" in the way that Mary Douglas defined the ambiguous, fearful possibilities of "pollution," "impurity," and "dirt"—a fertile chaos, a liminality awaiting birth.

If we shift our lenses for a moment and adopt the work of Peter Homans, we might render the same process in more emotional and psychological terms, as a process of cultural mourning:

> The [psycho]analyst agrees with the historian [of religions] that every interpretation begins as an act of love; but to this the analyst adds—as the historian does not—that every interpretation—whenever it is done with sentimentality—separates the interpreter from his text, his love object. And then the analyst goes on to note—which the historian cannot do—that such renunciation builds self-enhancing psychological structures. For this reason it must be said that interpretation is a healing all its own. But it is the inverse of religious healing [which incorporates the individual back into a precritical identity with the symbolic system]. And so, sad as it may seem—it is not really sad—it is necessary not to be religious in order to understand religious expressions psychologically.[25]

Thus, if the historian does not love the textual world, he will not sufficiently invest himself and his energies in the interpretive project, but if he does not also mourn the loss of that same world, he cannot critically understand the religious object as object, as truly other. He loses himself, as it were, along the *methodos* or path, and the quest that is the history of religions ends in what amounts to a spoken or unspoken conversion that in most cases can only silence the critical voice. But perhaps even in this mourning, the historian of mysticism strangely resembles the mystical writer, for both, as de Certeau writes, can write only within the space of our second palace, the palace of absence: "Thus it is that the historian of the mystics, summoned, as they are, to say the other, repeats their experience in studying it: an exercise of absence defines at once the operation by which he produces his text and that which constructed theirs."[26]

Certainly in this, the historian of mysticism very much resembles what Wasserstrom has so eloquently described as the historian of religions preaching and practicing a "religion after religion": "*Religion after religion,* the operating theory underlying the History of Religions... is itself religious, even as it is postreligious; it is itself a paradox, perhaps a *coincidentia oppositorum,* and, indeed, may be one of the most productively stimulating ideas for students of religion in this century. Lezak Kolakowski made a fundamental point concerning students of religion, which may help us understand *religion after religion* as *coincidentia oppositorum:*

'Thus we notice a strange convergence between the cognitive attitude of a radical mystic and that of a radical skeptic. By virtue of a *coincidentia oppositorum* the mystic and the skeptic turn out to be twin brothers in epistemology.'"[27] Such a position is certainly not without its problems, and I accept Wasserstrom's call to historians of religions to opt for an uncompromising intellectual integrity and openness over esoteric dissimulation and academic lying, to struggle with the essentially paradoxical nature of their methodological "religion after religion," and to address squarely the ethical dimensions that lie at the heart of both the religious traditions themselves and their own work on these traditions. Accordingly, I have revealed some of the psychological, sexual, ethical, and political complexities of my own life and work, not to resolve these tensions, much less to deny their presence, but rather to *exaggerate* them, and this with the hope, foolish or no, that they might lead me somewhere worth going if I follow them with a critical, self-reflexive honesty. Fortunately or unfortunately, depending upon one's perspective, this road has brought me to the doorstep of a thoroughgoing methodological and existential paradox, where remaining on the outside of a mystical tradition allows one, *precisely by virtue of that same distance,* to go deeper inside than even the insider will allow himself to go. Too often scholars parrot the obvious truth that every method, every (Western) cultural perspective, distorts and limits what we can see about another culture. This, no doubt, is true. But why must every concave and convex curve in our vision distort? Why is this metaphor always used to pathologize or deny a scholar's perspective? Concavity and convexity, after all, can also be used to *correct* vision, and lenses can focus and magnify as easily as they can distort. Perhaps our cultural distance, our own farsightedness, gives us a focus, a vision that the other does not, *cannot* have, just as the other's own nearsighted focus gives it a similar, if very different, advantage. Surely we need both in our attempts to achieve in-sight.

One might say that the superior hermeneutics is the one that can encompass and understand and even at times explain (God forbid) the most data, not the one that insists on denying, censoring, reducing, or scapegoating that which it cannot or does not want to see. More specifically, I am proposing a whole series of seemingly paradoxical positions: that we not fear to see the truly sexual in the genuinely spiritual, with all this implies about the roles that gender, sexual orientation, and human physiology play in religious experience; that we not assume that "enlightened" states of consciousness and psychopathology are mutually exclusive; that we not lock mystical experiences away in some airtight categorical safe (like "purity" or "perfection") to protect them (and ourselves) from the moral, cross-cultural, and political issues of antinomianism, authoritarianism, misogyny, and censorship that appear in these mystical traditions with such troubling consistency; and that, finally and most important, we challenge the dichotomy between insider and outsider and not assume *either* that the historian, psychologist, or anthropologist who seems to be on the outside—and in many senses truly is—does not also know and appreciate something of the shimmering truths of which the insider so passionately speaks *or* that the insider, however devoted to an ideal, cannot also see clearly and bravely something of the actual of which the scholar tries to speak. Scholars are not always religiously inept, and disciples are seldom stupid.

Perhaps in the end, as many of the mystical traditions themselves teach, there really is no inside or outside, no *nirvāṇa* or *saṁsāra*, no either-or on which to hang our dichotomous categories and concerns. Perhaps everything, at least here, really is a reflection in the double mirror of ourselves and the perceived world, each reflecting the other in a world turned doubly inside out by the gazes of the mystic and the hermeneut.[28]

The Seventh Palace: Hermeneutical Union

My best guess, however, about how historians of mysticism routinely have transforming religious experiences across spatial and temporal boundaries (recall that this was the basic hermeneutical question with which I began the present study) is that the "paradox" of the insider and the outsider in the sixth palace is not a genuine paradox at all but rather a function of the discursive metaphors that we use with such misplaced and ultimately mistaken faith. In the end, there is no inside or outside, and we are already one. Consider, for example, Jennifer Nedelsky's feminist critique of George Lakoff and Mark Johnson's classic work on metaphor, *Metaphors We Live By*. Lakoff and Johnson had identified the metaphor of the container as basic to how humans experience both their bodies and the world: the world is "outside" the physical container, and subjectivity exists "inside" it (of course, it is this same deep metaphor that creates the secondary metaphors of the "insider" and "outsider" in the study of religion). But this, Nedelesky argues, is only one possible metaphor, and one not particularly convincing to a wide range of human experiences, to which we could certainly add any number of conceptions of the mystical that make it their main aim to deny explicitly and radically the appropriateness of the insider/outsider metaphor as cosmically groundless, including Nedelsky's reference to Susan Griffin on the common human experience of cosmic interconnectedness: "For the part of the mind that is dark to us in this culture, that is sleeping in us, that we name 'unconscious,' is the knowledge that we are inseparable from all other beings in the universe. Intimations of this have reached us."[29] Here again, the psychoanalytic and the mystical collapse into one another.

What if, for example, we conceive, with Don Kulick, the embodied self not as a stable container with a clear inside and outside, but as an always-evolving set of incomplete narratives that promiscuously interact and combine with other narratives? The "paradox" of the insider and the outsider quickly dissolves and we get an almost immediate sense of the profundity and even mystical potential of studying texts. Texts can transform us *because we ourselves are texts*. This, I think, is a much better way of explaining how it is that scholars of mysticism, the vast majority of whom are textualists, can have mystical experiences within another cultural frame. Instead of bouncing billiard-ball ego containers hopelessly cut off from one another, or solipsistic Kantian minds locked into their own inherited categories, or, worse yet, cultural thieves "stealing" or "borrowing" beliefs or myths from another culture (as if they were stable, quasi-physical "things" that one could "own"), what we really have here is a stunning collection of mutually interacting texts and narratives that can and *do* combine in an almost infinite number of ways: life mocks all imagined boundaries. After all, if the self is indeed a kind of narrative, then, by definition, it must be both partial in itself and at least potentially open to other self-narratives: "The knowing self," Donna Haraway writes, "is partial in all its guises, never finished, whole, simply there and original; it is always constructed and stitched together imperfectly, and *therefore* able to join with another, to see together without claiming to be another."[30] Hence the cross-cultural, cross-religious mystical experiences of scholars of mysticism.

Hermeneutical theory, pioneered in the nineteenth century by Friedrich Ast, Schleiermacher, and Dilthey and more recently developed and radicalized by such thinkers as Hans-Georg Gadamer, Jürgen Habermas, and Paul Ricoeur, can deepen further this basic textual insight into how historians of mysticism can mystically experience the texts they study. The nineteenth-century model saw texts as objectified crystallizations of mind or spirit *(Geist)* that have the potential to reactivate the same kinds of spirit experiences in readers who know the original grammars and vocabularies: language has the power to transmit spirit, or better, awaken that which is already in us. Dilthey could thus write of "reexperiencing" *(Nachfühlen)* alien states of mind through a process of interpretive "reconstruction" *(Nachbildung)*,[31] define understanding *(Verstehen)* as "that process by which we intuit, behind the sign given to our senses, that psychic reality of which it is an expression,"[32] and describe the hermeneutical art as "an exegesis or *interpretation of those residues of human reality preserved in written form.*"[33] This, of course, is an essentially romantic vision based on a faith in a shared and universal humanity (for "both have been formed upon the substratum of a general human nature, and it is this which makes possible the communion of people with each other in speech")[34] that sees as its goal the attempt to reexperience the spiritual modalities and forms of consciousness embedded in the grammar and concepts of the received text.

More radically still, for Dilthey—who accepted, long before Freud, the "doctrine of unconscious creation"[35]—the ultimate goal of hermeneutics is not only to reexperience an alien form of consciousness crystallized in the text, but also to know and understand that modality of awareness better even than the author of the text.[36] But how? As I have tried to demonstrate throughout this work, any hermeneutical union that lays claim to an absolute identity or naive objectivism must be resisted, for we can never fully "become one" with the *Geist* of any historical manifestation or mystic. But we *can* still commune with a mystic through his or her texts as crystallized forms of mystical experience that have the power to catalyze similar meaning events in us. Moreover, we *can* know something about the historical mystic that the mystic himself or herself probably never knew.

Strangely, it is our very distance (our second palace of wisdom) that makes this possible. Such an idea has found its most striking and helpful image in Gadamer's notion of "horizons" of meaning and their partial "fusion" in the dialogic moment of hermeneutical understanding, developed most famously in his *Truth and Method*.[37] With Gadamer's fusion of horizons we can see quite easily just why the hermeneut may in fact understand the text "better" than its original author or speaker: in effect, the historian's present life world and categories provide probes or techniques of analysis that were simply nonexistent in the meaning horizon of the text's past. This present horizon of meaning fusing with the past horizon of the text produces a third, unprecedented, space in which new meanings and possibilities of insight can appear. Hence, Gadamer can write that the "meaning of a text goes beyond its author, not only occasionally, but always. Understanding is therefore not merely reproductive but also productive."[38] In the terms of our present project, we might say that the modern study of mysticism extends and radicalizes the history of mysticism through the various fusions of horizons that it enacts in its own texts and critical practices. Zaehner can thus use insights from psychiatry, Jungian psychology, and the comparative study of mysticism to analyze ancient and medieval Hindu and Muslim mystical texts, Bharati can employ psychoanalysis and analytic philosophy to discuss contemporary Indian holy men, and Wolfson can draw on French feminism and postmodern philosophy to shed new light on medieval Jewish visionary experience.

In his criticisms of Gadamer, Habermas has reminded us that such a hermeneutical practice inevitably calls into question the prejudgments of tradition and its authority, since language is always imbued with power structures that will not question themselves and thrive instead on active dissimulation. Indeed, there is every reason "to assume that the background consensus of established traditions and of language-games may be a forced consensus which resulted from pseudo-communications."[39] Ironically, then, to deepen and extend the past into the present and future through a hermeneutical practice is also to call into question that past and to engage in what amounts to a critique of ideology. This is perhaps most powerfully shown in psychoanalysis (or Marxism), where social communications (not to mention oneiric visions and ecstatic states) are shown to be systematically distorted and censored forms of expression; hence Habermas's call for what he calls, inspired by Freud, a "depth-hermeneutic," that is, a hermeneutical practice that does not take tradition on its own terms but exposes it to Enlightenment critiques and social-scientific methods.[40] We remember our sixth palace even in our seventh.

Always conscious of these deconstructive, apophatic dimensions, we can still accurately call this seventh and final palace the palace of hermeneutical union, certainly not in any clear or naive ontological sense, as if we had somehow reached the Godhead or the cosmic substratum of all that exists or achieved an absolute identity of meaning with some historical mystic, but in that more humble and qualified sense of a self-reflexive, textually mediated, human communion. Here we need only accept three premises, namely, (1) that we share, by virtue of our shared genetic makeup and common biocosmic environment, a great deal, even across times and cultures; (2) that the religious experiences (which are, in the end, always psychophysical experiences) we encode in our texts have the power to awaken similar experiences in the bodies and minds of those who engage these texts deeply; and (3) that these historical experiences are in turn radicalized and deepened further by the future horizons of meaning of their readers. It is in this kind of union, a hermeneutical union across space and time between human beings within an always renewable and developing form of critical consciousness, that our roads of excess finally end. If we have reached anything worthy of the names "palace" and "wisdom," it is here.

The Poetry of the Road: Toward an Infernal Method

[T]he notion that man has a body distinct from his soul is to be expunged; this I will do by printing in the infernal method by corrosives, which in Hell are salutary and medicinal, melting apparent surfaces away, and displaying the infinite which was hid.

William Blake, *The Marriage of Heaven and Hell*, plate 14

A book on a library shelf is like a Last Judgment in cold storage, waiting for a reader to energize it.

Editors' notes to plate 13 of *The Marriage of Heaven and Hell*, *William Blake: The Early Illuminated Books*

What, then, finally, is the road *(hodos)* after which *(meta)* we have followed to arrive at our final palace of union? How might we best define the method that has been as much a result of as a map for our excessive travels? Mircea Eliade once suggested that a good history of religions book should have the power to awaken in its readers something of the religious experience that is its subject.[41] This captures well the positive, conservative dimensions of what we have tried to accomplish here. But what of the "negative," deconstructive dimensions? Certainly the study of mysticism and the broader study of religion of which it has always been a part have contributed more than a little to an apocalypse, a necessary and perhaps even ultimately healing eschatological event, but an apocalypse nonetheless. Or is Zaehner's metaphor of rot more correct, and would we do better to see the study of religion as a kind of cultural fungus growing on the decomposing undergrowth of religion, now rendered defunctly "dead" by our modern and postmodern revolutions? Whichever metaphor we choose—renewal or rot—we would, I think, do well to take this apocalyptic aspect of our hermeneutical mysticism more seriously.

For my own part, I choose to be more hopeful and positive than Zaehner, even as I recognize that something of ominous proportions routinely takes place in our scholarship and classrooms that few seem to notice or, if they do notice, are willing to admit. In the end, perhaps it is only religious, mythological, or poetic language that can adequately capture the ambiguous power and haunting beauty of this process we so mundanely call "reading," "thinking," and "writing." Blake put it as weirdly, and yet somehow as accurately, as any in his "Memorable Fancy" of finding himself in a printing house in hell:

> I was in a Printing House in Hell & saw the method in which knowledge is transmitted from generation to generation.
> In the first chamber was a Dragon-Man, clearing away the rubbish from a caves mouth: within, a number of Dragons were hollowing the cave.
> In the second chamber was a Viper folding round the rock & the cave, and others adorning it with gold silver and precious stones.
> In the third chamber was an Eagle with wings and feathers of air, he caused the inside of the cave to be infinite, around were numbers of Eagle like men, who built palaces in the immense cliffs.
> In the fourth chamber were Lions of flaming fire raging around & melting the metals into living fluids.
> In the fifth chamber were Unnam'd forms, which cast the metals into the expanse.
> There they were receiv'd by Men who occupied the sixth chamber, and took the forms of books & were arranged in libraries.[42]

We need not lose ourselves in a full exegesis of this passage to recognize one thing clearly enough: Blake saw something of mythological proportions in the creative process and something terrifyingly violent and yet mysteriously beautiful in the art and business of conceiving, writing, and publishing books. Perhaps we should too. For many, including and especially us, our books are indeed Last Judgments in cold storage, waiting for readers to energize them.

And then what? Fortunately (or unfortunately?), this Last Judgment is effectively hidden, distributed as it is in thousands upon thousands of books "arranged in libraries," the whole of which no human being, however accomplished or well trained, will ever be able to read, much less understand. Our communal gnosis is far greater than any one of us can possibly assimilate. A certain esotericism thus returns through the sheer fact of our finitude and the temporal, financial, and emotional limitations that render any desire to acquire and appropriate the full power of our own

Last Judgment futile at best. We are spared. But we glimpse enough, and we know. We have received and eaten what Zaehner so appropriately called the serpent's gift. We may feel guilty about this. We may choose not to admit it. But it is so. We stand naked.

Very much related to Blake's "Memorable Fancy" of witnessing the creative process "in a Printing house in Hell" was his understanding, announced on the plate immediately preceding this "Memorable Fancy," of what he liked to call his "infernal method" (see the frontispiece). A reference to the chemical, and literally acidic, process by which Blake actually created his illuminated books, the phrase also carried mystical connotations of a certain poetic deconstruction that ends in a revelation in which "the whole creation will be consumed and appear infinite and holy whereas it now appears finite & corrupt." "This," Blake tells his readers, "will come to pass by an improvement of sensual enjoyment." Little wonder, then, that his paintings are filled with naked human forms, sensually strewn about and between his prose in postcoital collapse and various sexual positions, and that, for him, the Devil and Hell are the embodiments of all creative and revolutionary energies beyond the cold, stunted boundaries of Reason and Heaven. Blake's is quite literally an erotic devilish text, and a richly illustrated one at that, a kind of poetic porn. Such an eroticism served an ontological purpose for the visionary, both of which were linked to his poetic art. "But first," before our sensual enjoyment can be improved and usher in a vision of the universe's essential holiness, "the notion that man has a body distinct from his soul is to be expunged; this I will do by printing in the infernal method by corrosives, which in Hell are salutary and medicinal, melting apparent surfaces away, and displaying the infinite which was hid."[43] Perhaps it is also not a coincidence that he illustrates this same "infernal" plate with a naked, seemingly sleeping man (or is he dead?) being aroused into life by a fiery female figure hovering over him. We have seen this before.

Many of us would no doubt be uncomfortable with Blake's specific ontology, but is the "infernal method" that he so beautifully describes and paints here really so different from what we have practiced, honed, and perfected in our own twentieth-century disciplinary arts? Whether we practice a transformative psychoanalysis[44] that uncovers the sexual and aggressive roots of religious experience even as it attempts to engage dialectically the ontological ground of mystical forms of subjectivity—our own "Memorable Fancy"?—or a materialist sociological or postmodern analysis that denies the existence of any and all such grounds, our conclusions are equally "infinite," and equally terrifying, to the vast majority of believers, who fancy in their own specific ways that their doctrines and religions somehow protect them, "save" them as they often say, from the infinity of a universe about which we know more, and know more bizarrely, each day. As a number of postmodern writers have noted, mystical infinity and modern materialism, traditional apophaticism and contemporary atheism, easily collapse into one another.[45] Certainly such thinkers are not alone here, for such a position finds more than a little support in the history of mysticism, which returns again and again to powerful and often macabre images of death, annihilation, and nothingness—what Bataille, a modern nihilistic mystic if ever there was one, liked to call, rather euphemistically I think, the desire for ontological continuity. And, if I may speak confessionally again for a moment, certainly one of the defining emotional features of my Calcutta rapture was a terrifyingly clear sense that I was being sucked into a nothingness, imploded into a great void. At the center of my being, I was, and still am, not.

This dialectical notion of a Blakean "infernal method," of radical deconstruction and romantic art, of categorical apocalypse and mystical affirmation accomplished through a specific erotics, captures especially well my own methodological road as it has been tentatively mapped and stumblingly followed in the previous pages. I realize fully, and from experience, that readers will seize upon what they want to seize upon here in order to deal with their own, always contextualized, always specific emotional and intellectual responses to this hermeneutical art that is also a mystical practice. Some will see it as overly reductive and rational. Others will see it as inappropriately confessional and ecstatic. And they all will be half right. The fuller truth, however, is much richer, more paradoxical and poetic, if always admittedly infernal.

NOTES

Preface

1. Sissela Bok, *Secrets: On the Ethics of Concealment and Revelation* (1983; reprint, New York: Vintage Books, 1989); and Roger Shattuck, *Forbidden Knowledge: From Prometheus to Pornography* (San Diego: Harcourt, Brace, 1996).

2. Sissela Bok, *Lying: Moral Choice in Public and Private Life* (New York: Pantheon Books, 1978).

3. Michel Foucault was perhaps the first, and certainly the most eloquent, to see the clear connections among the Christian practice of confession, the *ars erotica* of the Catholic mystical life, and the later secular discipline of psychoanalysis. See especially Foucault, *An Introduction,* vol. 1 of *The History of Sexuality* (New York: Vintage Books, 1990), 57–73.

4. Such esoteric practices can often be read not as expressions of a desire to preserve boundaries or increase differentiation, but as necessary social mechanisms to protect the desired fusion or collapse of boundaries from the larger social world in which the practices take place and which they so often "offend."

5. Rudolf Otto, *The Idea of the Holy: An Inquiry into the Non-rational Factor in the Idea of the Divine and Its Relation to the Rational* (London: Oxford University Press, 1950).

6. See Georges Bataille, *Erotism: Death and Sensuality* (San Francisco: City Lights Books, 1986), especially pt. 1, "Taboo and Transgression."

7. Don Cupitt, *Mysticism after Modernity* (Oxford: Blackwell, 1998), 3.

8. Foucault, *An Introduction,* 34–35.

9. Quoted in Bok, *Secrets,* 105.

Introduction

1. "I learned the inestimable virtues of Silence, which initiates call 'the discipline of the arcane' (*Ketman* in Persian). One of the virtues of this Silence was to be put in solitary company alone with my invisible Shaykh, Shihaboddin Yahya Sohravardi, who died a martyr in 1191, at the age of 36, the very age that I was at that time" (Henry Corbin, quoted in Steven Wasserstrom, *Religion after Religion: Gershom Scholem, Mircea Eliade and Henry Corbin at Eranos* [Princeton, N.J.: Princeton University Press, 1999], 146).

2. Mircea Eliade, "The Secret of Dr. Honigberger," in *Two Strange Tales* (Boston: Shambalah, 1970).

3. For a powerful study of James's mystical experiences and their role in his psychology of mysticism, see G. William Barnard, *Exploring Unseen Worlds: William James and the Philosophy of Mysticism* (Albany, N.Y.: SUNY Press, 1997).

4. For eloquent discussions of Freud's understanding of mysticism, its genesis in Freud's correspondence with Romain Rolland, and its relationship to Freud's own "mystical" experiences, see William B. Parsons, *The Enigma of the Oceanic Feeling: Revisioning the Psychoanalytic Study of Mysticism* (Oxford: Oxford University Press, 1999).

5. For a discussion of Scholem and his reflections on the possibility of a modern Jewish mysticism, see my article "The Visitation of the Stranger: On Some Mystical Dimensions of the History of Religions," *CrossCurrents* 49, no. 3 (1999): 367–386.

6. Jeffrey Hopkins, *Sex, Orgasm, and the Mind of Clear Light: The Sixty-four Arts of Gay Male Love* (Berkeley: North Atlantic Books, 1998), 74.

7. Robert K. C. Forman, *Mysticism, Mind, Consciousness* (Albany, N.Y.: SUNY Press, 1999), 138–146.

8. See Hugh B. Urban, "A Dance of Masks: The Esoteric Ethics of Frithjof Schuon," in *Crossing Boundaries: Essays on the Ethical Status of Mysticism*, ed. G. William Barnard and Jeffrey J. Kripal (New York: Seven Bridges Press, 2001).

9. Frits Staal, *Exploring Mysticism* (Berkeley: University of California Press, 1975), xix, 123, 127.

10. Wendy Doniger, "Time, Sleep, and Death in the Life, Fiction, and Academic Writings of Mircea Eliade," in *Mircea Eliade e le Religioni Asiatiche*, ed. Gherardo Gnoli (Rome: Istituto Italiano per il Medio ed Estremo Oriente, 1989; offprint), 12 n. 32. See also her *Other Peoples' Myths: The Cave of Echoes* (New York: Macmillan, 1988).

11. Doniger, "Time, Sleep, and Death," 2.

12. Mircea Eliade, *Ordeal by Labyrinth: Conversations with Claude-Henri Rocquet* (Chicago: University of Chicago Press, 1982), 120.

13. The metaphor comes from Mircea Eliade, who uses it to talk about both the bewildering complexity of the history of religions and his own search "for a center" within that history (see ibid.).

14. This book presents itself in the name of an incompetence: it is exiled from that which it treats (Michel de Certeau, *La Fable mystique*, vol. 1 [Paris: Gallimard, 1982], 9; my translation).

15. Ram Chandra Datta, *Śrīśrīrāmakṛṣṇa Paramahaṁsadever Jīvanavṛttānta* (Calcutta: Jogodyan, 1935), 93.

16. Michael A. Sells, *Mystical Languages of Unsaying* (Chicago: University of Chicago Press, 1994), 9.

17. Ibid.

18. Ibid.

19. Don Cupitt, *Mysticism after Modernity* (Oxford: Blackwell, 1998), 9.

20. It is significant, I think, that Cupitt focuses on the "hard core mystical writers" of radically apophatic texts to make his postmodern case (ibid.). If one focuses instead on the erotic components of mysticism, such an absolute relativism, like Yeats's center, "does not hold." *All* mystics, after all, had bodies, which in turn shared a set of biologically and culturally shaped sexualities. Here in the sexual body, I would argue, lives what Doniger has called with respect to the study of mythology the "implied spider," that common embodied humanity that has

woven and continues to weave the mythologies and mysticisms of our many worlds (Wendy Doniger, *The Implied Spider: Politics and Theology in Myth* [New York: Columbia University Press, 1998]).

21. Cupitt, *Mysticism after Modernity*, 3.

22. Mark A. McIntosh, *Mystical Theology* (Oxford: Blackwell, 1998), 131.

23. Ibid., 130.

24. See below, chapter 1, for a summary of de Certeau's thesis. For an eloquent discussion of the "unchurched mysticism" that this deracination has made possible, see William B. Parsons, "Unchurched Mysticism," in *The Unknown, Remembered Gate: Religious Experience and Hermeneutical Reflection,* ed. Elliot Wolfson and Jeffrey J. Kripal (New York: Seven Bridges Press, forthcoming). See also below, chap. 5, n. 21, on Gershom Scholem.

25. Jean-Pierre Jossua, *Seul avec Dieu: L'Aventure mystique* (Paris: Gallimard, 1996).

26. I leave open the question whether this deracination is an opportunity to welcome and celebrate or an unfortunate corruption to mourn and ultimately reject.

27. I have necessarily refashioned, added to, and edited these journals into a coherent, readable narrative, and this of course has changed them. I have also changed or left out names in order to honor the assumed wishes of those who did not choose to appear in this self-narrative.

28. Nirad C. Chaudhuri, *Scholar Extraordinary: The Life of Friedrich Max Müller* (Delhi: Orient Paperbacks, 1974), 277.

29. See, for example, Diana L. Eck, *Encountering God: A Spiritual Journey from Bozeman to Banaras* (Boston: Beacon Press, 1993).

30. See, for example, the work of Rita Gross, particularly her essay "Religious Experience and the Study of Religion: The History of Religions," in her *Buddhism after Patriarchy: A Feminist History, Analysis, and Reconstruction of Buddhism* (Albany, N.Y.: SUNY Press, 1993).

31. See especially Michael Eigen, *The Psychoanalytic Mystic* (Binghamton, N.Y.: ESF Publications, 1998). Consider also Alan Roland's essay on contemporary psychoanalysts who weave some form of traditional meditative practice into their psychotherapy and theorizing: "Psychoanalysis and the Spiritual Quest: Framing a New Paradigm," in Wolfson and Kripal, *The Unknown, Remembered Gate.*

32. See especially Judith Okely and Hellen Callaway, eds., *Anthropology and Autobiography* (London: Routledge, 1992).

33. David E. Young and Jean-Guy Goulet, *Being Changed by Cross-Cultural Encounters: The Anthropology of Extraordinary Experience* (Peterborough, Ont.: Broadview Press, 1994).

34. See especially Don Kulick and Margaret Willson, eds., *Taboo: Sex, Identity and Erotic Subjectivity in Anthropological Fieldwork* (London: Routledge, 1995); and Tony Larry Whitehead and Mary Ellen Conaway, eds., *Self, Sex and Gender in Cross-Cultural Fieldwork* (Urbana: University of Illinois Press, 1986).

35. Sarah Caldwell, *Oh Terrifying Mother: Sexuality and Violence in the Worship of the Goddess Kāḷi* (New Delhi: Oxford University Press, 1999).

36. I borrow the expression from Benjamin Clark, who used it to describe the

manner in which Massignon's earlier studies of conservative mystics revolved around the "flaming target" of his fascination with the death of al-Hallāj and, by implication, with his own mystical experience of al-Hallāj's sacrificial intercession for him ("Translator's Introduction," in *Essay on the Origins of the Technical Language of Islamic Mysticism,* by Louis Massignon, trans. Benjamin Clark [Notre Dame, Ind.: University of Notre Dame Press, 1997], xxvi).

37. Don Kulick, "Introduction: The Sexual Life of Anthropologists: Erotic Subjectivity and Ethnographic Work," in Kulick and Willson, *Taboo,* 5; italics in original.

38. I am indebted for this line of thought to Diana Hume George, *Blake and Freud* (Ithaca, N.Y.: Cornell University Press, 1980), 149, 173. Indeed, although my own Freudian/Blakean convictions were formed long before encountering George's work, I have found it to be an especially effective means to think through many of the issues explored here. George's revision of Freud through Blake and her conviction that Blake's work not only anticipated Freud's "but that his mapping of psychic processes actually subsumes Freud's in several identifiable respects" (17) I believe to be essentially correct. Such claims confirm for me a thesis I have advanced in numerous contexts, namely, that there is something impressively analogous about psychoanalytic thought and traditional mystical traditions; see, for example, *Kālī's Child: The Mystical and the Erotic in the Life and Teachings of Ramakrishna,* 2d ed. (Chicago: University of Chicago Press, 1998), where I attempted a similar revision of Freud through Śākta Tantra; "Remembering a Presence of Mythological Proportions: Psychoanalysis and Hinduism," in *Religion and Psychological Studies: Mapping the Terrain,* ed. Diane Jonte-Pace and William Parsons (London: Routledge, 2000); and "Teaching Hindu Tantrism with Freud: Transgression as Critical Theory and Mystical Technique," in *Teaching Freud in Religious Studies,* ed. Diane Jonte-Pace (New York: Oxford University Press, forthcoming). This thesis, it should be pointed out, is hardly new. For a discussion of its history in twentieth-century psychoanalytic discourse, see below, chapter 5, n. 25.

39. The phrase, which became famous in medieval Christian thought, was first penned by Gregory the Great (d. 604) as *amor ipse notitia est.* For a discussion of Gregory's understanding of the expression and its later history in medieval thought, see Bernard McGinn, *The Growth of Mysticism,* vol. 2 of *The Presence of God: A History of Western Christian Mysticism* (New York: Crossroad, 1994).

40. Kulick, "Introduction," 5.

41. Ibid., 12.

42. Here my approach can best be described as "transformational" in Parsons's sense, that is, as a method that engages the critical powers of psychoanalysis but is "open to the possibility that the mystical element in religious traditions transcends the purely developmental and maps levels of consciousness which can, in a general sense, be designated by the label *primordial.* The latter term is used to point to the existence of deep, archaic, and mystical levels of being without implying that those levels are necessarily primitive, regressive, childish, or defensive" (William B. Parsons, "From Milan to Ostia" [unpublished manuscript], 23).

43. *The Letters of Evelyn Underhill,* ed. Charles Williams (London: Longmans, Green, 1943), 199.

44. For an important critique of this trichotomy, see Eve Kosofsky Sedgwick, *The Epistemology of the Closet* (Berkeley: University of California Press, 1990), 27–35.

45. David Halperin, *One Hundred Years of Homosexuality and Other Essays on Greek Love* (New York: Routledge, 1990), 25.

46. For an instructive summary and analysis of the essentialist-constructionist debate over sexual orientation, see Edward Stein, ed., *Forms of Desire: Sexual Orientation and the Social Constructionist Controversy* (New York: Routledge, 1992).

47. Elliot Wolfson, *Circle in the Square: Studies in the Use of Gender in Kabbalistic Symbolism* (Albany, N.Y.: SUNY Press, 1995), 79.

48. It is not, however, simply a matter of gendered symbolic systems. There is also the crucial element of social organization and institutional practice, and here I do not think it is coincidental that one of the most usual institutional practices in both Western and Asian mysticisms involves the creation of same-sex communities. The present study, however, will focus only on the first, symbolic or structural, argument.

49. Gananath Obeyesekere, *The Cult of the Goddess Pattini* (Chicago: University of Chicago Press, 1984), 428–440.

50. Wolfson, *Circle in the Square,* 223 n. 145.

51. This, of course, is an ongoing debate among historians of sexuality that has developed out of Michel Foucault's epistemological rupture and lexicalization theses (see n. 46 above), namely, the arguments that stable homosexual identities appeared in the West only with modern medical and psychological discourse (the rupture thesis) and that, since premodern cultures lacked sophisticated terms with which to talk about homosexualities, they could not have made possible stable homosexual identities (the lexicalization thesis), a position best articulated today by such thinkers as David M. Halperin *(One Hundred Years of Homosexuality)* and John J. Winkler (*The Constraints of Desire: The Anthropology of Sex and Gender in Ancient Greece* [New York, 1989]). On the other side, John Boswell, arguing that "homosexual" and "heterosexual" are categories that most historical societies would have implicitly recognized as meaningful, used the term "gay" as a historically defensible category for antique and medieval Christian materials (John Boswell, *Christianity, Social Tolerance, and Homosexuality: Gay People in Western Europe from the Beginning of the Christian Era to the Fourteenth Century* [Chicago: University of Chicago Press, 1980]), and more recently the contributors to the collection edited by Murray and Roscoe used Islamic materials to question the Eurocentric bias and historical correctness of Foucault's theses (Stephen O. Murray and Will Roscoe, eds., *Islamic Homosexualities: Culture, History, and Literature* [New York: New York University Press, 1997]). For the sake of honesty and open disclosure, I should say that, largely because of my interaction with mystical texts and communities, I consider the constructionist position to be heuristically invaluable (that is, its recognition of real difference

makes for better scholarship) but too extreme in its claims. Historical mystics, it seems to me, were in fact often aware of their sexual differences and so went to great lengths to form communities and symbolic cultures to express (and repress) these. But this is only a "working hunch," an intuition which may very well turn out to be simply a product of my own socially generated worldview, intuition and all (Halperin, *One Hundred Years of Homosexuality*, 44, 53).

52. Mark Jordan, *The Silence of Sodom: Homosexuality in Modern Catholicism* (Chicago: University of Chicago Press, 2000), 197–198.

53. I have in mind the nervous critical literatures surrounding my own work and that of Elliot Wolfson. For a discussion of the latter, see below, chap. 5. For a discussion of the former, see Jeffrey J. Kripal, "Mystical Homoeroticism, Reductionism, and the Reality of Censorship: A Response to Gerald James Larson," *Journal of the American Academy of Religion* 66, no. 3 (1998), "Pale Plausibilities," preface to the second edition of *Kālī's Child*, and "Secret Talk: Sexual Identity and the Politics of Scholarship in the Study of Hindu Tantrism," *Harvard Divinity Bulletin* 29, no. 4 (winter 2000/2001).

54. Modern egalitarian homosexuality, in which two partners of roughly the same age or status engage in sexual acts of mutual consent and form a stable public identity out of this activity, does indeed seem to be a recent Western phenomenon that can be read back into other periods or cultures only with great difficulty. When voices from non-Western cultures, then, object to contemporary gender or queer studies with the claim that "there are no homosexuals in our culture," they are partly correct, at least to the extent that we identify "homosexual" with "modern egalitarian homosexual" or "gay" and restrict ourselves to the past (since modern gay identities are quickly developing across the planet under the impact of globalization). But this, of course, is to unduly restrict our vision, our histories, and our humanity. Once we abandon such a simplistic conflation and adopt instead a broader and more precise terminology, we find quite the opposite, namely, that homosexualities are omnipresent in human cultures.

55. In Murray and Roscoe, *Islamic Homosexualities*, chap. 2.

56. In Pierre Teilhard de Chardin, *Toward the Future* (New York: Harcourt Brace Jovanovich, 1975). I consider this essay to be one of the most remarkable of Christian mystical literature, not only because Teilhard hints at his own sexual activity in its pages (60, 80, 84–85), but, more radically, because in it he attempts to advance an explicitly heterosexual Christian mysticism. This he accomplishes with a psychoanalytically informed understanding of "the spiritual power of matter" and the body as essentially passionate, capable of transfiguration, and a generator of spirit that must be stimulated, mastered, and transformed rather than repressed and denied (80). God looks very different here as well, experienced now not as the male bridegroom of the female soul, but as the "hyper-centre" that each lover knows in the other (76–77): a kind of mystical heterosexuality enacted within a bisexual Godhead. By working through (instead of escaping from) the evolutionary and essentially creative energies of human sexuality to the hyper-centre of God (and eventually, to the "delayed gift" of chastity and a "convergence at a higher level" [84]), man and woman thus reenact what looks remarkably like a traditional Hindu Tantric worldview.

57. Quoted in Halperin, *One Hundred Years of Homosexuality*, 40.
58. Ibid., 38.
59. Serena Nanda, *Neither Man nor Woman: The Hijra of India* (Belmont, Calif.: Wadsworth, 1990).
60. Wendy Doniger O'Flaherty, *Women, Androgynes, and Other Mythical Beasts* (Chicago: University of Chicago Press, 1980); Robert P. Goldman, "Transsexualism, Gender, and Anxiety in Traditional India," *Journal of the American Oriental Society* 113, no. 3 (1993): 374–401.
61. See n. 56 above.
62. See below, chap. 5.
63. See Arthur Versluis, *Wisdom's Children: A Christian Esoteric Tradition* (Albany, N.Y.: SUNY Press, 1999), especially chaps. 1–4, 20.
64. See below, chap. 2.
65. See, for example, *The Gospel of Thomas* 114, where Jesus promises to turn Mary into a man, "[f]or every female who makes herself male will enter heaven's kingdom" (*The Gospel of Thomas: The Hidden Sayings of Jesus*, trans. Marvin Meyer [San Francisco: HarperSanFrancisco, 1992]); and Diana Paul, *Women in Buddhism: Images of the Feminine in Mahāyāna Tradition* (Berkeley: University of California Press, 1979), especially chap. 5, "The Bodhisattvas with Sexual Transformation."
66. Robert M. Baum, "Homosexuality in the Traditional Religions of the Americas and Africa," in *Homosexuality and World Religions*, ed. Arlene Swidler (Valley Forge, Pa.: Trinity Press International, 1993); Will Roscoe, *The Zuni Man-Woman* (Albuquerque: University of New Mexico Press, 1991).
67. Paul Gordon Schalow, "Kukai and the Tradition of Male Love in Japanese Buddhism," in *Buddhism, Sexuality, and Gender*, ed. Jose Cabezon (Albany, N.Y.: SUNY Press, 1992). See also Bernard Faure, *The Red Thread: Buddhist Approaches to Sexuality* (Princeton, N.J.: Princeton University Press, 1998), especially chap. 5.
68. Bernard of Clairvaux, *Sermones super Cantica canticorum*, in *Sancti Bernardi, abbatis primi claraevallensis, opera genuina, juxta editionem monachorum Sancti Benedicti*, vol. 3, *Sermones de diverses et in cantica complectens* (Lyon: Ancienne Maison, 1854), sermons 9–10; for a good translation, see *Bernard of Clairvaux on the Song of Songs*, vol. 1, trans. Kilian Walsh, O.C.S.O. (Kalamazoo, Mich.: Cistercian Publications, 1981).
69. See Paul, *Women in Buddhism*, chap. 5.
70. Matthew 19.11–12. This, of course, is the locus classicus for the practice of Christian celibacy. But, once read in its original historical context, the saying is also much more, given the facts that *(a)* eunuchs were often absolutely central to the administration of ancient kingdoms (among many other good reasons, because they could produce no children to advance their dynastic ambitions); *(b)* eunuchs were often believed to function as passive homosexuals; and *(c)* castration was condemned by Jewish law and eunuchs were despised by pious Jews as deformed, impure, and unholy (see Will Roscoe, "Precursors of Islamic Male Homosexualities," in Murray and Roscoe, *Islamic Homosexualities*). Obviously, as with his parable of the good Samaritan (Samaritans were another fiercely hated

class of people), Jesus is trying his best to scandalize his audience here and no doubt hint, in the process, at the mystico-erotic dynamics of what he liked to call "the kingdom of heaven." Another, even more striking, scene appears in *The Secret Gospel of Mark*, where Jesus initiates a nearly naked young man into the kingdom in a secret midnight ritual: "And going out of the tomb they came into the house of the youth, for he was rich. And after six days Jesus told him what to do, and in the evening the youth comes to him, wearing a linen cloth over his naked body. And he remained with him that night, for Jesus taught him the mystery of the kingdom of God" (Morton Smith, *The Secret Gospel: The Discovery and Interpretation of the Secret Gospel According to Mark* [New York: Harper and Row, 1982], 78).

71. I prefer a human referent for these ontic claims (that is, I am speaking of "human being" and remain agnostic about any objective extrahuman referent for these kinds of experiences) and in the end opt for an aesthetic reading of mysticism as a kind of art (see below, "Conclusion"). For a fuller discussion of this "mystical humanism," see my "Debating the Mystical as the Ethical: An Indological Map," in Barnard and Kripal, *Crossing Boundaries*.

72. In terms of my own self-understanding, the most accurate reading of my method so far is that of William B. Parsons, who discusses it at some length as an example of what he calls an emerging "transformational school" of psychoanalysis. A transformational psychoanalytic method retains both the reductive insights of the "classical school" and the positive, therapeutic readings of the "adaptive school" but moves on from there to engage the ontological ground of mystical subjectivity itself as worthy of consideration; see Parsons, *The Enigma of the Oceanic Feeling*.

73. George, *Blake and Freud*, 141.

74. Quoted in ibid.

75. Ibid., 144.

76. Ibid., 143.

77. Again, I am indebted to George for this Freudian reading of Blake (ibid., 123).

78. Mahendranath Gupta, *Śrīśrīrāmakṛṣṇakathāmṛta*, 31st ed. (Calcutta: Kathamrita Bhaban, 1987), 1:247.

79. Hugh B. Urban, "Religion for the Age of Darkness: 'Tantrism' in the Works and Lives, Methods and Paths of the History of Religions," in Wolfson and Kripal, *The Unknown, Remembered Gate*.

80. See James R. Horne, *The Moral Mystic* (Waterloo, Ont.: Wilfrid Laurier University Press, 1983), and *Mysticism and Vocation* (Waterloo, Ont.: Wilfrid Laurier University Press, 1996).

81. Swedenborg's ability to hear angelic voices, see visions, and know clairvoyantly all came to a sudden end three months before he died, immediately after he suffered a stroke. Though still quite alive, "his spiritual sight of nearly 30 years was entirely gone." "More telling . . . is the apparent fact that the cerebral accident that deprived him of his spirit voices did not rob him of his own, allowing us to infer after all that these messages originated in his 'nondominant'

hemisphere" (David M. Wulff, *Psychology of Religion: Classic and Contemporary*, 2d ed. [New York: John Wiley and Sons, 1997], 108).

82. Kripal, *Kālī's Child*, chap. 2.

83. Louis Massignon, "Visitation of the Stranger: Response to an Inquiry about God," in *Testimonies and Reflections: Essays of Louis Massignon*, ed. and trans. Herbert Mason (Notre Dame, Ind.: University of Notre Dame Press, 1989), 40.

84. William Blake, *The Marriage of Heaven and Hell* (Oxford: Oxford University Press, 1985), plate 7.

85. I originally thought the title witnessed only to an analogous mystico-erotic approach to religious practice in Blake and the Tantric texts. I have since learned, through the work of Marsha Keith Schuchard, that the analogy runs much deeper and in places approaches historical diffusion. Blake scholars have known for years that Blake's *Marriage of Heaven and Hell* was deeply influenced by Emanuel Swedenborg. Schuchard has now shown that Swedenborg was influenced by magico-sexual ideas, including those connected to Moravian circles that sent missionaries to Asia, where they became familiar with Tantric practices (see her "Emanuel Swedenborg: Deciphering the Codes of a Celestial and Terrestrial Intelligencer," in *Rending the Veil: Secrecy and Concealment in the History of Religions*, ed. Elliot Wolfson [New York: Seven Bridges Press, 1998]). Blake's *Marriage of Heaven and Hell*, then, really is in some sense an "English Tantra."

86. See especially Peter Akroyd, *Blake: A Biography* (New York: Ballantine Books, 1995).

87. For a helpful discussion of the term and its history in medieval Christian mysticism, see Denys Turner, *Eros and Allegory: Medieval Exegesis of the Song of Songs* (Kalamazoo, Mich.: Cistercian Publications, 1995), 75–77.

88. For this idea I am indebted to Richard King (*Orientalism and Religion: Postcolonial Theory, India and "the Mystic East"* [London: Routledge, 1999], 5), who borrowed it from Paul Rabinow, "Representations are Social Facts: Modernity and Post-modernity in Anthropology," in *Writing Culture: The Poetics and Politics of Ethnography*, ed. James Clifford and George E. Marcus (Berkeley: University of California Press, 1986), 234–261.

89. Huston Smith, *Cleansing the Doors of Perception: The Religious Significance of Entheogenic Plants and Chemicals* (New York: Jeremy P. Tarcher and Putnam, 2000).

Chapter 1

1. Plotinus, *Enneads* 1.6.8; quoted in Christopher J. R. Armstrong, *Evelyn Underhill (1875–1941): An Introduction to Her Life and Writings* (Grand Rapids, Mich.: William B. Eerdmans, 1975), 49.

2. Louis Bouyer, "Mysticism: An Essay on the History of the Word," in *Understanding Mysticism*, ed. Richard Woods (Garden City, N.Y.: Image Books, 1980), 42–55.

3. Michel de Certeau, "Mysticism," *Diacritics* 22, no. 2 (1992): 14.

4. William James, *The Varieties of Religious Experience* (New York: Modern Library, 1929), 31.

5. If never, at least until the very end, quite political. For a political critique of Underhill's life and writings, particularly with reference to gender and social justice issues, see Grace Jantzen, "The Legacy of Evelyn Underhill," *Feminist Theology* 4 (1993): 79–100.

6. The book appears as a historical fossil beside such works as Bernard McGinn's recent five-volume work, *The Presence of God: A History of Western Christian Mysticism* (New York: Crossroad, 1991, 1994, 1998, forthcoming); and Paulist Press's Classics of Western Spirituality series.

7. Armstrong, *Underhill*, 109.

8. See *Evelyn Underhill: Modern Guide to the Ancient Quest for the Holy*, ed. Dana Greene (Albany, N.Y.: SUNY Press, 1988) for an excellent bibliography of sources both by and about Underhill.

9. Underhill, of course, continued to write about mysticism and the spiritual life throughout her life, producing in the end some forty books in a thirty-nine-year writing career. None, however, would have the influence of her *Mysticism*.

10. Evelyn Underhill, *Mysticism: A Study of the Nature and Development of Man's Spiritual Consciousness* (London: Methuen, 1911; reprint, London: Bracken Books, 1995); henceforth cited as M.

11. One could write an entire essay, and a rather delightful one at that, on Underhill's feline reflections; see, for example, *The Letters of Evelyn Underhill*, ed. Charles Williams (London: Longmans, Green, 1943), 73–74, 77, 86, 104, 114–115, 205, 233, 269, 278, 280–282, 333; henceforth cited as L.

12. Margaret Cropper, *Evelyn Underhill* (London: Longmans Green, 1958), 5–6. This is a particularly valuable text, as it includes much of Underhill's correspondence with Baron von Hügel, which was unavailable when the Williams collection was published.

13. Cropper, *Underhill*, 18.

14. Armstrong, *Underhill*, 34–35. It is not clear when Underhill formally left the group (ibid., 38).

15. Ibid., 38.

16. This piece is reprinted in *Underhill: Modern Guide*.

17. Letter to Father Robert Hugh Benson, n.d., quoted in Cropper, *Underhill*, 29.

18. Quoted in Cropper, *Underhill*, 72.

19. "As I understand the matter," she wrote to Father Benson, a convert from Anglicanism to Catholicism, priest, and writer on mysticism, "before one can become a Catholic, and for me Catholicism is the only possible organized faith, one must get into the state of mind which ignores all the results of the study of Comparative religions, and accepts, for instance the Ascension, in as literal and concrete a spirit as the Spanish Armada. Is this really so?" (n.d., quoted in Cropper, *Underhill*, 29). As Underhill aged, she would come to accept such traditional doctrines more on their own terms, but never perhaps as literally true; hence her acceptance of much of historical criticism (the priority of the Gospel of Mark, the

literary nature of the Magnificat, the ahistorical nature of the infancy narratives, etc. [L, 141–142]) and her consistent counsel to her advisees not to fret unduly over doctrines like the Virgin Birth.

20. Armstrong, *Underhill,* 55–56.

21. Of particular relevance was her correspondence with Father Benson, a self-described "violent defender of the Cardinals against Galileo" who argued that the church's first responsibility was to "Christ's lambs," most of whom, as spiritual children, would be scandalized by Evelyn's historical-critical truths (she had raised the example of the single authorship of Isaiah). Why protect the "brilliant young men" and sacrifice the masses for the sake of intellectual truths which may not even be true? Evelyn, fortunately, was not convinced (Armstrong, *Underhill,* 58).

22. Cropper, *Underhill,* 81.

23. The phrase occurs in her novel *The Lost Word,* cited and discussed in Armstrong, *Underhill,* 69.

24. Letter to Baron von Hügel, quoted in Cropper, *Underhill,* 72.

25. Jantzen, "The Legacy," 92.

26. Armstrong, *Underhill,* 90–91. Also of great relevance here were Underhill's three supernatural novels—*The Grey World* (1904), *The Lost Word* (1907), and *The Column of Dust* (1909), in which, according to Armstrong's readings, Underhill worked out the problem of "the two worlds" and its resolution in the mystical sacrifice of the divine world for the human one (see Armstrong, *Underhill,* chap. 4, for a lucid discussion of this theme). We can reasonably assume, Armstrong concludes, that these novels were "very much about Evelyn's life and her practical decisions" (ibid., 87).

27. Peter Homans, *The Ability to Mourn: Disillusionment and the Social Origins of Psychoanalysis* (Chicago: University of Chicago Press, 1989). See also his *Jung in Context: The Making of a Modern Psychology* (Chicago: University of Chicago Press, 1979).

28. Quoted in Armstrong, *Underhill,* 138.

29. For an example, see Cropper, *Underhill,* 23. In the same spirit, she dedicated her *Practical Mysticism* "To the Unseen Future" and began it with Blake's "If the doors of perception were cleansed . . . " No single line, I believe, has had a longer run in the modern study of mysticism.

30. I owe this reading of Underhill's love of Blake to Cropper, *Underhill,* 17.

31. Letter to Father Benson, quoted in Cropper, *Underhill,* 29.

32. Dana Greene, *Evelyn Underhill: Artist of the Infinite Life* (New York: Crossroad, 1990), 34.

33. One of Underhill's more daring moves is to interpret the obvious psychophysical sufferings and illnesses of the mystics, against the psychologists, as signs of the body suffering under an advanced form of consciousness to which it is not yet adapted. Thus, psychophysical pathology, far from detracting from the mystics' relevance and value, becomes yet another sign of their glory, a cosmic marker of some mysterious evolutionary adjustment (M, 62). This, of course, stands in marked contrast to the then dominant psychological readings

of such sufferings, which tended to interpret them as signs of psychopathology, hysteria, or, later, regressive returns to "archaic" and "primitive" levels of psychic functioning.

34. See also Armstrong, *Underhill*, chap. 6, "The Mystical Revival."

35. This idea has had a long and fruitful run in twentieth-century psychological thought. Consider, for example, Arthur Deikman's notion of meditative training as a kind "deautomatization" that can deprogram the mind's developmentally determined and perceptually restrictive organization: "If the automatization underlying that organization is reversed or temporarily suspended, aspects of reality that were formerly unavailable might then enter awareness." Unity may thus "in fact be a property of the real world that becomes perceptible via the technique of meditation and renunciation, or under special conditions, as yet unknown, that create the spontaneous, brief mystic experiences of untrained persons" (Arthur Deikman, "Deautomatization and the Mystic Experience," in Woods, *Understanding Mysticism*). Aldous Huxley adopted a similar "filtering" metaphor to explain how hallucinogens might work on the brain to produce ontologically genuine mystical experiences (see below, chap. 3).

36. Baron Friedrich von Hügel, *The Mystical Element of Religion as Studied in Saint Catherine of Genoa and Her Circle of Friends*, 2 vols. (London: J. M. Dent and Sons, 1908).

37. This same strategy of calling on Sufi polemics to do one's dirty work will be used later in the century, in an almost identical fashion, by R. C. Zaehner, who employed it to attack Hindu monistic mysticism (see below, chap. 3).

38. Quoted in Armstrong, *Evelyn Underhill*, 104. The notion of "over-beliefs" is Jamesian.

39. It should be noted that Underhill later moved away from this perennialism under the influence of von Hügel and became more and more Christocentric (and occasionally exclusivistic, if not intolerant) in her understandings of non-Christian religions. She could thus write around 1927: "When they bring out all the stuff about Christ being a World Teacher, or the parallels of the Mystery religions, the high quality of Buddhist ethics, etc., I just feel what shallow boring, unreal twaddle it is! But feeling that doesn't win souls for God" (quoted in Charles Williams, "Introduction," in L, 27). Christianity for Underhill was absolutely unique among all other systems of thought (L, 204) and so quite literally incomparable.

40. This again would change, and rather dramatically so, later on. For example, she would interact with the Bengali poet Rabindranath Tagore as a living mystic (even if she wanted to legitimate his poetry by comparing it to the writings of a long list of Christian mystics and a single Sufi [Armstrong, *Evelyn Underhill*, 140]).

41. Interestingly, and rather ironically, I can locate only one reference to Freud in *Mysticism*, and this in a discussion of Pratt's use of his dream theory to argue for a nonpathological reading of visionary phenomena (M, 288). Perhaps she had her own tome in mind when, years later, she reviewed McDougall's *Outline of Psychology* with the following barb: "A work of 450 pages which contains,

according to the index, only two references to Freud as against eight to apes, and none at all to auto-suggestion or the subconscious mind, must instantly attract us" (quoted in Cropper, *Underhill,* 114).

42. Underhill continued to struggle with psychology after *Mysticism.* See especially *The Life of the Spirit and the Life of Today* (1922; reprint, Harrisburg, Pa.: Morehouse Publishing, 1994). As with the rest of the essay, however, I will restrict my comments to *Mysticism.*

43. See, for example, James H. Leuba, *The Psychology of Religious Mysticism* (London: Kegan Paul, 1925); Theodore Flournoy, "Une Mystique moderne," in *Archives de Psychologie* 15 (1928): 1–224; Pierre Janet, *De l'angoisse à l'extase: Études sur les croyances et les sentiments,* 2 vols. (Paris: Félix Alcan, 1926–1928); and Joseph Maréchal, *Studies in the Psychology of the Mystics* (Albany, N.Y.: Magi Books, 1964); my thanks to William B. Parsons for pointing these sources out to me.

44. Underhill is a bit more forthcoming in her letters, where she describes, among other things: a "vision splendid" that leads to a kind of natural detachment from the world (L, 78–79); another vision, this one walking down the Notting Hill main road and seeing something indescribably beautiful and sublime in the sordid world of traffic and urban life now "energized by the invisible" (L, 80); and her experience of a healer who one day visited her after she had given a retreat — as the healer laid her hands on her back and head, she felt "a stream of warm energy" go through them into her body (L, 214).

45. Bernard McGinn, "Visions and Critiques of Vision in Thirteenth-Century Mysticism," in *Rending the Veil: Concealment and Secrecy in the History of Religions,* ed. Elliot Wolfson (New York: Seven Bridges Press, 1998).

46. Hans Jonas, "Myth and Mysticism: A Study in Objectification and Interiorization in Religious Thought," *Journal of Religion* 49 (1969): 328–329.

47. This is not to say, however, that experience is *only* interpretation. I would thus go much further along the constructivist arc than Underhill but not as far as Katz, whose Kantian epistemology, it seems to me, lands us squarely in a kind of dysfunctional, and ultimately unbelievable, solipsism. I am much more comfortable with a *via media* here that can incorporate the important insights of constructivism without denying the presence of cross-cultural patterns and the possibility of genuine confluence (for a more detailed discussion, see Jeffrey J. Kripal, *Kālī's Child: The Mystical and the Erotic in the Life and Teachings of Ramakrishna,* 2d ed. [Chicago: University of Chicago Press, 1998], 14–22).

48. For a discussion of this, see Elliot Wolfson, *Through a Speculum That Shines: Vision and Imagination in Medieval Jewish Mysticism* (Princeton, N.J.: Princeton University Press, 1994), 103–104 n. 135.

49. Underhill is certainly aware of one possible theological reason to include the body, even the sexualized body, within the domain of mysticism — the Incarnation, which, we are told, makes possible "the personal and passionate aspect of the Infinite Life" (M, 355). But again, she will not extend such reasoning to the messy details of any actual, physical sexuality. The Incarnation, it seems, stops just above the waist.

50. Denys Turner, *Eros and Allegory: Medieval Exegesis of the Song of Songs* (Kalamazoo, Mich.: Cistercian Publications, 1995), 25.

51. Ibid., 37.

52. Ibid., 84. Turner points out as well that the Latin Vulgate translation of the Song, which was normative for most of Christian mysticism, never refers to the male lover as *sponsus* and only rarely refers to the female lover as *sponsa* (124 n. 2).

53. I find Turner's stated disinterest in psychoanalytic categories puzzling. In an otherwise excellent study, which rightfully points out that any adequate approach to mystical eroticism will have to advance on numerous levels (hermeneutical, liturgical, doctrinal, institutional; ibid., 38, 162), he goes out of his way (17, 28) to avoid some rather obvious psychosexual conclusions (that is, about the homoerotic structure of this male celibate mysticism), although he does become a bit more open to psychological thought in his discussion of Denys the Carthusian, who gives Turner "the impression that fear of sex drives a compulsion to negate its human reality by means of displacement and that the fear is carried over in the displaced form of it" (167). I am not suggesting that we draw the same conclusions as other writers—as Turner points out, many of these medieval writers were quite conscious of the sublimation they were accomplishing and seem relatively unconflicted about its dynamics (18)—only that the thesis of a homoerotic structure goes a long way indeed toward answering Turner's most basic question, that is, why celibate male mystics insisted on employing sexual language to talk about their erotic encounters with (a male) God. It also, I think, has something important to add to Turner's helpful thesis that such a mystical eroticism was a creative synthesis of biblical and eschatological theology with Neoplatonic metaphysical theories of eros stemming from Plato's *Symposium* (21, 42). Is it not significant, for example, that the latter tradition possessed a definite (and seemingly practiced) homoerotic dimension?

54. Mark Jordan, *The Silence of Sodom: Homosexuality in Modern Catholicism* (Chicago: University of Chicago Press, 2000), 132.

55. Quoted in Bernard McGinn, "The Language of Love in Christian and Jewish Mysticism," in *Mysticism and Language,* ed. Steven Katz (New York: Oxford University Press, 1992), 203.

56. See Georges Bataille, *Erotism: Death and Sensuality* (San Francisco: City Lights Books, 1986), 225, 247.

57. Underhill, of course, is not referring to homosexuality here, but to Christianity as the normative mystical tradition of European culture. I am creatively misreading her.

58. This hunch is humorously strengthened when we encounter a pious youth in Underhill's text who, in an effort to protect his chastity, has shut himself up in the household cupboard lest he see his mother pass by (M, 216).

59. Consider, for example, her delightful description of a visit to Volendam: "Personally I nearly died of suppressed laughter," she wrote to a friend, "especially when one matron said, a propos of the cupboard-beds where all the family

sleep together: 'But of course the boys and girls do not sleep in the same bed?' and our informant replied, 'Oh yees, zey do: till zee boys begin to go after zee girls, zen they must go and sleep in the boats" (L, 136).

60. Armstrong, *Underhill*, 52.

61. Turner, *Eros and Allegory*, 79.

62. Prologue to Bernard's commentary on the Song of Songs, quoted in ibid., 131.

63. Quoted in Turner, *Eros and Allegory*, 151.

64. Ibid., 151. I would, of course, question the degree to which males in fact have a "choice" in directing their sexual energies to a male God or to human females.

65. Ibid.; italics his.

66. There is another major presence in Underhill's *Mysticism* who fits this same mystical heterosexual heretical pattern—the English poet William Blake. But Underhill never discusses Blake's eroticism, perhaps because, unlike Böhme's, it could be quite graphic and concrete (and beautifully illustrated). Interestingly, Underhill herself links these two anomalous figures, whose heteroerotic preferences could not be "mapped" by the existing homoerotic models: "At other times the maps have embarrassed him [the mystic], have refused to fit in with his description. Then he has tried, as Boehme did and after him Blake, to make new ones" (M, 104).

67. Cropper, *Underhill*, 51.

68. Ibid., 63.

69. Ibid., 44.

70. There are, however, important recent moves in this direction. McGinn, in *The Presence of God,* for example, draws rather explicitly on von Hügel (among many other thinkers) and accordingly understands the mystical not as a series of extraordinary subjective "experiences," but as a process enacted within the exegetical, liturgical, doctrinal, and ascetic practices of historical Christianity. This is certainly a better way to understand the history of Christian mysticism, which, as McGinn has convincingly shown, only rarely speaks of personal mystical experience before the twelfth century, but I suspect that it would need to be modified somewhat were we to approach twentieth-century constructions of "mysticism" in the academy and a religiously plural Western culture, all of which developed after the modernizing and psychologizing processes of which de Certeau has written and which we are exploring here.

71. Quoted in Cropper, *Underhill*, 78–79.

72. Quoted in ibid., 108.

73. Quoted in ibid., 107.

74. Quoted in ibid., 72.

75. Quoted in ibid., 108.

76. Quoted in ibid., 87.

77. Quoted in ibid., 106. Typically, Underhill does not tell us what the voice said.

78. Quoted in ibid., 82.
79. For an important feminist critique of this aspect of Underhill, see Jantzen, "The Legacy."
80. Armstrong, *Underhill,* xv.
81. Ibid., 82
82. Ibid., xxii.

Secret Talk: The Vajrāśva Vision

1. Contemporary research, by the way, lends more than a little support to the family's connection of a Gypsy background and distant Indian origins. For a helpful synopsis of this research, see Isabel Fonseca, *Bury Me Standing: The Gypsies and Their Journey* (New York: Vintage, 1995), especially chap. 2, "Hindupen." According to Fonseca, scholars have known about the Indian origins of eastern Europe's Gypsies since the eighteenth century through comparative linguistics (the Gypsies speak a dialect quite close to modern Hindi). The Roma, as they call themselves, may be related to the Indian caste of Doms, who were and are known especially as low-caste wandering musicians, scavengers, or menial workers (and, I might add, because of their marginal status, have often been connected with different types of Tantric practice). Most historians place the Gypsies' exodus from India sometime in the tenth century, when their presence in Persia was noted by the Persian historian Hamza. The reason for their departure from India remains a mystery. The cultural parallels, however, are many and impressive. Among them, we might list their sense of ritual purity and food-handling practices; their castelike social structure; an ancient, now defunct practice of "lustering," in which a dead man's widow was sacrificed on his funeral pyre; their use of the term *treshul* (a word of Indian origin for Śiva's trident) for the Christian cross; and their identification of the cult of Saint Sara with that of the Hindu goddess Kālī. Indeed, today Hindu statues, especially of Kālī, can often be found in Gypsy homes, and the hypothesis of an Indian origin has become part of a cultural movement for ethnic identity (at times financially supported by the Indian government) that Isabel Fonseca has dubbed "Hindupen."
2. Sigmund Freud, *Civilization and Its Discontents,* standard edition (London: Hogarth Press, 1955), 21:64–73. Later theorists would extend Freud's theorizing and posit intrauterine memories.
3. Ibid., 73.
4. I am indebted to Diana L. Eck for this line of thought; see her *Darśan: Seeing the Divine Image in India,* 3d ed. (New York: Columbia University Press, 1998), 63.
5. James H. Sanford, "Wind, Waters, Stūpas, Maṇḍalas: Fetal Buddhahood in Shingon," *Japanese Journal of Religious Studies* 24, nos. 1–2 (1997): 1–38.
6. .C. G. Jung, *Memories, Dreams, and Reflections,* ed. Aniela Jaffé (New York: Pantheon Books, 1973), 39–40.
7. Rudolph M. Bell, *Holy Anorexia* (Chicago: University of Chicago Press, 1985). It should be noted that such ascetic practices are quite common in early

adolescence, when they are often evoked as a defense mechanism against the forces released with the advent of puberty.

8. Jeffrey Kripal, "Dreaming Eros: On the Mythical Contours of a Student's Thought," paper written for the course "Theory of Myth and Symbolism," University of Chicago Divinity School, spring 1987.

9. "The anima is conservative and clings in the most exasperating fashion to the ways of earlier humanity. She likes to appear in historic dress, with a predilection for Greece and Egypt" (Carl G. Jung, *The Archetypes* [Princeton, N.J.: Princeton University Press, 1980], 28). I cannot say for sure, but as I do not wish to claim any transcendent atextual nature for these experiences, it is important that I point out that it is quite likely that I was reading Jung at this time.

10. Odell Shepard, *The Lore of the Unicorn* (New York: Harper and Row, 1979), 49–50.

11. Historically speaking, this makes a good deal of sense, since the Marian cult was in its origins partially a development of pagan goddess mythologies (see especially Stephen Benko, *The Virgin Mother: The Pagan and Christian Roots of the Marian Cult* [Leiden: Brill, 1984]). Somehow my unschooled psyche "knew" this bit of religious history. For an excellent sociological and psychoanalytic analysis of Marian apparitions, see Michael P. Carroll, *The Cult of the Virgin Mary: Psychological Origins* (Princeton, N.J.: Princeton University Press, 1986).

12. I am indebted to Sudhir Kakar for these two points (personal communication, September 2000).

13. This deification of the erotic was hinted at in the earlier ithyphallic Jesus fantasy; it was the god-man, after all, who possessed the erection.

14. David Gordon White, *The Alchemical Body: Siddha Traditions in Medieval India* (Chicago: University of Chicago Press, 1996), 204. Obviously, I ran across White's work much later.

15. Ibid., 232.

16. Ibid., 233–234.

Chapter 2

1. Herbert Mason, "Foreword to the English Edition," in *The Passion of al-Hallāj: Mystic and Martyr of Islam*, by Louis Massignon, trans. Herbert Mason, 4 vols. (Princeton, N.J.: Princeton University Press, 1982), 1:xix; *The Passion* is henceforth cited as PH.

2. Herbert Mason, *Memoir of a Friend: Louis Massignon* (Notre Dame, Ind.: University of Notre Dame Press, 1988), 120.

3. Louis Massignon, "Visitation of the Stranger: Response to an Inquiry about God," in *Testimonies and Reflections: Essays of Louis Massignon,* ed. and trans. Herbert Mason (Notre Dame, Ind.: University of Notre Dame Press, 1989), 40. The original French versions of most of these essays can be found in Louis Massignon (with Vicent-Mansour Monteil), *Parole donnée* (Paris: Seuil, 1983). The most complete collection (205 essays in all) can be found in Louis Massignon,

Opera minora, ed. Youakim Moubarek, 3 vols. (Paris: Presses universitaires de France, 1969).

4. "Burnt essays" is an adaptation of Massignon's own language, which described the "burnt monotheism" of an Arab tribe as a faith that burned itself out in death for the love of God (PH, 1:348).

5. Jim Wafer, "Vision and Passion: The Symbolism of Male Love in Islamic Mystical Literature," in *Islamic Homosexualities: Culture, History, and Literature,* ed. Stephen O. Murray and Will Roscoe (New York: New York University Press, 1997), 108.

6. The category was frequently used by Massignon himself (e.g., PH, 1:366, 1:343, and *Essay on the Origins of the Technical Language of Islamic Mysticism,* trans. Benjamin Clark [Notre Dame, Ind.: University of Notre Dame Press, 1997], 32; hereafter cited as EO). Massignon offers a theological critique of the notion in his *Les Trois Prières d'Abraham* (Paris: Éditions du Cerf, 1997), 44-45 (henceforth cited as TP), where he calls the attempt to sublimate profane love a "moving myth" but also an illusion and an impossibility, since only mystical union and the unique, transnatural love of God, which comes from God alone and delights only in God, can bring a creature to eternal life. He also wants to assert categorically that God is not a "loved object" of any sort (TP, 56).

7. It should be noted that others have commented on the importance of homosexuality in understanding the religious life of Louis Massignon. One of the most forthright treatments is the essay of Jean Moncelon, "Spirituality in the Life of Massignon" (in French), which was originally given at an international conference on Massignon at the University of Notre Dame, "Louis Massignon: The Vocation of a Scholar" (2–5 October 1997) and is now available on the web at http://jm.saliege.com/SPIRITUALITY/htm (17 December 2000).

8. Mary Louise Gude, for example, refers to him as a "Christian mystic" in her biography (*Louis Massignon: The Crucible of Compassion* [Notre Dame, Ind.: University of Notre Dame Press, 1996], ix; henceforth cited as LM), Seyyed Hossein Nasr calls him a Catholic "mystic" in a memoir ("In Commemoration of Louis Massignon: Catholic, Scholar, Islamicist and Mystic," in *Présence de Louis Massignon: Hommages et témoignages,* ed. Daniel Massignon [Paris: Maisonneuve et Larose, 1987]: 50–61), and Anne-Marie Schimmel describes him as "a man who conformed to what most of us would call a 'saint,' whose whole being was transformed by faith and love, and in whose presence we, other seekers, would be unable to utter a word" ("Remembering Louis Massignon," in ibid., 272).

9. Nasr breaks down the most common criticisms into four groups: an overemphasis on suffering and sacrifice; a neglect of later Sufism, particularly the theosophy of Ibn al-ʿArabī and his school; an academically inappropriate "existential" engagement with Islamic mysticism and spirituality; and an overemphasis on mysticism ("In Commemoration"). Massignon, I must add, was also heavily criticized for his refusal to support Israeli nationalism in 1948 (more on this below). I will add my own reservations at the end of the present essay.

10. Louis Massignon, letter 33, 8 Dec. 1934, in *L'Hospitalité sacrée,* ed. Jacques Keryell (Paris: Nouvelle Cité, 1987), 195; quoted in LM, 138.

11. Such Christian authors would have a rather profound, and sometimes unrecognized, influence on his interpretations of Hallāj. Carl Ernst and, following him, Benjamin Clark, for example, insightfully note that Massignon was thinking of John of the Cross's *locución* to translate Hallāj's *shaṭḥ* ("ecstatic speech") as *locution théopathique* (EO, xxiii n. 9, citing Ernst, *Words of Ecstasy in Sufism* [Albany, N.Y.: SUNY Press, 1985]).

12. Vincent-Mansour Monteil, "Entretiens," in L. Massignon, *Parole donnée,* 30; quoted in LM, 21.

13. Vincent-Mansour Monteil, *Le Linceul de feu* (Paris: Vegapress, 1987), 30; quoted in LM, 21.

14. I am following and developing Gude here (LM, 23).

15. Louis Massignon, letter 112, 29 Aug. 1912, in *Paul Claudel, Louis Massignon (1908–1914),* by Paul Claudel and Louis Massignon, ed. Michel Malicet (Paris: Desclée, 1973), 195; quoted in LM, 24. Gude notes that this comment was edited, that is, censored, in the Claudel-Massignon letters from which it is taken. And indeed, different forms of censorship, from mild and polite silences regarding difficult topics (like the scholar's homosexuality) to the actual destruction of correspondence and other documents, is common in the literature (for examples, see LM, 59, on the disappearance of Boullan's *le cahier rose* or "pink notebook," which Massignon sent to Rome to be studied; 63, on the destruction of Massignon's letters to Foucauld by Foucauld; 66, on Claudel's request to omit his account of Massignon's conversion from his published journals; 133, on the unavailability of the Kahil-Massignon correspondence). The secret of the mystical as the homoerotic is thus reproduced on the textual and historical level as a series of silences, indirections, and absences.

16. Louis Massignon, "Notes LM," quoted in Daniel Massignon, "Le Voyage en Mesopotamie et la conversion de Louis Massignon en 1908," *Islamochristiana* 14 (1988): 143; quoted in LM, 35–36.

17. Ibid., 144; quoted in LM, 38.

18. Ibid., 145; quoted in LM, 39. What was the shame here? Being executed by Muslims? Or acting on his homosexual desires? The passage is meaningfully ambiguous.

19. Louis Massignon, "Meditation of a Passerby on His Visit to the Sacred Woods of Ise," in L. Massignon, *Testimonies,* 167.

20. L. Massignon, "Visitation of the Stranger," 41.

21. L. Massignon, "Notes LM," quoted in D. Massignon, "Le Voyage," 148; quoted in LM, 45.

22. Ibid., 148–149; quoted in LM, 47.

23. Ibid., 149; quoted in LM, 47.

24. Ellis Hanson, *Decadence and Catholicism* (Cambridge, Mass.: Harvard University Press, 1998).

25. It is important to point out that there are similar linkages elsewhere in Sufi

history. Consider, for example, the famous case of Jalalūddīn Rūmī, who was initiated into the mystical-poetic life by his beloved Shamsuddīn. The passion of these two males became so intense that Shams was stabbed to death and thrown into a nearby well, perhaps by Rūmī's own son and disciples, after which Rūmī took another beloved (male) muse, the goldsmith Ṣalāhuddīn. Anne-Marie Schimmel connects Rūmī's subconscious memory of Shams's bloody death to the inspiration of a line strikingly similar to the quatrain that effected Massignon so: "This soil is not dust, it is a vessel full of blood, of the blood of lovers" (quoted in Schimmel, *Mystical Dimensions of Islam* [Chapel Hill: University of North Carolina Press, 1975], 320). Also related here is the Sufi tradition of commemorating the death of the saint as his *'urs,* or "wedding," to God (Anne-Marie Schimmel, "Eros—Heavenly and Not So Heavenly—in Sufi Literature and Life," in *Society and the Sexes in Medieval Islam,* ed. Afaf Lufti al-Sayyid-Marsot [Malibu, Calif.: Undena, 1979], 120) and what Wafer calls the "passion complex" of Sufism "in which the lover is wounded or killed by his beloved" ("Vision and Passion," 108): "This," Wafer writes, "is as close as Islam ever comes to giving a positive meaning to erotic passivity in males, although, of course, the imagery of the passion complex is sadomasochistic rather than coital. Since the killing of the lover is conventionally represented as a beheading [as with Hallāj's execution], it is not even necessary to engage too deeply in Freudian interpretation to see this death as symbolic feminization of the lover" (ibid., 108–109).

26. Jean Moncelon, "L'Extase et la grâce: Essai sur l'expérience intérieure de Louis Massignon," in *Louis Massignon: Mystique en dialogue* (Paris: Albin Michel, 1992).

27. Louis Massignon, letter 5, 31 October 1908, in Claudel and Massignon, *Paul Claudel, Louis Massignon,* 52–53; quoted in LM, 51.

28. Louis Massignon, "Les Modes de stylisation litteraire," in *Opera minora,* 2:371–372; quoted in LM, 53.

29. Louis Massignon, "The Three Prayers of Abraham," in L. Massignon, *Testimonies.* 14.

30. Ibid., 16. The themes of Mary's virginity and alleged adultery mingle in Massignon's writing, often with a decidedly anti-Semitic tinge. For example, he was furious with the Israelis when they captured Nazareth in 1948, since he considered this another mark of Jewish disrespect for the Virgin of Nazareth, whom, we are told, the Jewish tradition has blasphemously read as an adulteress (see, for example, Allen Harris Cutler's introduction to the appendices of Giulio Basetti-Sani, O.F.M., *Louis Massignon [1883–1962]: Christian Ecumenist, Prophet of Inter-religious Reconciliation* [Chicago: Franciscan Herald Press], 178). Blasphemous perhaps, but not entirely unreasonable once the infancy narratives are read beyond their mythological layers (Joseph, after all, assumed the same and was finally convinced to keep her not by a historical figure, but by a dream). Indeed, such a reading is ironically suggested when Massignon himself points out that "[w]omen represent the visitation of the Stranger, of the Sacred, in the life of mankind. . . . They substitute their own cognate genealogical kinship of the female line for the agnate genealogical kinship of the male line. They suspend that

legal kinship four times in the official genealogy of the Messiah in the first chapter of the Gospel of Matthew (Tamar, Rahab, Ruth, Bathsheba) before ending it with the virginal conception of Jesus by Mary" (L. Massignon, "Three Prayers," 187). As recent biblical scholarship has shown, Mary is in some very provocative and suggestive female company here: a woman who seduced her father-in-law into impregnating her by dressing up as a prostitute (Tamar), a professional prostitute (Rahab), a foreign woman who won her Israelite husband through a kind of sexual trick (Ruth), and the object of David's adultery (Bathsheba); indeed, Massignon himself makes all of these identifications in his " Three Prayers," 16. For a much more balanced and less hysterical treatment of the same topic, see also Jane Schaberg, *The Illegitimacy of Jesus: A Feminist Theological Interpretation of the Infancy Narratives* (New York: Crossroad, 1990). And this is hardly a digression, for all of these "adulterous," "blasphemous," and "scandalous" themes are explicitly linked in Massignon's thought through the use of the overdetermined expression "the visitation of the Stranger."

31. L. Massignon, "Visitation of the Stranger," 39.

32. Louis Massignon, "Was Avicenna, the Philosopher, Also a Mystic?" in L. Massignon, *Testimonies*, 111.

33. Louis Massignon, "Mystique et continence en Islam," L. Massignon, *Parole donnée*, 275.

34. Ibid., 273–274. Cf. PH, 2:89.

35. This is a line from al-Hallāj quoted by Massignon in his "Muslim and Christian Mysticism in the Middle Ages" (in L. Massignon, *Testimonies*, 133) that also functioned as a recurrent theme in both Massignon's personal mysticism and scholarship (see Dorothy C. Buck, "Le Thème du point vierge dans les écrits de Louis Massignon," in *Louis Massignon au coeur de notre temps*, ed. Jacques Keryell [Paris: Karthala, 1999]).

36. Louis Massignon, "Islam and the Testimony of the Faithful," in L. Massignon, *Testimonies*, 44.

37. Louis Massignon, "Charles de Foucauld," 25.

38. Ibid., 26.

39. L. Massignon, "Visitation of the Stranger," 39.

40. L. Massignon, "Muslim and Christian Mysticism," 127.

41. L. Massignon, "Visitation of the Stranger," 40.

42. Louis Massignon, "Aspects and Perspectives of Islam," in L. Massignon, *Testimonies*, 73.

43. Massignon, "Visitation of the Stranger," 41.

44. Massignon, "The Transfer of Suffering through Compassion," in L. Massignon, *Testimonies,* 160. Massignon also described the phenomenon as "heroic compassion" (ibid., 156).

45. Massignon, "The Transfer of Suffering," 156.

46. Massignon, "Charles de Foucauld," 26.

47. Massignon, "The Transfer of Suffering," 155.

48. Such a claim certainly had more than a little support in Sufi history, in which mystics routinely claimed initiatic and pedagogical contact with dead saints

and prophets (EO, 84). Consider, for example, the case of Attar, who was initiated into the mystical life by the "spiritual Hallāj" well after the latter's death (Schimmel, *Mystical Dimensions*, 305).

49. L. Massignon, "Meditation of a Passerby," 170.

50. L. Massignon, "The Transfer of Suffering," 158.

51. Ibid.

52. Ibid., 162. Massignon wrote this essay in English, which may help explain its stilted style.

53. Mason writes eloquently about how Massignon, following Huysmans, learned "the use of the autobiographical in 'correspondance' with the material of one's research" (PH, 1:xxvi).

54. L. Massignon, "Visitation of the Stranger," 41.

55. L. Massignon, "Meditation of a Passerby," 169.

56. This is a debate, by the way, which is still going on. For two recent installments, from opposite sides, see Julian Baldick, *Mystical Islam: An Introduction to Sufism* (New York: New York University Press, 1989), 35–37; and Michael Sells, "The Infinity of Desire: Love, Mystical Union, and Ethics in Sufism," in *Crossing Boundaries: Essays on the Ethical Status of Mysticism*, ed. G. William Barnard and Jeffrey J. Kripal (New York: Seven Bridges Press, 2001).

57. Pierre Rocalve, "Place et rôle de l'Islam et de l'Islamologie dans la vie et l'oeuvre de Louis Massignon" (diss., Sorbonne, 1990), 80; quoted in LM, 112.

58. Mary Louise Gude, "J. K. Huysmans, Louis Massignon, and the Language of Mysticism," *Religion and Literature* 30, no. 2 (summer 1998): 81–95.

59. Ibid., 82.

60. J.-K. Huysmans, *Là-bas I*, vol. 12 of *Oeuvres complètes de J.-K. Huysmans* (Paris: Editions G. Cres, n.d.), 1:32; quoted in Gude, "J. K. Huysmans," 88.

61. Compare Massignon's "Mystique et continence," in which he rejects a concept of celibacy that understands it as an Aristotelian virtue balancing between two extremes; on the contrary, virtues for Massignon are "heroic" and "dynamic," always oriented toward some teleological process (273). And the *telos* of continence? To die consumed *(mourir brule)* (280). Once again, love is death.

62. Gude, "J. K. Huysmans," 89.

63. Quoted in ibid.

64. Gude (ibid., 91) and Jacques Waardenburg have both made this point about Massignon's hermeneutical-mystical theory (Waardenburg, "Massignon, Louis," in *Encyclopedia of Religion*, ed. Mircea Eliade [New York: Macmillan, 1987]).

65. Gude, "J. K. Huysmans," 91.

66. Ibid., 93.

67. Wafer notes that it was the school of Basra in the early ʿAbbāsid dynasty in which the term *ʿishq* (denoting erotic passion) was first applied to the relationship between man and God. The term was deliberately chosen for its sexual connotations, Wafer notes, over the more neutral Qurʾanic *mahabba* (Wafer, "Vision and Passion," 110).

68. Schimmel, *Mystical Dimensions*, 288.

69. Anne-Marie Schimmel, *As through a Veil: Mystical Poetry in Islam* (New York: Columbia University Press, 1982), 68–69; quoted in Wafer, "Vision and Passion," 112.

70. Ibid.

71. Demonic possession was one of the models Hallāj's contemporaries used to understand and delegitimate his charisma, comparing it to "the way the demon expresses himself through the mouth of the possessed" (PH, 1:133; cf. 1:190, 2:226, 3:47 n. 156). Such an indigenous reading, minus the "demonic" valuation, deserves careful attention, especially in the light of recent anthropological research on possession states and their relationship to mystical systems of thought. Interestingly, Massignon sometimes uses the metaphor of the channel (cf. the contemporary American use of the term "channeling") to describe how God speaks through his saints (EO, 83–84).

72. This dualism appears throughout Massignon's corpus, but perhaps nowhere as clearly as in his "Mystique et continence en Islam," where he asserts, among many other remarkable things, that, although there is a certain *decalage* or shifting back and forth between continence and mysticism in Islam, the former can play only a preparatory role and never actually produce *(introduire)* the latter (273) (that he was resisting Freudian psychoanalysis here as much as Persian dialecticism is apparent when we get to the end of the article and find him stating explicitly that the medieval Islamic trope of courtly love or *hubb 'udhrī* was not "an artificial sublimation but the veil itself of an Attraction of Divine Desire" that slays [279]), that Islam has a "salutary horror" of mixing the purity of transcendence and the dirtiness of the material world (274), and that Christians have known since the Pentecost that marriage is only a "prefiguration of an absolutely chaste Union" (275). Massignon is honest and brave enough not to ignore the most obvious result of such thinking, that is, a misogyny that splits woman into a "symbol of the supreme paradisiacal ideal" and a conception that demeans and vilifies flesh-and-blood women as impure, a temptation, etc. (277), and even explores in the same article some truly disturbing mystical practices and doctrines (that flow, quite logically, out of this same misogynist sexual-spiritual dualism), but I frankly do not see him resolving this contradiction in his own thinking, at all.

73. L. Massignon, "Was Avicenna a Mystic? " 115.

74. There is an impressive and well-established literature on this aspect of Sufism. See, for example, Helmut Ritter, *Das Meer der Seele: Mensch, Welt und Gott in den Geschichten des Fariduddīn 'Attār* (Leiden: Brill, 1955); Schimmel, *Mystical Dimensions,* chap. 7, "The Rose and the Nightingale: Persian and Turkish Mystical Poetry," and "Eros"; William C. Chittick, *The Sufi Path of Love: The Spiritual Teachings of Rumi* (Albany, N.Y.: SUNY Press, 1983); Peter Lamborn Wilson, *Scandal: Essays in Islamic Heresy* (Brooklyn: Autonomedia, 1988), chap. 4, "The Witness Game: Imaginal Yoga and Sacred Pedophilia in Persian Sufism," and "Contemplation of the Unbearded: The Rubaiyyat of Awhadoddīn Kermanī," *Paidika* 3, no. 4 (1995): 13–22; Wafer, "Vision and Passion"; and Stephen O. Murray, "Corporealizing Medieval Persian and Turkish Tropes," in Murray and Roscoe, *Islamic Homosexualities.* For two fine collections of essays

on Islamic homoeroticism from the perspective of contemporary gender studies and cultural theory, see J. W. Wright, Jr., and Everett K. Rowson, *Homoeroticism in Classical Arabic Literature* (New York: Columbia University Press, 1997); and Murray and Roscoe, *Islamic Homosexualities*. In the preface to the former volume, Wright suggests that homoeroticism and masculine allusion "may be the two most pervasive themes in classical Arabic literature" (xv). There is no question, I think, that these are also the most pervasive themes in *The Passion*. Indeed, the very title can be read as a male homoerotic allusion.

75. For a linguistic analysis of *shāhid* in the Persian language, see Minoo S. Southgate, "Men, Women, and Boys: Love and Sex in the Works of Sa'di," *Iranian Studies* 17 (1984): 413–452; quoted and discussed in Murray, "Corporealizing Medieval Persian and Turkish Tropes," 139.

76. Quoted in Schimmel, *Mystical Dimensions*, 431.

77. Schimmel, "Eros," 130. For a fuller treatment of women and Sufism, see Schimmel, *Mystical Dimensions*, appendix 2, "The Feminine Element in Sufism."

78. The term is likely derived from Karl Heinrich Ulrichs, an early advocate for the rights of sexual minorities and the founder, in 1862, of the cult of Uranism, so named for Pausanias's hymn to uranian or "heavenly" *(ouranos)* pederasty in Plato's *Symposium* (David M. Halperin, *One Hundred Years of Homosexuality and Other Essays on Greek Love* [New York: Routledge, 1990], 16). A little later, in 1896, André Raffalovich would publish a lengthy defense of homosexuality under the title *Uranisme et unisexualité* (see Hanson, *Decadence and Catholicism*, 320–329, for a discussion of Raffalovich and his relationship to the decadent writers; my thanks to Steven Wasserstrom for pointing out the latter reference to me). We know that Massignon was familiar with Raffalovich, since he refers to him in *Les Trois Prières d'Abraham* (TP, 46 n. 1).

79. And what to do with Massignon's self-censorship and "untranslations," that is, those places in his text where he hints at some scandal (inevitably of a sexual nature) but will give no details or simply refuses to translate a passage or term that he believes to be too troubling? For a start, see PH, 2:31, on "certain disconcerting reminiscences" about Hallāj; PH, 2:123, on "a rather disgusting sexual perversion" of Sūlī; PH, 3:164, on an untranslated *hadīth* that inspired stories of marriages with *hūrīs* in paradise; PH, 3:194, on the Qarmathian practice of eating the *rajī'* (some sort of bodily fluid or waste product?) of others as "pure"; and PH, 3:239–242, on his vague descriptions of mystico-erotic practices within certain Nusayrī, Druze, and Sunnite initiatory circles.

80. Louis Massignon, "L'Amitié et la présence mariale dans nos vies," *Opera minora*, 3:767; quoted in LM, 82.

81. Mark Jordan, *The Silence of Sodom: Homosexuality in Modern Catholicism* (Chicago: University of Chicago Press, 2000), 92–93.

82. Paul Claudel, entry for Holy Saturday, April 1925, in *Journal*, 2 vols. (Paris: Pleiade, Gallimard, 1968), 1:668; quoted in LM, 139.

83. Solange LeMaître, "Louis Massignon," in *Cahiers de l'Herne*, ed. Jean-François Six (Paris: Editions de l'Herne, 1970), 443; quoted in LM, 151.

84. Even given the anecdotal and oral nature of the story (both of which I freely admit and note), the story rings true in that it fits in quite well with Massignon's

famous candid nature. Herbert Mason is clear: "The problem for discretion in Massignon's case is that he never kept anything about himself secret during his own lifetime. It is only his surviving disciples who are embarrassed. Massignon was open, available, present whenever anyone asked sincerely about any aspect of his life, and he often volunteered information even when not asked" (PH, 1:xxiii).

85. Louis Massignon, "Le Problème des réfugiés arabes de Palestine," in *Opera minora,* 3:518; quoted in LM, 165.

86. For some important philosophical and political critiques of Massignon's scholarship, particularly in reference to Islam and Judaism, see Edward Said, *Orientalism* (New York: Vintage, 1979); and Steven Wasserstrom, "The Quest for a Transcendent Unity of Religions: French Catholic Orientalists and the Turn to Islam" (unpublished paper, 2000). With Wasserstrom, I find Massignon's relationship to Judaism, not to mention Islam, every bit as conflicted and contradictory as his relationship to his homosexuality. Sometimes, moreover, the two Massignonian contradictions—Judaism and homosexuality—appear side by side, as in his "Three Prayers of Abraham," in which all the usual anti-Semitisms (e.g., legalism, fossilization, and racism) appear (15–16) alongside some deeply disturbing comments on male and female homosexuality, linking it with antisocialism and "extra-legal conspiratorial and revolutionary groups of coolies, convicts, spies, initiates, and mediums" (11).

87. Raoul Girardet, *L'Idée coloniale en France, 1871–1962* (Paris: La Table Ronde, 1972), 224–225; quoted in LM, 215.

88. François Mauriac, *Le Nouveau Bloc-notes, 1961–1964,* entry for 6 November 1962 (Paris: Flammarion, 1968), 207; quoted in LM, 248.

89. Louis Massignon, "Les Trois Prieres d'Abraham," in L. Massignon, *Parole donnée,* 263; my translation.

90. This text includes both his essay "La Prière sur Sodome" of 1949 and his essay "Les Trois Prières de'Abraham: Père de Tous les Croyants" of 1962 (which also appears in *Parole donnée* and is translated by Mason in L. Massignon, *Testimonies*), along with an elaborate historical discussion of these essays' private distribution during Massignon's life.

91. It is interesting that Massignon himself almost never uses the term "homosexuality." I could find the word used only once in "The Prayer for Sodom," and this in a footnoted book title of another scholar, Edward Carpenter's *Beziehungen zwischen Homosexualität und Prophetentum* of 1911 (TP, 38 n. 1). Massignon's more usual terms are the nominal forms "uranism," "inversion," "sodomy," "Platonism," "Angelicism" (strangely, there is more than a little sex going on between humans and fallen angels, succubi, incubi and other demonic presences in Massignon's text [TP 37, 48, 49]), "the ephebe," and "'udhritic love," along with their adjectival forms.

92. And a crime. Massignon explicitly connects homosexuality with criminal activity here (TP, 35, 46) and in "The Three Prayers of Abraham: Father of All Believers" (7, 11).

93. For the sake of our own intertextual musings, it is perhaps worth pointing out that Massignon cites Rimbaud's "Saison en enfer" as a clear example of this

"categorical conclusion" of homosexual suicide (TP, 41). This will become significant in our next chapter, where we will see R. C. Zaehner, who, like Massignon, struggled with his own homosexual desires in the context of a pious Catholicism, having his first mystical experience while reading this very poem.

94. "The Three Prayers of Abraham," in L. Massignon, *Testimonies,* 12.

Secret Talk: Heroic Heretical Heterosexuality

1. Bernard of Clairvaux, *Sermones super cantica canticorum,* sermons 2–4; for a good translation, see *Bernard of Clairvaux on the Song of Songs,* vol. 1, trans. Kilian Walsh, O.C.S.O. (Kalamazoo, Mich.: Cistercian Publications, 1981).

2. Saint John of the Cross, *The Living Flame of Love,* in *The Collected Works of St. John of the Cross,* trans. Kieran Kavanaugh and Otilio Rodriguez (Washington, D.C.: ICS Publications, 1979), 2.9–10.

3. John Boswell, *Christianity, Social Tolerance, and Homosexuality: Gay People in Western Europe from the Beginning of the Christian Era to the Fourteenth Century* (Chicago: University of Chicago Press, 1980); Mark Jordan, *The Silence of Sodom: Homosexuality and Modern Catholicism* (Chicago: University of Chicago Press, 2000).

4. My own experience of these patterns has been made more conscious, and dramatically confirmed, by reading Jordan's *Silence of Sodom.*

5. Howard Eilberg-Schwartz, *God's Phallus and Other Problems for Men and Monotheism* (Boston: Beacon Press, 1994), 99.

6. Ibid., 195.

7. My argument here is purely anecdotal, that is, autobiographical, but my conclusions are more than supported by a remarkable literature of historical, sociological, and psychological studies on homosexuality and the priesthood. For a summary of these, see Jordan, *The Silence of Sodom.* For two major historical treatments and an overwhelming fund of ancient and medieval support for this ancient thesis, see Boswell, *Christianity, Social Tolerance and Homosexuality;* and Mark Jordan, *The Invention of Sodomy in Christian Theology* (Chicago: University of Chicago Press, 1997).

8. Since I wrote these lines, the situation has changed considerably, catalyzed largely by the appearance of Donald B. Cozzens's remarkable book *The Changing Face of the Priesthood,* published by an enlightened Benedictine press (Collegeville, Minn.: Liturgical Press, 2000). Cozzens, president-rector and professor of pastoral theology at Saint Mary Seminary and Graduate School of Theology in Cleveland, writes honestly and "from the inside" about the significance of homosexuality among Catholic seminaries, draws on historical scholarship to suggest that this has likely always been the case (even as he contextualizes the present crisis in a post–Vatican II American Catholicism that has seen twenty thousand [no doubt mostly heterosexual] priests leave the ministry to marry), worries out loud about the effects a largely gay seminary culture might have on heterosexual men interested in the priesthood, and calls for more open discussion about whether the Catholic priesthood has become a "gay profession." His closing lines of chapter 7 appear prophetic to me: "The priesthood's crisis of soul, and by extension,

the Church's crisis of soul, is in part a crisis of orientation. Sooner or later the issue will be faced more forthrightly than it has in the closing decades of the twentieth-century. The longer the delay, the greater the harm to the priesthood and to the Church" (110). "A crisis of orientation"—that is precisely what the present work is all about, extended well beyond the present vocational crisis into the theological and mystical depths of the tradition.

9. Sudhir Kakar, *The Inner World* (New Delhi: Oxford University Press, 1978), 173.

10. Shashibhushan Dasgupta, *Obscure Religious Cults* (1946; 3d ed., Calcutta: Firma KLM, 1976), 126, 130.

Chapter 3

1. Michael Dummett, introduction to *The City within the Heart,* by R. C. Zaehner (New York: Crossroad, 1981), xii; *The City within the Heart* is henceforth cited as CWH.

2. The only extensive study of Zaehner's writings of which I am aware is William Lloyd Newell, *Struggle and Submission: R. C. Zaehner on Mysticisms* (Washington, D.C.: University Press of America, 1981). Newell's book succeeds, I think, in explaining Zaehner's main theses regarding the comparative study of mysticism and their implications for a comparative theology of religions. Newell describes his work as "not so much . . . a work in the History of Religions as a work in Roman Catholic Spiritual Theology" (viii). Interestingly, and quite relevant to our present concerns, Newell notes that his two years of study with Zaehner at Oxford convinced him that "one's own interiority had to be involved in judging the other," which in turn led him to ask: "How could my Catholic interiority go out, become vulnerable to the objects of my study, change me and then return to me to be judged theologically?" (vii). My own approach to Zaehner is much more psychological than theological but will pay special attention to these same practices of spiritual interiority and religious engagement with the other in Zaehner.

3. Lee Siegel, personal communication, 2000.

4. R. C. Zaehner, *Concordant Discord: The Interdependence of Faiths, Being the Gifford Lectures on Natural Religion Delivered at St. Andrews in 1967–1969* (Oxford: Clarendon Press, 1970), 11; henceforth cited as CD.

5. Zaehner borrowed the expression from Richard M. Bucke's *Cosmic Consciousness* (1901; reprint, New York: E. P. Dutton, 1969).

6. I am indebted to Lee Siegel (personal communication) for this theme.

7. The summary that follows is based on interviews with former students and colleagues and two obituaries: Ann K. S. Lambton, obituary for R. C. Zaehner, *Bulletin of the School of Oriental and African Studies* 38 (1975): 623–624; and George Morrison, obituary for R. C. Zaehner, *Iran* 13 (1975): iv. I am indebted to Prof. John Gurney of Wadham College for both references.

8. R. C. Zaehner, *Hinduism* (Oxford: Oxford University Press, 1962).

9. Yudhishthira, a saintly king and incarnation of his father, the god Dharma himself, is the eldest of the five brothers and leader of the Paṇḍava clan in the

epic, where he comes to stand against the deceptions, violence, and genocide of the warrior's ethical code or dharma he hears proclaimed and justified all around him. In his *Hinduism,* Zaehner made Yudhishthira the focus of his chapter "Dharma" and, in his title for chapter 8, described Mahatma Gandhi's remarkable appearance in the twentieth century in two poignant words: "Yudhishthira Returns." Not surprisingly, he returned to his beloved hero Yudhishthira again in his ninth Gifford Lecture, "The Greatness of Man and the Wretchedness of God" (CD, chap. 9). The jarring title is a reference to the epic story itself, in which the saintly king Yudhishthira struggles to preserve the sacrality and integrity of his own conscience before the almost overwhelming pressures of his family, the traditional dharma, and the absolute authority of the divine Kṛṣṇa, who does not hesitate to proclaim the rightness of the war and the inevitability of the fate *(daiva)* it mercilessly plays out.

10. Lambton, obituary, 624.

11. R. C. Zaehner, *Zen, Drugs and Mysticism* (New York: Pantheon Books, 1972), 196.

12. Lee Siegel, personal communication, 26 April 2000.

13. Peter Wright, *Spy Catcher: The Candid Autobiography of a Senior Intelligence Officer* (New York: Viking Penguin, 1987), 244.

14. Ibid., 246.

15. Peter Homans, *The Ability to Mourn: Disillusionment and the Social Origins of Psychoanalysis* (Chicago: University of Chicago Press, 1989).

16. CD, 36; Zaehner, *Zen, Drugs and Mysticism.*

17. Aldous Huxley, *The Doors of Perception and Heaven and Hell* (1954; reprint, New York: Harper and Row, 1963), 13–14.

18. "In the intervals between his revelations the mescalin taker is apt to feel that, though in one way everything is supremely as it should be, in another there is something wrong" (Huxley, *The Doors of Perception,* 41). Still, Huxley insists that mystics who are in touch with such realities can act as "conduits" for the world at large; in the end, even they are socially useful, if in indirect and mysterious ways (ibid., 44).

19. R. C Zaehner, *Mysticism Sacred and Profane* (Oxford: Clarendon Press, 1957), xi; henceforth cited as MSP.

20. R. C. Zaehner, *Hindu and Muslim Mysticism* (New York: Schocken Books, 1969), 87.

21. Zaehner would later expand this tripartite typology into four stages in CD and *Zen, Drugs and Mysticism,* but the basic theoretical model remained the same.

22. Zaehner prefers this term to the more traditional "pantheism," asserting that the latter is incorrect because, technically speaking, there is no "God" present in such experiences (MSP, 28).

23. Kay Redfield Jamison, *Touched with Fire: Manic-Depressive Illness and the Artistic Temperament* (New York: Free Press, 1993).

24. See, for example, MSP, 43–49, 63, 65, 78, 101, 106, 108, 118, 125, 136, 144, 148.

25. Kristen E. Kvam, Linda S. Schearing, and Valarie H. Ziegler, *Eve and Adam: Jewish, Christian, and Muslim Readings on Genesis and Gender* (Bloomington: Indiana University Press, 1999).

26. Elaine Pagels, *The Gnostic Gospels* (New York: Vintage Books, 1979), 64.

27. Certainly one of the most striking and humorous examples of Zaehner's allegorical thought is his essay "Hosea's Wife" (CD, chap. 18), in which he allegorically reads the prophet Hosea's prostituting wife as Catholicism and her three unfaithful children as Luther, Calvin, and the Church of England (CD, 376)! This may all be tongue in cheek (at least I hope so), but it nevertheless demonstrates clearly Zaehner's ability to make a serious point in a playful manner. It is also, I should point out, a good example of the hypersexualization of Zaehner's thought, which I will treat at some length below.

28. R. C. Zaehner, *Evolution in Religion: A Study in Sri Aurobindo and Pierre Teilhard de Chardin* (Oxford: Clarendon Press, 1971).

29. Quoted in Elaine Pagels, *Adam, Eve, and the Serpent* (New York: Vintage Books, 1988), 69.

30. Kvam et al., *Eve and Adam*, 88.

31. Consider, for example, the medieval kabbalist Abraham Abulafia: "Intercourse is called the Tree of Knowledge of good and evil and it is a matter of disgust and one ought to be ashamed at the time of the act" (quoted in David Biale, *Eros and the Jews: From Biblical Israel to Contemporary America* [Berkeley: University of California Press, 1997], 109).

32. Pagels, *Adam, Eve, and the Serpent*, 109.

33. Zaehner, *Evolution in Religion*, 17.

34. Zaehner, *Hinduism*, chap. 6.

35. Zaehner, *Hindu and Muslim Mysticism*, 85.

36. My technical uses of the term "the erotic" and its specific dialectical connotations, which I have developed and employed elsewhere (*Kālī's Child: The Mystical and the Erotic in the Life and Teachings of Ramakrishna*, 2d ed. [Chicago: University of Chicago Press, 1998]), are not reflected in Zaehner's language (which loosely collapses "sex," "sexuality," and "mysticism"), although they are reflected, and quite closely, in his Marxist-Teilhardian-inspired sanctification of sexuality as the meeting place of spirit and matter (more on this below).

37. For Zaehner, Christianity synthesizes the two great forces of the world religions, the ethical-prophetic and the contemplative-mystical; hence, he writes: "For Christians Jesus is God made man, and this makes it impossible to treat Christianity simply as a prophetic religion. From the very beginning a mystical element is present, and it is this, if anything, that entitles Christianity to speak of itself as unique. It cannot be broadly classified as either prophetic or mystical: it falls somewhere between the two" (CD, 24). He had earlier developed this idea in *The Convergent Spirit: Towards a Dialectics of Religion* (London: Routledge and Kegan Paul, 1963).

38. Although Zaehner despised Paul Tillich and the entire liberal Protestant tradition—"I confess that I have never been clear as to what Tillich understood by this 'eternal Protestant principle,' unless he meant himself" (CD, 11)—both

Zaehner's understanding of eroticism and his critique of ascetic Christianity are remarkably close to Tillich's (ironically) Platonic understanding of eros and critique of Nygren's agape-eros dichotomy (see Alexander C. Irwin, *Eros toward the World: Paul Tillich and the Theology of the Erotic* [Minneapolis: Fortress Press, 1991]). It is significant, I think, that both thinkers relied on intellectual traditions technically outside Christian thought to make their defenses of eroticism (Marxism and Bergsonian philosophy in Zaehner's case, Platonism and psychoanalysis in Tillich's).

39. James H. Leuba, *The Psychology of Mysticism* (London: Kegan Paul, Trench, Trubner, 1925), 119. Related here is Turner's observation on medieval commentaries on the Song of Songs: "[W]hy is it that not one mediaeval Song commentary makes anything at all of the theological topic the text throws in the commentator's face: the theology of sexuality and of marriage? Search the catalogue of mediaeval Song commentaries for even a hint of this theological interest. Result, zero" (Denys Turner, *Eros and Allegory: Medieval Exegesis of the Song of Songs* [Kalamazoo, Mich.: Cistercian Publications, 1995], 40).

40. The religious dimensions of drunkenness appear in Zaehner's marginalia as well, for example, in his highlighting of two of Ramakrishna's sayings, one comparing the social indifference of the true devotee to that of the true drunk and a second comparing the necessity of practicing devotion in order to see God to the necessity of ingesting hemp in order to get intoxicated (repeating the word "hemp" will get you nowhere, the saint points out) (Ramakrishna, *Sayings of Sri Ramakrishna: The Most Exhaustive Collection of Them, Their Number Being 1120* [Mylapore: Sri Ramakrishna Math, 1949], 114, 65).

41. It is interesting to note that Zaehner had no trouble with the sexual components of this *conjunctio* but rejected it when it was applied to ethics.

42. In another line of gender-bending reasoning, quoting, and comparing, Zaehner moves, within a single page, from the autoerotic to the heteroerotic and back to the autoerotic again, without seeming to recognize it at all. The texts are again Hindu. Although he admits that such language is rare in the Upaniṣads (CD, 107), he nevertheless insists on treating it and indeed highlighting the only two passages he can find on (1) the self enjoying intercourse with the Self, (2) this same state compared to the annihilation a man experiences while sexually embracing his wife, and (3) the pleasure the self feels playing and copulating with the Self (CD, 86). This "sacred marriage with this supreme Self," we are told, "is not at all unlike the spiritual nuptials between Christ and the soul that was to become a commonplace among the Christian mystics" (CD, 105).

43. Ellis Hanson, *Decadence and Catholicism* (Cambridge, Mass.: Harvard University Press, 1997), 17.

44. And this is appropriate, since Balzac's Illuminist mysticism was itself materialistic, arguing for the physiological base of "miracles" and parapsychological events as misunderstood natural phenomena (see Philippe Bertault, *Balzac and "The Human Comedy"* [New York: New York University Press, 1963], chap. 6, "The Occult Meaning of Balzacian Mysticism").

45. Honoré de Balzac, *Seraphita, A Daughter of Eve and Other Stories,* translated by Clara Bell and R. S. Scott (Philadelphia: Gebbie, 1899), 134.

46. Ibid., 138.
47. Ibid., 134.
48. R. C. Zaehner, *Our Savage God* (London: Collins, 1974).
49. All of these themes—Zen, drugs, and mystically justified violence—were part of Zaehner's previously published book, *Zen, Drugs and Mysticism*. Only Manson was missing.
50. Lee Siegel, personal communication, 2000.
51. Wendy Doniger, "Time, Sleep, and Death in the Life, Fiction, and Academic Writing of Mircea Eliade," in *Mircea Eliade e le Religioni Asiatiche*, ed. Gherardo Gnoli (Rome: Istituto Italiano per il Medio ed Estremo Oriente, 1989).

Secret Talk: Writing Out (of) That Night

1. I am also very much aware that the experience resembles at least three well-documented phenomena from other fields: the medieval legends of the succubus and the incubus, the condition known as sleep paralysis in contemporary sleep research, and the near-death experience (NDE). A full exegesis of the ecstatic vision would have to take each of these analogous cultural models into account.
2. Quoted in David Biale, *Gershom Scholem: Kabbalah and Counter-history* (Cambridge, Mass.: Harvard University Press, 1982), 31.
3. Jacques Waardenburg, "Massignon, Louis," in *Encyclopedia of Religion,* ed. Mircea Eliade (New York: Macmillan, 1987).
4. Mark S. G. Dyczkowski, *The Doctrine of Vibration: An Analysis of the Doctrines and Practices of Kashmir Shaivism* (Albany, N.Y.: SUNY Press, 1987), 217.

Chapter 4

1. See the issue of *Syranthropy* dedicated to his life and work: *Syranthropy: Journal of the Anthropology Department, Syracuse University* (spring 1993).
2. *Sandhā-bhāṣā,* as we will see below, is a Tantric use of language that played a major role both in Bharati's understanding of the Tantric traditions and in his own use of language; traditionally, the technique works through double-entendres as an "intentional language" *(sandhā-bhāṣā)* that "intends" both a sexual-physical and a mystical-spiritual meaning at the same time in order to collapse the ordinary dualisms of the religious mind.
3. Agehananda Bharati, *The Ochre Robe* (1960; reprint, Santa Barbara, Calif.: Ross-Erikson, 1980), 11; henceforth cited as OR.
4. Agehananda Bharati, *Dear Lalita* (first words of text, which I use as its title), 1962 (title and publication details all missing), 54–55; see below for a discussion of this text and its possible origins; henceforth cited as DL.
5. Agehananda Bharati, "Śākta and Vajrayāna: Their Place in Indian Thought," in *Studies of Esoteric Buddhism and Tantrism,* ed. Gisho Nakano (Koyasan, Japan: Koyasan University, 1965), 90.
6. Agehananda Bharati, "Broad, Noeticness and Other Guentheriana," *Kailash: A Journal of Himalayan Studies* 5, no. 2 (1977): 185.
7. Quoted in Warren Berger, "Agehananda Bharati: The Life and Times of a Hindu Monk," *Vantage,* October 1979, 9.

8. Bharati, "Broad, Noeticness and Other Guentheriana," 186.

9. Vinod Dhawan, "The Pugnacious Scholar-Swami," *Hindustani Times*, 18 January 1985.

10. His books *The Light at the Center, The Ochre Robe,* and *The Tantric Tradition* were particularly popular. They were read widely, reviewed in such periodicals as *Time* (13 September 1976), and translated into other languages.

11. The line was originally spoken by Lord Darlington in Wilde's *Lady Windermere's Fan*, act 1. I am assuming that Bharati was aware of the cultural and legal scandals surrounding Wilde's homosexuality. My thanks to Mark Jordan for both directing me to the original source and suggesting the latter line of thought.

12. Agehananda Bharati, *Indology and Science: Towards a Hermeneutical Coalition* (Calcutta: Roy and Chowdhury, 1989).

13. See also Agehananda Bharati, *The Light at the Center: Context and Pretext of Modern Mysticism* (Santa Barbara, Calif.: Ross-Erikson, 1976), 74; henceforth cited as LC.

14. Bharati, "Śākta and Vajrayāna," 87.

15. Ibid., 86–87; Agehananda Bharati, "The Future (if Any) of Tantrism," *Loka: A Journal from Naropa Institute* (1975), 129.

16. See also Agehananda Bharati,"Techniques of Control in Esoteric Traditions of India and Tibet," in *The Realm of the Extra-human: Ideas and Actions*, ed. Agehananda Bharati (The Hague: Mouton, 1976); and Bharati, "Śākta and Vajrayāna," 91–93.

17. See also Agehananda Bharati, "Hinduism, Psychotherapy, and the Human Predicament," in *Religious Systems and Psycho-Therapy*, ed. Richard H. Cox (Springfield, Ill.: Charles C. Thomas, 1973), and "Śākta and Vajrayāna," 95–98.

18. Bharati discusses the same in his "Techniques of Control."

19. Bharati, *Indology and Science*, 43 n. 17. See also his reviews of *Dreams, Illusions, and Other Realities* in *Journal of Asian Studies* 44, no. 4 (1985): 871–872, and of *Tales of Sex and Violence* in *American Anthropologist* 88, no. 4 (1986): 991–992.

20. Bharati loved Obeyesekere's *Medusa's Hair* and *Pattini*, both hermeneutically indebted to a psychoanalytic method. See his review of *Pattini*, "Pattini: The Anthropological Consummation of a Goddess," *American Anthropologist* 87, no. 2 (1985): 364–369, and of *Medusa's Hair, Mentalities/Mentalités* 1, no. 1 (1983): 39–40. See also Agehananda Bharati, "Speaking about 'That Which Shows Itself': The Language of Mysticism and the Mystics," in *Religious Experience and Scientific Paradigms: Proceedings of the IASWR Conference, 1982,* comp. Christopher Chapple (Stony Brook, N.Y.: Institute for Advanced Studies of World Religions, 1985), 238.

21. See Bharati's review of *The Great Universe of Kota*, by G. M. Carstairs, in *Annals of the American Academy of Political and Social Science* (September 1976): 141–142.

22. See also Bharati's reviews of Philip Spratt's *Hindu Culture and Personality* in *Journal of Asian Studies* 26 (May 1967): 519–520, and *American Anthropologist* 70, no. 1 (February 1968): 142.

23. Bharati, "Śākta and Vajrayāna," 93–94.

24. Joseph Campbell, *Baksheesh and Brahman: Indian Journal, 1954–1955,* ed. Robin and Stephen Larsen and Antony Van Cowering (New York: Harper-San Francisco, 1995).

25. Agehananda Bharati, "Religion for the Thinking Person," *New Delhi* 2, no. 14 (29 October 1974): 74.

26. Agehananda Bharati, "True and False Prophets of Today's Hinduism," *Asia,* November/December 1979, 36–37.

27. Bharati, "Hinduism, Psychotherapy, and the Human Predicament," 178.

28. Berger, "Agehananda Bharati," 8.

29. See also Bharati, "Hinduism, Psychotherapy, and the Human Predicament," 168.

30. See, for example, Agehananda Bharati, "Hindu Scholars and the Third Reich," *Quest* 44 (winter 1965): 74–77, "Bose and the German Ina: An Unexplored Chapter," *New Quest,* vol. 26 (March–April 1981), and "Hindu Faschismus," *Forum,* 30 September 1986, 29–35.

31. Bharati, "Bose and the German Ina," 84.

32. Consider one of his many great one-liners: "You don't learn ethical behavior through yoga and meditation any more than you learn loving your neighbors by playing poker or cello" (LC, 179).

33. The prophet and the mystic represented two opposing categories for Bharati: whereas the former often feels called to preach the objective truths of his visions or voices, the latter does not. Prophets can easily become totalitarians. Wise mystics, who make no ontological claims for their experiences, cannot; quite the contrary, they stand radically opposed to the establishment in both their intimate methods and in the equally intimate content of their experiences.

34. Bharati considered this popular text to be particularly dangerous, as it was full of "blatant moral contradictions" (quoted in Dhawan, "The Pugnacious Scholar-Swami") and could have (and may have) been used by Hitler (LC, 199).

35. Bharati, "The Future (if Any) of Tantrism," 37.

36. Bharati, "True and False Prophets," 130.

37. This, of course, flatly contradicts the usual orientalist distinction between the "spiritual East" and the "materialistic West," a stereotyping that Bharati despised. Once again, in true Bharatian style, the swami sought to turn a traditional trope on its head.

38. Bharati mercilessly lambasted the dichotomous and naive orientalisms of the Hindu Renaissance and contemporary American devotees for depicting India as the spiritual, mysterious balm that could solve the West's problems ("Hinduism, Psychotherapy, and the Human Predicament," 173–174), but he did seem to accept that there were real cultural differences, and he was explicit about his desire for a different kind of cultural synthesis, a humanistic-mystical synthesis that made no delusional claims about saving the world (or even the soul) but that concentrated instead on making human life richer, more sophisticated, more rational, and, above all, more aesthetically pleasing.

39. The term is carefully chosen, and it is Bharati's; see below for a discussion.

40. Bharati, "Śākta and Vajrayāna," 91, and "Techniques of Control."

41. Bharati, "Śākta and Vajrayāna," 94–95.

42. Ibid., 99.

43. Kathleen Taylor, "Arthur's Avalon: The Creation of a Legendary Orientalist," in *Myth and Mythmaking*, ed. Julia Leslie (Richmond, U.K: Curzon, 1996), 144–146.

44. Andre Padoux, "Tantrism: An Overview," in *Encyclopedia of Religion*, ed. M. Eliade (New York: MacMillan, 1986), vol. 14; and Hugh B. Urban, "The Extreme Orient: The Construction of 'Tantrism' as a Category in the Orientalist Imagination," *Religion* 29 (1999): 123–146.

45. I am not sure why Bharati does not mention the Bengali literary historian Shashibhushan Dasgupta here, whose *Obscure Religious Cults* (1946; 3d ed., Calcutta: Firma KLM, 1976), a quite remarkable study of vernacular Bengali Tantric traditions, is as impressive in its scholarship and as comfortable in its sexual discourse as anything that Western scholars had written at this time.

46. Accordingly, and quite faithfully, one of his disciples, Prem Saran, himself an initiated Tāntrika, published *Tantra: Hedonism in Indian Culture* (New Delhi: D. K. Printworld, 1994). Saran dedicated the book to Bharati, "My *icchā-guru* [self-chosen guru] and mentor."

47. Agehananda Bharati, "Making Sense out of Tantrism and Tantrics," *Loka 2: A Journal from Naropa Institute* (1976), 53; cf. Bharati, "Techniques of Control."

48. Bharati, "Śākta and Vajrayāna," 87.

49. Bharati, "Religion for the Thinking Person," 70.

50. Bharati, "Hinduism, Psychotherapy, and the Human Predicament," 171. These controls were defined as controlling the "threefold flow" *(tridhāra)* of breath, mind, and seminal emission; once accomplished, these "three jewels" *(triratna)* or this "threefold nectar" *(amṛtatraya)* would produce the experience of *yuganaddha,* or the binding together *(naddha)* of the previously opposed poles *(yuga)* of reality (Bharati, "Techniques of Control").

51. Agehananda Bharati, "Fictitious Tibet: The Origin and Persistence of Rampaism," *Tibet Society Bulletin* 7:4.

52. Bharati, "The Future (if Any) of Tantrism," 128.

53. Bharati, "Śākta and Vajrayāna," 75.

54. Ibid.

55. Bharati, "Religion for the Thinking Person," 37.

56. "I was falling asleep , when the whole world turned into one: one entity, one indivisible certainty. No euphoria, no colours, just a deadeningly sure oneness of which I was at the center—and everything else was just this, and nothing else" (LC, 39).

57. Berger, "Agehananda Bharati," 9. Such lines suggest that Bharati's much-advertised antinomianism could often be eclipsed by a quite conservative and equally touted cosmopolitanism that prided itself on the elite accomplishments of high culture and looked down on more popular (and much more transgressive) movements, such as rock-and-roll.

58. Agehananda Bharati, "Speaking about 'That Which Shows Itself': The Language of Mysticism and the Mystics," in *Religious Experience and Scientific*

Paradigms: Proceedings of the IASWR Conference, 1982, comp. Christopher Chapple (Institute for Advanced Studies of World Religions, 1985), 232–233.

59. It is important to point out that Bharati was against any ritual or belief that harmed another human being or which operated through compulsion or force.

60. Bharati, "The Future (if Any) of Tantrism," 130.

61. Bharati, "Making Sense out of Tantrism and Tantrics," 53.

62. Ibid.; italics his. For an insightful discussion of this same theme, see Hugh B. Urban, "The 'Poor Company': Secrecy and Symbolic Power in the Kartābhajā Sect of Colonial Bengal" (Ph.D. diss., University of Chicago, 1998), 126–139.

63. Bharati, "Fictitious Tibet," 2–3.

64. Ibid., 2.

65. Or sometimes six (Berger, "Agehananda Bharati," 9).

66. Bharati's polemical stance against modern Hindu swamis, gurus, and neo-Hindu thinkers (that is, against the modern tradition itself) colored practically everything he wrote. For his most extended and sophisticated treatment of this theme, see Agehananda Bharati, "The Hindu Renaissance and Its Apologetic Patterns," *Journal of Asian Studies* 29, no. 2 (1970): 267–288. Contemporary scholars (myself included) are uncomfortable with Bharati's notion of "authenticity" applied to these figures. For an excellent example of such a critique, see Brian A. Hatcher, *Eclecticism and Modern Hindu Discourse* (New York: Oxford University Press, 1999). Hatcher strikes a remarkable, self-consciously dialectic balance between reading Hindu eclecticism (with Salman Rushdie) as a kind of postmodern poiesis that can selectively create a renewed sense of identity out of the cultural bits and pieces that it finds at its disposal and seeing it (with Bharati) as a kind of false consciousness that must deny real difference to assert an illusory sameness or unity. In the process, he seriously questions, in a postmodern spirit, Bharati's handling of "authentic" and "inauthentic" spiritual leaders. Without denying such insights, I would also read Bharati's obsession with this theme as a projection of his own marginal status within the tradition and his subsequent search for some sort of cultural legitimation.

67. These four arms are most likely a reference to Kālī, a four-armed, eroticized goddess prevalent in numerous Tantric sects.

68. William Blake, *The Marriage of Heaven and Hell* (Oxford: Oxford University Press, 1975), plate 11.

69. Bharati, "The Future (if Any) of Tantrism," 128.

70. Ibid., 36.

71. I am frankly skeptical about this aspect of his argument. After all, much of Tantra's soteriological "punch" seems to derive precisely from its ritual transgression of strong cultural taboos, which are in turn tied to ego identity (and hence to its transcendence). The mystical experience of "power" *(śakti)*, in other words, flows largely from the rubber-band-like stretching and releasing of emotion and identity produced by an exaggeration and then a transgression of taboos and their control over the boundaries of subjectivity. But if one removes (or lacks altogether) such boundaries, how can one experience the euphoria of crossing them?

72. Agehananda Bharati, *The Tantric Tradition* (1965; reprint, Garden City, N.Y.: Anchor Books, 1970), 299; Bharati, "Making Sense," 54–55.

73. Bharati, *The Tantric Tradition*, 299.

74. Bharati, "The Future (if Any) of Tantrism."

75. Hence the subtitle of *The Light at the Center: Context and Pretext of Modern Mysticism.*

76. Bharati, *The Tantric Tradition*, 299.

77. Compare Bharati, "Religion for the Thinking Person," 70. Bharati's total rhetorical rejection of syncretism seems especially problematic, if not hypocritical, and this for at least two reasons: (1) he himself advanced a type of syncretism between Asian Tantra and Western humanism; and (2) historically speaking, *all* religions are the products of cultural, religious, and social syncreticism. I thus cannot help reading this aspect of Bharati's thought as a kind of defensive mechanism against his own radically syncretistic past and persona, as an attempt, if you will, to construct some kind of fictional cultural and religious purity for himself that could legitimate and authorize his own highly idiosyncratic, almost unprecedented place in the world. In Bharati's defense, it is also good to keep in mind that he lived in an era that witnessed the sale of millions of copies of such books as *The Third Eye,* a fantastic account of Tibetan theosophy written by a certain Lama Lobsang Rampa, a living Tibetan saint who, it turns out, was actually an Irish plumber fraudulently passing himself off as a psychic lama (Bharati, "Fictitious Tibet," 7–8; for an excellent treatment of this bizarre episode, see Donald Lopez, *Prisoners of Shangri-La* [Chicago: University of Chicago Press, 1998]).

78. After the mimetic paradigm of orgasm and sexual pleasure, psychedelic states are invoked the most often by Bharati as inducers and reflectors of the mystical (e.g., LC, 34, 38, 39–40, 43–44, 47–48, 52, 58, 62–63, 66, 69, 100, 112, 126, 140, 147, 185, 192, 193, 202–203, 207–208, 212, 215; "Techniques of Control"): "The analogy between the psychedelic and the mystical universe of discourse must be brought home with vigor," he asserted (LC, 208). After sex and drugs came the aesthetic experiences of classical music, poetry, or art, which constituted a very distant, probably because less euphoric, third (LC, 37, 19, 47–48, 75, 81, 101–102, 208, 218).

79. James R. Horne, *The Moral Mystic* (Waterloo, Ont.: Wilfrid Laurier University Press, 1983).

80. Bharati is by no means alone in this judgment. For a very similar position, see Frits Staal's call for a "rational mysticism" in his *Exploring Mysticism* (Berkeley: University of California Press, 1975).

81. Bharati, "Speaking about 'That Which Shows Itself,'" 217–218.

82. See Edward C. Dimock, Jr., *The Place of the Hidden Moon: Erotic Mysticism in the Vaiṣṇava-sahajiyā Cult of Bengal* (Chicago: University of Chicago Press, 1989); and Urban, "The 'Poor Company.'"

83. But see Bharati, "Speaking about 'That Which Shows Itself,'" 210.

84. Bharati, "Broad, Noeticness and Other Guentheriana," 189–190.

85. Bharati, "The Future (if Any) of Tantrism," 129; italics his. Cf. OR, 237, and Bharati, "Religion for the Thinking Person," 73.

86. Bharati, "The Future (if Any) of Tantrism," 130.

87. This refusal of ontology is complicated somewhat by Bharati's rejection of Freudian reductionism. It seems apparent that Bharati is assigning some sort of ontological substratum to mystical experience (or postulating such a substratum), especially of the erotic type; otherwise, why would he object to Freud's libidinal reductionism, which clearly rejects all objective, nonpsychological referents, and state his own admiration for Jung's understanding of the nature of mystical eroticism, which does seem to carry ontological implications (OR, 219)?

88. Bharati, "Speaking about 'That Which Shows Itself,'" 219; cf. Bharati, "Broad, Noeticness and Other Guentheriana."

89. Bharati, "Religion for the Thinking Person," 73.

90. Bharati, "Hinduism, Psychotherapy, and the Human Predicament," 179.

91. Personal communication with Roxanne Gupta, 3 October 1999.

92. Bharati, "The Future (if Any) of Tantrism," 128.

93. Bharati, *Indology and Science*, 18–20, 38.

94. But again, never at the same time; he rejected scholars, such as the Tibetologist Herbert Guenther, who confused the two and so practiced a kind of recommendation under the cloak of descriptive translation (Bharati, "Broad, Noeticness and Other Guentheriana"). Such critiques would cost Bharati his friendship with Guenther. He expressed similar reservations about the ethnography of E. Evans Pritchard, in whose texts he could not distinguish between the etic strategies of Pritchard, Freud, and Victor Turner and the emic beliefs of the Azande (Bharati, "Speaking about 'That Which Shows Itself,'" 219).

95. Bharati, "Śākta and Vajrayāna," 75.

96. See also Bharati, "Speaking about 'That Which Shows Itself,'" 230.

97. Bharati deeply admired Stace and his work. Stace, he wrote, was easily the finest mind at understanding the mystical from the outside (LC, 60). Not surprisingly, Bharati's personal copy of Stace's *Mysticism and Philosophy* was one of the most annotated books that I found in his library.

98. Robert K. C. Forman, ed., *The Problem of Pure Consciousness: Mysticism and Philosophy* (New York: Oxford University Press, 1990).

99. Bharati, "Speaking about 'That Which Shows Itself,'" 237.

100. Bharati, "Religion for the Thinking Person," 71.

101. Bharati, *The Tantric Tradition*, 219.

102. Yoga, by the way, cannot effect it either. For Bharati, the almost infinite variables and idiosyncratic nature of mystical experience render it impossible to predictably effect such a state; the mystical experience comes to whom it does, "regardless of what they do." It also might come to those who exert themselves over a long period of time, but this is rare (LC, 65).

103. Bharati, *The Tantric Tradition*, 299.

104. Bharati is always careful to make clear that mystical experience alone can never generate discursive, rational knowledge; only intelligence and study can ("Śākta and Vajrayāna," 74–76).

105. See also Bharati, "Hinduism, Psychotherapy, and the Human Predicament," 175.

106. Bharati, "Techniques of Control."
107. Bharati, "Speaking about 'That Which Shows Itself,'" 220.
108. Ibid., 222.
109. Ibid., 221.
110. Bharati, "Śākta and Vajrayāna," 76.
111. See Bharati, "Techniques of Control."
112. Bharati, paraphrasing "a tantric Bengali teacher of the last century," explains that an advanced adept's behavior and experience cannot be understood by those who have not had the experience, just as sexual pleasure cannot be understood by a child and a narcotic high cannot be explained to someone who has not taken the drug ("Techniques of Control"). Bharati is obviously quoting Ramakrishna; I am not sure why he wants to suppress his name here.
113. Mircea Eliade, *Yoga: Immortality and Freedom* (Princeton, N.J.: Princeton University Press, 1958), 250.
114. Sudhir Kakar, *Shamans, Mystics and Doctors: A Psychological Inquiry into India and Its Healing Traditions* (Delhi: Oxford University Press, 1982), 156–157.
115. Bharati, "Techniques of Control."
116. Bharati, "Making Sense," 52.
117. Two (very different) exceptions are worth noting: Brian Hatcher's excellent *Eclecticism and Modern Hindu Discourse* and Fred M. Frohock's fascinating *Lives of the Psychics: The Shared Worlds of Science and Mysticism* (Chicago: University of Chicago Press, 2000), which briefly employs Bharati's understanding of mysticism (Frohock knew Bharati at Syracuse), among many other more developed models, to examine alternative medicine and psychic practices in America and England.
118. For the contents of this paragraph I am indebted to Roxanne Gupta (personal communication, 2 October 1999).

Chapter 5

1. Elliot Wolfson, personal correspondence, 22 August 1996.
2. The biographical details of what follows are based, almost exclusively, on personal communication that took place in the fall of 1999.
3. This is the title of one of Elliot Wolfson's collections of essays: *Along the Path: Studies in Kabbalistic Myth, Symbolism and Hermeneutics* (Albany, N.Y.: SUNY Press, 1995). Wolfson may also intend erotic connotations, since, as he has pointed out, the act of God's walking with the righteous in paradise can function in kabbalistic thought as a euphemism for sexual intercourse, based as it is on the biblical understanding of the foot as phallic; see Wolfson, "Images of God's Feet: Some Observations on the Divine Body in Judaism," in *People of the Body: Jews and Judaism from an Embodied Perspective,* ed. Howard Eilberg-Schwartz (Albany, N.Y.: SUNY Press, 1992).
4. Pinchas Giller, "Elliot Wolfson and the Study of Kabbalah in the Wake of Scholem," *Religious Studies Review* 25, no. 1 (1999): 23.

5. Elliot Wolfson, personal communication, 21 August 1999.
6. Giller, "Elliot Wolfson and the Study of Kabbalah," 24.
7. Ibid.
8. Elliot Wolfson, "Circumcision and the Divine Name: A Study in the Transmission of Esoteric Doctrine," *Jewish Quarterly Review* 78 (1987): 77–112.
9. Elliot Wolfson, "Circumcision, Vision of God, and Textual Interpetation: From Midrashic Trope to Mystical Symbol," *History of Religions* 27 (1987): 189–215.
10. This early period of Wolfson's writings was captured in two collections of essays that he published shortly after *Speculum,* his *Along the Path* and *Circle and the Square: Studies in the Use of Gender in Kabbalistic Symbolism* (Albany, N.Y.: SUNY Press, 1995); henceforth cited as CS.
11. Giller, "Elliot Wolfson and the Study of Kabbalah," 24.
12. Ibid., 26.
13. Ibid. 27.
14. Elliot Wolfson, personal communication, 22 August 1999.
15. Wolfson originally presented "Lying on the Path" at a conference on religious experience and hermeneutical reflection that he and I codirected at New York University, the proceedings of which will appear as Elliot Wolfson and Jeffrey J. Kripal, eds., *The Unknown, Remembered Gate: Religious Experience and Hermeneutical Reflection* (New York: Seven Bridges Press, forthcoming). The manuscript for "Lying on the Path" from the forthcoming book is henceforth cited as LP.
16. Conversation with Elliot Wolfson during the third annual New York University Conference on Comparative Religion, "Method as Path: Religious Experience and Hermeneutical Reflection," New York University, 16–18 April 1999.
17. I am thinking in particular of Steven Katz, who edited an entire volume toward this goal, for which he wrote the lead essay, "The 'Conservative' Character of Mystical Experience" (*Mysticism and Religious Traditions* [Oxford: Oxford University Press, 1983]), although the same "taming pattern" can be seen in any number of other theorists, including, as we have seen, Evelyn Underhill.
18. Elliot Wolfson, *Through a Speculum That Shines: Vision and Imagination in Medieval Jewish Mysticism* (Princeton: Princeton University Press, 1994), 122; henceforth cited as S.
19. Wolfson has continued to develop his understanding of esotericism since publishing *Speculum,* exploring in particular its paradoxical or dialectical nature, with every revealing implying a concealing and every concealing implying a revealing: "[C]oncealment and disclosure are inseparably linked in dialectical tension" (Elliot Wolfson, "Occultation of the Feminine and the Body of Secrecy in Medieval Kabbalah," in *Rending the Veil: Secrecy and Concealment in the History of Religions,* ed. Elliot Wolfson [New York: Seven Bridges Press, 1998], 147).
20. Ibid., 147–148.
21. Gershom Scholem had said much the same: "[T]here is no such thing as mysticism in the abstract. . . . There is only the mysticism of a particular religious system, Christian, Islamic, Jewish mysticism and so on" (*Major Trends in Jewish*

Mysticism [New York: Schocken, 1961], 5). Later in life, however, he came close to reversing himself, hinting at the changed social circumstances of modernity and the subsequent virtual inevitability of a mysticism which is "a basic human experience, connected to the very nature of man" (*On the Possibility of Jewish Mysticism in Our Time and Other Essays,* ed. Avraham Shapira, trans. Jonathan Chipman [Philadelphia: Jewish Publication Society, 1997], 19). Here too he invoked the poetry of Walt Whitman and the "cosmic consciousness" of the Canadian psychologist Richard Bucke as possible hints of a future "secular mysticism." "These are things," he concludes, "which may perhaps allude to the possibility of a mystical embodiment in nontraditional forms" (ibid., 19). Similarly, Wolfson should not be misread here, as he takes a firm position in the middle, affirming both universal and particular processes of religious imagination and mystical experience.

22. William C. Chittick, "The Paradox of the Veil in Sufism," in Wolfson, *Rending the Veil,* 60. Chittick's dialectical understanding of esotericism seems particularly close to Wolfson's. More recently, Wolfson has made a very similar point with the reference to the unlimited/delimited nature of divinity in Kabbalah (particularly with reference to the Lurianic notion of *tsimtsum,* or "contraction") and, with it, the problem of evil and suffering in the Godhead (see Elliot Wolfson, "Divine Suffering and the Hermeneutics of Reading: Philosophical Reflections on Lurianic Mythology" [unpublished manuscript, 2000]). Here again "the secret is re/covered" (16) only in the paradox of what Solomon Alkabets called the "secret of inversion," where "the disclosure is concealment and the concealment disclosure" (13). This is a difficult point, but one absolutely central to Wolfson's dialectical hermeneutics.

23. For his response to one such critic, see Elliot Wolfson, "Coronation of the Sabbath Bride: Kabbalistic Myth and the Ritual of Androgynisation," *Journal of Jewish Thought and Philosophy* 6 (1997): 335 n. 89.

24. To take just one of many examples, consider the following: "R. Yose said, Why is it written, 'And the Lord will pass over the door *(ha-petaḥ)*' (Ex. 12:23)? . . . 'Over the door,' over that very opening *(ha-petaḥ mamash),* that is, the opening of the body *(petaḥ ha-guf).* And what is the opening of the body? That refers to [the place of] circumcision" (CS, 40). Consider also antique Jewish and gnostic Christian readings of the inner sanctum of the Temple as the womb of God's wife or as the bridal chamber wherein the sexes are redemptively united (S, 20 n. 42); the explicit linking in German Pietistic sources between the transmission of the divine name and the sublimation of sexual desire for a woman (S, 239 n. 202); the sefirotic gradation of *Yesod* (explicitly associated with the divine phallus by the kabbalists) symbolized by a cosmic pillar or ladder (S, 307); and the analogous prohibitions against viewing the sexual organ (upon which the sign of the covenant is inscribed in circumcision) and viewing the rainbow as the sign of the covenant in the clouds (S, 337 n. 40; S, 340). It bears repeating that we did not have to wait for Freud to see sexual meanings in the most innocent and holy of places. Mystical traditions from around the world have long seen and capitalized on as much.

25. David Bakan, *Sigmund Freud and the Jewish Mystical Tradition* (Boston:

Beacon Press,1958). Bakan was not the first to advance such a thesis. Abraham Roback, as early as 1918 and again in 1929 in his *Jewish Influence in Modern Thought*, argued that Freud's method is "strongly reminiscent" of Kabbalah, and that "[p]sychoanalysis, on the whole, contains a mystical tendency" (quoted in David M. Wulff, *Psychology of Religion: Classic and Contemporary,* 2d ed. [New York: John Wiley and Sons, 1997], 265). Although Freud himself objected strongly to Roback's thesis, calling it "nonsense" (quoted in Wulff, *Psychology of Religion,* 266), one wonders if there is not indeed something to it. Also relevant here are Suzanne Kirschner's study of the religious structure and romantic "naturalized supernaturalism" of psychoanalytic thought, seen again as a type of secularized mysticism (*The Religious and Romantic Origins of Psychoanalysis: Individuation and Integration in Post-Freudian Theory* [Cambridge, Mass.: Harvard University Press, 1996]), and William Parsons's most recent work on the correspondence of Freud and Romain Rolland with its important thesis that Freud's psychoanalysis, pace the usual assumptions, possesses, hidden within both its structure and history, profound and respectful engagements with mystical forms of subjectivity (*The Enigma of the Oceanic Feeling: The Freud-Rolland Correspondence and the Revisioning of the Psychoanalytic Theory of Mysticism* [New York: Oxford University Press, 1999]).

26. Wolfson treats the phallic natures of writing and creation in, among other places, his "Erasing the Erasure/Gender and the Writing of God's Body in Kabbalistic Symbolism," in CS, 49–78. Circumcision, on the other hand, is the focus of his "Circumcision, Vision of God, and Textual Interpretation: From Midrashic Trope to Mystical Symbol," *History of Religions* 27 (1987): 189–215 (reprinted in CS, 29–48). The discussion that follows will rely upon these two pieces.

27. Elliot Wolfson, "Eunuchs Who Keep the Sabbath: Becoming Male and the Ascetic Ideal in Thirteenth-Century Jewish Mysticism," in *Becoming Male in the Middle Ages,* ed. Jeffrey Jerome Cohen and Bonnie Wheeler (New York: Garland, 1997), 156–157.

28. Quoted in "Divine Suffering and the Hermeneutics of Reading," 29–30.

29. This feminization of the Torah and its historical development from a biblical or rabbinic metaphor to a hypostasized mythical being was an early focus of Wolfson's scholarship. See, for example, his 1989 essay "Female Imaging of the Torah: From Literary Metaphor to Religious Symbol," reprinted in CS.

30. Richard E. Palmer's etymological reflections on the term "hermeneutics" or "Hermes process" seem particularly apt in the context of our present concerns: "The Greek word *hermeios* referred to the priest at the Delphic oracle. This word and the more common verb *hermeneuein* and noun *hermeneia* point back to the wing-footed messenger-god Hermes, from whose name the words are apparently derived (or vice-versa?). Significantly, Hermes is associated with the function of transmuting what is beyond human understanding into a form that human intelligence can grasp. . . . The Greeks credited Hermes with the discovery of language and writing—the tools which human understanding employs to grasp meaning and to convey it to others" (Richard E. Palmer, *Hermeneutics: Interpretation Theory in Schleiermacher, Dilthey, Heidegger, and Gadamer* [Evanston, Ill.: Northwestern University Press, 1969], 13).

31. Wolfson can write, for example, of the "lure of psychoanalytic reductionism" (S, 118) and criticize scholars who he feels have been so tempted (S, 114). This is not to say that Wolfson rejects a psychoanalytic hermeneutic; far from it indeed. For example, he generously employs the psychoanalytic interpretation of dreams as an apt analogy for the particular and universal structures of visions (S, 66), and it goes without saying that his general hermeneutic of finding sexual meanings in kabbalistic sources (not to mention his Irigaray-inspired ocular phallocentrism thesis) is suffused with what I would call a mystically inclined psychoanalytic spirit. Also important here is Wolfson's careful treatment of rationalistic and psychologistic understandings of visions in the Jewish sources themselves (S, chaps. 3–4).

32. See especially Wolfson, "Circumcision, Vision of God, and Textual Interpretation."

33. Elliot Wolfson, "Weeping, Death, and Spiritual Ascent in Sixteenth-Century Jewish Mysticism," in *Death, Ecstasy, and Other-Worldly Journeys,* ed. John Collins and Michael Fishbane (Albany, N.Y.: 1995), 207–247, and "Beautiful Maiden without Eyes: *Peshat* and *Sod* in Zoharic Hermeneutics," in *The Midrashic Imagination,* ed. Michael Fishbane (Albany, N.Y.: SUNY Press, 1993).

34. Wolfson, "Eunuchs Who Keep the Sabbath," 161.

35. Very much relevant here is the work of Howard Eilberg-Schwartz, who detected a similar phallic object in the ancient Jewish prohibition against seeing the front side of God; see his *God's Phallus and Other Problems for Men and Monotheism* (Boston: Beacon Press, 1994). Eilberg-Schwartz's thesis about the consequent homoerotic anxiety this caused the ancient rabbis and scriptural writers is also significant, given both my own working hypothesis about the general homoerotic nature of male mysticism and Wolfson's reflections on the homoerotic implications of his ocular phallocentrism thesis (discussed below).

36. Specifically, Wolfson refers to both Irigaray's *Speculum of the Other Woman,* trans. Gillian C. Hill (Ithaca, N.Y.: Cornell University Press, 1985), and *This Sex Which Is Not One,* trans. Catherine Porter with Carolyn Burke (Ithaca, N.Y.: Cornell University Press, 1985), as particularly important to the genesis and development of his specular thesis (S, 5 n. 7).

37. This final vision of the Godhead, I must add in a distinctly Indological key, bears a remarkable resemblance to the Indian *liṅga-yoni,* that is, the god Śiva's divine phallus *(liṅga)* inside the goddess's vagina *(yoni),* which is worshiped as the perfect expression of the divine biunity within the Śaiva traditions and experientially attained, especially in the Tantric traditions, through reversing the flow of the semen from its downward flow into the genitals back up into the brain, where it can blossom out into ecstatic mystical experience. Wolfson himself, always appreciative of comparative insights, has noted and commented at some length on these kabbalistic-Tantric parallels in his "Eunuchs Who Keep the Sabbath" (163–165).

38. Consider, for example, the rainbow that can be coded female or male (S, 334 n. 30).

39. Wolfson, "Eunuchs Who Keep the Sabbath," 164.

40. Little wonder, then, that there was a restriction on seeing the divine form.

For Wolfson, this traditional prohibition arose not from the vision's impossibility (for numerous kabbalists claimed to have seen the divine and most of their sefirotic speculations were all about such vision), but from its content, "the mythic dynamic of copulation in the Godhead" (S, 339), a copulation, moreover, that was the very theurgic intention of the kabbalist's ritual acts and prayers as set out in the Zohar: "There is another hidden secret: at the moment one prays in his worship he intends the true unity, and the action that a person does below causes an act above, resulting in the copulation and union above" (S, 341). Provocatively, this same divine copulation was best represented not in a male-female union of equals, but in an androgynous incandescent phallus, the "splendor" *(zohar)* of the Presence itself.

41. Wolfson, "Eunuchs Who Keep the Sabbath," 154.
42. Ibid.
43. Ibid., 166.
44. Ibid., 167.
45. Ibid., 165. See also S, 373–377.
46. Cf. CS, 102, for a discussion of phallic tower-breasts.
47. Wolfson, "Eunuchs Who Keep the Sabbath," 169.
48. Ibid., 170–171.
49. Consider also Solomon ibn Gabirol, who "records in several poems dreams he had that he considered a form of prophetic revelation, for through them he heard the divine voice and received a particular mission or disclosure of secrets" (S, 176). Or Azriel's nearly perfect description of that Night and its drawing down of the energetic efflux: "[T]he vision is fixed in his mind and inscribed in his intellect and burns in him like fire. . . . The vision that the soul sees occurs at the time that a person sleeps, and his soul ascends and draws down from above the life force" (S, 299).
50. This is similar to Wolfson's own position (S, 279).
51. As Irigiray writes: "In fact, the refinements of theory brought to bear upon the ontic qualities of mirrors are not systematically carried over to the status of the being himself. The notion that, like a mirror, he might be *passed through* and have a *silver backing,* that he might reflect and be reflected in different ways, is in some sense denied" (*Speculum of the Other Woman,* 149).
52. Wolfson's balanced position between constructivism and structuralism, I must add, would predict precisely this. We are both different and similar, both present to and absent from the historical mystics we study. Given that we share a common neurophysiology *and* live in radically different cultures and times, how could it be any different?
53. "Occultation of the Feminine."
54. Jeffrey J. Kripal, *Kālī's Child: The Mystical and the Erotic in the Life and Teachings of Ramakrishna,* 2d ed. (Chicago: University of Chicago Press, 1998), 230–231.

Secret Talk: Svapna-Siddha

1. I constructed an essay on Sharada Devi, Ramakrishna's wife, around this same autobiographical theme; see my "Perfecting the Mother's Silence: Dream,

Devotion and Family in the Deification of Sharada Devi," in *Seeking Mahādevī: Constructing the Identities of the Hindu Great Goddess,* ed. Tracy Pintchman (Albany, N.Y.: SUNY Press, 2001).

2. I am indebted to William E. Paden for this insight; see his *Religious Worlds: The Comparative Study of Religion* (Boston: Beacon Press, 1988), especially chap. 3, "Worlds."

3. The foot as a phallic-mystical organ has figured prominently in my work on Ramakrishna from the beginning. I was thus fascinated to learn from Schuchard that Blake's Milton-channeling foot is likely derived from Swedenborg's kabbalistic-tantric code, in which an occult sexual channel connects the undersole, the big toe of the left foot, and the erect penis (Marsha Keith Schuchard, "Emmanuel Swedenborg: Deciphering the Codes of a Celestial and Terrestial Intelligencer," in *Rending the Veil: Concealment and Secrecy in the History of Religions,* ed. Elliot R. Wolfson [New York: Seven Bridges Press, 1999], 206–207).

Conclusion

1. Northrop Frye, *Fearful Symmetry: A Study of William Blake* (Princeton, N.J.: Princeton University Press, 1969), 7–8.

2. Ibid., 8.

3. Moshe Idel, *Kabbalah: New Perspectives* (New Haven, Conn.: Yale University Press, 1988), 12.

4. Elliot Wolfson, "Divine Suffering and the Hermeneutics of Reading: Philosophical Reflections on Lurianic Mythology" (unpublished manuscript, 2000), 42.

5. William B. Parsons, *The Enigma of the Oceanic Feeling: Revisioning the Psychoanalytic Theory of Mysticism* (Oxford: Oxford University Press, 1999), 51.

6. I am indebted for this line of thought to Anthony Storr, *Feet of Clay: Saints, Sinners and Madmen: A Study of Gurus* (New York: Free Press, 1996).

7. Sudhir Kakar, *The Analyst and the Mystic: Psychoanalytic Reflections on Religion and Mysticism* (Chicago: University of Chicago Press, 1991), 29.

8. David Halperin, *One Hundred Years of Homosexuality and Other Essays on Greek Love* (New York: Routledge, 1990), 29.

9. I am also following here Toril Moi's reading of Lacan in her *Sexual/Textual Politics* (London: Routledge, 1985).

10. Kaja Silverman, *Male Subjectivity at the Margins* (New York: Routledge, 1992), 4.

11. See Sigmund Freud, *New Introductory Lectures to Psycho-Analysis,* standard edition (London: Hogarth Press, 1955), 22:79–80, and *Civilization and Its Discontents,* standard edition (London: Hogarth Press, 1955), 21:64–73.

12. Irigaray argued that mystical experience is defined by a dramatic loss of subjectivity; hence its tapping by female mystics under patriarchal systems as both a place of accomplishment and potential power (see Luce Irigaray, *Speculum of the Other Woman,* trans. Gillian C. Hill [Ithaca, N.Y.: Cornell University Press, 1985], "La Mysterique," 191–202).

13. Silverman, *Male Subjectivity,* 3.

14. W. La Barre, *The Ghost Dance: The Origins of Religion* (New York: Delta, 1972), 111. I am indebted, as I am for so many things psychological, to David Wulff's magisterial *Psychology of Religion: Classic and Contemporary,* 2d ed. (New York: John Wiley and Sons, 1997), for pointing this reference out to me.

15. *The Gospel of Thomas: The Hidden Sayings of Jesus,* trans. Marvin Meyer (New York: HarperSanFrancisco, 1992), verse 22, p. 35.

16. See Jacques Lacan, "On Jouissance" and "God and W~~oman~~'s Jouissance," in *On Feminine Sexuality, The Limits of Love and Knowledge, Book XX, Encore 1972–1973,* ed. Jacques-Alain Miller, trans. Bruce Fink (New York: W. W. Norton, 1998), esp. 6–7, 74, 76.

17. I use this term deliberately, fully aware of its Christian connotations and its specifically mystical uses by early Christian writers, particularly from the Orthodox tradition, as the goal of Christian prayer, ascesis and divinization *(theosis).* It goes without saying that, both biblically and monastically speaking, the Transfiguration was an entirely male affair, with the male body of Jesus revealed by the Father in secret to an intimate circle of male figures.

18. Steven Wasserstrom, *Religion after Religion: Gershom Scholem, Mircea Eliade and Henry Corbin at Eranos* (Princeton, N.J.: Princeton University Press, 1999), ix.

19. Ibid., chap. 2.

20. Jeffrey J. Kripal, *Kālī's Child: The Mystical and the Erotic in the Life and Teachings of Ramakrishna,* 2d ed. (Chicago: University of Chicago Press, 1998), 302–304, 317.

21. *The Gospel of Thomas,* verse 113, p. 65.

22. *Tao Te Ching,* trans. Stephen Addis and Stanley Lombardo, (Indianapolis: Hackett, 1993), poem 5.

23. Russell T. McCutcheon, *The Insider/Outsider Problem in the Study of Religion: A Reader* (London: Cassell, 1999), 3. I have found McCutcheon's historical and theoretical synopsis of the insider/outsider problem particularly helpful in thinking through my own tentative resolution of it.

24. My metaphor of the tensive spiral promises no final resolution or release from the tension; quite the contrary, it implies that the closer we move to the mythical "center," the tighter the spiral becomes and, with it, the greater the tension between these two competing forces.

25. Peter Homans, "Once Again, Psychoanalysis, East and West: A Psychoanalytic Essay on Religion, Mourning, and Healing," *History of Religions* 24, no. 2 (1984): 133–154.

26. Michel de Certeau, *The Mystic Fable* (Chicago: University of Chicago Press, 1992), 11.

27. Wasserstrom, *Religion after Religion,* 78–79.

28. Much of the above was inspired by Stephen Butterfield, *The Double Mirror: A Skeptical Journey into Buddhist Tantra* (Berkeley: North Atlantic Books, 1994), a beautifully written, hilarious, touching, and shockingly honest study of Chogyam Trungpa. Butterfield speaks of his own double-mirrored journey through Trungpa's Vajrayana as a fiction necessary for transformation, at once

"fate, faith, and fraud" (26), "just like a blind man finding a jewel in a heap of dust" (92). For more on Butterfield's book and my own methodological nondualism, see my "Inside-Out, Outside-In: Existential Place and Academic Practice in the Study of North American Guru-Traditions," *Religious Studies Review* 25, no. 3 (1999): 233–238.

29. Quoted in Jennifer Nedelsky, "Law, Boundaries, and the Bounded Self," *Representations* 30 (1990): 178–179; I am indebted to Don Kulick for this reference, discussion, and quote ("Introduction: The Sexual Life of Anthropologists: Erotic Subjectivity and Ethnographic Work," in *Taboo: Sex, Identity and Erotic Subjectivity in Anthropological Fieldwork,* ed. Don Kulick and Margaret Willson [London: Routledge, 1995], 16–17).

30. Donna J. Haraway, *Simians, Cyborgs, and Women: The Reinvention of Nature* (London: Routledge, 1991), 193; emphasis in original; quoted in Kulick, "Introduction," 18.

31. Wilhelm Dilthey, "The Rise of Hermeneutics," trans. Fredric Jameson, in *The Hermeneutic Tradition: From Ast to Ricoeur,* ed. Gayle L. Ormiston and Alan D. Schrift (Albany, N.Y.: SUNY Press, 1990), 102.

32. Ibid.

33. Ibid., 103; italics in original.

34. Ibid., 112.

35. Ibid., 113.

36. Ibid. Schleiermacher had argued the same (ibid., 93).

37. Hans-Georg Gadamer, *Truth and Method,* 2d, rev. ed., trans. and rev. Joel Weinsheimer and Donald G. Marshall (New York: Continuum, 1997).

38. Quoted in ibid., 224.

39. Jürgen Habermas, "The Hermeneutic Claim to Universality," in Ormiston and Schrift, *The Hermeneutic Tradition,* 270.

40. Ibid., 263, 269–270.

41. Mircea Eliade, *The Quest: History and Meaning in Religion* (Chicago: University of Chicago Press, 1969), 62. The title metaphor seems especially appropriate for such a claim.

42. William Blake, *The Marriage of Heaven and Hell* (Oxford, Oxford University Press, 1985), plate 15.

43. All this takes place, by the way, on the very same plate (plate 14) of *The Marriage of Heaven and Hell*—we are back to a mystical eroticism again—from which Huxley borrowed his "doors of perception" trope.

44. The term was coined and defined by William Parsons, who used it to describe my psychoanalytic hermeneutic in his *Enigma of the Oceanic Feeling.*

45. To take just one scholarly example, Wasserstrom has pointed out that Scholem's personal interest in mysticism often became virtually indistinguishable from nihilism and was recognized as such by some of his contemporaries (Wasserstrom, *Religion after Religion,* 227–230, "Nihilism as a Religious Phenomenon").

BIBLIOGRAPHY

Akroyd, Peter. *Blake: A Biography.* New York: Ballantine Books, 1995.
Armstrong, Christopher J. R. *Evelyn Underhill (1875–1941): An Introduction to Her Life and Writings.* Grand Rapids, Mich.: William B. Eerdmans, 1975.
Bakan, David. *Sigmund Freud and the Jewish Mystical Tradition.* Boston: Beacon Press,1958.
Baldick, Julian. *Mystical Islam: An Introduction to Sufism.* New York: New York University Press, 1989.
Balzac, Honoré de. *Seraphita, A Daughter of Eve and Other Stories.* Translated by Clara Bell and R. S. Scott. Philadelphia: Gebbie, 1899.
Barnard, G. William. *Exploring Unseen Worlds: William James and the Philosophy of Mysticism.* Albany, N.Y.: SUNY Press, 1997.
Basetti-Sani, Giulio, O.F.M. *Louis Massignon (1883–1962): Christian Ecumenist, Prophet of Inter-religious Reconciliation.* Chicago: Franciscan Herald Press.
Bataille, Georges. *Erotism: Death and Sensuality.* San Francisco: City Lights Books, 1986.
Baum, Robert M. "Homosexuality in the Traditional Religions of the Americas and Africa." In *Homosexuality and World Religions,* edited by Arlene Swidler. Valley Forge, Pa.: Trinity Press International, 1993.
Bell, Rudolph M. *Holy Anorexia.* Chicago: University of Chicago Press, 1985.
Benko, Stephen. *The Virgin Mother: The Pagan and Christian Roots of the Marian Cult.* Leiden: Brill, 1984.
Berger, Warren. "Agehananda Bharati: The Life and Times of a Hindu Monk." *Vantage,* October 1979, 9.
Bernard of Clairvaux. *Sermones super cantica canticorum.* In *Sancti Bernardi, abbatis primi claraevallensis, opera genuina, juxta editionem monachorum Sancti Benedicti,* vol. 3, *Sermones de diverses et in cantica complectens.* Lyon: Ancienne Maison, 1854. Translated by Kilian Walsh, O.C.S.O., as *Bernard of Clairvaux on the Song of Songs* (Kalamazoo, Mich.: Cistercian Publications, 1981).
Bertault, Philippe. *Balzac and "The Human Comedy."* New York: New York University Press, 1963.
Bharati, Agehananda. *Indology and Science: Towards a Hermeneutical Coalition.* Calcutta: Roy and Chowdhury, 1989.
——. Review of *Tales of Sex and Violence,* by Wendy Doniger O'Flaherty. *American Anthropologist* 88, no. 4 (1986): 991–992.
——. "Hindu Faschismus." *Forum,* 30 September 1986, 29–35.
——. Review of *Dreams, Illusions, and Other Realities,* by Wendy Doniger O'Flaherty. *Journal of Asian Studies* 44, no. 4 (1985): 871–872.

———. "Pattini: The Anthropological Consummation of a Goddess." *American Anthropologist* 87, no. 2 (1985): 364–369.

———. "Speaking about 'That Which Shows Itself': The Language of Mysticism and the Mystics." In *Religious Experience and Scientific Paradigms: Proceedings of the IASWR Conference, 1982,* compiled by Christopher Chapple. Stony Brook, N.Y.: Institute for Advanced Studies of World Religions, 1985.

———. Review of *Medusa's Hair,* by Gananath Obeyesekere. *Mentalities/Mentalités* 1, no. 1 (1983): 39–40.

———. "Bose and the German Ina: An Unexplored Chapter." *New Quest* 26 (March-April 1981): 73–78.

———. *The Ochre Robe.* 1960. Reprint, Santa Barbara, Calif.: Ross-Erikson, 1980.

———. "True and False Prophets of Today's Hinduism." *Asia,* November/December 1979.

———. "Broad, Noeticness and Other Guentheriana." *Kailash: A Journal of Himalayan Studies* 5, no. 2 (1977): 185–200.

———. *The Light at the Center: Context and Pretext of Modern Mysticism.* Santa Barbara, Calif.: Ross-Erikson, 1976.

———. "Making Sense out of Tantrism and Tantrics." *Loka 2: A Journal from Naropa Institute* (1976), 52–55.

———. Review of *The Great Universe of Kota,* by G. M. Carstairs. *Annals of the American Academy of Political and Social Science* (September 1976), 141–142.

———. "Techniques of Control in Esoteric Traditions of India and Tibet." In *The Realm of the Extra-human: Ideas and Actions,* edited by Agehananda Bharati. The Hague: Mouton, 1976.

———. "The Future (if Any) of Tantrism." *Loka: A Journal from Naropa Institute* (1975), 126–130.

———. "Religion for the Thinking Person." *New Delhi* 2, no. 14 (29 October 1974): 69–74.

———. "Hinduism, Psychotherapy, and the Human Predicament." In *Religious Systems and Psycho-Therapy,* edited by Richard H. Cox. Springfield, Ill.: Charles C. Thomas, 1973.

———. "The Hindu Renaissance and Its Apologetic Patterns." *Journal of Asian Studies* 29, no. 2 (1970): 267–288.

———. *The Tantric Tradition.* 1965. Reprint, Garden City, N.Y.: Anchor Books, 1970.

———. Review of *Hindu Culture and Personality,* by Philip Spratt. *American Anthropologist* 70, no. 1 (February 1968): 142.

———. Review of *Hindu Culture and Personality,* by Philip Spratt. *Journal of Asian Studies* 26 (May 1967): 519–520.

———. "Śākta and Vajrayāna: Their Place in Indian Thought." In *Studies of Esoteric Buddhism and Tantrism,* edited by Gisho Nakano. Koyasan, Japan: Koyasan University, 1965.

———. "Hindu Scholars and the Third Reich." *Quest* 44 (winter 1965): 74–77.

———. *Dear Lalita.* N.p., 1962.

———. "Fictitious Tibet: The Origin and Persistence of Rampaism." *Tibet Society Bulletin,* 7:1–10.
Biale, David. *Eros and the Jews: From Biblical Israel to Contemporary America.* Berkeley: University of California Press, 1997.
———. *Gershom Scholem: Kabbalah and Counter-history.* Cambridge, Mass.: Harvard University Press, 1982.
Blake, William. *William Blake: The Early Illuminated Books.* Edited by Morris Eaves, Robert N. Essick, and Joseph Viscomi. Princeton, N.J.: William Blake Trust and Princeton University Press, 1993.
———. *The Marriage of Heaven and Hell.* Oxford: Oxford University Press, 1975.
Bok, Sissela. *Secrets: On the Ethics of Concealment and Revelation.* 1983. Reprint, New York: Vintage Books, 1989.
———. *Lying: Moral Choice in Public and Private Life.* New York: Pantheon Books, 1978.
Boswell, John. *Christianity, Social Tolerance, and Homosexuality: Gay People in Western Europe from the Beginning of the Christian Era to the Fourteenth Century.* Chicago: University of Chicago Press, 1980.
Bouyer, Louis. "Mysticism: An Essay on the History of the Word." In *Understanding Mysticism,* edited by Richard Woods. Garden City, N.Y.: Image Books, 1980.
Buck, Dorothy C. "Le Thème du point vierge dans les écrits de Louis Massignon." In *Louis Massignon au coeur de notre temps,* edited by Jacques Keryell. Paris: Karthala, 1999.
Bucke, Richard M. *Cosmic Consciousness.* 1901. Reprint, New York: E. P. Dutton, 1969.
Bulkeley, Kelly. *Spiritual Dreaming: A Cross-Cultural and Historical Journey.* New York: Paulist Press, 1995.
Butterfield, Stephen. *The Double Mirror: A Skeptical Journey into Buddhist Tantra.* Berkeley: North Atlantic Books, 1994.
Caldwell, Sarah. *Oh Terrifying Mother: Sexuality and Violence in the Worship of the Goddess Kāḷi.* New Delhi: Oxford University Press, 1999.
Campbell, Joseph. *Baksheesh and Brahman: Indian Journal, 1954–1955.* Edited by Robin and Stephen Larsen and Antony Van Cowering. New York: HarperSanFrancisco, 1995.
Carroll, Michael P. *The Cult of the Virgin Mary: Psychological Origins.* Princeton, N.J.: Princeton University Press, 1986.
Certeau, Michel de. "Mysticism." *Diacritics* 22, no. 2 (1992): 11–25.
———. *The Mystic Fable.* Chicago: University of Chicago Press, 1992.
———. *La Fable mystique, 1.* Paris: Gallimard, 1982.
Chaudhuri, Nirad C. *Scholar Extraordinary: The Life of Friedrich Max Müller.* Delhi: Orient Paperbacks, 1974.
Chittick, William C. "The Paradox of the Veil in Sufism." In *Rending the Veil: Secrecy and Concealment in the History of Religions,* edited by Elliot Wolfson. New York: Seven Bridges Press, 1998.

———. *The Sufi Path of Love: The Spiritual Teachings of Rumi.* Albany, N.Y.: SUNY Press, 1983.
Clark, Benjamin. "Translator's Introduction." In *Essay on the Origins of the Technical Language of Islamic Mysticism,* by Louis Massignon, trans. Benjamin Clark. Notre Dame, Ind.: University of Notre Dame Press, 1997.
Claudel, Paul, and Louis Massignon. *Paul Claudel, Louis Massignon (1908–1914).* Edited by Michel Malicet. Paris: Desclée, 1973.
Cozzens, Donald B. *The Changing Face of the Priesthood.* Collegeville, Minn.: Liturgical Press, 2000.
Cropper, Margaret. *Evelyn Underhill.* London: Longmans Green, 1958.
Cupitt, Don. *Mysticism after Modernity.* Oxford: Blackwell, 1998.
Dasgupta, Shashibhushan. *Obscure Religious Cults.* 1946. 3d ed., Calcutta: Firma KLM, 1976.
Datta, Ram Chandra. *Śrīśrīrāmakṛṣṇa Paramahaṁsadever Jīvanavṛttānta.* Calcutta: Jogodyan, 1935.
Deikman, Arthur. "Deautomatization and the Mystic Experience." In *Understanding Mysticism,* edited by Richard Woods. Garden City, N.Y.: Image Books, 1980.
Dhawan, Vinod. "The Pugnacious Scholar-Swami." *Hindustani Times,* 18 January 1985.
Dilthey, William. "The Rise of Hermeneutics." Translated by Fredric Jameson. In *The Hermeneutic Tradition: From Ast to Ricoeur,* edited by Gayle L. Ormiston and Alan D. Schrift. Albany, N.Y.: SUNY Press, 1990.
Dimock, Edward C., Jr. *The Place of the Hidden Moon: Erotic Mysticism in the Vaiṣṇava-sahajiyā Cult of Bengal.* Chicago: University of Chicago Press, 1989.
Doniger, Wendy. *The Implied Spider: Politics and Theology in Myth.* New York: Columbia University Press, 1998.
———. "Time, Sleep, and Death in the Life, Fiction, and Academic Writings of Mircea Eliade." In *Mircea Eliade e le Religioni Asiatiche,* edited by Gherardo Gnoli. Rome: Istituto Italiano per il Medio ed Estremo Oriente, 1989.
———. *Other Peoples' Myths: The Cave of Echoes.* New York: Macmillan, 1988.
Dyczkowski, Mark S. G. *The Doctrine of Vibration: An Analysis of the Doctrines and Practices of Kashmir Shaivism.* Albany, N.Y.: SUNY Press, 1987.
Eck, Diana L. *Darśan: Seeing the Divine Image in India.* 3d ed. New York: Columbia University Press, 1998.
———. *Encountering God: A Spiritual Journey from Bozeman to Banaras.* Boston: Beacon Press, 1993.
Eigen, Michael. *The Psychoanalytic Mystic.* Binghamton, N.Y.: ESF Publications, 1998.
Eilberg-Schwartz, Howard. *God's Phallus and Other Problems for Men and Monotheism.* Boston: Beacon Press, 1994.
Eliade, Mircea. *Ordeal by Labyrinth: Conversations with Claude-Henri Rocquet.* Chicago: University of Chicago Press, 1982.
———. "The Secret of Dr. Honigberger." In *Two Strange Tales.* Boston: Shambalah, 1970.

———. *The Quest: History and Meaning in Religion.* Chicago: University of Chicago Press, 1969.
———. *Yoga: Immortality and Freedom.* Princeton, N.J.: Princeton University Press, 1958.
Ernst, Carl. *Words of Ecstasy in Sufism.* Albany, N.Y.: SUNY Press, 1985.
Faure, Bernard. *The Red Thread: Buddhist Approaches to Sexuality* Princeton, N.J.: Princeton University Press, 1998.
Flournoy, Theodore. "Une Mystique moderne." *Archives de Psychologie* 15 (1928): 1–224.
Fonseca, Isabel. *Bury Me Standing: The Gypsies and Their Journey.* New York: Vintage, 1995.
Forman, Robert K. C. *Mysticism, Mind, Consciousness.* Albany, N.Y.: SUNY Press, 1999.
———, ed. *The Problem of Pure Consciousness: Mysticism and Philosophy.* New York: Oxford University Press, 1990.
Foucault, Michel. *An Introduction.* Vol. 1 of *The History of Sexuality.* New York: Vintage Books, 1990.
Freud, Sigmund. *New Introductory Lectures to Psycho-Analysis.* Standard edition, vol. 22. London: Hogarth Press, 1955.
———. *Civilization and Its Discontents.* Standard edition, vol. 21. London: Hogarth Press, 1955.
Frohock, Fred M. *Lives of the Psychics: The Shared Worlds of Science and Mysticism.* Chicago: University of Chicago Press, 2000.
Frye, Northrop. "The Keys to the Gate." In *Modern Critical Views: William Blake,* edited by Harold Bloom. New York: Chelsea House, 1985.
———. *Fearful Symmetry: A Study of William Blake.* Princeton, N.J.: Princeton University Press, 1969.
Gadamer, Hans-Georg. *Truth and Method.* 2d ed., rev. Translated and revised by Joel Weinsheimer and Donald G. Marshall. New York: Continuum, 1997.
George, Diana Hume. *Blake and Freud.* Ithaca, N.Y.: Cornell University Press, 1980.
Giller, Pinchas. "Elliot Wolfson and the Study of Kabbalah in the Wake of Scholem." *Religious Studies Review* 25, no. 1 (1999): 23–28.
Girardet, Raoul. *L'Idée coloniale en France, 1871–1962.* Paris: La Table Ronde, 1972.
Goldman, Robert P. "Transsexualism, Gender, and Anxiety in Traditional India." *Journal of the American Oriental Society* 113, no. 3 (1993): 374–401.
The Gospel of Thomas: The Hidden Sayings of Jesus. Translated by Marvin Meyer. San Francisco: HarperSanFrancisco, 1992.
Greene, Dana. *Evelyn Underhill: Artist of the Infinite Life.* New York: Crossroad, 1990.
Gross, Rita. *Buddhism after Patriarchy: A Feminist History, Analysis, and Reconstruction of Buddhism.* Albany, N.Y.: SUNY Press, 1993.
Gude, Mary Louise. "J. K. Huysmans, Louis Massignon, and the Language of Mysticism." *Religion and Literature* 30, no. 2 (summer 1998): 81–95.

———. *Louis Massignon: The Crucible of Compassion.* Notre Dame, Ind.: University of Notre Dame Press, 1996.

Gupta, Mahendranath. *Śrīśrīrāmakṛṣṇakathāmṛta.* 31st ed. Calcutta: Kathamrita Bhaban, 1987.

Gupta, Roxanne Poorman. "Kali Mayi: Myth and Reality in a Banaras Ghetto." In *Encountering Kali: In the Margins, at the Center, in the West,* edited by Rachel Fell McDermott and Jeffrey J. Kripal. Berkeley: University of California Press, forthcoming.

Habermas, Jürgen. "A Review of Gadamer's *Truth and Method.*" In *The Hermeneutic Tradition: From Ast to Ricoeur,* edited by Gayle L. Ormiston and Alan D. Schrift. Albany, N.Y.: SUNY Press, 1990.

Halperin, David. *One Hundred Years of Homosexuality and Other Essays on Greek Love.* New York: Routledge, 1990.

Hanson, Ellis. *Decadence and Catholicism.* Cambridge, Mass.: Harvard University Press, 1997.

Haraway, Donna J. *Simians, Cyborgs, and Women: The Reinvention of Nature.* London: Routledge, 1991.

Hatcher, Brian A. *Eclecticism and Modern Hindu Discourse.* New York: Oxford University Press, 1999.

Homans, Peter. *The Ability to Mourn: Disillusionment and the Social Origins of Psychoanalysis.* Chicago: University of Chicago Press, 1989.

———. "Once Again, Psychoanalysis, East and West: A Psychoanalytic Essay on Religion, Mourning, and Healing." *History of Religions* 24, no. 2 (1984): 133–154.

———. *Jung in Context: The Making of a Modern Psychology.* Chicago: University of Chicago Press, 1979.

Hopkins, Jeffrey. *Sex, Orgasm, and the Mind of Clear Light: The Sixty-four Arts of Gay Male Love.* Berkeley: North Atlantic Books, 1998.

Horne, James R. *Mysticism and Vocation.* Waterloo, Ont.: Wilfrid Laurier University Press, 1996.

———. *The Moral Mystic.* Waterloo, Ont.: Wilfrid Laurier University Press, 1983.

Huxley, Aldous. *The Doors of Perception and Heaven and Hell.* 1954. Reprint, New York: Harper and Row, 1963.

Huysmans, J.-K. *Là-bas I.* Vol. 12 of *Oeuvres complètes de J.-K. Huysmans.* Paris: Editions G. Cres, n.d.

Idel, Moshe. *Kabbalah: New Perspectives.* New Haven, Conn.: Yale University Press, 1988.

Irigaray, Luce. *Speculum of the Other Woman.* Translated by Gillian C. Hill. Ithaca, N.Y.: Cornell University Press, 1985.

———. *This Sex Which Is Not One.* Translated by Catherine Porter with Carolyn Burke. Ithaca, N.Y.: Cornell University Press, 1985.

Irwin, Alexander C. *Eros toward the World: Paul Tillich and the Theology of the Erotic.* Minneapolis: Fortress Press, 1991.

James, William. *The Varieties of Religious Experience.* New York: Modern Library, 1929.

Jamison, Kay Redfield. *Touched with Fire: Manic-Depressive Illness and the Artistic Temperament.* New York: Free Press, 1993.
Janet, Pierre. *De l'angoisse à l'extase: Études sur les croyances et les sentiments.* 2 vols. Paris: Félix Alcan, 1926–1928.
Jantzen, Grace. "The Legacy of Evelyn Underhill." *Feminist Theology* 4 (1993): 79–100.
John of the Cross, Saint. *The Collected Works of St. John of the Cross.* Translated by Kieran Kavanaugh and Otilio Rodriguez. Washington, D.C.: ICS Publications, 1979.
Jonas, Hans. "Myth and Mysticism: A Study in Objectification and Interiorization in Religious Thought." *Journal of Religion,* vol. 49 (1969).
Jordan, Mark. *The Silence of Sodom: Homosexuality in Modern Catholicism.* Chicago: University of Chicago Press, 2000.
———. *The Invention of Sodomy in Christian Theology.* Chicago: University of Chicago Press, 1997.
Jossua, Jean-Pierre. *Seul avec Dieu: L'Aventure mystique.* Paris: Gallimard, 1996.
Jung, Carl G. *Memories, Dreams, and Reflections.* Edited by Aniela Jaffé,. New York: Pantheon Books, 1973.
———. *The Archetypes and the Collective Unconscious.* Princeton, N.J.: Princeton University Press, 1980.
Kakar, Sudhir. *The Analyst and the Mystic: Psychoanalytic Reflections on Religion and Mysticism.* Chicago: University of Chicago Press, 1991.
———. *Shamans, Mystics and Doctors: A Psychological Inquiry into India and Its Healing Traditions.* Delhi: Oxford University Press, 1982.
———. *The Inner World: A Psycho-analytic Study of Childhood and Society in India.* New Delhi: Oxford University Press, 1978.
Katz, Steven. "The 'Conservative' Character of Mystical Experience." In *Mysticism and Religious Traditions,* edited by Steven Katz. Oxford: Oxford University Press, 1983.
Keryell, Jacques, ed. *L'Hospitalité sacrée.* Paris: Nouvelle Cité, 1987.
King, Richard. *Orientalism and Religion: Postcolonial Theory, India and "the Mystic East."* London: Routledge, 1999.
Kirschner, Suzanne. *The Religious and Romantic Origins of Psychoanalysis: Individuation and Integration in Post-Freudian Theory.* Cambridge, Mass.: Harvard University Press, 1996.
Kripal, Jeffrey J. "Teaching Hindu Tantrism with Freud: Transgression as Critical Theory and Mystical Technique." In *Teaching Freud in Religious Studies,* edited by Diane Jonte-Pace. New York: Oxford University Press, forthcoming.
———. "Perfecting the Mother's Silence: Dream, Devotion and Family in the Deification of Sharada Devi." In *Seeking Mahādevī: Constructing the Identities of the Hindu Great Goddess,* edited by Tracy Pintchman. Albany, N.Y.: SUNY Press, 2001.
———. "Secret Talk: Sexual Identity and the Politics of Scholarship in the Study of Hindu Tantrism." *Harvard Divinity Bulletin* 29, no. 4 (winter 2000/2001).

———. "Re-membering a Presence of Mythological Proportions: Psychoanalysis and Hinduism." In *Religion and Psychological Studies: Mapping the Terrain,* edited by Diane Jonte-Pace and William Parsons. London: Routledge, 2000.

———. "Debating the Mystical as the Ethical: An Indological Map." In *Crossing Boundaries: Essays on the Ethical Status of Mysticism,* edited by G. William Barnard and Jeffrey J. Kripal. New York: Seven Bridges Press, 2001.

———. "Inside-Out, Outside-In: Existential Place and Academic Practice in the Study of North American Guru-Traditions." *Religious Studies Review* 25, no. 3 (1999): 233–238.

———. "The Visitation of the Stranger: On Some Mystical Dimensions of the History of Religions." *CrossCurrents* 49, no. 3 (1999): 367–386.

———. "Mystical Homoeroticism, Reductionism, and the Reality of Censorship: A Response to Gerald James Larson." *Journal of the American Academy of Religion* 66, no. 3 (1998): 627–635.

———. *Kālī's Child: The Mystical and the Erotic in the Life and Teachings of Ramakrishna.* 2d ed. Chicago: University of Chicago Press, 1998.

———. "Dreaming Eros: On the Mythical Contours of a Student's Thought." Paper written for the course "Theory of Myth and Symbolism," University of Chicago Divinity School, spring 1987.

Kulick, Don, and Margaret Willson, eds. *Taboo: Sex, Identity and Erotic Subjectivity in Anthropological Fieldwork.* London: Routledge, 1995.

Kvam, Kristen E., Linda S. Schearing, and Valarie H. Ziegler. *Eve and Adam: Jewish, Christian, and Muslim Readings on Genesis and Gender.* Bloomington: Indiana University Press, 1999.

La Barre, Weston. *The Ghost Dance: The Origins of Religion.* New York: Delta, 1972.

Lacan, Jacque. *On Feminine Sexuality, The Limits of Love and Knowledge, Book XX, Encore 1972–1973.* Edited by Jacques-Alain Miller. Translated by Bruce Fink. New York: W. W. Norton, 1998.

Lambton, Ann K. S. Obituary for R. C. Zaehner. *Bulletin of the School of Oriental and African Studies* 38 (1975): 623–624.

LeMaître, Solange. "Louis Massignon." In *Cahiers de l'Herne,* edited by Jean-François Six. Paris: Editions de l'Herne, 1970.

Leuba, James H. *The Psychology of Mysticism.* London: Kegan Paul, 1925.

Lopez, Donald. *Prisoners of Shangri-La.* Chicago: University of Chicago Press, 1998.

Maréchal, Joseph. *Studies in the Psychology of the Mystics.* Albany, N.Y.: Magi Books, 1964.

Mason, Herbert. *Memoir of a Friend: Louis Massignon.* Notre Dame, Ind.: University of Notre Dame Press, 1988.

———. "Foreword to the English Edition." In *The Passion of al-Hallāj: Mystic and Martyr of Islam,* by Louis Massignon, translated by Herbert Mason. 4 vols. Princeton, N.J.: Princeton University Press, 1982.

Massignon, Daniel. "Le Voyage en Mesopotamie et la conversion de Louis Massignon en 1908." *Islamochristiana* 14 (1988): 127–199.

Massignon, Louis. *Essay on the Origins of the Technical Language of Islamic Mys-*

ticism. Translated by Benjamin Clark. Notre Dame, Ind.: University of Notre Dame Press, 1997.

———. *Les Trois Prières d'Abraham.* Paris: Éditions du Cerf, 1997.

———. *Testimonies and Reflections: Essays of Louis Massignon.* Edited and translated by Herbert Mason. Notre Dame, Ind.: University of Notre Dame Press, 1989.

——— (with Vicent-Mansour Monteil). *Parole donnée.* Paris: Seuil, 1983.

———. *The Passion of al-Hallāj: Mystic and Martyr of Islam.* Translated by Herbert Mason. 4 vols. Princeton, N.J.: Princeton University Press, 1982.

———. *Opera minora.* Edited by Youakim Moubarek. 3 vols. Paris: Presses universitaires de France, 1969.

Mauriac, François. *Le Nouveau Bloc-notes, 1961–1964.* Paris: Flammarion, 1968.

McCutcheon, Russell T. *The Insider/Outsider Problem in the Study of Religion: A Reader.* London: Cassell, 1999.

McGinn, Bernard. "Visions and Critiques of Vision in Thirteenth-Century Mysticism." In *Rending the Veil: Concealment and Secrecy in the History of Religions,* edited by Elliot Wolfson. New York: Seven Bridges Press, 1998.

———. *The Flowering of Mysticism: Men and Women in the New Mysticism, 1200–1350.* New York: Crossroad Herder, 1998.

———. *The Growth of Mysticism: Gregory the Great through the Twelfth Century.* New York: Crossroad, 1994.

———. "The Language of Love in Christian and Jewish Mysticism." In *Mysticism and Language,* edited by Steven Katz. New York: Oxford University Press, 1992.

———. *The Foundations of Mysticism: Origins to the Fifth Century.* New York: Crossroad, 1991.

McIntosh, Mark A. *Mystical Theology.* Oxford: Blackwell, 1998.

Moi, Toril. *Sexual/Textual Politics.* London: Routledge, 1985.

Moncelon, Jean. "L'Extase et la grâce: Essai sur l'expérience intérieure de Louis Massignon." In *Louis Massignon: Mystique en dialogue.* Paris: Albin Michel, 1992.

Monteil, Vincent-Mansour. *Le Linceul de feu.* Paris: Vegapress, 1987.

———. "Entretiens." In *Parole donnée,* by Louis Massignon. Paris: Seuil, 1983.

Morrison, George. Obituary for R. C. Zaehner. *Iran* 13 (1975): iv.

Murray, Stephen O., and Will Roscoe, eds. *Islamic Homosexualities: Culture, History, and Literature.* New York: New York University Press, 1997.

Nanda, Serena. *Neither Man nor Woman: The Hijra of India.* Belmont, Calif.: Wadsworth, 1990.

Nasr, Seyyed Hossein. "In Commemoration of Louis Massignon: Catholic, Scholar, Islamicist and Mystic." In *Présence de Louis Massignon: Hommages et témoignages,* edited by Daniel Massignon. Paris: Maisonneuve et Larose, 1987.

Nedelsky, Jennifer. "Law, Boundaries, and the Bounded Self." *Representations* 30 (1990) 162–189.

Newell, William Lloyd. *Struggle and Submission: R. C. Zaehner on Mysticisms.* Washington, D.C.: University Press of America, 1981.

Obeyesekere, Gananath. *The Cult of the Goddess Pattini.* Chicago: University of Chicago Press, 1984.

O'Flaherty, Wendy Doniger. *Women, Androgynes, and Other Mythical Beasts.* Chicago: University of Chicago Press, 1980.

Okely, Judith, and Hellen Callaway, eds. *Anthropology and Autobiography.* London: Routledge, 1992.

Otto, Rudolf. *The Idea of the Holy: An Inquiry into the Non-rational Factor in the Idea of the Divine and Its Relation to the Rational.* London: Oxford University Press, 1950.

Paden, William E. *Religious Worlds: The Comparative Study of Religion.* Boston: Beacon Press, 1988.

Padoux, Andre. "Tantrism: An Overview." In *Encyclopedia of Religion,* edited by Mircea Eliade. New York: MacMillan, 1987.

Pagels, Elaine. *Adam, Eve and the Serpent.* New York: Vintage Books, 1988.

———. *The Gnostic Gospels.* New York: Vintage Books, 1979.

Palmer, Richard E. *Hermeneutics: Interpretation Theory in Schleiermacher, Dilthey, Heidegger, and Gadamer.* Evanston, Ill.: Northwestern University Press, 1969.

Parsons, William B. "Unchurched Mysticism." In *The Unknown, Remembered Gate: Religious Experience and Hermeneutical Reflection,* edited by Elliot Wolfson and Jeffrey J. Kripal. New York: Seven Bridges Press, forthcoming.

———. *The Enigma of the Oceanic Feeling: Revisioning the Psychoanalytic Study of Mysticism.* New York: Oxford University Press, 1999.

———. "From Milan to Ostia." Unpublished manuscript.

Paul, Diana. *Women in Buddhism: Images of the Feminine in Mahāyāna Tradition.* Berkeley: University of California Press, 1979.

Rabinow, Paul. "Representations Are Social Facts: Modernity and Post-modernity in Anthropology." In *Writing Culture: The Poetics and Politics of Ethnography,* edited by James Clifford and George E. Marcus. Berkeley: University of California Press, 1986.

Ramakrishna. *Sayings of Sri Ramakrishna: The Most Exhaustive Collection of Them, Their Number Being 1120.* Mylapore: Sri Ramakrishna Math, 1949.

Ritter, Helmut. *Das Meer der Seele: Mensch, Welt und Gott in den Geschichten des Fariduddīn 'Attār.* Leiden: Brill, 1955.

Rocalve, Pierre. "Place et rôle de l'Islam et de l'Islamologie dans la vie et l'oeuvre de Louis Massignon." Diss., Sorbonne, 1990.

Roland, Alan. "Psychoanalysis and the Spiritual Quest: Framing a New Paradigm." In *The Unknown, Remembered Gate: Religious Experience and Hermeneutical Reflection,* edited by Elliot Wolfson and Jeffrey J. Kripal. New York: Seven Bridges Press, forthcoming.

Roscoe, Will. *The Zuni Man-Woman.* Albuquerque: University of New Mexico Press, 1991.

Said, Edward. *Orientalism.* New York: Vintage, 1979.

Sanford, James H. "Wind, Waters, Stūpas, Maṇḍalas: Fetal Buddhahood in Shingon." *Japanese Journal of Religious Studies* 24, nos. 1–2 (1997): 1–38.

Saran, Prem. *Tantra: Hedonism in Indian Culture.* New Delhi: D. K. Printworld, 1994.
Schaberg, Jane. *The Illegitimacy of Jesus: A Feminist Theological Interpretation of the Infancy Narratives.* New York: Crossroad, 1990.
Schalow, Paul Gordon. "Kukai and the Tradition of Male Love in Japanese Buddhism." In *Buddhism, Sexuality, and Gender,* edited by José Ignacio Cabezón. Albany, N.Y.: SUNY Press, 1992.
Schimmel, Anne-Marie. "Remembering Louis Massignon." In *Présence de Louis Massignon: Hommages et témoignages,* edited by Daniel Massignon. Paris: Maisonneuve et Larose, 1987.
——. *As through a Veil: Mystical Poetry in Islam.* New York: Columbia University Press, 1982.
——. "Eros—Heavenly and Not So Heavenly—in Sufi Literature and Life." In *Society and the Sexes in Medieval Islam,* edited by Afaf Lufti al-Sayyid-Marsot. Malibu, Calif.: Undena, 1979.
——. *Mystical Dimensions of Islam.* Chapel Hill: University of North Carolina Press, 1975.
Scholem, Gershom. "On the Possibility of Jewish Mysticism in Our Time (1963)." In *On the Possibility of Jewish Mysticism in Our Time and Other Essays,* edited by Avraham Shapira, translated by Jonathan Chipman. Philadelphia: Jewish Publication Society, 1997.
——. *Major Trends in Jewish Mysticism.* New York: Schocken, 1961.
Schuchard, Marsha Keith. "Emanuel Swedenborg: Deciphering the Codes of a Celestial and Terrestrial Intelligencer." In *Rending the Veil: Secrecy and Concealment in the History of Religions,* edited by Elliot Wolfson. New York: Seven Bridges Press, 1998.
Sedgwick, Eve Kosofsky. *The Epistemology of the Closet.* Berkeley: University of California Press, 1990.
Sells, Michael A. "The Infinity of Desire: Love, Mystical Union, and Ethics in Sufism." In *Crossing Boundaries: Essays on the Ethical Status of Mysticism,* edited by G. William Barnard and Jeffrey J. Kripal. New York: Seven Bridges Press, 2001.
——. *Mystical Languages of Unsaying.* Chicago: University of Chicago Press, 1994.
Shattuck, Roger. *Forbidden Knowledge: From Prometheus to Pornography.* San Diego: Harcourt, Brace, 1996.
Shepard, Odell. *The Lore of the Unicorn.* New York: Harper and Row, 1979.
Silverman, Kaja. *Male Subjectivity at the Margins.* New York: Routledge, 1992.
Smith, Huston. *Cleansing the Doors of Perception: The Religious Significance of Entheogenic Plants and Chemicals.* New York: Jeremy P. Tarcher and Putnam, 2000.
Smith, Morton. *The Secret Gospel: The Discovery and Interpretation of the Secret Gospel According to Mark.* New York: Harper and Row, 1982.
Southgate, Minoo S. "Men, Women, and Boys: Love and Sex in the Works of Sa'di." *Iranian Studies* 17 (1984): 413–452.

Staal, Frits. *Exploring Mysticism.* Berkeley: University of California Press, 1975.
Stein, Edward, ed. *Forms of Desire: Sexual Orientation and the Social Constructionist Controversy.* New York: Routledge, 1992.
Storr, Anthony. *Feet of Clay: Saints, Sinners and Madmen: A Study of Gurus.* New York: Free Press, 1996.
Syranthropy: Journal of the Anthropology Department, Syracuse University (spring 1993).
Tao Te Ching. Translated by Stephen Addis and Stanley Lombardo. Indianapolis: Hackett, 1993.
Taylor, Kathleen. "Arthur Avalon: The Creation of a Legendary Orientalist." In *Myth and Mythmaking,* edited by Julia Leslie. Richmond, U.K.: Curzon, 1996.
Teilhard de Chardin, Pierre. *Toward the Future.* New York: Harcourt Brace Jovanovich, 1975.
Turner, Denys. *Eros and Allegory: Medieval Exegesis of the Song of Songs.* Kalamazoo, Mich.: Cistercian Publications, 1995.
Underhill, Evelyn. *Evelyn Underhill: Modern Guide to the Ancient Quest for the Holy.* Edited by Dana Greene. Albany, N.Y.: SUNY Press, 1988.
———. *The Letters of Evelyn Underhill.* Edited by Charles Williams. London: Longmans, Green, 1943.
———. *The Life of the Spirit and the Life of Today.* 1922. Reprint, Harrisburg, Pa.: Morehouse, 1994.
———. *Practical Mysticism.* 1914. Reprint, Guildford, Surrey: Eagle, 1991.
———. *Mysticism: A Study of the Nature and Development of Man's Spiritual Consciousness.* London: Methuen, 1911. Reprint, London: Bracken Books, 1995.
Urban, Hugh B. "Religion for the Age of Darkness: 'Tantrism' in the Works and Lives, Methods and Paths of the History of Religions." In *The Unknown, Remembered Gate: Religious Experience and Hermeneutical Reflection,* edited by Elliot Wolfson and Jeffrey J. Kripal. New York: Seven Bridges Press, forthcoming.
———. "A Dance of Masks: The Esoteric Ethics of Frithjof Schuon." In *Crossing Boundaries: Essays on the Ethical Status of Mysticism,* edited by G. William Barnard and Jeffrey J. Kripal. New York: Seven Bridges Press, 2001.
———. "The Extreme Orient: The Construction of 'Tantrism' as a Category in the Orientalist Imagination." *Religion* 29 (1999): 123–146.
———. "The 'Poor Company': Secrecy and Symbolic Power in the Kartābhajā Sect of Colonial Bengal." Ph.D. diss., University of Chicago, 1998.
Versluis, Arthur. *Wisdom's Children: A Christian Esoteric Tradition.* Albany, N.Y.: SUNY Press, 1999.
von Hügel, Baron Friedrich. *The Mystical Element of Religion as Studied in Saint Catherine of Genoa and Her Circle of Friends.* 2 vols. London: J. M. Dent and Sons, 1908.
Waardenburg, Jacque. "Massignon, Louis." In *Encyclopedia of Religion,* edited by Mircea Eliade. New York: Macmillan, 1987.
Wafer, Jim. "Vision and Passion: The Symbolism of Male Love in Islamic Mystical Literature." In *Islamic Homosexualities: Culture, History, and Literature,*

edited by Stephen O. Murray and Will Roscoe. New York: New York University Press, 1997.
Wasserstrom, Steven. *Religion after Religion: Gershom Scholem, Mircea Eliade and Henry Corbin at Eranos.* Princeton, N.J.: Princeton University Press, 1999.
White, David Gordon. *The Alchemical Body: Siddha Traditions in Medieval India.* Chicago: University of Chicago Press, 1996.
Whitehead, Tony Larry, and Mary Ellen Conaway, eds. *Self, Sex and Gender in Cross-Cultural Fieldwork.* Urbana: University of Illinois Press, 1986.
Wilson, Peter Lamborn. "Contemplation of the Unbearded: The Rubaiyyat of Awhadoddīn Kermanī." *Paidika* 3, no. 4 (1995): 13–22.
———. *Scandal: Essays in Islamic Heresy.* Brooklyn: Autonomedia, 1988.
Wilson, Peter Lamborn, and Bernd Manuel Weischer. *Heart's Witness: The Sufi Quatrains of Awhaduddīn Kirmānī.* Tehran: Imperial Iranian Academy of Philosophy, 1978.
Winkler, John J. *The Constraints of Desire: The Anthropology of Sex and Gender in Ancient Greece.* New York: Routledge, 1989.
Wolfson, Elliot. "Divine Suffering and the Hermeneutics of Reading: Philosophical Reflections on Lurianic Mythology." Unpublished manuscript, 2000.
———. "Occultation of the Feminine and the Body of Secrecy in Medieval Kabbalah." In *Rending the Veil: Secrecy and Concealment in the History of Religions,* edited by Elliot Wolfson. New York: Seven Bridges Press, 1998.
———. "Coronation of the Sabbath Bride: Kabbalistic Myth and the Ritual of Androgynisation." *Journal of Jewish Thought and Philosophy,* vol. 6 (1997).
———. "Eunuchs Who Keep the Sabbath: Becoming Male and the Ascetic Ideal in Thirteenth-Century Jewish Mysticism." In *Becoming Male in the Middle Ages,* edited by Jeffrey Jerome Cohen and Bonnie Wheeler. New York: Garland, 1997.
———. "Weeping, Death, and Spiritual Ascent in Sixteenth-Century Jewish Mysticism." In *Death, Ecstasy, and Other-Worldly Journeys,* edited by John Collins and Michael Fishbane. Albany, N.Y.: SUNY Press, 1995.
———. *Circle in the Square: Studies in the Use of Gender in Kabbalistic Symbolism.* Albany, N.Y.: SUNY Press, 1995.
———. *Along the Path: Studies in Kabbalistic Myth, Symbolism and Hermeneutics.* Albany, N.Y.: SUNY Press, 1995.
———. "Erasing the Erasure/Gender and the Writing of God's Body in Kabbalistic Symbolism." In *Circle in the Square: Studies in the Use of Gender in Kabbalistic Symbolism.* Albany, N.Y.: SUNY Press, 1995.
———. "Beautiful Maiden without Eyes: *Peshat* and *Sod* in Zoharic Hermeneutics." In *The Midrashic Imagination,* edited by Michael Fishbane. Albany, N.Y.: SUNY Press, 1993.
———. *Through a Speculum That Shines: Vision and Imagination in Medieval Jewish Mysticism.* Princeton, N.J.: Princeton University Press, 1994.
———. "Images of God's Feet: Some Observations on the Divine Body in Judaism." In *People of the Body: Jews and Judaism from an Embodied Perspective,* edited by Howard Eilberg-Schwartz. Albany, N.Y.: SUNY Press, 1992.

———. "Circumcision and the Divine Name: A Study in the Transmission of Esoteric Doctrine." *Jewish Quarterly Review* 78 (1987): 77–112.

———. "Circumcision, Vision of God, and Textual Interpetation: From Midrashic Trope to Mystical Symbol." *History of Religions* 27 (1987): 189–215.

Wolfson, Elliot, and Jeffrey J. Kripal, eds. *The Unknown, Remembered Gate: Religious Experience and Hermeneutical Reflection.* New York: Seven Bridges Press, forthcoming.

Wright, J. W., Jr., and Everett K. Rowson. *Homoeroticism in Classical Arabic Literature.* New York: Columbia University Press, 1997.

Wright, Peter. *Spy Catcher: The Candid Autobiography of a Senior Intelligence Officer.* New York: Viking Penguin, 1987.

Wulff, David M. *Psychology of Religion: Classic and Contemporary.* 2d ed. New York: John Wiley and Sons, 1997.

Young, David E., and Jean-Guy Goulet. *Being Changed by Cross-Cultural Encounters: The Anthropology of Extraordinary Experience.* Peterborough, Ont.: Broadview Press, 1994.

Zaehner, R. C. *The City within the Heart.* New York: Crossroad, 1981.

———. *Our Savage God.* London: Collins, 1974.

———. *Zen, Drugs and Mysticism.* New York: Pantheon Books, 1972.

———. *Evolution in Religion: A Study in Sri Aurobindo and Pierre Teilhard de Chardin.* Oxford: Clarendon Press, 1971.

———. *Concordant Discord: The Interdependence of Faiths, Being the Gifford Lectures on Natural Religion Delivered at St. Andrews in 1967–1969.* Oxford: Clarendon Press, 1970.

———. *Hindu and Muslim Mysticism.* New York: Schocken Books, 1969.

———. *The Convergent Spirit: Towards a Dialectics of Religion.* London: Routledge and Kegan Paul, 1963.

———. *Hinduism.* Oxford: Oxford University Press, 1962.

———. *Mysticism Sacred and Profane.* Oxford: Clarendon Press, 1957.

INDEX

A
Abdāl, 140
Abraham, 141
Absence or distance, 269, 308–10, 321
   and ability to enter deeply into tradition, 322
   and Gadamer, 325–26
Abulafia, Abraham, 359n. 31
Abû Nuwās, 98
Academy
   and debate with pious community over making esotericism public, 266
   and "esotericism," 25
   secrecy in, 26
   and Wolfson's call for those outside tradition and without mystical experiences to be regarded as authoritative, 271
Acton, Lord, xiv
Adam and Eve, 172–75
Advaita Vedānta
   and Bharati, 227
   and Zaehner, 170, 177, 188
Age-defined homoeroticism, 20
Altmann, Alexander, 263
"Anāl'l-Haqq," 101
Analytic language philosophy, 239
Anastase, Père, 107
Angela of Foligno, 49
Anorexia, holy, 91, 346–47n. 7
Anthropology
   and Bharati, 212
   "of extraordinary experience," 11
Apophatic language, 7
Aristotle, 196–98
Armstrong, Christopher, 83–84

   and engaged nature of *Mysticism*, 35–36
   and Underhill's involvement in occult, 39
   and Underhill's marriage to Moore, 42
Art, 310–11, 338n. 71
   and mysticism and Underhill, 61–62
Ast, Friedrich, 324
ʿAttār, Farīduddīn, 104, 171, 351–52n. 48
Augustine, St., 54, 175, 183
Aurobindo, Sri, 173
Aurora (Böhme), 59
Automatic writing, 63
Awahad al-Din, 147
Azriel of Gerona, 199
Azzai, Ben, 284, 288–89

B
Badaliya community, 137
Bāḍava, 95
Bailey, Harold, 159
Bakan, David, 273
Balzac, Honoré de, 164–65, 182, 194–96, 360n. 44
Banū ʿUdhrā, 127, 128
Bataille, Georges, xiii, 109, 184, 330
Bāyezīd Bistāmi, 101
Bell, Rudolph, 91
Bengali Vaiṣṇava tradition, 7, 153–54
Benjamin, Walter, 268
Bergson, Henri, 44, 45, 173
Bernanos, Georges, 158, 163
Bernard of Clairvaux, St., 16, 19, 27, 33, 86
   sexual language of, 70–71, 78, 148

391

Berreman, G. D., 240
Bhagavad Gītā, 171, 197, 220, 363n. 34
Bhagavān, Bhāgavata and *bhakta*, 7
Bharati, Agehananda, 207–49
 and anthropology, 212
 and asceticism and celibacy, 207, 212–13, 215, 222
 and Christianity, 207, 208, 215–16
 and *Doors of Perception*, 30, 166
 and the esoteric, 238–39
 hermeneutic strategies of, 242–46
 and language from inside and outside, 238–42
 and letter to Lalita, 246–48
 life summary of, 210–12, 214
 and LSD and drugs, 225–26, 227–28, 232, 366n. 78
 and meeting of East and West, 221, 222, 363n. 37, 363n. 38
 and modern Hindu Renaissance and swamis, 228–29, 365n. 66
 and mysticism, 227–34; as a "mixed mystic," 237; amoral model of, 218–21; distance from required to create culture, 309; future of, and modern intellectual, 235–38; and its infilling rest of life, 243; and monism, 226; and personal experiences of, 225, 231–32, 364n. 56
 and Nazism and fascism, 208, 215–17
 and offense with popularizations, 235
 and phenomenology, 241
 and postulation, 240–41
 and privileging scholars with mystical experiences, 244
 and prophets and mystics, 220, 363n. 33
 and psychoanalysis and Freud, 213–14, 215, 367n. 87
 roots of his antinomianism, 213–17
 and Śaṃkarāchārya of Govardhanapīṭha, 207, 213, 222–23
 and *sandhā-bhāṣā*, 208, 229, 244–46
 scholarly-historical neglect of, 248
 and "singular reading" of traditional texts, 243–44
 and social wisdom and Western wise men, 221
 and standing a tradition on its head, 212
 and syncretism, 235, 366n. 77
 and Tantra; definition of, 224–25; and excess, 307; and experimentation, 225, 228; healing power of, 250; and hedonism, 207, 228, 229, 246; and initiation, 211, 231–32; and its establishment in the West, 232–34, 249, 365n. 71; sexual encounters of, 230–31, 247; and sexuality, 222, 227–28, 247–48; and sexualizing of practically everything, 229–30; and "Tantric tradition," 209, 224–27, 315; and theorizing out of the erotic, 221–34; and transgression, 217–18
 and theism and dualism, 226
 and Watts, 236–37
 and Wittgenstein, 209, 211, 221, 239
 and Zaehner, 207–8, 236, 237
 and zero-experience, 219, 220, 230, 241–42
Blake, William, 87, 231, 314, 327, 328–29, 374n. 3
 and automatic writing, 63
 and creation, 19, 31
 and criticism of fascism, 216–17
 and Evelyn Underhill, 42–43, 356n. 55
 "infernal method of" and eroticism, 329–30
 and intellect fueled by sexual energy, 250

and male inspiration and sexuality, 12
not fitting map of Christianity, 48
and poetry as mysticism, 308–9
as quoted by Wolfson, 258, 280, 290
and "road of excess," vi, 28–29, 308, 339n. 85
and roots of eros, 22
spirit of, in *Roads of Excess,* 28–31, 306
Blake and Freud (George), 250
Bodhicitta, 222
Böhme, Jakob, 19
  and automatic writing, 63
  as heteroerotic mystic, 79–81
  not fitting maps of Christian dogma, 48
Bok, Sissela, ix, x–xi, xiii
Bonaventure, St., 71–72
Bose, Subhas Chandra, 216
Boswell, John, 148
Boullan, Joseph-Antoine, 140
Bourignan, Antoinette, 77
Bowra, Morris, 160
Bratslav, Nahman, 262
Bridal mysticism. *See* Marriage, mystical
Brown, Norman, 235
Bucke, Richard, 164, 173, 174, 370n. 21
Buddhism, 230, 239
Budick, Sanford, 272
Butterfield, Stephen, 375–76n. 28

C
Caitanya, 188
Caldwell, Sarah, 11–12
Campbell, Joseph, 214
Carstairs, G. M., 214
Catherine of Alexandria, 76
Catherine of Genoa, 66, 77
Catherine of Sienna, 50, 76
Catholicism
  and alternative sexualities symbolically nurtured, 149
  glorified sexual pleasures of in Bible and saints, 193
  and imagined scenarios for gay and heterosexual males, 150–51
  and limits on what can be said, xi–xii
  See also Christianity
Celan, Paul, 261
Changing Face of the Priesthood, The (Cozzens), 356–57n. 8
Chatelier, Alfred le, 137
Cherub, 33, 57, 67
Chittick, William C., 370n. 22
Chomsky, Noam, 242
Christianity
  and Adam and Eve myth and original sin, 175
  and Bharati, 207, 208, 215–16
  and Blake, 48
  and bridal mysticism, 94, 122–23, 149
  and Divine as male, 73
  dogma of, and Underhill, 45
  essence of mystical as Underhill's method, 46–52
  failures of and rise of comparative religion, 163
  gendered and sexed lines of, 19–20
  and homoerotic structure of male mysticism, 19–20, 70, 72–73, 98–99, 149
  and homosexuality, 73, 108, 142, 314
  and lack of symbolic resources to reconcile spirituality and sexuality, 94–95
  and matter and redemptive process, 194
  as synthesis of prophetic and mystical according to Zaehner, 359n. 37
  and term mysticism, 34
  and Zaehner's critique of ascetic, 182–85

394 Index

Circumcision, 260, 277, 285
"Circumcision, Vision of God, and Textual Interpretation" (Wolfson), 263
"Circumcision and the Divine Name" (Wolfson), 263
City in the Heart, The, 197–98
Clark, Benjamin, 114, 333–34n. 36
Claudel, Paul, 136, 138
Cleansing the Doors of Perception (Smith), 30
Cloud of Unknowing (Hilton), 68
Comparative approach to study of twentieth-century mysticism, 4
    and publication of *Mysticism Sacred and Profound*, 160
    See also Scholars of mysticism
Comparative erotics of mysticism, 15–23, 312
Concordant Discord (Zaehner), 157, 181–93, 194
    and Adam and Eve myth, 174
    and autobiographical discourse, 161
    outline of text of, 181–82
Confucianism, 174
Contemplation, 63–64
Contextualism, 282
Corbin, Henry, 1, 299, 317, 333n. 1
Cosmic Consciousness (Bucke), 164, 370n. 21
Cozzens, Donald B., 356–57n. 8
Cropper, Margaret, 36, 39, 81–82
Crowning, 288–89
Cuardra, Luis de, 103–4, 107
    and conversion to Islam, 108
    Massignon's desire to save, 141
    suicide of, 109–10
Cupitt, Don, and mysticism and language, xiii, 8, 332–33n. 20
Cusa, Nicholas, 185
Custance, John, 177, 178

D
Dante, 19
Darwin, Charles, 173
Datta, Ram Chandra, 199
De Ars, Curé, 49
De Certeau, Michel, 6, 10, 34, 82, 321
Deikman, Arthur, 342n. 35
Delacroix, Eugène, 55
De Leon, Moshe, 265
Desire, 119–21, 126
Dhū'l-Nūn, 130
Dilthey, Wilhelm, 305, 324, 325
Dionysius the Areopagite, 33, 57, 67
Discourse on Thinking (Heidegger), 262
Doctrine of Vibration (Dyczkowski), 204
Doniger, Wendy, 214, 332–33n. 20
    and author, 92, 204–5
    and myths lived by scholars, 3
Doors of Perception (Huxley), 30, 156, 165–69
    and brain as filter, 167
    Eastern underpinnings of, 166
Double Mirror, The (Butterfield), 375–76n. 28
Douglas, Mary, 320–21
Dreams
    and author's dream choice for heterosexuality, 154
    and author's Night vision in Calcutta, 201–3
    and effects on dreamer and dreamed, 300
    initiatory and bringing reality of into life, 299–300
    teachings received in, 299
    without objectively real meaning, 301
Drugs, 307
    and Bharati's legitimizing of LSD, 207
    and Bharati's use of LSD, 225–26, 227–28, 232, 366n. 78
    and Charles Manson, 197
    and *Doors of Perception*, 165–69
    and Massignon, 116

and Zaehner's criticism of experiences using as equation with mystical experiences, 167–68
and Zaehner's mescaline experiment, 178–80
Dualism, 121, 148, 183, 226, 353n. 72
Dummett, Michael, 156, 157
Dyczkowski, Mark, 204

E
Eckhart, Meister, 51, 189
Ecstasy
as a form of writing, 62
and art, 62–63
Zaehner's ethical rejection of, 144
Ecstatic speech, 116
Eilberg-Schwartz, Howard, 149–50
Eliade, Mircea, 87, 224, 241, 317, 332n. 13
mystical experiences of, 1, 2, 203
and risks on the way, 299
and *sandhā-bhāṣā*, 244–45
and text having power to awaken experience in reader, 327
Emic speech, 239–40, 241, 244
Enigma of the Oceanic Feeling (Parsons), 376n. 44
Epistemology, and mystical and erotic, xiv
Erotic
comparative mystical study of, 15–23, 312
complexities, 21
definition of, 21–22, 200, 205, 359n. 36
and ethnography of foreign cultures, 13
and hermeneutical insight, 12
as jouissance and refashioning of masculine, 315–16
mystical, and similarity of author's and Wolfson's analysis of, 297
mystical, as sublimation of sexual instincts and absence of sexual-familial life, 158
and need for masculine transfiguration, 313–16, 375n. 17
nondual, 205
palace of, 311–16
subjectivity, 12, 13
See also Sexuality
Esotericism, x, 331n. 4
and Bharati, 238–39
made public only at risk, 266–67
and Sufism, 129
and Underhill, 64
and Wolfson, 267, 369n. 19, 370n. 22
Essay on the Origins of the Technical Language of Islamic Mysticism (Massignon), 86, 114
Essentials of Mysticism, The (Underhill), 81
Ethics
and amorality of mysticism for Bharati, 218–21, 318
critique of by Zaehner, 175–80
erasure of by mystocentric focus of history of religions, 317, 322
and mystical, 318, 319
and mystical humanism, 319
and mystical not based on, 318
palace of, 316–19
and questions raised by this book, 317–18
and sexual ignorance, xiv–xv
Etic speech, 239–40, 241, 244
Eunuchs, 21, 337–38n. 70
Eve and Adam, 172–75
Evola, Julius, 24
Evolution and Adam and Eve myth, 172–75
Evolution in Religion (Zaehner), 174
Excess, 29–30, 117, 306–8
Experience as interpretation, 66–67, 343n. 47

F
Female, heteroerotic symbolisms in *Mysticism*, 75–77
Feyerabend, Paul, 244

Forman, K. C., 2
Forman, Robert, 241
Foucauld, Charles, 102, 136, 220
Foucault, Michel, xiv, 331n. 3
   and homosexual identities, 335n. 51
   and sex and truth, ix
Francis of Assisi, 49
François De Sales, St., 182, 184, 191
Frauwallner, Erich, 210
Freud, Sigmund, vi, 12, 22, 23
   and art, 310
   and Bharati, 213–14
   and Blake, 334n. 20
   and dreams as wish fulfillment, 300
   and intellect fueled by sexual energy, 250
   and kabbalah, 273, 371n. 25
   and mystical experience, 88–89, 313
   oedipal theory of, 28, 91–92, 313–14
   and sexuality as foundation of culture and consciousness, 22
   and Zaehner, 185
Frye, Northrop, 305, 308–9

G
Gadamer, Hans-Georg, 268, 324, 325–26
Gandhi, Mohandas K., 137
"Garden of Love, The" (Blake), 87
Gardet, Louis, 170
Gender, 15, 17
   crossing of identities in kabbalah, 290–92
   of the Divine, 78
   and mystical texts as venue for alternative, 17–21
   and phallocentric ocularism, 287–88
   and phallus as male androgyne, 288
   of soul, 73–74

   and Tantra, 226–27
   and *Upaniṣads*, 294–95
   and Zaehner, 184–85, 187–89, 190–93, 195–96
George, Diana Hume, 22, 250, 334n. 20
Ghazālī, Abū Ḥāmid al-, 49, 191
Ghazālī, Ahman, 143
Giller, Pinchas, 261, 263
Girardet, Raoul, 139
God
   and Divine autoeroticism, 292, 360n. 42
   love of Himself, 132–33
   mystical experience of, 7
   and witness practice, 126–27
Gospel of Thomas, The, 21, 314, 319, 337n. 65
Greene, Dana, 43
Gregory the Great, 334n. 39
Grey World, The (Underhill), 42
Griffin, Susan, 324
Gude, Mary Louise, 102, 106–7, 117, 140
   and death of Massignon, 139
   and defining strands of Massignon's life, 136
   and Massignon's parents' beliefs, 103
Guenther, Herbert, 211, 224, 367n. 94
Gupta, Roxanne, 249
Guyon, Madame, 37, 50, 77
Gypsies, 88, 346n. 1

H
Habermas, Jürgen, 324
Halbfass, Wilhelm, 302
Hallāj, Ḥusayn ibn Manṣūr al-
   ban on publication of works of, 130
   execution of for speaking esoteric publicly, 130
   and manifestation of the Presence, 134

and "mystic love and true sacrifice," 135
as outlaw-saint, 101
and proclamation "I am the Truth," 101
Shibilī's reproach of homosexuality of, 141
as summation and crystallization of Sufism, 114
See also *Passion of al-Hallāj*
Halperin, David, 16–17, 20, 312
Hananel, 279
Hanson, Ellis, 108, 193
Hānswī, Jamāl, 123
Haraway, Donna, 324
Ḥasan al-Baṣrī, 129
Hedonism, 228, 229, 246
Heidegger, Martin, 262, 269, 281
Hekhalot mysticism, 278
Hercule Barbin (Foucault), ix
Hermeneutical process
   and allowing its address of all issues, 322–23
   and Bharati, 242–46
   community of, 9
   "depth" process of Habermas, 326
   and distance, 325
   and erotic subjectivity, 11–13
   and etymology and Hermes, 281, 371n. 30
   as kind of mysticism, 293
   and metaphors, 323–24
   and mystical changes both hermeneut and the interpreted, 304
   and mystical experience and God or religion, 7
   mystical experience as, 5–9
   and mystical marriage, 192–93
   palace of, 323–27
   and reading and writing of text as a double mirrors, 296, 297–98
   and reading as erotic activity, 289–90
   and texts as crystallizations available to reader, 324–25
   theories of, 324–26
   as union, 302, 326–27
   visionary and Wolfson, 283–84
   and warning against absolute identity or naive objectivism, 325
Hermeneutical revenge, 268, 308
Hermes, 281, 371n. 30
Hermetic Society of the Golden Dawn, 39
Hero (*vīra*) tradition in Tantrism, 153
Heterosexual mystics and mystical theologies, 15, 18, 19
   and al-Hallāj, 124
   and author's quest for, 151–52, 311–12, 313
   and Bharati, 217–18
   and Blake, 19, 345n. 66
   female, 75–77
   heroic heretical, 147–55, 297
   and Hindu goddess traditions, 152
   and Ibn ʿArabī, 123
   and Jacob Böhme, 79–81
   and Kabbalah, 259–60
   male, 79–81
   and male nature of God, 94
   nonexistence of stable case of, 312
   and Sahajiyā tradition, 153–54
   and Tantric traditions, 20–21, 96
   and Teilhard de Chardin, 336n. 56
Hildegard of Bingen, 28, 62
Hilton, Walter, 68
Hindu and Muslim Mysticism (Zaehner), 171
Hindu goddess traditions, 152
Hinduism
   and author, 151–52, 255, 302–3
   and hedonism and Bharati, 228
   and Massignon, 144–45
   and Underhill, 50
   and Zaehner, 163, 176–77, 184–85, 194

Historians of religion and mysticism. *See* Scholars of mysticism
Holocaust, 261
Homans, Peter, 42, 163, 321
Homoerotic
  definition of term, 17–19
  desire, rightly ending in death, 134
  gaze as "witnessing practice," 101, 121–23, 124–25, 129, 132, 191
Homoerotic structure of male mysticism, 14, 15, 17–21, 79–81, 98–99, 187
  and actual homosexuality, 18–19, 335–36n. 51
  age- or status-defined, 20
  and Christianity, 19–20, 70, 72–73, 149
  and classic Arabic literature, 353–54n. 74
  as final structure of kabbalistic vision, 290–92
  and *Passion of al-Hallāj*, 123–25
  and sexual fluids, 71–72
  and similarity of author's and Wolfson's analysis of, 297
  and Western monotheistic traditions, 17–18
  and Zaehner, 187
Homosexuality
  and Christianity, 73, 108, 142, 314, 356–57n. 8
  and death, 135
  and Hallāj, 131
  history of and religion according to Massignon, 141–42
  and homoerotic language, 18–19, 72
  identities of and history, 335–36n. 51
  Massignon's conflict relative to, 108, 135
  modern egalitarian notions of, 19, 336n. 54
  in mystics, 72, 98–99

Hopkins, Jeffrey, 2
Horne, James, 26, 237
Horse, flaming, 95
Humanism, mystical, 319
Husserl, Edmund, 262, 281
Huxley, Aldous, 30, 156, 165–67, 225
  and brain as filtering mechanism, 167, 342n. 35
  and Zaehner's mescaline experiment, 178–80
Huysmans, J.-K., 103, 117, 118, 140

I
Ibn ʿArabī, Muḥyīuddīn Muḥammad, 114, 123
Ibn ʿAtā, 125, 143
Ibn Dāwūd, 125–29, 130–33
Ibn Jāmīʿ, 130
"Ideal typical situations," 18
Idel, Moshe, 309
Imaginary, 314, 315
Imagination, 281–82, 293
Incarnation, progressive, 84
India and Europe (Halbfass), 302
Inside/outside
  and analysis of experience, 237–38
  and speaking authoritatively, 271, 322
Intuitions of Lovers (Ghazālī), 143
Irigiray, Luce, 264, 287, 313, 373n. 51, 374n. 12
Isaiah and burning-winged seraph, 67

J
Jacobs, Hans, 165
James, William, 2, 34, 56, 262
  and conversion, 53
  and his own mystical experiences in his writings, 52
  and Philo, 63
Jamison, Kay Reed, 170
Jantzen, Grace, 42
Jefferies, Richard, 175
Jerusalem (Blake), 31, 304

Jesus of Nazareth, 337–38n. 70
   author's vision of ithyphallic, 90–92, 252
   and becoming "eunuchs for the kingdom of heaven," 147
   and "kiss of the mouth," 71
   "love of," 149
John of the Cross, 54, 78, 94, 148, 281
   and Massignon, 103, 349n. 11
   and Zaehner, 186
Johnson, Mark, 323
Jonas, Hans, 65
Jordan, Mark, 18, 71, 147, 148
Joseph of Hamadan, 286
Jossua, Jean-Pierre, 10
Judaism
   and Adam and Eve myth, 175
   and dilemma of male heterosexuals, 149–50
   study of and outsiders, 271–72
Julian of Norwich, 28, 54, 75
Junayd, Abū'l-Qāsim Muḥammad al-, 130, 142, 171
Jung, C. G., 173, 185, 236

K
Kabbalah
   and auditory phenomenon, 281
   and esotericism through received tradition, 295
   and Freud, 273, 371n. 25
   and gender, 290–92
   and heterosexual mysticism, 259–60
   and imagination, 281–82
   and phallocentric ocularism, 264, 273, 284–88
   and psychoanalysis, 273, 371n. 25
   and sexuality as defining feature of, 263–64
   visionary experience in, 280–82
   and writing, creation, and circumcision, 274–78
   See also *Through a Speculum That Shines*
Kakar, Sudhir, 13, 153, 245, 311
Kālī, 153, 200–206, 346n. 1
Kalighat, 200
Kālī's Child: The Mystical and the Erotic in the Life and Teachings of Ramakrishna (Kripal), xii
   and author's replication of texts in his own body, 256
   and Night vision and dream in Calcutta, 201–3
   and psychoanalysis as analogous to traditional mystical traditions, 334n. 20
Kartābhajās, 238
Katz, Steven, 241, 343n. 47, 369n. 17
Kearney, Richard, 282
Kiss, 71
Kitagawa, Joseph, 138, 241
Knowledge, 57–58, 64
Kohut, Heinz, 13
Kolakowski, Lezak, 321–22
Kripal, Jeffrey
   and anorexia, 91–92
   and belief that profound religious experience requires asceticism, 147
   and choice of India and Hinduism for study and practice, 95, 151–52, 255, 302–3
   and the descent, 250–57
   and dialectical nature of work resting on mystical, 256–57
   and dream choice for heterosexuality, 154
   and early gender dilemma, 90
   and erotic mystical experiences in Calcutta, 199–200
   as exile from Catholicism by virtue of heterosexuality, 151
   familial background of, 87–88, 90
   and heroic heretical heterosexuality, 147–55, 297

Kripal, Jeffrey (*continued*)
  and homosexual identities, 335–36n. 51
  and Kālī, 200–206, 303–4, 313
  and *Kālī's Child,* 200–206, 256
  and memory of being in womb, 88–89
  mystical experience in sleep, 1
  and mystical experiences and life, 257
  and mystical vs. erotic, 93–94
  and name "Kripal," 88, 255, 346n. 1
  and Night experience of November 4 in Calcutta, 201–6, 301, 302, 312; and the descent, 250–57; and implosion into great void, 330; and *liṅgams,* 253–54, 313; metaphysical reading of, 251; personal meanings of, 251–52
  and noetic-erotic force, 254–55
  and participation in life and work as double mirror, 297–98
  and psychoanalysis, 91, 96–97
  and purposes in writing *Roads of Excess,* 31, 305–6
  and quest for tradition of heteroerotic male mysticism, 151–52, 311–12, 313
  and Ramakrishna, 152, 255–56, 303–4
  and reading himself into *Through a Speculum That Shines,* 293–96
  and relationship to Virgin Mary, 155, 252
  and spiritual direction, 94–95, 96
  and *svapna-siddha,* 299–304
  and training in and writing about secrets, xi, xiii
  and use of Śākta Tantric universe, 25
  and *vajrāśva* vision, 92–97
  and vision of ithyphallic Jesus, 90–92, 252
  and visit to Kalighat, 200
  and writing of "Secret Talk," 11, 13, 334n. 42
Kris, Ernst, 55
Kṛṣṇa, 153–54
Kulick, Don, 12, 13, 324
Kuṇḍalinī, 95

L
La Barre, Weston, 314
Lacan, Jacques, 250, 313, 314
Lakoff, George, 323
Lambton, Ann, 160
Language
  apophatic, 7
  as determiner of religious experience, 8, 332–33n. 20
  and ecstatic speech, 116
  erotic in Zaehner, 187
  homoerotic, 18–19, 72–73, 98–99
  and Kabbalah and primordial autoerotic act, 276
  of love of God in West as erotic, 69–70
  mysticism of and Massignon, 114, 115–17
  and reading and writing as mystical experience, 118
  religious as symbolic, 44–45
  and scholars of mysticism, 243
  sexualization and genderization of, 15
  and speaking inside and outside the light (Bharati), 238–42
"La Prière sur Sodome" (Massignon), 141
Leadbeater, Charles, 227
Leary, Timothy, 166, 225
Le Comédie humaine (Balzac), 164
LeMaître, Solange, 138
Les Trois Prières d'Abraham (Massignon), 141

Leuba, James, 186, 191
Light at the Center, The (Bharati), 208
   and amorality of mysticism, 218–19
   and call for American-Tantric approach, 234
   and eroticism, 222, 231
   and mysticism, 227
Līlāprasaṅga (Saradananda), 254
Llama de amor viva (John of the Cross), 148
Long, Charles, 241
Love
   dying of, 127
   and Ibn Dāwūd and Hallāj, 131
   and superiority over knowledge, 57–58
   '*udhritic*, 126–29
LSD and Bharati, 207, 225–26, 227–28, 232, 366n. 78
Lwanga, Charles, 109
Lydwine de Schiedam, 140
"Lying on the Path: Translation and the Transport of Sacred Texts" (Wolfson), 258, 265, 272, 295–96, 369n. 15

M

Mādhyamika Buddhism, 170
Mahānirvāṇa Tantra, 245
Maistre, Joseph de, 140
Male
   and dilemma of in Judaism, 149–50
   and imagined scenarios for gay and heterosexual in Catholicism, 150–51
   inspiration and sexuality (Blake), 12
   mystical marriage, 77–79, 94, 148–49
   mystics in Western monotheistic traditions, 17–18
   nature of God and impossibility of male heterosexual approach, 94
   phallus as male androgyne, 288
   See also Homoerotic structure of male mysticism
Male mystics in Christianity, 17–18
   and bridal mysticism, 77–79, 94, 148–49
   dilemma of, 149
   and homoerotic language, 72–73, 98–99
Mallarmé, Stéphane, 117, 118
Manson, Charles, 197–98
Map, Walter, 71
Marcuse, Herbert, 235
Marriage, mystical, 73–74, 76–77, 121
   and homoeroticism in Christianity and Sufism, 122–23
   male, 77–79, 94, 148–49
   and psychoanalytic and feminist hermeneutical perspectives, 192–93
   seen anthropologically, 193
   and Underhill, 315
   and Zaehner, 171–72, 187–89, 190–93, 195–96, 315, 360n. 42
Marriage of Heaven and Hell (Blake), 29, 30, 147, 338n. 85
Masculinity, socially defining character of, and its transfiguration, 313–16, 375n. 17
Mason, Herbert, 99–100, 354–55n. 84
Maspero, Henri, 138
Massignon, Louis, 98–146, 151
   and art, 310–11
   and Badaliya community, 137
   becoming ordained priest, 140–41
   called Christian mystic and saint, 102, 348n. 8
   and canonization of Ugandan martyrs, 109
   and continence, 353n. 72

Massignon, Louis (*continued*)
  criticism of, 348n. 9
  and de Cuadra, 103–4, 107, 109–10, 141
  and excess, 117, 307
  and Gandhi, 137
  and guest and friend, 111
  and Hindu mysticism, 144–45
  and homosexuality, 315; and agnosticism, 108; conflict of, 104, 144–45, 355nn. 86, 91; and death, 134–35; history of, 141–42; and homoerotic gaze, 101; and sacrificial atonement, 141; and sublimation of homoeroticism, 101, 110, 126, 127, 128, 348n. 6
  and Huysmans, 117
  and Israel and Judaism, 138–39, 348n. 9, 355n. 86
  and language, 114, 115–17
  and lecturing at Eranos Conference, 137
  life of, 102–13, 135–40
  and Mallarmé, 118
  maxim beginning religious life of, 104–5
  and mystical life and sacrifice and asceticism, 109, 120, 135, 143
  mystical method of, 114–18
  and mystical substitution, 140
  and parables of mystics, 86
  personality and qualities of, 138, 348n. 8
  and personal relationship to Hallāj, 98, 112, 113
  political and diplomatic life, 133–37, 138–39
  and reading and writing as religious experience, 118
  self-censorship and "untranslations," 354n. 79
  and "testimonial style," 28
  and Virgin Mary, 110–11, 350–51n. 30
  and "Visitation of the Stranger," 105–8, 203; and analysis of conversion experience, 108–10; and belief in as reality, 303; and conversion, 1, 2, 105–8, 120; and virginal conception of scholarship, 110–13
  and "vision" and "passion" complexes, 101
  and "witness practice," 101
  and worth of mystic in actions, 115
  writing style of, 99–100
McGinn, Bernard, 60, 345n. 70
McIntosh, Mark, 9
"Meaning event," 7, 28, 44
Mechthild of Hackborn, 75
Mehta, J. L., 229
"Memorable Fancy" (Blake), 328
Memorial of the Saints ('Attar), 104
Merkavah mysticism, 278
Merleau-Ponty, Maurice, 281
Merton, Thomas
  and Kanchenjunga, 255
  and LSD trips with Bharati, 225–26
Metaphors We Live By (Lakoff and Johnson), 323
Mirror, reading as a double, 258, 270, 293, 295–96, 297–98
Monism
  and absolute absorption, 50–51
  and Charles Manson, 197
  and ethics, 207–8
  Hindu as challenge to Massignon's sacrificial vision, 144–45
  and sacrifice and love, 120, 143–44, 188
  testimonial and existential, 120–21, 363n. 71
  traditions of and nonuse of sexual language, 188
  and Zaehner's ethical rejection of, 144

Montini, Monsignor (Pope Paul VI), 137
Moore, Hubert Stuart, 41, 42
Moses, 279–80
Mourning, 42, 163, 321
Müller, Max, 11
Muller-Ortega, Paul, 256
Muriac, François, 139–40
Murray, Stephan, 19
Mystical Element of Religion, The (von Hügel), 47, 52, 82
Mystical erotic. *See* Erotic
Mystical experience and mysticism
    always interpretation, 66–67
    and creativity, 311
    and denial of difference, xii
    does not grant ontological status upon its content (Bharati), 239–40
    and esotericism, 267
    as excessive, 29–30, 306–8
    free study of all dimensions of, 322–23
    as hermeneutical process, 5–9
    and heterosexual symbolism forbidden in monotheistic tradition, 149
    as historically secret, 33–34
    and implicit universalism, 10
    not ethical or amoral, 218–21, 318
    often induced via violent means, 307, 318–19
    poets and, 309
    as psychic probe, 313
    psychologizing of, 10, 34
    and sacrifice and Massignon, 143
    of scholars of mysticism, 3
    as secret (*mustikon*), xii, xiii, 9
    and terms as adjective or noun, 34
    and Underhill, 64–67
    writer of, maintaining space on, 164–65
Mystical humanism, 319
Mystical substitution, 140
Mystical texts. *See* Reading of sacred texts
"Mystic Fact," 58
Mysticism (Underhill), 5–6, 33–86
    aesthetic hermeneutics of, 62
    and avoidance of body, 68
    and avoidance of Hinduism and Buddhism, 50
    and Christian dogma, 45
    and condemnation of "eccentric," 66
    engaged nature of, 35–36
    and "essence of mystical Christianity," 46–52
    and her own mystical experience, 59–62
    and male homoerotic symbolisms, 77–79
    and modern ecumenical mysticism, 51
    and monistic or absolute absorption, 50–51
    and mystical experience as interpretive, 66–67
    as mystical text and road map, 43–64
    and *Mystical Element of Religion*, 52
    and mystics not fitting Underhill's model, 48–49
    ontology of, 46
    and perennialism, 51
    and problem of "experience," 64–67
    reading of, and awakening of mystical experience, 59
    and religious language as symbolic, 44–45
    and sexuality, 67–81; avoidance of subject, 67–68; and female heteroerotic symbolisms, 75–77; language to describe, 69–70; and love, 72; and male mystical heteroeroticisms, 79–81
    stage model of, 48

Mysticism (continued)
   and style of quoting other authors, 59–60
   and superiority of love over knowledge, 57–58
   and traditional and psychological framings, 34–35, 52–57
   and the Trinity and the Incarnation, 47–48, 343n. 49
   and Underhill's evaluation of saints qualities, 49–50
Mysticism Sacred and Profane (Zaehner), 157, 158, 307
   and Adam and Eve story, 173
   and *Doors of Perception*, 167–68
   and Zaehner's mescaline experience, 178–80
Mystic Way, The (Underhill), 81
Myth, and Adam and Eve, 172–75

N
Nammalvar, 187
Narcissism, 13
Narcissus flower, 133–34
Narendra (Swami Vivekananda), 254
Naropa Institute, 224, 233
Nasr, Seyyed Hossein, 348nn. 8, 9
Nedelsky, Jennifer, 323–24
Neoplatonism, 148, 183
Newell, Lloyd, 357n. 2
Niftawayh, 130–31, 132

O
Obeyesekere, Gananath, 18, 214, 362n. 20
Objectivity, scientific ideal of complete, 26
"Occultation of the Feminine and the Body of Secrecy in Medieval Kabbalah" (Wolfson), 267–68
Ochre Robe, The (Bharati), 208, 212, 216
Oedipus complex, 28, 91–92, 313–14
Oh Terrifying Mother (Caldwell), 11–12

Omar Khayyām, 104
Origen, 78
Otto, Rudolph, ix, xiii
Our Savage God (Zaehner), 197

P
Padoux, Andre, 223
Pagels, Elaine, 172
Palaces of wisdom, 305–27
   and absence, 308–10, 321
   and art, 310–11
   and the erotic, 311–16
   and ethical criticism, 316–19
   and excess, 306–8
   and hermeneutical union, 323–27
   and paradox, 319–23
Paradox
   and historians of mysticism and devotees of traditions, 320–21
   palace of, 319–23
   and two interpretive traditions of historians of mysticism, 320
Parsons, William B., 13, 310, 334n. 42, 338n. 72, 376n. 44
"Passion complex," 101
Passion of al-Hallāj (Massignon), 5–6, 98, 100, 114, 118–35
   and body of al-Hallāj on gibbet, 101
   and Dāwūd, 125–33
   and desire and divine essence, 119–21, 356n. 67
   and divine unity, 121
   ending of, and sacrifice, 143
   and execution and heteroerotic gaze, 124
   and exoteric and esoteric, 129
   and Hallāj as the Presence, 134
   and homoerotic; desire and death, 134; structure of, 123–25; sublimation, 101, 126, 127, 128, 348n. 6)
   and homosexual love as gaze into "cloudy mirror," 131

and Massignon's conversion, 120
and passion of union of researcher
    and researched, 113
and secrecy, 129–31
and sexual-spiritual dualism,
    72n. 72, 121
and ʿudhritic love, 126–29
Patañjali's Yoga Sūtras, 144, 236
Patmore, Coventry, 45, 73–74, 79
Paul the Apostle, 148
Perennialism
    and Underhill, 51, 66, 342n. 39
    Wolfson's rejection of, 282
    and Zaehner's criticism of, 157
Phaedrus (Plato), 205
Phallocentric ocularism, 264, 284–89,
    372n. 35, 372n. 37, 372–73n. 40
    and phallus as that which sees,
        imagines, and knows, 285–86
    and Shekhinah as means by which
        to see, 287
Phenomenology, 241
Philo, 63
Philology, 304
Pius X, 41
Pius XII, 140
Plato, 205
Plotinus, 33
Postulation, 240–41
Practical Mysticism (Underhill), 81
"Proverbs of Hell" (Blake), 22,
    28–29
Pseudo-Dionysius, 281
Psychoanalysis
    as analogous to mystical tradi-
        tions, 334n. 38
    and collapse with mystical, 324
    hermeneutical perspective of and
        Zaehner, 192
    and Kabbalah, 273, 371n. 25
    and secrecy, xi
    transformational school of,
        338n. 72
Psychologizing of mysticism, 10, 70,
    82, 345n. 70

Psychology of Mysticism (Leuba),
    186
Psychology of religion
    and Underhill's Mysticism, 52–57,
        295, 341–42n. 33, 342–43n. 41
    and Zaehner, 185–87
Purusha, 184, 188, 192

Q
Qurʾān, 114
Qushayrī, Abū'l-Qāsim, 171

R
Rādhā, 153–54
Radhakrishnan, Sarvepalli, 156
Raffalovich, André, 354n. 78
Ramakrishna, xii, 28, 254, 255,
    256–57
    and Guhya Kathā, 11
    homoeroticism of, 152
    and initiation or "perfection" in
        dreams, 299–300
    and Śākta Tantra, 23
    and the womb, 80
Rāmānuja, 171, 177–78
Rampa, Lobsang, 366n. 77
Raphael, 62
Reading of sacred texts
    and absence or contraction, 309
    as a double mirroring, 258, 270,
        293, 295–96, 297–98
    and alternative sexualities and
        genders, 17–21
    and author's experiences through
        reading Speculum, 293–96
    and dialectic of distance and inti-
        macy, 270
    and experiencing of what is read
        about, 203–4, 283–84
    and fundamentalist possession of
        text, 270
    as intensely erotic experience,
        289
    and Massignon, 118
    and mystical experience, 8–9, 243

Reading of sacred texts (*continued*)
and necessity for both revealed and concealed, 269–70
and normative claims on our lives, xiv
and Sufi veils, 269
and temptation to read oneself into the text, 258, 295–96
and "un-covering" of meaning by unfolding of layers, 269–70
and Underhill, 59
and Wolfson, 265–72
Relativism, 282, 332–33n. 20
Religion after Religion (Wasserstrom), 316–17, 321–22
"Religion for the Thinking Person" (Bharati), 240
Religiosity, 25–26
Rich, Adrienne, 20
Ricoeur, Paul, 324
Rimbaud, Arthur, 168, 176, 177, 311, 355–56n. 93
Roback, Abraham, 317n. 25
Robinson, Margaret, 51
Roche, Pierre (Fernand Massignon), 103, 117
Roclave, Pierre, 115
Rolland, Romain, 2
Rolle, Richard, 68, 78
Rose flower, 133–34
Rosenzweig, Franz, 263, 268
Ṛṣyaśṛṅga, 95
Rūmi, Jalāluddīn, 133, 349–50n. 25
Rupert of Deutz, 70, 71–72
Russell, Bertrand, 221, 236
Ruysbroeck, John, 47, 70, 78, 79

S
Sacrifice, theology of, 120
Sahajiyā tradition, 153–54, 238
Saison en Enfer (Rimbaud), 168
Śaiva Siddhānta, 188
"Śākta and Vajrayāna: Their Place in Indian Thought" (Bharati), 244, 250

Śākta Tantra, 23–24
Śaṅkara, 233, 236
Śaṃkarāchārya of Govardhanapīṭha, 207, 213, 222–23
Sāṃkhya, 170–71
Sandhā-bhāṣā, 208, 229, 244–46, 361n. 2
Saradananda, Swami, 254
Schimmel, Anne-Marie, 119–20, 348n. 8
Scholars of mysticism
as both gnostic and skeptic, 319–20
and cultural mourning required in critical interpretation, 321
and insider-outsider discussion relative to study of a tradition, 271, 322
modern and implicit universalism and psychologizing, 10
as mystical tradition, 3
and personal mystical experience, 3; and abilities with language, 243; and determining who is writing from, 59; historical significance of, 27–28; and impossibility of separation from academic method, 4–5, 6–7; and insistence that must have had in order to be authoritative, 271; and kabbalistic texts, 283–84; and Underhill, 58; and Zaehner, 164–65
and quadruply enfolding esoteric rhetorical structure, 14–15
and reading and writing and absence, 309
as sexual beings who can be studied, 99
two broad interpretive traditions of, and paradoxical tension, 320
use same hermeneutical processes in present as historically, 302

Scholem, Gershom, 2, 203, 263, 281, 317
  and necessary context of mysticism, 369–70n. 21
  training of, 261
Schuchard, Marsha Keith, 339n. 85
Schuon, Frithjof, 2
Second Vatican Council, 137, 145
Secrecy
  dynamics of, 272
  ethics of, x–xi
  and "forbidden knowledge," x
  and the mystical, xii, 9
  and *Passion of al-Hallāj*, 129–31
  scholars' revealing of, 266–68, 272
  and sex and the sacred, ix–xv
Secret Gospel of Mark, The, 337–38n. 70
"Secret of Dr. Honigberger, The" (Eliade), 1, 203
Secrets: On the Ethics of Concealment and Revelation (Bok), ix
"Secret Talk" (*Guhya Kathā*), 11, 14
Sefer ha-Yihud, 286
Self as always partial narrative, 324
Sells, Michael, 7–8, 9, 44
Seraph, burning-winged, 33, 57, 67
Seraphita (Balzac), 195–96
Sermones super cantica canticorum (Bernard of Clairvaux), 70–71, 86
Seul avec Dieu: L'Aventure mystique (Jossua), 10
Sexuality
  and Bharati's legitimizing of Tantra, 207
  and Christian doctrine of its opposition with mystical experience, 147–48
  definition of, 16–17
  and ecstasies of male mystics producing sexual fluids, 72
  and the erotic and Zaehner, 180–93, 359n. 36
  and female heteroerotic symbolisms, 75–77
  and the Imaginary, 314, 315
  language of, in Western Christian tradition, 70
  and male mystical heteroeroticisms, 79–81
  and male mystical homoeroticisms, 77–79
  and mystical communities and literatures and alternative modes, 17–21
  and *Mysticism*, 67–81
  and nonexistence of stable heterosexuality in spiritual traditions, 312
  and oedipus complex, 313–14
  religious ignorance relative to, xiv–xv
  and secrecy, ix–x
  suffering of as trigger for mystical study, 317–18
  and truth, ix
  See also Erotic; Gender
Sharada Devi, 299–300
Shattuck, Roger, x
Shekhinah
  as corona of phallus, 287, 288, 289, 290
  as empty in itself, 281
  and heterosexual mysticism, 260
  and homoerotic bonding, 291–92
  and leading from feminine to masculine, 290, 291–92
  as object of mystic's passage, 278
  as optical apparatus revealing vision of phallus, 287
  and seeing reflection of mystic's own divine soul, 293
Shiblī, 101, 124–25, 130, 133, 141
Shingon Buddhism, 89
Siegel, Lee, 160, 189–90
Silence of Sodom (Jordan), 147
Silverman, Kaja, 313, 314, 315
Smart, Ninian, 226, 241

Smith, Huston, 30
Society of Tantric Studies conference, 249
Sodom, 141
Song of Songs, 69, 70, 79, 94, 199, 360n. 39
Sophia, 79–80
Soul
  becoming a virgin before God, 111, 350–51n. 30
  as feminine in Zaehner, 187–88
  gender of, 73–74
Speculation, xiii
Spiro, Melford, 212
Spratt, Philip, 214
Staal, Frits, 3
Stace, W. T., 165, 241, 244, 367n. 97
Status-defined homoeroticism, 20
Struggle and Submission: R. C. Zaehner on Mysticisms (Newell), 357n. 2
Sublimation, 22, 73, 101, 151, 348n. 6)
Sufism
  and blood and death, 108–9, 349–50n. 25
  and "passion complex," 349–50n. 25
  Persian and mystical poetry and love of human boys, 190–91
  and secrecy, 129–31
  and "witness practice," 100–101, 121–23, 124–25, 191
Suso, Henry, 67, 77–78
Suzuki, D. T., 166
Svapna-Siddha, 299–304
Swedenborg, Emanuel, 27–28, 374n. 3, 338–39n. 81, 339n. 85

T
Tantra
  author's study of, 152
  as category in Bharati's thought, 209, 223–24
  definition of, 223
  and establishment within America, 232–33, 249
  goddess tradition within, 153
  and the hero (*vīra*), 23–24, 153
  and heterosexual assumptions, 20–21, 96, 152
  traditional, as sexist and nonromantic, 226–27
Tantric Tradition, The (Bharati), 208, 244
Taoism, 174
Tao Te Ching, 319
Tauler, Johannes, 78
Teilhard de Chardin, Pierre, 19, 336n. 56
  and Underhill, 44
  and Zaehner, 173, 182, 194, 195, 196
Teresa of Avila, 55, 62, 76, 94
  and automatic writing, 63
  and entering into states of prayer as they are written about, 283–84
  and her transverberation, 75–76, 186–87
Texts. See Reading of sacred texts
Theravāda Buddhism, 188
"Three Prayers of Abraham" (Massignon), 355n. 86
Through a Speculum That Shines (Wolfson), 273, 278–92
  and Blake, 258, 280, 290
  book itself as seven-staged process, 279–80
  as both historical study and living present work, 258
  and crowning, 288–89
  and final vision in seventh palace, 282–88
  and hermeneutical mysticism as both method and object of study, 259, 279
  and imagination, 281–82, 293
  kabbalistic vision as homoerotic, 290–92
  and mirroring of mystical experiences, 292–98; objective pole, 296–98; and subjective pole or author's reading himself into

text, 293–96; and Wolfson's
own mystical experiences,
293
and passage to erotic encounter
with Shekhinah, 278, 280
and phallocentric ocularism,
284–88
and visionary experience, 280–88
and vision of phallus in moment
of coitus, 286–88
Tikkun (repair), 272
Tillich, Paul, 359–60n. 38
Torah, 309, 371n. 29
as Shekhinah and corona of penis,
277
study of as illuminative, 288
Tradition
and necessity for ongoing critique
and reflection, 270
reception of through textual reading, 295
and reconstruction through continuous displacements, 271–72
and study of without restriction,
322–23
Traite de l'amour de Dieu (de Sales),
182
Transfiguration, 313–16, 375n. 17
"Transformational school" of psychoanalysis, 329, 338n. 72
Treatise on Purgatory (Catherine of
Genoa), 66
Triadic Heart of Siva, The (Muller-Ortega), 256
Trinity doctrine, 47–48
Truth and Method (Gadamer), 325
Turner, Denys, 70, 78–79, 344n. 53
Tyrrell, George, 41

U
ʿUdhritic love, 126–29, 132, 142
Ulrichs, Karl Heinrich, 354n. 78
Underhill, Evelyn, 33–86, 266
and art, 310
and brain as kind of filter, 45–46,
342n. 35
and Christian dogmas, 40, 340–41n. 19
conversion experience of, 40
and definition of mystics, 52
and excess, 306, 307
spiritual experience of, 58–62,
343n. 44
and homoeroticism of Christian
bridal mysticism, 315
life of, 38–43, 81–84, 340n. 9
and "Mystic Fact," 58, 295
and mysticism as practical, 306
and occultism, 39
and idea that "only a mystic can
write about mysticism," 16, 33
and place at borderland, 43
and progressive incarnation,
81–84
and "psychic tricks" of induced
mystical states, 121
and psychology and mysticism,
52–57, 295, 341–42n. 33, 342–43n. 41
squeamishness of, relative to sexuality, 76, 343n. 49
and Teilhard de Chardin, 44
and ties to institutional religion,
35, 39–50, 83
and vision, 281
and von Hügel, 35, 40, 47, 65,
81–83
and William Blake, 42–43,
345n. 66
Unicorn, 92–93, 95
Upaniṣads, 144, 176–77, 184–85
Uranism, 126, 354n. 78
Urban, Hugh, 24, 223

V
Vajra, 87, 93
"*Vajrāśva* Vision, The," 87, 93–97
Varieties of Religious Experience, The
(James), 34, 35, 52, 56
Virgin Mary or Mother, 93, 142
author's relationship to, 155,
346n. 11

Virgin Mary or Mother (*continued*)
  as soul penetrated by God, 110–11, 350–51n. 30
"Visionary complex," 101
Visionary experience, 280–88
  as form of art, 62
  Underhill's psychological interpretation of, 55–56
Visvananda, Swami, 211, 248
Von Hügel, Baron Friedrich, 35, 40, 47
  and church before mystic, 65
  and Underhill, 81–83
  See also *Mystical Element of Religion*

W
Waardenburg, Jacques, 203
Wafer, Jim, 101, 120, 349–50n. 25, 352n. 67
Waite, Arthur, 39
Wasserstrom, Steven, 316–17, 321–22, 355n. 86, 376n. 45
Watts, Alan, 236–37
Whitman, Walt, 182–83, 190, 370n. 21
Wilde, Oscar, 212, 362n. 11
"Witness practice," 100–101, 121–23, 124–25, 191
  with God, 126–27
Wittgenstein, Ludwig, 209, 211, 221, 239
Wolfson, Elliot, 258–98
  as "along the path," 260–61, 264, 368n. 3
  and context of text, 269, 370n. 21
  and discerning between homosexual practice and homoerotic structures in mystical texts, 18
  and esotericism, 267, 369n. 19
  and ethical critique of mystical eroticism, 318
  and excess, 307–8
  and Freud and psychoanalytic hermeneutic, 261–62, 273, 370n. 24, 372n. 31
  and gender, 17
  as guide for reader, 280
  and Heidegger, 262, 269
  and hermeneutical act analogized as art form, 311
  and the Holocaust, 261
  and Jewish orthodoxy, 262–63, 264
  and Judaism as a textual community, 264
  life of, 260–64
  and reading of sacred texts, 265–72; as danger and challenge to academic and practitioner, 265–66; and double mirroring, 258, 270, 293, 295–96; and focus on sexuality and gender, 266; and process of distancing, 270–71; and publication of what is esoteric, 266–67; and reading oneself into text, 258, 295–96; and scholar's historicizing methods, 266; and "uncovering" of meaning by unfolding of layers, 269–70; and "uninterupted listening," 268
  and sexual revelations, 267; and erasure of feminine through symbolic and theological strategies, 267; and exposing of kabbalistic masculine world, 315; and kabbalah and androcentric phallocentrism, 273–74; offense to and ostracizing by orthodox, 264; and phallocentric ocularism, 264, 285–89, 372n. 35, 372n. 37, 372–73n. 40; and sexuality as defining feature of Kabbalah, 263–64
  and similarity of analysis of mystical eroticism to author's, 297
  and writing, creation, and circumcision in Kabbalah, 274–78; and circumcision and opening and vision and the eye, 277–78;

and medieval ritual of preparation for writing, 277; and primordial autoerotic act and language, 276; and universe's emanation, 275; and writing as erotic penetration, 275; and writing as uniting of male and female, 277
writing style of, 274
Womb, 89
Woodroffe, John, 223
Worship (Underhill), 81
Wright, Peter, 161–62
Writing
and absence, 309
as a form of ecstasy, 62–63
as a form of sacred activity, xiii
and creation and circumcision in Kabbalah, 274–78
and creative imagination (Zaehner), 194
and mystical experience, 243
and reading as religious experience, 118
of text as a double mirror, 296, 297–98

Y
Yazīd, Abū, 171
Yoga, Massignon's critique of, 144
Yoga-Sūtras of Patañjali, 144
Yudhishthira, 160, 357–58n. 9

Z
Zaehner, R. C., 156–98
and Adam and Eve as evolutionary myth, 172–75
and art, 311
and Balzac, 164–65, 182, 194–96, 360n. 44
and Bharati, 207–8, 236, 237
and Bucke, 164
character of, 157, 159
and Christianity, 359n. 37; failures of, and comparative religion, 163; and flesh becoming Word or mystical body of Christ, 194–96; and gnostic interpretations of dogma, 173; and ontological critique of ascetic, 182–85; and Roman Catholicism, 156; and Tillich, 359–60n. 38
comparative typology model of, 169–72; and isolation of self or mysticism of isolation, 170–71, 176–77; and panenhenic experience, or nature mysticism, 169–70, 175–76; and return of self to God or mysticism of love, 171–72, 177–78
and denial of euphoric core of mysticism, 229
and *Doors of Perception,* 30, 156, 165–69
and drunkenness, 140, 360n. 40
and the erotic, 180–93, 359n. 36; and allowance of matter or "the flesh," 183, 193–94; and Catholicism and Zaehner's own homosexuality, 189–92; and defense of homoerotic practice, 190–91; and gender, 184–85, 187–89, 190–93, 195–96; and inability to deal with homoerotic structures of Christian bridal mysticism, 315; and monistic traditions, 188–89; and mystical and worldly spill over into each other, 182–83, 186, 187–88; and mystical eroticism as sublimation, 158; and mystical experiences akin to those of sexual union, 171–72; and mystical marriage, 171–72, 187–89, 190–93, 195–96, 360n. 42; and sexual intercourse and surrender to Divine, 187–88; and writing and creative inspiration, 194

Zaehner, R. C., (*continued*)
  ethical critique of, 175–80; and final ethical ideas of, 197–98; and rejection of ecstatic and monistic, 144
  and excess, 307
  and Freud, 192
  and Hindu mysticism, 163
  Last Judgment vision of, 196
  life and training of, 156, 159–62
  and Charles Manson, 197–98
  mescaline experience of, 178–80
  and monism, 121, 156–57, 158
  and mystical experiences, 168–69; and analogies between mystical states and manic-depressive illness, 170; Zaehner's own, at age twenty, 168; as "mystical critic," 159; writers of mysticism having, 164–65
  and perennialism, 162
  and psychoanalytic and feminist hermeneutical perspectives, 192
  and psychology of religion, 185–87
  and sense of humor, 160–61
  as Spalding Professor of Eastern Religions and Ethics, 156–57, 160, 161, 162
  and study of mysticism as a rot, 327
  and the truth, 162
  and universalism, 157
  and Zoroastrianism, 156
Zalman, Elijah ben Solomon (Gaon of Vilna), 286
Zen, Drugs and Mysticism (Zaehner), 160
Zen Buddhism, 188, 197, 262
Zimmer, Heinrich, 24
Zohar, 28, 274–75, 277, 284
Zoroastrianism, 183, 194

www.ingramcontent.com/pod-product-compliance
Lightning Source LLC
Chambersburg PA
CBHW070804300426
44111CB00014B/2422